DYNAMICS OF AMERICAN POLITICS

dynamics of

second edition

RAYMOND E. WOLFINGER

MARTIN SHAPIRO

FRED I. GREENSTEIN

american

politics

Library of Congress Cataloging in Publication Data

WOLFINGER, RAYMOND E
   Dynamics of American Politics

   Bibliography: p. 581
   Includes index.
   1. United States—Politics and government.
I. Shapiro, Martin M., joint author. II. Greenstein,
Fred I., joint author. III. Title.
JK274.W72 1980   320.4′73   79-19546
ISBN 0-13-221143-2

second edition
dynamics of american politics
Raymond E. Wolfinger, Martin Shapiro, Fred I. Greenstein

© 1980, 1976 by Raymond E. Wolfinger, Martin Shapiro, Fred I. Greenstein

Printed in the United States of America

10 9 8 7 6 5 4 3 2 1

Editorial/production supervision by Colette Conboy
Interior design by Judith Winthrop
Photo research by Roberta Guerette
Cover photograph by Bill Agee
Manufacturing buyer: Harry P. Baisley

Part opening photo credits:
    J.P. Laffont/Sygma, page 1
    Wide World, pages 119 and 511
    J.P. Laffont/Sygma; Suva, DPI, page 301

PRENTICE-HALL INTERNATIONAL, INC., *London*
PRENTICE-HALL OF AUSTRALIA PTY. LIMITED, *Sydney*
PRENTICE-HALL OF CANADA, LTD., *Toronto*
PRENTICE-HALL OF INDIA PRIVATE LIMITED, *New Delhi*
PRENTICE-HALL OF JAPAN, INC., *Tokyo*
PRENTICE-HALL OF SOUTHEAST ASIA PTE. LTD., *Singapore*
WHITEHALL BOOKS LIMITED, *Wellington, New Zealand*

To Barbara,
with love from all of us

abbreviated contents

preface   xvii
acknowledgments   xxi

PART ONE   the setting of american politics
1   introduction   3
2   the social context of american politics   18
3   the constitutional context of american politics   40
4   civil rights and liberties   56
5   federalism   75
6   the intellectual context of american politics   95

PART TWO   individual and group political activity
7   public opinion   121
8   voting   149
9   political participation   188
10   interest groups   225
11   political parties   263

PART THREE   national governmental institutions
12   how congress is elected and organized   303
13   congress in action   350
14   the presidency   391
15   the politics of administration   436
16   the courts   477

PART FOUR   the policy process
17   public policymaking   513
18   evaluating the american political system   543
appendix: the constitution of the united states   565
glossary   575
bibliography   581
index   595

contents

preface *xvii*

acknowledgments *xxi*

PART ONE the setting of american politics

CHAPTER 1 introduction 3

POLITICS: MANAGING CONFLICT 4   *Scarcity 4*   *Value Conflict 5*
Politics as a Source of Conflict 6
POLITICS: ORGANIZING COLLECTIVE EFFORT 8
THE ART OF DOING POLITICS 10
AMERICAN NATIONAL POLITICS 11   *The Dynamics of American Politics 12*
Political Evaluation 12
PLAN OF THE BOOK 13   *The Context of American Politics 13*
Individual Political Action 14   *Collective Political Action 15*   *Government 16*
Policymaking 17   *Evaluation 17*

CHAPTER 2 the social context of american politics 18

WEALTH AND THE DISTRIBUTION OF INCOME 19
ETHNICITY AND RACE 21   *National Origins 21*   *Black Americans 25*
People of Spanish Origin 27
RELIGION 28
AGE 30
OCCUPATION 31
SOCIAL CLASS 34
WHERE DO AMERICANS LIVE? 36
THE MAKEUP OF THE AMERICAN PEOPLE: BASES OF FACTION 38
SUMMARY 39

CHAPTER 3

the constitutional context of american politics 40

THE IDEAS BEHIND THE CONSTITUTION 41
THE INTENT OF THE FRAMERS 42
ARTICLE I: THE LEGISLATIVE POWER 45   *Representative Democracy* 45
The Independence of Congress 46   *The Powers of Congress* 46   *Limitations* 48
Impeachment 48   *Veto* 49   *Three Parts of Government with Overlapping Powers* 49
ARTICLE II: THE EXECUTIVE POWER 50
ARTICLE III: THE JUDICIAL POWER 51
ARTICLES IV TO VII 53   *The Amendments* 54
CONSTITUTIONAL LEGITIMACY 54
SUMMARY 55

CHAPTER 4

civil rights and liberties 56

FREEDOM OF SPEECH 57   *The Content of Speech* 58
Other Aspects of Freedom of Speech 59
RELIGION 61
RIGHTS OF ACCUSED PERSONS 62   *Other Rights of Accused* 65
Constitutional Rights and the States 65   *Habeas Corpus* 67
THE RIGHT TO VOTE 67
PRIVACY 67
CIVIL RIGHTS 68   *The Civil War Amendments* 68   *School Desegregation* 69
Affirmative Action 70   *Due Process* 73
THE EXPANSION OF RIGHTS 74
SUMMARY 74

CHAPTER 5

federalism 75

WHAT IS FEDERALISM? 76
THE SUPREME COURT AND FEDERALISM 77
THE DIVISION OF POLITICAL AUTHORITY: ADVANTAGES AND DISADVANTAGES 78
Greater Access to Power 78   *Local Experimentation* 80
Local Majorities and National Majorities 81
THE NEW FEDERALISM 83   *Grants-in-Aid* 83
Grants-in-Aid in the 1960s and 1970s 85   *Revenue Sharing* 86
FISCAL FEDERALISM 87
WELFARE: FEDERALISM AT WORK 90   *(Box) CETA* 93
SUMMARY 94

CHAPTER 6

the intellectual context of american politics 95

DEMOCRACY 96   *Representation and the Consent of the Governed* 96
Popular Sovereignty 99   *Direct Democracy and the Fear of Big Government* 99
Political Participation 101   *Majority Rule* 102   *American Thoughts on Democracy* 102
INDIVIDUAL RIGHTS 103   *The Liberal Tradition* 103
The Doctrine of Laissez Faire 104   *Private Property and Laissez Faire* 104
Economic Interests 105   *Negative and Positive Rights* 106
THE ROLE OF THE CONSTITUTION 107   *Majority Rule and Minority Rights* 107
Factions 108   *Majorities of the Moment* 110
EQUALITY 111   *Political Equality* 111   *Social Equality* 111
Equality of Opportunity 112   *Racial Equality* 113
JUSTICE AND THE RULE OF LAW 113
CONSENSUS 115
SUMMARY 116

PART TWO individual and group political activity

CHAPTER 7 public opinion 121

SURVEY RESEARCH 122 *Choosing a Sample 122* *Questions and Answers 123*
Validity: Evaluating Results 124
AWARENESS AND INTEREST: HOW MUCH DO AMERICANS KNOW? 125
THE SHAPE OF AMERICAN PUBLIC OPINION 128
Belief in the American Creed: Freedom and Racial Tolerance 128
Left or Right: It All Depends 129 *Ideological Self-Identification 130*
Interrelationships of Opinions 132
WHO HAS WHAT OPINIONS? 134 *Education and Occupation 134*
Racial Differences 136
HOW ATTITUDES ARE LEARNED 136 *Learning National Loyalty 137*
Learning about National Government 137 *Learning about Equality 139*
HOW ATTITUDES ARE SHAPED 140 *The Role of Leadership 140*
THE MASS MEDIA 142 *Leaks to the Press 144*
WHAT KINDS OF OPINION COUNT? 146
SUMMARY 147

CHAPTER 8 voting 149

VOTER TURNOUT 150 *Election Laws 150* *Who Votes? 153*
Abstentation: A Plague on Both Your Houses? 155 *Why Is Voter Turnout Falling? 156*
PARTY IDENTIFICATION 157 *The Stability of Party Identification 157*
The Social and Economic Bases of Faction 162 *The Two Parties: An Ideological Portrait 169*
The End of the American Party System? 171
CANDIDATE APPEAL 173
ISSUE VOTING 179 *Looking Backward 182*
ELECTIONS MANDATE 185
SUMMARY 186

CHAPTER 9 political partici participation 188

HOW MANY CITIZENS PARTICIPATE IN POLITICS? 189
WHY DO PEOPLE PARTICIPATE 191 *Policy-Oriented Participation 192*
Patronage-Based Participation 194 *Ideological Participation 198*
Sociability, Prestige, and Friendship 200
GIVING MONEY 202 *The Revolution in Campaign Finance 203*
Who Gives Money and Who Gets It? 206 *The Direct Mail Revolution 210*
HOW MONEY WORKS 212 *Does Money Buy Elections? 212*
Does Money Buy Political Influence? 213 *Future Issues in Campaign Finance 216*
WHO PARTICIPATES IN POLITICS? 218 *Activists Are Better Off 218*
The Ideology Gap 219
IMPLICATIONS AND CONSEQUENCES 222
SUMMARY 224

CHAPTER interest groups *225*

WHAT IS AN INTEREST GROUP? *227*
AMERICAN INTEREST GROUPS: NUMBERS AND DIVERSITY *228*
Who Belongs to Groups? 229   *Types of Interest Groups 231*
Economic Interest Groups 233   *Business Groups 233*   *Labor Unions 236*
Professional Associations 240
SOLIDARITY GROUPS *241*   *Ethnic Groups 241*   *The Women's Movement 244*
PUBLIC INTEREST GROUPS *245*   *Common Cause 246*
WHO GOVERNS INTEREST GROUPS? *248*
SELFISH INTERESTS OR CONCERNED CITIZENS? *250*
INTEREST GROUP TACTICS *251*   *Unplanned Effects and Anticipated Reactions 251*
Lobbying 252   *Litigation 255*   *Confrontation Strategies 258*
SUMMARY *261*

CHAPTER political parties *263*

WHAT THE PARTIES DO: THE TWO-PARTY SYSTEM *265*   *The Parties' Functions 265*
Why Two Parties? 267
PARTY MEMBERSHIP *270*   *Party Activists: Regulars, Purists, Hybrids 271*
HOW THE PARTIES ARE ORGANIZED *273*   *National Structures 274*
State and Local Parties 276
NOMINATING A PRESIDENTIAL CANDIDATE *278*   *The Legal Framework 278*
Routes to the Nomination 281   *The National Convention 286*   *Evaluating the Results 289*
CAMPAIGNING FOR OFFICE *290*
THE ELECTORAL COLLEGE *292*
HOW DIFFERENT ARE THE PARTIES? *294*
SUMMARY *298*

PART THREE national governmental institutions

CHAPTER how congress is elected and organized *303*

THE BASES OF REPRESENTATION *305*   *The Constitution 305*
Legislative Apportionment 306
CONGRESSIONAL ELECTIONS *307*   *The Advantages of Incumbency 309*
Party Images and Presidential Coattails 311   *Dynamic Factors in Congressional Elections 312*
Nominations 313   *Sources of Support 314*   *Popular Accountability 317*
WHO IS ELECTED TO CONGRESS? *319*   *What Do They Want? 320*
WORKING CONDITIONS *321*   *Perquisites of Office 323*   *Social Life 325*
Congressional Ethics 326
THE COMMITTEE SYSTEM *329*   *Committee Assignments 331*
House-Senate Differences 332   *Committee Chairmen and the Seniority System 334*
Changing Biases of the Seniority System 335   *The Revolt against Seniority 337*
PARTIES IN CONGRESS *339*   *Party Organization 340*   *Party Programs 344*
OTHER WAYS TO ORGANIZE *346*   *State Delegations 346*   *Ideological Groups 347*
SUMMARY *348*

CHAPTER 13 congress in action 350

FROM BILL TO LAW: THE LEGISLATIVE PROCESS 353   The Committee Stage 353
Bringing the Bill to the Floor 355   Debate and the Filibuster 357
Conference Committees 358   Party Voting 360   The Conservative Coalition 361
Veto Politics 363   Overview: A Bias against Action? 363
MINORITY RULE 364   Limits on Minority Rule 365   Subgovernments 367
The Appropriations Process 368
COORDINATING LEGISLATION 370   The New Congressional Budget Process 371
GATHERING INFORMATION 372   Information Sources 373
REPRESENTATION 377   How Members of Congress Learn What Constituents Want 379
What Americans Want from Their Representatives 381
Members of Congress vs. Congress 382
LEGISLATIVE CONTROL OF THE EXECUTIVE BRANCH 383   Legislative Oversight 384
Reorganization 386   Confirmation 386   Foreign Policy 388
SUMMARY 389

CHAPTER 14 the presidency 391

CONSTITUTIONAL POWERS 394
WHAT THE PRESIDENT MEANS TO AMERICANS 396   The Symbolic President 396
Presidential Popularity 398
THE MAN AND THE OFFICE 399   Who Are the Presidents? 399
The Presidential Role 402
THE PRESIDENT AS PARTY LEADER 407
THE PRESIDENT AND CONGRESS 408   The President as Chief Legislator 409
The President's Policy Stance and Initiative 410
Legislative Liaison: The Presidential Lobby 412
The President's "Vote" in Congress: The Veto Power 415
THE PRESIDENT AND THE EXECUTIVE BRANCH 415   Presidential Appointments 415
The Cabinet 421
THE INSTITUTIONALIZED PRESIDENCY 423   The White House Staff 424
Advising the President 427
THE UPS AND DOWNS OF PRESIDENTIAL POWER 428
The Power To Use Military Force 429   Executive Privilege 430   Impoundment 431
THE VICE-PRESIDENCY 432   How Vice-Presidents Are Chosen 432
What the Vice-President Does 433
SUMMARY 435

CHAPTER 15 the politics of administration 436

THE ORGANIZATION OF THE ADMINISTRATIVE BRANCH 440   The Line Agencies 440
Independent Regulatory Commissions 444   Indirect Federal Administration 445
Outside Contractors 447
ACCESS TO GOVERNMENT EMPLOYMENT 450   The Civil Service 450
Government Executives 453   Members of the Professions as Civil Servants 457
CLIENTELISM 457   Clientele Agencies 457   Interest Groups and Administration 461
ADMINISTRATORS AND GOVERNMENTAL DECISION-MAKING 462
Limitations on Hierarchial Control 463   Agency Overlap and Competition 464
THE POLITICS OF ADMINISTRATIVE REORGANIZATION 466
A Case Study in Government Reorganization: A Separate Department of Education 467
THE BUDGET: KEY TOOL OF POLICY COORDINATION 469
AN OVERVIEW OF ADMINISTRATION AND POLICY 473
SUMMARY 476

CHAPTER 16

the courts *477*

THE SUPREME COURT AS COURT *479*
The Third Person *480*   *Lawmaker* *480*
Instrument of Government *481*   *Highest Court* *481*
SHOULD THE SUPREME COURT ACT? *484*
The Court and Democracy *484*
The Finality of Court Decisions *487*
THE JUSTICES *488*
THE WORK OF THE COURT *491*   *The Lower Federal Courts* *491*
Policymaking in the District and Circuit Courts *495*
Routes to the Supreme Court *496*
The Workload of the Supreme Court *498*   *The Decision-Making Process* *500*
SUPREME COURT OPINIONS *501*
THE ROLES OF THE SUPREME COURT *503*
Maintaining Constitutional Boundaries *503*
Defender of Civil Liberties *503*   *The Court and the Rights of the Accused* *504*
The Court and Elections *506*   *Race Relations* *506*
The Court and Economic Rights *508*
THE COURT TODAY: AN OVERVIEW *508*
SUMMARY *509*

PART FOUR

the policy process

CHAPTER 17

public policymaking *513*

GOALS AND PRIORITIES *514*
DECISION-MAKING STYLES *515*   *The Synoptic Approach* *515*
The Incremental Approach *517*   *"Rational" Policymaking* *518*
A Bias toward the Status Quo? *519*   *Uncontrolled Spending* *520*
DISTRIBUTIVE AND REDISTRIBUTIVE POLICIES *522*   *Distributive Policy* *522*
Zero-Sum or Redistributive Policies *523*
Politicians' Preference for Distributive Policies *524*
The Role of the Political Entrepreneur *527*
INFORMATION AND POLICYMAKING *527*   *Popular Ignorance* *527*
Technical Ignorance *528*   *Unanticipated Consequences* *528*
POLICY IMPLEMENTATION *529*
Overload and Implementation *529*
Ease of Administration *530*
THE EFFECTIVENESS OF POLICY *532*
Auditing *533*   *Policy Analysis* *533*
FOREIGN AND DEFENSE POLICY *536*   *Intelligence* *536*
Continuity and Crisis: Inventing Alternatives *537*
Secrecy *539*   *Coordination* *540*
Foreign and Domestic Policy *540*
SUMMARY *542*

CHAPTER 18 evaluating the american political system 543

LOOKING AT POLITICS FROM INSIDE 544
WHAT'S GOOD FOR THE PEOPLE VS. WHAT THE PEOPLE WANT: THE ROLE OF THE EXPERT 545
WHAT GOVERNMENT CAN AND SHOULD DO 546   *Governmental Responsibility* 547
Governmental Capacity 547   *Limiting Conflict* 548
POLITICS AS A CORRECTIVE IN POLITICAL EVALUATION 549
COMPARATIVE ANALYSIS 550
AMERICANS' EVALUATION OF THEIR POLITICAL SYSTEM 552
MANAGING CONFLICT 555
EQUALITY 556
THE TENSION BETWEEN FREEDOM AND EQUALITY 562
SUMMARY 563

appendix: the constitution of the united states 565

glossary 575

bibliography 581

index 595

preface

This book expresses our belief that political scientists now know a good deal about how and why American politics works, and that this knowledge can be clearly communicated to students in an interesting way. All three of us are working scholars whose research covers most of the topics in this book. Each of us has twenty years of experience teaching introductory American politics in schools ranging from private colleges to huge state universities. Both sorts of experience — as teachers and as researchers — are reflected in this book. The title indicates what we have tried to accomplish. Rather than treating the political system as set in concrete, we see it in a state of continual evolution, constrained by two centuries of American history. The themes of change and continuity are intertwined throughout the book. We believe that describing and explaining what actually happens is at least as important as presenting our views of what ought to happen. Before people can make informed judgments about American politics, they should know how it works. Thus we describe and explain the nuts and bolts of each element in the system, and show the connections between those elements. We do not think politics is a matter of good guys versus bad guys. Our goal is to describe and explain, not to praise or condemn. We will not announce what tax laws Congress should enact in 1981, but we will explain why the House Ways and Means Committee is central to whatever laws will be enacted. We do not tell students what to think, but we do try to provide the tools for them to come to their own conclusions about the American political system.

Above and beyond this approach, what we are after is a good book. To us that means puncturing the untrue cliches and not being afraid to affirm the cliches that we have tested and found to be true. It means doing our own research when necessary, rather than using outdated or irrelevant figures and examples. It means giving readers facts and ideas that they can use to understand American politics now and in the future, rather than basing our book on the issues and controversies of 1979. We do not believe that introducing college students to the study of American politics is a matter of asking them to memorize the names of all the committees in Congress. Nor do we believe that students should be bored with the unresolved methodological difficulties and ideological disputes in political science. We have tried to avoid these pitfalls.

This edition, like the first, assumes that a textbook can be successful without compromising the intellectual standards of good political science scholarship. Before beginning this revision, we consulted a number of Washington reporters and academic specialists. Through our publisher, we received detailed comments on the first edition by thirteen anonymous professors who had taught with that book at schools ranging from community colleges to private universities. These reactions pointed us toward many substantive improvements and helped us clarify our presentation. Many chapters were thoroughly revised and the last part of the book was completely reorganized. Throughout we reduced unnecessary elaboration, tightened our presentation of important concepts, and provided many more concrete examples to aid understanding of abstract material. Most chapters are shorter, some by as many as ten pages. This general tightening, plus the elimination of one chapter, made room for new chapters on federalism and on civil rights and civil liberties.

The whole book has, of course, been brought up to date. (Doing so, we were pleased to see that recent events and scholarship did not contradict the general propositions we presented the first time around.) For example, the material on voting and campaign contributions includes the 1978 elections; our discussion of congressional ethics covers developments in 1979; our discussion of presidential nomination is based on the new rules for the 1980 election. In addition, important terms are shown in boldface in color within the text and are collected and defined in a Glossary at the end of the book.

Our focus is on *how* the political system works, not *what* it produces. Nevertheless, we have discussed many policy issues to illustrate how institutions work. There are several case studies ranging up to three pages in length and dozens of "boxes" scattered throughout the text to provide examples and to bring controversies into the open so students can discuss them. Sometimes we use a single issue area to highlight a variety of general points. For example, federal policy toward the handicapped is discussed in Chapter 5 as an example of federalism, in Chapter 15 as an example of congressional delegation of rulemaking to bureaucrats, and in Chapter 18 to illustrate two different definitions of equality: should the government spend the same amount of money on each person, or should it spend any amount necessary to give everyone the same degree of access to public facilities? Racial minorities and civil rights policies are discussed in eight different chapters.

We begin by showing why politics is a necessity in civilized society. The next five chapters then set forth the social, legal and intellectual context of American politics: socioeconomic cleavages in contemporary America, the constitutional foundation of politics, civil rights and liberties, federalism, and the enduring themes and contradictions in American political thought. In Part Two the focus shifts to individual political behavior in chapters on public opinion, voting, and participation. This leads to consideration of the organizations — interest groups and parties — that link individuals to government. The next step, in Part Three, is to the national governmental institutions: Congress, the presidency, the bureaucracy, and the courts. In analyzing each one, we are concerned with its roots in the political process, the motivations of its officials, and the interplay of conflict and cooperation among institutions. In Part Four we move from the structure of government to its functioning as a political entity — from anatomy to physiology. We analyze common themes in policymaking and then conclude with a chapter that gives students the tools to evaluate the political system for themselves.

Accompanying the text are additional tools for instructors. For the student we have a *Study Guide and Workbook* that provides outline summaries of each chapter, suggestions for how to approach the material, and questions on the text material and on the issues or points of controversy. There is an *Instructor's Manual* that suggests teaching strategies, provides resources for supplementary reading and additional lectures, supplies an outline of the major points in each chapter, and provides discussion questions and topics for research projects. A separate *Test Item File* contains approximately 1000 questions: multiple choice, true-false, and short-answer.

acknowledgments

We have profited from the criticism and suggestions of dozens of people. Many of the most perceptive and influential comments came from thirteen anonymous professors who used the first edition. We are equally indebted to a number of scholars and journalists for commenting on smaller portions of that book: Herbert E. Alexander, Dom Bonafede, Richard A. Brody, Richard E. Cohen, Leon D. Epstein, James W. Fesler, Louis Fisher, Joel B. Grossman, Ted Robert Gurr, Joel Havemann, Charles E. Lindblom, J. Donald Moon, Benjamin I. Page, David W. Rohde, Steven J. Rosenstone, Robert H. Salisbury, David O. Sears, Stephen Simpson, Paul M. Sniderman, and Aaron Wildavsky. After drafting this edition, we were aided by comments from Herbert E. Alexander, Matthew Pinkus, Austin Ranney, Steven J. Rosenstone, and several anonymous readers.

Much of the research we did for this edition reflects the assistance of Victor Crain and Richard A. McIntosh. Eric L. Davis and Marian Smiley helped prepare the bibliography.

Many people at Prentice-Hall had a hand in making this book from our manuscript. We are particularly indebted to Colette Conboy for capably managing the book's production, and to Stan Wakefield, whose executive talents brought our book to completion.

R.E.W.
M.S.
F.I.G.

DYNAMICS OF AMERICAN POLITICS

the setting
of american politics

PART ONE

introduction

Politics is inevitable because people live together and because they have different material desires and personal ideals. It is also inevitable because both resources and power must be shared according to some kind of rule. Politics is a way to express and resolve conflicts and differences. At the same time, it is a way to organize people to do together what they could not do alone. We will look first at the many roles politics plays in a nation's life and then at the way this book analyzes American politics.

CHAPTER 1

A great deal of politics consists of bargaining and compromise designed to give conflicting interests enough of what they want so that they will continue to cooperate with each other. The farmers of an area may want a new irrigation project. They will not be able to get it without the support of the environmentalists, who want to preserve the same land as a park. Without the farmers' support, there will be no park. So both groups cooperate to back a combined irrigation and park project. Both settle for less than they originally wanted. Each gets more than it could have gotten if they had not joined forces. The farmers get a smaller irrigation project than they could have had if there were no park with which to share the land, but they do get some land irrigated. The environmentalists have a small park instead of none at all. Sometimes a conflict can actually be resolved. Two groups, each strongly backing its own candidate for office, may discover a third candidate whom they can both support with more enthusiasm than either had for the other two.

How successful politics can be at settling conflict frequently depends on whether the conflict comes in little or big pieces. Let us imagine a society composed solely and in equal parts of factory workers and farmers. Let us also suppose that this society was one in which all the factory workers were poor, black, Protestant, city-dwelling, and uneducated. All the farmers were wealthy, white, Catholic, country-dwelling, and educated. Nearly any issue in the society would pit 50 percent of the people against the other 50 percent. More important, each and every issue would pit the *same* 50 percent against the same other 50 percent. Whether the issue was urban renewal or farm subsidies or aid to parochial schools, all the farmers would always be opposed by all the factory workers.

To a large extent, whether a political system works depends on whether conflicts can be broken down into small enough parts so that *everyone* can have something. If so, everyone will sometimes win and sometimes lose. Everyone will sometimes be a political ally of some people and sometimes of other people. In the United States, for example, if a farm subsidy bill passes, all farmers may be happy. But only some of the rich and some of the poor, some Protestants and some Catholics, some of the well-educated and some of the uneducated will be happy. We have rich and poor, Protestant and Catholic, educated and uneducated farmers. When aid to parochial schools is proposed, the Catholic and Protestant farmers who fought together on farm subsidies may find themselves on opposite sides. The Catholic farmers will be allied with Catholic factory workers who fought against the farm subsidy law. The saying that "politics makes strange bedfellows" reflects this pattern.

Scarcity Sometimes conflict can be resolved by giving everyone what they want. We can have Mother's Day and Father's Day, St. Patrick's Day and National Eat More Peanuts Day and Support Your Local Police Day, because any one day can be two or three different ceremonial days at once. But we cannot resolve most of our political conflicts this way because a basic fact of politics is scarcity: many of the things people want do not exist in sufficient quantity

SCARCITY

Thousands of Americans have diseases that will kill them unless they can hook up to kidney machines at intervals. These machines are very expensive; there are not enough to go around. Panels of doctors decide which patients get to use the machines and which do not. Those who do not, die. These are literally life and death decisions that someone must make because of scarcity.

America is rich enough to buy enough kidney machines, but if it did it would have to buy less of something else. Each year cities that could buy more kidney machines choose instead to spend their tax dollars on educating children, or keeping streets clean, or subsidizing symphony orchestras. Is it preferable to spend more money on keeping more people alive? Apparently we do not think so, or there would be enough kidney machines. Does the fact that most of those who die are people so ill that their lives could be prolonged for only a few months even with the machine make you feel differently about what should be done about this particular scarcity?

to satisfy everybody. The case of the irrigation project and the park is an excellent example. There simply was not enough land to give both farmers and environmentalists as much as they wanted. There probably was not enough money, either. Time also is in scarce supply. Most politicians cannot spend as much time listening to the problems of their constituents as some of the constituents might want. A president and Congress faced with an urgent nationwide problem like energy do not have the time to spend a day with a group seeking a solution to a strictly local issue.

Indeed, politics at its best may be the art of finding compromises where none seems to exist. For example, liquor prohibition would seem to be an all-or-nothing proposition. If the prohibitionists get what they want, the drinkers get nothing to drink. And if the drinkers get their drink, then the prohibitionists do not get prohibition. But it is possible to allow the sale of liquor and still give the prohibitionists *something* of what they want. This is done in some states by confining the sale of alcoholic beverages to a few state-run stores.

Value Conflict One type of difference, however, is almost impossible to work out. Some people have such intense beliefs about what a society ought to be like that they have little room to maneuver in the political arena. Radical socialists, extreme right-wing conservatives, and militant ethnic separatists may refuse to compromise on their visions of the ideal society. The socialist may reject as "capitalist hypocrisy" every government policy that aids the poor but does not help bring about the government ownership of industry that is an essential feature of the ideal socialist state. Some black militants may reject government programs that aid poor blacks but do not contribute to the creation of totally self-sufficient black communities. Some ideologies that do not require reorganizing society may still be so extreme that they dominate everything else. Before the Civil War, the most fervid Abolitionist or slaveowner may have had no vision of an ideal society, but he was certain it was better to have a bloody civil war than allow the country to continue half-slave and half-free.

When an issue taps deep emotions among some people, the secret of conflict resolution sometimes lies in keeping the issue out of politics. This is why the Constitution prohibits laws "respecting an establishment of religion." It may lie in forcing militants to keep quiet. Or it may lie in major changes in the political, social, and economic structure to meet the demands of those who feel most deeply. In many instances, however, people who have conflicting values or belief systems can be brought together. Those who disagree about what is good in the long run may be able to agree on what is best for the moment. Thus, socialists and capitalists may agree that the government should build highways. Some things can be done to pursue one ideal that do not conflict with the pursuit of others. The government can often act neutrally toward two competing belief systems; for instance, it can give tax exemptions to both Protestant and Catholic churches. A lot of politics consists of inventing ways for people with conflicting values or basic beliefs to live together.

Politics as a Source of Conflict

In speaking of politics as a method for conflict resolution, we must not forget that politics is itself a major *source* of conflict. One of the things politics is about is who shall govern. Individuals, groups, and political parties seek political power both for its own sake and to use that power to pursue their other interests. Obviously, there is not enough political power to go around. There are two major political parties, but only one presidency. Only one party at a time can win a presidential election. Like other scarcities, scarcity of political power also leads to conflict. Conflict arises not only about who should govern, but about basic political ideas and values. Some people believe "That government is best that governs least." Others think a good society should provide for the poor and want government to take on this responsibility. Others may value national security very highly. They may want a big Department of Defense and a small Department of Health, Education and Welfare. Each group will disagree with the others about how big government should be and what it should do.

At the time of the American Revolution, those who felt that the colonies should be politically independent shot at those who believed otherwise. Later, those who believed that the new Constitution should be adopted talked and voted against those who opposed adoption. In the 1960s and 1970s, those who believed the government was fighting an unjust war in Vietnam demonstrated and sometimes battled against that policy. Women's groups fighting for the Equal Rights Amendment have urged people not to buy things produced in states whose legislatures refuse to vote for the amendment. Whenever people have different ideas about what kind of government is best and what goals it ought to pursue, there will be political conflict.

Keeping that conflict to an acceptable level is an important function of a nation's political system. Without mechanisms for sharing and transferring power, conflict can result in revolution and civil war. In the United States there are many

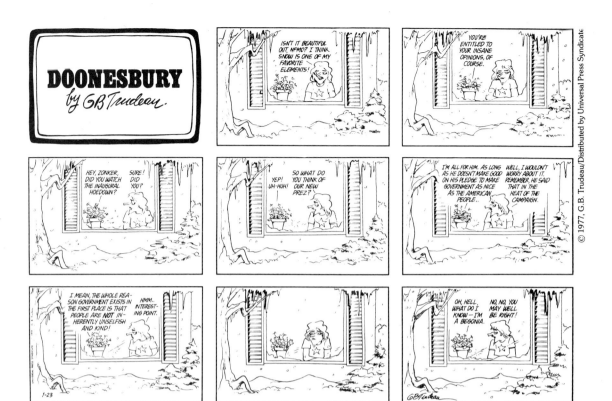

devices for accomplishing this task. The best known is our great number of governing bodies, political offices, and places of political power in nongovernmental organizations. There are fifty state governments, and thousands of county, city, and town governments. We have one president, nine Supreme Court Justices, hundreds of federal judges, 535 members of Congress, and several thousand high-level federal executives. In addition, there are millions of officers of political parties and private organizations ranging from the secretary-treasurer of a local PTA to the president of the American Bar Association. Thus, while not everyone who wishes to hold a position of power can do so, a great many can. And while only one party can hold the presidency at a given time, the other can hold many congressional seats, governorships, and so on.

Perhaps even more important than the large number of political offices is the American consensus on the rules of the political game. One of the things that reduces tension in American politics is the fact that the losing party knows it will get another chance in the next election. As we can see from newspaper and TV reporting of events in less stable parts of the world, politics can be a bloody business in nations where the winning party outlaws the losing party and executes its leaders as traitors. In the United States, our commitment to a democratic electoral process and to rotation of political offices among large numbers of politicians is a major way of reducing the conflict that arises from politics itself.

POLITICS: ORGANIZING COLLECTIVE EFFORT

So far we have emphasized the negative role of politics, its role in reducing or avoiding conflict. But politics also has a positive side. One of its major functions is to organize collective effort to achieve social goals that individuals or private groups find it difficult to achieve by themselves. Governments respond to practical, material needs: They build dams, create parks, give aid to the needy, and provide national defense forces. Governments also meet such nonmaterial needs as desires for group recognition and for a sense of identification with one's fellow citizens. Group recognition is achieved, for example, by appointing representatives of a group to prestigious positions. There are no natural or required activities for government. At various times in history, there have been private armies and postal services. Many small towns still have volunteer fire departments. Today we often see government-owned hospitals and schools operating alongside privately owned institutions providing the same services. Government is one means of operating collective enterprises and of focusing social resources to deal with a problem—but it is not the only means. For instance, in the United States we pay for the planes and warships that defend us through taxes, but we make most of them in private factories.

Just how much the government should own, operate, regulate, or plan, and just which and how many new collective enterprises it should undertake are themselves political questions giving rise to conflict. But there has never been a feeling in America that the government ought to do nothing at all. Activities aimed at improving the quality of life do not necessarily mean government ownership or operation; subsidies, such as grants or loans to keep symphony orchestras or railroads going when they are in financial trouble, are also ways of accomplishing this goal. Government may also act by regulating private activity, such as requiring smog control devices to improve air quality.

THE CASE OF THE ACLU

The American Civil Liberties Union is one of the collective efforts we have been talking about in the last page or so. Its members contribute time and money to defending such rights as freedom of speech. Lawyers from the ACLU may find themselves in court one day helping the American Nazi Party to get a parade permit. The next day they may be helping in the defense of black civil rights workers arrested for protesting against racial bigotry. Earlier in this chapter we talked both about politics making strange allies and about some value conflicts being very deep. Would you donate money to an organization that helped Nazis? To one that helped Communists? Abortionists? Pornographic moviemakers whose stars are six-year-old children? To one that helped all of them? Perhaps you feel that defending all speakers is worth it even though there are some speakers you do not like. Perhaps you feel that, no matter what, you could not give money when some of it would go to help people who act in ways that you think are evil. (The ACLU, by the way, has not helped "child pornographers.")

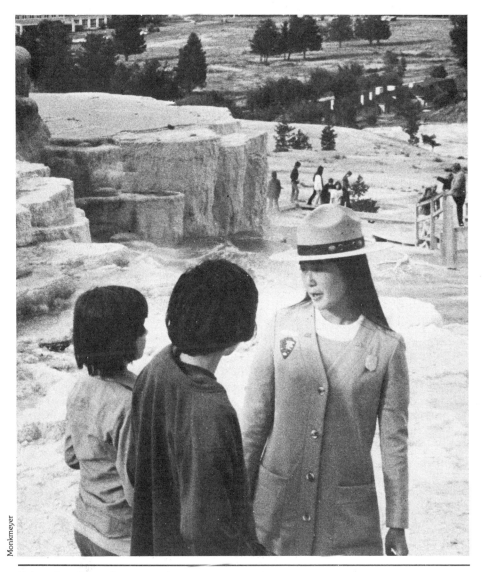

Monkmeyer

*Politics provides collective goods
that individuals cannot achieve
for themselves, such as this park.*

Political parties and government must expend a great deal of collective energy on internal processes — that is, on making government work. Campaigns must be organized, elections conducted, legislation deliberated, passed, and administered, court cases heard, and so on. Such collective political effort may also help to build a sense of political community among the people of a nation. It not only produces things they want, but also helps them to express their common beliefs and values in ways that foster mutual faith and support.

For all the positive benefits that result from politics and government, Americans frequently think of politics negatively. One of the ways the *Random House Dictionary* illustrates the word *politics* is with the sentence "The advocated reforms have become embroiled in politics." Or we say of someone we believe to be insincere or without principles, "he's just a politician." To label something "just politics" can mean that it is without real content, without any purpose other than to get someone reelected or to gain him some other advantage.

Throughout American history we have honored individual politicians such as Lincoln or Jefferson. At the same time we have expressed our contempt for politicians in general. Not all politicians are good public servants. Some of politics *is* self-serving, designed to save a politician rather than serve the people. But the reader must guard against unconscious negative feelings whenever he or she sees the word *politics*. In each instance, whether the politics is good or bad—nation-serving or self-serving—is an open question to be decided after a good look. Usually events in the political world contain a mixture of selfish and unselfish motives. Self-interest is one of the basic fuels of politics. It provides much of the energy that keeps politics going. But that does not mean that the sole purpose or product of politics is to improve the lot of politicians.

Much of our negative feelings about politics comes from our vision of politics as the self-serving manipulation of some people by others. On the other hand, whatever sympathy we have for political leadership and good government comes from our vision of politics as getting people to work together to solve their problems. Often these two visions are simply different ways of looking at the same thing.

Politics is, among other things, a set of skills through which people seek to in-

POLITICS

Suppose you were a senator who had written an air pollution bill that would help clean up the atmosphere. Another senator came to you and said he could not vote for the bill because if it were enacted, an important industry in his state would have to move elsewhere and thousands of jobs would be lost. Voters in his state cared about clean air, but they also cared about their jobs. If you inserted a clause in your bill exempting that particular industry in order to get the senator's vote, would that be politics in the good or bad sense?

In deciding, think about the following points: Without the extra vote, the bill might fail and an important chance to reduce pollution would be lost. But if every senator could exempt his or her pet polluters, the new law would leave the air as dirty as before. It might reduce health hazards if the polluting industry moved from your fellow senator's state to another state where its waste products would not bring pollution to dangerous levels. But what about the people who would lose their jobs? Politicians have to face questions like these all the time.

crease their influence over others in order to achieve their goals. As such, *politics* means far more than government and the selection of people to govern. At work we speak of the "office politician." At home we have become increasingly aware of the "politics" that governs relationships between husbands and wives or parents and children. As these usages indicate, one aspect of politics is gaining control over others or reaching a position of leadership or command. A person may seek such a position either for its own sake or for some substantive purpose, like making the family buy a new car or making the business more profitable. Here again, as in governmental politics, we usually encounter a mixture of desire for self-advancement and desire to do good.

Although we can often tell when political skills are being used, it is not easy to specify exactly what they are. A whole range of skills may be useful at various times and in various settings to get others to reduce their conflicts and work together. Anything from bursting into tears to proposing a new solution may turn the trick in a given instance. The same technique that has worked in one situation may fail in another. Thus, when we speak of someone as being "a good politician," we usually mean someone who knows which tool to pick and how to use it at the right moment.

Politics is often called the "art of the possible." As in all arts, the political artist must seek to create new things within the limitations imposed by tradition and the materials with which he or she works. As we have seen already, the art of politics often involves compromise. But political compromise is not necessarily built on giving everybody something or treating everyone equally. Political skill is skill at risking and channeling conflict, at accepting some risk and hostility in order to achieve goals. The politician must know when and whom to fight, when and in which direction to run, and how to move people.

AMERICAN NATIONAL POLITICS

Although we talk occasionally about family, business, religious, and other kinds of politics, this book is about politics in the narrower sense. We will be examining the activities of government and the processes by which the nation decides who shall govern. We will also be more concerned with national than state and local politics. But, because much of American *national* politics occurs at state, local, and nongovernmental levels, we must pay attention to these "lower" levels of political activity. For example, the mayor of Chicago has a certain amount of power within the city of Chicago. To the degree that the mayor is simply a political actor within Chicago, we are not interested in her. But she is also an actor on the national political level. In this capacity, she may influence the behavior of Illinois delegates to the national nominating convention of the Democratic party. She may influence the way the eight members of Congress from Chicago act and vote in the House of Representatives in Washington. And she may have a vital say in the way certain national programs, such as federal urban renewal, affect Chicago.

Similarly, we shall see that many policies of the national government are implemented or even initiated by state governments, or by private firms or groups to whom the central government "contracts out" its work. For example, the government in Washington may tell a state that it may have a certain amount of money if the state will repair a federal highway to meet federal standards. Or it may pay an aerospace firm in California to design a new missile for the Defense Department. To the extent that state and local governments and private organizations do the national government's business, they will concern us in this book.

The Dynamics of American Politics

In real life, things seldom work out exactly as their designers intended. Over the years, the living institutions of government grow and evolve. American politics is always changing, and along with it, our knowledge. For this reason, we cannot hope to present a final account of our political system. If it is to stay in touch with reality, political inquiry must always be a matter of continuing investigation, clarification, and revision.

Although our focus will be largely on what we know about how American politics actually works, the ideal or "ought" elements of politics will not be overlooked. For instance, in Chapter 3 we will treat the Constitution as one of the many factors setting the outer limits of political action. It tells politicians that although they can choose to do many different things, there are some they cannot do at all. Yet the Constitution is more than just a set of limits. Most American politicians, like most other Americans, have "internalized" the Constitution. Our sense of political right and wrong is largely shaped by our understanding of it. Thus it serves as a guide to action. If it were not for this belief, the Constitution would be little more than a historical document on display at the National Archives. Of course, we cannot understand a twentieth-century government just by reading an eighteenth-century document like the Constitution. On the other hand, we cannot really understand contemporary events without knowing the beliefs and expectations on which they are based.

Political Evaluation

In political analysis, a distinction is often made between *description* and *evaluation,* between accounts of a political system that show us how it works and those that pass judgment on it. For instance, we may ask "What is the impact of the seniority system in Congress?" Some observers may say it increases conservative influence in Congress. Others may say it does not. But the disagreement is about how the thing works in fact, not about whether it is good or bad. Indeed, we cannot tell whether it is a good or a bad thing until we know how it works.

One step from factual description is evaluation in terms of specific criteria. For instance, does the seniority system increase or decrease citizen control over political leaders? We need not agree on whether citizen control is good or bad in order to ask and answer this question. Basically, the question remains one of fact—how does the seniority system really work? But now it is a question of fact focused on a specific criterion of evaluation. It asks us to analyze how seniority works in terms of whether it turns out well or badly for a specific value—citizen control.

Farthest away from description is evaluation in the sense of broad judgments of value. Is citizen control over leaders a good thing? Social scientists have no special skills that enable them to make final judgments on such questions. They can, however, know enough about how politics really works to predict accurately whether a particular value will actually be achieved if we make a given change in our political process.

Of course, political scientists, including the writers of this book, do have their own political values.[1] No doubt these values color some of what we say. But on the whole, the evaluations offered in this book are most concerned with assessing the impact of a given political arrangement in terms of specific criteria. We will attempt to make "if . . . then" statements where we have the knowledge to do so. We leave to our readers decisions about basic questions as to what is ultimately good and bad. We have sought to provide only the kind of analysis of actual political dynamics that will help in answering these questions about the American political system.

PLAN OF THE BOOK

So far we have spoken about politics, political dynamics, and political evaluation without defining the word *politics*. Dictionary definitions of complex phenomena like politics are either circular or so abstract as to be of little use. Speaking in an obscenity case, a judge once said: "I can't define it, but I know it when I see it." The same is true of politics. When our readers have completed this book, they still may not know how to define American politics, but they should know it when they see it. At this point the reader will get less help from definitions than from a brief outline or roadmap of how this book describes the workings of American politics.

We begin with a description of the environment or context within which American politics operates (Chapters 2, 3, 4, 5, 6). Then we move to the level of individual political behavior (Chapters 7, 8, 9). Next come the ways people join together in groups and parties to do politics (Chapters 10, 11). We then move on to an account of the government (Chapters 12, 13, 14, 15, 16). In the remaining chapters, we describe the dynamic process of policymaking through which politics actually has its effect on society and offer some thoughts on how to evaluate the system we have described.

The Context   We start with the context or environment of politics because it
of American Politics   provides both the resources for and the limitations on how
much politics can do. Chapter 2 is devoted to the socioeconomic context of American politics. It describes the physical and economic re-

---

[1] If we were asked to classify ourselves as liberals or conservatives, two of us would pick the first label and one the second. Collectively we resemble all American political scientists, around 70 percent of whom call themselves "liberal" or "left." (As we will see in Chapter 7, self-imposed labels like liberal and conservative are only rough guides to the opinions individuals actually have on any single issue.) Political scientists' attitudes on particular issues generally are well to the left side of the ideological spectrum. Those of us who write books are more liberal than those who do not publish. See Seymour M. Lipset and Everett C. Ladd, Jr., "The Divided Professoriate," *Change*, 3 (May–June 1971); and Ladd and Lipset, *Academics, Politics, and the 1972 Election* (Washington: American Enterprise Institute, 1973), pp. 16–23.

sources available to the United States as well as its human resources, the people. Obviously, the physical and economic side of American life is important for its politics. If there were no deserts in the United States, for example, there would be no political action directed at getting the government to build irrigation projects. Conversely, if our whole country were desert that produced nothing, the government could not raise the tax dollars to build irrigation projects. The economic and physical resources of a country influence its foreign as well as its domestic policies. A small, poor country could not have won World War II and would not have been tempted to try to win a war in Vietnam.

The human context of politics may be even more important. Some Americans belong to the upper class and a great many more to the middle class. Some have much more education than others. Some live in poverty, others in plenty. Some are black and some are white. In politics people are not merely faceless votes; they are individuals. Obviously, all the human characteristics of a person influence what he or she feels about politics and wants out of politics. Individuals also fall into such larger categories as poor urban black, or white-collar suburbanite. Often politicians think about how people in one or another of these groups will react to some political action they are about to take.

In Chapter 3, we deal with the constitutional context of American politics. We examine the written Constitution and our beliefs about it as well as the general structure of government it establishes. The constitutional context is both a product of political actions and a major influence on them. In Chapter 4, we examine civil rights and liberties as part of that constitutional context. Federalism is another important feature of our Constitution. American politicians at the Constitutional Convention of 1789 made the decision to create a federal system of state and national governments. Today the central government finds it hard to make policy on the control of crime because most police officers work for the cities and states, not the government in Washington. Today's politicians must operate within this context, which was created by other politicians almost two hundred years ago. Because federalism is such a special and important feature of the American scene it is the subject of Chapter 5.

Chapter 6 is about the intellectual context of American politics. Here we will examine the general ideas held by Americans about how politics should be done and what its goals ought to be. Clearly, the intellectual context provides both restraints and resources for political action. For example, if most Americans think that everyone should be allowed to speak freely, then the president is going to have a hard time getting Congress to pass a censorship law. If Americans have a basic commitment to equality, this commitment can be harnessed to get Congress to support government food programs for the poor.

Individual Political Action From the environment or context of politics, we turn to the individual level of political action. Chapters 7 and 8, on public opinion and voting behavior, form a natural pair. Public opinion is the total of individual opinions, just as election outcomes are the total of individual votes. Moreover, data from public opinion polls and elections give us most of the knowledge we have about how individuals think and act in politics.

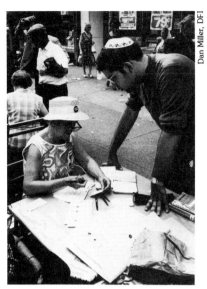

Voting is the foundation for all linkages between public opinion and government policy.

Although both opinion polls and elections give citizens an opportunity to express their political preferences, there are important differences between them. Public opinion is expressed continuously, not simply at election time. It is far more issue-oriented and fragmented than voting. There are usually only two or three candidates for an office, and the voter can choose only one of these. But there are hundreds of issues — abortion, social security, inflation, school integration, and so forth. Each individual can have an opinion on each issue. What is more, there are many positions on each issue. A person need not simply be for or against school integration, the way he or she must vote either for or against a candidate. For instance, a person may be for changing school boundaries but against busing to achieve integration.

Chapter 7 examines how people learn about politics and how they form their political opinions. It also examines the changing strengths and distributions of various opinions on various issues. It is these many opinions that we call "public opinion." Chapter 8 examines voting as the form of political action most common to all Americans. It describes who votes and examines why they vote the way they do.

Chapter 9, on political participation, forms a bridge between the chapter on voting and those on collective political action. In exploring forms of political participation other than voting, it addresses itself to the question of why some Americans move beyond voting to more active involvement in politics and what forms that involvement takes.

Collective Political Action   Many Americans do not confine their political activity to the individual level. They also act collectively through *interest groups* and *parties*. Interest groups seek to organize and focus the political desires of their constituents. Parties seek votes. Chapters 10 and 11 examine the ways in which individual political preferences are brought together and organized so that they can more effectively influence government.

Earlier, we stressed that politics came about because people of differing and sometimes conflicting interests and beliefs sought to live and work together. People sometimes can express their interests and beliefs through their votes and through other individual acts such as writing public officials. They also band together with others who share the same interests. Chapter 10, on interest groups, examines the organized political effort of various interests to achieve their goals. Interest groups are a more collective, more organized expression of interests than individually expressed opinions or votes. They are a smaller-scale, more specialized form of interest expression than the political parties, which seek to collect or cut across numerous interests.

Chapter 11 examines political parties in America. The American party system is one of the principal means we have of collecting, compromising, and integrating individual and group interests in the society so that they can work together to win

15

elections. We choose who will govern through the system of parties and elections. In this sense, parties serve as a transmission belt between all the individual and group politics discussed earlier in the book and the government, which will be discussed later. Because they must get many people together to wage electoral campaigns, and then must get even more voters together to win elections, parties are, like government itself, among the basic American mechanisms for channeling and consolidating conflict among various interests and beliefs and organizing people for action.

Government   Chapters 12, 13, 14, 15, and 16 examine the institutions of the national government. Chapter 12 is closely linked to Chapter 11 because it begins with a discussion of how members of Congress are elected and how Congress is organized. Chapter 13 shows how these factors produce legislation.

Chapter 14 is on the presidency. Within the government, the president faces in three directions. He must deal with Congress in the passage of new laws. He heads the federal bureaucracy which does the day-to-day work of the executive branch of government. He must be concerned with how the judiciary interprets the laws made by Congress and the actions of the executive branch, including his own actions. Thus, the chapter on the president occurs after those on Congress and before those on the bureaucracy and the federal courts.

In its examination of the administration of the federal government, Chapter 15 goes considerably beyond the civil servants in Washington. Today the business of the federal government is done not only in Washington, but in field offices scattered across the country, in state and local government agencies which administer many federal programs, and in private organizations which are paid to do all sorts of research, development, and administrative chores for the government. Chapter 16 on the judiciary is especially attentive to the courts' relations to the other parts of government described in Chapters 12, 13, 14, and 15.

Each part of government acts on all the others and, in turn, is acted on by them. No one can fully understand Congress until he has studied the presidency because the president is an important source of the legislation Congress considers. And no one can fully understand the presidency without studying Congress. A president who is not on friendly terms with Congress leads a very different political life from one who has strong support on Capitol Hill. Nor can we understand the president unless we understand his relationship to the vast federal bureaucracy. The bureaucracy, in turn, sits at the intersection between the power of the president, who is theoretically its boss, and Congress, which provides it with money and new programs. Nor can the Supreme Court be understood in isolation. The nature of the Court is fundamentally shaped by the president who nominates its members and the Senate which must confirm them. Yet this influence, too, runs in both directions. One of the basic jobs of the Supreme Court is to review the laws enacted by Congress as well as the decisions and actions of the president and the federal bureaucracy.

For this reason, some patience is required in reading Chapters 12 through 16.

It is not possible to say everything all at once. Yet until everything is said about the government, nothing is complete or even completely clear. Because the flow of change runs through many interconnected parts, it is necessary to grasp the whole pattern. But the beginner who does not look at one part at a time will become hopelessly confused. Thus, we take up the parts of government one at a time. But as we do so, we try from the beginning to stress the interconnections. When the student has finished these chapters, he or she should have a distinct feel for each of the parts of the government and some sense of their interactions.

Policymaking   The major purpose of Chapter 17, which is devoted to policymaking, is to assist the student in putting the parts of government back together again. This chapter describes features of the policymaking process that are found in all governmental institutions. It is concerned with how solutions are devised, the stages in making and implementing decisions, and different types of policy.

Evaluation   Chapter 18 is about political evaluation. It seeks to provide a new perspective on everything the reader has seen earlier in the book. The person who is absolutely sure that something is "totally" good or bad often is the person with superficial knowledge of the thing being evaluated. By the time readers reach Chapter 18, we hope they will know enough about American politics to make them hesitant to accept the easy slogans of the Right or of the Left. Chapter 18 does not offer the authors' own evaluations. It does point out various modes of arriving at political evaluations and the advantages and pitfalls of each. It is about asking political questions, and about how to answer them. But it does not *give* the answers. It provides what we hope is an appropriate nonconclusion to an introductory text, because political evaluation does not end with one book or one course.

the social
context
of american
politics

about to begin a detailed examination of the
ple come from. What do they do for a living?
major social strain the political developments
increase or decrease the number of

CHAPTER 2

American government must respond to the needs of a population that was 220 million in 1979 and increases by more than a million people each year.[1] Americans come from every part of the world. Within the country they are continually on the move, as they have been since the nation's founding. Occupations range from cowboy to astronaut; incomes go from virtually nothing to millions of dollars a year. With a huge, interdependent population, government acquires countless responsibilities and is exposed to innumerable demands. It must cope with conflicting opinions about taxes, air pollution, energy, poverty, national defense, abortion, and so on.

Such ethnic, social, and economic diversity has an enormous impact on politics. Of course, political conflict is not simply an extension of social differences. But these differences are major sources of political interests. They are the bases of conflicts and alliances, and they provide the resources for political influence. Rich and poor often have dissimilar interests and vote differently, as do people with different ethnic backgrounds and ways of making a living.

In this chapter we will examine the anatomy of American society: the distribution of income among various segments of the population; immigration, nationality group identification, race, and religion; the age structure of the population; how jobs are changing; what Americans think of social class; and where they live. We are especially interested in how these features affect both the nature of the political system and how that system operates.

WEALTH AND THE DISTRIBUTION OF INCOME

Compared to other large countries, the most striking thing about the United States has been its phenomenal wealth. American economic development was based on a huge, resource-rich, and almost unpopulated continent. When the first Europeans arrived, the area was sparsely peopled by Indians who had had little impact on the land or its resources. These native Americans were overcome by the technology, numbers, and organization of the newcomers.

The Atlantic Ocean permitted direct contact with Europe and therefore allowed the entry of European goods and settlers. But it was enough of a barrier to prevent Americans from being overwhelmed by Old World ways of thinking and doing things. Americans thus were able to form a distinct culture. The ocean barrier fostered democracy by making a large standing army unnecessary. Moreover, resources that might have been drained by military spending could be turned to economic growth. The abundance of two basic raw materials of the Industrial Revolution, coal and iron, also contributed to the growth of a uniquely wealthy nation. So did the ready availability of western lands for agricultural expansion. By the end of the nineteenth century, the United States led the world in **Gross National Product**

---

[1] This figure includes only legal residents. Anywhere from 6 to 12 million people are in the United States illegally. Unless otherwise indicated, the statistics used in this chapter are from the latest available edition of the annual *Statistical Abstract of the United States* (Washington, D.C.: Government Printing Office).

(GNP)— the total value of the goods and services produced in a country. We were also the wealthiest nation per capita. The United States continues to be the world's richest country by a vast margin. In the past few years, however, we have been exceeded in per capita income by Sweden, Switzerland, and a couple of tiny, oil-rich nations in the Middle East.

How is the country's wealth reflected at the individual family level? The most common measure is **median family income,** which was $16,009 in 1977. The median is the midpoint in a distribution, separating the top and bottom halves. Here we mean that in 1977, half of all American families had incomes of more than $16,009, and the other half had less than this amount. Median family income has been increasing about $1,000 a year, largely because of inflation.

Prosperity has risen dramatically since the Great Depression of the 1930s. And between 1950 and 1970, there was an 84 percent increase in **real income**— that is, in purchasing power, which takes inflation into account. Most Americans came to consider a steady increase in real income natural and inevitable. But in the 1970s inflation almost canceled rises in income; we have more money, but each dollar is worth less. As a result, the average American's buying power changed little in the past few years. Many people are distressed at the lack of economic advances. This reaction was an important reason for President Ford's defeat in 1976.

More political insights come from looking beyond median income to statistics on how income is distributed. Figure 2.1 shows this breakdown for 1977. Families earning over $20,000 a year comprised more than a third of all families. In contrast, 12 percent of all American families had incomes below the federally defined pover-

Figure 2.1
Distribution of Family Income in 1977

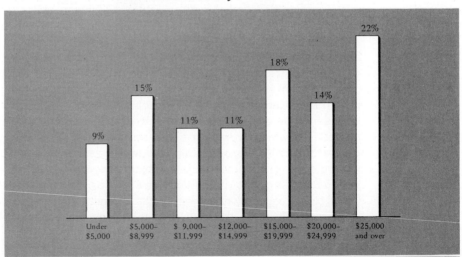

Source: U.S. Bureau of the Census, *Statistical Abstract of the United States 1978* (Washington, D.C.: Government Printing Office, 1978). p. 453.

ty level, an estimate of the budget necessary for the basic necessities of life.[2] These figures help us to understand an important aspect of the current American poverty problem. In the American past—and in most of the world still—the poor were "the masses." In modern America, prosperity for the majority means that the smaller proportion who are poor cannot rely only on their own voting power to influence the government. The poor have become a minority who lack the traditional political weapon of the underprivileged—numbers. More than ever, they need allies. They have some in middle-class liberals working through the sorts of public interest groups we will discuss in Chapter 10. They also benefit from direct interest-group activity by social categories with large numbers of poor people, such as blacks and the aged.

ETHNICITY AND RACE

National Origins   With the exception of less than a million American Indians, every American is descended from immigrants. Official records on immigration were first kept in 1820. Between then and the 1970 census, over 45 million people moved to the United States, about 80 percent of them from Europe. In addition, several million blacks were brought here forcibly as slaves, almost all before 1820. The peak of immigration was reached in the first decade of the twentieth century, when the population was swollen by about 9 million migrants, mostly from southern and eastern Europe.

During the first half-century of American nationhood, free Americans were mainly English-speaking Protestants. This sameness made it easy to conclude that the United States would be a "melting pot" in which people from any part of the world would lose their original identities and become Americans. In the 1840s, immigrants who were not Protestant and in many cases not English-speaking began to arrive. The idea that everyone would "melt" into a common whole soon began to prove false. Many of the newcomers were Irish Catholics escaping the potato famine in their homeland. Arriving just as America was beginning to industrialize, the unskilled Irish found plenty of work at manual jobs. They also encountered ruthless economic exploitation and religious bigotry. Failing to receive recognition as full-fledged "Americans," they found it emotionally rewarding to maintain their sense of Irish identity. They lived in Irish neighborhoods, attended Irish churches, and formed Irish social and civic associations. The same pattern was repeated with successive waves of immigrants from central, southern, and eastern Europe. The first generation usually was poor and uneducated. But even when their children went to school and attained some measure of prosperity, they continued to experience discrimination from Americans of English-speaking Protestant stock—and from the earlier immigrants. These second-generation Americans retained memories of their rejection, and passed them to their children. The consequence has been to maintain to this day a strong sense of nationality-group consciousness among

---

[2] In 1977 this figure was $6,191 for a nonfarm family of four. Like all income figures, this does not include noncash assistance, such as food stamps and medicare.

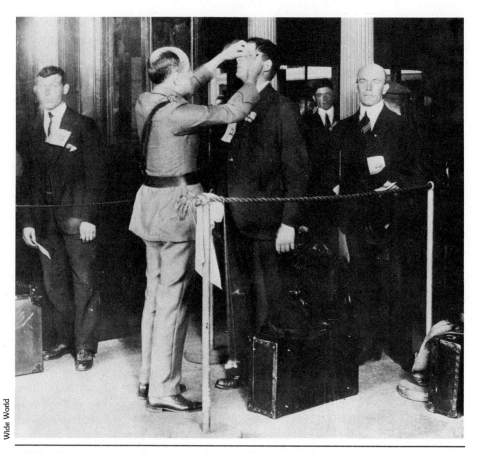

*Immigrants before World War I got their first view
of America on Ellis Island, New York City.
Here, new arrivals are lined up
for examination by physicians.*

many millions of Americans. To the degree that this consciousness is psychologically important to a group's members, providing them with a source of self-identification and a sense of belonging, national origins become a basis for what social psychologists call **reference groups.** We all belong to various reference groups. Depending on the context, we may think of ourselves as Americans, students, professors, radicals, conservatives, blacks, whites, and so on. Different reference groups are important in different contexts.

National origin reference groups have the most political impact once a group begins to become prosperous. Usually immigrants do not produce political leaders until they have developed a middle class. These leaders then symbolize the aspirations of the group and make group membership more politically relevant. Millions of nationality-group members may vote for candidates of "their own kind" in preference to other candidates, crossing party lines if necessary when an election causes them to think in terms of ethnic solidarity. And there are distinct tendencies for members of particular nationality groups to identify with one political party or another.

Partly in response to the great flood of immigration in the first decade of the twentieth century, in 1924 Congress passed the National Quota Act to restrict the flow. The new law created quotas that favored northern Europe, held down the number of southern and eastern Europeans who could settle here, and continued the virtual bar that had existed since the 1880s on immigration from Asia. The 1924 law did not restrict immigration from within the Western Hemisphere, however. Consequently, until the law was revised in 1965, most immigration was from Canada and Latin America. During the National Quota Act period, Canadian immigration was gradually dwarfed by that from Latin America. Special provisions temporarily relaxed the Quota Act in order to admit European refugees from the German and Italian dictatorships in the 1930s, people left homeless as a result of the dislocations of World War II, and refugees from Communist regimes. (About a million political refugees entered in the 30 years after World War II. Vietnamese fleeing their country's Communist regime added another 175,000 by the end of 1978.) The 1965 legislation eliminated restrictions against southern and eastern European immigration and the bar against immigration from Asian nations. But, partly in response to the rapidly growing Latin American immigration, restraints on Western Hemisphere immigration were introduced.

In all, there has been a continuous, if much moderated, flow of immigrants into the United States since 1924. In 1920, 28 percent of the population consisted of immigrants and their children; in 1970, it was 16 percent. The composition of the immigrant population has been affected by the changes in the regulations. It also has been affected by social and historical factors. There was, for example, very little immigration in the depression decade of the 1930s, when the United States could not employ many of its own citizens. Each recent decade has been quite different in its source of immigration. Of the 2.5 million immigrants in the 1950s, 59 percent were European, a third were from the Americas, and a mere 157,000 were from Asia. During the 1960s, there were 3.3 million immigrants, with Asians accounting for 445,000. Since 1970, more Asians than Europeans have come, and immigration from the Western and Eastern Hemispheres has been roughly equal.[3] The effect of these trends will be a gradual lessening of the historic European predominance in our ethnic composition and perhaps new bases of political coalition and conflict.

Nationality groups and other population categories such

Politicians traditionally include ethnic activities in their campaigning. Here, presidential nominee George McGovern tries his hand at bocce in an Italian neighborhood.

Wide World

[3] Hispanic migration is not fully reflected in immigration records because movement from Puerto Rico to the mainland United States is not classified as immigration, Puerto Rico being a part of the United States.

as young or old are not automatically politically influential in proportion to their numbers. Indeed, whether members of a nationality group even think of themselves that way is significant for political mobilization. Figure 2.2 shows the results of a special Census Bureau survey in 1973 asking people to report their national origins. About 26 million Americans identified themselves as being of British stock, 20.5 million had German origins, 12 million were Irish, 10 million Hispanic (including 6 million from Mexico and 1.5 million Puerto Ricans), 7 million Italian, and 3.6 million Polish.

These reports are not the same as politically significant ethnic consciousness. Few of those with German or British origins, for example, still think that this is a basis for political demands. On the other hand, small nationality groups can be influential if they have active leaders, devoted members, and enough political resources. For instance, in 1974 representatives of the small but active Greek-American community persuaded Congress to curtail aid to Turkey. (Turkey had invaded the ethnically divided Mediterranean island of Cyprus, siding with Cyprus's Turkish minority against its Greek majority.) In addition, politically relevant ethnicity does not stem only from national origins. The most politically important American ethnic group—the blacks—is not a nationality group; the great bulk of blacks are descendants of slaves transported from Africa long before that continent became divided into independent nations. Jews are a politically significant ethnic minority who im-

Figure 2.2
Americans' Reports of Their Ethnic Backgrounds (1973)

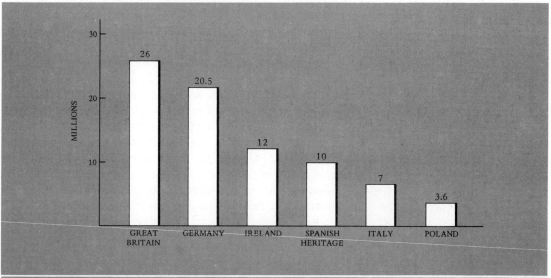

Source: Statistical Abstract of the United States 1978.

migrated from a number of nations. In short, groups are not important simply because they have identifiable national origins. It is reference groups that are potentially politically significant, whether or not they are also nationality groups.

Some Misconceptions about Nationality Groups. In recent years, European nationality groups have been "rediscovered," and there has been much speculation about their social and political characteristics. Perhaps the most common beliefs about ethnics are that they are predominantly blue-collar workers, always on the point of abandoning their traditional loyalty to the Democratic party, prejudiced against blacks, and belligerently patriotic in foreign policy. Sociologist Andrew M. Greeley has shown that these beliefs are *not* true.[4] They are no more than myths, although they are among the most prominent myths of our times. For example, European ethnics are *not* the core of the blue-collar working class. On the contrary, they are relatively prosperous. Of the three most numerous relatively unassimilated nationality groups, Irish Catholics are more likely than the average American to hold white-collar jobs, Italian-Americans are at about the national average in this respect, and Polish-Americans are only slightly below the average. All three are well above the national mean on income. The most prosperous ethnic groups in the country are Jews, Japanese-Americans, Irish Catholics, and "British Protestants." The least prosperous groups are Indians, blacks, people of Spanish heritage, and Irish Protestants.

Members of almost all European ethnic groups have made extraordinary progress in the last twenty years. If we look at those aged 60 or more, we see that Americans of Italian, Polish, and other Slavic ancestry are well below the national average in income and education. But members of the same ethnic groups below the age of 30 rank *above* the national averages in these categories. Greeley has also shown that, far from being "hard hats," Irish Catholics, Italians, and Poles were no more likely than Protestants to be hawks on the Vietnam war. And members of these groups are just as favorable as other groups to racial equality, generous welfare payments, the 18-year-old vote, conservation, and other liberal policies.

Black Americans   Blacks are now the largest self-conscious ethnic group in America: about one American in nine is black. Blacks have fared less well than any of the other ethnic groups we have discussed so far. They have less education, worse jobs, and lower incomes. The median income of black families was only $9,563 in 1977, a dismal contrast to the white median of $16,740. In 1977, 29 percent of all blacks were below the poverty line, compared to just 9 percent of whites. Virtually every statistic that can be mustered adds to the portrait of blacks as a major group that has not experienced the traditional rise from poverty to prosperity.

[4] Andrew M. Greeley, *Why Can't They Be More Like Us? America's White Ethnic Groups* (New York: Dutton, 1975).

Figure 2.3
Socioeconomic Characteristics of the White,
Black, and Spanish-Origin Population, 1975

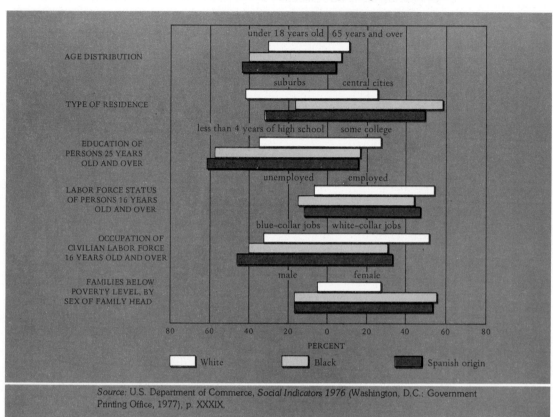

Source: U.S. Department of Commerce, *Social Indicators 1976* (Washington, D.C.: Government Printing Office, 1977), p. XXXIX.

A significant minority of blacks, however, are fairly propserous; 17 percent of black families had annual incomes of more than $20,000. The political implications of a growing black middle class are double-edged. On the one hand, this group provides most of the leaders who have contributed to the improvement in black social and economic conditions. But there is a less promising aspect to the circumstances of blacks in the late 1970s. Education and professional skills are increasingly important in an economy that has little need for unskilled labor. Thus, poor blacks are deprived of the opportunity available to ethnic groups that achieved economic mobility in the past—a chance to exploit their muscle power. Particularly for unemployed youths in central city ghettos, a stratum of economically successful brothers and sisters may be a source of frustration rather than satisfaction.

People of Spanish Origin   The Census Bureau uses the label "persons of Spanish origin"
to refer not just to the few Spaniards who immigrated to the
United States, but to all people from places where Spanish is the dominant language. The 6 percent of the population in this category consists mainly of Mexican-Americans, called Chicanos in many parts of the country (58 percent), and of Puerto Ricans (16 percent). Because of both immigration and high birth rates, Hispanic-Americans are now the country's fastest growing minority group and may well outnumber blacks by 1990. Although most people of Spanish origin were quite poor when they first came here, this is not true of the Cubans, most of whom were middle-class refugees from the Castro regime. As a category, Hispanic-Americans have somewhat higher incomes than blacks, but are well below whites. People from Cuba and Spain are considerably better off than Chicanos and most other Latin Americans, who in turn are much more prosperous than Puerto Ricans. Social and economic differences between whites, blacks, and Spanish-heritage people are summarized in Figure 2.3.

The various Spanish-origin groups also resemble blacks in the extent to which their self-consciousness and level of political organization have increased since the 1960s. But unlike blacks, they have not formed a single reference group. Nationali-

WHO THE CENSUS MISSES

Some kinds of people are difficult to count accurately — or to count at all: people with something to hide, those with no fixed residence, and those who live in places that census takers may find disagreeable or dangerous. The Census Bureau estimates that it missed about 5.3 million people in 1970, of whom perhaps 1.9 million were black.

Undoubtedly a big share of those who went uncounted were foreigners who had entered this country illegally. Such illegal aliens (or "undocumented workers," as they are sometimes delicately called) became increasingly numerous throughout the 1970s and now are a major social problem. For obvious reasons, it is difficult to get an accurate measure of their numbers. Estimates of the total range from 6 to 12 million and it is generally believed that the amount of illegal immigration is double that of legal immigration. In 1977, over a million foreigners in this country illegally were arrested and returned to their homelands.

Most of the illegal aliens are Mexicans, and most settle in a few big cities or do agricultural work near the border. Unless the federal government takes action far more drastic than now seems likely, the illegal aliens will be with us for a long time to come, although uncounted by the census and so not officially a part of the population. Hence they will be deprived of the benefits of local residence, such as food stamps and unemployment insurance. They will be exploited by employers, and they will take jobs away from Americans. Just how many jobs, however, is as uncertain as almost every aspect of this problem — except its growing dimensions.

ty seems to have prevented unity based on common language and many common cultural traditions. In the 1970s, federal equal opportunity regulations required institutions using federal funds (such as universities and government contractors) to employ people from stipulated minority groups. This led to many possibilities for conflict between Chicanos and Puerto Ricans about whether one or the other group might benefit more from "affirmative action." Moreover, there was no effective organization of other Latin American groups, with the exception of Cubans. And the latter are organized mainly with reference to their dislike of the present Cuban government. Fortunately for the cause of ethnic harmony, however, the greatest concentrations of different Spanish-origin groups are in different parts of the country. The Puerto Ricans live mostly in the cities of the Northeast; Cubans have settled largely in southern Florida; and Chicanos are most numerous in both rural and urban areas from California to Texas. These groups will probably best achieve national political influence through their individual impact on regional political officials.

RELIGION

Religion has often been a powerful source of political conflict. It still is today in places like Lebanon and Northern Ireland where religious conflict is a continuous source of bloodshed. In milder forms, disputes about religion, or between believers in different faiths, shape politics in many countries. Religious affiliation can combine with other group differences in ways that increase or diminish the chances of conflict. Social cleavages can coincide and thus reinforce a society's potential for basic disagreement: the poor can belong to one church and the rich to another; farmers can all be Protestants and workers all Catholics; and so on. Alternatively, religion can contribute to cross-cutting cleavages. That is, it can be a basis for self-identification that does not match other bases: farmers will be both Protestant and Catholic, and so will workers. Thus, people who are divided on economic matters will be united on issues involving religion — abortion and private schools, for example.

The Bureau of the Census has long been barred from asking people about their religious affiliation. Fortunately, an annual survey conducted by the American Institute of Public Opinion (the Gallup Poll) gives us an excellent portrait of American religious characteristics.[5] Sixty percent of Americans call themselves Protestants, 28 percent are Catholics, 2 percent are Jews, and the remaining 10 percent are evenly divided between smaller denominations and no religious preference. About 15 percent of Protestants and 4 percent of Catholics are nonwhites.

The first settlers were almost all Protestant. Later immigrants were more likely to be Catholics and Jews. We can see the historic pattern of immigrant settlement in the present geographic distribution of people according to religion. Thirty-nine percent of American Catholics and 65 percent of Jews, but only 20 percent of Protestants, live in the Northeast. The Midwest and especially the South are the most

---

[5] Gallup Opinion Index, *Religion in America, 1977–78*.

TWO MINORITIES

The condition of two small minorities—American Indians and Asian-Americans—illustrates the complexities of the American social mosaic.

American Indians, or Native Americans as some have recently begun to call them, numbered 792,730 in 1970, three times as many as in 1900, and not far short of the total population before Columbus. Indians are the poorest of the poor in America: They earn slightly less than blacks and have considerably lower levels of education and life expectancy. Their poverty reflects the poor quality of the reservation land on which nearly a third still live, inferior schools, racial discrimination, and the vast gap between their cultures and that of white America. Government policy has been consistent only in its inconsistency. The land grabbing of frontier days was followed by neglect and then by a baffled alternation between encouraging Indians to assimilate and encouraging them to remain culturally isolated. As a result, their future is clouded and uncertain.

Asians, once excluded by racist immigration bars, now come in numbers equal to those of Europeans. Between 1960 and 1970, their numbers increased 55 percent to 1.4 million. People from China and Japan at one time were subject to a variety of discriminatory laws; in California, for example, they could not own land. The forced removal of 110,000 Americans of Japanese origin from the West Coast during World War II was a shocking act of prejudice. Since that time there has been an end to government policies against Asian-Americans and a drastic lessening of private discrimination. Today Americans of Chinese, Japanese, and Filipino backgrounds have twice as many college graduates per capita as the white population, median family incomes over $1,000 higher, and an apparently secure and prosperous future.

Protestant regions. Catholics and Jews are also likelier to live in big cities. Forty-three percent of Catholics and 68 percent of Jews are in cities with more than half a million residents, compared to only 23 percent of Protestants.

Protestants and Catholics differed greatly in social status during the nineteenth and early twentieth centuries. Today these groups provide perfect examples of cross-cutting cleavages, since they are almost identical with respect to income, occupation, and education. We can thus be confident that political differences among them do not reflect underlying economic cleavages. Jews in particular have made remarkable economic and educational strides in the New World. Forty-three percent of all Jews make more than $20,000 a year, and 58 percent have graduated from college. Here is an important clue to their ability to exercise political influence beyond their numbers, notably in maintaining American support for Israel. In addition, we will see that Jews are far likelier to be liberals than are other Americans of comparable economic achievement, and so are a major source of financial support for liberal causes and candidates.

Both ends of the adult life cycle—youth and age—are of particular interest to observers of American politics. From the 1950s through the end of the 1960s, the focus was on "the youth generation." In the 1950s, the emphasis was on their political passivity. During the Kennedy years, it was the reforming idealism stimulated by programs such as the Peace Corps. In the late 1960s, student protest against the Vietnam war and extensive publicity given "new life styles" (rejection of economic achievement, use of drugs, more permissive views about sex roles and sexual activity) made young people the object of still more attention. During this last period it was sometimes taken for granted that there was a single bloc of Americans who could accurately be thought of as *the* young and who were the potential vanguard of revolutionary change.

Behind these many images there was at least one firm reality: The middle years of this century had witnessed a dramatic increase in the number and proportion of young people. During the Depression, birth rates were low. The return of World War II veterans in 1945 and the accompanying national prosperity brought the postwar baby boom. The postwar babies were the young people who crowded first primary and secondary schools and then colleges in the 1950s and 1960s. But the children of the baby boom had little in common other than age; their political opinions were not much different from those of their elders. As Figure 2.4 shows, the largest single chunk of the population consists of people who in 1977 were be-

Figure 2.4
Age Distribution of the Adult Population
in 1977

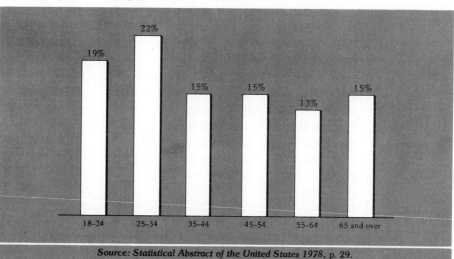

Source: Statistical Abstract of the United States 1978, p. 29.

tween 25 and 34 years old. Within a few years, the "youth generation" will have become the "middle-aged generation." The second largest age group is the children of the 1950s, those who were 18 to 24 in 1977. Together, these two young cohorts amount to 41 percent of the adult population. The baby boom, however, is over. Birth rates have declined steadily since 1965. The enormous proportion of young people is a passing phenomenon. Now the population is becoming older.

People over 64 accounted for 15 percent of the adult population in 1977. That share will grow as the baby boom generation passes through the life cycle and life expectancy rises. Because women outlive men by about eight years, they outnumber men in the over-64 category by a ratio of three to two. In contrast to young people, who do not have clear, age-related interests, the elderly as a group have certain political goals, including higher social security benefits, old-age tax exemptions, and subsidized medical care. To a much greater degree than younger generations, old people have achieved a good deal of group consciousness. And like so many other newly-aware social groups, the old are gaining political aggressiveness and skill. They also have invaluable allies in their demands on government, for their children share their desires for public policies that will provide more financial aid at the end of careers. The political power of old people is reflected in the fact that they received over 30 percent of the entire 1979 federal budget. In ten years, the proportion of the elderly with incomes below the poverty level fell from 28 to 14 percent.[6] The growth in federal benefits to old people has far outdistanced their increased numbers.

OCCUPATION

In 1900, about three-quarters of the people in the labor force worked with their hands; they were farmers, miners, factory workers, and so forth. By 1978, the occupational makeup of the nation had been transformed, as Figure 2.5 shows. Over half the jobholders were in white-collar occupations. These were about evenly divided into lower-status clerical and sales jobs, and the high-status managerial and professional positions (doctors, lawyers, and the like). A mere third of Americans were in blue-collar jobs, ranging from foremen and artisans to factory workers and unskilled laborers. Tilling the soil has become the work of less than 3 percent of the people, although the United States is still the world's leading exporter of farm products. The final 14 percent were in service occupations — bus drivers, police officers, and so on. These figures show why the United States is sometimes called a postindustrial society. Less than two-fifths of the labor force actually produce anything; the rest provide services of one kind or another.

People in the upper middle class, which comprises about a quarter of the population, are far from a unified "business class." More than half of them are not business people at all, but professionals. These do not mostly think of them-

---

[6] Robert J. Samuelson, "Busting the U.S. Budget — The Costs of an Aging America," *National Journal*, February 18, 1978, pp. 256–60.

Figure 2.5

Occupations of Employed People in 1978

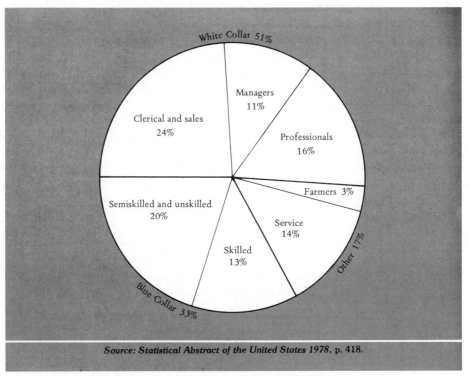

Source: Statistical Abstract of the United States 1978, p. 418.

selves as being "in business," but as lawyers, engineers, professors, or what have you. Many are self-employed, and many others identify more with their profession than their employer. Millions work for or are dependent on the government for financial support through grants to schools, nonprofit corporations, research projects, and the like. The biggest single "industry" in America is education. There were almost 3.3 million classroom teachers in 1978, and another 300,000 educational administrators and principals.[7]

The other half of those with white-collar jobs are salespeople or clerks who often make less money than many who work with their hands. Nevertheless, such people's outlook on political questions is usually different from that of manual workers. Politically, they tend more to resemble the upper middle class. "Workers" in the traditional blue-collar meaning of the term are a distinct minority in the United States and will become an increasingly smaller one in the future. These changes in the occupational structure explain why political theories (like Marxism) that assign a special historical role to the "working class" are not very relevant to the United States.

[7] *Higher Education and National Affairs,* September 1, 1978, p. 1.

Another major trend in employment is the enormous expansion in the number of public employees. Nearly one American in six works for a government agency of some sort, and in the last fifteen years the number of government employees has risen by nearly 6 million. This increase, however, occurred almost entirely at the state and local levels; the number of civilian federal employees has held fairly steady at about 2.8 million. The size of the armed services rises and falls with international events and American reactions to them. Currently, the United States has about 2 million men and women in uniform, the lowest level since 1950, and down from the Vietnam war peak of over 3.5 million.

The number of public employees is likely to grow faster than the labor force as a whole. In many places, public employee unions are successful advocates for higher salaries and fringe benefits. Thus, at all levels of government budgets have increased to pay for this growing and influential population of public servants (Figure 2.6). Pay for government jobs generally compares favorably with

Figure 2.6
The Growth in Public Employment,
1960–1977

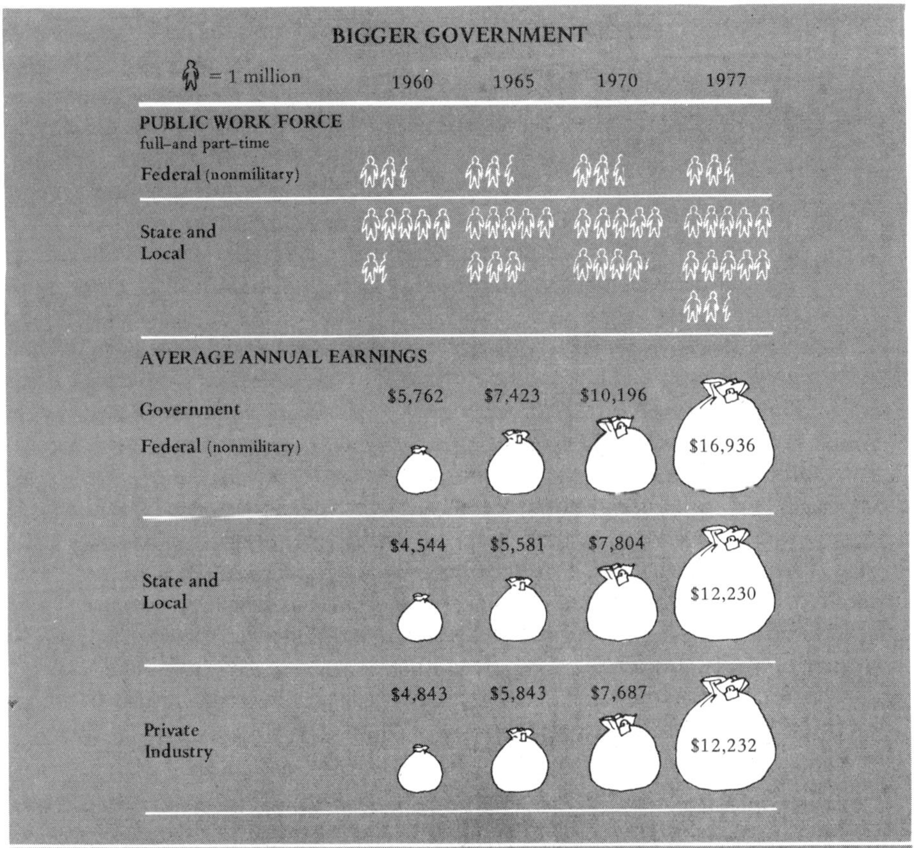

BIGGER GOVERNMENT

= 1 million

	1960	1965	1970	1977
PUBLIC WORK FORCE full–and part–time				
Federal (nonmilitary)				
State and Local				

AVERAGE ANNUAL EARNINGS

	1960	1965	1970	1977
Government Federal (nonmilitary)	$5,762	$7,423	$10,196	$16,936
State and Local	$4,544	$5,581	$7,804	$12,230
Private Industry	$4,843	$5,843	$7,687	$12,232

Source: Statistical Abstract of the United States 1978.

corresponding private employment except at the top levels, where the private sector is much more generous. Few public officials earn more than $60,000 a year, but salaries far above this level are commonplace in the higher reaches of private employment.

Also of political importance is the growing proportion of women in the workforce. In 1960, 37 percent of women worked; in 1977, it was 48 percent. Women are concentrated in clerical and sales jobs, and if they work at similar tasks, often are paid less than men. Resentment at such differences helped account for such movements as the drive to pass the Equal Rights Amendment to the Constitution.

About a quarter of the labor force belong to labor unions. Union membership is not keeping pace with the growth in population. Nearly 30 percent of nonagricultural workers were unionized in 1964, compared to 28 percent in 1970 and 26 percent in 1974, the most recent year for which figures are available. The kinds of jobs traditionally likely to be unionized — the blue-collar jobs — are a shrinking share of the economy. Organization of teachers and government employees advanced in the 1970s, but in general the signs seem to be for a declining unionized segment of the workforce. The trend could have momentous long-run consequences, since unions are a major force in American politics.

SOCIAL CLASS

If we look at the distribution of occupations in terms of the class structure of American society, we find the following. The upper class and the upper middle class, consisting of professionals, executives, and administrators, make up 27 percent of the working population. The lower middle class, consisting of sales and clerical workers, accounts for 24 percent. And the working class, including foremen, craftsmen, factory workers, and service workers, weighs in with 47 percent.[8] Looked at in this way, social classes are **categorical groups.** That is, they are groups by virtue of the fact that the people in them share one or more characteristics. In this case, however, the characteristics are exceptionally vague. They include such factors as the status or prestige attached to an occupation as well as the income it produces. For many occupations, high status tends to coincide with high income, and vice versa. But there are exceptions. For example, teachers are classified as middle-class professionals despite the fact that most of them earn less than skilled workers. Similarly, a physician with a general practice in a poor community might have a very high

---

[8] Farmers are a thorny problem for this sort of classification because they include millionaire ranchers and impoverished sharecroppers.

status but a modest income. Because of these exceptions, we cannot really say that categorical groups like this constitute bases for political action.

Most modern class theorists argue that what is important is not the category to which people belong, but how they identify themselves. It is not their class but their **class consciousness** that matters. Would a plumber vote on the basis of his "objective" position in the working class or on the basis of an income of $25,000 a year? What is more important to a typist, a $9,000 income or a white-collar job? We would have to know whether the plumber and the typist identified primarily with their incomes or with the ways they earned them. On some issues, they might identify one way and on other occasions they might feel that their interests were represented by the opposite identification.

It might be more useful to regard social class as a reference group than as a categorical group. This is another way of asking to what extent Americans in various occupations think of their jobs as the basis for identification with a social class. In some societies, there is a great deal of class consciousness. People in blue-collar jobs and their families consider themselves members of the working class; white-collar employment brings with it a sense of middle-class membership. Americans traditionally have not thought of themselves in these terms. Directly confronted with a question about whether they think of themselves as belonging to one social class or the other, about a third answer that they do not think of themselves in these terms at all. The remainder sort themselves fairly evenly into "middle class" and "working class." Most of those who deny a class identity will, when pressed by an interviewer, say that one or the other term best describes them.

How deeply felt are these social class identifications? Public opinion surveys have found many Americans expressing puzzlement about the very language of social class. Moreover, many people do not identify themselves with the class that is "correct" for their occupation. A third of people with white-collar jobs, for example, call themselves "working class." And roughly the same proportion of blue-collar workers and their families describe themselves as middle class.[9] It is not surprising, therefore, that most Americans do not consider social class a basis for differences in political beliefs. In a 1972 survey (Table 2.1), 40 percent of the people took the view that class makes no difference. Only 7 percent thought that the two classes always agreed and less than 2 percent thought that they were consistently in disagreement.

In short, we can speak of differing levels of income, education, and social prominence in the United States. These levels are real and they have real political consequences. But we cannot easily lump them into two or three neat, distinct, and definite classes whose identity determines political behavior and attitudes. In this sense, there is no clear class structure or class conflict in the United States, although

---

[9] These figures on social class consciousness are from the 1976 National Election Study conducted by the Center for Political Studies of the University of Michigan. Throughout this book we use findings based on our analyses of data from Michigan election studies, made available by the Inter-University Consortium for Political and Social Research. In no instance is the Consortium or the Center for Political Studies responsible for our analyses or interpretations.

Table 2.1

**Do Workingmen and the Middle Class Usually
Agree or Disagree on Important Issues?**

RESPONSE	PERCENTAGE
Always agree	7%
Usually agree	11
Sometimes agree	15
Neither agree nor disagree	40
Sometimes disagree	12
Usually disagree	3
Always disagree	2
Don't know	11
	101%

Source: Computed by the authors from data from the 1972 National
Election Study of the University of Michigan Center for Political Studies.

there is a great deal of political, social, and economic inequality, as well as conflict
over that inequality.

WHERE DO AMERICANS LIVE?

The fifty American states differ so greatly in population that some of them are larger
than most of the countries represented in the United Nations and others have fewer
residents than middle-sized cities. Over half of all Americans live in nine states. In
contrast, the thirteen states with the smallest populations account for only 4 percent. Nearly three-quarters of all Americans live in 272 Standard Metropolitan
Statistical Areas (SMSA) defined by the Census Bureau as a central city and its
surrounding suburbs. About 40 percent live in SMSAs with populations of more
than a million. But a great many others live in smaller SMSAs like Modesto, California, or Lima, Ohio, that do not represent the same sort of living experience as New
York or Chicago.

Within SMSAs, about four people live in suburbs for every three in central cities. The older central cities are losing population and becoming increasingly poor
and black; fourteen of the country's twenty largest cities lost population between
1970 and 1975. Growth has occurred in the suburbs.[10] More prosperous people,

---

[10] Another trend in population movement is much newer: many small towns and rural areas are
growing. By 1974, fully a quarter of all SMSAs were losing population. This does not mean a return to farming, but a search for more relaxed life styles by people fleeing the unpleasantness of
urban life and able to exploit the decentralization of many forms of work. It is too early to know
whether this is a passing fad or a significant new development. See William Alonso, "Metropolis
Without Growth," *The Public Interest,* fall 1978, pp. 68–86.

The movement of white Americans to the suburbs has left many of the nation's central cities with increasingly nonwhite populations.

along with businesses, have moved to the suburbs. Much of metropolitan area life is now located outside city centers. The stores that once brought customers downtown are moving to shopping centers. Postindustrial businesses—engineering and research organizations using computer technology or electronics, light manufacturing plants, and investment firms—now locate in the suburbs. Even major corporate headquarters are deserting big cities for their outskirts. Today suburban shopping centers offer the same lure to campaigning politicians that once was provided by the squares of central cities.

Between 1960 and 1970, central cities grew by only 5.9 million, whereas their suburbs grew by 16.6 million. Between the 1960 and 1970 censuses, the proportion of blacks in central city populations grew most in central cities in the East and the Midwest. The black population of Newark increased from 34 to 54 percent; that of Detroit, from 29 to 44 percent; and that of Cleveland from 29 to 38 percent. The political rewards to blacks have not been slow in coming. Atlanta, Cleveland, Detroit, Los Angeles, Newark, New Orleans, and Oakland all elected black mayors in the 1970s and most sent black representatives to Congress as well.

What is the impact of population shifts on politics? At first glance, it might seem to be slight. Most people who move to the suburbs do not change their political outlook along with their address. A person from a small town tends to remain a Republican when moving to the city; a central city Democrat keeps the same party after a move to the Republican suburbs. But these population shifts do have another kind of political effect. As the nation's cities are drained of much of their white middle-class population, they also lose much of their Republican voting strength and become Democratic strongholds. This has increased the number of safe Democratic seats in the House of Representatives, and these new safe seats represent crowded urban neighborhoods rather than rural southern backwaters. The representatives with the most seniority will increasingly be liberals representing working-class constituencies, whether black or white. This is a marked change from the recent past, when the overwhelming bulk of safe seats tended to be in placid, conservative rural areas. Thus, one consequence of suburban growth is to enhance the power of liberal Democrats in Congress and to reduce the power of conservative southerners. Concurrent social and economic changes in the South are hastening this process by affecting the other side of the equation. Republicans are now being elected in what used to be called the "solid South," reducing the number of conservative southern Democrats from "safe" districts who can easily build up seniority.

THE MAKEUP OF THE AMERICAN PEOPLE: BASES OF FACTION

Many Americans object to group analyses of political behavior. They consider it alien to their way of thinking or even "Marxist" to think of politics in terms of groups rather than individuals. In fact, such analyses have been part of our political tradition since before the adoption of the Constitution. The ways in which groups affect politics were a major consideration to the Founding Fathers who designed our governmental structure. Groups as a source of political behavior are lucidly discussed in *The Federalist Papers,* a collection of essays written to persuade Americans to adopt the Constitution.[11] Describing groups that seek to influence government as "factions," James Madison in *Federalist 10* observed that the "diversity of the faculties" (that is, personal qualities) of humans was the basic cause of factions. The Founding Fathers were particularly attuned to the political effects of economic differences. *Federalist 10* goes on to say that

> The most common and durable source of factions has been the various and unequal distribution of property. Those who hold and those who are without property have ever formed distinct interests in society. Those who are creditors, and those who are debtors, fall under a like discrimination. A landed interest, a manufacturing interest, with many lesser interests, grow up of necessity in civilized nations, and divide them into different classes, actuated by different sentiments and views.

In contemporary America social differences cross in many overlapping ways and do not always translate into political differences. Madison recognized the existence of noneconomic divisions. He also realized that what we today call different ideologies ("a zeal for different opinions") affected political divisions, as did attachments to different political leaders. The modern social structure of the United States makes economic differences between "haves" and "have-nots" less likely to be *the* major source of faction than the Founding Fathers expected. American politics is a vehicle for expressing and satisfying a wide range of unevenly distributed human needs and desires.

In a nation of such exceptional size and diversity, there are many kinds of needs and desires and therefore many factions. There are also, of course, some common interests that tend to unite most of the nation and to consolidate particular groups. All the unemployed, for example, have unemployment in common. All blacks and all poor people have blackness or poverty in common. But the unemployed tuna fisherman may want something different from what the unem-

[11] There are many editions of *The Federalist Papers.* A particularly useful version is the paperback edited by Clinton Rossiter and published by the New American Library (New York: 1961).

"How would you like me to answer that question? As a member of my ethnic group, educational class, income group, or religious category?"

Drawing by Dana Fradon;
© 1969 The New Yorker Magazine, Inc.

ployed steelworker wants. The fisherman might be hoping for relaxation of the laws protecting porpoises, while the steelworker may want to restrict the importation of foreign steel. Similarly, although all nonwhites may feel themselves to be the victims of discrimination, this does not necessarily mean that blacks, Chicanos, and American Indians want the same things or would be happy if treated the same way by government. Nor do all the poor view all issues the same way, despite the fact that they have many interests in common. The working poor may seek a higher minimum wage, but that means little to the unemployed poor.

We should not be surprised if the American political system does a better job of serving some needs than others. Nor should it startle us that the politics of such a diverse society is composed of countless different parts interacting in countless different ways. Rather, we should expect that any two parts may interact differently with one another at different times, depending upon what needs and desires come to the fore at a given moment. The following chapters introduce a great number of political people, processes, and institutions that act in a variety of ways to meet the diverse demands of thousands of factions. At the same time, they provide some insight into the common aspirations of the American people as a whole. Precisely because of the diversity of American life, we can rarely offer a clear, simple rule or law of politics that specifies exactly how any part of the political process will work. A tolerance for complexity is necessary if we are to learn about American politics.

SUMMARY Part of a nation's politics is governed by that nation's social context: the size and composition of the population; the amount and distribution of wealth and physical resources; the class structure; whether the population is urban or rural; whether living patterns are shifting or stable. The United States, examined in these terms, is a large, wealthy, and heterogeneous society in which social and economic differences overlap in many different ways. Clear and unchanging lines of division, such as those between the "haves" and "have nots," are seldom important politically. Rather, there is a wide range of unevenly distributed needs and desires, and therefore a wide range of shifting alliances and conflicts. Common interests will unite people for a particular purpose, but any given person or group may be connected to and involved in any number of other groups of different composition at the same time. The result of these cross-cutting divisions is a politics as shifting and complex as the nation's population.

the constitutional context of american politics

CHAPTER 3

THE IDEAS BEHIND THE CONSTITUTION

In one sense, the Constitution is interesting because it records the political ideas of a particular time and the concerns that stamped the character of a new nation. One of these was the idea that a constitution placed limits on government.

From England, the American colonists had imported the liberal philosophy of John Locke, which taught that government was essentially the result of a contract freely entered into by individual citizens. The Constitution was and is viewed as a contract between the people and their government. It specifies what powers the government shall have and what limits are placed on those powers. When we say an act of government is unconstitutional, we say it is legally null and void, because anything the government does that violates its contract has no legal force.

The philosophy of Locke and the other English liberals also drew on the idea of **natural law.** Since Roman times, philosophers had argued that there was a "higher law" than human law. This higher law, which ultimately derived from God, was inherent in nature. Human beings could understand it through the exercise of their reason. According to this tradition, any human law that violated the natural law was not law at all. Americans have always viewed the Constitution as a kind of higher law. An unconstitutional law violates the contract of government and also violates this higher law.

A third English heritage behind our Constitution is the tradition of **common law.** The common law was a mass of court decisions, old statutes, legal maxims, and lawyers' lore passed on from generation to generation. By the seventeenth century, most people believed that the common law embodied the collective, traditional wisdom — the "right reason" — of the English people. Indeed, many saw it as a kind of higher law against which new government actions should be measured. Most Americans came to see the Constitution as our equivalent of the common law, embodying the wisdom and right reason of our people. Here again it follows that a law which violates the Constitution is not a law at all — this time because it runs against the collective wisdom of Americans.

All three conceptions of the Constitution — contract, natural law, and common law — came together to give us two overriding ideas. First, *the Constitution is higher law.*[1] Whenever there is a conflict between the Constitution and a law passed by Congress or another government, the new law must be wrong and the Constitution must be right. Second, *the Constitution is based on reason,* so that any government act which is unreasonable must be unconstitutional.

These powerful traditions behind the American Constitution make it more than a document written at a particular moment by particular men. It is a symbol or code word for whatever our current ideas are about what government ought and ought not do, about what is or is not reasonable public policy. It is in this sense that we speak of "the living Constitution." For example, Americans do not find it peculiar to debate the constitutionality of the government's licensing television stations, although the men who wrote the Constitution could not have imagined television.

---

[1] Edward S. Corwin, *The Higher Law Backgrounds of the Constitution* (Ithaca: Cornell University Press, 1956).

The British speak of their constitution even though they have no specific written document like ours. By "constitution," the British simply mean their basic arrangements and procedures of government. In many ways, the constitution of American government does not square with what is described in the written constitution. For example, two fundamental features of our politics—parties and the bureaucracy—are not mentioned in the written document (parties will be discussed in Chapter 11 and the bureaucracy in Chapter 15). Nor does the document itself mention the Supreme Court's power to declare laws unconstitutional, which is discussed in Chapter 16. Even more important, it does not precisely define the relation of president to Congress, discussed in Chapters 13 and 14. Indeed, throughout our history the balance of power between Congress and president has shifted back and forth. Each change in this balance has been greeted by critics who denounced it as "unconstitutional." But who can say which of the many balances is the truly constitutional one? Was President Jefferson behaving constitutionally when he dominated the House of Representatives? Was Congress acting constitutionally when it threatened President Andrew Johnson with impeachment because he did not want to treat the South harshly after the Civil War?

Our written Constitution is not and never has been a detailed and specific blueprint for government. And life has grown far more complex in the centuries since it was written, so there are bound to be differences between the written and the living constitutions. How can these differences be resolved? How can we tell whether an act of government is constitutional or unconstitutional? One of the ways for dealing with such questions is to try to find out what those who drew it up intended to do. By analyzing their ideas about government, we can make some educated guesses about how they would have looked at the issues that arise today. In this way, we can keep our contemporary interpretations more or less consistent with the principles upon which the nation was founded.

THE INTENT OF THE FRAMERS

What do we know about the intent of those who wrote the Constitution? The men who met in Philadelphia in 1789 were representatives of the wealthier and better educated segments of colonial society. For a number of reasons, they were dissatisfied with the weak central government established by the Articles of Confederation and headed by the Continental Congress. First, the Confederation government did not have sufficient power to prevent a state from blocking the flow of business across state lines and preventing the growth of a national economy. Second, a confederation of separate states could not establish a single, firmly backed national currency. A sound dollar, acceptable everywhere, was a key to the expansion of interstate and international trade. And third, the confederation could not speak and act with unity in international affairs.

Moreover, several of the state governments were subject to strong pressure, perhaps even control, by small farmers who were heavily in debt and wanted new laws favoring debtors over creditors. A national government would be far less likely to come under the control of these local interests. A relatively strong central govern-

We the People

Article I

ment also might help ensure that the big states, like Massachusetts and Virginia, did not dominate the smaller ones. Above all, a stronger central government might ensure that the political experiment begun by the Revolution would succeed. Without it, the new nation might disintegrate in the squabbling of thirteen states.

There was substantial agreement among the Framers on a moderately strong central government. But most of them were loyal to their states as well as to the ideas of Locke and other liberals. They wanted a national government strong enough to ensure international security, national economic and political development, and the security of traditional property rights. But they also wanted to create a government that would not be able to tyrannize its citizens. Political thinkers from

DOES THE CONSTITUTION ENFORCE ITSELF?

Often we assume that if something is unconstitutional, somebody will put a stop to it. But will they? Article I, Section 6 provides that "no person holding any office under the United States shall be a member of either House during his continuance in office." A number of members of the House of Representatives and Senate hold commissions in the Army, Navy, and Air Force reserves. To be an officer in the armed forces is clearly to hold office under the United States. A group of Vietnam war protesters brought suit that these members of Congress had violated the Constitution. The Supreme Court refused to decide the case because it found that the protesters had not been personally injured by the alleged violation of the Constitution. (Normally, one may not sue someone else unless he or she has been injured.) The members of Congress stayed in Congress *and* kept their commissions. Even if the Supreme Court refused to act, couldn't Congress or the president have acted? Yes. Congress could have expelled these members. The president could have taken steps to terminate their commissions. But Congress and the president did not do these things, apparently because they viewed what these members of Congress were doing as a patriotic act only technically in violation of the Constitution.

Locke all the way back to the ancient Greek philosopher Aristotle had preached mixed government as a solution to this problem. A mixed government was one in which power was divided among a number of governing institutions. It was also one in which both the masses of people and the wealthier and better educated had some say. One branch of government would check the others and prevent them from abusing their powers. One segment of the population would balance the other to keep the interests of one group from dominating. The Framers embodied these ideas in the Constitution, but they were not content with divided powers as the sole guarantee against tyrannical government. They also sought to impose specific limitations on the powers of that mixed government.[2]

This pattern of granting limited powers to a mixed government is reflected in the very structure of the Constitution. Articles, I, II, and III establish the basic framework of government. They divide it into three parts: the Congress (Article I), the executive (Article II), and the courts (Article III).[3] Let us look at each of these in turn.

---

[2] Much material on the convention, as well as other information on the background of the Constitution, is summarized in Broadus Mitchell and Louise Pearson Mitchell, *A Biography of the Constitution of the United States* (New York: Oxford University Press, 1961). One of the most important collections of original documents relating to the Constitution is Max Farrand, ed., *The Records of the Federal Convention of 1787,* 4 vols. (New Haven: Yale University Press, 1911).

[3] An extremely valuable guide to reading the Constitution is Edward S. Corwin, ed., *The Constitution of the United States of America: Analysis and Interpretation* (Washington, D.C.: Government Printing Office, 1953). See also the latest edition of *The Constitution and What It Means Today* (Princeton: Princeton University Press, 1954), originally written by Corwin and periodically brought up to date by other authors.

ARTICLE I: THE LEGISLATIVE POWER

The Capitol Building went through several designs before it was completed in the form familiar to most Americans. Construction of the Capitol began in 1793.

The Framers were more concerned about the legislature than the other two branches because they felt it had the most potential for uncontrolled expansion. Thus, they not only provided for a division of power among the three branches, but also divided the legislative branch into two parts, the House of Representatives and the Senate. Each part was supposed to check the other. A bill could become a law only with the assent of both. The House of Representatives was to be the "popular" wing of the legislature, directly elected by the people and representing their interests. The House alone was to have the power to initiate *revenue* (tax) bills. Such bills would also have to be passed by the Senate after they were passed by the House, and the Senate was allowed to amend them. This special role for the House with regard to money was based on British tradition. In England, the principal control that the people had over the Crown was the ability of the House of Commons to withhold new taxes needed by the king until he had responded to their complaints.

The very name of the Senate suggests age and its corollary, wisdom. The senate of the ancient Roman Republic was to be a body of wise elders. The Framers intended the Senate of the United States of America to be a mature, rather aristocratic check on the popular enthusiasms of the House. The number of House seats assigned to each state is decided by population, so that the more populous states have larger delegations. But in the Senate all states are equal. Each has two senators. House members had to be at least 25 years old, but the minimum age for senators was set at 30. (Both minimum ages may seem young today, but given the lower life expectancies in colonial America and the fact that revolutionary governments are usually staffed by young men, 30 seemed old at the time.) The House was to be elected every two years, so that it would reflect the opinion of the moment, but senators were to have six-year terms. One-third of their number was to be elected every two years. This arrangement of staggered terms meant that at most only a third of the Senate could be turned out at any one time. This was further insurance against the Senate's yielding to sudden bursts of popular sentiment. Most important, senators were not to be chosen directly by the people, as were members of the House. Instead, they were elected by the state legislatures, an arrangement that remained in effect until 1913. Then ratification of the Seventeenth Amendment provided for direct popular election of senators.

Representative Democracy

The Framers believed that representation, as opposed to direct rule by the mass of people, was itself a device for mixing aristocratic with popular government. They were confident that the people would elect the most responsible, the most educated, the most qualified among them. Representative government would place the actual power of day-to-day governing in the hands of the better sort. The name "House of Representatives" thus had a nondemocratic connotation that we tend to forget today. Indeed, one of the basic motives for locating the national capital far from where most citizens lived was that such a government required representatives. It could not be run like town meetings or local assemblies of the people. This nondemocratic strain in the thinking of the Framers was further emphasized by the special powers of the Senate. It was not only given an equal share in lawmaking with the House, but also was assigned special responsibilities: to advise on and consent to major matters of executive government, including the appointment of cabinet members, Supreme Court justices, and other high officers, and the approval of treaties with foreign powers. The part of the legislature least dependent on changing public opinion was to be the one with a special vote in major decisions affecting the nation and its future.

The Independence of Congress

Learning from the English struggle to defend Parliament from the interference of the king, Americans gave Congress power to regulate its own elections, make its own internal rules, elect its own officers, and set the pay of its members.[4] Members of both houses were also given special protection from arrest, libel suits, and other forms of harassment. They were forbidden to hold executive office while in Congress or even to resign in order to accept an executive office that had been created or whose salary had been increased while they were in Congress. These measures were intended to maintain a free and independent legislature not subject to either threat or bribery by the executive. But these provisions also prevented the evolution of the sort of Parliament-cabinet government that was developing in England at the same time. The English form of government is based on the fact that members of the cabinet (that is, the executive branch of government) are simultaneously members of the legislative branch.

The Powers of Congress

The core of Article I of the Constitution is to be found in Section 8, which specifies the powers of Congress. It begins by enumerating a series of taxing, spending, borrowing, commerce, bankruptcy, monetary, postal, patent, and copyright powers designed to allow the new government to encourage a prosperous national economy. Then comes a series of law enforcement and war powers designed to make the new government strong enough to ensure national security against foreign powers and domestic insurrection. This is followed by a clause providing for a national capital.

The long list of enumerated powers in Article I, Section 8 reflects still another division of powers intended by the Framers—the division between the central government and the states. The central government was to have only those powers specifically enumerated in the Constitution. All other powers were to be retained by the states—although, as we shall see in a moment, there are constitu-

---

[4] Although Congress was empowered to regulate its own elections, election procedures for the House were left to the states unless Congress chose to intervene.

WHAT DOES THE CONSTITUTION SAY?

There are many important provisions of the Constitution that we know little about even after nearly two hundred years of experience. In 1972, Congress passed a resolution by a two-thirds vote in each house proposing the Equal Rights Amendment. Congress provided that the amendment would come into effect if ratified by three-fourths of the state legislatures within seven years. By the end of that time, only 35 of the needed 38 states had ratified. Four of these state legislatures later voted to withdraw their ratification. In October 1978, Congress passed a resolution to extend the deadline for ratification by 39 additional months. This new resolution was passed by simple majority vote, not by two-thirds vote.

Now turn to the back of the book and read Article V of the Constitution. Can you answer the following questions?

1. Can a state withdraw its ratification of an amendment? (If not, the ERA needed only three more state ratifications.)

2. Can Congress set a time limit for ratification? (If not, then there was no need to extend the time limit and the ERA "stays alive" indefinitely.)

3. Can Congress extend the time limit by simple majority vote, or must there be a two-thirds vote in each house as there must be to propose an amendment? (If there must be a two-thirds vote, the time extension is invalid.)

4. If three more states ratify, will the ERA become part of the Constitution? If seven more? What does the Constitution say?

tional grounds for arguing that the central government should have very broad powers. Nevertheless, the idea that all powers not specified in the Constitution are reserved for the states is one of the chief reasons the Constitution has played so large a role in our history. Most governments can introduce a new program on the assumption that they have the general power to govern. When the United States government wants to introduce a new program, no such general assumption exists. Instead, the government must find some specific authority in the Constitution for what it wants to do.

To some extent, the idea that the government is limited to the powers actually enumerated in the Constitution is offset by the last clause in Section 8, the famous "necessary and proper clause." It says that in exercising the enumerated powers, Congress is permitted to "make all laws . . . necessary and proper" for carrying out these powers. This is one of the central creative ambiguities of the Constitution, but there are two other key ambiguities in Section 8. One is the power to "lay and collect taxes . . . to . . . provide for the . . . general welfare." The other is the power to "regulate commerce . . . among the several states." The broad and rather vague wording of the general welfare and commerce clauses is easily combined with the implications of the "necessary and proper" clause. The powers of the central government are far broader and far more capable of step-by-step expansion than the strictest theory of constitutional enumeration would imply. Over the years, the central government has managed to amass many powers not mentioned specifically in the Constitution. It has defended most of them on the ground that they involved interstate commerce, were aimed at the general welfare, or were necessary and proper for exercising those powers the Framers did enumerate.

Limitations   The Constitution was designed not only to divide and mix powers, but also to limit them. Article I is full of specific limitations. Most of the limitations on Congress are to be found in Section 9, although others are included in Sections 2 and 8. The bulk of them ensure that Congress will not discriminate for or against any particular state in its tax and commerce laws. Section 9 also contains three important protections for individuals against government repression. The first prohibits **bills of attainder,** laws that punish a particular individual and his or her family. The second prohibits **ex post facto laws,** laws making an act criminal after it has been committed, so that a person could be punished for doing something that had not been criminal when it was done. The third forbids the government to suspend the **writ of habeas corpus.** This writ allows an imprisoned person to demand to be brought before a judge so that the judge can determine whether the imprisonment is legal. Article III, Section 2, provides for the right to trial by jury. Article VI provides that a person need not be of any particular religion in order to hold public office.

Section 8 also creates several prohibitions growing out of the English struggle between king and Parliament. The executive is forbidden to draw money from the treasury except on the basis of an appropriation law. And no titles of nobility are to be allowed. This is to ensure that politicians will not be bribed into betraying the people.

Section 10 of Article I contains a number of limits on the states designed to ensure that the new central government will have sole control over the national economy and national defense. A key phrase forbids the states from "impairing the obligation of contracts" — that is, from tampering with debtor-creditor agreements to favor the debtors.

Impeachment   Article I contains two of the most famous constitutional "checks and balances" between Congress and president. The impeachment power was certainly not intended to be used as a routine device for checking the president, but the provisions establishing this power are broadly worded to allow Congress plenty of leeway. Although the House may *impeach* (that is, indict or accuse) the president by a simple majority vote, the impeachment trial takes place in the Senate, where a two-thirds vote of the members present is required to convict the president and remove him from office. Article II, Section 4 specifies that impeachment shall be for "treason, bribery or other high crimes and misdemeanors."

The impeachment provisions jumped into sudden prominence during the Watergate scandal in the early 1970s. In the entire history of the nation, they had been employed only once against a president. Abraham Lincoln's successor, Andrew Johnson, was impeached by the House but not convicted in the Senate. Despite the fact that impeachment procedures had not been employed in over a century, no one questioned the right of Congress to proceed with the Nixon impeachment. The words of the Framers endowed this almost unprecedented course of political action with great legitimacy. But here, as in many other spheres of political action, the words themselves gave little specific guidance. The phrase "high crimes and misdemeanors" can be interpreted in various ways. It may mean only legal crimes for which an ordinary citizen could be sent to jail. Or it may be interpreted to include presidential abuse of the powers of office or failure to enforce the laws. It is reasonable to assume the Framers intended that impeachment could be used against a president who clearly violated some specific provision of the Constitution.[5] For instance, a president who signed a treaty without the advice and consent of the Senate could be impeached for such an act even though it is not a crime for which a private citizen could be tried and sent to prison. On the other hand, it is not clear just when a president has abused his vast discretionary powers so much that he is guilty of a "high crime." Nixon's resignation in 1974 ended the proceedings that had begun in the House and that had resulted in a committee recommendation favoring impeachment. Nearly all commentators agreed that the resignation was better for the nation than a lengthy impeachment trial would have been.

Veto   A second major check in Article I is the veto power provided in Section 7. The president can veto a bill by returning it to Congress. In this case it does not become a law unless the veto is overridden by a two-thirds vote in each house. Section 7 also provides for the **pocket veto.** If the president neither signs nor vetoes a bill within ten days of its passage by Congress, it becomes law without his signature unless Congress adjourns within the ten days. Thus, at the end of a congressional session, when bills normally pile up for signature, the president may veto simply by not signing.

The veto power of the president is introduced in Article I rather than Article II because it is a lawmaking and not an executive power. It fits with the Article I description of the legislative process. When one person's "no" vote on a bill is worth more than the "yes" votes of two-thirds minus one of the House and Senate, that person is certainly a powerful legislator. In all, only about 4 percent of the roughly 2,300 vetoes cast by presidents since George Washington have been overridden by Congress.

Three Parts of Government   The placement of the veto power in Article I is an important
with Overlapping Powers   clue to the often misunderstood intentions of the Framers with regard to the "separation of powers" among the three branches. It shows that the Framers quite deliberately gave the president a very important share of the lawmaking power. They intended to make it extremely difficult for Congress to pass laws without the cooperation of the president. The idea that

[5] See Raoul Berger, *Impeachment* (Cambridge: Harvard University Press, 1974).

American government is based on a system of separation of powers with checks and balances does *not* mean that the Constitution gives all lawmaking power and nothing but lawmaking power to Congress, all executive power and nothing but executive power to the president, and all judicial power and nothing but judicial power to the courts. Power is given to three branches of government. But each branch checks and balances the others because each *shares* lawmaking, executive, and judicial powers with the other two. Separation of powers really means *sharing* of powers.

All three branches share judicial power. Articles I and III give Congress power to establish the lower federal courts and to determine what the appellate jurisdiction and rules of the Supreme Court shall be. Article II gives the president the power to appoint the justices with the advice and consent of the Senate. All three branches share executive power. Article II, Section 2 gives Congress the power to set the basic executive structure of the United States. It specifies that executive departments shall be established "by law" — that is, by act of Congress. It is Congress that determines whether there shall be a Department of Defense or a Department of Energy at all.

President Jimmy Carter delivers his State of the Union message to a joint session of Congress. Behind him are the presiding officer of the Senate, Vice-President Walter Mondale, and Thomas P. O'Neill, Jr., Speaker of the House of Representatives.

Article III is not specific in assigning legislative or administrative powers to the Supreme Court. The Court's power to declare acts of administrative officers illegal or unconstitutional allows it to block actions of the executive branch. As we have already seen, all three branches share legislative power. The Court's ability to declare laws unconstitutional makes it a factor in the legislative process, just as the veto power gives the president a key role as a legislator. Roughly, Article I is about Congress, Article II is about the president, and Article III is about the Supreme Court. But lawmaking, executing, and judging are scattered throughout the Constitution, just as they are divided and shared by the three branches.

ARTICLE II: THE EXECUTIVE POWER

Article II, Section I begins with one of the broad ambiguities for which the Constitution is famous. It says "The executive power shall be vested in a President of the United States," but it does not define "executive." It then goes on to describe the procedures for electing the president. We know that the Framers saw the presidency as a dangerous institution. They had just fought the Revolution to overthrow a king and become a republic, and a president was a potential king. Yet they saw that the absence of a strong executive was a key factor in the failure of the government established by the Articles of Confederation. They therefore designed the elaborate electoral college mode of electing the president. The electoral college is another variation on the notion of using the principle of representation to purify democracy. The people would not choose the president directly; instead, they would choose prominent persons to be *electors*. These electors would then choose a president. The hope was that these special electors would be far less likely than the people as a whole to make a potential tyrant president. As we shall see in Chapter 11, the growth of political parties has meant that this electoral mechanism has worked far differently than the Framers thought it would.

Article II, Section 2, which states the powers of the president, consists of only three short paragraphs. Yet the vast, complex powers of the modern executive branch have grown from these few words. Read them and you will see how little the general language of the Constitution tells us about the actual operations of modern government.

Chiefly, Sections 2 and 3 give the president four broad kinds of power. (1) He is the commander-in-chief of the armed forces and the chief of our relations with foreign nations. (2) He appoints the principal officers of government. (3) He gathers and disseminates information about the "state of the nation" — that is, what the government is doing and what it ought to do. (4) "He shall take care that the laws be faithfully executed" — that is, he has some sort of general administrative power.

Article II also includes many checks and balances on the power of the president. Although the president is commander-in-chief of the armed forces, the power to declare war is vested in Congress. Although the president has responsibility for foreign policy, the Senate must advise and consent to treaties negotiated by the president or they do not become law. Similarly, the fact that the departments of the executive branch are to be created by congressional statute means that the organization of the branch headed by the president is to be dictated by Congress. Indeed, the president's principal power is defined as carrying out the laws passed by Congress rather than pursuing his own policies.

Nevertheless, the commander-in-chief, chief diplomat, and chief executive roles are potentially very powerful ones. The Framers did not take nearly so many precautions in limiting the president as they did in limiting Congress. In part, this was because they did not foresee the rise of an international situation in which defense and diplomacy, and thus the president, would become the central concerns of government. Also, the Framers saw the lawmaking power as the central power of government, and therefore the power most in need of limitation. Chapters 13 and 14 describe the shifting modern balance of lawmaking power between Congress and president and the growth of the president's foreign affairs powers. Chapter 15 describes the growth of the executive branch bureaucracy, which has played a fundamental role in shifting a great deal of the lawmaking power from Congress to the executive branch.

ARTICLE III: THE JUDICIAL POWER

Article III vests "the judicial power of the United States" in "one supreme court" and whatever lower federal courts Congress chooses to establish. This provision is one of the compromises for which the Framers are famous. Many of the Founding Fathers were concerned about states' rights. They feared that a network of lower federal courts in the states would interfere in the legal affairs of the states. For this

WHAT DOES THE CONSTITUTION MEAN—TREATIES AND EXECUTIVE AGREEMENTS

Article II, Section 2 of the Constitution says that the president shall have the power to make treaties with the advice and consent of two-thirds of the Senate. Beginning quite early in our history, however, presidents have made agreements with foreign countries that have not been called treaties. The Supreme Court has ruled that where such "executive agreements" have been backed by House and Senate resolutions passed by simple majority vote (that is, one more vote than half rather than a two-thirds vote), they have the same legal force as treaties. Should the Court be able to get around the clear constitutional requirement that a treaty becomes law only by a two-thirds vote of the Senate simply by calling a treaty something else? Whether it should or not, it has.

In 1979, the United States reached agreement with the Soviet Union in the SALT (Strategic Arms Limitation) negotiations. The draft Salt II treaty was one of the most important and risky international agreements ever concluded by the United States. The lives of millions of Americans and the very survival of the nation might be at stake in the promises we made to limit our capacity to attack the Russians and defend ourselves from their attacks in return for similar promises from them. A debate raged for months in Washington over the draft to congress, whether the president would submit it in the form of a proposed treaty or an executive agreement. Since the president was not sure of getting a two-thirds vote in the Senate, many of his advisers pressed for the executive agreement route. Finally, under great Senate pressure, he announced that he would submit a SALT agreement as a proposed treaty. So what does Article II, Section 2 mean? Does it mean that the president has a choice between a two-thirds vote or a simple majority vote? Or does it mean that he has such a choice unless the Senate yells and screams? Or does it mean that when something is really important, it must be called a treaty and not an executive agreement?

reason, they preferred to limit federal judicial power to one court in the capital. Those who desired strong central government wanted a full system of federal courts to spread federal law throughout the states. They compromised by leaving to Congress the authority to establish lower federal courts. Indeed, so much of the judicial system is *not* specified in the Constitution that the Judiciary Act of 1789 is considered almost a part of the Constitution itself. It was passed by the First Congress to fill in the constitutional gaps. Eventually, a full system of lower federal courts was established. This system is described in Chapter 16.

Much of Article III is devoted to spelling out the jurisdiction of the Supreme Court and lower federal courts. The Constitution goes into considerable detail about what kinds of cases federal courts can and cannot take. However, the power of judicial review—that is, the power of the Supreme Court to declare laws unconstitutional—is not mentioned in the Constitution at all. Nevertheless, it has become

President Roosevelt appeared before Congress on December 8, 1941, to ask for a declaration of war in response to Japan's attack on Pearl Harbor.

one of the important checks and balances of the Constitution. It is also a major factor in determining the division of powers between the federal government and the states. We know from various debates, documents, and letters that most of the Framers probably favored some sort of judicial review, but it is not clear how much of this power they wanted the Supreme Court to have. In Chapter 16 we will see how this power gradually evolved out of the Court's interpretations of the Constitution.

ARTICLES IV TO VII

Article IV is largely devoted to adjusting the relations of the new federal government to the states. It is one of the several places in the Constitution where specific concessions are made to the institution of slavery in the southern states. Article V sets out the procedures for amending the Constitution. The Framers made the working of the Constitution broad and flexible enough to allow for changing interpretations as circumstances changed. When formal amendments are needed, however, Article V requires that they be proposed by both houses of Congress and ratified by the legislatures of three-fourths of the states. (Article V also provides for an alternative method, constitutional convention. This method has been used only once, for the ratification of the Twenty-first Amendment.) Thus, it is difficult to amend the Constitution.

Article VI contains a number of important miscellaneous provisions. One, designed to improve the international credit of a struggling new nation, guarantees that the new national government will take over the debts owed by the old. Here again, we see the special concern for the rights of creditors to be found in several places in the Constitution.[6] Most important, Article VI contains the *supremacy clause.* It provides that the "constitution . . . the laws . . . and treaties . . . of the United States, shall be the supreme Law of the Land." It is this provision that changes the former colonies from a confederation of thirteen equal, sovereign states into a federal system in which the central government is supreme within its own sphere. The supremacy clause means that the Supreme Court can strike down state laws which conflict with valid federal laws.

Article VII, which provides for the ratification of the Constitution, is not of much relevance today. But it does provide us with a good insight into the thinking of the Framers, for it contains a truly revolutionary maneuver. Article VII stipulates that the new government will come into existence as soon as any nine of the thirteen members of the old confederation ratify the document. That is, the vote of nine states would bind all thirteen.

[6] See Robert E. Brown, *Charles Beard and the Constitution* (Princeton: Princeton University Press, 1956); Forrest McDonald, *We the People: The Economic Origins of the Constitution* (Chicago: University of Chicago Press, 1958).

The Amendments   At the time of the Constitutional Convention, one of the great arguments against ratification was that the Constitution did not contain enough specific limitations on the powers of government. Nevertheless, the Constitution was ratified. Three years later, in 1791, these objections were answered when the first ten amendments to the Constitution were adopted. Known collectively as the Bill of Rights, these amendments guarantee a variety of individual rights ranging from freedom of speech through a prohibition on excessive bail. They have been interpreted and reinterpreted in hundreds of Supreme Court decisions, so that what they mean in practice today can barely be guessed from reading the original wording.[7] We will look in detail at these protections for the individual in the next chapter.

After the adoption of the Bill of Rights, subsequent amendments were rare, with the exception of the three that followed the Civil War, when amendments were adopted to end slavery and to protect those newly freed. In all, only sixteen amendments have been adopted since 1791. Except for the Bill of Rights and the Civil War amendments, most of the others were designed to cure omissions in the original document or to reverse particular Supreme Court interpretations of specific constitutional provisions.

CONSTITUTIONAL LEGITIMACY

On reading the Constitution, we realize that the effort to discover the "intent of the Framers" is in some respects a false search. The Constitution is the product of a large body of men with differing purposes. It was written in broad, general language and frequently embodies compromises designed to bridge conflicting viewpoints. What is more, on many issues that are important to us now, the Framers had no intentions at all or deliberately sought to avoid commitment. Where the language of the document is not clear, the debates of the Convention of 1787 usually reveal differing intents from various speakers. No single clear intent emerges.

On most current questions of constitutional interpretation, appeals to the "intent of the Framers" or the "true meaning" of the Constitution can be misleading. From the words of the document itself, it is impossible to tell precisely what kinds of laws the Framers thought might be "necessary and proper." We have no way of knowing whether "commerce among the several states" was intended to include manufacturing as well as transportation. Nor can we tell whether the Framers, in conferring the commander-in-chief power on the President, intended to authorize operations such as the undeclared wars in Korea and Vietnam.

Nevertheless, it is easy to understand why politicians want to enlist the Framers on their side and why they try to phrase modern political preferences in old constitutional language. The Constitution is perhaps the central aspect of the American

---

[7] The current meaning of the Bill of Rights and the Civil War amendments is discussed at greater length in Chapters 4 and 16. See also Henry J. Abraham, *Freedom and the Court*, 2nd ed. (New York: Oxford University Press, 1972); Samuel Krislov, *The Supreme Court and Political Freedom* (New York: The Free Press, 1968); and Richard E. Morgan, *The Supreme Court* and *Religion* (New York: The Free Press, 1975).

political context. Americans believe that the Constitution does and ought to set the rules by which politics is played. In this sense, it is the Constitution that confers *legitimacy* on the government. Americans feel that political decisions reached by following constitutional rules deserve their respect and obedience. We feel this way as a people not because we are forced, and not necessarily because we agree with the decisions, but because we support the constitutional rules and procedures that produced them.

SUMMARY One of the factors setting the outer limits of political action is the Constitution, both the written document and the general structure of government it establishes. And behind the document itself are powerful traditions that make it a symbol for ideas about what is or is not reasonable public policy. This is why we can speak of a document that is almost two centuries old as "living": it is a blueprint, not a rulebook, and what we make of the blueprint at any time becomes the "constitution" of that time.

The way the blueprint is constructed has much to do with the intentions of those who framed it. Two central ideas run through American constitutional experience. One is that the Constitution is a contract of government or higher law. Thus, any action of government that violates the Constitution is illegal and void. The second is that the Constitution distributes powers among a large number of governing bodies and so limits the power of each of those bodies. The result is a system of checks and balances that structures the interactions between executive, legislative, and judiciary—and also, through the amendments, between government and people. The amendments, which guarantee individual civil rights and liberties, thus serve as another limit on what government can and cannot do. Together, all these aspects of our Constitution—the written document, the amendments, and the supporting ideas—set the boundaries for American politics.

civil rights
and liberties

This book is about constitutional politics. One might say it is about how the game is played. So far we have described some of the rules of that game. The rules dealing with the major players like Congress and the president, just describe the rules of the game. These are the rights and liberties guaranteed by the Constitution. What makes these so special is that they are the rules about how the government plays its part of the game in relation to the individual citizen. That is why they are phrased in terms of what the government cannot do. In the context of, and limitations on, the power of government. For example, the First Amendment of the Constitution says "Congress shall

CHAPTER 4

make no law . . . abridging the freedom of speech . . . ," it creates a "right" to free speech. Such a right is a limit on how far those active in the political process can go in using government to tell people what they can and cannot say.

This view of civil rights and civil liberties as rules of the game or limitations is not complete, however. Civil rights and liberties not only form part of the context of politics, they are also outputs or policies of government. How much freedom of speech we have, for instance, is not wholly predetermined by the words of the First Amendment. It is also determined by the degree to which various individuals, groups, and government institutions act politically to broaden or narrow this right. As you read about specific rights and liberties in this chapter, you will see that each has expanded and contracted at various times in our history. Those expansions and contractions have been the result of political action. Just as our agricultural or defense policies change in response to political action, so do our civil rights and liberties. This is a game in which part of the play is directed to changing the rules themselves. Thus, the rules in this chapter are constantly being changed by the political processes described in the rest of the book.

We use the term **civil rights** to refer to the rules about racial discrimination and **civil liberties** to refer to all the other constitutional guarantees of individual freedom. In this chapter we will take up civil liberties first and then go on to civil rights.

FREEDOM OF SPEECH

The First Amendment says "Congress shall make no law . . . abridging the freedom of speech, or of the press; . . ." Nevertheless, the Supreme Court has held that such laws are sometimes constitutional. The Court will balance the interest in freedom of speech against the interest that a given law seeks to protect. If the interests furthered by that law are important enough, the Court will uphold the limitation on speech. The 1976 case of *Buckley* v. *Valeo*[1] used this **balancing test**. The Court upheld the part of the Federal Election Campaign Act that limited the amount of money any one person could contribute to political campaigns. The Justices said the provisions were designed to prevent corruption or the appearance of corruption in politics. They agreed that contributing to campaigns was a right protected by the First Amendment. But they felt it was proper to abridge the right because preventing undue influence by big contributors was so important to democratic politics. They also declared another portion of the act unconstitutional. This portion limited the total amount an individual could spend on his or her own campaign. The Justices said that no interest served by this provision was strong enough to outweigh the right to free speech. That right included the right to spend money to bring one's speech to more listeners—for instance, by buying television time.

Today the First Amendment means that Congress may make laws abridging freedom of speech if the Supreme Court thinks the laws are necessary to protect

[1] 421 U.S. 1 (1976).

the nation against serious evils. Usually, however, the Court will strike down attempts by government to limit freedom of speech. The core of the First Amendment seems to be that government may not pick and choose who gets to speak freely on the basis of whose ideas it likes and dislikes. It may reasonably regulate the time, place, and manner of speech so long as those regulations treat all speakers alike, no matter what opinions they wish to express. Government may forbid all parades in the downtown business district on weekdays; it may not forbid Socialists to parade while allowing Republicans to do so.

The Content of Speech   Another way of putting this is to say that the government may not regulate the content of speech. It may not reward good ideas and punish bad ones. This principle is firm enough so that neither federal nor state governments have often tried to suppress ideas as such. It is a bit frayed at the edges, however. During the late 1940s and 1950s, most Americans were deeply concerned with the worldwide struggle between communism and liberal democracy. In those years, a majority of Americans seemed to believe there should be no absolute freedom of speech for Communists and their sympathizers. For if the Communists won, they would take away everyone else's freedom of speech. In general, many Americans seem to believe that there should be freedom of speech for the good guys, and even for the not so good guys, but not for the really bad guys. In the 1950s the really bad guys were the Communists. In the 1970s they are Nazis, or racists, or the people who want to advertise sugar-soaked cereals to the children who watch Saturday-morning TV.

In such famous cases as *Dennis* v. *United States,*[2] *Yates* v. *United States,*[3] *Barenblatt* v. *United States,*[4] and *Scales* v. *United States,*[5] the Supreme Court said that the laws making Communist speech a crime did not violate the First Amendment. It was in these cases that the balancing test we have already described was created. The Court found Communists such a threat to our national security that the government's interest in security outbalanced the Communists' interests in freedom of speech. In these and in other earlier and later cases, the Court has also agreed that speech may be punished when it is really a part of or very closely connected to criminal action. Communist speech, so the Court argued, was closely tied to organizing and planning the overthrow of our government. "Incitement to riot" statutes are constitutional when applied to situations in which the speaker says: "Okay you guys, let's go burn down the jail and hang the prisoners. Charlie, you get the gasoline; Jane, you get the rope." Often, however, the examples are not so clear. What if a white man carries a sign

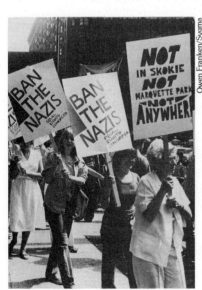

Owen Franken/Sygma

[2] 341 U.S. 494 (1951).
[3] 354 U.S. 298 (1957).
[4] 360 U.S. 109 (1959).
[5] 367 U.S. 263 (1961).

down a street that forms the boundary between a white neighborhood and a black one. The sign reads: "Mongrelizing of the races will destroy our country. White women for white men only." What if an enraged black man takes a swing at him? Should the sign carrier be arrested for incitement or the black man for assault? Should both be arrested? What if twelve white men come out of their houses and march down the street with him, shouting "Blackie, stay out of our neighborhood"? Where free speech ends and incitement begins is a judgment call.

Other Aspects of Freedom of Speech   Aside from this core problem of when speech itself may be punished, a number of other aspects of the right to freedom of speech have been very important in recent years.

Prior Restraint.   Prior restraint means censorship—that is, prohibiting someone from saying something. Subsequent punishment is punishing someone after he or she has said it. The Supreme Court has been particularly opposed to prior restraint. For instance, in *New York Times* v. *United States*,[6] the government sought a court order prohibiting a newspaper from publishing certain secret government documents. The Supreme Court refused because such an action would be a prior restraint, and only the most vital government interests could justify it.

Symbolic Speech.   Is draft card or flag burning or wearing a black arm band a form of speech protected by the First Amendment? The Supreme Court has upheld some forms of symbolic speech in cases like *Tinker* v. *Des Moines*,[7] but avoided upholding others.

The Geography of Speech.   The *Tinker* case involved children who wore black arm bands to school to protest the war in Vietnam. Given that they had a right to free speech, did the students have that right only on the street or could they carry it into school? In this and a dozen or so other cases, the Supreme Court seems to have said that an individual's speech rights do not travel onto the private property of others. They do travel onto government property as long as they do not disrupt the functioning of that property. The student may wear the arm band, but he may not deliver an antiwar speech during math class.

Indirect Punishment.   People may not be fired from government jobs or have other government benefits withdrawn because the government does not like their speech.[8] Here again a balancing approach is used; the government may prohibit employees from engaging in political activity that interferes with their duties.[9]

[6] 403 U.S. 713 (1971).

[7] 393 U.S. 503 (1969).

[8] *Keyishian* v. *Board of Regents*, 385 U.S. 589 (1967).

[9] A good general treatment of free speech and other civil liberties and civil rights questions is Henry Abraham, *Freedom and the Court* (New York: Oxford University Press, 1977).

"I'm so proud of you—imagine having your hair defended by the American Civil Liberties Union!"

Donald Reilly, © 1968 Saturday Review, Inc.

The Scope of Freedom of Speech. In recent years, many new kinds of First Amendment claims have been heard. Newspapers have claimed they have a First Amendment right not to have their offices searched even with a search warrant. Individuals have claimed they have a right to free television time to reply to statements made on television with which they disagree. Reporters claim they have a right not to reveal their sources because they could not gather the news effectively without being able to promise people anonymity. Private citizens claim they have a right not to be watched by government intelligence agencies because knowing they are being watched makes them afraid to speak out against government. There are so many of these claims they cannot be presented even in box score form. The courts have accepted some and rejected others. The clearest expansion in the scope of freedom of speech is that movies, television, and still pictures and paintings have been held to be speech.

Vagueness. A vague statute prohibiting speech, like a prior restraint, seems a particularly bad way of limiting even dangerous speech. For instance, the Supreme Court has struck down a statute making it a crime "wantonly to curse or revile or to use obscene or opprobrious language toward" a police officer.[10] It reasoned that almost anything said in an argument with a police officer might or might not be criminal under the statute. A speaker had a right to know more precisely when he or she risked jail by arguing with a police officer.

Anita Sabarese, DPI

Obscenity. The Supreme Court holds that obscenity is not protected by the First Amendment, but speech about sex is. It has found it impossible to draw a clear line between the two.[11] As a result, films, pictures, and magazines that clearly would have been criminal fifty years ago are now either clearly legal or only doubtfully illegal.

Libel. Much speech that injured another person's reputation used to be considered libel and unprotected by the First Amendment. In recent years, most such speech directed against public officials (but not against private citizens) has been held to be protected by the First Amendment.[12]

Freedom of Association. The Supreme Court has derived from freedom of speech a freedom to associate with others

[10] *Lewis* v. *New Orleans*, 415 U.S. 130 (1974).
[11] See *Miller* v. *California*, 413 U.S. 5 (1973).
[12] *New York Times Co.* v. *Sullivan*, 376 U.S. 254 (1964).

CONFLICTS OF CONSTITUTIONAL RIGHTS:
FREE SPEECH AND FAIR TRIAL

The First Amendment guarantees freedom of speech and of the press.
Reporters often say they cannot report the news properly unless they can
keep their sources secret. They learn a lot by talking to people who will
speak only "if you keep my name out of it." So reporters claim they have a
constitutional right not to name their sources. Suppose a reporter has
interviewed a witness to a crime. The prosecutor needs to know the name
of the witness, because her eyewitness testimony would nail down the
conviction of the criminal. Should the reporter be ordered by the judge to
reveal the source? If your answer is "No," how about a slightly different
situation? Suppose the witness is the only person who can give the
defendant an alibi. Without it, there is an overwhelming case against her
and she surely will be convicted. Should the reporter be ordered to reveal
the source? Should the defendant's right to a fair trial guaranteed by the
due process clauses of the Fifth and Fourteenth Amendments or the
reporter's right to freedom of speech be considered more important? See
Branzburg v. Hayes, 408 U.S. 665 (1972).

to further one's speech. The basic feature of the right of association is the right
of *anonymous* association. For instance, in *NAACP* v. *Alabama,*[13] the Supreme
Court held that a state could not require the NAACP to give up its membership
lists. The Court argued that once the names were known, members might be
subject to harassment by those who did not want desegregation. This right has,
however, also been subject to the balancing approach. In the *Buckley* case, discussed at the beginning of the section on freedom of speech, the Court upheld
a statute providing that those who gave over $50 to a political campaign must
make their names a matter of public record.

RELIGION

The First Amendment has two clauses about religion. The first guarantees the free
exercise of religion. Suppose a religious group believed its children should not salute the flag or say the pledge of allegiance because to do so would be to worship
false gods and graven images. In this case, the Supreme Court struck down a state
law requiring all children to perform the flag salute. It argued that such a law invaded the children's free exercise rights.[14]

The other religion clause forbids an "establishment" of religion. Basically, this
means that government may not make one religion the official religion of the country. The Supreme Court has held it also means that government may not aid reli-

[13] 357 U.S. 449 (1958).
[14] *West Virginia Board of Education* v. *Barnette,* 319 U.S. 624 (1943).

HOW MUCH FREEDOM OF RELIGION DO WE WANT?

The First Amendment says that government shall not make laws interfering with the "free exercise" of religion. Suppose a new religious sect is founded. Each year a member of the sect volunteers to be a human sacrifice. The volunteer is killed on the high altar of the "Great God of Life and Death" by two priests of the sect. Would their convictions for murder be unconstitutional as a violation of their right to exercise their religion?

Common sense would seem to say "No." Courts have usually said that where neither the purpose nor intent of a law was to limit religion, and the law applies equally to all persons no matter what their religion, it could be enforced for everyone. The purpose of the law against murder is not to interfere with religion. Nor was that the intent of the legislators who passed the law. The murder law is enforced against everyone, not only those of certain religious faiths. So we would normally argue that even though the law did have the incidental effect of limiting the particular religious beliefs of the two priests, their convictions would not violate the First Amendment.

Now let us try another example. Suppose a state had a law requiring parents to send their children to school, either public or private, until age 16. As a matter of religious principle, the Amish believe their children should go to school only until the age of 14. Neither the purpose nor the intent of the school attendance law is to limit religious freedom. Its purpose and intent are to make sure that all children get an education. And the law is enforced not only against people who keep their children out of school for religious reasons, but against all people who keep their children out of school. Is forcing the Amish to send their children to school unconstitutional? What do you think? In *Wisconsin v. Yoder*, 406 U.S. 205 (1972), the Supreme Court said it violates the First Amendment. Why? Is it only because keeping children out of school for two years is not as bad as murdering them?

gion. Thus, the Court has held unconstitutional a number of laws that provided government money for Catholic and other religious schools.[15] It has also struck down laws that provided for religious instruction, prayers, and Bible reading in schools. Released time programs, in which students are permitted to leave school early to go to religious instruction, and the study of the Bible in courses on religion or literature do not violate the establishment clause.[16]

RIGHTS OF ACCUSED PERSONS

Search and Seizure. The Fourth Amendment protects people against "unreasonable search and seizure." It is not always easy to say what kinds of searches are reasonable and what kinds unreasonable. In general, the

---

[15] See *Commission for Public Education and Religious Liberty v. Nyquist*, 431 U.S. 756 (1973).

[16] See Martin Shapiro and Douglas Hobbs, *American Constitutional Law* (Cambridge, Mass.: Winthrop Publishers, 1978), pp. 245–64.

An Amish parent being sent to jail for refusing to send his child to public school.

Supreme Court has said that the police must have a search warrant issued by a judge before they can search a person's home. But there are exceptions. Usually the police may search automobiles without a warrant. They may search a person they are lawfully arresting without a warrant. They need not have a warrant to seize evidence that is in plain sight. They may enter a house "in hot pursuit" of a suspect they are chasing. If they have stopped a suspicious person to speak to him or her, they may "pat down" that person to discover concealed weapons.[17]

Self-Incrimination. The Fifth Amendment forbids self-incrimination. Basically, that means that a defendant may not be forced to testify at his or her trial. Nor may an accused person be tortured to get a confession. The Supreme Court has held that a confession may not be obtained by psychological coercion. It has also held that the police must warn those they arrest that they have a right to remain silent and a right to have a lawyer present when they speak to the police.[18]

Right to Counsel. The Sixth Amendment guarantees the "right to counsel." This used to mean only that a person had a right to hire a lawyer for a criminal trial. The Court now holds that the "right to counsel" includes the right to be informed that one is entitled to counsel and the right to free legal services if the criminal defendant cannot afford to hire a lawyer. It also.includes the right to have a lawyer present at all crucial stages before the trial as well as at the trial itself.[19]

Exclusionary Rule. The Supreme Court has been enforcing the rights against unreasonable search and self-incrimination and the right to counsel by the exclusionary rule. The Court has held that confessions or evidence that have been obtained in ways that violate these rights must be excluded from trial. If evidence of this sort has been admitted at a trial, the resulting conviction must be struck down. The defendant may then be tried again, but this time without the admission of the illegally obtained evidence or confession.[20]

There has been much unhappiness with the exclusionary rule because it punishes the police by letting the criminal go

Prayers such as these in public schools have been delcared unconstitutional by the Supreme Court.

[17] See Martin Shapiro and Rocco Tresolini, *American Constitutational Law,* 5th ed. (New York: Macmillan, 1979), Chap. 15.

[18] *Miranda* v. *Arizona,* 384 U.S. 436 (1966).

[19] *Gideon* v. *Wainwright,* 372 U.S. 335 (1963); *Coleman* v. *Alabama,* 399 U.S. 1 (1970).

[20] *Mapp* v. *Ohio,* 367 U.S. 643 (1961).

At the time of the American Revolution, England had an official state church, the Church of England. It was supported by special taxes collected by the government. It is clear that the clause of the First Amendment which forbids the "establishment of religion" was meant to prohibit tax-supported religion. So the Constitution would seem to forbid the use of tax money to support Catholic and other religious schools.

On the other hand, those who send their children to religious schools argue that they are unfairly treated. They face a hard choice. If they send their children to public schools, those schools will provide them with an education that is at best godless and at worst openly skeptical about religious beliefs. Five days a week of education that explains everything in nonspiritual ways can hardly be balanced by a few hours of Sunday school instruction. On the other hand, if they send their children to religious schools, they must pay for education twice—once in the tuition they pay to the religious school and again in the taxes they and everyone else pays to support the public schools. Many simply cannot afford the double payment.

In recent years, Catholic schools in most big cities have been in very bad financial shape. It is often argued that if they go under, their students will be dumped into the public schools, which are already hard-pressed financially to handle the students they have now. So wouldn't it be both fairer and better for even the public schools to send a little tax money into the religious schools?

A number of states invented clever schemes for getting that money into parochial and other religious schools without openly violating the establishment clause. One solution was to allow parents to take tuition payments to private schools as tax deductions. Money that otherwise would have gone to the state in taxes was saved by the parent and could be used to pay part of the tuition. No money was paid directly by the state to the school, but of course the state was allowing some money that would normally have come to it to go to the religious schools. Is it any more constitutional for the state to say "Don't send us the taxes, send the money direct to the religious school," than it is to say "We'll tax you and then send part of what we get to the school"? The Supreme Court has said "No." It has held that so long as money that would have gone to the state ends up in the religious school, the establishment clause is violated. See *Commission for Public Education* v. *Nyquist*, 413 U.S. 756 (1973).

Does this seem right to you? It may seem true to the establishment clause, but does it answer the arguments of many people that they are being forced to send their children to schools which do not provide adequate religious training and so are being deprived of their freedom of religion?

free. If the police conduct an unconstitutional search, they are not prosecuted and sent to jail. Instead, the evidence they have obtained is excluded from the trial. As a result, the criminal may be set free because the jury has not seen the evidence against him or her. Even the body of a murdered child to which the accused had led the police has been excluded and the murder conviction reversed by the Supreme Court. Nevertheless, there may not be any other effective way to avoid a situation in which the police violate the Constitution and the courts condone that constitutional violation by accepting the evidence.

Other Rights of Accused   The Fourth, Fifth, Sixth, Seventh, and Eighth amendments also guarantee other rights involving the legal process. Each of them may become important at times. For instance, the prohibition of cruel and unusual punishments in the Eighth Amendment has been the basis of Supreme Court decisions striking down the death penalty statutes of most states. The states have been forced to give up the death penalty or to provide for very limited use of the penalty under strict procedural rules.[21] The right to a speedy trial guaranteed by the Sixth Amendment has been the basis of Supreme Court attacks on the long delays that sometimes occur in the criminal courts.[22] The Supreme Court also has held that the Constitution forbids discrimination by race or sex in the selection of juries.[23] Some of the other legal process provisions, such as those guaranteeing the defendant the right to know the charges against him or her, and to have a trial by jury, have not been the basis for many leading Supreme Court decisions.

The **double jeopardy** provision of the Fifth Amendment says that no one shall be tried twice for the same offense. But there are exceptions. Sometimes an appeals court overturns a conviction because the trial court made a procedural error. The defendant may then be tried again. When a single act, like bank robbery, is a violation of both federal and state law, the offender may be tried and punished twice.[24]

Constitutional Rights and the States   The first ten amendments originally limited only the federal government. Between the 1920s and the 1970s, however, the Court ruled that one after another of them was binding on the states as well. Only the provision of the Fifth Amendment requiring indictment by grand jury has not been held binding on the states to some degree. One result has been that all the freedom of speech and religious rights contained in the First Amendment are binding on state governments even though the First Amendment begins "Congress shall make no law. . . . " Even more important, however, incorporation has drastically changed the basic rules of state criminal procedure and subjected those procedures to a single, uniform, national set of standards. Perhaps

[21] See *Furman* v. *Georgia,* 408 U.S. 238 (1972).
[22] See *Barker* v. *Wingo,* 407 U.S. 514 (1972).
[23] See *Alexander* v. *Louisiana,* 405 U.S. 625 (1972).
[24] *United States* v. *Lanza,* 260 U.S. 377 (1922).

THE VAGUE COMMANDS OF THE CONSTITUTION: CRUEL AND UNUSUAL PUNISHMENT

The Eighth Amendment bans "cruel and unusual punishment." It was ratified in 1791. At that time, all the states imposed the death penalty for murder. Many used it for other offenses as well, including rape. Few people at that time seem to have thought that execution was in and of itself cruel and unusual. Many did think that torture or such things as cutting off the hand of a thief were. In 1972 and subsequent years, the Supreme Court struck down many existing state statutes providing the death penalty for murder. The Justices argued that beliefs about what was or was not cruel and unusual changed from time to time, and the Constitution should reflect current American beliefs, not those of almost two hundred years ago. The Court held, however, that if the states rewrote their statutes to ensure high levels of procedural protection for the accused, such statutes would not violate the cruel and unusual punishment clause.

In 1977 the Court struck down a state statute that did provide such procedures but authorized the death penalty for rape as well as murder. The Court ruled that because the death penalty was "grossly disproportionate" punishment for the crime of rape, it was "cruel and unusual" punishment within the meaning of the Constitution. Do you think that when the Constitution says "cruel and unusual," it means "grossly disproportionate"? Do those two phrases say the same thing?

In defense of its position, the Court said: "Life is over for the murder victim; for the rape victim, life may not be nearly so happy as it was, but it is not over and normally is not beyond repair. We have the abiding conviction that the death penalty is an excessive penalty for the rapist. . . ." Do you agree? Even if you do, do you think the meaning of The Constitution should be set by the "abiding conviction" of the Justices?

Would your views be changed by the following facts? The man sentenced to death in this case had raped and killed a woman in 1971. Less than seven months later, he had raped another woman, beaten her with a club, and dragged her into a woods, where he left her for dead. He was sentenced to three consecutive life terms in prison for these offenses. He escaped from prison and promptly raped another woman in the presence of her husband, abducted her, and threatened her with death. It was for this offense that he was sentenced to death. See *Coker* v. *Georgia, 97 S.Ct.* 2861 (1977).

the most dramatic change has been in the area of right to counsel. State and local governments must now spend millions of dollars each year providing a lawyer for every criminal defendant who is poor and wants one. Unless that person receives legal assistance, the state may not convict him or her of any serious crime or even send him or her to jail for a minor offense.

Habeas Corpus   A few important constitutional rights of the accused are contained in the main body of the Constitution. For instance, Article I, Section 9 guarantees the right to **habeas corpus**. A writ of habeas corpus is issued by a judge, and orders that a prisoner be brought before the court. The judge will then determine whether the prisoner is being held legally. If the imprisonment is not legal, the prisoner must be released. Federal judges frequently use the writ to release prisoners whose arrests and trials involved violations of their constitutional rights.

THE RIGHT TO VOTE

The Fifteenth Amendment and various civil rights statutes guarantee blacks the right to vote. Women and those between 18 and 21 have had their right to vote secured by constitutional amendment. In recent years, perhaps the most important constitutional provision for the right to vote has been the equal protection clause of the Fourteenth Amendment. The Supreme Court has used this provision to attack the problem of malapportionment. The significance of these developments in voting rights is discussed in Chapter 8.

PRIVACY

The Supreme Court has recently created a new constitutional right—the right to privacy—which is not mentioned in the Constitution at all. It was announced in *Griswold* v. *Connecticut*,[25] a case involving birth control. At least in its initial form, this right to privacy has been concerned almost entirely with birth control and abortion. Women are held to have a particular right to make their own private decisions about conception and giving birth, free from unreasonable governmental interference. In *Griswold* and subsequent cases, the Court has held that states may not prevent women from learning about and obtaining birth control drugs and devices. In *Roe* v. *Wade*,[26] the Court dealt with the right to abortion. It divided pregnancy into three, three-month segments. During the first three months, a woman has a right to an abortion without state interference. During the last three months, she may be subjected to state regulations designed to prevent abortions. Even in that three months, the state may not prohibit abortions necessary to preserve her life and health. During the middle three months, the state may forbid only those abortions that threaten the woman's health.

The abortion decisions have been the subject of great controversy. They do protect the privacy rights of pregnant women; they do not acknowledge that the fetuses have any rights. If you view the abortion decisions as depriving one person (the fetus) of a right to life in order to give another person (the pregnant woman) a right to privacy, then the Court's decisions are surely wrong. The "right to life"

[25] 381 U.S. 479 (1965).
[26] 410 U.S. 113 (1973).

67

movement has become an important political force in the United States. If you view the abortion decisions as acknowledging a woman's right to control her own body, then they are right. The struggle between pro- and anti-abortion forces reminds us that rights and politics are closely interrelated.

CIVIL RIGHTS

The Civil War Amendments   The Thirteenth, Fourteenth, and Fifteenth Amendments were passed after the Civil War to ensure the rights of the newly freed slaves. Over the years, they have been used to expand or create a great many rights for everyone. For instance, we just noted that much of the Bill of Rights had been applied to the states. The Supreme Court did this by finding that the **due process clause** of the Fourteenth Amendment "incorporated" these rights — that is, it made them binding on the states. That clause says that no state may deprive any person of life, liberty, or property without due process of law. The words *due process* do not have any very clear or fixed meaning and have been used by the Supreme Court to protect all sorts of rights and liberties. One important feature of these three amendments is that the final section of each authorizes Congress to enforce it by legislation. The Supreme Court can enforce the amendments by its case decisions, but Congress can also enforce them by passing laws.

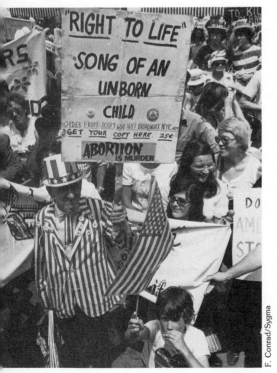

Often the words of these amendments have been stretched very far. For example, the Thirteenth bans "slavery" or "involuntary servitude." The Court has upheld a congressional law forbidding racial discrimination in the sale or rental of housing by arguing that such discrimination was a "badge" of slavery.[27]

The Fifteenth Amendment forbids the states to practice racial discrimination in their voting laws. The Supreme Court has struck down state measures designed to forbid or discourage voting by minorities in regular elections. It has also acted to ensure equal rights to minorities in the primaries and party conventions in which candidates are chosen.[28] In addition, Congress has passed a series of voting rights laws based on the Fifteenth Amendment. They forbid various state practices that discriminate against minority voters. They also provide special ways in which federal officials can make sure that states are not discriminating.

One of the most important clauses of the Fourteenth Amendment is the **equal protection clause** which has been used to strike at all kinds of racial discrimination. It is the basis for the famous school desegregation decision, *Brown* v. *Board of Education.*[29] It is also the foundation of court rulings and laws that forbid discrimination in all publicly owned facili-

[27] *Jones* v. *Alfred H. Mayer Co.,* 392 U.S. 409 (1968).
[28] *Smith* v. *Allwright,* 321 U.S. 649 (1944).
[29] 349 U.S. 294 (1955).

ties. The Fourteenth Amendment says "No State shall . . . deny . . . equal protection. . . ." Thus, it does not reach purely private discrimination by one person
against another. Congress, however, has passed a series of Civil Rights Acts that
forbid private discrimination in "public accommodations" — that is, hotels, motels,
restaurants, and similar places. Since the Fourteenth Amendment may not authorize such a statute, Congress used its power to regulate commerce as the basis for
these laws. Using a combination of the Thirteenth, Fourteenth, and Fifteenth
amendments and various civil rights laws, Congress and the Supreme Court have
made racial discrimination illegal in all but the most private parts of life.

School Desegregation The story of the struggle against racial discrimination is a complex one that can be presented here only in brief outline. After
the Civil War, the South gradually built up a system of laws that segregated blacks
from whites. This segregation by law was approved by the Supreme Court in *Plessy*
v. *Ferguson,*[30] which held that laws requiring separate facilities for whites and blacks
were constitutional so long as the facilities were "separate but equal." (In point of
fact, the segregated facilities for blacks were almost always inferior to those for
whites. This violation of the "separate but equal" doctrine was not successfully
challenged until a few years before the *Brown* decision.) Meanwhile, in both North
and South much racial segregation occurred not because the law required it, but
simply because as an everyday matter of social life many whites would not mix
with blacks.

General American sentiment against segregation did not reach a very high
level until after World War II — which we fought with a segregated army and navy.
The decision of the Supreme Court in *Brown* v. *Board* in 1954 overturned *Plessy* v.
Ferguson. It forbade governments to segregate schools *by law.* (Later Supreme
Court decisions extended the basic principle of the *Brown* decision to forbid other
kinds of officially segregated public facilities, such as parks and swimming pools.)
It did not require integration — that is, that whites and blacks be required to inter-
mix. After *Brown* v. *Board,* however, a peculiar story played itself out in the
South. The southern state governments had seen all their *laws* requiring segregation swept away. But white and black children had been going to separate schools.
They could be kept in those separate schools by various devices and maneuvers
even after the laws were gone. For instance, blacks and whites usually lived in
separate neighborhoods. By requiring children to go to their "neighborhood
school," some schools would remain all white and others all black even though the
segregation law was gone.

Federal courts trying to enforce *Brown* got tired of all this. They said, in effect:
In the past you set up dual school systems by segregation (**Jim Crow) laws.** Those
laws were unconstitutional. You must dismantle the dual school systems. And the
only evidence we will accept that you have really done so is the sight of black and
white faces in the same school room. Thus **integration** — that is, blacks and whites
actually being together — came to be demanded by courts not on its own, or be-

[30] 163 U.S. 537 (1896).

cause they agreed that the Constitution required integration. Instead, integration was of value only as evidence. It was demanded as proof of **desegregation** — that is, as proof that the old laws requiring racial separation had really been wiped out. For this reason, there never really has been a full-scale debate in the United States about whether integration as such is a good thing or a constitutional right.

One major problem has been northern schools. Southern schools had been forced to integrate to prove they had undone their segregation laws. In the North, there had been no segregation laws. So there was no need to undo them, nor any constitutional duty to integrate. There seems something hypocritical about federal courts requiring the South but not the North to integrate. Some northern states have interpreted their own state constitutions to require integration; others have passed state laws requiring integration. In many instances, federal courts have found that northern school districts pursued deliberate policies of segregation even though there were no segregation laws. Instead of laws, northern school districts used rules, regulations, and policies to achieve segregation. Courts have ruled that such official government practices in the North are just as much segregation by law as were the South's Jim Crow laws. Where a northern school district has practiced such de jure segregation (*de jure* means "by law"), it too is under a constitutional duty to integrate. What about a northern district that shows only de facto segregation? De facto segegation exists where *in fact* some schools are all white and some all black, but the segregation is not the result of deliberate government policy. Such de facto segregation often exists not because of government action, but because all the white people live in one part of town and all the blacks in another. A northern school district that shows only de facto segregation is under no federal constitutional duty to integrate.

Although the Supreme Court has not spoken very often or very clearly on these subjects, the distinctions between de facto and de jure segregation and between desegregation and integration are extremely important. They mean that, at least outside the South, each city and school district must be treated individually. Some have a duty to integrate and some do not.[31]

Affirmative Action   The positive side of the drive for civil rights began with courts demanding that actions be taken to make up for the effects of past segregation. Thus, courts ordered busing to integrate formerly segregated schools. Congress and the executive then moved from the problem of segregation to the broader problem of discrimination — treating people unequally on the basis of race. By statute, executive action, and court decision, most government, business, educational, and charitable organizations in the United States today are under a legal duty not to discriminate. Many are under a legal duty to go further, to take positive steps to make up for past discrimination. And many organizations not under any legal obligation are nonetheless trying to compensate for past discrimination in the society as a whole.

Applying congressional statutes, the executive branch demands that those

[31] See Richard Kluger, *Simple Justice* (New York: Vintage, 1976).

HOW AFFIRMATIVE SHOULD AFFIRMATIVE ACTION BE?

Let us suppose that a company had previously hired very few minority workers. Now it has an affirmative action program and encourages minority workers. Let us suppose that three workers are caught stealing from the company supply room. Two of them are white and one is black. The company fires the two whites, but retains the black. It argues that black workers ought to have every possible chance to make good. Has the company been guilty of racial discrimination, or has it practiced affirmative action? In such a case, the Supreme Court said the company had discriminated [*McDonald* v. *Sante Fe Trail Transport Co.,* 427 U.S. 273 (1976)].

Now let us change the example slightly. Suppose a company had a rule that those with over five years' seniority would be fined rather than fired for a first offense and those with under five years' time on the job would be fired. Suppose the company had refused to hire blacks until two years ago. Now let us take two white workers and one black caught stealing. Under the rule, the two white workers are fined because they have worked for the company for six years, and the black is fired because he has been at work only a year. Is this discrimination?

Finally, take the same company and the same rules. Now take two workers who steal, one black and one white, each of whom has been on the job a year. The company fires the white but retains the black. It argues that since the black could not have been hired five years ago and therefore could not have five years seniority, he should not be penalized for not having the seniority. Is this discrimination or affirmative action?

who receive government grants or contracts file **affirmative action** plans. Such plans must provide for special recruiting of minorities and other measures to move minorities into more and better jobs. They usually specify "targets," or how many minorities should be in what jobs by certain future dates. These plans are based on the idea that in the past minorities have been deprived of decent educations and job opportunities. This past mistreatment leaves them handicapped in economic competition with whites. To take a clear example, let us suppose that until this year a business refused to hire minorities at all. Now it says that to be a supervisor, a worker must have had five years' experience with the company. Even if the company no longer discriminates, no minority person can possibly become a supervisor for at least five years. Under an affirmative action plan, the company might promise to consider minorities for the supervisor's job even though they had not worked for the company for five years.

It is this positive aspect of civil rights policy that has caused the most controversy. Its defenders argue that without it, blacks and others could make little real progress in overcoming the great weight of so many years of past mistreatment. Its opponents argue that the government should not force people into integration, as in "forced busing." And they argue that "targets" are really racial quotas which force employers to give jobs to minority persons that more qualified whites deserve. What seems like a necessary tool for gaining racial equality to some seems like reverse discrimination to others. Those who use the term reverse discrimination argue that practicing job and other discrimination against whites now is no more fair than past discrimination against blacks.

The Supreme Court faced this issue in the *Bakke*[32] case. It involved a state medical school that had reserved a certain number of places in each entering class for minority applicants. Bakke, a white, argued that if some places had not been reserved for minorities, he would have been admitted. Instead, minority persons with much lower test scores and college grades had been admitted. The Justices split badly in their response. They ordered Bakke admitted, indicating that at least some affirmative action programs under some circumstances went so far as to constitute reverse discrimination. On the other hand, they also held that race could be taken into account in making admissions decisions in order to ensure the presence of more minority persons in the class. An important factor in *Bakke* was that there was no charge that the medical school had discriminated in the past. In many instances where courts have found past discrimination, they have ordered rigorous affirmative action. A police department that is found to have discriminated against minorities in past promotions may be under a court order to promote one minority patrol officer to sergeant for every white one it promotes.

Perhaps the basic problem of affirmative action is that it looks good or bad depending on where we focus. First let us focus on the organization that discriminated in the past. Why shouldn't it make up for its past evils by affirmative programs even if those programs impose costs, inconveniences, and inefficiencies on the organization? On the other hand, let us focus on the individual. Why should a young white male, who may never have discriminated against anyone, have to give up his place in medical school or his promotion to sergeant because some organization has discriminated in the past? Is the following answer entirely satisfactory? Someone has to suffer. Minorities had to suffer in the past. Now it is the turn of whites to suffer until the minorities have caught up.

Blacks, Hispanic-Americans, American Indians, Asian-Americans, and Company.   Because we traced the civil rights movement historically from the Civil War onward, our attention was focused on blacks. That movement flourished, however, under the equal protection clause of the Fourteenth Amendment. Whatever its historical origins, the equal protection clause now protects all racial minorities. Indeed, it is a bit hard to state just who it does and does not cover. It certainly covers Eskimos as well as other native Americans—that is, American Indians. It covers Asians, but in certain areas of the country where Japanese- or Chinese-Americans have achieved high levels of income and education, they may have no claim to affirmative action consideration in areas like admission to graduate school. The Spanish-surname or Spanish-speaking or Hispanic minority is not a racial minority. There are Cuban-Americans who are white, and Latin Americans

[32] *Board of Regents* v. *Bakke* (1978).

who are of every possible racial mixture. Yet we cannot say that linguistic minorities as such or ethnic minorities are specially protected by the equal protection clause. The Italian speakers of the North End of Boston and the Yiddish-speaking Jews of Brooklyn are simply whites as far as the government is concerned.

When we speak of minorities in connection with the equal protection clause, we are speaking less in precise terms of race or language than in terms of a distinguishable group of Americans that has been historically disadvantaged and continues to suffer the ill effects of past and present discrimination.

Women, the Aged, the Handicapped, and Company. For this very reason, the notion that minorities were entitled to affirmative action in order to achieve equal protection has now spread to include well over a majority of Americans. The civil rights statutes and many Supreme Court decisions ban sex discrimination just as they ban race discrimination. The proposed Equal Rights Amendment would go even further in banning sex discrimination. The elderly and the handicapped have successfully argued that they too have been the victims of discrimination. Recent federal legislation gives them new rights to equal treatment. About the only category that has not recently acquired new constitutional and statutory guarantees of equality are non-elderly white males who are not war veterans. The equal protection clause and the basic concept of civil rights—nondiscrimination—have come a long way since Civil War days. In practice, what this means is that nearly all the "personnel" decisions—hiring, firing, promotion, school admissions—that used to be made independently by private organizations or state and local governments are now subject to review by the federal bureaucracy and judiciary to ensure that discrimination has not occurred. This is a new equal protection far broader than the Fourteenth Amendment's concern for the former black slaves.

Due Process The expansion of civil rights has occurred in another direction as well. The second major clause of the Fourteenth Amendment is the "due process" clause. We have already seen that the rights of criminal defendants to proper procedures, contained in the Bill of Rights, are part of due process. Today, the amendment reaches much further than the procedures and processes of criminal law. No one holding a government job or receiving a government benefit, like welfare, can be deprived of what the government gives him or her without proper procedures. Indeed, courts now hold that the government cannot take any action which directly hurts the interests of any individual or group without at least notifying them in advance and giving them a chance to be heard. Due process basically does not involve the right to any particular decision by government. Instead, it involves the right to demand that government use fair procedures in arriving at its decisions. Those decisions must be based on correct evidence and good reasons. Since the Fifth Amendment has a due process clause binding on the federal government, most Fourteenth Amendment due process arguments apply to federal as well as state governments. Due process rights have been extended so far in recent years that we sometimes speak of a "due process revolution." Previously only those accused of crime thought much about due process. Now, with nearly every American receiving some benefits from the government, the right not to be deprived of those benefits arbitrarily is important to all.

THE EXPANSION OF RIGHTS

Using a combination of equal protection and due process arguments, the federal courts have become more and more involved in every aspect of government administration, from running prisons to granting broadcasting licenses for TV stations. Many things that used to be thought of as economic, social, or political interests are being turned into legal rights. When people want something from the government or want to stop it from doing something, they frequently go to court and sue it. Or they sue a private person or group claiming that it violated some statute, regulation, or court decision. Today going to court to assert one's "rights" is a normal form of political action. Many Americans would list their right to enjoy a healthy and beautiful environment as an important civil right. There seems to be no end in sight for the expansion of the concept of rights to cover more and more aspects of political and social life.

SUMMARY   In the American context, civil rights and civil liberties are not only part of the political rules of the game, they are also government policies. How these rights and liberties have been interpreted and enforced depend not only on the wording of the amendments to the Constitution on which they are based, but on the interpretations of courts and legislatures and the changes in those interpretations over the past two hundred years.

Civil liberties are all the constitutional guarantees of individual freedom except those relating to the rules against racial discrimination, which we call civil rights. Our civil liberties include freedom of speech and religion, the rights of an accused person in criminal cases, the right to vote, and the right to privacy. By its decisions, especially those of the past three decades, the Supreme Court has redefined and expanded many of our civil liberties. It has also extended the protections of the Thirteenth, Fourteenth, and Fifteenth Amendments to address all forms of inequality and to include any distinguishable group that has suffered or suffers discrimination—blacks, Hispanic-Americans, native Americans, women, the aged, and the handicapped.

federalism

In 1977 in the midst of the energy crisis, the United States was anticipating a natural gas shortage. It was also awaiting the first flow of crude oil from Alaska, which was to be shipped by tanker to West Coast ports. There were rumors that the governor of California was threatening to refuse the necessary permits for building receiving facilities at California ports. First he wanted promises from the federal government that California would receive a larger share of the nation's supply of natural gas. At the same time city governments, local port authorities, state and local air pollution authorities, and the California Coastal Commission

CHAPTER 5

The Alaska Pipeline.

were all holding hearings or inquiries about the potential dangers and benefits of new oil terminals. The U.S. Navy, the U.S. Coast Guard, the Federal Power Commision, the Department of Transportation, and the newly formed Department of Energy were also involved. Oil company executives and lawyers spent hours and hours with officials of federal, state, and local agencies. Would the Alaskan oil flow at last? And would more natural gas flow west? Probably, but only after many governments and interest groups had had their say.

Federalism is a significant concept in American political thought. It is also an extremely important aspect of the everyday world of American politics. It would be impossible to understand the national parties, congressional voting patterns, the organization of the executive branch, the construction of the federal budget, or many other features of national politics without some understanding of the powers and jurisdictions of the various levels of state and local government. To a large extent, local political units are the building blocks out of which the national parties are built. They are also the operating agencies through which many national policies are carried out.

WHAT IS FEDERALISM?

Technically defined, **federalism** is division of political power among a number of governments sharing the same territory. There is one central government with jurisdiction over the whole territory of the nation. A number of other governments each control some part of that territory. Thus the United States government ("the federal government") has jurisdiction over all United States territory. Each state government controls the land and people within its boundaries. The basic legal characteristic of federalism is that both federal and state governments enjoy independent legal powers. We often speak of "sovereign" states to stress that their *legal* authority is just as complete and just as clearly and directly derived from the people as that of the federal government.[1]

Different federal systems use different ways of dividing power between federal and state governments. The Canadian constitution assigns specific powers to the states or provinces and leaves everything else to the federal government. The United States Constitution gives enumerated powers to the federal government; all powers not specifically mentioned in the wording of the document are left to the states. For instance, Article I, Section 8 of the Constitution lists a number of specific powers of the federal government, including the power to regulate commerce among the states, coin money, and raise an army and navy. The specific powers of the states are not given. We usually say that the states retain the general "police

---

[1] For general treatments of federalism, see William H. Riker, "Federalism," in Fred I. Greenstein and Nelson W. Polsby, eds., *Handbook of Political Science*, vol. 5 (Reading, Mass.: Addison-Wesley, 1975); and Daniel J. Elazar, "Federalism," in David L. Sills, ed., *International Encyclopedia of the Social Sciences,* vol. 5 (New York: Macmillan, 1968).

power'' — the power to do whatever contributes to the health, safety, morals, and welfare of the people of the state.

The Constitution gives the states themselves representation in the central government. No piece of federal legislation can pass without the consent of the Senate. The Constitution originally called for senators from each state to be elected by the state legislature. The Senate was something like an international conference to which each sovereign state sent delegates. But once elected, senators did not take orders from the state legislatures on how to vote. In this sense, the Senate was an independent part of the national government rather than a servant of the states. The Seventeenth Amendment (1913) provided for the popular election of senators, thus cutting their direct tie to state governments.

The biggest influence the states have directly within the federal government occurs because members of both the House and the Senate are elected by state. Each state has one or more congressional districts, and none of these districts overlaps into two states. So no member of Congress is elected by voters from more than one state. On issues that clearly benefit or hurt a particular state, all the representatives and senators from that state usually vote together. A new federal salmon spawning laboratory would mean more federal jobs and more federal money for the state of Washington. Thus, when Congress is considering a bill to establish such a laboratory, that state's congressmen would vote for it.

More generally, the interests of the states are protected by the belief of members of Congress and presidents that federalism is a good thing. Ultimately the states are protected less by specific constitutional safeguards than by the commitment of Americans to their preservation. Many Americans believe in states rights. They believe it is important that some of the government be close to the people rather than all of it being centralized in Washington. As a result, even national programs often leave a lot of elbow room for the states.

THE SUPREME COURT AND FEDERALISM

Of all the agencies of the central government, the Supreme Court has the most direct connection with the federal system. Remember that the basic model of federalism is based on clear boundaries between the central government and the states. Some mechanism is necessary to settle the boundary disputes that are bound to arise as each level of government responds to changing social needs. Thus the Supreme Court has become a referee between the states and the federal government.

Many of the Supreme Court's most famous and controversial constitutional decisions are about these boundary problems.[2] In the earliest period of American history, the Court was an important instrument in expanding the powers of the central government. From the 1890s to the 1930s, however, the Court very often announced the importance of keeping both national and state governments strictly

[2] John R. Schmidhauser, *The Supreme Court as Final Arbiter in Federal-State Relations, 1789–1957* (Chapel Hill: University of North Carolina Press, 1958).

within their traditional boundaries. For the last thirty years or so, the Supreme Court has itself been the national government agency that most dramatically and consistently expands national authority at the expense of the states. The Thirteenth, Fourteenth, and Fifteenth Amendments, passed after the Civil War, were intended primarily to provide national protection for former slaves. Recently, the Court has interpreted the equal protection and due process clauses of the Fourteenth Amendment to limit the power of the states. Among other things, the Court has held that most of the provisions of the Bill of Rights, which originally limited only the central government, are "incorporated" into the due process clause of the Fourteenth Amendment. Thus, they become binding on the states also.

In recent years, the Supreme Court has imposed many national rules on the states. These include rules about voter qualifications, the size of election districts, education, and racial discrimination in the use of public facilities and in public employment. For instance, as the result of a Supreme Court decision, local school authorities everywhere in the United States must talk to a student, listen to his or her side of the story, and explain what they are doing before they can expel the student from school. The Court has also made national rules about censorship of obscene literature and movies, police and court procedures, jury selection, legislative investigations, loyalty oaths, anti-Communist security measures in state employment, libel prosecutions, and welfare and unemployment compensation practices. More major demands have been made by the central government on the states in the area of racial discrimination than any other, and the principal agent of the central government in enforcing desegregation has been the federal courts, as we saw in Chapter 4.

THE DIVISION OF POLITICAL AUTHORITY: ADVANTAGES AND DISADVANTAGES

Of course the United States has many other political units besides the national government and the states. Each state has county and city governments. Many state constitutions and statutes give these subunits a great deal of independent authority, particularly over things like education and police. The whole nation is covered also with a web of overlapping federal and state special purpose districts. Among the most important of these are the state, county, and city electoral districts (the wards and precincts), and state legislative and congressional districts. But there are also flood control districts, water use districts, junior college districts, and hundreds of others.

Greater Access to Power   The division and redivision of governing authority into hundreds of parcels has many important effects on American politics.[3] A political party that has fallen very far from national majority status, for

---

[3] The importance of dividing power geographically is discussed in Arthur Maass, *Area and Power: A Theory of Local Government* (New York: Free Press, 1959).

IS REGIONAL FEELING STILL ALIVE?

Fifty years ago, American politics often was talked about in terms of "the Middle West", the "South", "New England", and so on. Today issues seem to be more and more national—but not all issues.

In order to conduct many kinds of physics research, a special facility that boosts subatomic particles to enormous speeds must be used. These accelerators or cyclotrons are very expensive. The national government usually pays the construction bills and so decides where the building is to be located. By the early 1970s, modern reactor facilities of this kind existed on the East and West coasts but not in the Middle West. Scientists were pushing for the building of one last reactor. It might seem reasonable to put the new facility in the place closest to the largest number of scientists who might use it. That place would have been either New York or California. The new facility was built instead in a small town in Illinois. Why?

Scientists at middle-western universities argued that unless the new reactor were put in the Middle West, the great universities of the region would lose out to northeastern and California universities in the race for scientific prestige, for they would have no place to do the experiments that brought fame. Was it better to serve the immediate interests of the many scientists on the two coasts or to ensure that a great region of the country could maintain its share of scientific accomplishment? Congress decided that the regional interest should be served.

instance, may continue to flourish on the power, offices, and patronage of local governments in areas where it still enjoys local majorities. The Democratic base in the South in the lean years after the Civil War played a major part in that party's eventual recovery. Locally based interest groups may be able to use the resources of local government to resist or lead national sentiment. In California, antipollution groups managed to get antismog measures through the state legislature; this success was then used to push Congress into action. The railroads, the labor movement, the cooperative movement, the farmers, and various consumer groups have often found it possible to exert a great deal more influence over some local governments than they can on the national scene. The existence of so many government units creates a lot of chances for small victories, so that American politics is not a desperate all-or-nothing game. It is not necessary to have a revolution or a civil war in order to effect change, and competing groups can all have power somewhere. A geographic division of powers has other advantages. Several federal systems, including those of the United States, Switzerland, Canada, and Australia, have been created out of clusters of preexisting political units. In 1789, for instance, most Americans probably thought of themselves as Virginians or Rhode Islanders first and Americans second. Under such circumstances, federalism is a bridge between local and national sentiment. It may be the only way a big enough national government can be created to provide effective military, economic, and political security.

The idea of federalism is closely linked with that of the separation of power among the three branches of the central government. In practice, there is little doubt that the existence of the federal system has sometimes frustrated local or national majorities on specific issues, particularly in the spheres of business and labor regulation. In the 1880s, for instance, several midwestern states were dominated by farmers and small businessmen who felt they were being exploited by the railroads. These groups pressed their state legislatures to pass laws regulating the railroads. The Supreme Court then invalidated a number of these new statutes on the ground that railroad traffic was interstate commerce and thus under the jurisdiction of the federal government. Congress subsequently passed legislation that corrected some of the worst abuses but was far more favorable to the railroads than some state legislatures had been. In another case, the fairly clear national majority against child labor was thwarted for many years by a Court interpretation that assigned labor regulation to the states as part of the general pool of police powers left to them after the federal government received its enumerated powers.[4] During this period, state laws varied widely; some sharply limited the hours and working conditions of children, others permitted employers to set the rules.

Federalism ought not to be seen, however, solely in negative terms of blocking action by the central government. Southern blacks, who repeatedly found themselves politically overwhelmed in their own states, were eventually able to recruit national majorities willing to use the instruments of the federal government to get them better treatment from their own states in voting, education, employment, and housing. And in many instances, federal conservation practices have saved natural beauties that local interests wanted to develop to provide local prosperity. It is, of course, not always clear who the good guys are. Faced with nationwide concern for ecology, many of the citizens of Alaska argue that all the other states, having used their natural resources to increase the standard of living of their citizens, now want to preserve Alaska as a sort of primitive museum while its citizens go jobless.

Local Experimentation   Federalism has certainly provided for flexibility and variation in government policies. It is often argued that the states are "little laboratories" in which new policies can be tried out on a small scale and the successful ones then transferred to the whole country. Much federal regulation of business, labor, and natural resources was first introduced in individual states and later more or less copied by the federal government.[5] For instance, long before the federal government did so, many cities and states had created public defender offices

---

[4] *Hammer* v. *Dagenhart,* 247 U.S. 251 (1918); overruled in *United States* v. *Darby,* 312 U.S. 100 (1941).

[5] For arguments that the states retain this innovative role, see Kenneth C. Olson, "The States, Governors, and Policy Management: Changing the Equilibrium of the Federal System," *Public Administration Review,* 35 (1975), pp. 764–70; and Aaron Wildavsky, "A Bias toward Federalism: Confronting the Conventional Wisdom on the Delivery of Governmental Services," *Publius,* 6 (1976), pp. 95–108.

A civil rights worker explains voter registration.

to provide free legal services to poor persons accused of crime. On the other hand, some state governments allowed persons to be sent to prison after trials in which they had been given no lawyer long after federal courts had insisted that those accused of federal crimes must have lawyers. On balance, it is difficult to say whether federalism has resulted in a better or worse body of American public policies than would have occurred if we had adopted a nonfederal system.

On the whole, however, at least since the turn of the century, we have been much more accustomed to seeing the federal government engage in innovations, pulling and hauling along the reluctant states. This has been particularly true in social security, transportation, resource planning, and labor regulation. But it may also be true in health, education, criminal law, and a number of other areas. At least it is very frequently true that although a few states may be well in advance of the federal government, the remainder only follow their lead as a result of federal pressure. Particularly since World War II, there has been a general tendency to dismiss "flexibility" as an excuse for arbitrary and unenlightened state performance. Instead, there is much insistence on national standards in fields from health to criminal trials. Such standards are often seen as the best means of ensuring an acceptable economic, social, and political environment.[6]

This tendency toward nationalization is counteracted by the advantages of increased participation in a federal system. Under federalism there are more governments, and most of them are closer to home. Federalism provides vastly more political leadership posts than would a centralized system. State and local politics are the training grounds for almost all congressional candidates and for a substantial fraction of the president's appointees to the upper levels of the executive branch. A great many federal judges are also political veterans — almost always in the party of the president who appoints them to the bench. But although state and local governments are often said to be "closer to home," they do not really seem to be closer to the mass of the people. More Americans vote in national than in state or local elections, and the available evidence suggests that national politics generally attracts more attention, emotional involvement, and participation.[7]

Local Majorities and National Majorities The principal impact of federalism is to increase the power of local majorities to oppose national majorities. But even this power is rather arbitrarily distributed. In the United States, certain social and economic interests are geographically concentrated. They often find local majorities that can use federalism to achieve their goals. Other interests are

[6] Herbert Jacob and Kenneth N. Vines, *Politics in the American States,* 3rd ed. (Boston: Little, Brown, 1976).

[7] Robert A. Dahl, *Democracy in the United States: Promise and Performance,* 3rd ed. (Chicago: Rand McNally, 1976), pp. 263–66.

more or less distributed across the land and cannot concentrate their power. For instance, Air Force contracts are concentrated in half a dozen states; Army contractors are spread all over the nation. Federalism enhances the political punch of one but not the other. Thus, federalism is not only a tool for limiting the power of government in general; it is also a tool that enhances the national power of some kinds of interests but not others.

With this qualification in mind, it remains true that federalism has worked roughly as the Founding Fathers expected it to — as a constraint on national majorities. Some observers have applauded this constraint. Others have condemned federalism for fostering sluggishness in the central government and failure to provide national solutions to national problems, such as the plight of the cities, health care, and poverty.[8]

As opinions have shifted on these questions, the nature of American federalism has also changed. There is no single correct, constitutional version of American federalism. From the earliest days of the Republic, each faction remolded its ideal federalism to meet its current needs. The South was for strong central government and the Abolitionists were states-righters when the federal Fugitive Slave Laws returned escaped blacks from Massachusetts to the South. Then the central government seemed likely to end slavery. At that point, the Abolitionists were for saving the union while the slaveowners liked states rights. Pro-business forces were federalist in the first years of the Republic and again during the period when Progressivism and Populism swept a number of states into liberal policies. Business interests rediscovered the glories of the states as Wilson, Roosevelt, and other presidents put the central government to the task of regulating business.[9]

This constant fluidity is possible because American federalism consists of a series of very open devices for mutual control which do not exactly specify who has just how much authority over whom. The levels and qualities of controls each level of government wields over others are subtle and constantly changing. In general, the federal government has the advantage of greater resources, dominant authority in the realm of foreign and defense policy, and the ability to dramatize whatever issues it chooses. The states, however, provide the bulk of government services immediately visible to citizens, such as roads and police protection. They retain their traditional role as representatives of local interests. Above all, they retain the strong voice within the central government that is generated by a system of elections, party organization, and congressional representation that continues to use the states as its basic building blocks.

---

[8] Martin Diamond, "What the Framers Meant by Federalism," in Robert A. Goldwin, ed., *A Nation of States* (Chicago: Rand McNally, 1963); Morton Grodzins, "The Federal System," in President's Commission on National Goals, *Goals for Americans* (Englewood Cliffs, N. J.: Prentice-Hall, 1960); and Grodzins, *The American System* (Chicago: Rand McNally, 1966).

[9] On the historical stages of federalism, see Daniel Elazar, *The American Partnership: Intergovernmental Cooperation in the Nineteenth-Century United States* (Chicago: University of Chicago Press, 1962); Harry Scheiber, "Federalism and the American Economic Order, 1789–1910," *Law and Society Review*, 10 (1975), pp. 57–89; and Samuel Beer, "Modernization of American Federalism," *Publius*, 3 (1973) pp. 49–74.

Since about 1930, the United States has been in a phase often called "the new federalism." The new federalism relies largely on cooperation and shared effort between state and national governments. In contrast, the old federalism relied more on each level of government working independently within its own constitutionally defined areas of authority.[10]

In the new federalism, the American states not only retain their "sovereignty" in constitutional theory, but remain major governments. They have large budgets, provide many essential services, and retain a major share of public policymaking. Yet Americans have increasingly come to look to the central government for the solution of many problems once considered local. We have adopted a number of devices for bridging the gap between a traditional concern for maintaining the safeguards of federalism and a desire to employ national resources in the solution of economic, educational, health, housing, transportation, welfare, social security, police, and other problems.[11] Many federal laws provide for federal advice, technical assistance, and minor centralized support to state agencies. The FBI, for instance, provides conferences and instruction in police methods for local officials, gathers nationwide crime statistics, and provides a nationwide fingerprint identification service. In many instances, legislation provides for federal assistance to local authorities while clearly leaving the initiative in their control. For example, Congress has made fleeing across state lines to avoid capture by state authorities a federal crime. The statute allows the FBI to seek out violators of state law because they have technically committed a federal offense. But once caught, these people are almost always turned over to state authorities for prosecution.

Grants-in-Aid The most important devices of the new federalism, however, are grants-in-aid and federal contracts. Grant-in-aid legislation typically provides for a grant of federal funds to a state or local government for some specific purpose like vocational education. Such grants do strengthen the states by increasing their ability to serve their citizens. It has become customary, however, to attach increasingly complex federal regulations, standards, and reporting requirements to the grants. Recipients must obey detailed federal instructions contained in the statutes and in the regulations and policies of the federal agencies that administer the grants. In this way, a state agency that is theoretically independent may become little more than a field office for the federal agency which passes out the grants. In some instances, the federal government employs contracts, in which a state agency provides a service, such as educational research, for a fee.

---

[10] Michael D. Regan, *The New Federalism* (New York: Oxford University Press, 1972); and James T. Patterson, *The New Deal and the States: Federalism in Transition* (Princeton, N.J.: Princeton University Press, 1969).

[11] See, for example, George M. Smerk, *Urban Mass Transportation: A Dozen Years of Federal Policy* (Bloomington: Indiana University Press, 1974); and Harvey Lieber, *Federalism and Clean Waters: The 1972 Water Pollution Control Act* (Lexington, Mass.: Lexington Books, 1975).

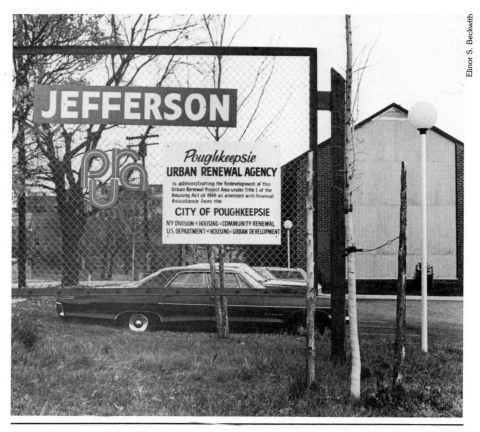

*The Housing Act of 1949 referred to
in the sign is federal legislation
providing money for urban renewal.
Here, federal, state, and local governments
cooperate in the construction of new housing.*

Like any other federal contractor, the state must abide by the terms of the contract, which frequently involve detailed federal controls.

Many federal grants also require "matching" by state or local government. In order to get a dollar of federal money, the state must spend a dollar or fifty cents of its own money on the same program. Or the state must agree to bear the administrative costs. The federal government provides the "big" money, but the state must pay for the local office rent, the paper clips, and the secretaries' salaries. Frequently a federal grant covers only the first few years of a new program's operation; if it wants the program to continue, the local government must pay all the costs. Many state and local governments find that they must agree to spend millions of dollars of their own money in order to get tens of millions of federal dollars. Often they would have chosen to spend their own money differently if it were not for the lure of "free" federal dollars. Indeed, the aim of many federal grants-in-aid is to encourage states to undertake programs they would not choose to carry out on their own.[12]

Because many city governments feel that unsympathetic state agencies have retained too much control, they frequently press for direct links between Washington and the cities rather than funneling Washington money through state government. For instance, when New York City fell so deeply into debt that it had no money to pay its employees, the mayor appealed directly to the president and Congress for financial help that he could not get from the state government. The states argue that this undermines federalism, and they have often succeeded in convincing Congress and the president.[13]

Grants-in-Aid in the 1960s and 1970s During the presidency of Lyndon Johnson, a marked change in the tempo and style of federal grant and contract spending occurred. The Johnson administration announced a "war on poverty" in order to create the "great society." A new Office of Economic Opportunity had been created. The Department of Housing and Urban Development (HUD) played a leading role with its Model Cities program. Earlier federal grants had typically been relatively small, piecemeal attempts to aid the states in performing traditional functions like providing schools and highways. Now federal grants were more massive and more consciously directed at achieving *national* goals and policies. They were often designed to do things the states had never attempted, like rebuilding central cities. State governments were frequently bypassed; HUD preferred to deal directly with mayors. In many instances, the federal government encouraged local people to set up their own organizations outside existing local government structures. These organizations would then receive federal contracts. Thus, HUD might be giving the city government of Detroit a federal grant to improve its parks. At the same time, the Detroit Fight for Jobs Corporation might have been formed by local groups and have a federal contract to train teenagers to be park workers.

Sybil Shelton, Monkmeyer

The Johnson war on poverty was not an overwhelming success. Even at its height, the older type of grant-in-aid-continued alongside the newer one, and both are still in use. Under the "new federalism" the central government continues to deal with the states as legal, political, and administrative units. Sometimes it assigns them new powers. For instance, recent federal regulations require that any new hospital construction

[12] Russell Harrison, "Federal Categorical Grants and the Stimulation of State-Local Expenditures," *Publius*, 5 (1975), pp. 123–36.

[13] Donald H. Halder, *When Governments Come to Washington* (New York: Free Press, 1974); Roscoe Martin, *The Cities and the Federal System* (New York: Atherton, 1965); and Richard D. Feld and Carl Grafton, eds., *The Uneasy Partnership: The Dynamics of Federal, State, and Urban Relations* (Palo Alto, Calif.: National Press, 1973).

In Wauwatosa, Wisconsin, a suburb of Milwaukee, a developer proposed an ambitious plan for subsidized housing for the elderly and low-income families. The townspeople exploded and the city Planning Commission sat on the project for months.

On October 27 [1977] the area director for the federal Housing and Urban Development Department warned not only of a cutoff of current community development funds but also of a denial of $955,000 for the coming year.

On November 7 the Planning Commission approved the developer's proposal and Mayor James Benz said recently he expects the Wauwatosa Common Council to give final approval. "It's hard for us to ignore a million dollars," he conceded.

Source: San Francisco Chronicle, December 28, 1977.

using federal funds be reviewed by a state committee. Such committees will approve the construction only if they find that the region of the state where construction is proposed needs more hospital facilities. The federal government now sometimes bribes the states, sometimes threatens them, and sometimes ignores them. It nearly always requires them to do things the way the federal government wants them done if they want the federal money. And it moves state and local governments into patterns of spending, professional staffing, and hiring they would not have undertaken on their own.

Often federal grant programs initially designed to assist state and local governments result in quite different kinds of federal influence. For instance, concern for crime led to the creation of the Law Enforcement Assistance Administration, which makes grants to state and local police departments to beef up their crime fighting capacities. The threat of withdrawing these grants is a major federal weapon in forcing police departments to recruit more women and minorities. LEAA grants have had far more impact on police personnel policies than they have on the crime rate.

Revenue Sharing   Many defenders of states rights have expressed concern that federal grants were undermining the "sovereignty" of the states. The states were, so it was argued, in danger of becoming mere administrative field offices for federal agencies. President Nixon's administration responded to these worries with what it called **revenue sharing.** In 1972 Congress passed legislation that provided over $4 billion a year of federal funds to the states above and beyond grants that were tied to specific programs. One-third of the money was to go directly to state governments for spending on whatever they pleased. Two-thirds went directly to local governments. About 38,000 government units received revenue-sharing money. There were some limits on what they could use the money for, but in general they had broad discretion over how to spend it. Revenue sharing is a welcome addition to state and local treasuries. By 1978, the amount had risen to $6.8 billion. Nevertheless, this was still less than 10 percent of all federal payments to state and local governments.

FISCAL FEDERALISM

From all that has been said so far, it is clear that contemporary federalism is largely a matter of the flow of money between the nation and the states. Three things about this flow stand out. First, largely because of the federal income tax and its borrowing powers, the national government has overwhelmingly greater financial resources than state and local governments, many of which currently face financial crises. Thus, the national government is necessarily the senior partner in federal-state relations. Federalism today is largely about how much federal money will flow to the states and how the federal government may use that flow to tell the states what to do.

Second, each state has been far more concerned with how much federal money it will get than with protecting itself against federal control. The problem of state shares is complex because several opposing principles are involved. The people and businesses of each state pay large sums of money into the federal treasury each year. It would seem fair that those states which pay the most taxes to Wash-

THE FEDERAL WHIP

A recent act of Congress requires local school districts to make an individual educational plan for every handicapped student. The school district must then provide whatever special facilities are needed to carry out each plan, such as science labs in which wheelchair students can work comfortably. The federal law also requires that parents be consulted in making the plans and that every effort be made to follow their wishes. For instance, if a father and mother want their mentally retarded child to be taught in special classes for the retarded, the district should provide such classes. If the parents want their retarded child to be taught in the same class with the nonretarded, then the district should do so. If some parents want one and some the other, the district should do both. For many districts, the costs of doing all these things for the handicapped will be very high. So far Congress has provided almost no federal money for doing them. Yet if the districts do not do them, they risk losing whatever federal money they get for other purposes. And if Washington officials do not feel that a local plan is good enough, they may order it changed. So federal officials in Washington will ultimately decide how much the taxpayers of Tulsa, Oklahoma, must spend on a new Braille library for a high school. On the other hand, it is clear that a great many school districts had not been giving handicapped children anything like a fair chance and probably would not do so without federal pressure.

"All yours, boy."

ington get the most back in the form of grants and revenue sharing. No state wants to pay more to Washington in taxes than it gets back in benefits, particularly if another state gets more back than it pays in.

On the other hand, why should individuals receiving federal aid receive more money if they live in a rich state that pays a lot of taxes to the federal government than if they live in a poor state? Why should a blind person in California receive a larger monthly check than a blind person in Mississippi? Shouldn't they be treated equally? Indeed, shouldn't federal grants give more money to poor states than to rich states in order to equalize the ability of all states to help needy citizens?

But there is yet another consideration. Suppose a state like New York uses its own money to pay a deserted mother $100 per month for the support of her child, and Mississippi pays such a mother $20 a month. Then let us use a federal grant to "equalize" the treatment of the two mothers by specifying that federal funds will go to every state to bring their payments up to $105 for every child. Then New York will get 5 federal dollars for each child of a deserted mother and Mississippi will get 85 dollars of federal money. Why should the states that do least on their own to help their people be rewarded with big federal payments and the states that make the biggest effort be punished?

We have seen that a major protection of the states is that both senators and representatives are elected by states or districts within a state. When Congress is considering grant or revenue-sharing legislation, the bitterest battles are usually about the distribution formula—that is, how to determine how much money each state gets. Using one or a combination of the three considerations we have just sketched out, the congressional delegation from each state battles for the formula that will help its state most. For instance, when the Senate considered revenue sharing in 1972, it came up with a formula based on each state's population, relative need, and tax effort—that is, how much it was taxing itself. This formula favored smaller states without large cities. The House came up with a formula based on population, proportion of persons living in cities, per capita income, the amount of income tax collected in the state, and state tax effort. This formula favored richer, larger, more urban states. The final law required that each state's allocation be figured by both formulas, and it be given whichever amount was higher. This is an increasingly common solution. When deciding on a formula to allocate grants, each member of Congress thinks less about justice than about a computer printout showing the projected payments to his or her constituency.

There is considerable disagreement over the total impact of grants and revenue sharing.[14] Some people argue that the entire pattern of federal spending should

---

[14] Richard P. Nathan, Allen D. Manuel, and Susannah E. Calkins, *Monitoring Revenue Sharing* (Washington: The Brookings Institution, 1975); J. Maxwell and J. Aranson, *Financing State and Local Government,* 3rd ed. (Washington: The Brookings Institution, 1977); and Comptroller General of the United States, *Revenue Sharing: Its Uses by and Impact on Local Government* (Washington: Government Printing Office, 1974).

Figure 5.1
**How Federal Aid to States and Cities
Has Grown**

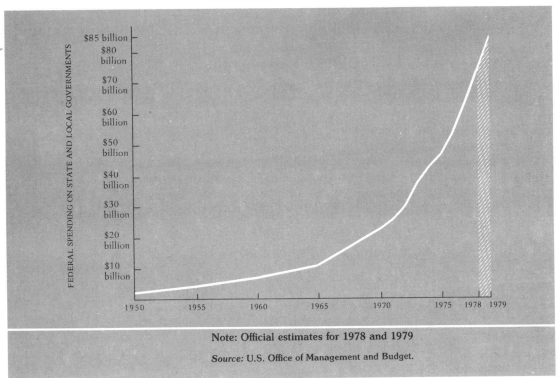

Note: Official estimates for 1978 and 1979

Source: U.S. Office of Management and Budget.

be taken into account in calculating a fair distribution. Price-support payments to farmers funnel billions of dollars from urban to rural areas; water resource projects take money from the rest of the country for the benefit of the arid West; and so on. These expenditures are as large as grants and revenue sharing. The urban states of the Northeast and Midwest are the losers in the exchange — they pay more in federal taxes than they get back in federal benefits. Therefore, they claim, their portion of grants and revenue sharing should reflect this overall imbalance. But so far they have not had much luck with this argument in Congress.

A third major theme in fiscal federalism is the enormous and fairly recent expansion in the number of purposes for which federal grants are made, the amounts of money involved, and the dependence of state and local budgets on the federal treasury. There are over a thousand different grant programs — forty-two in the field of transportation alone. Federal payments to states and cities increased from $11 billion a year in 1965 to $82.1 billion in 1979 (Figure 5.1). Federal money accounted for over a quarter of state and local budgets. At the same time, state and local taxes and expenditures have also been rising. Fiscal federalism has not been simply a shift in taxing and spending from the states to the federal government. Instead, both state and federal programs have been expanding. While state dependence on

FEDERAL AID JUNKIES

Money from the federal treasury has become so important to some
financially hard-pressed cities that they have been called "federal aid
junkies." Although much of the total flow of federal dollars began only in
the last ten years, cutting off the supply to the "high fiscal strain" cities
would plunge them into disaster. It is estimated that St. Louis, Newark,
Buffalo, Cleveland, Baltimore, Philadelphia, and Detroit each receives from
the federal government at least half as much as they collect in local taxes.
This trend will continue in the future, and cities in this position will become
increasingly dependent on the federal government—and increasingly
vulnerable to federal guidelines.

Source: Information, but not conclusion, from *National Journal,* February 18, 1978, p. 281.

federal funds may have increased, the states themselves are also raising and spending more money than they ever have before.

WELFARE: FEDERALISM AT WORK

We conclude this chapter with a brief sketch of the welfare system as an illustration
of the complexity of modern federal-state relations.[15]

Social Security is basically a set of retirement, disability, survivor, and death
benefits for workers. It is a federal program, supported by special payments made
by employers and employees directly to the federal government. It is administered
by the Social Security Administration in Washington and in its hundreds of field
offices throughout the United States.

Unemployment compensation provides payments to workers who have lost
their jobs while they are actively seeking new ones. The federal government pays a
substantial share of the costs, although the states do pay a part. The federal government sets the general rules on eligibility. The states administer the program through
offices that determine the eligibility of individuals, make the payments, and aid the
unemployed in finding new jobs.[16] Each state decides for itself how high the payments will be. During times of high unemployment, Congress sometimes extends
the benefits from the normal 26 weeks to up to 65 weeks. When it does so, the
costs are paid by the federal treasury.

Until recently there has been a whole series of special federal grants to the
states to aid the handicapped and the elderly not on social security. The states
shared the costs and administered the programs, and each determined how much it

---

[15] See the "Special Issue on Income Maintenance," *Public Policy,* 25 (1977).

[16] The actual legal arrangement is very complex. There is a federal payroll tax which need not be
paid by employers if comparable payments are made to the state and if the state's unemployment program meets federal standards. All states have such programs. Most states use a system
under which the fewer workers an employer lays off, the less tax the employer pays.

wanted to spend. As a result, a blind or disabled person in one state might receive two or three times as much as a similar person in another state. In 1974 a new federal program, Social Security Increment (SSI), took effect. It provided federal money to establish minimum annual total benefits for some of the aged, blind, and disabled. This program has somewhat reduced the range between the size of payments made by the most and least generous states. The SSI program is operated and paid for entirely by the federal government. The states, however, are allowed to supplement the benefits. As a result, about 27 percent of SSI payments now comes from the states.

The Aid For Dependent Children program provides payments to mothers who are raising children in the absence of a father. The costs are shared by the federal and state governments. The greater the per capita income of the state, the smaller the percentage of the total payment that comes from the federal government. But the state sets the total amount of payment per child and per family, although the general rules for eligibility are federal. State social welfare agencies administer the program and determine individual eligibility. The amount paid per child varies widely from state to state, as does toughness in determining who is eligible and the proportion of potentially eligible mothers who actually apply for and receive benefits. Many states once forbade payments to a mother so long as there was an adult male living in the household, but the Supreme Court finally forced them to stop using the man-in-the-house rule. A number of states have reduced their benefits in recent years; others have raised theirs. Congress has changed some of the rules for calculating the benefits to encourage mothers on AFDC to seek work. There is also a special federal provision for AFDC-UF, aid for dependent children when the father is living at home but is unemployed. Twenty-seven states have chosen to participate in this program; the others have not.

The Food Stamp program was begun by the federal government, which pays the full cost of the benefits—stamps that are exchanged for food by poor people. Eligibility rules are also set by the federal government. States actually distribute the stamps, determine whether applicants are eligible, and split the administrative costs with Washington. Local resistance to the program was so great in some places that lawsuits were required to get things started. Some of the backing for food stamps comes from farm-state conservatives who see it as a way to get rid of agricultural surpluses. Whatever the motivations, it has turned into a major welfare program that helps about 16 million people and will cost over $7 billion a year by 1980.

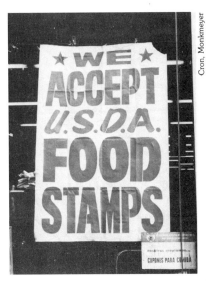
Cron, Monkmeyer

When Congress considered Medicare for persons on social security, there were criticisms that it did not help the younger poor. Congress then enacted Medicaid, which now provides nearly $20 billion annually in federal funds for medical care to the poor. Each state could decide for itself whether to create a Medicaid program, and whether only the poor on welfare or all the poor would be included. Each state had to share the costs, and each state decided what medical services would be covered and what the schedule of fees would be. All

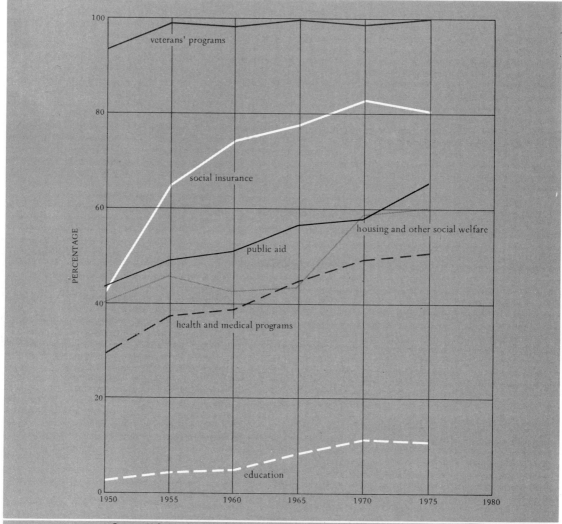

Figure 5.2

Federal Funding as a Percentage of Total
Public Social Welfare Expenditures,
1950–1975

Source: U.S. Department of Commerce, *Social Indicators 1976* (Washington: Government Printing Office, 1977), p. 107.

states now have Medicaid programs. Twenty-nine cover all the poor, not only those on welfare programs. Virtually all cover people on AFDC. Medicaid costs to many of the states far exceed their AFDC costs.[17] Many other federal programs provide some housing, transportation, and education aid to the poor, disabled, and

[17] Barry L. Friedman and Leonard J. Hausman, "Welfare in Retreat: A Dilemma for the Federal System," *Public Policy,* 25 (1977), pp. 25–48.

A CETA job training program.

elderly. Most state and local governments also provide assistance or welfare payments to those in extreme need who do not qualify for any of the federally mandated programs. Most of the money for this general assistance is the states' own, although there are some federal sources that can be used. As Figure 5.2 shows, the proportion of the federal contribution to total social spending differs vastly from one program to the next. Veterans benefits, for example, come almost entirely from Washington. Education, on the other hand, is still largely funded at the state and local level; despite recent increases, the federal contribution remains under 20 percent. In social insurance (pensions, disability, unemployment), the federal role has expanded greatly.

The general pattern is typical of American federalism: A mix of federal and state funding, administration, and policy-making. The federal government requires some programs; others come into existence as the states respond to the lure of federal dollars. In some programs Washington makes the rules; in others, matters like eligibility and matching funds are left to the states. State and local governments do much of the detailed administration and thus make it harder or easier for individuals to collect benefits. States often must spend a great deal of their own money in order to get federal aid, but some programs are close to a free ride. In some programs, there is national uniformity; in others, there is wide variation from state to state.

CETA

In 1973 Congress passed the Comprehensive Employment and Training Act to provide training and temporary jobs for the unemployed. The Department of Labor oversees the program and passes the funds to about 450 state and local governments, each of which runs its own CETA program. Usually a local government hires some CETA workers directly but allocates much of the money to nonprofit groups, public and private, for "public service employment" as well as training in assorted skills. Money might go to schools and little theaters, as well as a variety of civic and community action groups. CETA jobs are outside civil service. If patronage is important in filling regular government jobs, it is likely to figure in CETA hiring as well. In many cities, some of the groups getting CETA funds engage in open political activities. Often mayors and city councils wrangle about who will have how much control of CETA money.

As some cities administer the program, CETA is another form of revenue sharing. In some places, over one-fourth of all municipal employees are CETA workers. Few of these are the hard-core unemployed for whom the program was intended. In 1979, 625,000 public service jobs were funded. Other CETA programs involve over half a million more people, bringing the total cost to more than $10 billion.

SUMMARY   Federalism is part of American political thought; it is also part of everyday political life. We have a federal structure; both national and state governments have independent legal powers. But we have no fixed set of rules for American federalism. Rather, there is a whole series of devices for sharing policymaking, financing, and administration among central, state, and local governments. And these devices keep changing, along with the balance between those that promote national minimum standards and those that leave local problems to local discretion. Congress and the president push new national initiatives but they are also concerned with protecting the states' control. The Supreme Court usually intervenes on the side of national standards. The welfare area is an excellent illustration of how American federalism has become fiscal federalism. The flow of money is its most important aspect. In welfare federalism, both state and national activities are expanding. Welfare mirrors the general balance of power between national and state governments. The federal government clearly has the resources to call many of the shots. The states do so much of the work, however, that they remain significant participants in policymaking.

the intellectual context of american politics

This chapter is about the basic ideas, such as *equality*, *freedom*, and *democracy*, that Americans use when they think about their own politics. All nations and peoples mix ultimate ideals with concerns about immediate problems. This chapter is devoted to American political thought because the ideas Americans have about politics affect their actual behavior. These ideas are loosely interconnected. They cannot be neatly separated into a series of building blocks, because that is not the way people really think. This chapter is organized into several main parts, each of which examines a number of overlapping ideas. The first is about

CHAPTER 6

American ideas of *democracy,* and the second about *individual rights.* The third is about our *constitutional ideas* because this is where our notions of democratic majority rule are combined with our concern for individual rights. Then follow sections on *equality* and *justice,* two of the basic values of most Americans. Finally, there is a concluding section on the vision Americans have of their country as a unique political achievement.

In examining the intellectual context of American politics, we will find that there is no such thing as *the* American political theory. The best we can do is identify the dominant features of a mass of differing and often contradictory ideas. This chapter describes what ideas are in the air. To find out what the American public actually believes, we must turn from the study of political thought to the study of public opinion—the subject of Chapter 7.

DEMOCRACY

*Representation and the
Consent of the Governed*

Abraham Lincoln said our political system was a "government of the people, by the people, for the people." We all know what "of the people" and "for the people" mean, but it is not so clear what "by the people" means. It does not seem to mean actual popular participation in government, in the manner of a town meeting, for that obviously is not the way the American system works. Yet our political system is a government *by* the people in the sense that our government depends upon the *consent of the governed.* Although the people do not actually make the government's decisions, they consent to the decisions made by those who do govern.

*Looking over the shoulder
of a political candidate
translating ultimate ideals
into immediate promises.*

Katrina Thomas, Photo Researchers, Rapho Division

How do they express this consent? They do it by electing representatives to run the government. This is the central democratic feature of the Constitution, which provides for the election of Congress and the president. Most Americans identify these elections as the most important guarantee of rule by the people. The rationale for representative government is that most individuals do not have the time or the desire to run the government themselves. What is more, in a large country such as ours, it would be physically impossible for all the people to come together to run the government. So the people elect some of their number to represent them in governing.

What do we mean, though, when we say that we elect certain individuals to *represent* us in government? Actually, there are at least two distinct theories of representation. Most Americans more or less accept both. The first is the simplest and the most democratic theory. According to this view, the representative's job is simply to express the wishes of those who sent him or her to Washington. In this sense, the representative is the *means* through which the people govern. The idea

"Just one thing more.
If he invokes Lincoln before I invoke Lincoln,
who the hell do I invoke?"

seems to make sense: when an election campaign is dominated by one issue, for example, it is tempting to claim that the people are voting on the issue rather than the candidates. They are saying that they favor school busing or oppose it, that they favor abortion law reform or oppose it, and so forth. And they should have every reason to expect that the person they send to Washington will work to carry out the wishes they expressed.

Elections rarely fit this theory of representation, because campaigns seldom are devoted to a single issue. Each candidate usually talks about a number of different issues. If a candidate has been pro-busing and anti-abortion, how can we tell whether a vote for that candidate was a vote for busing or against abortion, or both? The voter may not have cared much about either issue, but liked the candidate's personality. So the winner will go off to Congress without a specific set of instructions from his or her constituents. When casting their ballots, the voters may simply have said, "We think candidate X will do a better job of looking after our interests than candidate Y." If they voted on this basis, they were following the second theory of representation. According to this theory, the representative does not merely carry out the wishes of the voters. Rather, the voters choose a representative in whom they have confidence, and the representative is then supposed to decide what is best for his or her constituents and for the nation as a whole.[1]

In the first of these two theories of representation, the wisdom that goes into political decision-making is assumed to reside in the people themselves. In the second, political wisdom is assumed to reside in the legislators; it is the people's job "to make in general a good choice of persons to represent them, and having done so, to leave to those whom they had chosen a liberal discretion."[2]

Most of the men who wrote the Constitution generally thought of representative government in this second way. They saw representation as a device to filter and elevate public sentiment rather than simply to express it. They hoped the common people would choose the best minds among them as their representatives. Most members of Congress and presidents who are admired did not always follow the moods of the voters. We sometimes praise politicians because they "rise above" mere "politics" and seem genuinely to pursue what they think is best for the nation, even at the cost of popular support.

To the extent that we ask our politicians to rise above politics, to resist pres-

Town meeting democracy: a kind of political participation
the Founding Fathers did not include
in the Constitution.

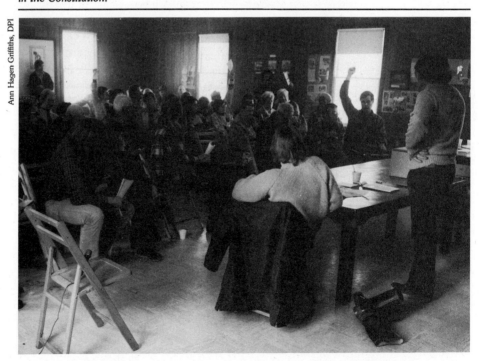

Ann Hagen Griffiths, DPI

[1] Hanna Pitkin, *The Concept of Representation* (Berkeley: University of California Press, 1967).
[2] John Stuart Mill, *Autobiography* (New York: Columbia University Press, 1924), p. 74.

sure, to solve problems, to do what is best, we seem to be endorsing this second theory of representation. The election of representatives becomes essentially a means of popular consent. By electing one set of people rather than another, we give our consent in advance to what they will do in office. Then, if we do not like what they do, we can withdraw our consent at the next election and give it to another set of people. Although Americans do not adopt consent of the governed as their sole democratic theory, one of the central interpretations of American elections rests in part on such notions. American elections usually do not present the people with a clear choice between alternative future policies. Instead, they permit the people to choose leaders in whom they have confidence and also to throw out leaders whose past policies they dislike.

Popular Sovereignty   Closely related to the idea of the consent of the governed is our notion of *popular sovereignty*. Americans tend to believe that all political power comes from the people and ultimately "belongs" to them. In the sixteenth and seventeenth centuries, the idea became prevalent that each nation possessed some complete ruling power called *sovereignty*. This sovereignty usually was held to reside in the king, who was often called the sovereign.

The men who set down the words "We, the People . . ." in the preamble to the Constitution meant to say that in the United States the people were the sovereign. The people replace the king as the source of all the powers wielded by the government. They retain the ultimate political power.

It is clearer now than it was in the seventeenth century that power is not a thing like a rock or a horse that can belong to someone. Neither the king nor the people can be sovereign in the sense of owning all the power. Power is a relationship, not an entity — a relationship in which one individual or group is influenced by another. The power wielders are the individuals who actually make the decisions about what the government does and does not do. As the idea of sovereignty becomes less convincing, popular sovereignty becomes merely a slogan. However, it can be effective when used by those who seek more political power. Such persons try to justify their demands for greater participation in government decisions by identifying themselves with "the people." When we hear that a candidate is a "man of the people" or that a party is the "people's party," we are hearing echoes of the old idea of popular sovereignty.

Direct Democracy and the Fear   A belief in the value of popular participation in government is
of Big Government   one of the major strands in American political thought. The New England town meeting, in which citizens debated and decided every major question of government, is an old reality and a continuing dream. This style of government is often described as **direct** as opposed to **representative democracy**. Provisions for the participation of the poor in the management of poverty programs reflect this ideal of the people governing themselves rather than having government imposed upon them from above. Much of the criticism of big government and bureaucracy is based on loyalty to the principle of

direct democracy. So is the insistence on maintaining the strength of local government. The appeal of keeping government "close to the people" rests on the assumption that citizens can participate more directly in the government of their own town and state than in a government way off in Washington. Such an assumption may no longer be correct, given the large size of the local communities in which most Americans live. Indeed, most Americans seem to pay more attention to national than to local politics. Even so, the hope that big government can wither away, that people can live a simpler political life of face-to-face cooperation, is a recurrent theme of Western civilization.

Jacksonian Democracy.   This side of American democratic thought was made explicit during the period of Jacksonian democracy, from about 1820 to the Civil War. The Jacksonians believed that the representative should reflect and faithfully follow the views of his constituents rather than try to purify and elevate them. The idea was to elect common people rather than gentlemen to office. The "folksy" politician is still a popular figure, as illustrated by baby-kissing and similar gimmicks. Many of the pictures of campaigning politicians in this book show them trying to depict themselves as close to "the people" in general or to some category of Americans specifically.

The Jacksonians were not content simply with putting common people in the legislature. They also wanted to achieve direct popular participation in administration. They argued that the tasks of the bureaucracy were simple. In their view, a government job was a way of taking money *from* the government, not working *for* it. Not only was every citizen qualified to do what little had to be done, but every-

Candidate Jimmy Carter showing himself to the people.

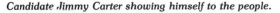

Arthur Grace/Sygma

101
CHAPTER 6
the intellectual
context
of american
politics

one was entitled to a turn at the public trough. To the victorious party at each election, then, should go the spoils. Whenever the party in power was voted out of office, incumbent government workers should be turned out and replaced by the party faithful on the winner's side. This philosophy of public service was known as the **spoils system.** It let a large number of citizens be rotated through office. In a fully developed spoils system there would be no such thing as a body of government officials separate from the people. Both the legislative and administrative branches would literally embody the principle of government by the people.

Democracy and Efficiency.   After the Civil War, as government became larger and more complicated, the ideal of democratic public administration began to conflict with another element in American thought—the desire for efficiency and technological excellence. The traditional American solution to a difficult task has been specialization and improving professional and technical qualifications. We do not hire a farmer to build a space station. All these approaches conflict with the philosophy behind the spoils system, which assumes that any citizen can do any government job for a short time and then go back to private life. In the late nineteenth century, efficiency began to replace participation as a value. The result was the merit or **civil service system.** This system stressed technical qualification for each of thousands of specific and permanent government jobs. The goal of the civil service reform movement was to take public employment out of politics and create a professional force of career administrators. They would do the business of government effectively and efficiently. Though these reforms ended the corruption and inefficiencies of the spoils system, they also spelled the end of direct democracy. Administration was to be done largely by professional employees whose full-time, lifelong business was government service.

American political thought has never successfully resolved this conflict between the demand for efficient government service and the yearning for direct democracy. Most of today's talk about alienation, the "establishment," and popular participation echoes an earlier generation's complaints about bureaucratic red tape. Yet the notion of democratic participation is itself a screen for an even deeper question in American thought.

Political Participation   Just how much participation by how many and what kind of citizens do we really want? Although the United States was established on democratic principles, the Founding Fathers distrusted democratic participation even in elections. Of all elected officials, only members of the House of Representatives were to be chosen directly by popular vote according to the scheme originally set forth in the Constitution. And House elections were conducted under state laws, most of which limited voting to those owning a certain amount of property. Growing support for democracy can be seen in the step-by-step broadening of the electorate which began with the elimination of property qualifications in the states. It continued in the post-Civil War amendments barring racial restrictions on voting. The Seventeenth Amendment, ratified in 1913, provided for the popular election of senators, and there has been a push

Eighteen-year-olds registering to vote.

to abolish the electoral college. The Nineteenth and Twenty-sixth Amendments extended suffrage to women and to eighteen- through twenty-year-olds. In the 1960s, Supreme Court decisions and voting rights legislation put teeth in the constitutional barrier against racial restrictions in voting. Many of the states provide for direct voting on proposed legislation through the initiative and referendum.

But our desire for democracy is not complete. We continue to use the word "demagogue" to describe candidates who appeal to voters' baser sentiments — to prejudices and fears. Thus, we temper our belief in democracy with a fear that the people can be easily misled or converted into an ugly mob. Similarly, our belief in the value of strong presidential leadership may be taken as an indication that we think the people are not always capable of choosing the best policies without help from "above."

Majority Rule The concept of majority rule is probably the most widely shared and deeply held element of American political thought. We see it at work from the smallest informal group trying to decide what movie to see to the Supreme Court of the United States deciding the most solemn constitutional questions. Having voted eight yea and five nay, it is hardly conceivable that a group of Americans would then say, "The nays have it," except under such special circumstances as the two-thirds majorities required in the Senate for treaty ratification or a jury vote in a criminal case.

Yet Americans continue to doubt that the will of the majority is always what is best for the country. Long ago the French philosopher Jean-Jacques Rousseau, who was read by some of the Founding Fathers, drew a sharp distinction between the will of the people, which he called the *general will,* and the will of the majority. The will of the majority, he said, is often merely the sum of the selfish desires of individual voters. It is not necessarily the same as what would be best for the people as a whole — that is, what would be in the public interest. Rousseau's thinking is echoed in the suspicion that there can be good majority decisions and others that are not so good. Some Americans tend to reserve special praise for politicians who stand up for the public interest in the face of hostile public opinion. Whenever we do so, we are saying that a particular policy would be good for the people even though a majority of them did not particularly want it.

American Thoughts on Democracy Americans, then, have a number of different ideas about democracy. They believe that no government is legitimate that does not enjoy the consent of the governed. They believe that the people are in some vague way the ultimate source of political power. They want the people to participate in government both directly and through their elected representatives. They believe in majority rule. But at the same time, they acknowledge that the mass of citizens cannot themselves directly run large and complex governments. And they suspect that what the majority of the people may want at any given moment is not always what would be best in the long run for the country as a whole.

INDIVIDUAL RIGHTS

The Declaration of Independence proclaims the "self-evident" truth that all men had been endowed with "certain inalienable rights." Our continued allegiance to the concept of *rights* is a major check on the equally self-evident truth of majority rule.

The Liberal Tradition   The dominant school of American historians argues that from the beginning our country was so steeped in the political ideas associated with the English Whig, or liberal, philosophy that to this day American thought is almost exclusively liberal.[3] In the next chapter we will look at liberal and conservative political ideologies. The point here is that Americans who think of themselves as liberal and those who think of themselves as conservative share a common set of beliefs. This set of beliefs derives from a historical body of thought described as *liberal* because it emphasizes the rights of the individual against the powers of government.

Echoing earlier Greek and Roman writers, the thirteenth-century philosopher St. Thomas Aquinas taught that there was a hierarchy of law, with divine law at the top. **Natural law,** which could be discovered by human reason, was a reflection of divine law. It followed that positive law—the laws people made and wrote down in statute books—ought to be a reflection of natural law. In this way, a standard quite apart from the wishes of the sovereign was created for determining which laws were good and bad. God-fearing persons should obey the real laws. They need not obey false laws. Only reasonable laws—that is, laws in accord with natural law—were real laws. We inherit this notion in our concept of unconstitutionality. As we saw in Chapter 3, a law that is not in accord with the higher law of the Constitution is null and void, not a real law at all.

In seventeenth-century England, the philosophy of natural law underwent a significant change. The emphasis now fell on the idea of *natural rights*. Since God had given every person reason, each individual had the right to make his own decisions and to live his own life freely, according to the dictates of his own reason. Those who defended the idea of natural rights did not believe their ideas would lead to anarchy or lawlessness. As they saw it, if society were governed by the principle of natural rights, all people would live under the natural law, the law of reason. Even under the rule of natural law, government would not be abolished. Man-

---

[3] Daniel Boorstin, *The Genius of American Politics* (Chicago: University of Chicago Press, 1953); and Louis Hartz, *The Liberal Tradition in America* (New York: Harcourt Brace Jovanovich, 1955).

made laws were needed to control some aspects of human behavior because people were not totally rational. Government would provide certain added protections to the natural rights of the individual that he or she could not fully protect unaided. But a government that infringed on the rights of the individual had violated its very reason for being.

The Doctrine of Laissez Faire

The philosophy of natural rights in which the Founding Fathers so strongly believed was essentially a philosophy of individual freedom. It stressed the limitations that should be placed upon government; in most things, people should rule themselves. In late nineteenth-century America, this individualism was expressed in the doctrine of *laissez faire,* a French term meaning "leave alone." Essentially, the **laissez faire doctrine** was based on the principle that the government should interfere as little as possible with the "natural" workings of society. In the economic realm, for example, it was believed that if the government would only "leave things alone," the system of free competition in the open market and the laws of supply and demand would automatically correct any temporary imbalances. The role of government should be limited to providing basic police services to ensure the safety of the individual and the security of private property.

As those who believed in laissez faire saw it, the main threat to the rights of the individual came from the state. The idea that a person has a right to do something meant chiefly that the government should not be allowed to stop that person from doing it. It did not mean that the government should take positive steps to help him. For example, today many people believe that each citizen has a right to earn a decent living. Many of us take this to mean that the government should set minimum wage standards, that it should take steps to correct the economy when there are not enough jobs, and so on. In the heyday of laissez faire, however, the right to earn a living meant the right to be free from government legislation requiring that a person work for no more than so many hours or less than some minimum wage.

In other words, the laissez faire thinkers defined rights in negative terms. To say that a citizen had a right to do something was chiefly a way to indicate what the government should not be allowed to do. In many areas we still think of rights in this negative way. Freedom of speech and religion, our First Amendment rights, mean that we may speak and worship where, when, and how we please, free from government interference.

Private Property and Laissez Faire

From the time of the Founding Fathers, one fundamental individual right has been the right to hold private property. The Declaration of Independence substituted "pursuit of happiness" for "property" in the traditional English slogan, "Life, liberty and property." For the founders, the advantage of the new phrase was only that it covered a little more ground than "property" alone. They certainly thought that the accumulation of wealth through the institution of private property was the central vehicle for the pursuit of happiness. The old phrase reappears in the Fourteenth Amendment:

105
CHAPTER 6
the intellectual
context
of american
politics

"Nor shall any State deprive any person of life, liberty, or property, without the due process of law."

The American commitment to private property and individual economic initiative has been so strong that Marxist ideologies, which swept so much of the world, hardly have made a dent here. The highest vote ever achieved by a socialist party in a presidential election was 926,000 in 1912. Although our anticommunism is no longer as intense as it was in the 1950s, it is still a fundamental part of American political opinion.

All this is not to say that the American commitment to property rights is complete and unquestioning. In the first place, an unlimited right to private property conflicts with the commitment to equality, which we will examine later in this chapter. Gross inequalities in the distribution of property have always been an issue in American politics. Fear of the "money power," "the trusts," the "big corporations," "Wall Street," and "the banks" has been a constant theme of American life. Indeed, one of the most interesting features of American thought is the way it reconciles the belief in private property with the belief in equality. Often, the people who push programs of business regulation and progressive taxation are staunch believers in private property. They want social reform to ensure that major concentrations of family and corporate wealth cannot economically enslave "the little person." They believe that everyone should at least be guaranteed a job so that he or she can earn enough to get some property. Most Americans are so deeply committed to the value of private property that this issue rarely even rises to the level of political consciousness. But arguments over what distribution and regulation of property are desirable are a constant part of day-to-day politics. In a sense, then, American economic thought consists of a series of constantly readjusted compromises between our commitment to private property and our commitment to equality.

Economic Interests   Laissez faire never became the exclusive economic theory of the United States. In the period after the Civil War, which was the heyday of the laissez faire philosophy, strong political movements arose which we usually lump together under the title **Populism**. These movements were aimed at preserving the individual freedom of the small farmer, businessperson, and worker. As the Populists saw it, the freedom of these people was threatened by the trusts, the banks, and the railroads. For them, freedom did not mean freedom from government interference; they wanted the government to play an active role in protecting their rights. They demanded legislation to protect the individual from enterprises that had become so large and powerful that their exercise of complete freedom threatened the freedom of others.

Thus, by the early twentieth century, the idea of liberal government took on a new meaning. The government would protect the liberty of the people not by leaving them alone, but by settling the clashes that arose between the rights claimed by various individuals and groups. We began to speak less of rights and more of **interests**, each of which was entitled to government protection. By interest we meant anything people wanted or valued, from an interest in freedom of speech to an interest in a new house. Gradually, we came to see rights less as negative protections *against* government interference and more as positive claims for governmental services that would protect and foster individual freedom. Particularly during the New Deal of the 1930s and World War II, the concept of rights took on more and more positive meaning. Minimum wage laws came to be seen as part of a government guarantee of a right to work rather than as interference with the individual's right to work for low wages. After the war, under the terms of the Employment Act of 1946, the government was given the moral obligation to promote full employment. And since then the positive role of government as a promoter of conditions of economic opportunity for all citizens has continued to grow.

Negative and Positive Rights   Obviously, all these different concepts of rights can conflict with one another, even though they are all grounded in the same ideas about the fundamental worth of the individual. The government may ensure a right to pure air by prohibiting smoking. But in doing so, it interferes with the freedom of the smoker. If the government is going to assure its citizens the positive right to a job, the right to eat, the right to medical care, the right to education, it must have more and more control over their lives. Their negative rights to be free of government interference must be reduced. For example, an increase in the worker's right to a job means a decrease in the employer's right to hire or not hire whomever he wishes. Similarly, we cannot guarantee all our citizens the right to medical care without curtailing the medical profession's right to dispense its services as it sees fit.

WHO IS HURT BY VICTIMLESS CRIME?

One example of the tension between negative and positive rights may be seen in the area we sometimes call "victimless crime." If someone wants to drink himself to death, doesn't he or she have a right to do so free of government interference? The basic negative right, after all, is the right to be left alone. For this reason, many people urge that drunkenness and drug-taking not be treated as crimes.

On the other hand, many Americans now feel they ought to have a positive right to government-provided health care—at least when they cannot afford such care. Millions of Americans now do have a right to health care. The alcoholic and drug addict want to be left alone while they are poisoning themselves. But afterward they may want medical care. Should they have a negative right to make themselves sick and then a positive right to free medical services? There is a victim in many "victimless crimes"—the taxpayers who have to pay the rehabilitation bill. On the other hand, we may believe so strongly in the right to be left alone that even those who abuse it ought neither to be punished nor deprived of positive rights.

107
CHAPTER 6
the intellectual
context
of american
politics

Negative and positive concepts of rights coexist uneasily in contemporary American political thinking. Nevertheless, we retain a strong commitment to preserving our negative rights. We continue to believe that certain fundamental individual rights ought to be absolutely protected from government interference. And we continue to look to the Constitution and the working political system to protect these rights. We do so even if we do not know exactly how to draw the boundaries between one person's rights and those of another.

THE ROLE OF THE CONSTITUTION

As we already have noted, one of the basic ingredients in American political thought is the belief that ours is a government "by the people." This idea has many complex meanings. Central to them all is the conviction that our democratic government works on the principle of *majority rule*. We also have observed that a second important element in American thought is our belief that every individual enjoys certain *inalienable rights*. These two beliefs—the belief in majority rule and the belief in individual rights—are the bedrock on which American political thinking rests.

It is easy to see that, in the abstract, these two principles provide good guidelines for government action. Yet it is also easy to see that they can readily come into conflict. In any given time or place, the majority may not want to respect the rights of the minority. In that case, one of the two principles must suffer. Either the belief in individual rights will win and the majority will not have its way, or the principle of majority rule will win and the minority will lose its rights. Nazi Germany was a tragic example of what can happen when a majority of the people feels it is entitled to disregard the rights of a minority. Throughout much of American history, the treatment of blacks, American Indians, and other racial and ethnic minorities serves as a sad reminder that a government based on the principle of majority rule does not guarantee that the rights of all persons will be respected.

The Constitution is the point of intersection between belief in rule by the people and belief in individual rights. Let us briefly examine some of the ways in which the Constitution reconciles these two potentially conflicting strains in American political thought.

Majority Rule and Minority Rights   Americans frequently face the following problem: If you believe in majority rule, then you must believe that the majority can do what it pleases, including taking away the rights of minorities. If you believe in minority rights, then you must believe that the minority may sometimes block the majority. But if the minority can block the majority, you have minority rule.

The standard answer is based on our faith in the Constitution. The majority rules, but its rule is not absolute. The majority may not deprive individuals of their constitutional rights. Freedom of speech and the right to vote, for instance, are guarantees of the rights of minorities to participate in the political process. The Supreme Court traditionally has been seen as a major means of protecting individual rights. In this sense, then, minority rights do not mean that the minority has the right to block the majority. It means that the minority has the right to participate in the democratic process. The only thing the majority may not do is block the access of minorities to that process. Thus, minority rights do not contradict the principle of majority rule; they simply allow everyone a fair chance at becoming part of a winning majority.

Factions   So far, we have been discussing ways in which the Constitution protects the rights of minorities against the will of *the* majority. In a sense, this is an oversimplification, for the Constitution was actually designed to produce a political system in which there was no such thing as *the* majority.[4] James Madison, one of the Founding Fathers, expressed this idea most clearly in *The Federalist Papers,* and his thinking has continued to be one of the major strands in American political thought.[5]

As Madison saw it, the nation was divided into a number of *factions,* each of which would pursue its own interests. Farmers had somewhat different interests than merchants, creditors than debtors, shipowners than manufacturers, northerners than southerners, gentlemen than common men. As long as none of these factions was dominant, the government would have to operate on the principle of compromise. In the long run, no single faction could dominate by itself, each faction would get some of what it wanted, and no faction would ever have its way entirely.

The problem, of course, is how to put Madison's principles into practice. How can a government be set up in such a way as to keep any single faction from ever becoming a majority, and thus dominating the political process?

Geographical Diversity.   The first part of the answer to this question lies in the tremendous geographic diversity of the United States. Today, the nation spans the entire continent, but even the original thirteen states were immense by European standards. When the United States of America first came into being, it was almost twice the size of France and almost four times the size of Great Britain. This huge area contained many different sorts of people in many different occupations. Madison recognized that in this diversity lay the key to the type of government he wanted. With so many different groups, it was unlikely that enough of them could ever find enough in common to form a permanent ruling majority.

Elections.   The Founding Fathers designed an electoral system that would take maximum advantage of the natural diversity of American society. For example, the Framers permitted the states to set their own rules for House

[4] Max Farrand, *The Framing of the Constitution of the United States* (New Haven: Yale University Press, 1965).

[5] Clinton Rossiter, ed., *The Federalist Papers* (New York: New American Library, 1961

109
CHAPTER 6
the intellectual
context
of american
politics

elections. Each state, regardless of size, was to elect two senators. Thus the voice of the few big states would not dominate the Senate. Different terms of office were established for representatives, senators, and presidents. Representatives serve for two years, the president for four years, and senators for six years. The Supreme Court was not elected at all; justices are appointed for life terms. Thus, it seemed highly unlikely that a single faction would ever control all at the same time a majority of House and Senate seats, the electoral college which selected the president, and the Supreme Court.

How does this system prevent the emergence of a dominant majority? First, virtually all representatives were chosen in small, single-member districts. This means that geographically concentrated minorities have a good chance of electing some members of the House. For example, a state may be largely rural, with only a few sizable towns. If representatives were elected on a statewide basis, obviously the rural vote would predominate. But with single-member districts, the chances are that the people in the towns will be the majority in a few districts, so that they can control some House seats. No American ethnic minority is large enough to win a statewide election. But in a number of House districts, a majority of the voters come from a single ethnic background and can send "one of our own" to the House.

The staggered terms of senators also serve to blunt the force of temporary opinion. For example, imagine that the majority of Americans became very excited during one of the oil crises of the 1970s and decided that war with the oil-producing nations was the only solution. Wherever they could, they would vote for senators and representatives who were pledged to a militant oil policy. As a result, the House would tend to support these militant views. (Even here, though, the victory would not be complete, thanks to the geographic diversity we have just discussed. Farm states, for example, might not feel the oil crisis very acutely, and so they would not side with the nationwide majority. Or farm communities within industrial states might vote for representatives who did not agree with the opinions expressed by the statewide majority.) But even granting that the House would come to be dominated by representatives who were swept along with the majority opinion, the Senate would be relatively immune to such short-term passions. Only a third of the senators are up for election in any election year. Even if those wanting war swept twenty-five of the thirty-three Senate seats up for election, this would give them only a quarter of the votes in the Senate. Two years later, when the next third of the Senate runs for reelection, the passions raised by the issue may have calmed down; and four years later, when the final third runs for office, the issue may be dead. So the staggered terms of senators prevent temporary majorities from controlling the political process.

Checks and Balances.   For Madison and some of the other Founding Fathers, the most crucial check on the rise of a dominant majority was what is commonly called the system of **checks and balances.**

As we saw in Chapter 3, the Constitution is designed so that each branch will do some legislating, some administering, and some judging. It is because their functions overlap that the branches can check and balance one another. For instance, for a new law to come into effect, Congress must pass it and the president must sign rather than veto it. The Supreme Court must declare it constitutional if it is challenged in court. The three branches can check one another because no law can be passed and enforced unless all three cooperate in using the lawmaking power they *share*. Because it was unlikely that all three would be in the hands of the same faction for any length of time, no single faction—no matter what its numerical strength—could use the government to its sole advantage. Any operation of government would require cooperation and compromise between the various factions. Faith in the separation of powers remains a major element of American political thinking.[6] Few people would be willing to concentrate all the powers of government in any one of the branches.

Majorities of the Moment

The Constitution does contain devices for avoiding dominance by a single faction. But it also presupposes majority voting in the House and Senate as well as the majority principle through the election process. It is the candidate who gets the most votes who gets elected. The Founding Fathers were afraid of what would happen if the government fell into the hands of a dominant majority. Instead, they wanted a system in which decisions would be made by what have been called **majorities of the moment.**[7] Such a majority is a combination of a number of factions that find themselves in momentary agreement on a specific issue. They combine to form a voting majority in Congress, and they gain the cooperation or at least neutrality of the president. This combination may dissolve again as soon as what it wants becomes law. Having achieved the single purpose that the member groups or factions shared, there is nothing further to hold them together. As new issues arise, new majorities of the moment form.

In the American political process, there are many points where a small group can block government action. A prospective majority will have to win the support of a good number of such groups in order to get what it wants. In this way, the chance of every group frequently being a member of the winning majority is maximized. There is a risk, however, in strengthening the position of small groups in order to ensure that they will be included. Some disgruntled group may then always be strong enough to block the majority of the moment. If this happens, we will have what amounts to minority rule. This danger is a very real one, since the power to block a majority is the power of a minority to rule in favor of the status quo. The American system of dispersed power has the disadvantage of making decision difficult, since the power to decide major issues rarely is in the same hands. Thus, the reverse side of the system's protection of minority interests is a bias toward inaction. At any given time there is bound to be a fairly large number of Americans who are convinced that one faction or another is obstructing the political process and blocking the majority.

The existence of majorities of the moment helps explain the widespread loyalty to the American political process. Because the United States contains so many

---

[6] Ralph Gabriel, *The Course of American Democratic Thought* (New York: Ronald Press, 1956).

[7] Arthur Holcombe, *Our More Perfect Union* (Cambridge: Harvard University Press, 1950).

111
CHAPTER 6
the intellectual
context
of american
politics

minorities with so many overlapping interests, most people can be relatively confident that they will sometimes find enough others willing to cooperate with them to form a majority of the moment. It is this confidence that encourages those who lose a vote to abide by the majority decision. After all, the next time they may be part of the majority.

What would happen, however, if there were a permanent minority, one that loses *every* vote, that is never in a winning majority? Who would be fool enough to believe that he has a stake in democracy if he *never* gets what he wants out of his right to participate? This is not merely a hypothetical question. Racial minorities have always provided American democracy with its most significant failures, including a civil war. For long periods of time, they were permanent minorities who were not even admitted to the political process. Or, once admitted, they saw themselves as permanent minorities who always lost. Those who see themselves as members of a permanent minority that always loses may interpret their condition as a case of majority tyranny and may look to revolution as the only way out. It is for this reason that both the most self-satisfied white and the most militant black are equally products of American political thought. The white may praise our democratic processes. The black may say that these processes always yield white majorities that never allow black minorities to get what they want.

EQUALITY

Political Equality The idea of equality is one of the great traditional themes of American thought. The Declaration of Independence announces that "all men are created equal" even before it explains that they are endowed by·their Creator with "certain inalienable rights." This close association between belief in equality and commitment to individual rights has continued throughout American history. Indeed, ideas about equality and ideas about individual rights are really two sides of the same coin. If all men are equal, then each man is equal to every other. If each is equal to every other, then each has rights all others are bound to respect. Equality in the American setting implies individual autonomy, the freedom of each person to make his or her own decisions.

When the Declaration of Independence says that "all men are created equal," it is talking about *political equality*. This idea is echoed in the Constitution, which says that every citizen has a right to "the equal protection of the laws."

Social Equality Legal political equality, as protected in the right-to-vote guarantee of the Fifteenth Amendment, is actually the only type of equality the Constitution specifically mentions. Nevertheless, other types of equality are important to Americans. For example, most Americans believe in the principle of social equality. Of course, many people in this country think quite highly of themselves and look down at their social "inferiors." Nevertheless, judged by European standards, America is a remarkably unsnobbish nation. In the 1830s, the great French social commentator Alexis de Tocqueville commented on the fact that in America the owner of a factory and his hired hands treated each other as equals when they met after working hours. In Europe, this type of relationship would have been unthinkable.

Equality of Opportunity   In twentieth-century America, there has been a growing concern about still another kind of equality. Increasingly, government takes on the task of guaranteeing a certain minimum of food, housing, education, and health care to every American, as well as seeing that guarantees of political equality actually are enforced. For the last seventy years, Americans have been debating about just how much government ought to do in these areas. What is not up for debate, however, is the idea that there must be equality — at least in the sense that everyone must be assured the necessities of life and some chance for their children to better themselves. This type of equality is known as *equality of opportunity*. Although most Americans believe in equality, they are willing to tolerate enormous differences in wealth between the richest and the poorest segments of the population. Americans often explain this seeming contradiction in terms of equality of opportunity. Believing in equality of opportunity does not necessarily mean believing that all people should be equally well off. It does not even mean believing that someday, when everyone has been given a fair chance, the inequalities will even out and the wealth of the nation will be equally distributed. Equality of opportunity simply means that every individual should have an equal chance to become

FREEDOM AND EQUALITY

We do not often talk much about it, but one of our basic rights or freedoms is the freedom to raise one's own children rather than having them taken away and raised by the government. Yet some American families are far wealthier, far better educated and/or far more caring about their children than others. Can we really say that a child whose father is a drug addict and whose mother is a streetwalker who beats him really enjoys equality of opportunity with a child whose father is a lawyer and whose mother is a doctor and who gets a lot of kind attention from both? As long as children are raised by their own families, there are bound to be inequalities in society. Yet few of us think that the government should force families to give up their children so that they can be raised equally in state institutions.

We can, however, adopt policies that reduce the conflict between the freedom to raise children and our belief in equality. Inheritance taxes reduce the differences in wealth between families. Free public education for all reduces the educational advantages of wealthy families. Welfare payments and other social services to the poor are aimed at giving their children a better chance. There is a continuing debate about how much government should do to overcome the head start that some children get because we believe in family freedom.

113
CHAPTER 6
the intellectual
context
of american
politics

wealthy. In other words, *we all are entitled to an equal opportunity to become unequal.*

By applying the principle of equality of opportunity, Americans in the second half of the twentieth century have taken some steps toward eliminating inequalities in our society. For example, the Civil Rights Act of 1964 prohibited discrimination that denied racial minorities an equal opportunity to get jobs, education, and access to public facilities. Nevertheless, in many respects the idea of equal opportunity rests on a naive misunderstanding of social and political reality. Even if we could eliminate all the formal and legal barriers that deny some people an equal opportunity, the poor would still stand less of a chance for success than the middle-class members of society. To mention just a few factors, the middle-class child lives in an environment which places a high value on education and encourages ambition; he is probably surrounded by successful adults who can serve as role models for him as he grows up. The poor child may have none of these advantages. To say, then, that these two children have equal opportunities simply because there are no formal, legal barriers blocking the poor child's way is obviously wrong.

Racial Equality   The most troubling aspects of the American commitment to equality are related to racial equality. Indeed, it is the depth of our attachment to equality that makes American racism such a deeply frustrating phenomenon to its opponents. Contemporary American racism rarely rests on an open, conscious, and deliberate assertion of racial superiority. It is accompanied by massive doses of guilt generated by the knowledge that the plight of racial minorities does violate a basic belief. Our allegiance to equality is clearest on the political level. Depriving someone of the vote on racial grounds, for instance, was the most unpopular form of prejudice. And official, social discrimination by law, such as racially segregated public facilities, was also rejected by most Americans some time ago. But when white Americans confront the social and economic consequences of past racism, they are not sure what steps they want to take to correct them. They are not sure what sacrifices they are willing to make in order to provide racial minorities with more jobs, more money, more housing, and more education. The greatest problem of American politics today is whether legal equality for racial minorities will, in turn, produce enough social and economic gains to satisfy them. If such gains are not achieved, and many of them may come to see themselves as the kind of embittered permanent minority we mentioned earlier.

JUSTICE AND THE RULE OF LAW

The idea of justice is closely related to the idea of equality. One of the oldest definitions of justice is giving equality to equals.[8] We also think of justice as being intimately connected with the rule of law. We would prefer that a law be announced in advance and spell out how all people in the same situation will be treated. This is

[8] Carl J. Friedrich and John W. Chapman, eds., *Justice* (New York: Atherton, 1963).

because we feel that uniform, equal treatment will yield better results across the board for all individuals than special treatment for each individual.

Thus, one component of the idea of justice is equal treatment. A second is fair procedure. If two people are having a dispute and go before a judge, we expect that both will get a chance to tell their side of the story. If the court used rules and procedures that prevented one side from talking, we would say that the court was not giving both sides a fair hearing and thus not doing justice. We also think that justice should be not only equal and procedurally fair, but good. Let us imagine a proposed law for the extermination of the mentally retarded. It might provide for equal treatment in the sense that it would treat all the mentally retarded exactly alike. It might be fair in the sense that it set up fair procedures, complete with lawyers, expert witnesses, and scientific tests, to determine who was and who was not mentally retarded, giving everyone a fair chance to prove that he was not retarded. But we would not call such a law *just* because we believe that killing people because they are handicapped violates their fundamental human rights. Or to put it another way, such a law violates our fundamental beliefs about how a good society should treat its citizens.

THE JUSTICE OF DRAFT LAWS

There are so many considerations in deciding whether a law is just or unjust that it is impossible to spell them all out. Often we feel that we know an unjust law when we see one even though we cannot say exactly what a just one would be. Do you think that a draft law is just? Consider the following points:

1. A draft law is passed by a majority of the people to force some of them to fight and perhaps die for their country's security. Is it just to require some people to die so that others may live the way they want to?

2. Most proposed draft laws are limited to the young. Is it just to allow older people, who know they will not be drafted, to vote on such laws? Would it be just to say that only those who would be directly affected by a draft law should vote on it? (Perhaps by a national vote of those between 18 and 25 instead of by vote in Congress, where all of the members are 25 or older.)

3. Would a draft law be more just if it required the old as well as the young to serve even though we know that young people make better soldiers?

4. Would a draft law be more just if it chose by lottery or if it chose those who would make the best soldiers and exempted those who could contribute most to the country in other ways? Should a great violinist or quarterback be exempted? How about a great tank designer?

5. Is the more just draft law the one that picks and chooses in such a way as to maximize our chances of winning a war or the one that most equally distributes the risk of dying?

6. Let us suppose—for the sake of argument—that we could prove men would not make as good combat soldiers as women. Would a law that drafted only women be just?

*A campaign sign
for presidential candidate
Barry Goldwater.
The slogan reflects the notion
that politics is about good
and evil as well as about
immediate interests.*

Americans on the whole place a great deal of confidence in the ability of our legal system to provide fair and equal treatment for everyone. What is more, Americans generally believe that the surest way of attaining justice is through the legal system. But this does not mean we believe that law and justice are synonymous. On the contrary, the idea that justice is a higher value than law has long been a feature of American thinking. We use the concept of justice as a critical check on our faith in law.

But even where they disagree with particular laws, Americans remain deeply committed to the principle of *the rule of law*. This is why theories of civil disobedience, violence, resistance, and rebellion have never played a dominant role in American political thinking. Instead of resisting or rebelling against unjust laws, Americans traditionally direct their efforts toward changing them. They try to use the law to correct whatever injustices the law has created. When we praise the rule of law, we do not mean that all our laws are necessarily good. We mean only that it is better to be governed by a system of laws that apply equally to everyone than by a ruler who can do whatever he pleases, whenever he pleases, to whomever he pleases.

CONSENSUS

It is often argued that a nation cannot have democratic politics unless it enjoys a strong consensus or agreement on basic political ideas. For if the majority and minority of the moment had fundamentally different ideas about political good and evil, the minority would not yield gracefully to the majority. It would fight for its basic principles rather than let evil triumph until the next election.

Sometimes the consensus argument is put a little differently. Perhaps the citizens of a democracy need not agree on all fundamentals. Some may be Catholic and some atheist. Some may be socialists and some capitalists. But they still can operate a democracy if they all believe in the same rules of the game. If there is a consensus across all groups on free elections, majority rule, freedom of speech, and the preservation of the individual's right to participate in politics, then democratic politics is possible. In other words, if people can agree on the procedures of politics, they can cooperate democratically even if they disagree on what goals politics should be seeking to achieve. For example, socialists have a fundamental belief in government ownership of the means of production. Capitalists have a fundamental belief in private ownership. But so long as both share the belief that the people should decide the issue through free elections, then socialists and capitalists can live together in a democracy.

This argument can be related very specifically to the United States. The people of the United States come from different ethnic, religious, political, and economic backgrounds. We might expect them to be in conflict over many major and fundamental issues. Yet so long as most of them subscribe to the fundamental rules of the game, it is possible for the United States to maintain a democratic political system.

In the final analysis, however, we do not know how correct this argument is. In public opinion surveys, many Americans do not express great support for such democratic rules of the game as freedom of speech for people with unpopular opinions. There is greater consensus on the rules of the game among the better-educated. Since they are more active in politics and in leading public opinion, perhaps their consensus is the crucial one for the functioning of democratic government.[9]

There is a kind of chicken and egg situation here. A democratic nation may avoid projecting fundamental conflicts into politics. Then it can continue to have consensus on the democratic rules of the game. It can do so because it never has to test just how deeply that consensus runs in the hearts of its people by asking them to choose between the rules and something they want very much. People may be persuaded to keep basic conflicts out of politics in order to preserve the apparent consensus on the rules of the game. On the whole, except for the Civil War, the United States has done quite well at fostering and proclaiming a liberal democratic political theory and avoiding the kind of crises which would put that theory to ultimate tests.

SUMMARY In their politics, all nations and people mix ultimate ideals with concerns about immediate problems. Some basic political ideas affect everyday political behavior in America: ideas of democracy, individual rights, constitutionality, equality, and justice form an interconnected and sometimes conflicting basis for politics. Since some people hold some of these ideas more strongly than others, there is no such thing as a single American political theory.

We believe in democracy and representative government—yet we have two ideas of what representative means. We also believe in popular sovereignty and direct democracy, but at the same time we believe in efficiency. We believe in majority rule, yet we also believe in the public interest and in individual rights. We believe in private property and individual economic initiative—but more and more we also believe in equality of opportunity, and in each person's right to a job. We look at government as the protector of individual freedoms and as the judge of which (or whose) rights will prevail when there is conflict.

We believe in both majority rule and minority rights: everyone must have a fair chance to participate. The Constitution itself promotes this equality of access. The Founders designed an electoral system that would prevent the emergence of a dominant and permanent majority, as well as a structure of government based on shared powers and checks and balances. Their aim was

---

[9] Herbert McClosky, "Consensus and Ideology in American Politics," *American Political Science Review,* 58 (June 1964), 361–82; and Robert W. Jackman, "Political Elites, Mass Publics, and Support for Democratic Principles," *Journal of Politics,* 34 (August 1972), 753–73.

117
CHAPTER 6
the intellectual
context
of american
politics

rule by majorities of the moment rather than permanent majorities, so that groups and factions could constantly combine and dissolve, depending on the issue. We believe not only in legal and political equality, but in social equality, equality of opportunity, and racial equality—although how all these ideas are to be realized is often a source of conflict. We also believe in justice and the rule of law as the way to adjust and resolve conflict.

These beliefs and theories are the fundamental rules of the American political game. Without some agreement that we will all follow them, we could not maintain a democratic political system.

individual and group
political activity

PART TWO

public opinion

In the last chapter we surveyed the ideas that form the basis of the American ideology. But ideas do not tell us what ordinary Americans really think about politics, and how and why they think what they do. Now we will focus not on the background to current politics, but on the political process itself. We will look at the present, not the past, at actual political behavior, not ideas about politics, and at the political world, not its social context.

We begin with the raw material of individuals and their beliefs about politics. How aware of their government are most Americans? What do they think about the

CHAPTER 7

basic elements of the democratic creed? What kinds of people have liberal and conservative opinions about political and social deviants, minorities, drugs, taxes, and the like? To what extent do Americans think ideologically? How do children learn about the political world? What is the role of the mass media?

Social scientists have learned a good deal about questions like these through **survey research,** or public opinion polls. We have already drawn on surveys in Chapter 2, and we will be using this material frequently in later chapters. First, however, we need to understand how public opinion polls are taken. We need to know how we gather the information on which we rely.

SURVEY RESEARCH

In election campaigns, candidates and the mass media rely on polls. Government agencies use surveys to gather information about social and economic conditions. Once every ten years (every five years beginning in 1985), the Census Bureau tries to contact everyone living in the United States. In between these periodic nose-countings, the Census Bureau gathers data by asking questions of samples. The monthly unemployment figures for example, are a product of survey research. Almost all the material on income, occupations, and other population characteristics presented in Chapter 2 was based on the Census Bureau's survey research. In the private sector, major marketing decisions are made with the guidance of polls about consumer habits and preferences in products and services.

Although scientific survey research did not begin until the 1930s, there is nothing new about asking people their opinions and voting intentions; it was done by newspaper reporters as early as the election of 1824. Straw polls, as they were then called, were common throughout the nineteenth and early twentieth centuries. The most famous one was conducted by the *Literary Digest,* a magazine that for many years accurately predicted the outcome of presidential elections. But in 1936 the *Literary Digest* claimed that Alfred M. Landon would defeat the incumbent Democratic President, Franklin D. Roosevelt. Roosevelt's record-breaking majority buried both Landon and the *Literary Digest,* which soon went out of business. That election also made the reputation of a young pollster named George Gallup.

Choosing a Sample How can pollsters claim to know what 150 million American adults are thinking after asking questions of only 1,500 to 2,700 people? The *Literary Digest* based its prediction that Landon would defeat Roosevelt on replies from 2.4 million people. Unfortunately, these people were not representative of the whole electorate. Most of the names were drawn from the magazine's subscription list and from automobile registration records, both highly unrepresentative groups in the Depression years. By polling the relatively prosperous, the *Liberary Digest* exaggerated the Republican vote.

What is important about a survey is less the size of the sample than *how it is chosen.* **Probability sampling** is the technique used by academic survey analysts

and many commercial pollsters. In a probability sample, everyone in the population being surveyed has a known chance of being chosen to be in the sample. A national probability sample is drawn by establishing anywhere from 70 to 450 primary sampling units. These are voting precincts or similar small geographical areas chosen randomly throughout the country. Within each unit, a specified number of interviewees (generally called **respondents**) are chosen by statistical procedures that do not give the interviewer any say in whom to interview. This rules out a tendency to skip hard-to-find or "unattractive" respondents.

Such a cross-section faithfully represents the group from which it is drawn within a narrow range of what is technically called **sampling error**—the extent to which the sample is likely to differ from the entire population. The sampling error in most polls reported in newspapers and conducted by academics is plus or minus 3 percent. In other words, a Gallup Poll result that a candidate is favored by 43 percent of the population means the candidate's "real" support is almost certainly somewhere between 40 and 46 percent. Because increasing the size of a sample will not reduce the sampling error very much, most national survey pollsters use a sample of 1,500 to 2,700 people.

Questions and Answers An important key to interpreting survey findings is understanding the effect of differences in how questions are worded and asked: the kind of question will often determine the results. Many of the problems are not mere technical difficulties—they reflect the underlying ways Americans think about politics, with all their quirks and inconsistencies. In short, a look at the limitations of polls is also a good introduction to the study of public opinion.[1]

If a poll question asks for a "yes-no" or "approve-disapprove" response, the results may be quite different from those gotten with multiple-choice or open-ended questions. If a question makes it easy to answer "I don't know," or "I haven't thought about that," many people will take one of these options. Not everyone has a position on every political topic, but people are often reluctant to say so. In fact, they may not have thought about the problem until an interviewer shows up in their living room. Some opinions may be so lightly held that they shift with every passing item of news. Thus, polls can exaggerate the depth and extent of public opinion by taking these "nonattitudes" seriously.

In the late 1960s, during the furious debate about whether the United States should build a limited antiballistic missile (ABM) system, some pollsters reported that as much as 73 percent of the public favored development. The Gallup Poll was

[1] An especially good discussion of this problem is Seymour Martin Lipset, "The Wavering Polls," *The Public Interest,* spring 1976, pp. 70–89.

In December 1974 the Louis Harris organization asked:

As you know, the United States has sent planes, tanks, artillery, and other weapons to arm Israel. The Russians have sent similar military supplies for Egypt and Syria. In general, with the Russians arming Egypt and Syria, do you think the United States is right or wrong to send Israel the military supplies it needs?

Answering this question, 66 percent favored military aid to Israel.

In January 1975 the Gallup Poll asked:

What should the United States do if a full-scale war breaks out in the Middle East?

Only 16 percent favored military aid to Israel.

Source: Seymour Martin Lipset, "The Wavering Polls," *The Public Interest,* spring 1976, pp. 79–80.

more careful and first asked if the respondent had an opinion, before trying to measure it. The results: 25 percent favored the ABM, 15 percent opposed it, and 60 percent had no opinion.[2] The Center for Political Studies at the University of Michigan now adds "or haven't you thought much about this?" to questions asking for attitudes on issues like tax reform, busing, and unemployment. When given a chance to come clean, 10 to 20 percent always admit they really have not thought about the question. Even tiny changes in the way a question is phrased may produce dramatic shifts in poll results. Different results also may be obtained depending on whether the question provides some fact or lets the respondent answer on the basis of his or her existing level of information (see the above example about arms for Israel). Because wording is so crucial, answers to a question that has been asked only once are hard to interpret. Researchers therefore pay particular attention to (1) differences in answers to variations of the same basic question, (2) answers to the same question at different times, and (3) how groups in the population differ in their responses to the same question.

Validity: Evaluating Results Carefully designed and evaluated polls are the principal source of information about public opinion and other aspects of individual political behavior. We know their results are valid from the consistency over the years in responses on various topics and the resemblance poll results bear to those of the national census. And with the exception of the 1948 Truman-Dewey election outcome, pollsters have accurately predicted national election results for many years. But although polls can be useful, they do pose some problems:

[2] Leo Bogart, *Silent Politics: Polls and the Awareness of Public Opinion* (New York: Wiley-Interscience, 1972).

1. About 15 percent of the people in any national sample refuse to be interviewed, a figure that has increased in the past few years. Some pollsters believe this reflects an increasing amount of generalized distrust in American society. It certainly means that researchers must do without the information that can be gathered from these people. They can only hope that refusers distribute their opinions and votes more or less like those who are willing to be interviewed.

2. The only votes that count are those cast by people who appear at the polling place on election day. A substantial number of those polled may not even be registered to vote. Merely asking someone whether he or she is going to vote is not terribly reliable; people are embarrassed about not performing their civic duty and often say they will vote when they won't. It is possible that people who do not vote have different political preferences from those who do. Pollsters can predict with reasonable accuracy who will vote in general elections, but they still have difficulty with primary elections, where the turnout is much lower.

3. During campaigns, people change their minds in response to the campaign itself or to the pressure of events. A poll can only measure intention at the time the interview is conducted. The fall presidential contests see less vote shifting than other campaigns because the candidates are fairly well known and because party loyalties have a major effect on voting. But in other elections, when the candidates have not attracted much attention, turnout is low and party labels are irrelevant. Under these circumstances, prediction is hazardous. In presidential primaries, accuracy improves as election day approaches.

The survey data used in this book are drawn largely from academic survey organizations. The most important of these is the University of Michigan Center for Political Studies, which has conducted careful nationwide studies of every presidential and congressional election since the early 1950s. Unless otherwise indicated, the survey data used in this book are from the CPS.[3] We have also used findings from the National Opinion Research Center of the University of Chicago, as well as from commercial polling organizations such as George Gallup's American Institute of Public Opinion and Louis Harris and Associates.

AWARENESS AND INTEREST: HOW MUCH DO AMERICANS KNOW?

In the winter of 1973–74, motorists had to wait in long lines to buy gasoline. The shortage was caused by an oil embargo by the Arab nations, which then quadrupled the cost of imported oil, driving up prices for all petroleum products. Since

[3] The Michigan data were made available by the Inter-University Consortium for Political and Social Research, and analyzed by the authors. Neither the Michigan Center for Political Studies nor the Consortium is responsible for our analyses or interpretations of the data. Unless otherwise indicated, the data in this chapter are from the 1976 Michigan CPS National Election Survey.

then the Ford and Carter administrations have been trying—without much success—to limit and direct American energy consumption. Much of the problem is
rooted in simple ignorance: only 60 percent of the American public knows the basic
fact that we cannot produce all the oil we consume (in fact, nearly half of the oil
used in this country is imported).[4] About half the population can name their representative in Congress, and a few more know the name of one of their senators. In
1972, the voters elected a Democratic Congress and at the same time reelected the
Republican president, Richard M. Nixon, by a landslide. Scarcely half the people
knew that the Democrats had maintained their control of Congress in 1972. Many
similar examples (see Table 7.1) could be presented to show how little Americans
know about politics.[5]

   This level of ignorance exists because the workings of the government are
usually remote from the day-to-day lives of most people. Politics seems complex,
abstract, and irrelevant: Supreme Court decisions, Middle East politics, China, are
not real issues for most people. Thirty percent of adult Americans say that they pay
attention to politics "only now and then" or "hardly at all." About the same number see anything about politics on television or in newspapers rarely, if at all. In fact,
barely more than a quarter of the population say they "frequently" read about national politics in a newspaper.

   Sometimes, however, a political event is so sensational that everyone is aware
of it. During a single week at the height of the Watergate scandal, nearly nine out of
ten adults watched the televised Senate hearings.[6] In the 1976 presidential cam-

Table 7.1

**What the American People Know
about American Government**

	ADULTS WHO KNOW THE RIGHT ANSWER (PERCENTAGES)
How many times can an individual be elected president?	74%
Which party had the most members in the House of Representatives before the election?	64
Which party elected the most members to the House of Representatives in the election?	56
How long is the term of office for a member of the House of Representatives?	32
How long is the term of office for a United States senator?	30

Source: Unless otherwise indicated, data in this chapter has been
computed by the authors from the University of Michigan Center for
Political Studies, 1972 National Election Study.

[4] *Gallup Opinion Index,* August 1978, pp. 26–29. People who knew the facts were more favorable toward President Carter's proposals. In 1979, during another gasoline shortage and after
the decline of oil production in Iran, only 46 percent said that the United States has to import
some oil from other countries. (*San Francisco Chronicle,* May 21, 1979, p. 5.)

[5] Americans are better informed about politics than the citizens of England, Germany, and Italy.
See Gabriel A. Almond and Sidney Verba, *The Civic Culture* (Princeton, N.J.: Princeton University Press, 1963), p. 96.

[6] *Gallup Opinion Index,* September 1973.

paign, 83 percent saw at least one of the Ford-Carter debates. And in a general way, everyone is aware of issues such as the Vietnam war and inflation. It is not that public opinion is nonexistent; there are always *some* people who know and care about almost any political subject. Widespread apathy and ignorance should not lead us to conclude that *no one* cares.

The American electorate, then, is not a single thing: it is as varied as American society. At one extreme is a largely uneducated core of 20 to 30 percent who are chronic political know-nothings, who seldom think at all about politics. Near the other extreme are college graduates, the best-informed segment of the population. In 1977, however, only 14 percent of all Americans over the age of 17 had completed four or more years of college. Less than half of all 17- and 18-year-olds were in college, and less than a third of people aged 20 and 21. Fully 33 percent of all adults had not graduated from high school, and 17 percent had not even gone beyond the eighth grade (see Figure 7.1). In short, most Americans do not have the educational experience of the readers of this book. As a result, their view of the world differs from the view of those who have had such experiences. Like everything else we acquire, information has costs. Learning something requires giving up time that could be spent doing other things. Naturally, the cost of information is higher for people who have little experience reading complex and often abstract material.

The bulk of the electorate falls between the two extremes. These people are not strongly interested in or informed about politics, but they can be roused over certain issues. They are believers in the "American creed" — but find defining that creed in terms of concrete issues difficult.

Figure 7.1
Educational Levels of Americans Age 18 and Over, 1977

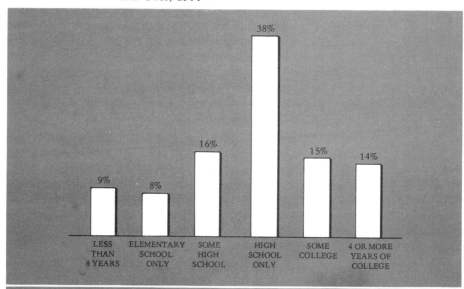

Source: Current Population Reports, Series P-20, No. 314, December 1977.

Belief in the American Creed:
Freedom and Racial Tolerance

Freedom is an idea that is clear and uncontroversial in the abstract, and muddy and controversial in the concrete. Our belief in freedom has frequently been compromised by our unwillingness to give it to people holding unpopular views. A policy which to one person is a matter of freedom — for example, permitting a public lecture to be held in which it is claimed that blacks are racially inferior — may be interpreted by others as an intolerable assault on the equality of all Americans. Others might let a racist speak but draw the line at an atheist, or at pornography. Does freedom of speech include the right to present sexually explicit films, despite the wishes of the community? In short, a great many people who are in favor of freedom of speech as a general proposition are not, when it comes down to cases, willing to say that Communists, atheists, and so on should be allowed to express their opinions in public. Since the early 1950s, a series of polls has traced tolerance of unpopular minorities. Willingness to grant free speech has grown considerably over this period. At the outset, only 37 percent of the public would let an atheist speak in their community, and just 27 percent would grant this freedom to "an admitted Communist." By 1977, fully 62 percent said they would let an atheist speak, and 55 percent would be tolerant of a Communist. But substantial minorities still opposed making the Bill of Rights a reality for atheists and Communists.[7]

Attitudes toward blacks also have changed in a liberal direction over the years. Many popular stereotypes about blacks have been rejected by almost everyone. Support for racial equality in specific areas of life has risen since the 1960s, when much of the press was claiming inaccurately that a great "white backlash" was building.[8]

Nevertheless, there is still much variation from issue to issue in white beliefs on issues that are explicitly racial — like busing — or that have particular relevance to blacks — like unemployment. For example, only one person in twelve said that whites have a right to keep blacks from moving into their neighborhoods. At the same time, busing children to schools outside their neighborhoods in order to achieve racial integration was opposed by an overwhelming majority. Fully 62 percent of all Americans said they were "strongly opposed" to busing, another 12 percent were against it, and only 9 percent were in favor. Unlike most issues, the proportion of people who said they hadn't thought about the issue or had no opinion was very small.

By the late 1970s, most American whites thought that persisting social and economic inequalities were due not to racial discrimination but to blacks' lack of job skills. In their view, further black advances should come from individual efforts rather than racial militancy or special governmental assistance. Only 10 percent of the entire population (and 27 percent of nonwhites) favored giving women and minori-

[7] Samuel A. Stouffer, *Communism, Conformity and Civil Liberties* (Garden City, N.Y.: Doubleday, 1955), pp. 29–42. We calculated the 1977 findings from the 1977 NORC General Social Survey.

[8] D. Garth Taylor et al., "Periods of Change in American Racial Attitudes," unpublished paper, National Opinion Research Center, 1977.

ties special preference in jobs and education. There was no difference on this point between men and women.[9] Numerous polls show strong support for reducing welfare, a step that would have a negative effect on blacks. At the same time, over two-thirds of the public believes "the federal government should see to it that *every* person who wants to work has a job."[10] Such a job program would, of course, be most beneficial to blacks, who suffer much higher unemployment than do whites.

These contrasting findings show the difficulty of deducing opinions on one issue from attitudes toward another issue. If we look just at busing, the American public seems very hostile to a leading civil rights measure — but predominant sentiment on jobs would lead to the opposite conclusion. Are Americans liberal or conservative?

Left or Right: It All Depends

At any particular time, it is easy to find evidence that the American public is conservative, but moving to the left. At the same time, one could with equal ease find evidence that the American people are liberal, but moving to the right. Depending on the issue, one can prove that most Americans are very liberal, very conservative, or anything in between. One way to describe public opinion, then, would be to present a laundry list of poll findings. Many of these findings would, however, change in response to events in the political world. Another approach is to talk about the structure of differences in public opinion: from issue to issue, group to group, and time to time.

Much debate by American political leaders and theorists divides into two channels that can be broadly described as **liberal** and **conservative.** Conservatives emphasize the freedom of individuals and corporations to pursue their own economic interests. Liberals pay more attention to seeing that no one starves and that everyone is protected from too much private power. On matters of personal expression, on the other hand, the liberal position stresses freedom, while conservatives are more likely to favor government regulation. Here we are concerned about the importance of liberalism and conservatism to the average American. They are examples of **ideology,** which we define as an internally consistent pattern of general beliefs that leads to specific attitudes about political issues.

What role does ideology play in the formation of political opinions in America? If most Americans had well-developed ideological outlooks and took them seriously, then liberals would always take the liberal position and conservatives would always adopt the conservative solution whenever a new issue arose. Ideology would be a substitute for information in opinion formation. If this were the case, the widespread

Drawing by Weber; © 1976, The New Yorker Magazine, Inc.

"I guess I'm a conservative, if you mean do I put up a lot of jams and jellies."

[9] *Gallup Opinion Index,* June 1977, p. 22.

[10] E. J. Dionne, Jr., "The New Politics of Jobs," *Public Opinion,* March – April 1978, p. 52.

Depending on the issue, the American public is conservative:
   74 percent oppose busing*
   73 percent oppose abortion on demand
   only 23 percent favor legalizing marijuana*
Or liberal:
   77 percent think that big business has too much influence
   69 percent want federal job safety rules for business
   only 23 percent say women's place is in the home*
   only 18 percent emphasize law and order over treating the causes
      of urban unrest*
Or halfway in between:
   34 percent want to increase the tax rate for high incomes and
      37 percent want the same tax rate for everyone*

*The remaining respondents include many who have no opinion or whose opinion is neutral.

lack of information about current events would be less important because people would make decisions on the basis of ideology.

Liberal and conservative are handy labels many people use in talking about politics. Commentators often talk about public opinion and election results in these ideological terms: "America is moving to the right" or "The outcome of the election revealed a pronounced liberal shift among the voters." Most such interpretations are out of touch with the real world, although, of course, some people *do* have a general political philosophy that could properly be called ideological. These people are **ideologues.** They base their conclusions about particular issues and candidates on their ideologies. By knowing the attitudes of such people on one issue, we can predict how they will respond on others. It is also true that any individual's attitude on any specific issue could be labeled radical, liberal, conservative, reactionary, or what have you. *But the vast majority of Americans do not have ideological perspectives, or even internally consistent clusters of attitudes.* Let us examine this conclusion more fully by exploring three questions about the role of ideology in American politics. How many Americans identify themselves in ideological terms? How many Americans actually know the meanings of words like "liberal" and "conservative"? To what extent are the opinions people hold on a single issue related to the opinions they hold on other issues?

Ideological Self-Identification When Americans are asked "How would you describe yourself—as very conservative, fairly conservative, middle-of-the-road, fairly liberal, or very liberal?" almost all will use one of these terms. But a different picture emerges if a more sensitive question is asked. In some studies, instead of pushing people to give themselves labels, researchers ask questions such as these: "We hear a lot of talk these days about liberals and conservatives. I'm going to show you a seven-point scale on which the political views that people might hold are arranged from extremely liberal to extremely conservative. Where would you place yourself on this scale, or haven't you thought much about this?"

We have arranged answers to this question in Figure 7.2, which shows that less than 3 percent of the population call themselves either extremely liberal or extremely conservative. About 7 percent call themselves liberal, another 8 percent slightly liberal, 12 percent slightly conservative, and 11 percent conservative. Counting the number of people on the liberal and conservative sides of the midpoint in Figure 7.2, we can see that about 16 percent of the population put themselves on the Left, compared to 25 percent on the Right. More significant is the fact that 34 percent say they really have not thought much about locating themselves ideologically, or they just plain do not know. Another 25 percent call themselves moderates or middle-of-the-road, which may be another way of ducking the problem altogether. Thus, 59 percent of Americans either do not define themselves ideologically or make the wishy-washy statement that they are moderate.

These findings about self-identification lead us to conclude that most Americans have a very low level of ideological consciousness. Only about half the adults in this country even know what the words "liberal" and "conservative" mean.[11] This is more than not knowing a definition. At the heart of conservative thought in

Figure 7.2

How Americans Locate Themselves on a Scale from "Extremely Liberal" to "Extremely Conservative"

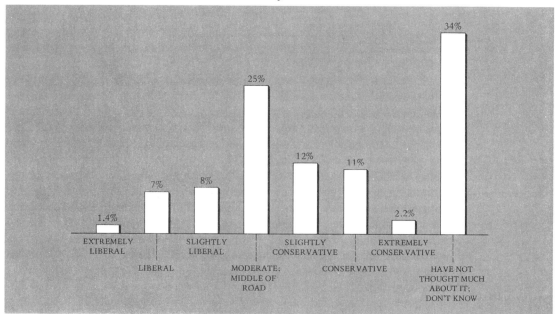

[11] Herbert McClosky and Charles A. Bann, "On the Reappraisal of the Classical Conservatism Scale," *Political Methodology,* (spring 1979).

Table 7.2

How Americans Classify Themselves, Liberals, and
Conservatives on Whether the Government Should
See That Everyone Has a Job and a Good
Standard of Living

OPINION	OWN POSITION	MOST LIBERALS	MOST CONSERVATIVES
"See to it that every person has a job and a good standard of living"	24%	34%	13%
Halfway in between	17	11	11
"The government should just let each person get ahead on his own"	38	14	37
Don't know own position or haven't thought much about the issue	20	20	20
Don't know where most liberals or conservatives stand	–	21	19
	99%	100%	100%

America is a preference for individual initiative rather than governmental intervention. Liberals, on the other hand, look to government to ensure a basic standard of
living for everyone. But this simple distinction is understood by only one American
in three. The 1976 Michigan respondents were asked for their own views on the
proper governmental role in providing welfare, and what they thought liberals and
conservatives believed about this basic policy question. Twenty percent had no
opinions of their own on this issue, and another 20 percent said they did not know
the liberal or conservative position. About one person in four got it backward or
said that liberals and conservatives were neutral on the welfare issue, leaving just
about a third who knew the answer (Table 7.2).

What is more, people who call themselves conservatives often do not take
conservative positions on specific issues, just as self-professed liberals may take positions that cannot be called liberal. For example, 28 percent of those who called
themselves liberals preferred private to governmental solutions to the health care
problem, while 23 percent of self-identified conservatives favored federally funded
insurance over private plans. Although people who call themselves conservatives
outnumber those who claim to be liberals, the number of people in favor of liberal
policies is often greater than the number opposed. This is more true of economic
than social issues (abortion, drugs, marijuana, gay rights), where the conservative
position is generally more popular. In other words, Americans tend to see themselves as more conservative than liberal, but their opinions on many issues are
more liberal than conservative.

Interrelations of Opinions   Perhaps we are being too demanding, perhaps it is not fair to
test for ideological consciousness by asking people to label
themselves. The American people may not feel comfortable with abstractions, but
may have a kind of folk wisdom that serves to distinguish left and right. The best

way to look for this sort of inarticulate ideology is to see how the position people take on one issue is related to their positions on other issues. If opinions are derived from some general political outlook, we would expect them to be related to each other in a consistent pattern.

Over the past half-century, one of the major disputes in American politics has been the extent to which the government should take responsibility for meeting the basic needs of every citizen. Among the most important of these needs are a job, a decent standard of living, and good health. The liberal position on these issues is that the government should see that everyone has a job and medical care. Conservatives argue that individuals should be responsible for getting their own jobs and obtaining their own medical care. Of those who have opinions about whether the government should finance medical care and whether it should see that everyone has a job, only 57 percent were consistently liberal or conservative on these two issues. The other 43 percent were either liberal on one issue and conservative on the other, or did not give unqualified answers to both questions.

Do economic liberals tend to be liberals on civil rights, civil liberties, foreign policy, or environmental issues? There is a modest tendency toward consistency, with some clusters of opinions in related areas, and other cases where there is no relationship at all. Look, for example, at the connection between opinions on the welfare state and on protecting the rights of the accused. Some people, liberals on this issue, say they are "primarily concerned with doing everything possible to protect the legal rights of those accused of committing crimes." Other people, conservatives on this issue, "feel that it is more important to stop criminal activity even at the risk of reducing the rights of the accused."

How many people who are liberal on the rights of the accused also take the liberal position on government job policy? The answer is in Table 7.3, which shows the combinations of opinions on these two issues. Due process liberals are about evenly split between liberal and conservative positions on the welfare state: 38 percent of them think the government should see that everyone has a job, and 42 percent think the government should let each person get ahead on his own. Conservatives on law and order are a bit more consistent. Less than a quarter of them are

Table 7.3

Relationship between Opinions on Due Process and on Welfare

POSITION ON WELFARE	POSITION ON DUE PROCESS		
	Protect the Rights of the Accused	*Middle of the Road*	*Stop Crime Regardless of Rights*
Government should see that everyone has a job and a good standard of living	38%	22%	23%
Middle of the road	20	31	21
Government should let each person get ahead on his own	42	47	57
	100%	100%	101%

liberal on jobs for everyone, while more than half support the laissez-faire notion that everyone should take care of himself. No matter what combinations of issues we examine, the results are the same. Ideology and "consistency" may be important in speeches and to activists, but they play a very small role in the perspectives of the mass public. Even among college graduates, ideological awareness and opinion consistency are far from overwhelming.[12]

The failure of the population to divide into neatly defined ideological groups brings us back to the discussion in Chapter 2 about **cross-cutting social cleavages.** Lines of ethnicity, religion, and social class in the United States run across each other; they do not build into a series of cumulative antagonisms. The political consequences of such a mixture were described this way by one political scientist:

> People do not divide into two camps, with members of one group in agreement on one side of all domestic economic issues and united to oppose the other group united within itself in opposition on the same issues. . . . Instead, the liberal-conservative cleavage divides the population along different lines, depending on the matter at issue. . . .
>
> Enemies on the burning issues of today may be allies on the foremost questions of tomorrow. Antagonists will, in short, have common interests, and the mixture of antagonism and alliance may induce restraint in conflict.[13]

Although the existence of overlapping, inconsistent belief systems keeps us from bitter political conflict, it also makes it difficult for us to form alliances based on common attitudes. Thus, the low level of ideology helps explain why the government often finds it difficult to reach decisions about policy.

WHO HAS WHAT OPINIONS?

As we have just seen, most Americans cannot be described as liberal or conservative. But on an opinion-by-opinion basis, it is possible to generalize about what kinds of people have what sorts of opinions. The two personal characteristics most strongly related to differences in political opinion are *occupation* and *education*. These two factors are not the only lines along which political differences occur, but they are the most important.

Education and Occupation   In a very rough way, we can talk about two kinds of liberals and conservatives. One sort of liberal favors government intervention in the economy and the provision of certain kinds of benefits to individuals. This "pork-chop liberalism" focuses on income distribution, taxes, labor-manage-

---

[12] For a time it was believed that the American people became more ideologically consistent as a result of political turmoil in the 1960s. A closer look at the evidence revealed that nothing had changed except the questions asked by survey researchers. See George F. Bishop et al., "Effects of Question Wording and Format on Political Attitude Consistency," *Public Opinion Quarterly*, 42 (spring 1978), pp. 81–92.

[13] V. O. Key, Jr., *Public Opinion and American Democracy* (New York: Knopf, 1961), p. 164.

ment relations, regulation of business, minimum wages, social security, medical insurance, public works, federal aid to education, and the like. The most important determinant of attitudes on such topics is occupation. Business and professional people are most opposed to government action in these areas, clerks and salespeople are somewhat more liberal, and blue-collar workers are most liberal of all.

On a wide variety of other issues, however, opinions differ more by education than by occupation. Race relations is one such area. The more schooling a white person has, the greater the likelihood of racial tolerance. This does not mean that all college graduates are tolerant and all unschooled people are bigots. It means only that the proportion of tolerant people is higher among the better educated. In fact, willingness to accept "different" people and behavior generally is greater among those with more education. Better educated people are more sympathetic to abortion, the women's movement, gay rights, and drugs. Since people with better educations tend to have better jobs, the pattern of liberalism on these life-style issues runs opposite to that on economic issues. People earning over $25,000 a year are almost twice as favorable toward abortion as those making under $5,000. Over half the poorest group and only a fourth of the richer one say they would turn in their own child if they caught him or her smoking marijuana.[14]

Educational differences are particularly striking on the "American creed" issues discussed previously. As Table 7.4 shows, people with more schooling are much more willing to grant free speech to those who advocate unpopular causes. By overwhelming majorities, college graduates are tolerant of Communists, atheists, and advocates of military dictatorship. Although less educated people are equally ready to pay lip service to freedom in the abstract, they are far less likely to support granting it to people whose causes they find distasteful.

Table 7.4

Education and Support for Freedom of Speech

	PERCENTAGE WILLING TO ALLOW VARIOUS TYPES OF INDIVIDUALS TO SPEAK					
	General Public	College Graduates	Some College	High School Graduates	Some High School	Grade School or Less
An advocate of abolishing elections and setting up a military government	51	78	62	53	41	23
An opponent of churches and religion	62	83	79	67	55	30
An admitted Communist	55	81	70	59	44	25
A homosexual	62	82	77	68	52	31

Source: National Opinion Research Center, General Social Survey, 1977.

[14] "Who Opposes Social Change?" *The Public Interest,* spring 1974, pp. 126–27; and Peter Skerry, "The Class Conflict over Abortion," *The Public Interest,* summer 1978, p. 75.

Educated people are more tolerant of free speech because they are more likely to understand the importance of civil liberties to the functioning of democratic government. Furthermore, since they have the highest levels of political activity, they have a vested interest in free speech. The greater political influence of such people helps explain why we continue to have a fairly high degree of political freedom despite the large number of people who are not committed to civil liberties. Since the educated are more influential, their political views have a greater chance of success than the views of the uneducated.

Racial Differences   As groups, blacks and whites do not disagree much on most issues, particularly when we take educational differences into account.[15] Not surprisingly, however, major gaps occur concerning the condition of blacks and what should be done about it. The sharp decline in white prejudice has not been accompanied by a widespread conviction that blacks are still badly hurt by discrimination or that federal policy should guarantee blacks the same level of jobs and prosperity as whites. Blacks, on the other hand, are more likely to favor such measures. In 1976, for example, the vast majority of blacks thought that the government should guarantee school integration, a position taken by less than a quarter of the white population. Moreover, whites were twice as likely to say that they had not thought much about this issue.

On the other hand, it would be a mistake to assume that blacks always support measures undertaken to achieve racial equality. Most blacks, for example, join the overwhelming majority of whites in opposing school busing. And as we saw earlier, the prevailing black view opposes preferential treatment of minorities and women. So far, we have looked at what American opinions are. Now let us look at how they are learned and shaped.

HOW ATTITUDES ARE LEARNED

Every society has rules of conduct that children learn as they discover the outside world. There are rules about how to address older people, younger people, or strangers; rules about appropriate behavior at home, in school, and so forth. Every society has some sort of political system, and therefore there are lessons about politics to be learned. Among the most important of these are general rules, such as equality or hierarchy, that are transferred to politics from everyday life.

Beginning with Plato, political observers have recognized the importance of each new generation's learning citizenship. Only recently, however, have social scientists done systematic studies of how political learning takes place. What they have found is that much of a person's political education is done in childhood.

[15] Blacks are the only racial minority numerous enough to provide enough respondents in a national survey sample to give us reliable information on their political opinions. The enormous samples used by the Bureau of the Census will let us say something in the next chapter about the voting rates of Chicanos and Puerto Ricans. Other valid data on the political behavior of these minorities are very scarce.

Courses in civics and American government are required of public school students in almost every state. But the schools are only part of the larger process known as **political socialization.** Many of the experiences that motivate the behavior of both leaders and citizens happen in early childhood, before the first civics course. Let us examine some of the steps though which most Americans, in the course of growing up, are introduced to the political world.

Learning
National Loyalty
In the modern world, one's nation commonly is an important reference group. From the early days of the United States, foreign visitors have often commented on our outspoken pride in being Americans. Even in the 1960s and 1970s, when many more people were expressing political cynicism, being an American still seemed to be a source of pride for most citizens.

It is not surprising, therefore, that a sense of nationality is one of the first political ideas. Early in elementary school, children begin to think of themselves as Americans. When children were shown pictures of the flags of different nations and asked which they liked most, kindergarten pupils most often preferred the Thai flag, which at the time of the research pictured an elephant. But first-graders rejected the flag of Thailand in favor of the American flag — a triumph of patriotism over a childish love of zoological wonders.[16] Apparently the kindergarten children saw the flags simply as pictures or patterns. The first-graders understood that the flag is a symbol of America, that they are Americans, and that being American is *good.*

The development of national loyalty in children begins before they can understand the meaning of the political symbols they accept.

Ann Hagen Griffiths, DPI

Learning about
National
Government
Political Figures and Institutions. The president is the first element of the government to come to the child's attention. Indeed, throughout the school years, most children have a presidency-centered view of the federal government. As Table 7.5 shows, by age 13 almost everyone can name the president but only one other official was known by more than a fifth of the children studied.

During the Eisenhower, Kennedy, and early Johnson administrations, children considered the president a "benevolent leader." When asked to describe the president, children often answered with praise. A typical response was that the president's job is "to make people happy . . . he helps other people in other countries too and tries to make things better for everyone."[17] What happens to this benign view when the president falls into public disfavor? Children then adopt their

16 Edwin D. Lawson, "The Development of Patriotism in Children: A Second Look," *Journal of Psychology,* 55 (1963), pp. 279–86.

17 Fred I. Greenstein, "The Benevolent Leader Revisited: Children's Images of Political Authority in Three Countries," *American Political Science Review,* 69 (December 1975), pp. 1371–98.

Table 7.5

Political Information of Children and Young Adults

OFFICIAL	PERCENTAGE WHO KNOW THE NAME OF EACH OFFICIAL		
	13-Year-Olds	*17-Year-Olds*	*Young Adults*
President	94	98	98
Vice-president	60	79	87
Secretary of state	2	9	16
Secretary of defense	6	16	24
Speaker of the House of Representatives	2	25	32
Senate majority leader	4	14	23
At least one senator from own state	16	44	57
U.S. Representative from own district	11	35	39

Source: National Assessment of Educational Progress, Report 2: Citizenship: National Results—Partial (Denver and Ann Arbor, July 1970), p. 37.

elders' negative views, although they still have an idealized view of the presidency itself. They also seem not to absorb the full intensity of public criticism. Early in the unfolding Watergate scandal, President Nixon's popularity among adults plunged in six months from about 75 percent to about 50 percent. At the same time, children's opinions of Nixon declined only slightly. Later, when only a quarter of adults supported Nixon, his popularity among children finally dropped sharply. In the Ford administration, however, children once again tended to see the president in a favorable light.[18]

In short, children normally tend to have an idealized view of the presidency and to organize their political awareness around this office. In many ways the American political system is in fact presidency-centered. The prominence both children and adults assign to the president is realistic, so belief and reality tend to reinforce one another. The fact that our system *is* presidency-centered reinforces our beliefs, and our beliefs in turn enhance our tendency to look to the president to establish the basic agenda of politics. But events in the world can reduce or eliminate idealization. Moreover, changes in a child's reference group environment can affect political socialization. At the peak of the civil rights movement in the mid-1960s, Presidents Kennedy and Johnson were very popular among black adults and were liked even more by black than by white children. But by the late 1960s many blacks had become distinctly hostile to the political system and its leaders. During this period, black children had more negative views of the president than did white children.

[18] *Ibid.;* and F. Christopher Arterton, "Watergate and Children's Attitudes toward Political Authority Revisited," *Political Science Quarterly,* 90 (fall 1975), pp. 477–96.

Party Preferences.   Many children consider themselves "Republicans" or "Democrats" at an early age, long before they know what the parties do or the differences between them. Like sports fans, they support a team because it is "theirs."

These loyalties are learned from parents and from sharing the parents' political and social environment. Few children depart from their parents' party loyalties. What is more, most young people who do not share their parents' choice of party fail to develop any party loyalties of their own. That is, they are Independents.

Learning about Equality   The family is the first political system to which we belong. Often our ideas about equality and authority were first formed in the little social system in which we grew up. Foreign visitors who commented on the nonauthoritarian nature of American families were also struck by the extraordinary sense of social and political equality that Americans expressed. The social and economic inequalities in early American society were slight compared to Europe. Later, these inequalities became much sharper. Nevertheless, the subjective reality—what people *believe* to be true—is as important as the objective situation. And Americans, from post-Revolutionary times to the 1970s, seem to have retained a strong belief in the principle of equality.

A sense of the way assumptions about equality can arise (or fail to arise) in childhood is conveyed by the following pair of interviews with an American and a French child. Both children were studied in a comparative inquiry into political socialization that explored spontaneous expectations about political behavior by asking children to finish incomplete stories. The stories were designed to pose standard dilemmas of social and political existence. Compare Michelle, the daughter of a French businessman, and Debbie, the daughter of an American doctor.

INTERVIEWER: One day the President was driving his car to a meeting. Because he was late, he was driving very fast. The police stopped the car. Finish the story.

Michelle	*Debbie*
M: First of all, it isn't true that General de Gaulle drives his own car. He has a chauffeur and can tell him to go very fast. If he is stopped by a policeman, the policeman will have to let him go because General de Gaulle commands everyone, because they all must serve France and they are there to see that order is maintained in France. They release him immediately, because General de Gaulle has a very important meeting, so they are forced to let him go.	D: The President asks him why he's stopping him and the policeman says, "You're going too fast." And he says, "Well, I'm going to be late for a meeting." And the policeman says, "I don't really care if you're President or anything, you've got to obey the rules of the country and if you don't you shouldn't be President." And then, of course, the President agrees, if he's smart enough to agree, so he believes him. And so he slows down. He's late for the meeting, but it was worth it.
I: What will the policeman say?	

M: "I apologize, *mon Général,* for
stopping you, but I didn't
recognize your car."

The investigators responsible for the study in which Michelle and Debbie were interviewed were struck by the many references by children like Debbie to the equality of all Americans:

It doesn't make a difference who you are in this country, you still have to obey the laws.

And the policeman says, "I don't really care if you're the President or anything, you've got to obey the rules of the country and if you don't you shouldn't be President."

The President is an American. He's just like anybody else, only he's got a high office.

Such ideas about equality were not expressed by all American children, however. The study found that although *white* children were considerably more likely than French children to refer to the equality of all citizens, the *black* children were *less* likely than any other group to employ this theme. Coming from a deprived segment of the population, these children have adopted a more cynical attitude than their white counterparts. Understandably, they find it hard to believe that all Americans are equal.

HOW ATTITUDES ARE SHAPED

Most people have *some* interest in politics and do have opinions about various issues and politicians. Their opinions may be weak and open to change with tomorrow's headlines, or they may be so solid as to be part of the individual's personality. How are such opinions formed and altered?

One of the most important sources of opinion is reference groups. Any group to which a person feels he or she belongs qualifies as a reference group if the person's sense of common identity with other group members helps define his or her self-image. A Jew might assess a foreign policy issue in terms of its impact on Israel, a traveling salesman might be concerned about how it would affect the price of gasoline, a farmer might think about its consequences for the demand for wheat, and a black might think about its impact on employment in the ghetto. But although group identifications play a great part in opinion formation, there are limits on their influence. In the first place, most people have several reference groups. A Jewish traveling salesman, for example, might favor aid to Israel, despite the fact that it would antagonize Arab states and thus raise the price of gasoline. The fact that he is also a salesman would not influence his opinion. What is more, many issues are not relevant for groups, and groups are often divided on issues.

Despite low public attention to politics, some events are noted by almost everyone, especially major historical changes that affect many personal lives. Wars, depressions, and severe domestic unrest all may shape views of politics long after they have ended. Such events by themselves are not a clear signpost for individual beliefs; usually it is political leaders who provide the "interpretations" that link societal earthquakes to personal seismographs. Many people may be dissatisfied with the economy; they find it hard to get jobs or are disturbed by the failure of others to do so. But the economy may not become an issue until the press and politicians interpret it as such. And even then, such attention may lack focus until solutions are advanced — although these may be nothing more than voting incumbents out of office.

The Role of Leadership   When an admired politician says or does something that conflicts with some followers' beliefs, they have a potential source of discomfort. Their problem can be resolved by any of these steps: (1) dropping support of the politician; (2) changing their mind on the issue; (3) misperceiving what the politician said; or (4) living with the discomfort. All four of these things happen all the time. In the psychologist's laboratory, where experimental subjects can be forced to confront inconsistent beliefs, this experience produces anxiety. In the real world, anxiety is minimized because one or the other of the inconsistent beliefs is often unimportant to the individual and fades into the background. Or perhaps the inconsistency causes the person to play down one of the beliefs. The "problem" may be handled by an unconscious "convenient memory."

Sometimes, of course, the response will be a loss of support for the politician. Much more common, however, is for supporters to change their opinion on the issue to bring it into conformity with his position. After all, few issues are as important as one's liking (or disliking) the president or another major figure. A good example of this occurred in early 1970. Shortly before Americans troops moved into Cambodia, only 7 percent of the public said they favored such a step. After the surprise invasion — which was the most unpopular episode of the Vietnam war — 50 percent said that President Nixon had done the right thing.[19] We can safely assume that Cambodia was not a major object of concern for most Americans, that few people thought about it, and thus that there was little investment in the subject one way or the other. This was not true about loyalty to one's party, nor about attitudes toward the president. With the double advantage of his office and his position as party leader, Nixon produced dramatic changes in public opinion by his action. Opinion about military action in Cambodia was much more subject to change than feelings about Nixon. As this example suggests, officials usually have more freedom in foreign than domestic policy, since public opinion about almost all international issues is weak enough to be changed by political leaders.

The war in Vietnam was more prominent and emotion laden than any other foreign policy issue of the past generation. Nevertheless, attitudes toward the war reflected not only the ups and downs of the conflict itself, but also the influence of more durable points of reference. There were three general sources of attitudes

[19] Milton Rosenberg et al., *Vietnam and the Silent Majority,* quoted in Lipset, "The Wavering Polls," pp. 86–87.

toward the war. One group consisted of *followers* who supported the president and what he was doing because he was the president. (Some people, of course, automatically oppose whatever the U.S. government does.) A second category consisted of *partisans* who supported or opposed Vietnam policy depending on the party of the person in the White House. During the Johnson administration, Republicans were most likely to think that the war had been a mistake. But by the time Nixon had been president for eight months, Republicans were more favorable to the war than Democrats. "Johnson's war" thus became "Nixon's war." Finally, there were *believers,* people who were moved chiefly by the substance of what was going on. These people made up their minds on the merits of the policy as they understood it, rather than on the basis of what party was in power or what the president was doing.[20]

Because believers are a small minority on most issues, a great deal of public opinion is determined not by perceptions of the issue itself, but by various factors associated with it, such as the people who are seen to be for and against it and the party positions of those concerned. People seek guidelines for evaluating the political world and for determining their own positions on issues. Often these guidelines are provided by personal and party loyalties that really have little to do with the issue itself.

THE MASS MEDIA

Most of what we know about national politics comes to us through the mass media. Newspapers and television are the primary source of information; radio and magazines are less important. Although magazine circulation is tiny compared to the other three media, magazine readership is concentrated among the most interested, active people. As a result, magazines have an impact out of proportion to their numerical readership. Television has overtaken newspapers as the most important source of political news; its coverage of politics is simpler, clearer, and more encouraging. In 1976, 64 percent of the population said they relied on it, compared to just 19 percent who named newspapers, and 17 percent who used the two media equally. Nearly three-quarters of the population say they read a daily paper, although only 28 percent say they "frequently" read about national politics, compared to 36 percent who say they often read crime news. It appears that both newspapers and TV network news are watched primarily for "nonpolitical" reasons, so a good deal of political information is acquired as a by-product.[21]

The media are a perennial political scapegoat. Almost

Most political ceremonies are staged with the mass media in mind. Here television technicians prepare to cover Gerald Ford's swearing in as president.

Suva, DPI

[20] These categories and the evidence for them are from John E. Mueller, *War, Presidents, and Public Opinion* (New York: Wiley, 1973), Chap. 5.

[21] Michael J. Robinson, "Television and American Politics: 1956–1976," *The Public Interest,* summer 1977, p. 17. The television news audience is somewhat less educated than newspaper readers.

all losing candidates complain that the press is against them, and even some winners do not seem happy about the media. Long before Watergate, President Nixon and other members of his administration felt that the press had a distinct bias to the Left. On the other side of the ideological spectrum, radicals consider the media part of the "establishment" that hoodwinks and oppresses "the people." Since there are newspapers and magazines to satisfy any conceivable political taste, from Maoist to Nazi, anyone complaining about press bias can make a case based on a careful selection of the evidence.

Although television and radio stations are prohibited by licensing laws and the Federal Communications Commission from advocating political viewpoints, no such restrictions apply to the print media. At election time, most newspapers publish editorials endorsing the candidates of their choice. It is the owners of the newspapers who decide which candidates to recommend, and most newspaper owners have a conservative outlook. Republicans are always favored over Democrats by a wide margin. In 1968, Richard Nixon got the editorial support of 80 percent of the nation's newspapers; this figure went up to 90 percent in 1972. Four years later, Gerald Ford enjoyed almost as big a margin of endorsements.

The conservative bias of most owners is only part of the story, however. There are major limits to the ability or willingness of owners to transfer their political opinions from the editorial page to the news columns. As businesspeople, their first interest is in selling their product. If they are too offensive politically, they may lose part of their audience. Moreover, most reporters and editors are sympathetic to liberal — and sometimes radical — causes. Thus, the conservatism of the owners is often balanced by the liberalism of the working press. In their actual news coverage of presidential campaigns, the nationwide press services, electronic media, and most newspapers seem even-handed in their treatment of the Democratic and Republican presidential nominees.[22]

A few publications are far more influential than the rest, however. The most important are the *New York Times, Washington Post, Wall Street Journal, Time,* and *Newsweek.* The *New York Times* and the *Washington Post* (in partnership with the *Los Angeles Times*) each has its own news service, which is received daily by hundreds of local newspapers. The *Post* also owns *Newsweek.* The detailed and sophisticated political coverage of these publications helps set the tone for the rest of the media, including television news. These strategic periodicals provide a major share of the stories read in local papers and seen on television. They are read by most national politicians, network executives, and newspaper editors. They are a central component of the political system. In short, their influence is far greater than their circulation figures would suggest.[23] Except for the *Wall Street Journal,* the owners and editors of these crucial organs are moderates and liberals. The people controlling television network news are also inclined to the liberal side of the spectrum.

All presidents complain about the press and have mixed relations with it. A

---

[22] Doris A. Graber, "Press and TV as Opinion Resources in Presidential Campaigns," *Public Opinion Quarterly,* 40 (fall 1976), p. 286.

[23] *The New York Times* has a circulation of about 850,000 on weekdays and 1.4 million on Sundays. Eighty-six copies of the *Times* are delivered to the White House every morning.

rather mild example is Carter's complaint that reporters overemphasize the "mechanics of policy and policy-making rather than the substance of policy."[24] Kennedy canceled the White House subscriptions to one paper that offended him and tried to get the *New York Times* to transfer a correspondent who wrote a story that displeased him. Eisenhower brought a Republican convention audience to its feet with a denunciation of "sensation-seeking columnists and commentators." Far from indicating that something is wrong, such complaints are a sign that the press is functioning as it should. The fact of the matter is that *all* politicians have a natural adversary relationship with the press because they have different interests. Politicians want to maintain their power and get their programs enacted. Media owners want to sell more papers or attract more viewers. They do this by looking for new material. The ambitions of individual reporters lead them in the same direction. They want to present new facts. They are, indeed, seeking sensations. This means that bad news is more interesting than good news. But bad news, of course, is unwelcome to politicians in power, no matter how happy it may make the opposition.

In addition to analyzing the various biases of the mass media, we might ask what difference they make. For the most part, researchers have been hard put to find much evidence of how the media have affected political opinions or behavior. In 1968 and 1972, some voters reading papers that endorsed Nixon were a trifle more inclined to vote for him than were readers of papers backing his opponents.[25] People who were interviewed right after the second Ford-Carter debate in 1976 thought that Ford had done better. But after exposure to the press outcry about Ford's claim that Eastern Europe was not dominated by Russia, viewers came around to the conclusion that Carter had "won" the debate.[26]

Leaks to the Press   The desire of the press to tell what's happening day after day tends to irritate officials, but it also makes the press dependent on them for information. One expert described the reporter's dilemma this way:

> Journalists are rarely, if ever, in a position to establish the truth about an issue for themselves, and they are therefore almost entirely dependent on self-interested "sources" for the version of reality that they report.[27]

At first glance, this seems to give the party in power an enormous advantage, since officials can release only as much information as they want. The facts that make the president and his policy look good can be announced with great fanfare, while the facts that point in the opposite direction can be passed over. In reality, however, the president cannot prevent members of his administration from "leak-

---

[24] *The New York Times,* December 4, 1977, p. 43.

[25] *Institute of Social Relations Newsletter,* winter 1974, p. 8.

[26] David O. Sears and Steven H. Chaffee, "Uses and Effects of the 1976 Debates: An Overview of Empirical Studies," in Sidney Kraus, ed., *The Great Debates: Ford vs. Carter, 1976* (Bloomington: Indiana University Press, 1979), p. 240.

[27] Edward Jay Epstein, "Journalism and Truth," *Commentary,* April 1974, p. 36.

"This is turning out to be such a high-minded meeting it would be a shame if someone didn't leak it to the press."

ing" information to the press. The American governmental system is exceptionally leaky. Secret information often finds its way into print, unless national security is involved. Almost all government employees are career civil servants who do not owe their jobs to the party in power. Although they cannot openly defy their political superiors, they can leak embarrassing information. The same is true of political appointees who differ with the president, or among themselves.

Political reporters devote a good deal of time to cultivating sources who can provide them with information that the president wants to keep confidential. Columnists specializing in exposes are particularly adept at developing networks of inside informants. The best known reporter of this kind, Jack Anderson, describes his methods:

> The most reliable sources are the professional, nonpolitical public servants whom the public never sees. Their first loyalty is to the citizens who pay them, not to their political superiors.
>
> I have been cultivating informers for twenty-five years; I know something about the psychology of one who has a dark secret and is teetering on the awful brink of disclosing it. His motive may be noble or base or just human; he may seek to protect the public from fraud, to advance a good cause, to discredit a rival, or to avenge a personal grievance.[28]

There is an obvious conflict between the public's right to know what the government is doing and the government's need to keep secrets for purposes of national security. The problem is complicated by an official tendency to classify material secret when disclosure would simply embarrass the administration but would not endanger the national interest. For this reason, some reporters argue that the government has no right to keep secrets, or that deciding to respect official secrecy should be a matter of individual conscience.

There are also "official leaks," material given deliberately by administration representatives to a friendly reporter for use without attributing it to the actual source. This technique is used to get an idea or a fact or an accusation into the media without taking responsibility for it. Reporters differ in their willingness to cooperate with politicians this way, depending on the nature of the material and the journalist's relations with the politician. Often, when we read that "sources close to the president revealed," the source may be the president himself. A leak attributed to "a high state department official" may actually come straight from the secretary of state.

Leaks are a peculiarly American practice. In almost all other democratic countries, it is a crime for government employees to reveal any official information. The American belief that one of the government's jobs is to provide information to the

[28] Jack Anderson, with George Clifford, *The Anderson Papers* (New York: Random House, 1973), pp. 7–8, 17.

public differs from the European conception that government business is not to be shared with the public. Complaints about excessive secrecy in Washington should be evaluated in light of the fact that the rest of the world is astounded at what seems to be the American practice of conducting government business in a goldfish bowl.

WHAT KINDS OF OPINION COUNT?

We can easily produce examples of the government's failing to conform to public sentiment on particular issues. For example, popular majorities favor handgun registration and permitting prayer in public schools. And large majorities oppose abortion, school busing, and preferential treatment for minorities. Yet the federal government has failed to adopt the first two measures, and it has adopted the latter three.

On the other hand, we can easily show that politicians do indeed respond to public opinion. Given the present state of knowledge in this area, we cannot be very precise about distinguishing between those areas where the government is responsive to popular pressure and those where it is not. At best, we can offer some generalizations about the relationship of public opinion to public policy. When people *do* care about an issue, or only *seem* to care about it, politicians are often quite responsive. The politician's problem is to find out what the public really wants. Here there is something of a dilemma, for most politicians know that people who write letters, demonstrate, or in some other way make their opinions known may not be representative of the public as a whole. A politician who favors a policy simply because mail runs strongly in favor of it may find he or she is supporting a vocal minority and displeasing most constituents, who dislike the policy but do not say so. On the other hand, articulate people who speak out strongly on an issue, even though they are only a minority, may be the very ones who care enough to change their votes if their representative displeases them, or even may contribute their time and money to defeat him or her.

It is easier for citizens to get their way politically if they know something about the issue and who their representives are. Outrage — whether by an average American, a union leader, or a millionaire — is not useful unless one knows how to direct it. Thus knowledge is a useful preliminary to influence. Information about politics is most common among better educated people. As we will see, the uninformed can move politicians, particularly through interest groups. Nevertheless, more specific and precise exercises of influence are possible only if one knows who the players are.

Although knowledge of the political process increases with education, even the best educated people are not informed about the complex specifics of government personnel and policy alternatives. Who, for example, knows the provisions of the president's annual legislative program, which committees in Congress consider which bills, and countless other crucial details of policymaking? Obviously, the answer is: Not very many people. A Washington lobbyist or correspondent might be informed about such matters, but the average American does not have the time or the resources required for keeping track of day-to-day political events.

Democracy simply cannot be the direct enactment by the government of the detailed policies the majority wants because in fact the majority seldom knows what alternatives are available, much less which ones it prefers.

Even when the people do have clear preferences, however, there is no guarantee that their opinions will be effective. Public opinion is largely irrelevant when people do not care very much about an issue. One of the most striking examples of public opinion favoring reform that does not seem likely to come about concerns the electoral college. Four out of five Americans would approve a constitutional amendment to "do away with the Electoral College and base the election of a President on the total vote cast throughout the nation."[29] Yet Congress has consistently failed to adopt such an amendment, and the chances of abandoning the electoral college do not seem bright. The failure of the American public to be concerned about abolishing the electoral college is undoubtedly explained by the fact that, while almost everyone expresses an opinion about the electoral college, only 35 percent of the public actually know what is is.[30]

In this chapter we have presented the raw material of individual political action — how Americans perceive the political world. In the following chapters, we will see how this raw material is mobilized and focused on the government, through the linkages provided by elections, participation, interest groups, and political parties. These mechanisms all simplify the diversity of individual opinions, rendering them more intelligible to the government. They also have considerable impact on what people think. Thus, public opinion is not formed in a vacuum; it both feeds and is shaped by the institutions that link it to the government.

SUMMARY Almost everything we know about public opinion comes from polls. One of the most important lessons is that careless polling can exaggerate impressions of Americans' political information and the clarity and stability of their opinions. In fact, politics is seldom very interesting to most people.

While almost everyone gives lip service to the Bill of Rights, a surprising number of people say they would not allow the public expression of unpopular views. Tolerance is growing in this area, however, as well as in acceptance of racial minorities.

The American people are mostly liberal on some issues, and largely conservative on others. As a general rule, the liberal viewpoint is more popular on economic issues than on social or "life-style" matters. Most Americans do not think about politics in ideological terms, do not know what liberalism and conservatism mean, and do not have opinions that are consistently liberal or conservative. People with better jobs are more likely to be conservative on economic issues, while better educated people are more liberal on social and life-style subjects.

As children become aware of the political world, they develop patriotic

---

[29] *Gallup Opinion Index,* October 1969, p. 22.

[30] Hazel Gaudet Erskine, "The Polls: Textbook Knowledge," *Public Opinion Quarterly,* 28 (spring 1963), p. 139.

attachment to the United States, an awareness of the president as the center of government, a belief that everyone should be treated equally, and identification with the Democratic or Republican party.

Because opinions on most political topics are less important personally than attitudes toward the president and presidential candidates, many people adjust their views on issues so as to make them consistent with what they think of a political leader whom they admire.

The mass media offer far more information and points of view than anyone can absorb. The media's most important bias is not toward one party, candidate, or ideology. Rather, the media are biased toward attracting audiences, which means that they simplify and sensationalize the news. The press is not dependent on the administration's version of events because of the availability of information leaked by officials who want to bring their side of the story before the public.

voting

Voting is the most common form of political action, the only way most people ever exert political influence. Voting is also the foundation for all other linkages between public opinion and government policy, such as interest groups and the political parties.

Elections are the mechanism by which government leaders are chosen. Almost 3 million civilians are on the federal payroll, but only 537 of them reach and hold their jobs by being elected. The president and vice-president are elected to terms of four years. Four hundred and thirty-five members of the House of Repre-

CHAPTER 8

sentatives are elected every two years. And 100 senators are elected to six-year terms, a third of them running every two years. These 537 men and women link "the people" and "the government." The processes that put them in and out of office are therefore fundamental to the functioning of the political system. They are also the major reason we call the United States a democracy.

In this chapter we will concentrate on the core of this process, the voting behavior of individuals. We begin by examining **voter turnout** — the number of people who go to the polls on election day. Then we look into how Americans decide how to vote as they do. This leads to an analysis of the lines of political cleavage, what election outcomes mean, and what can reasonably be expected of elections as a method for popular control of government.

Thanks to survey research, the study of voting behavior is a relatively advanced field in political science. We can talk about voting with more confidence than we can bring to topics where the facts are less accessible, such as the presidency or the Supreme Court. Nevertheless, it will soon be obvious that many things about voting remain mysterious.

VOTER TURNOUT

How many Americans vote, what kinds of people are most likely to vote, and in what circumstances? There are two sorts of answers to these questions. The first concerns **situational factors,** such as the voting laws and different types of election. The second involves the personal characteristics of citizens.

Election Laws The Constitution left the individual states free to determine the crucial question of who would be allowed to vote. At first, qualifications differed considerably from state to state, and only some men could vote. By the Civil War, the franchise had been extended to all adult white male citizens. Since then, federal action has expanded the electorate further. Constitutional amendments have restricted the states' autonomy by forbidding them to deny the right to vote on various grounds:

1. The Fifteenth Amendment, adopted in 1870, forbade the states to deny or limit the franchise because of "race, color, or previous condition of servitude."

2. The Nineteenth Amendment (1920) extended the vote to women.

3. The Twenty-fourth Amendment (1964) prohibited states from requiring voters to pay a special tax (poll taxes had been used in the South to discourage voting by poor people).

4. The Twenty-sixth Amendment (1971) forbade the states to deny the vote to anyone over 17 on the basis of age.

Despite the Fifteenth Amendment, by 1900 southern states prevented almost all blacks from voting, and continued to do so until recently. In 1940 a mere 5 per-

Twenty-thousand women march for suffrage on New York's Fifth Avenue in 1918.

cent of southern blacks were registered to vote. A combination of social change and legal and political pressure brought southern black registration to 27 percent by 1962. But some states still held out almost completely against democracy for blacks. In Mississippi only 5 percent of the black voting-age population was registered, and in Alabama only 13 percent. In 1965 the Voting Rights Act provided for replacement of local election officials by federal registrars in certain areas. The result was a dramatic expansion of black registration in the South, which rose to 65 percent between 1964 and 1974. The proportion of blacks registered in Mississippi increased tenfold.[1]

Although these steps expanded and guaranteed the right to vote, election turnout in America has been low for a long time. In the past fifty years the proportion of the voting-age population who actually cast a presidential ballot has never been as high as 65 percent. In off-year congressional elections, the average is under 42 percent. Figure 8.1 shows election turnout since 1952. The American performance compares badly with other democracies, where 75 to 90 percent of the population vote. This is a change from the past century, when Americans voted as much as anyone else.

In the days when Americans voted more, there were no registration requirements. This permitted a great deal of fraud, including repeat voting and voting by noncitizens. Around the turn of the century, states adopted laws requiring potential voters to register before the election, establishing that they were citizens and had been residents of the place for a specified period of time — in some places, up to two years.

Registration is an extra step, usually requiring a visit to a government office.

[1] Neal R. Peirce, *The Deep South States of America* (New York: Norton, 1974).

Figure 8.1
**Turnout in Presidential and House Elections,
1952–1978**

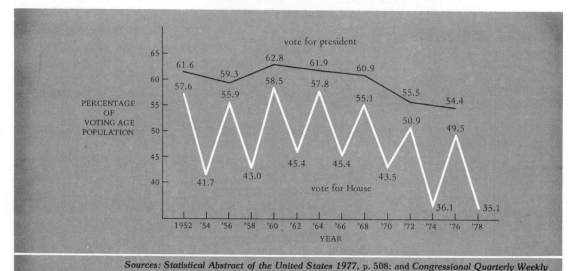

Sources: *Statistical Abstract of the United States 1977*, p. 508; and *Congressional Quarterly Weekly Report*, March 31, 1979, p. 574.

Most deadlines are some weeks before election day, when political interest is lower. Since a person registers in a particular voting precinct, almost any change of address involves re-registering. People who move have to find out all over again where and when to register. In contrast, almost all other democracies have automatic, national, permanent registration. Although Europeans are more likely than Americans to vote, they are *less* interested in politics. Most students of this problem have concluded that the lower turnout in America is due largely to the requirement that voters must register in advance of the election.[2]

Generalizations about American voting rates are risky. There are enormous differences from one state to the next, in part because of different state registration laws. In 1976, for example, turnout ranged from 72 percent in Minnesota to 42 percent in South Carolina. In Minnesota, any eligible voter can register at the polling place when he or she goes to vote on election day. South Carolina, like most southern states, makes registration difficult: the deadline is a month before the election, the offices are not required to be open after working hours, and there is no provision for registering by mail. If every state's registration laws were as liberal as in Minnesota and a few other states, nationwide turnout would increase by about nine percentage points. The biggest gains would be among the uneducated (who are

[2] Steven J. Rosenstone and Raymond E. Wolfinger, "The Effect of Registration Laws on Voter Turnout," *American Political Science Review*, 72 (March 1978), pp. 22–45. The timing of the registration deadline is the most important influence on turnout. One attempt to account for ill, ineligible, and other involuntary nonvoters produced an estimate that about 82 percent of the "legal, able electorate" voted in the 1960 election. See William G. Andrews, "American Voting Participation," *Western Political Quarterly*, 19 (December 1966), pp. 639–52.

most put off by demanding requirements) and in the South (which has lower educational levels and the least permissive laws). But these reforms would have virtually no political impact. If they were achieved, the voting population would be scarcely more liberal or Democratic than at present.[3]

In 1972 a Supreme Court decision imposed a maximum residency requirement of 30 days. The decision also had the effect of limiting the registration deadline to no more than a month before election day.[4] By 1976, several states permitted registration on election day. The following year, however, Congress rejected a national election-day registration bill drafted by the White House. The idea is not popular with the public and its immediate prospects are not bright, although a few more states may adopt it.

Registration laws are a prime example of a situational variable affecting turnout. Another such factor is the *kind* of election. Presidential contests are the most glamorous, exciting, and publicized races, and attract considerably more participation than congressional elections, as Figure 8.1 shows. Primary elections, held by each party to choose its nominees for the general election, are even less appealing to many voters. The turnout in primaries usually is about half as big as in the following general election, although once again the state-to-state variation is enormous.[5]

Who Votes? Voting rates can be analyzed according to many personal characteristics.[6] The two most important factors related to turnout are *age* and *education*. Figure 8.2 shows the relationship between age and turnout, calculated separately for men and women.[7] Voting is least frequent among the young. As age increases, so does voting. The high point for men is not reached until about the age of 70. Turnout of women, on the other hand, peaks before age 60. There is no difference in turnout between young men and women, and scarcely any until late middle age. The decline in voting by older women largely reflects two other characteristics of these age groups: (1) In earlier generations, many women were brought up to believe that voting was men's business. (2) Because women

---

[3] Rosenstone and Wolfinger, "The Effect of Registration Laws."

[4] *Dunn* v. *Blumstein,* 405 U.S. 330.

[5] Austin Ranney, *Participation in American Presidential Nominations, 1976* (Washington: American Enterprise Institute, 1977), p. 28.

[6] This section is based on Raymond E. Wolfinger and Steven J. Rosenstone, *Who Votes?* (New Haven: Yale University Press, 1980); and Steven J. Rosenstone et al., "Voter Turnout in Midterm Elections," paper presented at the 1978 annual meeting of the American Political Science Association.

[7] Up to this point, our measure of turnout has been the number of valid votes cast for a particular office, divided by the population of voting age. This *underestimates* the actual voting rate: (1) Millions of people are ineligible to vote because they are not citizens, are in prison, are ex-convicts, and so on. (2) Some voters spoil their ballots or do not vote for president. From now on, we will study voting with the findings of sample surveys, which *overestimate* turnout: (1) Surveys usually exclude about six million residents in institutions, who are mostly eligible to vote but unlikely to do so. (2) Surveys often miss types of people with very low turnout rates, particularly uneducated transients. (3) Some interviewees falsely claim to have voted. Comparisons with voting records show that this last factor inflated reported turnout by 11 percentage points in the 1976 election study. See Wolfinger and Rosenstone, *Who Votes?*, Appendix A.

Figure 8.2
Turnout by Age and Sex

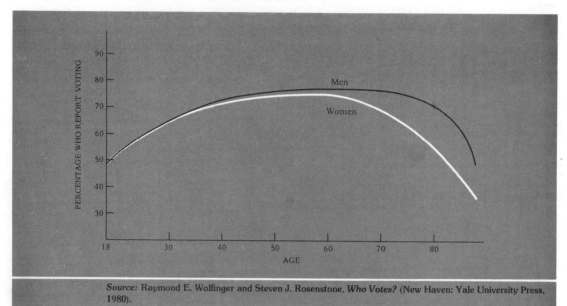

Source: Raymond E. Wolfinger and Steven J. Rosenstone, *Who Votes?* (New Haven: Yale University Press, 1980).

have a higher life expectancy, many more older women than men are left to live alone, and so are likelier to become socially isolated.

The low turnout of young people may come as a surprise. In fact, research for many years has shown consistently that the young vote less than their elders. In part, this reflects their tremendous mobility: In 1974, for example, 60 percent of everyone under the age of 32 had moved at least once in the past two years, triple the rate for those aged 37 to 69. People who have recently moved are far less likely to vote. Their turnout rate in 1974 was fully 20 percentage points lower than that of people who had lived at the same address for at least ten years.

The most important influence on turnout is education. The more schooling, the greater the probability of voting. Only 38 percent of people with less than five years of school voted in 1972, compared to 91 percent of those with five or more years of college. Although the young are less likely to vote than their elders, they are also, as a group, better educated. Obviously, then, these two major factors push in opposite directions. We can see that the least likely voters are the unschooled young. Those most likely to vote are middle-aged college graduates. Except for very recent graduates, almost everyone with a college degree votes, unless prevented by illness or ineligibility. Better educated people vote more because they are more confident in dealing with intangible subjects like politics and more experienced at overcoming the hurdles involved in registering. They are also more interested in politics. The more sense one can make of a subject, the greater probability of paying attention to it.

Of course, better educated people are also likely to make more money and to have higher prestige occupations. We would expect richer people and those with better jobs to vote more, and this expectation is correct. But do income or occupation themselves have much to do with turnout? This question can be answered because education does not fit perfectly with either income or occupation. There are millions of college graduates with modest incomes, and many affluent people who lack education. Moreover, almost everyone is finished with school by their early twenties, when earning power is relatively weak. Holding other factors constant reveals the importance of education.[8] Income has only a slight impact on turnout once people have risen above the poverty level. In general, the same is true for occupations; it is education that makes most of the difference. Blacks and Chicanos vote less than whites, but the difference reflects the lower age and educational levels of these minorities. When these factors are held constant, we find that, contrary to popular myth, black and Chicano turnout is the same as that of whites. In fact, blacks who live in the North vote a bit more than southern whites.

These facts are a major explanation for differences in political influence. Groups with very high rates of turnout are better able to use the ballot box to get what they want from government than groups with very low voting rates.

Abstention: A Plague on Both Your Houses?   We have said that nonvoting is a result of ignorance, confusion, and apathy. What about **principled abstention,** a refusal to vote because all candidates are distasteful or because there are no apparent meaningful differences between them? Could it be, as some commentators have suggested, that our low turnout level reflects popular revulsion at the available candidates?

One way to answer this question is to see if turnout has any relation to the extent of differences among presidential candidates. In 1968, the Vietnam war was the prime issue, and no candidate favored speedy withdrawal from Vietnam. There was some talk that many peace supporters would not vote because there was no candidate who expressed their views. On election day, nearly 61 percent of the voting-age population voted. Four years later, when there were major differences between Nixon and McGovern on most issues (including Vietnam), turnout was considerably lower. The lowest turnout in the past half-century (51 percent) was in the 1948 election, when voters had their choice of four major candidates representing a range of opinion from Henry Wallace's radicalism to Strom Thurmond's ultraconservative segregationist platform.

In any presidential election the ballot includes a variety of candidates expressing unorthodox points of view—libertarians, vegetarians, and an assortment of socialists—all of whom offer alternatives to the two major parties. These candidates seldom get more than a few thousand votes and never affect the outcome of the election. (Major third-party candidates like Wallace and Thurmond are another matter. They will be discussed in Chapter 11.) The failure of these fringe candidates is further evidence that the causes of voter apathy do not include the narrowness of the choices offered by the major parties.

Another approach is to ask whether people who dislike both candidates, or

[8] "Other factors" include age, education, income, race, mobility, sex, region, and the relevant voter registration laws.

who see no difference between them, are less likely to vote. The most recent and thorough survey of this subject finds that few people fit this pattern. Those who find both candidates unappealing, or equally attractive, vote at nearly the same rate as those who have strong favorites.[9] The differences are so small and inconsistent it seems safe to conclude that the public's ability to distinguish differences among presidential candidates has little to do with voter turnout.

The same is true of the many millions of "alienated" citizens who say they are suspicious of politicians and do not trust government. These self-proclaimed cynics vote at the same rate as people who express faith in the system and trust in the good intentions of politicians.[10] Either their cynicism is not real or their voting is more a habit than anything else. Perhaps the truth includes a bit of both explanations.

Turnout is lowered, however, by personal economic misfortune. Everything else being equal, the unemployed vote about 2 percent less than do Americans with jobs. Moreover, people who say they are worse off financially than a year earlier were about 10 percent less likely to vote than those who did not think they had suffered pocketbook miseries recently. Citizens of all ages, incomes, occupations, and levels of education responded in about the same way if they thought they were worse off financially. The political consequence of economic setbacks, then, is not a rush to protest at the polls. Instead, it seems that when people are preoccupied with personal economic problems, they are less inclined to vote.

Why Is Turnout Falling?

Figure 8.1 shows that American voting rates, never very high in the twentieth century, have fallen considerably in recent years. Presidential turnout declined from 61 and 63 percent in the 1960s to 54 and 55 percent in the 1970s. The drop in midterm elections was equally sharp. This trend is particularly puzzling because so many obstacles to voting have been eliminated. The modern peak of turnout was reached in 1960, when one- and two-year residency requirements, literacy tests, and poll taxes were common; and when maladministration of the laws kept millions of southern blacks from registering. Since then all these barriers have been removed, and yet turnout has fallen.

This is a subject of great interest, particularly at election time, when observers deplore the trend and offer explanations and remedies. Many "explanations" of the decline are really disguised propaganda for a point of view. Conservatives say that "the people" are rejecting the welfare state policies of both parties, the unbalanced budgets and social assistance programs that increase in both Democratic and Republican administrations. Radicals say that nonvoters are repudiating the capitalistic conspiracy that ensnares both major parties. There is precious little evidence for either of these notions. What we know about voting shows that people with such strong political opinions are *more* likely to vote, not less. Nor, as we have just seen, do the facts support the idea that people who have lost faith in politicians are

[9] Richard A. Brody, "The Puzzle of Political Participation in America," in Anthony King, ed., *The New American Political System* (Washington: American Enterprise Institute, 1978), pp. 306–12.

[10] Jack Citrin, "The Alienated Voter," *Taxing and Spending,* 1 (October 1978), pp. 1–7.

"Me, I vote the man, not the party. Hoover, Landon, Dewey, Eisenhower, Nixon, Goldwater, Nixon, Ford . . ."

any less inclined to vote. Giving the vote to people aged 18 to 20 is only a partial cause of falling turnout. If we excluded 18- to 20-year-olds from the 1972 electorate, the result would be an increase in turnout of only 1.2 percent. This is just a quarter of the total decline from 1968, when the minimum voting age was 21. The fact of the matter is that no one has produced an explanation of falling turnout that will withstand careful analysis.

So far we have discussed what kind of people vote, and in what circumstances, without saying anything about *how* they vote. We will devote the remainder of this chapter to trying to unravel this crucial, fascinating, and elusive topic.

PARTY IDENTIFICATION

It is part of our political mythology that Americans "vote for the man, not the party." Fully 84 percent of the population say this is how they decide on election day.[11] If you ask friends and relatives how they made up their minds, they will probably mention the personal qualities of the candidates or the issues that seemed most important. This may be accurate in some cases, but for most of us, the man (or woman) we like most is the one who belongs to our own party. In 1972, two-thirds of the voters admitted they had made up their minds about the presidential race by the time the nominating conventions chose the candidates, and 85 percent decided before the campaign got underway.[12]

The Stability of Party Identification Voting choices usually are not made anew for each election, but instead reflect a standing decision. This decision is based on a lasting identification with the Democratic or Republican party. Party preferences are relatively enduring, whereas issues and candidates change from one election to the next. In fact, people are more likely to change their minds on issues or their self-labeling as liberals or conservatives than they are to switch parties. This is true even now, when there is so much talk about the decline of the parties. As we will see, party affiliations are slipping a bit, but they still are the most durable political orientation.

The two parties have so many different functions that party "membership" has several meanings. Being a Republican or Democrat has a specific legal definition. In many states, an individual cannot vote or seek nomination in a party's primary election without registering as a member of that party (see Chapter 11). Here

[11] Richard M. Scammon and Ben J. Wattenberg, *The Real Majority* (New York: Coward, McCann & Geoghegan, 1971), p. 172.

[12] The source for these findings and all other unattributed data used in this chapter is the National Election Studies of the Center for Political Studies of the University of Michigan, obtained through the Inter-University Consortium for Political and Social Research. We computed these data and are solely responsible for the analysis.

we are concerned not with legality, but with personal identification. This intangible, psychological meaning of party membership is far more important than the legal meaning. Although American political parties are organizationally weak, they are a major force because they have a powerful influence on voter psychology.

It is useful to think of the parties as reference groups — sources of identification and self-definition for their "members." Political scientists commonly measure party identification by this simple question: "Generally speaking, do you usually think of yourself as a Republican, a Democrat, an Independent, or what?"[13] Almost two-thirds of the population say they consider themselves Republicans or Democrats. These people are then asked, "Would you call yourself a strong Republican (Democrat) or a not very strong Republican (Democrat)?" Those who answer the first question by calling themselves Independents are then asked, "Do you think of yourself as closer to the Republican or Democratic party?" Roughly two-thirds of those who initially label themselves Independents then admit being closer to one or the other party. These people are generally called "Independent Democrats" and "Independent Republicans." The remaining category is the "Pure Independents," those who insist they have no partisan attachment. This series of questions thus yields these seven categories of party identification:[14]

Strong Democrats
Weak Democrats
Independent Democrats
Pure Independents
Independent Republicans
Weak Republicans
Strong Republicans

Past studies generally combined all three varieties of Independent. But if each type of Independent is examined separately, instead of being lumped together, it is clear that they are very different from each other. Independent Democrats think and vote like other kinds of Democrats. Likewise, Independent Republicans are far more Republican than Independent.[15] Therefore, in this book we include the Independent Democrats with other Democrats, and classify the Republicans the same way. The only Independents will be the pure variety, who in 1978 amounted to 14 percent of the population. We will have more to say about Independents later in this chapter.

Figure 8.3 shows a breakdown of the electorate by party identification from 1952 through 1978. Partisan divisions were remarkably stable during this period of

[13] This series of questions has been used since 1952 in the biennial National Election Studies of the Michigan CPS and is the standard measure of party identification used in hundreds of books and articles. See Warren E. Miller, "The Cross-National Use of Party Identification as a Stimulus to Political Inquiry," in Ian Budge et al., eds., *Party Identification and Beyond* (New York: Wiley, 1976), pp. 21–32.

[14] So few people identify with third parties that minor party identifiers are insignificant in national samples. One to four percent of the population give essentially apolitical answers to the question about party identification.

[15] Bruce E. Keith et al., *The Myth of the Independent Voter* (Washington: American Enterprise Institute, 1980).

Figure 8.3
**Party Identification in the United States,
1952–1978**
Generally speaking, do you usually think of yourself
as a Republican, a Democrat, an Independent, or what?
(If Republican or Democrat):
Would you call yourself a strong Republican
(Democrat) or a not very strong Republican (Democrat)?
(If Independent): Do you think of yourself as closer to
the Republican or Democratic Party?

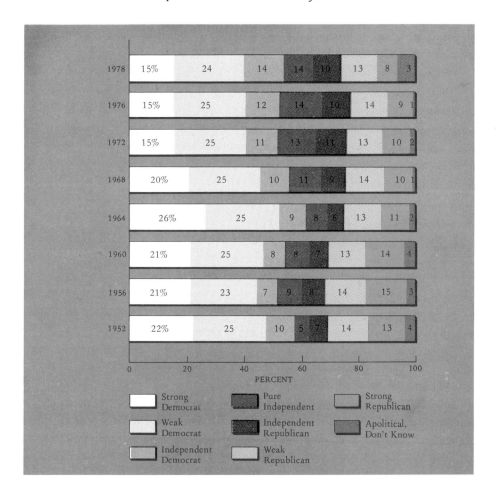

tumult and change. Party identification resists the passing of time, changing personal circumstances, and historical developments. It is more enduring than other political outlooks, including attitudes on issues, evaluations of politicians, and general political philosophy.[16] The *strength* of affiliation with a party may change in

---

[16] Philip E. Converse and Gregory B. Markus, *"Plus ça change . . . :* The New CPS Election Study Panel," *American Political Science Review,* 73 (March 1979) pp. 32–49.

response to passing events. Some Strong Democrats today may be "less strong" four or eight years later. But the *direction* of identification — Democratic or Republican — does not shift so readily. People who are Democrats this year are very unlikely to be Republicans four or eight years from now. Researchers who interviewed the same people in 1965 and again in 1973 found that only 8 percent of the adults in their study had switched party over this eight-year period.[17] Switchers generally are motivated by profound dissatisfaction with their old party's performance.[18]

Party identification is by far the best single predictor of an individual's vote. People who consider themselves Republicans tend to vote for Republican candidates, usually by overwhelming margins. The same is true for Democratic identifiers. Table 8.1 shows the proportion of the vote cast in presidential and House elections by Independents, defectors, and party identifiers voting for their party's candidate. The last category — party-line voting — always accounts for the vast majority of the electorate. There has been much talk in the last few years about the declining power of party identification. This trend has been exaggerated, as Table 8.1 shows. There is no clear tendency in presidential elections; the rate of defection in 1976 was no higher than in 1956.[19] Party loyalty has fallen somewhat in House elections, although more than 70 percent of all votes for House candidates are still cast along party lines.

Identifying with a party should not be confused with voting for its candidates in a particular election. Identification is an affiliation that often lasts a lifetime — a

Table 8.1

The Composition of the Vote in Presidential and House Elections: Party-Line Voters, Defectors, and Pure Independents, 1956–1978

	HOUSE ELECTIONS											
	1956	1958	1960	1962	1964	1966	1968	1970	1972	1974	1976	1978
Party-line votes*	82%	84%	80%	83%	79%	76%	74%	76%	75%	74%	72%	69%
Defection†	9	11	12	12	15	16	19	16	17	18	19	22
Pure Independents	9	5	8	6	5	8	7	8	8	8	9	9
	100%	100%	100%	101%	99%	100%	100%	100%	100%	100%	100%	100%

	PRESIDENTIAL ELECTIONS					
Party-line votes*	76%	79%	79%	69%	67%	74%
Defection†	15	13	15	23	25	15
Pure Independents	9	8	5	9	8	11
	100%	100%	99%	101%	100%	100%

*Votes by party identifiers for the candidate of their party.
†Votes by party identifiers for another party's candidate.

[17] M. Kent Jennings and Richard G. Niemi, "The Persistence of Political Orientations: An Over-Time Analysis of Two Generations," *British Journal of Political Science,* 8 (1978), p. 349.

[18] Richard A. Brody, "Stability and Change in Party Identification: Presidential to Off-Years," paper presented at the 1977 annual meeting of the American Political Science Association.

[19] The higher defection rates in 1968 and 1972 reflect the third-party appeal of George Wallace in 1968 and George McGovern's extraordinary unpopularity in 1972.

permanent "brand label" preference. Voting is a short-term act that *usually* reflects party identification, but not always. Republicans and Democrats can and do vote for the other party's candidate without changing their attachment to their own party. Crossing party lines is usually a temporary phenomenon, not the sign of a permanent conversion. Most defectors return to their party in subsequent elections. So a massive presidential victory by one party does not mean that the other party has suffered a *permanent* loss of support.

There have been four presidential landslides since World War II: In 1952 and 1956, the Republican candidate Dwight Eisenhower beat Adlai Stevenson. In 1964 Lyndon Johnson overwhelmed Barry Goldwater. In 1972 Richard Nixon crushed George McGovern. Each of these elections was followed by a flood of predictions that the losing party was about to fall apart. The predictions were wrong. Although a substantial fraction of one party's identifiers defected in each case, they rarely began to consider themselves members of the other party. For this reason, such contests are called **deviating elections.** The outcomes of these elections are *temporary* departures from ordinary party alignments, the result of such short-term forces as Eisenhower's striking popularity, the unpopularity of Goldwater and McGovern, or widespread disapproval of the incumbent party's performance, as in 1952.

Party identification is not the only factor in voting choice. If voting resulted *only* from party identification, the Democrats would always control the White House and would be guaranteed congressional majorities. Since election results are not this consistent, it follows that party loyalty is not always equally strong. When is party-line voting most common, and when do the parties have a weaker hold on voters? The more information about the candidates that is available to voters, the greater the likelihood that some voters will learn something that will cause them to cross party lines. Without any other information, party labels are the only possible basis for picking among the candidates.

People who are informed about the issues and candidates are more likely to defect, since they can take more into consideration than just party. Party labels make it easier for voters to evaluate candidates by providing them with a simple, familiar, and meaningful guideline. Abolishing party labels and party identification would mean voters would have to know more in order to make sense of the election. "Information costs" are lower for better educated people. The party label helps many uninformed citizens relate their limited knowledge to the political process and to the choices they can make in the voting booth.

Party identification helps explain the continued monopoly of the Democratic and Republican parties in the face of numerous protest movements and attempts to found other parties. With so large a proportion of the population committed to the major parties, would-be new parties have an almost insuperable obstacle to overcome. This contributes to the stability of American political institutions and processes.

Searching for the causes of individual loyalty to the Republicans or Democrats sheds light on a variety of important aspects of American politics, ranging from the private, personal meanings of politics to the public, historical convulsions that have shaped the course of American life for the past century. In tracing the roots of party identification, we gain insight into contemporary political behavior, and this helps us understand the potential for future changes.

A fundamental explanation for party loyalties is simply that most Republicans come from Republican families, while Democrats have Democratic parents. Children call themselves Democrats or Republicans long before they have any understanding of what political parties are. Most children identify with one or the other party at an age when these labels and the name of the president exhaust their fund of political information. Less than one high school senior in twelve identifies with a party different from that of his or her parents.[20]

Not only is party identification largely "inherited," but it persists long after any objective justification, even when the child's life circumstances change drastically from those of his or her parents. American society is highly mobile, both economically and physically. Education, better jobs, prosperity, depression, moving from one place to another — all these changes alter life styles. But life styles change more rapidly than party loyalties. Despite changes in their personal lives, most Americans retain their original affiliation. Perhaps this is because politics is not a continuing preoccupation for most Americans, so inertia helps stabilize party preferences. This interpretation is supported by the fact that the most common cause of individual party change is marriage, when one spouse converts to the other's party. Only 7 percent of married couples have a spouse in each party.[21] The only exception comes during very rare periods of social upheaval and party realignment.

The Social and Economic Bases of Faction   What kinds of people are Democrats and Republicans? How do the lines of partisan affiliation fit with economic, religious, racial, and ideological divisions? To put the question in the language used by James Madison in *The Federalist,* what are the "bases of faction" in modern America? This is one of the most important questions about any country. The answers help explain the strengths and weaknesses not only of the parties themselves, but of the political system in which the parties play such a major role. We will consider two kinds of answer to this question. First, we will look at how party identification is related to social groupings. Then we will examine how followers of the two parties differ in their beliefs on issues.

In some nations the parties so closely reflect societal cleavages (rich versus poor, farmers versus workers, workers versus factory owners, Catholics versus Protestants) that they have virtually no meaning outside the social categories they represent. The more that partisan lines correspond to economic and social divisions, the greater the chance that political conflict will be bitter and unrestrained. In other nations, however, political divisions cut across social alignments. In these countries, the parties tend to be coalitions of different interests, less capable of unity and singleness of purpose, but also more able to compromise.

---

[20] M. Kent Jennings and Richard G. Niemi, *The Political Character of Adolescence* (Princeton, N.J.: Princeton University Press, 1974).

[21] Richard G. Niemi et al., "The Similarity of Husbands' and Wives' Political Views," *American Politics Quarterly,* 5 (April 1977), p. 137.

American parties fall in the second category. Both Republicans and Democrats are coalitions embracing a variety of interests. Although each party is more popular than the other among certain social and economic groups, in virtually no case does one party enjoy a monopoly of support from a major American social group. Since the most important lines of division in any political system are generally economic, regional, religious, and racial, we will examine the American electorate in terms of each of these categories, and then look at the political loyalties of different age groups.

Economic Differences. The richer an American is, or the better the job he or she holds, the more likely that person is to be a Republican. As one goes down the status ladder, Democrats become increasingly more common. About 44 percent of business and professional people consider themselves Democrats, compared to 52 percent of clerks and salespeople, and 58 percent of manual workers. Democrats are especially scarce at the highest reaches of big business. Only about 10 percent of the heads of major corporations are Democrats. Compared to the leaders of big business, independently wealthy people are somewhat more sympathetic to the Democrats. Democrats outnumber Republicans among two other elite groups — high-ranking civil servants and executives and commentators in the mass media.[22] Whether social class is measured by income, self-identification, or occupation, the same results emerge: the higher the status, the greater the tendency for Republican affiliation. And, as you can also see in Figure 8.4, the greater the sympathy for the Republican party, the smaller the social grouping. Thus the Democrats' popularity among the larger social classes is offset somewhat by their lower turnout. As Figure 8.4 shows, no party even approaches a monopoly of any economic group. Moreover, these economic categories are large and overlap with other significant divisions of the population. The result is to prevent the kind of deep social and political cleavages found in many European countries.

The relationship between social class and party preference has weakened since the 1950s, and the two parties are now less divided along class lines than they once were. In particular, more middle-class people are now Democrats. Many descendants of poor immigrants who have become educated and prosperous have retained their Democratic allegiance as they rose in the world.[23] Major portions of the upper middle class are increasingly Democratic. Although most business executives remain Republican, this is not so true of professionals and executives in the communications industry and the growing world of nonprofit institutions (universities, foundations, civic action organizations). Republicans are scarce in the student bodies of elite colleges. For example, they are outnumbered six to one by Democrats at Harvard.[24] It seems likely, then, that the future will bring further weakening

---

[22] Charles G. Burck, "A Group Profile of the *Fortune* 500 Chief Executive," *Fortune,* May 1976; and Carol H. Weiss, "What America's Leaders Read," *Public Opinion Quarterly,* 38 (spring 1974), pp. 3–4.

[23] Paul R. Abramson, "Generational Change in American Electoral Behavior," *American Political Science Review,* 68 (March 1974), pp. 93–105.

[24] Everett Carll Ladd, Jr., *Where Have All the Voters Gone?* (New York: Norton, 1978), p. 11.

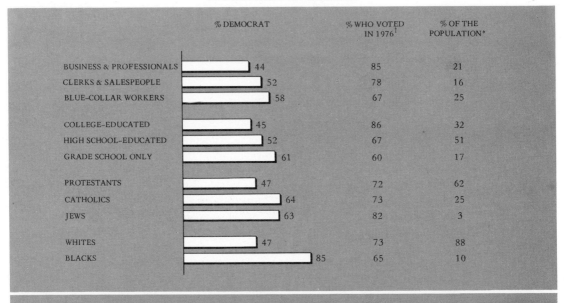

Figure 8.4

The Socioeconomic Sources
of Democratic Identification

	% DEMOCRAT	% WHO VOTED IN 1976[†]	% OF THE POPULATION*
BUSINESS & PROFESSIONALS	44	85	21
CLERKS & SALESPEOPLE	52	78	16
BLUE-COLLAR WORKERS	58	67	25
COLLEGE-EDUCATED	45	86	32
HIGH SCHOOL-EDUCATED	52	67	51
GRADE SCHOOL ONLY	61	60	17
PROTESTANTS	47	72	62
CATHOLICS	64	73	25
JEWS	63	82	3
WHITES	47	73	88
BLACKS	85	65	10

*These figures do not always add up to 100 percent
because certain categories are excluded. For example,
farmers and people not in the labor force are not included
in the "occupation" categories.

†Remember that some people being interviewed falsely
claim that they have voted, and that reported turnout in
1976 was 11 percent too high.

of the relationship between class and party as the older, more polarized generation
passes from the scene.

Regional Differences.   Among the most important cross-cut-
ting cleavages in American history have been the lines separating one geographical
area from another. At times in our past, issues have pitted section against section in
disputes that muffled, diverted, or submerged conflict between haves and have-
nots. The most important sectional antagonism was, of course, the Civil War. It
took the lives of almost a tenth of the adult male population and left a political legacy that still survives.

Because the Union was successfully defended by the first Republican president, the defeated South became almost entirely Democratic. The small-town,
Protestant, middle-class conservatives who elsewhere formed the backbone of the
Republican party were, in the South, fervent Democrats. The overwhelming Democratic loyalty of white southerners was even stronger in the middle class than
among workers. Until the 1950s the South was safely Democratic, with the single

exception of the 1928 election, when Democratic candidate Al Smith's member-ship in the Catholic Church drove many southerners temporarily into the Republi-can camp. In 1952, Republican presidential candidates began to win a substantial southern vote. From 1964 through 1972, the Republicans outpolled the Democrats in the South; and in 1976, Jimmy Carter took more than 57 percent in only two states in his native region. From a negligible share of the population in the 1950s, Republicans grew to a respectable minority by 1976.[25]

There are two main sources of Republican growth in the South: prosperous transplanted northerners and the younger generation of natives, who are less influ-enced by the traditions of the Solid South. Time is on the Republican side in the South. Both the continuing northern migration and the death of the old native gen-eration will sap Democratic voting power. But despite the Republican party's bright future in the South, its present popular base is weaker than in the North. Only 25 percent of all southerners were Republicans in 1976, compared to 36 percent in the rest of the country. This continued (if lesser) regional difference reflects the heritage of the Civil War, more than 110 years after Lee surrendered to Grant at Appomat-tox Courthouse.

Not only in the South, but throughout the United States, political alignments based on region often result from a historical legacy of past experience that has lost its relevance to contemporary political events but still leaves its mark on voting pat-terns. For example, the contrasting Democratic and Republican inclinations of many areas in the Midwest can be traced to distant antecedents. Those parts of Ohio and Indiana settled by New Englanders are still a good deal more Republican than the otherwise socially identical areas in the same states that were first occupied by southerners. Such regional divisions are fading somewhat, but other legacies remain as strong today as they ever were, notably differences in party affiliation based on religion.

Religious Differences.   Cutting across the class division of the electorate is a network of religious alignments. Catholics are more likely than Prot-estants to identify with the Democratic party and to vote for Democratic candidates. And Jews are as Democratic as Catholics. In 1976, 47 percent of Protestants identi-fied with the Democratic party, compared to 64 percent of all Catholics and 63 per-cent of Jews. These differences are not due to religious differences in income. As we saw in Chapter 2, Catholics and Protestants are equally prosperous, while Jews are considerably better off.[26]

The differences in party identification among the three major religious groups are reflected in their voting behavior. In 1976, for example, Carter got 47 percent of the presidential vote cast by Protestants, 58 percent of the Catholic vote, and 71 percent of the Jewish vote.

[25] Raymond E. Wolfinger and Robert B. Arseneau, "Partisan Change in the South, 1952–1976," in Louis Maisel and Joseph Cooper, eds., *Political Parties: Development and Decay* (Beverly Hills, Calif.: Sage, 1978).

[26] The most thorough analysis of the social bases of party identification found that religious dif-ferences were far more important than economic considerations. See David Knoke, *Change and Continuity in American Politics: The Social Bases of Political Parties* (Baltimore: The Johns Hop-kins University Press, 1976), p. 29.

Party loyalites based on religion, like loyalties based on regional considerations, often can be traced to historical causes. Before 1928, Catholics were not nearly as prone to vote Democratic as they have been since. In that year Governor Al Smith of New York was the Democratic presidential nominee. This was the first time a major party had nominated a Catholic as its presidential candidate. The campaign, which featured intense anti-Catholic sentiments, had a "backlash" effect that cost the Republican party millions of Catholic voters. These conversions proved to be quite durable. In 1960, when John F. Kennedy, the nation's second Catholic presidential candidate, was nominated by the Democrats, political-religious cleavages were reactivated. Catholics generally are 10 to 15 percent more Democratic than Protestants, but in 1960 fully 80 percent of the Catholic vote went to Kennedy, a sharp increase from the 50 percent who voted for Adlai Stevenson in 1956.[27]

The anti-Catholic campaign against Democratic presidential candidate Al Smith cost the Republican party millions of Catholic voters for generations after the 1928 election.

Party loyalties based on nationality are quite similar to religious cleavages. Consciousness of national origins is high and politically relevant in much of the Northeast and Midwest. In New England, for example, appeals to Irish and Italian sentiments often are a prominent feature of election campaigns. Even where national origins are not so obvious a feature of the political scene, the two parties often have very different appeal to voters according to the European roots of their ancestors. Generally speaking, people of Irish Catholic, Italian, and Slavic descent are a good deal more likely to identify with the Democratic party and to vote for Democratic candidates than are Americans whose ancestors came from Scandinavia, Great Britain, or Germany.

Ethnic and religious voting is not a function of underlying economic differences. In fact, it cuts across economic lines. Jews are the most prosperous ethnic group in the country, and are also, next to blacks, the most strongly Democratic. Further, ethnic and religious loyalties do not appear to be fading, even though the disappearance of ethnic voting has been predicted for generations. Consciousness of national origins seems to be important for many voters. Even when this consciousness itself fades, its political effects remain.[28]

Racial Differences.   As recently as 1956, about a third of all black adults did not identify with either party. Half of them called themselves Independents and the other half professed to have no interest in politics at all. But the civil rights movement, rising black political awareness, and federal action to protect

[27] V. O. Key, Jr., "A Theory of Critical Elections," *Journal of Politics,* 17 (February 1955), pp. 3–18; and Angus Campbell et al., *Elections and the Political Order* (New York: Wiley, 1966), pp. 87–88.

[28] Raymond E. Wolfinger, *The Politics of Progress* (Englewood Cliffs, N.J.: Prentice-Hall, 1974), Chap. 3.

the rights of southern blacks produced a dramatic change. By 1964, only one black in twenty-five claimed to be apolitical, and by 1976 this dwindled to a mere 1 percent.

Before the Roosevelt administration of the 1930s and early 1940s, blacks tended to vote Republican, largely out of gratitude to "the party of Lincoln." Since the New Deal they have voted Democratic, although the extent of black support for the Democrats has varied considerably. These shifts reflect events and the images of the two parties on civil rights, which changed from ambiguity to a more clear-cut differentiation in the mid-1960s. Adlai Stevenson, the Democratic presidential candidate in 1952 and 1956, seemed less than enthusiastic about proposed civil rights laws. Although President Eisenhower was not responsible for the Supreme Court school desegregation decision issued in 1954, he and his party benefited from it. In 1956, almost one black in five was a Republican, and Eisenhower got 39 percent of the black vote. Four years later, when Eisenhower's vice-president, Richard Nixon, ran for the presidency, he received a quarter of the votes cast by blacks.

In 1964, Republican nominee Barry Goldwater appealed to white southerners. In the Senate he conspicuously voted against the Civil Rights Act of 1964, a historic piece of legislation which had been the most prominent item in the legislative programs of Presidents Kennedy and Johnson. One result was a sharp divergence in the popular images of the two parties. For the first time, the Democrats were widely perceived as more liberal than the Republicans on civil rights. As a consequence, there was a marked change in black support of Democrats from a strong advantage to a near monopoly. Black identification with the Republican party fell to 6 percent in 1964 and has remained near this level ever since. Black Democratic affiliation rose to 83 percent in 1968 and 85 percent in 1976. Recent Republican presidential candidates have gotten only a handful of black votes. Some Republican candidates for other offices do better, but even so, fully 83 percent of the votes cast by blacks in the 1978 House elections went to Democrats. In contrast, 61 percent of Spanish-heritage citizens voted Democratic.[29] (This confirms the general belief that Americans of Spanish heritage are Democrats, but not overwhelmingly.)

Black loyalty to the Democratic party is clearly not a matter of blind commitment. In Baltimore, black wards that went 93 percent Democratic in the 1964 presidential election voted a mere 13 percent Democratic in the 1966 race for governor of Maryland, in which the Democratic candidate based his campaign on opposition to civil rights legislation.[30] This is a particularly good example of rational voting. The issue was clear, of paramount importance to the group, and not obscured by other concerns. An ironic footnote is the fact that the Republican candidate who benefited from his opponent's racism was Spiro Agnew. His political career ended in 1973 with his resignation from the vice-presidency in order to avoid having to face trial for corruption.

---

[29] *Public Opinion,* November–December 1978, p. 21.

[30] Walter Dean Burnham, "American Voting Behavior and the 1964 Election," *Midwest Journal of Political Science,* 12 (February 1968), p. 37.

Age Differences.   Although Democrats outnumber Republi-
cans in every age group, the elderly are more likely to be Republicans than are
younger people. This is not because people become Republicans as they grow older, but because many Americans who were in their late sixties or older in the 1970s
had always been Republican. They grew up before the New Deal, in the days when
the Republicans were the majority party. Having reached the age of political consciousness when Republicans dominated American politics, they were inclined to
take on what was then the prevailing partisan loyalty.

The Great Depression that began in 1929 has been the most durable source
of political realignment in modern America. At the depth of the Depression, a quarter of the labor force was unemployed. Since this catastrophe came during the
Republican administration of Herbert Hoover, he and his party were blamed. The
immediate consequence was Hoover's smashing defeat in 1932 by Roosevelt. The
long-term consequence was that the Democrats became the new majority party.
This did not happen because of wholesale conversions of former Republicans. Except among blacks and Jews, party switching was not especially common. Instead,
the Democrats gained by picking up the support of most of those who reached political consciousness for the first time during the New Deal: young people casting
their first votes and new citizens from the last great wave of immigration. The ratio
of Republicans to Democrats has shrunk steadily since the late 1930s. This Republican decline primarily reflects the death of generations that were predominantly
Republican, replaced by new generations in which Democrats predominate.[31] Contrary to popular belief, young voters are not particularly strong supporters of
Democratic presidential candidates. In 1976, for example, people under 30 voted
for Carter only a couple of percentage points more than the rest of the population.[32]

The party affiliations of young people seem somewhat more unstable than
those of their parents. That is, they are a bit more likely to change from Republican
to Independent to Democrat, and so on. (The large majority, however, are not party switchers.)[33] Since the early 1960s, the young have grown fonder of calling
themselves Independents; by the 1970s more than half of all whites under 30 were
in this category. (Blacks moved in the opposite direction, toward greater identification with the Democratic party.) But most of these Independents admit that they
lean to one party or the other. So in fact only about one out of six young people are
Pure Independents, without any attachment to a party.

[31] Kristi Andersen, "Generation, Partisan Shift, and Realignment: A Glance Back to the New
Deal," in Norman H. Nie et al., *The Changing American Voter* (Cambridge: Harvard University
Press, 1976), Chap. 5; Angus Campbell et al., *The American Voter* (New York: Wiley, 1960), pp.
153–60; and Norval D. Glenn and Ted Hefner, "Further Evidence on Aging and Party Identification," *Public Opinion Quarterly*, 36 (spring 1972), pp. 35–36.

[32] Robert Axelrod, "Where the Votes Come From: An Analysis of Electoral Coalitions, 1952–
1968," *American Political Science Review*, 66 (March 1972), pp. 16–17; and *Gallup Opinion
Index*, December 1976.

[33] Jennings and Niemi, "The Persistence of Political Orientations," p. 349.

The Two Parties: Scholars and journalists commonly consider the Democrats the
An Ideological Portrait liberal party and the Republicans the conservative party. Is this
picture reflected in the way rank-and-file Republicans and
Democrats think about themselves, about the issues, and about their parties? In
other words, do ordinary Democrats and Republicans have sharply divergent opinions about policy and philosophy, or are the ideological roots of the two parties as
mixed as their socioeconomic sources of support?

For the most part, the answer is that the differences between identifiers with
the two parties are *distinct but moderate.* As can be seen from Figure 8.5, when
members of the two parties are asked to locate themselves on a spectrum running
from "extremely liberal" to "extremely conservative," the most popular label for
both Republicans and Democrats is "moderate," or "middle of the road." There is
some tendency for Republicans to place themselves on the right side of the spectrum and for Democrats to be more toward the left. But we could hardly say that
the two parties are sharply divided by the ideological self-identification of their followers.

When opinions on specific issues are examined, the same blurring of differences is found. Many Republicans take the liberal position and many Democrats
the conservative one. On numerous issues there are no differences between follow-

Figure 8.5

**Ideological Identifications of Democrats and
Republicans in 1976**

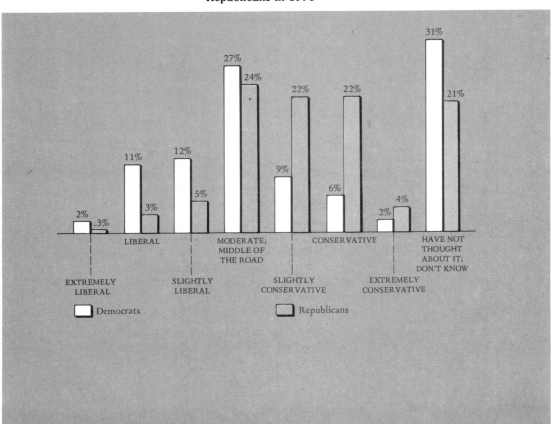

ers of the two parties. When Benjamin I. Page examined the views of ordinary Republicans and Democrats on 63 issues, he found *no* partisan differences on half of these issues.[34] Partisan differences are strongest on questions about the economic role of the federal government. This is clearly shown in Figure 8.6, which charts the relationship between party identification and opinions on five major political issues: jobs, health insurance, busing, legalizing marijuana, and sexual equality. Democrats are considerably more liberal on the first two issues, which typify the concerns that have traditionally divided the parties since the New Deal. Half of those who call themselves Strong Democrats believe the government should take an active part in providing jobs and a decent standard of living for everyone. This position is supported by less than one in ten Strong Republicans. The same is true for national health insurance, although the gap is much smaller. Just over half of all three varieties of Democrat take the liberal position here, compared to about a third of Weak and Independent Republicans, and a quarter of Strong Republicans.[35]

Figure 8.6
**Party Identification and Attitudes on Issues
in 1976**

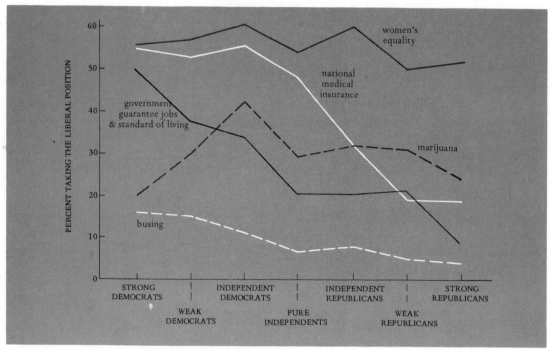

[34] Benjamin I. Page, *Choices and Echoes in Presidential Elections* (Chicago: University of Chicago Press, 1978), pp. 66–67.

[35] Notice also that on both issues the Independent Democrats are like the Weak Democrats, and the Independent Republicans closely resemble the Weak Republicans. This pattern, found on all issues where Republicans and Democrats differ, is further reason to believe that the Independent Republicans and Independent Democrats are really "closet partisans."

These pronounced partisan differences almost vanish if we look at social is-sues. As Figure 8.6 shows, problems like women's equality and legalizing marijuana cut across party lines. There are few differences in the ways that followers of the two parties think about these topics. The same is true of foreign policy. Republicans and Democrats rarely differ much on foreign policy *unless* the issue is posed in terms of approving the performance of a particular president. Then, ordinary Republicans tend to support what a Republican president is doing while Democrats support their president. Thus, Democrats were more favorable to the Vietnam war when it was being fought by Lyndon Johnson, and Republicans became more hawkish when Richard Nixon took over the White House—and the war.

Not only are individual Republicans and Democrats themselves not very far apart on the issues, but most people do not perceive differences between the par-ties. After decades of partisan wrangling among political leaders about federal aid to education, 40 percent of the public did not think that the two parties differed on this question.[36] This is about the normal amount of confusion. In 1976, only a third of the public could link the Republican party with its traditional laissez-faire position that "the government should let each person get ahead on his own." The same number did not have an opinion about where the Republican party stood on this issue, and the rest had an incorrect opinion.

Many voters are equally unclear about how the two parties differ in terms of basic ideology. Only 58 percent of the public thinks that one of the two parties is "more conservative" or "more liberal" than the other. Among those who claimed to see an ideological difference, one in five regarded the Democrats as the more conservative party. People who did not themselves perceive a difference between the parties were then asked which party was generally considered more conserva-tive. Only 18 percent thought the Republicans were publicly viewed as the more conservative.

In short, many Americans have strong party loyalties but weak, confused, or inconsistent ideas about what policies their parties actually stand for. Party identifi-cation is an important factor in its own right, not merely a mask for different opin-ions about what the government should do.

The End of the American Party System?

Although the United States has had the same two major parties for 110 years, almost every national election brings speculation that this state of affairs is about to end. Such claims reach new peaks whenever one party loses an election by more than a small margin. Since these claims have been with us for so long, there is a tendency for sophisticated observers to discount them, for much the same reason that the boy who cried "wolf" was ignored. But the wolf eventually did come, and in fact there have been significant shifts in the sources of support for each party in the past. We can reason-ably expect more realignments in the future. Therefore, some alternatives to our present party alignment need to be considered.

[36] Gerald M. Pomper, "From Confusion to Clarity: Issues and American Voters, 1956–68," *American Political Science Review*, 66 (June 1972), p. 418.

Third Parties.   Democrats and Republicans have dominated elections in the twentieth century. The only serious threat to their monopoly on voter attention has come from occasional "third party" presidential candidates. In 1912 Theodore Roosevelt, after failing to take the Republican nomination away from his successor in the White House, William Howard Taft, ran as the Progressive party candidate. Roosevelt outpolled Taft, but by splitting the Republican vote he put the Democrat Woodrow Wilson in the White House.

In 1924, disappointed by conservative candidates on both major party ballots, Senator Robert La Follette won almost 5 million votes on the Independent Progressive ticket. In 1948 there were two "third parties." Infuriated by the Democratic convention's adoption of a liberal civil rights platform, southern segregationists walked out and formed the States' Rights Democratic party, with J. Strom Thurmond, then governor of South Carolina, as their candidate. Nicknamed the "Dixiecrats," Thurmond's party got a little over a million votes and carried four southern states, where it appeared on the ballot as the official Democratic party. On the other side of the 1948 ideological spectrum was Henry Wallace, a former vice-president, who won about as many votes as Thurmond and cost Truman victory in New York. The most successful third-party movement in more than fifty years was headed by Governor George Wallace of Alabama in 1968. He gathered over 10 million votes — 13 percent — and carried five southern states.

Theodore Roosevelt was the only third-party candidate to outpoll one of the major party candidates. On only two other occasions, in 1924 and 1968, did a third party win as much as a tenth of the vote, and in neither case was the outcome affected by the presence of the third party. Each of these movements was the personal vehicle for the political ambitions of a single leader. No third party has ever run many candidates for offices other than the presidency, and none has tried to build grassroots organizations.

The probability, then, is that the Republicans and Democrats are here to stay. Some third-party movements, like George Wallace's, fade quickly because the passions they express subside. But if a third party threatens to be serious competition for more than a season, the two major parties borrow enough of its program to steal its thunder. As we will see, there are some elements of ideological rigidity in the two parties. The more important fact, however, is their instinct for survival, which generally provides the flexibility needed to adjust to popular sentiment.

Are Parties Becoming Irrelevant?   The weakening of party ties is one of those predictions that have been heard for at least a generation. Almost everyone has read about the phenomenal growth of Independents, a trend that is regarded as potentially lethal to the party system. But as we have noted already, there are three kinds of Independents: those who reject any affinity for one party or the other, and those who admit they are "closer" to the Democrats or the Republicans. The Pure Independents are only about a third of the total, 10 percent of the population in 1978. (They were 9 percent in 1956.) The others are Independent Democrats or Independent Republicans. Their political behavior does *not* support the notion that they are free from affiliation with one or the other party. Most important, they are very much inclined to vote for the candidates of the party toward which they lean. In fact, other than their initial preference for being called "Independents," there is very little reason to separate them from ordinary Democrats and Republicans.

Social scientists have been unable to identify the causes of the increase in either type of Independent. It is clearly not due to alienation from the American political system or cynicism about contemporary politicians. Although expressions of disillusionment became quite popular in the late 1960s and early 1970s, this growing disenchantment had nothing to do with the parallel growth in Independents. People who identify with a party are no less cynical than those who decline any partisan identification. The most alienated group in the country is blacks, who have the most reason to be dissatisfied with the status quo and distrustful of existing political institutions. Yet in 1976 only 8 percent of all blacks considered themselves Independents.

Another sign of weakening party ties is defection — voting for the other party's candidate. Defections in House elections have risen moderately, from 10 to 12 percent in the 1950s and early 1960s to 21 percent more recently. The best guess is that this represents an increase in the ability of incumbents to publicize themselves and thus attract some votes across party lines.[37]

Defection in presidential voting rose in 1968 and 1972, and then fell back to the level of the 1950s in 1976 (see Table 8.1). A major factor in the 1968 and 1972 elections was Vietnam and the so-called "social" and life-style issues (crime, race, abortion, marijuana, sexual equality). All these concerns cut across party lines. Since opinions on these issues were not related to party identification, individual voters who felt strongly about them were likelier to find the other party's candidate attractive. To the extent that the issues which capture voters' interest are unrelated to party, the probability of defections increases. After the 1972 election, however, economic issues pushed other concerns into the background. Voters' opinions on these problems were more closely related to their party identification. The result was, in 1976, a greater correspondence between party and vote — that is, more party-line voting. In the future, we can expect that if new issues coincide with party identification, party-line voting will continue.

CANDIDATE APPEAL

Elections are won and lost by a combination of long-term forces, such as party identification, and short-term-forces, such as issues and candidates. The most important short-term force is the positive and negative appeal of the candidates. The attraction of the other party's candidate or distaste for one's own party's candidate is stronger than issues in causing voters to cross party lines.[38]

---

[37] John A. Ferejohn, "On the Decline of Competition in Congressional Elections," *American Political Science Review,* 71 (March 1977), pp. 166–76.

[38] Richard W. Boyd, "Presidential Elections: An Explanation of Voting Defection," *American Political Science Review,* 63 (June 1969), pp. 498–514; and Donald E. Stokes, "Some Dynamic Elements of Contests for the Presidency," *American Political Science Review,* 60 (March 1966), pp. 19–28.

Republican presidential candidates have been much more appealing to the public than their Democratic opponents in most elections from 1952 through 1976. The only exceptions were Barry Goldwater in 1964 and Gerald Ford in 1976 (see Figure 8.7). Goldwater was the most unpopular major party candidate in this period. On balance, Ford had a faintly favorable public image, and was narrowly edged by Carter in this respect. Republicans have had so much success in presidential elections largely because they have nominated more attractive candidates.

Although a voter's opinion of a candidate is affected by party and views on issues, a candidate's appeal is somewhat independent of these other factors. This can be seen in an analysis of Dwight Eisenhower's remarkable political magnetism. Eisenhower was the most popular presidential candidate since World War II. His enormous personal appeal brought the Republicans back to the White House after twenty years of Democratic presidents. In addition to almost all Republicans, Eisenhower got most of the Pure Independent vote and a substantial fraction of Democrats as well.

His popularity was not simply a result of his positions on issues; in fact, as a career soldier Eisenhower had not taken positions on most issues. Part of his appeal came from the past: his role as the general who led the Allies to victory in Europe in World War II. But military heroism alone was not enough for political success, as was shown by Douglas MacArthur's futile pursuit of the presidency in the late 1940s and early 1950s. Another aspect of Eisenhower's appeal was his ingratiating, "unmilitary" manner. Liking Ike was a matter of liking his personal public image, not a matter of agreement with him on issues. To be sure, liberal Republicans were more favorably inclined toward him than conservative ones. In the general election, Republicans were more favorable than Democrats. But Eisenhower's appeal transcended partisan and ideological lines to a remarkable extent. Liberals who liked him thought he was a liberal. Conservatives who liked him thought he was a conservative. And people in the middle thought Eisenhower was right there with them.[39] Of course, the fact that Eisenhower was new to politics was a great help. Since he had spent his adult life in the army, he had no record from which voters could judge his positions on the issues. Eisenhower himself did not even decide whether he was a Republican or a Democrat until a year or two before he won the Republican nomination.

A candidate's appeal may be based on his nonpolitical record, as Eisenhower's was. It may be based on his political abilities, as in the case of Lyndon Johnson, who was thought of as a politician who could get things done. Or it may be based on his personal qualities, whether positive or negative, such as Goldwater's "impetuous" style or Kennedy's perceived vigor. Many of these characteristics do not have any ideological coloring; anyone can be impressed by vigor or alarmed by impetuosity. Yet as one political scientist observed, impressions of the candidates as human beings "do not fall on wholly unprepared ground."[40] For example, Demo-

---

[39] Herbert H. Hyman and Paul B. Sheatsley, "The Political Appeal of President Eisenhower," *Public Opinion Quarterly,* 17 (winter 1954–55), pp. 443–60. This sort of wishful thinking is common. Voters tend to see the candidate they prefer as having the same views on the issues that they do. See Page, *Choices and Echoes,* pp. 184–86.

[40] Stokes, "Some Dynamic Elements," p. 23.

Figure 8.7

Feelings Toward Presidential Candidates,
1952–1976*

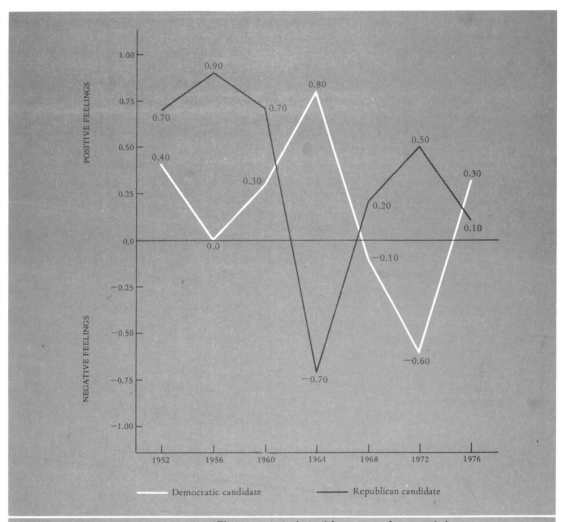

*The measure is derived from a set of open-ended
questions that ask the respondents whether there is
anything that would make them vote for or against either
candidate. The number of "negative" comments per
candidate are then subtracted from the number of
"positive" comments per candidate; the resulting mean of
this difference for the total sample is displayed in the
figure.

Source: Arthur H. Miller and Warren E. Miller, "Partisanship and Performance: 'Rational' Choice in the
1976 Presidential Election," paper presented at the 1977 annual meeting of the American Political
Science Association, p. 90.

Dwight Eisenhower's popularity as a presidential candidate reflected his image as a humane and humble military leader.

crats always take a more favorable view of the personal qualities of Democratic candidates than Republicans do, and vice versa.

When a candidate has some characteristic that seems politically relevant, it will be more important to some voters than to others. A particularly important aspect of John Kennedy's image in 1960 was his religion. Although Democrats were more likely to think well of Kennedy than Republicans, Catholics also tended to see him in a favorable light. Catholic Republicans were more favorable to Kennedy than Protestant Republicans. The same was true for Democrats. Democratic Protestants who never went to church voted loyally for Kennedy. But Protestant Democrats who were regular churchgoers were a good deal more uneasy. Almost 40 percent of them defected to Nixon. A milder version of the same thing happened in 1976. Carter's widely publicized experience of being a "born again Christian" seemed troubling to many Catholics, and he did rather poorly with Catholic voters compared to other Democratic candidates over the past twenty-five years.[41]

In 1964, Goldwater managed to create an exceptionally unfavorable personal impression of himself. As one student of that election wrote, "The detailed references to Goldwater are an impressive amalgam of doubts—a wild and erratic campaigner, muddled and unclear, unstable, poorly educated, and so on."[42] The next most unpopular candidate in the postwar era was Senator McGovern, who ran against Nixon in 1972. Like Goldwater, he was an underdog in the contest for his party's nomination who won with the dedicated work of many enthusiastic activists. Also like Goldwater, McGovern took—or seemed to take—the unpopular side of issues. Many Americans considered him an advocate of amnesty for draft resisters, legalization of marijuana, and other positions rejected by most voters.[43] In 1972, only 8 percent of the public considered themselves "liberal" or "extremely liberal," but fully 41 percent applied one of these labels to McGovern. Public perceptions of Nixon, on the other hand, much more closely resembled the public's own ideological profile.

An even greater handicap was McGovern's inability to convince voters of his stability, integrity, and intelligence. In part this was due to televised impressions of the Democratic National Convention, which seemed to be dominated by young radicals. Another contribution to McGovern's reputation was his inept response to the discovery that his vice-presidential candidate, Senator Thomas Eagleton, had

[41] Campbell et al., *Elections and the Political Order,* pp. 87–89; and *Gallup Opinion Index,* December 1976, p. 3.

[42] Philip E. Converse et al., "Electoral Myth and Reality: The 1964 Election," *American Political Science Review,* 59 (June 1965), pp. 330–31; and Stokes, "Some Dynamic Elements," p. 22.

[43] Arthur H. Miller et al., "A Majority Party in Disarray: Policy Polarization in the 1972 Election," *American Political Science Review,* 70 (September 1976), pp. 756–66; and Page, *Choices and Echoes,* Chap. 5.

"Frankly, Al, we feel it wasn't your style, your platform, or the people around you the voters wouldn't buy. What they wouldn't buy was you."

Drawing by Lorenz; © 1974 The New Yorker Magazine, Inc.

been hospitalized three times for nervous disorders.[44] By the end of the summer, McGovern was hopelessly saddled with a reputation for indecision, weakness, and bad judgment. In August a Gallup Poll revealed that more than twice as many people thought phrases like "sticks to principles" and "good judgment" described President Nixon rather than McGovern. Twenty percent considered McGovern an "extremist," compared to just 3 percent who put this label on Nixon.[45]

The voters became so distrustful of McGovern that they did not consider him preferable to Nixon on issues that traditionally had been the Democratic party's strongest suits. Nixon was far more successful in convincing the voters that he would keep "the big interests from having too much influence over the government" and would make "the government pay more attention to the problems of the working man and his family."[46] McGovern also failed to gain public recognition of his fundamental position—a speedy end to the war in Vietnam. Less than two-thirds of the people who supported withdrawal from Vietnam believed that McGovern also took this position. In contrast, almost everyone whose position on the war resembled Nixon's thought he agreed with them. The same was true on other issues. Many people who shared McGovern's views on particular topics did not think that he agreed with them. That is, they misperceived where McGovern stood. Nixon, on the other hand, had no trouble being seen as the advocate of their views by people who agreed with him. Nixon got almost half the votes of people with the most liberal views on social problems, those who were sympathetic to political protest and the counterculture and hostile to the military and "law and order" symbolism.[47]

Four years later, the contrast between the two candidates' images was very different. For one thing, Carter and Ford were not as far apart ideologically as the 1972 candidates had been. Only 19 percent of the public considered Carter "liberal" or "extremely liberal," compared to 41 percent who had put McGovern in one of these categories. Ford and Nixon were thought "conservative" or "extremely conservative" by about the same number of people—23 and 24 percent. Many observers complained that Carter was "fuzzy on the issues," and the public evidently agreed. Fully 40 percent could not place him ideologically. But Ford was not

---

[44] McGovern learned about Eagleton's psychiatric record from reporters who were on the point of publishing the story. When the story broke, McGovern's first response was a staunch defense of Eagleton: he supported his running mate "one thousand percent." Almost immediately, however, he began to undermine Eagleton, and forced him off the Democratic ticket within two weeks. This combination of public defense and private subversion—all fully reported in the press—made McGovern look both devious and incompetent. "One thousand percent" became a derisive taunt for the rest of the campaign.

[45] John G. Stewart, *One Last Chance: The Democratic Party, 1974–76* (New York: Praeger, 1974), pp. 20–21.

[46] Stewart, *One Last Chance,* pp. 25–26.

[47] Warren E. Miller and Teresa E. Levitin, *Leadership and Change: Presidential Elections from 1952 to 1976* (Cambridge: Winthrop Publishers, 1976), pp. 141–44, 158.

any easier to diagnose, for 39 percent said they could not classify him as liberal, conservative, or moderate (see Figure 8.8).

Issues and ideology were not the main concern of most voters in 1976; only 30 percent of the comments about Ford and Carter mentioned issues.[48] Overshadowing everything else was the public's interest in the personal qualities of the two candidates. This was a consequence of the Watergate scandals, which highlighted the importance of presidential character. Carter exploited this situation by trying to take advantage of what might otherwise have seemed a handicap: his lack of experience in national politics. He campaigned as an outsider, unconnected to the evils of Washington. Ford could hardly divorce himself from Washington; he had been in Congress since 1949. He too had to make a virtue of necessity. He tried to turn the tables on Carter by emphasizing his record of governmental service and success in restoring public respect for the presidency. As it turned out, both strategies registered with the electorate, who had generally favorable views of both candidates. Ford was evaluated for his competence, past performance, and trustworthiness as president. Carter, however, was more highly rated on such qualities as personal

Figure 8.8
How the Public Classified Carter and Ford
in 1976

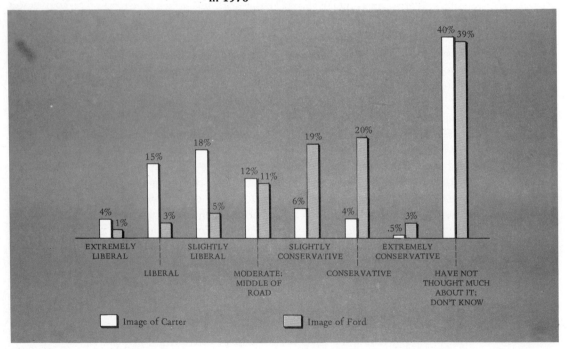

48 Arthur H. Miller and Warren E. Miller, "Partisanship and Performance: 'Rational' Choice in the 1976 Presidential Election," paper presented at the 1977 annual meeting of the American Political Science Association, p. 53.

THE 1976 CAMPAIGN DEBATES

The centerpiece of the 1976 presidential race was three nationally televised debates between Gerald Ford and Jimmy Carter. (A fourth debate featured the two vice-presidential candidates.) Eighty-three percent of the public watched one or more of these events.

Carter and Ford concentrated on issues in their debate presentations. Many viewers did learn something from watching, although they saw the debates principally as a demonstration of the two candidates' personal qualities. This style of reaction was encouraged by the press, which slighted what the candidates said in favor of how they said it and what personal impressions they projected. The most important "issue" seemed to be Ford's assertion that the Soviet Union did not dominate Eastern Europe. This blunder outraged many Americans of Eastern European descent, and astonished millions of other voters.

The media were preoccupied with pronouncing a "winner" for each debate. Viewers' reactions on this point largely reflected their previous preferences, although there was a faint leaning toward one or the other candidate as a result of his performance. The media's interpretations played a part in these verdicts, however. As we have seen, the unfavorable public response to Ford's emancipation of Eastern Europe did not occur until after several days of press attention. In short, citizens saw the debates through a double screen: first their own predispositions, and second what the media reported.

Source: Miller and Miller, "Partisanship and Performance," pp. 85–88; and David O. Sears and Steven H. Chaffee, "Uses and Effects of the 1976 Debates: An Overview of Empirical Studies," in Sidney Kraus, ed., *The Great Debates: Ford vs. Carter, 1976* (Bloomington: Indiana University Press, 1979), pp. 223–61.

warmth, honesty, intelligence, religious faith, and strength. By a narrow margin, he emerged as the more popular candidate.[49]

We have seen that much of a candidate's personal popularity is based not on the policies he or she advocates, but on his or her imagined personality or character, or past achievements. It follows, then, that a vote for a candidate is not necessarily a vote for some or all the positions that person takes. In order to explore directly what an election victory "means," we must turn to the most difficult problem in election research: To what extent are voting decisions determined by issues?

ISSUE VOTING

How close to reality is the textbook image of voters who judge candidates solely in terms of the policies the candidates stand for? Many politicians and political scientists think issues are not important. Instead, they stress candidate image, party loyal-

---

[49] Miller and Miller, "Partisanship and Performance," pp. 90–95.

ty, and get-out-the-vote drives. Others concede the strength of all these factors but argue that in recent years more and more people have come to base their choices on the closeness of fit between their own issue positions and the candidates' stands on policy.

We have already seen evidence for both points of view. The drastic switch of Baltimore blacks from 93 percent support of Lyndon Johnson in 1964 to 13 percent for the Democratic gubernatorial candidate in 1966 was based on their correct impression that George Mahoney's campaign for the governorship was based on racist appeals. The other side of the coin is repeated findings that many voters do not have opinions, or have only weak and unstable opinions, about most issues. Moreover, voters often are ignorant of the candidates' positions on issues. During the 1950s, only 18 to 36 percent of the American public had an opinion on major issues, knew what government policy had been on these issues, and saw differences between the two parties on them.[50] What of the 1960s and 1970s, when supposedly there was such a great increase in issue voting?

At first glance, this question seems easy to answer. Why not simply ask the voters their positions on the issues and what they think the candidates' positions are? One drawback to this approach is a widespread tendency for voters to rationalize their choice of candidate by misperceiving where a candidate stands. Many will "pull" their favored candidate toward them by mistakenly thinking that he or she agrees with their policy preferences. At the same time they "push" the other candidate away by imagining he or she disagrees with them even when this is not true. Furthermore, many voters will change their minds on issues to be consistent with the candidate they prefer. In other words, the candidate may be more important than the issue. Thus, it is difficult to tell if a vote is caused by one's position on an issue, or whether the position on the issue is caused by the vote intention.

Voters' perceptions on the issues are further clouded by the common desire of politicians to sit on the fence. The most thorough study of candidates' positions and public opinion concluded that in presidential campaigns, "policy stands are infrequent, inconspicuous, and unspecific."[51] The 1968 election presents a clear example of all of these points. Although the war in Vietnam was by far the biggest issue on voters' minds, neither Humphrey nor Nixon spent much time talking about the war, and each made it difficult for voters to understand where he stood. Not surprisingly, then, more than half the electorate could see no difference between the two on Vietnam. Those who did see a difference were likely to think that the candidate they favored shared their own positions:

> Those who saw a big difference between Humphrey and Nixon—a difference in either direction—were generally perceiving each candidate as standing wherever they wanted him to stand. They projected their own opinions onto their favored candidate. Among Republicans, who mostly favored Nixon, extreme hawks thought that Nixon was an extreme hawk; extreme doves thought he was an extreme dove; and those in the middle thought that Nixon stood in the

[50] Campbell et al., *The American Voter,* p. 182.
[51] Page, *Choices and Echoes,* p. 153.

middle! . . . Similarly, among Democrats, extreme hawks tended to think Humphrey was an extreme hawk; extreme doves thought Humphrey an extreme dove; and those in the middle thought he stood in the middle.[52]

Thus, many voters committed to an antiwar position were frustrated by the absence of a clear peace candidate in the general election.

In 1972 the picture seemed to change. Unlike Humphrey and Nixon, George McGovern struck most observers as a man of very pronounced views on many issues. He claimed to offer a meaningful choice instead of the lack of alternatives that sometimes faced the electorate. It is true that the people who voted for him had, on the whole, somewhat different opinions from those of Nixon's supporters. The Democrats who abandoned McGovern were more conservative than those who voted for him. But attempts to relate attitudes on particular issues to individual voting decisions have not been very successful. We have already seen that McGovern's personal unpopularity clouded many voters' perceptions of his policy stands, even when these were crystal clear. Issue by issue, many people who had the same position as McGovern did not think they were in agreement with him. Although his supporters were more liberal than Nixon's, the plain truth is that a great many liberals voted for Nixon.

The possibilities for issue voting in 1976 were reduced by the smaller and fuzzier differences between the candidates. Comparing their own preferences with their estimates of Ford's and Carter's positions, 40 percent of the public placed themselves equally distant from either candidate.[53] On some issues, like busing and abortion, there were no differences in the positions the two men were thought to hold. Even when the candidates did express clear differences, however, it did not always register on many voters. For example, in one debate Carter attacked Ford for the high unemployment rate and pledged himself to the traditional Democratic doctrine that the government should "see that everyone has a job." In response, Ford placed his reliance on free enterprise. Yet only 44 percent of the public associated Carter with the position that the government should see to jobs for everyone, and 21 percent put Ford in the same category.

We do not think that voters *never* decide on the basis of a candidate's policy proposals. But the possibilities of such issue voting are reduced by these inescapable facts:

1. Many voters do not have opinions on some or many issues.

2. Candidates do not often present clear alternative proposals about what they would do.

3. Even when a candidate does present a clear position, many voters may not know what it is, either out of simple ignorance or wishful thinking.

[52] Benjamin I. Page and Richard A. Brody, "Policy Voting and the Electoral Process: The Vietnam War Issue," *American Political Science Review*, 66 (September 1972), p. 987. Often a candidate's closest approach to discussing policy comes when he or she talks about goals, problems, and past performance—omitting the crucial point about *how* he would solve the problem or achieve the goal.

[53] Miller and Miller, "Partisanship and Performance," p. 59.

Finally, there are many issues in any election and only one vote. The voter must reconcile his or her issue positions with the need to make a single either/or decision about the candidates.

Looking Backward   We have defined issue voting as a choice of candidates based on the voter's preference for one policy alternative rather than another. In other words, *issue voting is concerned with what the government is going to do in the future.* This definition requires that the voter have opinions about future policy, know the candidates' positions on them, and vote accordingly. Now let us relax the definition and consider as issue voting *an occasion when citizens vote to express their estimate of the past performance of a candidate or party.* This does not require having a preference about policy for the future and knowing which candidate is closer to that preference. All it requires is a judgment on the past. It is a verdict, not a prescription.

Looked at this way, voters *did* exercise some judgment in 1968. A vote for Nixon was not necessarily a demand for more or less force in Vietnam. It was an unfavorable verdict on the Johnson administration's performance. For just this reason, Nixon left the door open for support by both hawks and doves by refusing to state his own intentions about the war. In a similar situation in 1952, Eisenhower avoided specific policy commitments and attracted both hawks and doves on the Korean war by making his famous pledge: "If elected, I will go to Korea." This committed him to nothing but a long trip.

Humphrey lost millions of votes in 1968 both from those who wanted to pull out of Vietnam altogether and those who wanted to "take a stronger stand even if it means invading North Vietnam." He did not lose votes from Democrats who agreed with administration policy. Thus, it was less important that most voters saw little difference between the two candidates than that they were predominantly disenchanted with existing American policy. Humphrey's greatest problem was his identification with Johnson. Since almost two-thirds of the public disapproved of LBJ's handling of the war, this meant that Humphrey, as Johnson's vice-president, was tied to an unpopular leader and a disliked policy.[54]

In any presidential campaign, a variety of issues is available for discussion by the candidates. Major attention goes to the current performance of the party in power.[55] That party's candidate will dwell on areas of success. A president running for reelection in a time of prosperity will talk about how he has brought good times. His challenger naturally will emphasize issues where the administration has been less successful. The candidates seldom engage in genuine debate. Instead, they talk past each other, each stressing those subjects where he thinks he has the more appealing side of the argument.

Since there are many issues, one way to establish their influence on the outcome of the election is to ask people what they consider the most important prob-

[54] Richard W. Boyd, "Popular Control of Public Policy: A Normal Vote Analysis of the 1968 Election," *American Political Science Review,* 66 (June 1972), p. 440; and *Gallup Opinion Index,* April 1968, p. 3.

[55] Page, *Choices and Echoes,* Chap. 7.

lem facing the government. As Figure 8.9 shows, there is considerable change on this point from one election to the next. In 1964, at the height of the civil rights movement, over 20 percent of the public thought that racial problems were the foremost issue. All domestic issues combined were at the top of the agenda for more than 60 percent of the population. Vietnam was important to only one out of eight Americans. By 1968, fully 43 percent thought that Vietnam was the most important problem facing the country. Civil rights was most important to only 9 percent, most of them black.

Unfortunately for Humphrey, the issue that was at the forefront of attention in 1968 was not one on which most people had confidence in the Democratic party. Of the 43 percent who thought Vietnam was the most important issue, only one out of five thought the Democrats would handle it better.

In 1964, the Democrats had enjoyed the advantage in public confidence as the party most likely to perform well on the issue most important to Americans. Whatever issue they chose, 43 percent of the people thought that the Democrats would do a better job on the issue most important to them, compared to 23 percent

Figure 8.9
Popular Views of the Country's Most Important Problem, 1960–1976

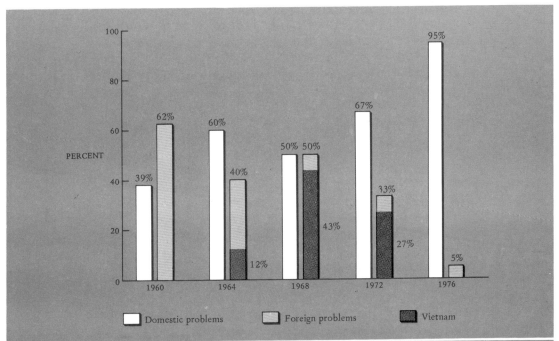

Sources: For 1960 and 1964, David E. RePass, "Issue Salience and Party Choice," *American Political Science Review*, 65 (June 1971), p. 392; for 1968, Alan A. Oldall, "Salient Issue Preferences and Voting Defections, 1964–1968," unpublished paper, University of California, Berkeley, 1973; for 1972, Mark Westlye, "The Role of Issues in Presidential Voting in 1972," unpublished paper, University of California, Berkeley, 1975; for 1976, computed by the authors from data from the 1976 National Election Study of the Michigan Center for Political Studies.

who chose the Republicans and 25 percent who said there was no difference between the parties. But in 1968, the proportion of people having confidence in the Democrats fell to 21 percent, whereas 31 percent thought the Republicans would do a better job (see Table 8.2).

One index of the erosion of confidence in the Democratic party between 1964 and 1968 is the fact that about one Democrat in six thought the Republicans were the better party on the crucial Vietnam issue. Only a quarter of these Democrats voted for Humphrey. A similar situation occurred with other issues.[56] As a result, many Democrats voted for Nixon because they thought the Republicans could do a better job on the issue that was most important to them. These Democratic defectors were not necessarily embracing the Republican solution to the problem, but they had lost confidence in the Democratic party's ability to solve it. In voting for Nixon they were not voting for his position; they were passing an unfavorable judgment on the Johnson administration's performance.

We have looked at the Vietnam issue in the 1968 election in two different ways in order to illustrate how issues affect voting. The 1968 election clearly was not a referendum where the voters chose which policy to follow in Vietnam. But it was an opportunity to pass judgment on the Johnson administration's performance in Vietnam and on other issues as well. Johnson did not rate highly in the eyes of the many voters who thought Vietnam was of paramount importance, including millions of Democrats and Independents. A substantial fraction of these disappointed Democrats deserted Humphrey because they associated him with an administration they judged to be a failure.

In 1976 the United States was experiencing unemployment, inflation, and little growth of real income. Not surprisingly, the state of the economy was on most

Table 8.2

**Preferred Party To Deal With the Most
Important Problem**

	1964	1968	1972	1976
Democrats best	43%	21%	24%	34%
Republicans best	23	31	25	12
No difference	25	39	42	46
Don't know	9	10	9	8
	100%	101%	100%	100%

Sources: For 1964, David, E. RePass, "Issue Salience and Party Choice," *American Political Science Review,* 65 (June 1971), p. 392; for 1968, Alan A. Oldall, "Salient Issue Preferences and Voting Defection, 1964–1968," unpublished paper, University of California, Berkeley, 1973; for 1972, Mark Westlye, "The Role of Issues in Presidential Voting in 1972," unpublished paper, University of California, Berkeley, 1975; for 1976, computed by the authors from data from the 1976 National Election Study of the Michigan Center for Political Studies.

[56] Alan A. Oldall, "Salient Issue Preferences and Voting Defection, 1964–68," unpublished paper, University of California, Berkeley, 1973.

voters' minds. Like Vietnam in 1968, the economic issue in 1976 was bad news for the incumbent administration. People who considered inflation or unemployment the country's most pressing problem were more likely to vote for Carter than were those interested in other issues. This was not a vote for any particular economic policies that Carter advocated. Rather, it was a vote of no confidence in Ford and an affirmation of the long-standing belief that the Democratic party is better able to bring prosperity to the country.[57]

If we think about issue voting in this way, there is less reason to be preoccupied about the accuracy of voters' perceptions, their ability to use political philosophies, or the internal consistencies of their beliefs. Even if the outcome of an election is not a choice by the voters among conflicting proposals about what the government should do in the future, it may well express a verdict on the adequacy of past performance. When an incumbent president is running for reelection, it is his performance that is likely to be evaluated. If incumbents are not candidates for reelection, the candidate of the incumbent's party is likely to be the beneficiary —or the victim—of the reputation the incumbent has established.

ELECTIONS AS MANDATES

After the votes have been counted, what does the outcome mean? People who win elections usually claim that their victory means that they have a "mandate" to carry out the policies they have advocated during the campaign. But is this true? In voting for a candidate, do the people vote for everything he or she has said? Clearly the answer is no, even though politicians and journalists alike persist in reading such mandates into election outcomes.

It is particularly tempting to regard a candidate's victory as popular affirmation of the most conspicuous campaign theme. Sometimes interpretations of this sort are grotesquely wrong. The first presidential primary in 1968 was in New Hampshire, where the only Democrat on the ballot was Senator Eugene McCarthy, running as a peace candidate opposed to Johnson's war in Vietnam. A write-in campaign brought Johnson more votes than McCarthy, but McCarthy still got over 40 percent. This was interpreted as a moral victory for him and a remarkable setback not only for Johnson but for his policy in Vietnam. Shortly thereafter, Johnson announced that he would not be a candidate for reelection. Closer analysis revealed that McCarthy had gotten more votes from hawks than doves. New Hampshire Democrats choosing McCarthy were voting not *for* his policy, but *against* Johnson's. Johnson was opposed from both sides—by hawks as well as doves— and McCarthy's candidacy presented an opportunity to register discontent with Johnson from all points of view. Indeed, many voters in New Hampshire did not

---

[57] Miller and Miller, "Partisanship and Performance"; and *Gallup Opinion Index*, December 1976. Individual reactions to the recession were shaped by party identification. At every income level, Democrats were far more inclined to report they were worse off financially than they had been a year earlier. When a Democrat is president, Republicans are more likely to claim that their personal financial fortunes are declining. See Edward R. Tufte, *Political Control of the Economy* (Princeton, N.J.: Princeton University Press, 1978), pp. 130–31.

seem as concerned about the war as about other issues. When they were dissatisfied with Johnson's performance, for any reason, they voted for McCarthy.[58] Thus, to the voters in the New Hampshire primary, the most important thing about McCarthy was not what he stood for, but the stark fact that he was an alternative to Johnson.

One political scientist observed that "The vocabulary of the people consists mainly of the words 'yes' and 'no'; and at times one cannot be certain which word is being uttered."[59] Each voter is limited to a single "Yes" or "No," although numerous issues are debated in the campaign and each issue has more than two possible answers. Different voters use their votes to answer "Yes" or "No" to different questions in the same election. Although blacks were more opposed to the Vietnam war than whites, they voted 97 percent for Humphrey in 1968. In doing so they were not expressing their opinions about the war; rather, they were indicating which candidate they considered most sympathetic to racial justice. An inherent limitation of elections is that they permit only one answer, no matter how many questions emerge in the campaign.

The purpose of voting is to group individual choices into a collective decision about which candidate will hold elective office. Voting is the only political activity for most people. Their preferences help determine who the candidates will be and what positions they will take, for politicians pay attention to what the voters will "buy." Nevertheless, the voters themselves do not produce the alternatives from which they will choose. Where do these alternatives come from? Up to this point we have said nothing about the processes that take place before candidates face the public in a general election. In the following three chapters we will examine parts of the political scene more specialized than voting. We will look into the roles of activists, interest groups, and the parties themselves.

SUMMARY   Voting is the basic link between people and government, between public opinion and government policy. How many Americans vote depends on election laws (ease of access to the ballot) and type of election as well as on the individual's personal characteristics. In the past fifty years, the vote in presidential elections has never been as high as 65 percent, and turnout in congressional and local elections is much lower. There are also great variations in voting rates from one state to the next because each state regulates access to the ballot through its own registration laws.

Who votes depends more on age and education than anything else; the older and the better educated, the more likely a person is to vote. Blacks and Chicanos vote less than whites as a group, but the difference reflects the younger ages and lower educational levels of these minorities. Turnout in American elections has fallen considerably in recent years, but as yet we have no explanation that can stand up to careful analysis.

[58]   Philip E. Converse et al., "Continuity and Change in American Politics: Parties and Issues in the 1968 Election," *American Political Science Review,* 63 (December 1969), p. 1085.

[59]   V. O. Key, Jr., *Politics, Parties, and Pressure Groups,* 5th ed. (New York: Crowell, 1964), p. 544.

How people vote depends more on party identification than on candidates or issues. Parties in America are sources of self-definition for their members. This identification resists the passing of time, changing personal circumstances, and historical events. The power of this identification is declining a bit, but it is still strong enough to keep American political institutions and processes stable and to prevent the formation of successful third parties.

American parties cut across economic, religious, racial, regional, and ideological divisions in the population. Although members of any such group may tend to be more Republican or Democratic than others, no party has a monopoly on any given social group. The Depression of the 1930s was the major modern source of political realignment, making the Democrats the new majority party.

Many Americans do not see clear differences between the parties on issues. As individuals, Democrats are somewhat more liberal on many economic issues, but otherwise there is usually little relationship between an individual's party's identification and beliefs on particular issues.

The most important source of change in elections is the personal appeal of the candidates. Voting on the basis of the candidates' issue positions is less important, because voters often do not have opinions themselves or lack an accurate idea of the candidates' positions. The more common kind of issue voting is a judgment on past performance rather than a choice of one or another promise about the future.

political
participation

CHAPTER 9

than others to participate. And not everyone becomes an activist for the same reasons. As we will see, the motivations for political participation, the characteristics of the participants, and the resources they bring to the political struggle all shape the nature of our political system. We will concentrate on campaign participation in this chapter and look at interest group activity in Chapter 10.

No area of political life has more conflicting moral overtones and offers more ambiguities — partly because contributing money is a prime method of exerting influence. Private individuals active in politics are often called "concerned citizens." But just as often they may be called zealots, fanatics, vested interests, ward heelers, or party hacks.

HOW MANY AMERICANS PARTICIPATE IN POLITICS?

Apathy is a universal characteristic of political life. From the Greek city-states to the present, most citizens have not become actively involved in public affairs. Even in such widely acclaimed models of civic virtue as ancient Athens and New England town meetings, there were penalties for absenteeism in order to get people to meetings. In contemporary America, people who are *interested* in politics are a minority. As we might expect, those who are *active* in politics are an even smaller minority.[1]

What do we mean by *active participation?* Participation consists of giving any sort of help to an election campaign or attempting to influence what the government does. It includes campaign contributions, licking envelopes, registering voters, going to conventions, writing speeches, raising money, and all the other actions connected with nominating and electing any of the more than 500,000 elected government officials in the United States. Influencing the government (which we discuss in the next chapter) might involve many of the same sorts of behavior, as well as communicating with officials and trying to get other people to do the same.

The most common forms of political activity are shown in Figure 9.1. The bars on the right side show how many adult Americans engage in each type of activity. The most common form of participation in 1976 — as in past campaigns — was giving money. Nine percent of the population supplied financial aid to at least one candidate or party in 1976. (This does not count those who checked off a dollar or two on their federal income tax returns.) Six percent went to some sort of campaign meeting or rally, and 4 percent did something else to help out. The total number of campaign workers is somewhat greater than the number who perform any single task, but there is a good deal of overlap because the most active workers are likely to do a variety of things for their candidate or party. All told, 14 percent of the sample worked in the 1976 campaign in one way or another.

This level of activity has been remarkably stable for at least twenty-five years. Every presidential election year, about one American in six works in a campaign in

---

[1] Although Americans vote less than citizens of other countries, they participate in politics at a much higher rate. For example, 16 percent report that they have tried to influence a decision of the federal government, compared to only 6 percent of the British and even smaller proportions in other European countries. See Kenneth Prewitt and Sidney Verba, *An Introduction to American Government* (New York: Harper & Row, 1974), pp. 164–65.

Figure 9.1
Rates of Political Participation

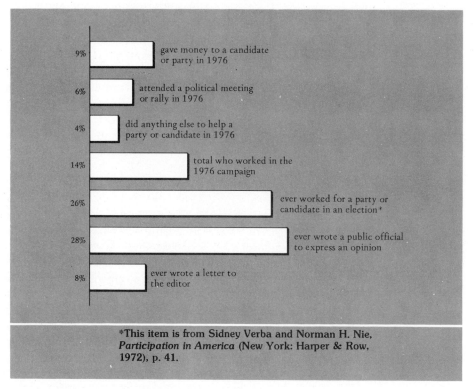

9%	gave money to a candidate or party in 1976
6%	attended a political meeting or rally in 1976
4%	did anything else to help a party or candidate in 1976
14%	total who worked in the 1976 campaign
26%	ever worked for a party or candidate in an election*
28%	ever wrote a public official to express an opinion
8%	ever wrote a letter to the editor

*This item is from Sidney Verba and Norman H. Nie, *Participation in America* (New York: Harper & Row, 1972), p. 41.

one way or another, although not necessarily in the campaign for the presidency. This is an interesting contrast to recent trends in turnout. In Chapter 8 we saw that the percentage of eligible Americans who vote has declined since the mid-1960s. But behavior that requires more involvement has not declined. Indeed, letter writing to public officials has increased considerably, from about a sixth of the population in the 1960s to the present level of 28 percent.

This suggests that what moves people to participate is not necessarily what moves them to vote. We find support for this theory if we divide the campaign activists into Democrats and Republicans. For the past twenty-five years, we have statistics that let us see whether the number of campaign workers a party has is related to the total number of votes the party's presidential candidate gets. They reveal that there is *no relationship between a candidate's share of the popular vote and the number of activists working in the campaign.*[2] In fact, the peak year for grassroots campaign participation by Republicans was 1964, which was a disastrous electoral year for that party. Although Senator Goldwater, the candidate, was a flop with the general public, he was an enormously appealing hero to Republican activists. The

[2] These calculations are from Carolyn K. Ban, "The Party Activist: 1956–68" (unpublished Ph. D. dissertation, Stanford University, 1975).

Wide World

Senator George McGovern was a presidential candidate who appealed far more to activists than to the general public.

1956 election presented the same picture for the Democrats. Adlai Stevenson, the Democratic candidate, did not make a good personal impression on the electorate, but he was an inspiration to millions of Democratic activists. The point is not that campaign work is worthless, for there is plenty of evidence to the contrary. But activists and voters do not always march to the same drummer. Causes and candidates that attract activist support may be unpopular with the general public. Conversely, candidates who get massive popular backing may not be able to inspire those who go in for active participation.

Figure 9.1 gives us one other important clue for understanding political participation. We can see from the graph that the proportion of people who worked in one campaign or another in 1976 is considerably smaller (14 percent) than the number who say they have ever worked in an election (26 percent). In fact, the amount of turnover is probably even greater than these figures indicate. Interviewing the same people in two consecutive elections reveals that over half of the people who participated in the 1972 campaign did nothing in 1976. *Although activists are always a minority, they are not always the same minority.* Instead, there is a good deal of coming and going.

The turnover in participation suggests that the important thing about participation is not the total amount of available resources, but whether or not those resources are mobilized. As political conditions change and new leaders, issues, and organizations emerge, the composition of the activist population changes. It also changes in response to the political skills of the candidates. All three Kennedy brothers, for example, have been known for their ability to recruit and organize volunteer campaign workers.

WHY DO PEOPLE PARTICIPATE?

People spend time and money on politics for many reasons. Differences in motivation are related to differences in the consequences of participation. People moved to participation by personal friendship will make very different claims on a candidate than those who are moved by a desire to raise the minimum wage or the price of oil. We assume that all human behavior is motivated by expectations of some sort of reward. By looking at motivations, we can learn a great deal about the consequences of participation. This also helps us to understand different sorts of party organizations, a subject we will consider directly in Chapter 11.

In this section we will describe four major categories of incentive for participation in politics.[3] As you read this material, remember that individuals seldom fit

[3] This typology is from Raymond E. Wolfinger, *The Politics of Progress* (Englewood Cliffs, N.J.: Prentice-Hall, 1974), Chap. 4.

neatly into any of these boxes; the same person may have several motivations and consequently may belong in more than one category. The categories are policy-oriented participation, patronage-based participation, ideological participation, and participation for sociability, prestige, and friendship.

Policy-Oriented Participation   When Jimmy Carter was campaigning for the 1976 Democratic presidential nomination, several maritime unions contributed over $100,000. They wanted a legal requirement that 9.5 percent of all oil imported to the United States be carried in American-flag tankers. The newly-elected President Carter urged Congress to pass such a law, despite advice that it would cost American consumers at least $600 million a year.[4] The unions wanted the requirement because it would guarantee jobs for the declining American merchant marine.

In 1978, labor unions gave $10.3 million to congressional candidates, almost exclusively to Democrats.[5] These expenditures are nothing compared to what organized labor did for Hubert Humphrey in the 1968 presidential election:

> . . . the ultimate registration, by labor's efforts, of 4.6 million voters; the printing and distribution of 55 million pamphlets and leaflets out of Washington and 60 million more from local unions; telephone banks in 638 localities, using 8,055 telephones, manned by 24,611 union men and women and their families; some 75,225 house-to-house canvassers; and on Election Day, 94,457 volunteers serving as car-poolers, materials-distributors, baby-sitters, poll-watchers, telephoners.[6]

This union activity was motivated by a desire to influence government policy. The unions are interested in such issues as federal medical insurance, a higher minimum wage, and amendment of the laws regulating unions. Their help was given to candidates whose votes they expected to be prolabor. Corporations and trade associations, also motivated by a desire to influence government policy, contributed over $21 million in the 1978 congressional elections.

Policy-motivated participation is the easiest kind of participation to understand. Millions of people want the government to enact laws or regulations to do all sorts of things: register guns, build freeways, limit grazing in national forests, include farmworkers under the National Labor Relations Act, prohibit abortions, give aid to Israel, and so on. All these goals — and thousands more — are supported by interest groups, which we will discuss in Chapter 10. Individuals who want the same goals, acting on their own or through organizations, also contribute vast amounts of money and time to political campaigns. The purpose behind these contributions, of course, is to put sympathetic officials in office and create an obligation toward the contributor. It is important to remember that the goals of policy-oriented political contributors are not necessarily economic.

[4] *San Francisco Chronicle,* September 20, 1977.
[5] *Congressional Quarterly Weekly Report,* June 2, 1979, p. 1043.
[6] Theodore H. White, *The Making of the President, 1968* (New York: Atheneum, 1969), p. 365.

THE TEN BIGGEST POLICY-ORIENTED CONTRIBUTORS IN THE 1978 ELECTIONS

	AMOUNT
1. *American Medical Political Action Committee (American Medical Association)*	$1,644,795
2. *Realtors Political Action Committee (National Association of Realtors)*	1,122,378
3. *Automobile and Truck Dealers Election Action Committee (National Automobile Dealers Association)*	975,675
4. *UAW Voluntary Community Action Program (United Auto Workers)*	964,465
5. *AFL-CIO COPE Political Contributions Committee (AFL-CIO)*	920,841
6. *United Steelworkers of America Political Action Fund (United Steelworkers of America)*	594,930
7. *Transportation Political Education League (United Transportation Union)*	557,603
8. *Machinists Non-Partisan Political League (Machinists and Aerospace Workers)*	536,538
9. *American Dental Political Action Committee (American Dental Association)*	510,050
10. *CWA-COPE Political Contributions Committee (Communications Workers of America)*	474,633

Source: Federal Election Commission; published in *Congressional Quarterly Weekly Report,* June 2, 1979, p. 1045.

Political activity of this type is aimed at influencing government policy. By its very nature, government policy usually affects all members of a particular category. For example, tax laws affect all taxpayers, price supports for wheat affect all wheat farmers, a ban on saccharin may affect all producers of diet drinks, and so on. We call these decisions *indivisible,* because, as Robert Dahl observes, they lead to benefits (or penalties) that "cannot be or ordinarily are not allocated by dividing the benefits piecemeal and allocating various pieces to specific individuals" or firms or places.[7]

[7] Robert A. Dahl, *Who Governs?* (New Haven: Yale University Press, 1961), p. 52.

Patronage-Based Participation   All government activity is not indivisible. Much of it concerns only a particular person, firm, organization, or place. Shall Jones be hired? Shall Smith be promoted? Shall a contract for building the new freeway be given to the X Construction Company or the Y Construction Company? Shall a new post office be built in Tucson now or in the indefinite future? Shall the post office be designed by this architect or that one? Shall the Gulf Oil Company be investigated for possible violation of any of the 417 laws, regulations, and guidelines that affect its operations? Of all the factories that are polluting the air, shall the Wonder Widget Company be fined?

Decisions of this sort are different from policy decisions in three important respects: (1) They are divisible; (2) they concern the routine operations of government; and (3) they depend on the discretion of individuals. That is, such decisions are not mandated by laws or regulations. Human beings make them by choosing one course of action rather than another. Given a choice of two people to hire, an official may pick the one who has worked for the winning political party. Confronted with four insurance brokers, each offering the same premium to insure public property, the official may pick the broker who contributed to the ruling party's campaign fund. These are examples of **patronage,** the practice of rewarding or stimulating political activity by the exercise of discretion on divisible matters of governmental routine. A few examples will make clear the range of patronage and its relevance to the national political system.

• A typist employed by the City of Chicago is assessed 2 percent of her salary by the Democratic organization in her ward. When a fund-raising dinner is held, she is expected to buy a $50 ticket. She explains her position:

> You can't tell the organization "no." If they say pay, you pay. Sure, there's a lot I don't like. But the organization got me the job when I couldn't find work anywhere else. I'm not exactly a great typist.[8]

The Democratic organization in Chicago has 35,000 patronage jobs at its disposal. It controls the nomination of several Chicago representatives, has a good deal to say about the Democratic senate nomination, and ordinarily picks much of the Illinois delegation to the Democratic National Convention. (The new mayor, Jane Byrne, is a veteran politician who had a falling out with her predecessor in city hall after many years of faithful service to the organization.)

• John V. Lindsay is elected Mayor of New York as an opponent of machine politics. His campaign stresses his dedication to good government and the merit system. Within five years, the number of "temporary" municipal jobs, which are exempt from civil service, multiplies ten times. Lindsay also finds that contracts with outside private consultants can be used for patronage. The city's expenditures on consultants increase 900 percent in Lindsay's first term. Consultants study traffic on

---

[8] Quoted in Martin and Susan Tolchin, *To the Victor . . .* (New York: Random House, 1972), p. 39.

the Queensboro Bridge five times in two years. New York City has a Neighborhood Youth Corps with 43,000 people on the payroll. Forty percent of the names on the payroll cannot be traced to actual human beings, although paychecks have been issued to these names and cashed.[9] In 1971, Lindsay switches from the Republican to the Democratic party and tries for its presidential nomination. New York municipal employees turn up as far away as Arizona to help his campaign.

• Congressman Morris K. Udall, a high-ranking member of the House Committee on Post Office and Civil Service and a liberal candidate for the 1976 Democratic presidential nomination, explains how the patronage system works:

> When a Post Office building was to be located in my district, I was notified that I could pick the architect. The congressman is always asked which architect he would like. One of the local Democrats was asked which architect he would like, and got a $2,000 campaign contribution from the architect he eventually selected. Now that Nixon is in power, I doubt that I'd have much to say.[10]

• Claude C. Wild, Jr., a vice president of the Gulf Oil Corporation — the eleventh largest company in the United States — explains his firm's $100,000 contribution to the 1972 Nixon reelection campaign. He was told by Nixon's secretary of commerce that a contribution of this size was expected from every large company. Wild said that he feared Gulf Oil could "be on a blacklist" if he didn't contribute, that sixty-one different federal agencies had jurisdiction over some aspect of his company's operations, and that "I just wanted someone [in the government] to answer my telephone calls once in a while." In other words, he felt he had no alternative, even though the contribution was from company funds and therefore illegal.[11] In any case, the legality of this particular contribution is beside the point. Most of the uses of patronage we have discussed do *not* involve illegal behavior. Even if all illegal practices were eliminated, the patronage system would remain virtually unchanged.

Fact and Fiction about Patronage. When most people think of patronage, they think of big cities and the Democratic party. This association is wrong on both counts, as some of our examples indicate. *The New York Times* says that "the most effective political machine east of Chicago" is the suburban Nassau County (New York) Republican organization. It gets much of its income from 17,000 public employees in Nassau County who pay it 1 percent of their annual salary.[12] Patronage seems to flourish in some parts of the country and to be far less common and less popular in other regions. The governor of New York, for example, can make 39,000 political appointments when he takes office. The governor of Pennsylvania can make 50,000, and the chief executives of Illinois, Indiana, and some other states are not far behind. In contrast, the governor of

---

[9] Tolchin and Tolchin, *To the Victor,* pp. 24, 61 – 64, 84.
[10] Quoted in Tolchin and Tolchin, *To the Victor,* pp. 219 – 20.
[11] *San Francisco Chronicle,* November 15, 1973, pp. 1, 6.
[12] *The New York Times,* July 7, 1974, Sec. E, p. 5.

"We're in the protection business. Your four-year-policy will be $100,000."

Oregon has less than a dozen patronage jobs, the governor of Wisconsin has about twice as many, and the governor of California has only a few hundred.[13]

Public opinion about patronage also seems to vary regionally. Eastern politicians believe that it is essential to the proper functioning of the party system. The Democratic leader in the Bronx told a reporter that he believed in patronage because "How can you ask a man to go out and give the time and energy [to politics] without any reward. . . . Lindsay would be ungrateful if he didn't reward the people who helped elect him."[14] People in the West and in parts of the Midwest regard this attitude as an immoral perversion of civic virtue. In California, paying precinct workers is considered scandalous. Nobody really knows the reason for so much regional variation in the prevalence of patronage. The old idea that patronage flourished in communities made up largely of immigrants and poor people can hardly hold water in view of ample evidence that political machines are also going strong in the suburbs and in rural areas.

Patronage in the Federal Government. Many Americans assume that federal patronage vanished with the civil service reforms of the late nineteenth century. This view is largely correct so far as job patronage is concerned. An incoming president can make fewer than three thousand appointments. Some of these are used to reward supporters, but the president also must worry about appointing able people who can help him control the immense federal bureaucracy. His success in office may depend on the quality of the people he appoints to some of these key positions, so he naturally will be reluctant to use these jobs to pay off political debts. As a result, the patronage value of federal jobs, although far from trivial, is far less than what can be found in many city halls and state capitols.

But patronage is not limited to jobs. The cases of the Gulf Oil executive and the congressman who could choose the architect to build a post office in his district suggest some of the other possibilities. The federal government is engaged in a vast number of regulatory activities and contractual relationships. Usually, decisions in these areas are not made on political grounds. But if officials in Washington want to, they can use their power to extract campaign contributions from businesspeople who fear retribution if they do not contribute, or who expect rewards if they do. The chairman of the board of directors of American Airlines admitted to *Fortune:* "A large part of the money raised from the business community for political purposes is given in fear of what would happen if it were not given."[15]

---

13. Tolchin and Tolchin, *To the Victor,* p. 96.

14. *The New York Times,* June 1, 1970, p. 30.

15. Quoted in *San Francisco Sunday Examiner and Chronicle,* August 19, 1973, Sec. B, p. 3.

Machine Politics and the Growth of Patronage.   A vast array of governmental decisions *can* be used as patronage if the people involved want to do so. Among the most common types of patronage are jobs, deposits of government funds, insurance, contracts, franchises, bankruptcy receiverships, guardianships of the estates of minors, and zoning variances. In the past, when patronage seemed to consist largely of city jobs passed out by local bosses, it was widely regarded as something for poor people, a sort of unofficial welfare system. Today, however, many of the spoils of government go to the middle classes. Poor people are not bidding for cable television franchises, or asking to be court-appointed referees for bankrupt businesses.

As government services have grown since the 1930s, the number of opportunities for favoritism also has expanded. The essence of **machine politics** is that every government decision is treated not as a matter of routine but as a favor. Naturally, the recipient of the "favor" is expected to repay it by contributing money or work. As its part of the bargain, the machine performs such services as interceding to speed the bureaucratic process along, to get special treatment for its favorites, or to cut through red tape. New federal welfare programs can be used as a source of patronage to supplement or compete with the established political powers. This is one of the reasons why local politicians were so eager to put control of antipoverty agencies in city hall.[16]

When political contributions are motivated by policy considerations, we assume that the contributor has bought influence with the gift. But with patronage, the opposite is the case. As we have seen, activity based on patronage is seldom voluntary. Patronage employees are assessed a percentage of their salary; they do not give because they want to. They work in the campaign for the same reason. Sometimes people who do business with the city, county, or state are told bluntly that they must contribute. Usually, though, this reminder is not necessary. This sort of contribution does not buy influence. It is simply a business expense that has to be paid if one wants to do business with the government. For example, Richard Cohen and Jules Witcover observed that "In Maryland, and especially in Baltimore, political contributions were considered part of the overhead, like the monthly bill from Baltimore Gas and Electric."[17] In other words, patronage is participation without influence.

Machine politicians take quite a dim view of participation based on any consideration other than financial gain: "You can't keep an organization together without patronage. Men ain't in politics for nothin'. They want to get somethin' out of it."[18] "Enthusiasm for causes is short-lived, but the necessity of making a living is permanent."[19] These judgments are just as inaccurate as all the predictions about

[16] Michael Johnston, "Patrons and Clients, Jobs and Machines: A Case Study of the Uses of Patronage," *American Political Science Review,* 73 (June 1979), pp. 385–98.

[17] Richard M. Cohen and Jules Witcover, *A Heartbeat Away* (New York: Bantam Books, 1974), p. 41.

[18] William L. Riordan, *Plunkitt of Tammany Hall* (New York: McClure, Phillips & Co., 1905), p. 51.

[19] Quoted in Martin Meyerson and Edward C. Banfield, *Politics, Planning and the Public Interest* (New York: Free Press, 1955), p. 71.

the end of patronage. As we shall see, among the various incentives for participation, "enthusiasm for causes" is at least as important as "the necessity of making a living."

Ideological Participation So far we have discussed incentives to political participation that involve expectations of a tangible reward. Now, let us turn to people who are not motivated by hopes of getting something tangible for themselves or achieving a particular policy goal. Instead, they are idealists, moved to action by their vision of the good, true, and beautiful. They are interested not so much in particular issues as in pursuing their vision of a better society. Occasionally, such a passion may find its momentary focus on a particular issue. This was the case in 1968 and 1972, when the peace issue drew many activists to the McCarthy, Robert Kennedy, and McGovern campaigns. In cases like this, the dividing line between ideologues and policy-oriented activists is fuzzy. The difference might be stated this way: the policy-motivated activists have finite goals. Achieving those goals provides their gratification. The ideologues may mention specific goals, but in fact they will never be satisfied until they achieve their ideal society.

Of course, ideologues are not limited to one party, one cause, or one side of the ideological spectrum. They are not limited to one social class, either, although they do come largely from the middle and upper classes. Regardless of whether they are left-wing or right-wing, political idealists are likely to be well educated and well-to-do. They have the time and money to give to the causes and candidates they favor. Because they are people who feel strongly about politics, they are capable of sustained attention to detailed and obscure tasks. Like patronage-motivated activists, ideologues are the kind of people who turn out to vote in primaries, attend caucuses in large numbers, pack meetings, go from door to door to register new voters, and perform all the tasks that generate political power in those aspects of election campaigns that do not get on television or in the headlines.

Although ideologues generally are deeply committed to their ideals, their attention to politics tends to be somewhat uneven. They are intensely active when a candidate or cause captures their interest, but at other times they just fade away. The machine politicians, on the other hand, always can count on a high level of activity from their followers because supporters know they will lose their jobs, contracts, or whatever if their candidate loses the election.

Ideologues are interested chiefly in national politics, particularly presidential elections. Even House and Senate contests often do not seem important enough to them. National politics, on the other hand, is not usually of great concern to machine politicians. The stakes for them are control of patronage, which is located in city hall or the state capitol. This means that the ideologues are left a somewhat clearer field than they would have if they were in competition with the patronage dispensers for control of national offices.

Ideological activists are particularly taken by candidates who seem to embody ideals. Adlai Stevenson, who ran for the presidency against Eisenhower in 1952 and 1956, was the first of these candidates in the postwar era. His eloquence and ability to articulate sophisticated commitment to civic virtue drew thousands of eager volunteers. Stevenson was a moderate, but his most conspicuous followers were to be found in the "intellectual" liberal wing of the party. In 1960, when Kennedy ran against Nixon, neither candidate seemed to ignite the same sort of intense ideologically-based adulation. But in 1964, ideological politics came to the fore again. This time the active ideologues were on the far right of the Republican party rather than on the left of the Democratic party. Hundreds of thousands of political newcomers actively supported Barry Goldwater's challenge to the bipartisan consensus about the welfare state and coexistence with the Soviet Union. In 1968, the idealistic "amateur" politicians were to be found on the left wing of the Democratic party. Legions of young people labored on behalf of Eugene McCarthy's unsuccessful campaign for the Democratic nomination. The left wing of the Democratic party was the scene of amateur activity again in 1972, when George McGovern captured the nomination on the crest of a wave of idealistic enthusiasm. McGovern's nomination was a stunning upset, but his landslide defeat by Nixon was quite predictable. Indeed, from Stevenson through Goldwater to McCarthy and McGovern, ideological candidates have compiled a track record that shows they can mobilize intense support among activists but are unable to achieve broad enough appeal to the electorate as a whole to win office.

All these candidates appealed to their supporters in ways that were very similar in style, if not in content. Political scientists who studied Goldwater and McCarthy delegates at their respective nominating conventions were struck by their similar approaches to politics, which they label "purist." Compare the following descriptions of Goldwater's and McCarthy's appeal:

> It was not so much his [Goldwater's] principles (though these were undoubtedly important) but the belief that he stuck to them that counted most with his supporters. "He can be trusted." "He is straightforward." "He does not compromise." "He doesn't pander to the public; he's against expediency." . . .
> The purists manifested amazingly little interest in specific issues. In our interviews at the convention, we simply could not get them to talk about anything concrete. . . .
> The purists did express strong belief in the importance of being interested in issues, but this is not equivalent to being interested in specific issues.[20]

> These political purists consider . . . compromise and bargaining, conciliating the opposition, bending a little to capture public support—to be hypocritical; their style relies on the announcement of principles and on moral crusades. Since it is difficult to make public policy or to win elections without compromising one's self in some way, there is an understandable tendency for purist political leaders to adopt a highly critical view of the main activities of American politics. . . .[21]

Criticizing "established powers" is something purists of all kinds seem fond of. The Goldwater enthusiasts of the 1960s and the Ronald Reagan fans of the 1960s and 1970s condemn "politics as usual" and depict themselves as outsiders trying to clean up a political system hopelessly corrupted by compromise. Indeed, when Reagan first ran for public office in 1966, he called himself a "citizen candidate" to

---

[20] Aaron B. Wildavsky, "The Goldwater Phenomenon: Purists, Politicians, and the Two-Party System," *The Review of Politics,* 27 (July 1965), 393–94, 402.

[21] Nelson W. Polsby and Aaron B. Wildavsky, *Presidential Elections,* 3rd ed. (New York: Scribner's, 1971), pp. 36–37.

EVERYONE'S AGAINST "THE ESTABLISHMENT"

When they talk, the New Right's members often sound like repackaged radicals.

They call their new coalition "The Movement," speak of "smashing the liberal power structure" and promise to "radicalize" ordinary citizens by "mobilizing" their anger and frustration over issues such as the Panama Canal treaties and abortion.

"We are different from previous generations of conservatives," said Paul M. Weyrich, director of the Committee for the Survival of a Free Congress. "We are no longer working to preserve the status quo. We are radicals, working to overturn the present power structure in this country. . . . Our enemies are not encroaching socialists [who are] taking away what's there. They have already succeeded. We are not in power, *they* are. We are the outsiders, . . . a group of young people coming in and saying, "What's here isn't right and we're going to change it.' "

Source: William J. Lanouette, "The New Right—'Revolutionaries' Out After the 'Lunch-Pail' Vote," *National Journal,* January 21, 1978, pp. 88–89.

differentiate himself from "ordinary politicians." Even after eight years as governor of California and one unsuccessful try for the Republican presidential nomination, he still insisted he was not a politician when he tried again for the nomination in 1976.

All this talk about being outsiders should not lead one to think that purists are actually outside the mainstream of American society. Purism is largely a middle-class phenomenon, and there are plenty of purist millionaires. The notion that the "big money" contributors are all on the conservative and Republican side is wrong. The left wing and the right wing both have their own financial angels. Consider the case of Nicholas H. Noyes, an heir to the Eli Lilly pharmaceutical fortune, who gave $7,000 to the Nixon campaign in 1972 while two of his grandsons gave McGovern $400,000.[22]

***Sociability, Prestige,
and Friendship*** Many organizations formed for a particular purpose produce social by-products for their members. Corporations, schools, churches, unions, and military units are not only organizations; they are also social groups. They provide a social environment from which people derive the pleasures that come from friendship and a sense of belonging. Political groups are no exception to this rule. Although some involve no face-to-face interaction, others provide opportunities for social relationships. This is true both of the so-called old-fashioned clubhouses based on patronage and the "amateur" clubs of trendy young ideologues. Amateur clubs in California stage dances, parties, boat

[22] *CQ Weekly Report,* October 6, 1973, p. 2658.

trips, and a variety of other social activities. Like college extracurricular activities, they are a way for men and women to meet. One of the most powerful ideological party organizations is the Democratic group in New York City's Greenwich Village. Yet the club is not all business; one of its subcommittees is devoted to planning charter trips to Europe for members.

Political organizations are an important social environment for some of their members. They become "special worlds" with their own sources of prestige and gratification. One of us once knew a party activist in New Haven who aspired to greater acceptance and prestige in the special world of the Democratic machine. To make himself seem more important, he told his friends that he could fix their parking tickets. In fact, he lacked the influence to do so. Instead, he paid his friends' tickets with his own money and gloried in his reputation as a fixer. This man is like many people who fill unpaid political positions out of a need for recognition or status. There are hundreds of thousands of such posts at every level of government. They do not confer money or power on the people who hold them, but they do

These symbolic rewards were mailed wholesale to Carter workers in the 1976 campaign. The "invitations" are meaningless—they were unnecessary for public events staged outside, and did not admit one to any of the highly prized balls and galas held inside.

The Inaugural Committee
requests the honor of your presence
and participation in the Inauguration of

Jimmy Carter

as President of the United States of America
and

Walter Mondale

as Vice President of the United States of America
on Thursday the twentieth of January
one thousand nine hundred and seventy-seven
in the City of Washington

We sincerely hope that you will be able to come to Washington and participate in the Inauguration of Jimmy Carter and Walter Mondale. You are entitled to view and take part in the two major Inaugural events: The Inaugural Ceremony, which will take place at 11:30 a.m., Thursday, January 20, and the Inaugural Parade on Pennsylvania Avenue, which follows at 1:30 p.m. January 20.
There are some Inaugural events which will require special tickets for admission. We deeply regret that, due to the limitation of space, this invitation cannot be honored at those events. We would like more than anything to be able to invite everybody to every Inaugural event, but we know that you understand and hope that you'll take advantage of the hundreds of things to see and do in Washington during Inaugural Week.
You're going to see a new openness and a new spirit in Washington. We hope that after you visit, you will take that spirit back to your home and help make it grow throughout this great country of ours.

confer status. In short, political activity provides public attention for people who crave recognition.

Political activity is also a path to association with celebrities. Americans seem to be of two minds about public life. On the one hand, "politics" and "politicians" have unfavorable meanings to most people. On the other hand, presidents, senators, representatives, governors, and mayors all find that their offices convey enormous prestige. Many people want very much to cultivate their friendship for reasons that have nothing to do with getting special treatment from the government. It is a genuine status symbol to have personal contact with a major political official, to call him by his first name, to be invited to a dinner or reception where other famous people will be present, to feel able to invite the official to one's own social affairs. There are people who value such symbols enough to pay for them by contributing money.

Some wealthy people like to cultivate the friendship of artists, to spend time with artists, and to be accepted by them as patrons of the arts. Others have the same feelings about actors, baseball players, authors, or even gangsters. And some rich people like to hang around with politicians, to be able to feel that they are "on the inside." Politicians know this, of course, and cater to these ambitions. A member of Congress describes his relationship with such a supporter:

> What he wants from me is attention. He's very powerful and very rich, and there's nothing I can do for him. He doesn't want anything from me but recognition. Human beings want to be recognized, no matter how powerful they are. . . . All he wants is to be able to say, "Oh, the Congressman was here Sunday afternoon," or "when I was talking to the Congressman Friday evening. . . ." That's all he wants. And so I talk to him every time I come home.[23]

The glamor and excitement of political life and the ties of friendship often combine to provide political candidates with surprisingly loyal organizations. The personal loyalties directed at political figures are often strong enough to survive fundamental changes in ideological direction. Representative Paul N. McCloskey, a maverick Republican from California, entrusted much of his fund-raising and constituency organizing to friends and neighbors with conservative beliefs. As McCloskey moved farther and farther to the left—even going so far as to run against Nixon for the 1972 Republican presidential nomination—many of these backers stayed loyal to him, thus choosing friendship over ideology.

GIVING MONEY

As we observed earlier, giving money is the most common form of political activity. In 1976, 9 percent of the adult population contributed to at least one party or candidate. The peak year for spending was 1972, when a total of $425 million was expended for elections at all levels, from president to dogcatcher. How should we

---

[23] Quoted in Richard F. Fenno, Jr., *Home Style: House Members in Their Districts* (Boston: Little, Brown, 1978), pp. 132–33.

judge this figure? It is a lot of money, but is it "too much"? It is less than 1/1,000 of the cost of government in 1972, or under $3 for every adult American. Is this too much to spend on choosing over 500,000 officials? Compared to other democratic countries, American campaigns are not terribly expensive.[24]

Suspicions that "money power" makes democracy meaningless are common. How important are campaign contributions? What limitations does the need for money impose on candidates? To what extent is political equality perverted by a need for contributions? If money were important, but relatively available, we would be less concerned about it. If money were more available to some candidates than to others, but not very important in deciding elections, we still would not be so concerned. But to the extent that money is both important *and* restricted, it could become a threat to the health of the political system. Participating in politics by giving money has been given much attention in recent years. Campaign contributions are now regulated by new laws that have radically changed some of the rules.

The Revolution in Campaign Finance

For generations, various laws limited the amounts of money that candidates could receive, required that contributions be reported, and prohibited corporations and unions from making donations in federal elections. But these provisions did not seriously interfere with anyone's desire either to get or to give campaign contributions, and such transactions often were concealed. Obviously, research in this field was limited in scope and precision, and our information about the impact of contributions on election success was haphazard.

The first major change came with the Federal Election Campaign Act (FECA) of 1971, which required that candidates report every expenditure and the source and amount of every contribution. For the first time, accurate and detailed records of campaign financing were available. The FECA Amendments of 1974 brought other major changes. They established:

1. Strict and timely reporting of contributions and spending
2. Limits on spending in presidential and congressional primary and general elections
3. Limits on contributions
4. Public financing for presidential candidates
5. A bipartisan Federal Election Commission (FEC) to administer the law

The constitutionality of the 1974 FECA Amendments was challenged by a coalition of liberals and conservatives, joined by the New York Civil Liberties Union and several other groups. Early in 1976, the Supreme Court upheld most of the new provisions in *Buckley* v. *Valeo.*[25] But the Court did prohibit, as unconstitutional restrictions on free speech, any limitations on campaign spending *unless* a candi-

---

[24] Herbert E. Alexander, *Political Financing* (Minneapolis: Burgess, 1972), pp. 33, 38–39.
[25] 424 U.S. 1 (1976).

date accepted public financing. For the same reason, the Court also struck down any limits on a congressional candidate spending his or her own money and on spending by organizations genuinely independent of a candidate or party. Finally, the Court held that the FEC was unconstitutionally appointed and therefore prohibited it from performing most of its duties. This last finding required speedy reconstitution of the FEC, which disbursed federal funds to all the presidential candidates.

Congress took advantage of the opportunity to adjust the 1974 legislation in various ways.[26] In 1977, President Carter requested public financing of congressional campaigning, but legislative attempts to deal with this topic were not successful. Thus, the 1980 elections probably will be conducted under the sweeping new rules created by legislation and court decision in 1974–76. We will examine these measures in some detail as background for a further consideration of campaign financing.

Limits on Contributions. Each individual can give no more than $1000 to a candidate in each primary and general election, $5000 per multi-candidate committee, and $20,000 to a party's national committee. No organization (except a party's national committee) may give more than $15,000 in any election. "In-kind" donations (goods or services rather than money) are treated as cash contributions.

Limits on Party Spending. Each major party has a $2.2 million spending limit for its presidential nominating convention, adjusted to the Consumer Price Index. Minor parties have a lower limit, but this is not a real restriction because, in fact, minor parties rarely have conventions.

National, congressional, and state/local party committees can each give $5000 to a candidate in the primary and again in the general election, for a grand total of $30,000. Moreover, national and congressional committees can each spend $10,000 *in behalf of* a candidate in the general election. The national party can also spend 2 cents per voting-age citizen (about $3.2 million) in a presidential election.

Actual party spending seldom reaches these limits; the parties contribute only a fraction of total campaign budgets. In 1976, for example, 12 percent of total expenditures by Republican House candidates, and just 4 percent by Democratic candidates, came from party committees. As this suggests, the Republican party is much better at fund raising. Before the 1978 campaign season began, Republican committees had raised $35.3 million, compared to $11.5 million for the Democrats. Most Republican money comes in amounts of less than $100, while the Democrats rely on big contributors.[27]

---

[26] Between them, Congress and President Ford took over four months to produce the FECA Amendments of 1976. Part of this delay reflected a desire to do more than merely put the FEC back on its feet. But the FEC could not pass out campaign funds until it had a new legislative charter. The unavailability of this money hurt some presidential campaigns more than others. This was an important reason for the four-month delay.

[27] *CQ Weekly Report,* March 18, 1978, p. 718; and June 24, 1978, p. 1608.

Public Financing of Campaign Expenses.   The provisions on public funding apply only to presidential elections and are optional. A party's nominee can raise money privately to pay for the general election campaign. But if he opts for public funding (as both candidates did in 1976), he cannot accept private contributions. Public funding covers all general election expenses for major party candidates up to a probable limit in 1980 of about $26.4 million. (The exact figure is tied to the Consumer Price Index.) Money for minor party candidates is proportional to votes received and is available after the election to candidates who get at least 5 percent of the vote. A minor party can obtain public funds before election day only if its presidential candidate won 5 percent of the vote four years earlier.

Before his party's convention, each candidate for a presidential nomination is limited to $13.2 million if he accepts federal funds. This support is on a matching basis. A dollar of public money is paid for every dollar raised privately. But to qualify for public support in a primary, each candidate must first raise on his own at least $5000 in each of twenty states, in contributions of $250 or less. This is intended to screen out frivolous or hopeless candidates so that public support goes only to serious contenders. (There were 207 presidential candidates in 1976, of whom 131 reported no campaign expenditures at all.) Some campaigns for the 1976 election began as early as 1973, but it was not until the election year itself that any candidates received federal funds. Thus there is still a need for fund-raising efforts in the early stages. The various contenders for the major party presidential nominations in 1976 spent a total of $64 million, of which just $24 million was supplied from federal funds.[28]

The money for public financing comes from the Presidential Election Campaign Fund, which is supplied by a checkoff on the federal income tax form. Any taxpayer can assign $1 of his or her federal tax (or $2 in the case of a joint return) to this fund. Between 25 and 30 percent do so.

Reporting and Disclosure.   Each candidate must form a single committee through which all expenditures and contributions on his behalf are reported. Contributors of $100 or more are asked to give their occupation and address, and this information is reported to the Federal Election Commission. Candidates are required to file several reports with the FEC during the campaign, and a comprehensive final report shortly after election day.

Enforcement.   The FEC receives reports, makes rules to implement the law, and oversees compliance. It consists of three Democrats and three Republicans, nominated by the president and confirmed by the Senate. At the peak of the 1976 campaign, the FEC received over 1000 calls a week requesting interpretations of the law. A sample inquiry: A Democratic congressional candidate wanted to produce a button featuring his name and Carter's and Mondale's. Would this be considered a contribution to Carter's campaign and therefore illegal, since Carter had accepted federal funding? The FEC pondered the issue and then ap-

[28] Herbert E. Alexander, *Financing Politics* (Washington: Congressional Quarterly Press, 1976), p. 249.

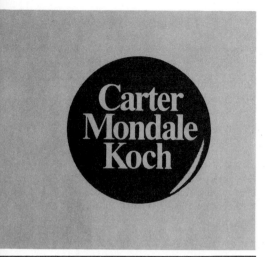

proved the button, but said that a billboard linking Carter's name with a congressional candidate would not be approved![29]

Political Action Committees. A major benefit of the new laws was the creation of a legal, aboveboard method for corporate and union financial contributions. The laws authorized unions, firms, trade associations, and other organizations to create political action committees (PACs). Corporate PACs can solicit contributions from executives and stockholders. In addition, they can solicit nonexecutive employees twice a year by mail. Unions' PACs can request money from members and their families without limit. No one may give more than $5000 to a PAC, and no PAC may give more than $5000 to a candidate per election.

These new provisions provided much more freedom to contribute money, and PACs have become the main way both labor and business participate in campaigns. PACs are the fastest growing political organizations in the country, particularly in the business community. Apparently a great many people are willing to contribute if they are asked to do so. With a single solicitation. Texaco raised $94,304, with no contribution over $100.[30] Over 1900 PACs were formed by the 1978 election.

The Federal Election Commission ruled that campaign buttons with the names of a Democratic House candidate and his party's national ticket was not a contribution to the Carter campaign, but it drew the line at a billboard with the same message.

They contributed $35.1 million, with labor accounting for just under a third and business and professional groups almost all the rest.[31]

Corporations and unions cannot give their own money to PACs, but they can use their funds to start and administer PACs, and for electioneering limited to internal audiences — executives and stockholders or union members. Such money can also be used for registration and get-out-the-vote drives that do not urge the election of particular candidates. These have been traditional labor techniques for generations, and labor is far ahead of management on these "nonpartisan" aspects of campaigning. Unions probably spend as much on such activities as they give in reported contributions. On the other hand, businesses have just begun to exploit their capacity to form PACs. Only 20 percent of the country's top 1000 industrial firms had PACs by 1978. The Republican party is encouraging more businesses to take the plunge.[32]

Who Gives Money and Who Gets It?   All congressional campaigns in 1976 combined accounted for $99 million. Party committees contributed $9 million of this amount, and PACs added another $22.6 million. This last figure is often called the "interest group" contribution. It would make more sense to

[29] *Minneapolis Tribune,* January 4, 1978, p. 5A.

[30] *Minneapolis Tribune,* January 5, 1978, p. 1A.

[31] *CQ Weekly Report,* June 2, 1979, p. 1043.

[32] Edwin M. Epstein, "The Emergence of Political Action Committees," in Herbert E. Alexander (ed.), *Political Finance* (Beverly Hills, Calif.: Sage Publications, 1979), pp. 175–85.

say that much of the individual contributions — which made up the remainder of the bill — were based on the same sorts of calculations as the PAC gifts.

Perhaps the most useful generalization about this subject is that generalizations are very difficult. Even the amount of money spent by candidates varies enormously. In 1976, Senator William Proxmire's reelection cost $697. Two years later, Senator Jesse Helms of North Carolina set a record by spending over $6 million to retain his seat. (His opponent, who had less than $500,000, called Helms "The Six Million Dollar Man.") Some House winners spend under $100, but in California's 27th District, two candidates each spent half a million dollars in 1976. In 1974, the average expenditure for all incumbents was $63,800; challengers running against incumbents averaged $40,200.[33]

Party and Incumbency.   Analysis of campaign finance records produces four different guides to the types of congressional candidates who do best in getting contributions. (1) Republicans get more than Democrats. (2) For nonincumbents, likely winners get more than people who are expected to lose. (3) Incumbents get more than challengers. (4) Incumbents raise money to match their opponents' spending. Everything else being equal, Republicans do better than Democrats because they usually have more wealthy supporters. In some congressional elections, however, Democrats have spent more money than Republicans. In 1974, for example, in all contested House and Senate races combined, Democrats spent a total of $38.4 million compared to $32.5 million for Republicans. The higher level of Democratic spending in 1974 reflects our second and third generalizations: incumbents and expected winners do better. The Democrats had a healthy majority in both houses of Congress before the election, and 1974 was widely and accurately considered a Democratic year. The average Democratic incumbent spent more than twice as much as his or her Republican challenger. Republican incumbents, on the other hand, had about a three-to-two financial advantage over their Democratic opponents.

Incumbents (who are mostly Democrats) do better than challengers because, being in office, they have more to offer potential contributors. The head of one powerful interest group explained why his organization would support friendly incumbents no matter how attractive their opponents looked: "We have no choice but to support those showing loyal service rather than those who show promise. A high seniority friend is better than a low seniority one."[34] Moreover, the statistical probability that an incumbent will be reelected is very high. Naturally, many potential contributors feel that money given to a loser is money wasted. In short, challengers suffer from being less known and less likely to win.

There are always some challengers whose chances of victory are brighter, and who can raise substantial campaign funds. Here the last of our four generalizations comes into play. The incumbents threatened by such challenges "are apparently able to adjust their level of spending to the gravity of a specific challenge; they spend more when challengers spend more, less when challengers spend less." The

[33] Gary C. Jacobson, "The Electoral Consequences of Public Subsidies for Congressional Campaigns," paper presented at the 1977 annual meeting of the American Political Science Association.

[34] Quoted in *CQ Weekly Report*, June 1, 1974, p. 1415.

incumbents who *lost* in 1974 spent an average of $101,645, compared to $63,800 for all incumbents.[35] The author of the only study of this subject summarizes his findings:

> Incumbent spending is *not* a positive function of the likelihood of victory at all; rather, the more certain they are of election, the less incumbents spend . . . incumbents sure of a victory feel no need for the money that is available. . . . Incumbents, then, acquire funds only in proportion to the felt necessity to do so.[36]

Wealth and Ideology.   Other significant factors affect the give and take of political finance. One of these, obviously, is the personal wealth of the candidate and his or her immediate family. A Kennedy or a Rockefeller is better off than, say, a Humphrey or a Nixon. The advantage of wealthy candidates has increased with the recent wave of reform; while individual contributions are limited to $1000, there is no limit on how much of his or her own money a congressional candidate can spend. Senator H. John Heinz III spent $2.5 million from his family's soup and catsup fortune in his 1976 campaign.

Most complaints about the role of money in politics assume that conservative candidates have an enormous advantage because most wealthy people tend to be conservative. Although this accusation contains a germ of truth, it misses so much of the reality of American politics as to be more misleading than helpful. The best way to make our argument is by example.

The two top spenders in the 1974 congressional elections were both incumbent liberal Democratic senators. Alan Cranston, a Democrat from California, the largest state in the country, spent $1,336,000 as he took 60 percent of the vote. This works out to about 33 cents for every vote Cranston received. The next biggest spender was George McGovern of South Dakota. Coming from one of the smallest states, McGovern spent $1,173,000 as he squeaked to a third term with 53 percent of the vote. McGovern spent $7.93 for every vote he got, by far the highest ratio in 1974. The bulk of his contributions came from outside South Dakota, motivated by the same ideological fervor that had made McGovern his party's presidential nominee in 1972.

These cases suggest an important generalization about money in politics. *There is no necessary connection between a candidate's ideological inclination and the size of the contributions he or she receives or the total amount of financial backing.* Rightwingers do not invariably enjoy huge campaign budgets, nor do liberals or radicals have to limp along with nickels and dimes contributed by "ordinary people." Barry Goldwater was unquestionably the most conservative politician to win a major party's presidential nomination in the modern era. His opponent, Lyndon Johnson, was responsible for the greatest increase in social welfare legislation in a generation. Yet Goldwater was the first candidate to develop broadly based fi-

---

[35] Gary C. Jacobson, "The Effects of Campaign Spending in Congressional Elections," *American Political Science Review,* 72 (June 1978), pp. 470, 474.

[36] Jacobson, "The Effects of Campaign Spending," p. 475.

nancial backing. Scarcely a fourth of his money was from donations of $500 or more, while 69 percent of Johnson's campaign funds came in such substantial chunks.[37]

George Wallace's presidential campaigns show that conservatives often draw their support from less prosperous groups. Although Wallace was certainly as far to the right as any recent presidential candidate, his financial backing was much more broadly based than any other candidate's. He raised about $7 million in 1968, far less than the liberal Eugene McCarthy, and he got it from five times as many contributors. Less than 15 percent of Wallace's financial backing came in contributions of $100 or more. The same pattern of broad-based support could be seen in Wallace's fund-raising for the 1976 presidential campaign. The average contribution he reported to the FEC in order to obtain federal matching funds was only $14.75, compared to $21.84 for Morris Udall, the leading liberal candidate, and somewhat higher amounts for Carter, Reagan, and Ford.[38]

How PACs Spend Their Money.   Both labor and business committees give about 60 percent of their contributions to incumbents and divide the rest between challengers and candidates for open seats (those without an incumbent running for reelection). Labor PACs give almost exclusively to Democrats, which is what we would expect. More surprising is the lack of similar devotion to Republicans on the part of business PACs. In 1978, 40 percent of their donations went to Democrats.[39] Where a Republican is the incumbent or a candidate for an open seat, he or she will get business support. But if a Democrat is in office, many firms feel that getting along with the incumbent is more important than trying—probably unsuccessfully—to replace a Democrat with a more sympathetic Republican. One lobbyist explained the situation faced by many businesses: "Most PACs are simply tools to solidify the position of a particular corporation's lobbyist with whoever the incumbent is. And in most cases he's a Democrat getting support from unions, too."[40]

PACs generally concentrate their attention on the members of Congress who are most concerned with their particular problems. For example, in 1976 PACs in the dairy industry (chiefly cooperatives) gave a total of $205,986 to seventeen Democrats and six Republican members of the House Committee on Agriculture. Two dozen Democrats on the House Committee on Merchant Marine and Fisheries took in $96,138 from maritime unions in 1976.[41] We will explore these networks of special interests in detail in Chapter 13.

---

[37] Herbert E. Alexander, *Financing the 1964 Election* (Princeton, N.J.: Citizens Research Foundation, 1966), pp. 70, 84.

[38] Federal Election Commission, *Annual Report 1976* (Washington, 1977), p. 16.

[39] *CQ Weekly Report,* June 2, 1979, p. 1044. These figures include both corporate and trade association PACs. Democratic candidates received 56 percent of all the contributions by PACs in 1978. This advantage was offset by the greater sums spent by Republican party committees.

[40] Quoted in the *Minneapolis Tribune,* January 5, 1978, p. 3A.

[41] Fred Wertheimer, testimony before U.S. Senate Committee on Rules and Administration, May 5, 1977.

The Direct Mail Revolution The $1000 limit on individual contributions forces fund-raisers to broaden their financial base rather than concentrating on a few big givers. One promising way to do this is direct mail solicitation of contributions. Barry Goldwater was the first to do this; he raised about half his funds from mail and televised appeals. The key to this introduction of techniques developed in advertising is the computer, which makes possible storing and classifying great amounts of data. The raw material comes from magazine subscription lists, records of donors to charities, organization membership rosters, and the like. Many businesses and organizations sell their memberships lists to direct mail advertisers or to "list brokers." An advertiser can direct an appeal to a tailor-made audience of people whose interests have been demonstrated by their previous purchases, contributions, or affiliations.

HOUSE OF REPRESENTATIVES
WASHINGTON, D.C.

MORRIS K. UDALL
ARIZONA

Dear Friend:

    Do you <u>really</u> mean it when you tell elected officials, like me, that you want to be told the truth?

    Do you <u>really</u> want us to give you the cold, uncompromising facts without sugar coating?

    Because... if I become President, I'm going to tell it exactly like it is. And for starters, I'll tell you right now that the only way you and I and all America will ever overcome our current economic and energy crises is to acknowledge the painful truth that <u>we must change our way of life</u>.

Dear Congressman Udall...

Enclosed is my investment in your campaign for the Presidency.

☐ $10 ☐ $25 ☐ $50 ☐ $100 ☐ $250 Other $_____

Name_____

Address_____   Make checks payable to:
                                      UDALL '76 COMMITTEE

City_____ State _____ Zip_____

Occupation and Employer's Name (This information is needed to comply with the Federal Election Campaign Act.)

☐ I would also like to volunteer some time for the campaign; call me at _____

Help Us Double Your Contribution.
    When you fill in the above information, your contribution—up to the first $250—will qualify for matching funds from the federal government under the new election reform laws.

Your Tax Benefit Is Now Doubled.
You can now deduct your contribution to the Udall '76 Campaign from your federal income tax in either of two ways:

1. You can subtract one-half of your contribution (up to a maximum of $50 on a joint return; $25 if you file separately) directly from your federal tax. This means you get back $1 for every $2 contributed regardless of your tax bracket because this is a credit to your final tax bill.

2. You can declare your contribution (up to a maximum of $200 on a joint return; $100 if you file separately) just as you would a charitable gift.

A copy of our report is filed with the Federal Election Commission and is available for purchase from the Federal Commission, Washington, D.C.

Politicians have always kept and jealously guarded their mailing lists, which contain the names of people who have given money in the past, have written a letter of complaint or praise, are known to be sympathetic, have gotten a favor, are related to a patronage employee, and so on. Computerizing these lists makes them infinitely more usable, and also lets the politician add, delete, and classify the names on the list far more easily.

Nixon's 1968 campaign followed up on Goldwater's success by raising almost $9 million by direct mail. The Democrats were slower to catch on to this new technique. In 1972, however, they far exceeded the Republicans in their use of direct mail. One of McGovern's greatest resources in his presidential campaign came from a chance encounter in 1971 with an Alabama lawyer named Morris Dees.

Richard E. Aaron/Thunder Thumbs; and Chuck Pulin © 1979

One result of the search for small contributors is the growing importance of benefit performances. The law permits entertainers to donate their services for concerts whose proceeds will go to a campaign fund. A single rock or country and western event can yield over $100,000 for a candidate with the right connections. This is one advantage of California Governor Brown's well-publicized relationship with rock singer Linda Ronstadt. Jimmy Carter began cultivating the popular music industry while he was governor of Georgia. In 1975, when Carter was still "Jimmy Who?" his campaign was saved financially by his friendship with the head of a Georgia-based record firm. The firm's star attraction, the now-defunct Allman Brothers, raised over $350,000 for Carter's campaign. Friendship or ideological affinity are not the only reasons for this kind of contribution. The businessmen who bailed out Carter later met with him in the White House to ask his help in a controversy over royalty payments, and in a federal investigation of bribery in the record industry.

Source: San Francisco Sunday Examiner & Chronicle, August 28, 1977, p. 14A; and Richard Reeves, *Convention* (New York: Harcourt Brace Jovanovich, 1977), p. 181n.

Having just sold his direct mail advertising business for several million dollars, Dees had a good deal of time on his hands. Deeply impressed by McGovern's positions on the issues, Dees joined the McGovern campaign and took charge of direct mail fund-raising. Thanks in good measure to Dees, McGovern's campaign escaped the financial anemia that had plagued Humphrey in 1968. The most famous practitioner of direct mail politics in the late 1970s is Richard A. Viguerie, head of a large firm in the Washington suburbs. A fervent conservative, Viguerie finds ex-President Ford too liberal for his taste. He will not accept any client who fails to pass his ideological test, and still sells his services to over 300 conservative groups and candidates. Viguerie's files hold the current addresses of nearly 2 million people who have given to right-wing groups or candidates, and he mails more than 2 million letters every week.

The greatest returns from direct mail have gone to candidates at the extremes of the ideological spectrum like Goldwater, Wallace, and McGovern. Some observers think it is not suited for more moderate causes, despite the success of Nixon and of the Republican campaign committees on Capitol Hill. In fact, direct mail is too new to permit conclusions about its importance. From any politician's standpoint, direct mail has the virtue of providing money without commitments to the donor. The average contribution is rarely over $25, and there is no continuing interaction between the candidate and the contributor.

HOW MONEY WORKS

Does Money Buy Elections? The obvious way to answer this question is to see whether better financed candidates are more likely to win. But until the strict new laws, the lack of reliable information kept the answers at the level of inspired guesswork. Another problem, of course, was sorting out cause and effect. Did Nixon win because he outspent McGovern two to one, or did he have so much money because he was a sure winner? Some contributors like to invest in winners. But political history provides many examples of well-financed losers, including the Republican opponents of Presidents Roosevelt, Kennedy, and Johnson.

The recent flood of detailed information on campaign financing provides far more satisfactory ways of learning the role of money in campaigns. In the 1976 Senate races, the candidate who outspent his or her opponent won just half the time. The same was true in House contests: the big spenders lost almost as often as they won. This is clear evidence that money is not everything in congressional elections. It does not mean, however, that money is unimportant. By far the best explanation of the impact of money comes from Gary Jacobson's study of the effect of campaign spending in the 1972 and 1974 congressional elections. He found that the consequences of spending are very different for incumbents and nonincumbents:

> . . . spending by *challengers* has a substantial impact on election outcomes, whereas spending by *incumbents* has relatively little effect. . . . campaign expenditures buy nonincumbents the necessary voter recognition already enjoyed by incumbents prior to the campaign. . . . Since nonincumbents have the most to gain from campaigning [because incumbents are already well known], it is not

surprising that their level of spending has a greater impact on the outcomes of elections than does that of incumbents.[42]

Incumbent senators and representatives are, on the average, much better known than their opponents. Thus they need less campaign money and usually have more. The challenger needs more and generally does not get it. When he or she does, the following scenario is likely: (1) The challenger becomes better known and hence more likely to win. (2) The incumbent raises money to meet the threat. (3) Spending this money does not do the incumbent much good. This situation is illustrated in Figure 9.2. As we have seen, incumbents who lose their seats spend much more than those who are reelected.

Money is more important in primaries than in general elections. These contests are more obscure and party identification – the major guideline in general elections – is not relevant. When several candidates contend for their party's nomination, none is likely to be known to most of the voters. The candidates with money can afford extensive publicity campaigns to bring their names to everyone's attention. In the 1970 Democratic primary in New York, four major candidates battled for the senatorial nomination. The winner was Representative Richard Ottinger, who spent around $2 million on his primary campaign, compared to a total of $353,200 spent by his three opponents. Although Ottinger may have bought the primary, he was unsuccessful in the general election, where he spent

[42] Jacobson, "The Effects of Campaign Spending," pp. 469, 489.

Figure 9.2

Campaign Spending and Candidate Familiarity in Elections to the House of Representatives, 1974

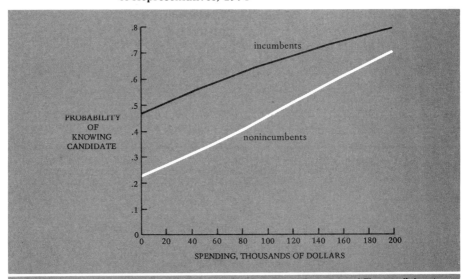

Source: Gary C. Jacobson, "The Effects of Campaign Spending in Congressional Elections," *American Political Science Review,* 72 (June 1978), p. 485.

another $2 million. If he did not get to the Senate, he at least had the distinction of having waged the most expensive Senate campaign in history up to that time. Ottinger could afford it, however. Most of his budget came from his family, the heirs to the U.S. Plywood Corporation fortune.

Of course, not all candidates have such splendid backing. Fortunately, there are substitutes for money. One is fame. Someone who is already well known does not have as much need for lavish advertising. And no matter how famous a candidate is or how much money he has, he cannot buy a political organization that reg-

A few months after his surprising election to the Senate in 1972, Joseph R. Biden, Jr., a Democrat from Delaware, testified in favor of public financing of election expenses before a Senate subcommittee:

. . . we all know how tough it is to raise money and we all know what we have to do to raise that money.

Let me give you a couple of examples. . . . I can recall in one instance going to a labor union who I knew was contributing $5,000 to a Senate campaign—to anyone they endorse—all above board, all honest, you know, by the numbers and it was a check, the full works. And we walk in and we sit down and start off the discussion very polite. He said, "Mr. Biden, would you like a cup of coffee?" We go through that routine, we have a cup of coffee . . . and then you really get down to it. Then, no one asks you to buy your vote or to promise a vote but they say things like this to me anyway. . . . , "Well, Joe, had you been in the 92nd Congress how would you have voted on the SST and while you're at it how would you have voted on bailing out Lockheed?" Now, I may be a naive young feller, but I knew the right answer for $5,000. I knew what had to be said to get that money.

The same thing occurred again when it looked like the polls started to narrow and Joe Biden is going to win . . . 13 multimillionaires invite me out to cocktails. . . . We sit down and we start off, only the only difference is they offer me a Bloody Mary instead of a Coke or a cup of coffee, and they're a little more frank about it. The spokesman for the group said, "Well, Joe, let's get right to it, looks like you may win this damn thing and we underestimated it. Now, Joe, I'd like to ask you a few questions. We know everybody running for public office has to talk about tax reform, Joe, and it's particularly capital gains. . . ." One fellow leans over and sort of pats me on the knee in a fatherly fashion and says to me, "Joe, you really don't mean what you say about capital gains, do you?" Now I knew the right answer to that one for $20,000 and quite frankly, were it not for the fact that I had a Scotch Presbyterian wife who had a backbone like a ramrod . . . and who I was more afraid of than those people I was talking to, I would have said on both occasions, "No, I didn't mean what I said about capital gains and yep I would have gone for the SST." Only because of her I didn't and I thought I lost it.*

*Quoted in *National Journal Reports*, November 10, 1973, pp. 1678–79.

isters voters and then gets them to the polls on election day. For these tasks he needs a dedicated army of supporters. Interpersonal campaigning of this kind has long been a favorite tactic of patronage-based machines and of labor unions. It is also one of the hallmarks of the "new politics" associated with ideological candidates from Reagan to McGovern.

Does Money Buy Political Influence? Some sorts of contributions do not provide much opportunity for influence. Money raised by direct mail, squeezed from patronage employees, or extracted from contractors as a condition of doing business with the government clearly does not earn any control over policy. Contributions by policy-oriented groups are another matter, at least in principle. Obviously such groups would like to influence policy. Nevertheless, the purpose of the contribution may not be so much to buy a friend as to elect one. Sometimes the two processes are difficult to separate, as Senator Biden's testimony illustrates.

On the other hand, sometimes one cannot even be sure that the candidate who gets a group's money is the one most likely to be sympathetic to it. As we have seen, business PACs give over a third of their contributions to Democrats who usually are less favorable to business goals. Since most incumbents are sure to be re-elected, the purpose of a contribution may be to gain access to the official, not to try to defeat him or her. Many lobbyists say, in effect, "our contributions buy the representative's ear, not his or her vote." One Democratic incumbent had this to say about a major interest group in his district: "If they oppose me in both the primary and general, they will have a hard time getting in the door to talk to me."[43]

It is important to realize that the initiative is more often with the official than the contributor. Many lobbyists say that they seldom offer contributions; rather, politicians ask for them. As we saw earlier, incumbents seem able to raise as much money as they need, which suggests that politicians are far from passive victims of moneyed interests. None of this is to say that contributions never buy influence, only that the picture is a complex one.

Politicians seem to be forever disappointing their contributors. One of Theodore Roosevelt's major financial backers early in this century was Henry C. Frick, the president of the United States Steel Corporation. Frick was not very happy with his investment in Roosevelt's presidential campaign, however. He felt that Roosevelt's progressive policies were a betrayal of the principles that led Frick to give his support. "He got down on his knees to us," Frick complained. "We bought the son of a bitch and then he did not stay bought."[44]

Perhaps the fundamental wisdom about money and politics is summed up in advice that Jess Unruh, the former Speaker of the California Assembly, gave some members of the state legislature: "If you can't eat their [the lobbyists'] food, drink their booze, . . . and then vote against them, you have no business being up here."[45]

[43] Quoted in *CQ Weekly Report,* January 28, 1978, p. 198.

[44] Quoted in Alexander, *Political Financing, p. 21.*

[45] Quoted in Lou Cannon, *Ronnie and Jesse* (Garden City, N.Y.: Doubleday, 1969), p. 101.

Future Issues in   The situation seems fairly stable for presidential elections.
Campaign Finance   Some of the consequences of the new order are these: Freed of
the need to raise money, the two major party candidates will
avoid some obligations and be able to concentrate more on the campaign. The
limits on monetary aid will shift influence to interests with greater amounts of other
resources: the mass media, and unions and other organizations that can mobilize

QUESTIONS WITHOUT ANSWERS

The difference between a campaign contribution and a bribe is often very
dim. Trying to explore the difference illustrates the ethical ambiguities that
surround this subject. The legal distinction is clear. If a politician uses a
contribution for professional expenses—either in the campaign or to
supplement an office budget—he or she does not have to declare it as
income and pay tax on it. If a politician takes money and uses it for
personal expenses, he or she has to declare it as income. To most people,
taking money to cover political expenses seems innocent enough, but taking
money for personal use smacks of corruption. But if a career is the most
important thing in the world to a politician, money for a campaign is much
more important than money for fast cars or fancy houses. Thus, despite the
tax laws, should not a campaign contribution be considered another form of
bribery?

On the other hand, don't citizens have the right to help elect the
candidate of their choice? One form of help is giving money. Can we
condemn representatives who vote a certain way because they expect to get
campaign contributions if they do? To be consistent, wouldn't we also have
to condemn the person or group that gave the contribution? But if we do,
aren't we denying the potential contributors their right to help the
candidate of their choice?

What is the morality of contributions motivated by ethnic solidarity?
Senator Abraham Ribicoff, a liberal Democrat from Connecticut, explained
that he could sponsor legislation opposed by Connecticut interests because
"My money comes from what I call emotional money, wealthy Jewish
liberals from New York who like to see a good Jewish boy in the Senate."*
Can we then say that the Jewish contributors from New York have bribed a
senator whose primary concern should be the interests of Connecticut?
James Abourezk of South Dakota was the first Senator of Arab descent. In
his first year in the Senate, he received $49,425 in speaking fees, largely
from Lebanese-American groups. Just four speeches to such bodies earned
him a total of $29,335.47. He used $30,000 of the proceeds of his lecturing
for office expenses.† Was he being bribed to take a pro-Arab position on
issues involving Middle Eastern affairs?

*Quoted in Tolchin and Tolchin, *To the Victor*, p. 241.
†Congressional Quarterly, *Financial Disclosures by Members of Congress* (Washington:
Congressional Quarterly, Inc., 1974), pp. 1, 4, 32.

campaign workers—important help that is not counted as money. Unions are far better suited than corporations for registration drives and other forms of "non-partisan" activity that are not restricted by the new laws.

The new rules will make things difficult for last-minute candidates for the presidential nomination, because of the time it takes to raise $5000 in each of twenty states. Federal matching funds will be unavailable to any presidential hopeful who fails to win 10 percent of the vote in two consecutive primaries in which he or she is a candidate. Taken together, these provisions will limit the number of politicians who can launch serious presidential bids. A dark horse candidate like Carter or McGovern will have a chance only if he succeeds from the start.

The outlook in congressional elections depends on the way Congress deals with the question of public funding. Jacobson analyzes the alternatives this way:

> . . . any increase in spending by both candidates will help the challenger. Public subsidies—or any other policy which gets more money into the hands of challengers—should therefore make House elections more competitive. . . . Incumbents will also get more money under such circumstances, but since for them raising money is not the problem it is for challengers and because their additional spending does not counterbalance the effects of greater spending by challengers, this will not work to their benefit.[46]

The situation is fluid because business and labor are still learning how to live with the new laws of the mid-1970s. The most explosive factor is the corporations' enormous capacity to form and fund PACs. If the business community exploits its financial advantage, it will outspend the unions many times over. If this happens, labor is likely to push harder to amend the laws again, probably to a combination of spending limits and public financing of congressional campaigns.

Many observers are concerned about the implications of campaign finance limits for freedom of speech. The reformers' goal is to equalize access to money and thus free candidates from restrictions based on their ability to attract contributions. Financial equality discriminates against people who have money to give to politics but no time, and favors people who have time but no money.[47] Restricting the political use of money while allowing full exploitation of nonmonetary resources gives advantages to some political interests at the expense of others. As is so often the case, "reform" is not neutral.

---

[46] Jacobson, "The Effects of Campaign Spending," p. 489.

[47] In June 1974 the voters of Berkeley, California, approved a referendum measure that prohibited corporations or labor unions from spending money in municipal elections. The forces behind this measure then put on the November ballot a proposal for the city government to take over the local gas and electric company. The proponents had no trouble publicizing their point of view, but the utility could not present its side of the case because of the law forbidding it to spend money in a local election. With the help of the American Civil Liberties Union, the utility went to court and won an injunction nullifying the no-spending provision as an unconstitutional restriction on free speech. *San Francisco Chronicle,* October 16, 1974, p. 4, and October 17, 1974, p. 6. In 1978 the U.S. Supreme Court affirmed the free speech rights of corporations in another campaign finance case.

The fundamental point is that limiting the ability to publicize one's views limits free speech. The right of free expression is meaningless without the ability to communicate that expression. An unamplified voice is just a cry in the wilderness. This is why the Supreme Court has removed limits on candidates' spending their own money and on the expression of opinion that is genuinely independent of a candidate's campaign. The Court approved limits on campaign spending only if the candidate accepted those limits by taking the option of public funding rather than soliciting his or her own funds. The future course of campaign finance legislation will be a tightrope walk between the goals of equality and freedom of speech.

WHO PARTICIPATES IN POLITICS?

In the final analysis, we are interested in political participation because the people who engage in such activities are more influential than those who do not. This is true for two reasons. First, candidates need money and campaign workers. Anyone running for office must attract at least a core of backers in order to be taken seriously. Unless some activists can be won over, a candidate cannot even get his or her name on the ballot. Thus activists are a constituency that must be wooed, just like the electorate as a whole. In places where one party's dominance makes its nomination tantamount to election, the minority that picks its party's nominee is all that matters. Second, activists are overrepresented among those people with whom politicians have contact and who provide them with many of their impressions of public opinion. It is the activists who write letters, go to meetings, ask officials for favorable consideration. In short, they are more visible to the politicians and thus count for more in political decisions.

Activists Are Better Off   As we said in Chapter 8, educated people are more likely to vote because they are more interested in politics, more comfortable with abstract issues, and more skilled at the minor administrative tasks required in registering. Participation is a more "demanding" activity than voting. Thus we would expect that the educated are even more overrepresented in the ranks of the activists than they are among voters. This is true: the more schooling someone has, the greater the probability that he or she will participate in politics. Since education is so strongly related to income, this means that the poor are least likely to participate. In every country, party, and organization about which scholars know anything, the finding is the same: leaders and activists are more likely to have better educations and better jobs. For the same reasons that they vote less, young people also participate less.

Table 9.1 shows the extent to which campaign activists come from the educated and prosperous. College graduates make up 13 percent of all Democrats but nearly a third of all Democratic activists. College graduates account for over a third of the Republican activists but only 24 percent of all Republicans. The same holds for occupation and income. The proportion of activists who are well-off and have business or professional jobs is much greater than the percentage of such people in the voting population as a whole.

Table 9.1

The Socioeconomic Composition of Party Activists in 1976*

	ALL DEMOCRATS (%)	DEMOCRATIC ACTIVISTS (%)	ALL REPUBLICANS (%)	REPUBLICAN ACTIVISTS (%)
Make over $20,000 per year	16	36	33	57
Graduated from college	13	31	24	37
Have business or professional job	21	38	34	55

*Activists are people who did anything to help a candidate get elected.

The Ideology Gap   The fact that activists are richer than other people leads some observers to the conclusion that this imbalance favors conservative interests. Not so. There are other, more interesting differences between activists and nonactivists. The most important of these concerns political awareness. Campaign workers are far more interested in and informed about public affairs than the average American. They are much more consistent in their opinions about political issues, in contrast to the unstructured pattern displayed by most citizens. By the same token, they are far more ideologically aware, less likely to have moderate opinions, and more frequently found at one or the other end of the ideological spectrum. As we saw in Chapter 7, most people refuse to identify themselves as conservatives or liberals. In contrast, activists take a stand, generally not in the middle of the road. This is shown in Figure 9.3, which compares the proportion of activists and nonactivists who apply ideological labels to themselves. For example, 13 percent of activists call themselves liberal or extremely liberal, while just 7 percent of those who did not participate in the campaign were willing to describe themselves in these terms. Similarly, 21 percent of the activists called themselves conservative or extremely conservative, compared to 13 percent of the less active. Finally, each party's activists are more "extreme" in their opinions than the ordinary voters. Republican activists are more conservative and Democratic activists are more liberal.

This gap between activists and ordinary party members fluctuates from year to year and party to party. Sometimes the gap is wider for Republicans and sometimes for Democrats. Once in a while both parties' activists are notably out of step with their rank and file.[48] This is not so much because people change their minds on the issues; rather, it is because different people are drawn to campaign activity from one election to the next. A particularly compelling issue or candidate draws certain kinds of people into the political arena and may discourage others. Sometimes a candidate who is particularly inspiring to activists may leave the mass of voters cold.

The most extreme illustration of these patterns was the 1972 election, when

[48] Norman H. Nie et al., *The Changing American Voter* (Cambridge, Mass., and London: Harvard Univeristy Press, 1976), pp. 203–4.

Figure 9.3

Activists Are More Ideological

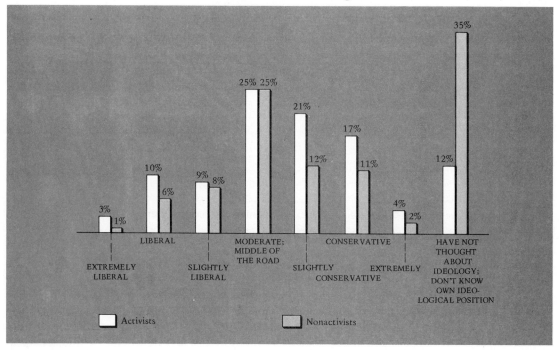

there was quite an ideology gap in the Democratic party. In that election, liberal and extremely liberal activists outnumbered conservative and extremely conservative activists by a ratio of about three to two. In fact, the conservatives were only slightly more active than people who claimed to be in the middle of the road. This increase in liberal participation reflected George McGovern's ability to mobilize millions of ideologically committed liberals, many of whom had sat out previous campaigns because of distaste for the Democratic presidential candidates.

The Democratic activists in 1972 were no poorer or uneducated than in other years, but they were a great deal more liberal. The most dramatic evidence on this point comes from research on the delegates to the two nominating conventions, who can be compared with each other and with the rank and file followers of the two parties. The Democrats had placed great emphasis on making the convention delegates representative of the party's mass membership. By using a quota system, the convention was opened up to women, blacks, and young people. Almost half the delegates were under 40, two-fifths were women, and 15 percent were black. But achieving representation for these three categories did not mean achieving it for other categories of people. In other respects, the Democratic delegates were quite unrepresentative. For example, 29 percent had graduate degrees and a total of 56 percent were college graduates. They were also an elite in terms of income. Fully

52 percent had incomes over $20,000, which was far ahead of the general population and not far behind the Republican delegates.[49]

Although the delegates to the two conventions were similarly prosperous and well educated, they were far apart in political outlook. The Republican delegates were generally—but not always—more conservative than all Republicans. The Democrats were vastly further to the left than rank and file Democrats on almost all topics. Indeed, on the issues most important in 1972, the opinions of the Republican delegates were closer to those of the Democratic voters. For example, the strongest possible antibusing position was taken by 81 percent of all Republicans, 71 percent of all Democrats, 64 percent of Republican delegates, and just 17 percent of Democratic delegates. Most of the Democratic delegates favored busing, a position not even supported by most black voters.[50] In short, the elite character of the two sets of delegates did not mean that they had similar views. Unlike the situation among the mass public, there is little relationship between activists' income or occupation and their views on the issues. Again in 1976, both parties had well-educated, well-to-do delegates; 65 percent in each party were college graduates. They were worlds apart on the issues, however (although not as far as in 1972). For example, 81 percent of the Democratic delegates favored a national health care plan, and 78 percent of the Republicans opposed it.[51]

We can reject the notion that the American political system is in the hands of an elite corps of activists who are conservative because they are prosperous. The activists *are* more prosperous, but their ideological commitments run in both directions. Moreover, a great many people are active in one election and then retire to the sidelines, to be succeeded by new, and often different, activists. There is no doubt about the advantages of money, energy, and determination in politics—as in every area of life. But no group or political faction in America has a monopoly on any of these resources. The amount of time and money expended for political purposes is only a tiny fraction of what could be spent. The amount of time and money devoted to politics depends more on one's motivation than on the absolute amount of time and money one has. The crucial factor, then, is not how much money or time is *available* to a particular cause, but how much is *used* and how effectively. In politics, potential power is far less important than the ability and will to mobilize that power.

Thus, our system is not firmly tipped toward one end of the ideological spectrum. Instead, we have a situation in which many activists in each party exert pressure to pull their party away from the center and toward the left or right. But neither party's activists are a solid bloc. Within each party, the ideologues are resisted by moderates and by politicians willing to compromise to appeal to the broader electorate. These struggles reach a climax every four years, when the parties select their presidential candidates, as we will see in Chapter 11.

---

[49] Jeane Kirkpatrick, *The New Presidential Elite* (New York: Russell Sage Foundation and The Twentieth Century Fund, 1976), Chap. 3.

[50] Kirkpatrick, *The New Presidential Elite,* Chap. 10.

[51] *San Francisco Chronicle,* August 17, 1976, p. 5. The gap between Democratic delegates and all Democratic identifiers also narrowed considerably in 1976.

IMPLICATIONS AND CONSEQUENCES

We have seen that differences between Republicans and Democrats are much sharper among activists than among ordinary voters. Activists are as important a constituency for candidates as the total electorate. Indeed, candidates' need for contributors and workers comes before their need for mass appeal because they must be nominated before they can even get to the general election. Activists are extremely important in the nominating phase because of the small turnout in primaries and the tremendous advantage of money and precinct workers in low-visibility elections. Moreover, the voters in primaries are more polarized by party than the people who vote in general elections. That is, Republican primary voters are likely to be more conservative and Democratic primary voters to be more liberal than Republicans and Democrats in general elections. As a result, Democratic candidates generally are more liberal than the average Democratic voter, while Republican candidates are more conservative than their voters. The candidates are pushed to the left and right, respectively, by the activists in their parties. And the fact that candidates are almost always recruited from the ranks of the activists further increases the likelihood that the people running for office will be somewhere toward the "extremes" of their parties.

Another factor that tends to push the parties apart is the unrepresentative character of the people who communicate with candidates and officials. Politicians need to get information about what the public thinks. The people with whom they come in contact are one obvious and important source of information. For example, during campaigns, candidates use the people they see at meetings as samples of the public. But the individuals who come to meetings and rallies are much more opinionated than the vast majority who refrain from such involvement.[52] The most common form of contact with politicians is through letter writing. This is something that over a quarter of the population has done. But here again, the people who write letters to public officials are not a representative selection of the public. Like the campaign activists, they are not only better educated and richer, but also far more ideologically oriented. Their opinions are likely to be located more on the left and right, and less in the middle of the road, than general opinion. Politicians who rely on the mail for their impressions of public sentiment may be grievously misled.

The 1964 election presents a dramatic example of this. Barry Goldwater won the Republican presidential nomination despite the fact that most Republicans preferred other candidates. However, Goldwater had the support of a majority of that fraction of Republicans who cared enough about politics to have written a letter to an official or newspaper. The letter writers were not only far more conservative than other Republicans but also more active. If the general election had been restricted to people who had written letters, Goldwater would have beaten Johnson by a comfortable margin. Unfortunately for him, his popularity among this select group was not matched by his appeal to the mass electorate. Goldwater's support among activists may explain why he persisted in ignoring the polls, which showed that his favorite ideas were highly unpopular. The very policies rejected by the mass public

---

[52] John W. Kingdon, *Candidates for Office: Beliefs and Strategies* (New York: Random House, 1966), pp. 91–101.

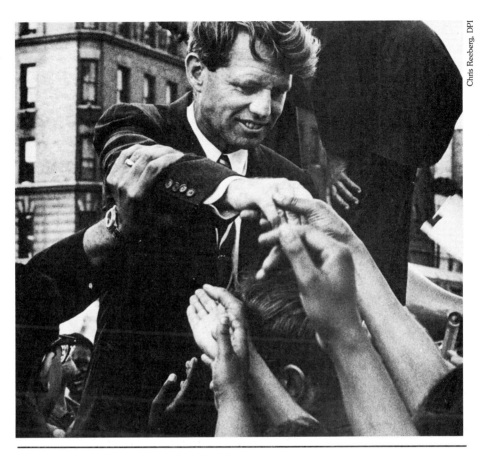

*The late Robert Kennedy appealed both
to the general public and to activists.*

were the ones most ardently held by the people who wrote letters. As a result, Goldwater may have been misled into overestimating his own strength because he relied on letters as an indication of public opinion.[53]

McGovern's nomination in 1972 was achieved much the same way as Goldwater's. A year before the convention that nominated him, McGovern was the choice of less than 5 percent of all Democrats. He was the first choice of only 6 percent of Democratic county chairmen, but these same leaders reported that McGovern's supporters were working harder than any other candidate's backers to win convention delegates.[54] By the time the convention rolled around, McGovern's popularity had risen dramatically, but he was still far from having a majority among all Democrats. He succeeded in winning the nomination because he was the overwhelming favorite of activist Democrats, just as Goldwater had been the favorite of activist Republicans eight years earlier.

[53] Philip E. Converse et al., "Electoral Myth and Reality: The 1964 Election," *American Political Science Review,* 59 (June 1965), pp. 333–36.

[54] *Gallup Opinion Index,* July 1971, p. 16.

Perhaps the best way to conclude our discussion of political participation is to consider an even broader implication of these findings about the gap between activists and the general public. There has been a great deal of rhetoric about the need to "increase popular participation" in political and civic life. The evidence about who actually engages in political action should make it clear that efforts at "increasing participation" usually end simply by increasing the influence of people who are not representative of the general public. Who goes to meetings? Who can write and speak effectively? Who knows how to raise money? Who is experienced in organization and in dealing with legal requirements? Obviously, not everybody. Nor does everybody care enough about politics to invest the time and energy to participate. Therefore, most methods of "increasing participation in decision making" will in fact increase the influence of the committed believers—those who are middle-class enough to be comfortable with political organization and committed enough to invest the necessary effort.

SUMMARY Individuals who participate in politics can expand their influence beyond their own votes. They do this by working in campaigns, by joining with others to try to influence policy, and by contributing money.

The proportion of those who participate has remained stable over the last twenty-five years: about 14 to 17 percent actively work in campaigns in each election. The same people do not participate in every campaign.

People participate for various reasons: to influence policy; because they have received or hope to receive patronage; because of ideology; and for sociability, prestige, and friendship.

Giving money has always been the most common form of campaign activism. It is now regulated by laws that set up requirements for accurate and timely reporting of contributions and spending; limits on the amount of individual contributions; public financing for presidential candidates; and a Federal Election Commission to administer the law. A major benefit of these laws was the creation of an open, legal way for corporations and unions to contribute. Political action committees (PACs) have now become the main way labor and business contribute to campaigns.

Republicans get more money than Democrats, but incumbents and expected winners get more than challengers and expected losers, and incumbents raise money to match challengers' spending. There is not much connection between ideology and the size of the contributions a candidate receives or the total amount of financial backing he or she has.

People who participate are more influential than those who do not, because candidates need money and campaign workers. Activists are older, better educated, richer, and better informed than nonactivists in their own party. Activist Democrats are more liberal than other Democrats; activist Republicans are more conservative than other Republicans. Presidential candidates who win their party's nomination by appealing to party activists may find themselves too liberal or too conservative for a majority of the voters.

interest groups

In 1977, the U.S. Food and Drug Administration (FDA) proposed to ban saccharin, the only commercially practical artificial sweetener, which is used in low-calorie foods, soft drinks, and many other products. This decision was based on the results of Canadian laboratory studies showing that some rats had contracted cancer after eating massive amounts of saccharin over long periods of time. In the FDA's judgment, any protracted human consumption of saccharin might increase the risk of cancer.

CHAPTER 10

Praise came immediately from one of Ralph Nader's organizations, the Public Health Research Group. At the same time, the FDA was condemned by the American Diabetes Association. Deprived of saccharin, diabetics would be faced with a choice between a diet with few sweet foods and potentially lethal use of sugar. Other health organizations also protested. The American Dental Association, for example, noted that saccharin is widely used to make toothpaste taste better; bad-tasting toothpaste would mean less brushing and more cavities. Dieters' groups complained that the FDA's proposal would make their goal more difficult, and that the health hazards of being overweight were far greater and more certain than the danger from saccharin.

Saccharin is the basis of a $2 billion annual market in foods and beverages. The producers, however, did not voice their alarm in economic terms. Instead, they spoke through an organization with a noncommercial name—the Calorie Control Council. The council bought ads urging people to protest the FDA's intention as both a medical threat and an attack on consumers' freedom of choice. More quietly, lobbyists made the same case on Capitol Hill, concentrating on members of Congress in whose districts food processing was important. The council also combed the scientific literature for evidence contradicting the Canadian results. The major producer of saccharin, the Sherwin-Williams Company, evidently took no part in the controversy. And on the other side, the sugar industry was equally inactive. The pro-saccharin coalition won. Moved by industry and consumer protests, Congress postponed any steps toward a ban until May 1979, and asked for a study and report from the National Academy of Sciences. The report was not clear-cut. Some scientists thought that saccharin use should continue; others urged total or partial controls. In 1979 Congress again delayed any action and the issue is sure to occupy Congress, the executive branch, the courts, scientists, and a diverse collection of individuals and groups for years to come.

From this example, we can see illustrations of several important points about interest groups:

1. Interest group conflicts often do not come down to clashes between "the public" and "special" or "vested" interests out to exploit the public. How were the claims of weight-watchers and diabetics less "special" than those of bureaucrats reaching for more power or self-appointed consumer groups that need scandals and exposés in order to attract financial support? The diet food manufacturers were motivated by profit, but scientific research may (or may not) prove their position to be entirely correct.

2. Organized groups represent a wide array of interests in a large and complex country where freedom of speech and association are important political traditions. As we will see, some of these groups have specialized interests and others have a broad agenda of issues.

226

3. Many individuals with a particular interest are not members of any organization advocating that interest. Few of the millions of diabetics belonged to any group working against the saccharin ban.

4. Groups formed for wholly nonpolitical purposes, such as dieters' clubs, can become political interest groups when it seems the government might do something they consider harmful to their common goal.

5. Sometimes those with strong interests at stake — like the sugar industry — do not participate in political struggles that could affect those interests.

WHAT IS AN INTEREST GROUP?

The many subdivisions into which a society can be classified (rich, poor, bald people, dieters, rich bald dieters, and so on), are **categoric groups.** Chapter 2 analyzed the bases of some major social and economic categoric groups — occupation, income, ethnicity, and religion, for example. Categoric groups do not become politically significant until at least some of their members begin to think of their common identity as a meaningful way of defining themselves — that is, until the categoric group is also a **reference group.** Overweight people are a categoric group — they all have fatness in common — but that fatness is a basis for reference group membership only for those people who think of themselves as fat. Even a reference group needs to begin thinking of politics as a way of expressing its common interest before it is an **interest group,** which we define as a collection of people making claims on the government on the basis of one or more shared attitudes. We consider that an interest group consists of all those who identify with it and who consider that identification in making political decisions. Thus, interest groups are not limited to organizations. The political preferences of individuals are often important whether or not they belong to a group, as we saw with the diabetics and weight-watchers.

Almost any category by which we describe human beings can be the basis for an interest group: age, sex, race, religion, occupation, sexual preference, nationality group, physical agility, hobbies, political beliefs. Thus, any of us "belongs" to many potential interest groups. Just as members of categoric groups may not be conscious of their group identity or see the political relevance of their group membership, different group identities come to the fore in different circumstances. When neighbors get together to campaign for a stop sign on a dangerous corner, they act on the basis of their common identity as neighbors. This identity may not be relevant to any other political action. It is not necessary that the people who want the stop sign share all political beliefs; they need to share only the beliefs that are the basis of their demand for the sign. Each one of them has other interests. When politicking for the stop sign, a man whose time is spent enjoying nature will not think of himself as an environmentalist, nor will his neighbor who designs freeways think of herself as a construction engineer. And when writing their senator for or against a new national park, these neighbors will not think of their common desire for the stop sign.

THE DIVERSITY OF AMERICAN ASSOCIATIONS

Business organizations:
Chamber of Commerce of the United States
National Association of Manufacturers
Business Roundtable
Automotive Advertisers Council
Air Traffic Control Association
American Apparel Manufacturers Association
Bow Tie Manufacturers Association
Woolen Hosiery Institute of America
National Armored Car Association
Art Dealers' Association of America
Paper Bag Institute
American Bakers Association
National Pretzel Bakers Association
American Bankers Association
Carbonated Beverage Institute
National Association of Wine Bottlers
Root Beer Institute
United States Brewers Association
Bicycle Institute of America
Cheese Importers Association of America
National Association of Chewing Gum Manufacturers
National Association of Home Builders
Dairy Industry Committee
Maine Sardine Council
Grocery Manufacturers of America
American Hotel and Motel Management Association

American Ladder Institute
National Macaroni Manufacturers Association
Academy of Motion Picture Arts and Sciences
New York Board of Trade
American Newspaper Publishers Association
American Petroleum Institute
American Association of Railroads
National Restaurant Association
Denim Council
Vinegar Institute

Agricultural organizations:
Farm Bureau Federation
National Grange
National Farmer's Union
Artichoke Advisory Board
American Breeders' Association
American Conservation Association
Future Farmers of America
4-H Program
National Maple Syrup Council
National Egg Council
National Pork Producers Council

Governmental organizations:
National Governors' Association
National League of Cities
National Association of Counties

Scientific, professional, and educational organizations:
American Bar Association
American Institute of Architects
American Society of Golf Course Architects
Association of Universities for Research in Astronomy
Society of Automotive Engineers
Users of Automatic Information Display Equipment
American Nuclear Society
Northeastern Bird-Banding Association
Radiation Research Society
Weather Modification Association
American Institute of Arts and Letters
Authors League of America
Council on Interracial Books for Children
American Association of Teachers of the Chinese Language
Modern Language Association of America
Public Library Association
American Institute for Marxist Studies
American Montessori Society
United Negro College Fund
National Science Teachers Association
Council for Advancement of Secondary Education
American Sociological Association
Association of Urban Universities

Groups become politicized as they see political relevance in their common situation. This is often the point at which they organize. The neighborhood residents might hold meetings and form a committee to press their demand for a stop sign. Sometimes such groups take on a life of their own and become fixed parts of the political landscape. With the stop sign installed, the neighborhood organization might live on and press for other advantages. It might work with similar bodies in other neighborhoods to develop a broader program, endorse candidates for the city council, and exert influence on a wider front.

AMERICAN INTEREST GROUPS: NUMBERS AND DIVERSITY

Americans seem to be particularly inclined to form organizations in order to pursue common interests. The classic statement of the importance of associations in American society was made by the most famous of all foreign commentators on America, Alexis de Tocqueville. Written in the 1830s, Tocqueville's portrait still rings true:

International Christian Youth
  Exchange
American Political Science Association

Public interest and consumer organizations:
Common Cause
Natural Resources Defense Council
Public Citizen, Inc.
Open Up the System (OUTS)

Social welfare organizations:
National Committee for the Prevention
  of Alcoholism
American Society for the Prevention of
  Cruelty to Animals
National Anti-Vivisection Society
Boy Scouts of America
Boys Clubs of America
Campfire Girls
Jewish Family Service
Foster Parents Plan
Indian Community Action Program
Citizens Committee for UNICEF
American Youth Hostels

Health and medical organizations:
American Society of Anesthesiologists
Braille Institute of America
Eye-Bank for Sight Restoration

Guide Dog Foundation for the Blind
Childbirth Without Pain Education
  Association
American Dental Association
American Diabetes Association
American Board of Internal Medicine
American Medical Association
American Psychiatric Association
American Psychoanalytic Association

Ethnic organizations:
American Arab Relief Agency
Catholic Workmen
Danish Brotherhood in America
American-Hungarian Federation
American-Italian Congress
National Association for the Advance-
  ment of Colored People
National Association of
  Polish-Americans

Religious organizations:
Fellowship of Christian Athletes
Society of Biblical Literature
Joint Commission on Church Music
American Jewish Congress
United Jewish Appeal
Americans United for Separation of
  Church and State

World Council of Churches
First Zen Institute of America

Veterans' and patriotic organizations:
American Legion
Bay of Pigs Veterans' Association
United States Flag Foundation
World War Tank Corps Association
Wives of the Armed Forces

Labor unions:
American Federation of Labor –
  Congress of Industrial
  Organizations
Negro Labor Committee
Actors' Equity Association
Airline Stewards and Stewardesses
  Association
International Brotherhood of
  Bookbinders
United Brotherhood of Carpenters and
  Joiners of America
International Brotherhood of Electrical
  Workers
International Longshoremen's and
  Warehousemen's Union
Brotherhood of Painters, Decorators,
  and Paperhangers of America
United Steel Workers of America
American Watchmakers Union

Americans of all ages, all conditions, and all dispositions, constantly form associations. They have not only commercial and manufacturing companies, in which all take part, but associations of a thousand other kinds — religious, moral, serious, futile, extensive or restricted, enormous or diminutive. The Americans make associations to give entertainments, to found establishments for education, to build inns, to construct churches, to diffuse books, to send missionaries to the antipodes; and in this manner they found hospitals, prisons, and schools.[1]

Who Belongs to Groups? In 1976 there were 13,583 national associations in the United States, devoted to everything from sports to religion to education to science to business.[2] Seventy-four percent of all American adults belong to at least one organization (not necessarily a nationwide one), and 57 percent are

[1] Alexis de Tocqueville, *Democracy in America*, trans. Henry Reeve (New York: Schocken, 1961), Vol. II, p. 128.

[2] *Encyclopedia of Associations*, Vol. I, *National Associations of the U. S.*, 10th ed. (Detroit: Gale, 1976).

Figure 10.1

Membership and Activity in Organizations by Americans with Different Amounts of Education

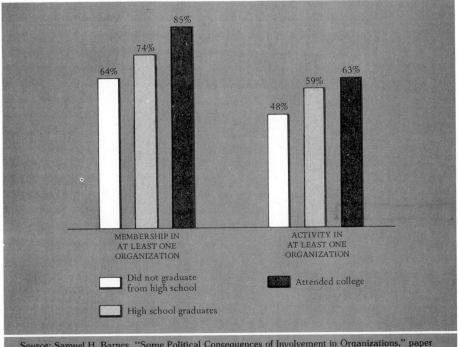

Source: Samuel H. Barnes, "Some Political Consequences of Involvement in Organizations," paper presented at the 1977 annual meeting of the American Political Science Association

active in at least one organization.[3] There is a strong relationship between education and belonging to and participating in organizations. As Figure 10.1 shows, only 64 percent of those who have not graduated from high school belong to an organization, and just under half are active in a group to which they belong. The proportion of members increases to three-quarters among high school graduates and fully 85 percent among those who have attended college. Active participation in an organization increases even more dramatically with education. Nearly two-thirds of those who have been to college report that they are active in at least one group to which they belong.

In all times and in all societies, joining and participating in organizations is more common among educated people, which means people with better jobs and higher incomes. Organizational activity is similar to knowing about politics, voting, and working in campaigns. The poor are less likely to do any of these things. Self-confidence, bureaucratic skill, and verbal ability are not a middle-class monopoly; but these qualities are scarcer among less-educated people, who are at a competi-

---

[3] Samuel H. Barnes, "Some Political Consequences of Involvement in Organizations," paper presented at the 1977 annual meeting of the American Political Science Association.

tive disadvantage in the interest group struggle, as they are generally. This is why some observers think that the interest group "chorus sings with a strong upper-class accent."[4]

This conclusion is true, but it is only part of the truth. All important issues do not pit rich against poor. Many issues are about things that have little to do with income. The controversy over saccharin, for example, found rich and poor diabetics on the same side, and for the same reason, a reason that had nothing to do with how much money they had. As we saw in Chapter 2, most people are neither rich nor poor. What is more, different kinds of poor people have different interests, and they often share those interests with those who are better off. The youthful poor do not worry about pensions; they are more interested in things like child care and jobs. Many people who are not poor want the same things. The elderly poor have little interest in day-care centers; they want pensions. Millions of Americans who are not poor also want income security in old age. The enormously increased social security benefits of the past few years reflect that concern, and help many poor people. Coalitions that include and benefit the poor often include unions and middle-class liberal organizations. Sometimes powerful economic interests profit from welfare programs. Food stamps, for example, are supported not only by unions and liberals, but by farmers and food processors. Once any government program to aid the poor is established, the officials who administer it have a vested interest in continuing and expanding its activities.

It is difficult to imagine anyone whose interests are not represented by organized groups. Even a hermit living in a cave would find his craving for solitude and pure air supported by conservationist groups, or his interest in pure food looked after by dozens of consumer lobbies. But that hermit would be dependent on others; he would not be looking after his own interests. This is the crux of the "class bias" in interest groups: The group struggle is a game that anyone can play, but everyone does not enter the game with the same partners, the same number of chips, and the same skills. As a famous singer once observed: "I've been rich and I've been poor, and rich is better."

Types of Interest Groups

One way to identify themes and patterns in group politics is to look at the types of interest groups (Figure 10.2). A useful way to do this is in terms of the motives or incentives that lead individuals to participate in and support groups: economic incentives, solidary incentives, and issue incentives.[5]

Few economic interest groups were formed with political activity in mind. Individual firms, trade associations, and labor unions perform a great many non-political services for their members. The American Medical Association, for example, was formed in part to distinguish academically trained physicians from what medical school graduates considered to be unqualified "quacks." The AMA gives

---

[4] E. E. Schattschneider, *The Semi-Sovereign People* (New York: Holt, Rinehart and Winston, 1960), p. 35.

[5] Adapted from James Q. Wilson, *Political Organizations* (New York: Basic Books, 1973).

Veterans organizations, which are often politically influential, are appealing to their members primarily as social clubs.

its members many nonpolitical benefits—medical journals, procedures for becoming affiliated with hospitals, professional conferences, and malpractice insurance. The AMA is also deeply engaged in politics. It illustrates the important point that actions of economic lobbies are frequently by-products of organizations "that obtain their strength and support because they perform some function in addition to lobbying for collective goods."[6]

This aspect of economic interest groups explains their substantial resources and leadership stability. Organizations formed for nonpolitical purposes have sometimes been restrained in their political activities because their executives must be attentive to the internal requirements of organizational harmony. On the other hand, leaders of such groups often have had great leeway for freewheeling political action. They do things that have not occurred to group members and would be opposed by many members if the members were aware of what was being done in their name.

Solidary groups—for example, ethnic associations—also draw on nonpolitical motivations in order to build organizational resources for political action. The sociability functions served by local chapters of veterans organizations illustrate this point. There is a rough division among solidary groups. Some concentrate on such face-to-face satisfactions of group membership as the local gatherings of veterans groups; in others, membership is more important as a way of developing reference group loyalty and pride. Organizations in the second category often have small formal memberships, but they may lead countless others who are not dues-paying members.

The third type, the issue incentive group, can be divided into two partially overlapping classes: those that seek to advance overall value positions bearing on a wide range of issues (notably generalized liberalism and conservatism), and groups with specific issue goals (for example, environmental groups and pro- and anti-abortion or gun control groups). The policies of both general and specific issue incentive groups often have economic implications. For this reason, a liberal group, such as Common Cause, is sometimes allied with an economic group such as the AFL-CIO. Nevertheless, the motivation is different for the partners in such coalitions. Many liberal groups are supported by activists who are not likely personally to profit (and may even lose) from the passage of liberal legislation. And conservative groups frequently have substantial support from individuals who are not particularly prosperous.[7]

---

[6] Mancur Olson, Jr., *The Logic of Collective Action* (Cambridge, Mass.: Harvard University Press, 1965), p. 132.

[7] During the period of student activism in the 1960s, the members of radical groups often came from more prosperous families than those of conservative groups.

Figure 10.2
Membership in Various Organizations
(percentage of population who belong)

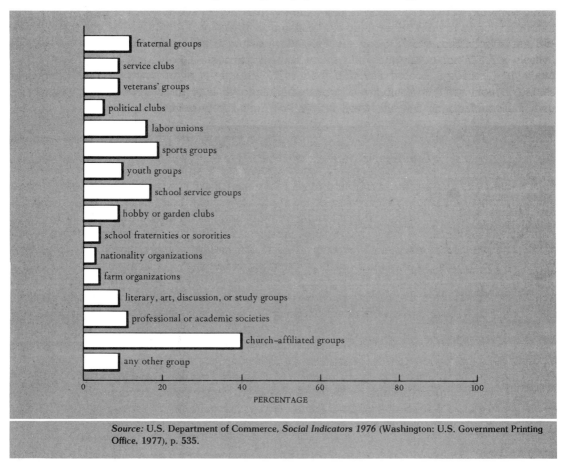

Source: U.S. Department of Commerce, *Social Indicators 1976* (Washington: U.S. Government Printing Office, 1977), p. 535.

ECONOMIC INTEREST GROUPS

Business Groups   Business interests have three advantages in dealing with the government. First, individual firms are already organized, so it is not necessary to form a group when a political issue arises. This is also true of trade associations. Formed for nonpolitical purposes, they have leaders, including attorneys and public relations staff, available for political purposes. Second, in dealing with government, business groups are on "home ground": they deal with familiar topics—their own economic specialities. This is not the same thing as being knowledgeable about politics, but it does give business an advantage not always shared by other groups. Further, public officials tend to find the views of individuals who are directly affected by a policy particularly important. When business groups move to general ideological advocacy, they are far less persuasive than when they confine themselves to issues bearing directly on their business. Third, business organizations, whether they are individual firms or trade associations, are able to spend money liberally to attain their political ends.

These considerations are advantages, not guarantees of success. Careful studies of the actual political activities of corporations show that often they do not muster the unity, interest, and skill to cope successfully with the political world. General Motors had no Washington lobbyist until 1969, and as late as 1976 had only one, despite an unbroken string of defeats on air pollution and auto safety legislation.[8] Some firms rely more and more on public relations consultants and Washington attorneys who specialize in dealing with the federal government. Even so, these experts cannot fully compensate for in-house political ability and often are called in only after a crisis has developed.

The business community generates the largest number of active interest groups. The several thousand nationwide trade and business associations range from the Associated Corset and Brassiere Manufacturers to the Latex Foam Rubber Council. Many of these organizations are quite specialized. There is a Paper Bag Institute, a Box Association of America, and an Envelope Manufacturers Association. Trade associations often find themselves on opposite sides of the fence. The Farmers and Manufacturers Beet Sugar Association wants the highest possible prices for sugar. But high sugar prices are not in the interests of big users like the National Association of Chewing Gum Manufacturers, the Chocolate Manufacturers Association of the United States, or the Flavor and Extract Manufacturers Association.

As some of these examples indicate, many issues pit different business groups against each other. But there are also concerns that they all have in common. The closest thing to an overall lobby for American business is the Chamber of Commerce of the United States. The chamber's membership includes over one thousand trade associations, about 2500 local, state, and regional chambers of commerce, and around 4600 firms and individuals. It employs about 400 people in its Washington headquarters and engages in a great variety of activities. It produces reports, magazines, memoranda, newsletters, and so on in great quantity. The chamber lobbies Congress and the executive branch on a variety of issues of general concern to the business community. Generally, it speaks only on issues with very broad relevance and remains silent on matters that affect a particular industry. Its flexibility is severely limited by its federal structure. The staff may not take action on a matter until a formal "policy" has been adopted by the chamber. This is a complicated process involving study by committees and adoption by the chamber's annual meeting. For this reason, the chamber is not very fast on its feet.

Equally prominent, but with somewhat more limited scope, is the National Association of Manufacturers. More than the chamber, this organization represents big business. The NAM's activities and limitations resemble those of the chamber. It too is hobbled by the need for formal policies adopted by the membership before it

---

[8] Norman J. Ornstein and Shirley Elder, *Interest Groups, Lobbying and Policymaking* (Washington: Congressional Quarterly Press, 1978), p. 168.

THE BUSINESS ROUNDTABLE

The inability of the Chamber of Commerce and the NAM to decide and act quickly led to the formation in 1974 of a new "umbrella" organization, the Business Roundtable. The Roundtable is an alliance of nearly 200 chief executive officers of major corporations, including General Motors, General Electric, DuPont, IBM, and American Telephone and Telegraph. This group has not sought broad publicity and usually does not speak out on general issues, but it has quickly acquired a reputation in Washington for high political influence. While much of the Roundtable's day-to-day work is done by a professional Washington staff, the group's basic strength is its ability to bring the top executives of the nation's biggest firms in direct and informal contact with officials. These executives, many of whom can easily get an appointment with the president, are articulate and well informed. The Roundtable has helped alert them to circumstances in which they might usefully make personal appearances. It also has been able to achieve some general agreement on issues broadly bearing on business; for example, government policy toward labor unions, and consumer protection. When Roundtable members find themselves in disagreement, the organization itself does not take a position. But even then a business's Roundtable membership is politically significant. The discussions alert individual firms to approach the government on their own.

Source: Congressional Quarterly Weekly Report, September 17, 1977.

can take action. Since the membership consists of industries that frequently have conflicting interests—for example, liberal versus restrictive import tariff levels—the NAM is often unable to take positions on significant economic issues. It may prove to be easy to achieve agreement on taxes or on an Alaska pipeline, but not on issues like federal pricing and allocation policies. The latter may affect different sectors of industry differently—for example, natural gas vs. gasoline interests, or Sunbelt state vs. Snowbelt state firms.[9]

Although some government policy applies to "business in general," most policy is more limited in focus. Topics of concern to particular categories of business are commonly handled by trade associations. An example is the Grocery Manufacturers of America (GMA), which represents the supermarket industry. A few years ago, the chairman and president represented Pepsi-Cola; the vice-chairman was from the H. J. Heinz Company; the secretary was the president of The Quaker Oats Company; the treasurer was the chairman of General Mills. Board members included representatives of Coca-Cola, Lever Brothers, and other manufacturers of products sold in grocery stores. GMA gives members of the grocery industry a way to

[9] The most up-to-date and detailed information on interest groups is contained in the weekly *National Journal*. For collections of case studies from that periodical, see *The Pressure Groups* (Washington: National Journal, 1971) and the annual *National Journal Reprints* pamphlet published at the beginning of each academic year and entitled *Interest Groups.*

"Our task then, gentlemen, is to persuade the government that the best way to solve a problem __still__ is to just throw money at it."

mobilize pressure on the government at many levels, from regulatory agencies like the Federal Trade Commission and the Food and Drug Administration through the Commerce Department to individual members of Congress. The executives and directors of the corporations that make up GMA have contacts in many, if not all, congressional districts. Therefore, the GMA can draw on a widespread network of personal connections and political contributors in attempting to make its case to the government on any issue. But an organization that represents all food interests cannot attain the unity to act in all areas. What is good for butter may be bad for margarine, and what is good for frozen foods may be bad for canned goods. Thus, conflicting interests often make agreement impossible. In these cases the GMA is paralyzed.

Some economic interests have no trouble at all expressing their political goals, because they are united on what they want. An example is the American Milk Producers, Inc., a dairy cooperative with more than 40,000 individual farmer members. AMPI is single-minded about what it most wants from government—a higher federal support price for milk. It succeeded in getting this in 1971 shortly after making a massive contribution to the Committee to Re-elect the President, a contribution which was one of the many issues that figured in the Watergate scandals.

There was a time when corporations' major political goal was to be left alone by the government. It is still true that businesses do not eagerly welcome more government regulation. But corporate political activity no longer consists just of crying out for unrestricted free enterprise. One political scientist put it this way:

> . . . as the regulatory and managerial apparatus of government has become an established part of our national life, important segments of business have made their peace with it, adapted themselves to it, and have even come to depend on it. A number of major corporations would collapse if their government contracts were cancelled tomorrow. Big business, quite as much as "big labor," "big science," and "big education," has become a claimant upon and beneficiary of the "service state" erected since the New Deal.[10]

Labor Unions   Labor is a much more centralized interest group—or set of groups—than business. The principal labor organization, the AFL-CIO, has 107 constituent unions, called *internationals,* which between them have about 13.6 million members.[11] Almost all internationals have their own Wash-

---

[10] Everett Carll Ladd, Jr., "The New Lines Are Drawn: Class and Ideology, Part II," *Public Opinion,* September–October 1978, p. 15.

[11] The AFL-CIO is the product of a merger between the American Federation of Labor (AFL) and the Congress of Industrial Organizations (CIO). The AFL was the traditional organization, composed largely of unions organized by particular skills, such as welders. The CIO was formed in the 1930s by people who believed that workers should be organized by the industry in which they worked, not by their skills. Thus all auto workers would be grouped in one union, all steelworkers in another, and so on. The two organizations were rivals until their merger in 1955.

ington headquarters, lobbyists, campaign workers, and political action committees (PACs). So do the major independent unions, such as the Teamsters (nearly 2 million members) and the United Automobile, Aerospace, and Agricultural Implement Workers (UAW for short), which has about 1.5 million members. This is not many organizations compared to the thousands of trade associations and hundreds of thousands of corporations that make up American business. The points of contact between labor unions and government are fewer than those between business and government. There is no counterpart in the labor movement to the innumerable minor, specialized problems that attract business interests to political activity.

The labor movement is not of one mind on political matters, however. Individual unions vary enormously in their ideological orientation, political involvement, and range of interests. Some unions stick closely to their own immediate concerns. The United Mineworkers, for example, concentrates on mine safety and health problems. The AFL-CIO itself, along with many of its internationals, pursues far more issues than any business organization. The unions are interested in matters that affect what they consider to be the well-being of workers, whether or not they belong to unions. Thus, labor is active and influential on more issues than any other single interest group.

Labor representatives are generally the most important lobbyists on social security, school aid, medical insurance, consumer issues, and civil rights. Labor favors policies to redistribute income and otherwise protect Americans in the lower reaches of society. Their traditional positions on economic and civil rights issues used to put the unions in the left wing of the Democratic party. But by the 1970s, liberalism was defined more by other sorts of issues: defense spending, detente with the Russians, the environment, and such life style problems as marijuana legalization and women's rights. These issues are more interesting to middle class people than to workers. Moreover, the liberal position on these issues seldom has much support from most labor leaders. The unions began to be viewed as a "conservative" political force. The most dramatic example was the failure of the national AFL-CIO to support George McGovern's presidential campaign, the first such defection from a Democratic presidential endorsement since labor began taking sides.

Although Jimmy Carter was not labor's first choice for the Democratic nomination, he was much more preferable than Gerald Ford and got strong labor support. The unions fielded 120,000 campaign workers and registered 6 million voters, as well as contributing over $8 million directly to candidates in 1976.[12] Unions have a ready-made source of campaign workers because their organizers and officials can easily become political activists. Some unions can perform most of the specialized tasks in a congressional campaign. They are particularly good at registering potential voters and then getting them to the polls on election day. Unions are the only interest group that can mobilize as many workers as political machines or—occasionally—the "new politics" ideologues. Although a substantial minority of union members are Republicans, labor's campaign efforts are almost always in behalf of Democratic candidates.

---

[12] James W. Singer, "Election Victories Mean Labor Can Come in from the Cold," *National Journal*, November 20, 1976, pp. 1655–56.

This is not to say that, once in office, Democratic politicians necessarily enjoy smooth relationships with labor. President Carter has been in hot water with labor leaders on economic issues. When the cost of living rises steeply, unions favor price controls but resist limits on wages. Since inflation was a problem throughout Carter's first term, he was often on the receiving end of heavy criticism from labor. Moreover, the more liberal unions — roughly those that supported McGovern in 1972 — were among those dissident Democrats who complained that Carter's domestic policies were too conservative. Despite these sources of friction, however, labor lobbyists often have been among the most important Capitol Hill advocates of Carter's legislative program.

Cargo Preference — Unions and Business in Alliance.   On May 25, 1976, Jimmy Carter promised Jesse Calhoon, the president of the National Maritime Engineers' Beneficial Association (a union), that as president he would work to "Enact and develop a national cargo policy which would assure our U.S.-flag merchant marine a fair share of all types of cargo."[13] In other words, Carter pledged support for "cargo preference," a requirement that some proportion of imports to this country be carried in American ships. Cargo preference would help America's declining shipping industry; it would benefit shipowners and shipbuilders as well as the workers who depend on a healthy merchant marine for jobs. Cargo preference united business and labor in a coalition based on common interest. Within a month after Carter's pledge to Calhoon, maritime corporations and unions had given $150,000 to his campaign. Once in the White House, Carter backed a bill to require that 9.5 percent of all imported oil be carried in American-flag tankers. The bill was approved by the House Merchant Marine and Fisheries Committee, whose chairman had received over $20,000 from maritime industry and union campaign funds.

In keeping his promise to one set of interests, Carter had antagonized others. The oil industry was outraged by the prospect of paying an extra half-billion dollars each year in transportation costs. Farm interests feared that their exports might be next on the preference list. Consumer groups opposed the impact of cargo preference on the cost of living. Other strong opponents included the U.S. Chamber of Commerce, Common Cause, and Ralph Nader. Carter's support of the cargo preference bill came after furious debate within his administration. His political promise was weighed against his economic advisers' view that cargo preference was a dreadful idea. Someone leaked the relevant memos, so the public could read this report to the president from Stuart Eizenstat, his chief aide on domestic policy:

> On the other side many members of our Administration, including Charlie Schultze [chairman of the Council of Economic Advisers], Mike Blumenthal [secretary of the treasury] and Dick Cooper [undersecretary of state for economic affairs], feel that *no* version of cargo preference is acceptable. *They feel that the principles involved — our commitments to free trade and to the fight against inflation —* cannot

---

[13] Our discussion of cargo preference is based on White House memoranda made available to us by Representative Paul N. McCloskey, Jr.; and on Richard E. Cohen, "Cargo Preference Faces Rough Waters in Congress," *National Journal,* September 24, 1977, pp. 1494–96.

June 24, 1977

MEMORANDUM FOR THE PRESIDENT

From: Ambassador Robert S. Strauss

Subject: Cargo Preference Legislation

Stu Eizenstat and I have met at length with
Senator Long on this issue. I have taken indirect soundings
of the leadership of the unions, and talked with others on
the Hill. Blackwell of the Maritime Administration believes
our labor soundings are accurate.

Politically, something in the way of a Cargo Preference
is going to be very hard to resist. Other options don't
serve or satisfy the political need, and might even be
counterproductive. The unions certainly feel that the
Administration is committed to a Cargo Preference Policy.

The Maritime unions claim that a Cargo Preference Act
is essential to the future of the U.S. Merchant Fleet and
the security of the United States. Other remedies such as
those proposed in the several option papers which have been
circulated, in their view, do not suit this purpose and are
seen either as entirely insufficient or a policy action contrary to their interests. They believe that the Cargo
Preference policy will protect seafaring jobs for U.S. sailors
and provide substantial on-shore employment in shipyards around
America. (They point to the substantial numbers of minority
employment in today's shipyards as evidence that the jobs
created on-shore would go where the need is greatest.)

What we have determined is that establishing the concept
of Cargo Preferences is more important than the percentage.
When Eizenstat and I met with Russell Long, we finally convinced
him of this and left him in the political posture of "anything
you fellows can satisfy Jesse Calhoun with, I will take and
support." I believe we can successfully sell less than ten
percent preferences stretched out over five or six years and
try to get the Hill and the Union committed to this if you
desire to go the Cargo Preference route. In short, what we
have accomplished is determining that the concept is far more
important than the percentage.

be breached. They argue that the economic costs of cargo preference outweigh its benefits. Moreover, they feel that even a modest cargo preference bill entails a dangerous precedent that may later be extended by Congress, or imitated by other nations.

Carter stuck to his campaign pledge despite the economists' arguments. But he was saved from having to live with his decision by the House of Representatives, which killed cargo preference decisively. Many opponents of the bill compared the shippers' campaign gifts to the milk interests' contributions during the Nixon administration.

Professional Associations   Labor unions became a strong political force in the 1930s as traditionally nonpartisan, politically cautious leaders were replaced by a newer generation who believed that unions should be active in politics. A similar process is occurring in some professional organizations. An example is the National Education Association (NEA). The NEA has long been the major organization representing schoolteachers. Until recently, it avoided political involvement. In 1972, the NEA formally decided to abandon this policy and plunge into politics. As its aggressive new executive secretary remarked, "The united teaching profession is on the brink of an unprecedented professional offensive. Its aim is to give teachers the decision-making authority, the public esteem, and the economic remuneration they deserve and must have."[14]

The NEA was something of a sleeping giant. Once it decided to get into politics, its tremendous resources immediately made it a heavyweight. It has 1.8 million members, an annual budget of nearly $50 million, and a staff in Washington alone of over 500 people.[15] One of its first projects was to rescue the reelection campaign of Senator Claiborne Pell, chairman of the Education, Arts, and Humanities Subcommittee of the Senate Committee on Labor and Human Resources. Pell is a strong supporter of more federal aid to education and so the teachers felt it important to keep him in office. Pell explained the result this way:

> My election is a victory for teacher power. Before the teachers began to help me, I was a two-to-one underdog. Now, thanks to an army of teachers who knocked on thousands of doors and made thousands of phone calls. I have won by more than 33,000 votes. This victory is a victory for education.[16]

One of the NEA's allies in the struggle for more federal aid and the right of public employees to strike is its rival, the American Federation of Teachers (AFT), an AFL-CIO union. The AFT competes with the NEA to represent teachers, and it may have been partly responsible for pushing the NEA into its new politically active role. Although the NEA and the AFT are allies on some issues, they are opposed on

---

[14] *Congressional Quarterly Weekly Report,* June 1, 1974, p. 1414; and *National Journal Reports,* August 30, 1975, p. 1246.

[15] Ornstein and Elder, *Interest Groups,* p. 43.

[16] Quoted in *CQ Weekly Report,* June 1, 1974, p. 1415.

others, such as the sales tax, which the NEA supports and the AFT opposes. The NEA manages to engage in political action even though its members are divided between Democrats and Republicans. Here, as with the unions, a strong organization overcomes divided political sentiments among its members.

SOLIDARY GROUPS

So far we have looked at groups based on economic relationships, and whose demands of the government are usually for economic policies of one sort or another. Economic demands are also made by other kinds of groups. Among the most important of these are **solidary groups,** which draw on feelings of common identity based on a shared characteristic, such as race, age, or sexual preference. The most important of these emphasize a common bond rather than the pleasures of face-to-face interaction. In other words, the basis of the group is a sense of kinship. The formal organization structure of a particular group may be just the tip of the iceberg—a few thousand card-carrying members representing (more or less accurately) millions of fellow members. Although solidary groups often seek to influence public policy in economic matters, they also seek recognition, protection, and favoritism. Frequently they have long existed as categoric groups; it takes external events or dynamic leaders to weld members into a politically focused reference group.

Ethnic Groups   European nationality groups illustrate how a category of individuals can become a politically meaningful group. Many of the southern and eastern Europeans who came to the United States were peasants. They often were illiterate, and in the old country their frame of reference did not go beyond the village. In some cases, the development of their language in written form had deliberately been discouraged by imperial rulers. America, rather than being a melting pot, became an instrument for bringing out, consolidating, and hardening ethnic loyalties. And ethnic loyalties in turn helped immigrants band together and find emotional, economic, and eventually political means for coping with their lives in the New World. The ethnic consciousness of some European nationality groups has faded, but others seem to be as aware of their ancestry as ever.

The most striking recent example of what has come to be called **consciousness-raising** (the increase of awareness and sense of one's stake in a group membership) is the experience of black Americans over the past two decades. Since the mid-1950s, blacks have won a series of important victories at the federal level, beginning with the landmark Supreme Court decision in 1954 outlawing school segregation and extending through a series of historic acts of Congress. Although the record of White House commitment to civil rights measures has been uneven, the effect of federal involvement on the racial front has been persistently in the direction of greater equality and opportunity. These victories by blacks reflect in large measure increasing black political awareness, the ability of blacks to hurt their enemies and help their friends, as well as the development in Washington of a powerful

GOVERNMENTS AS INTEREST GROUPS

The federal treasury provides more than $80 billion a year to lower levels of government, and along with federal money come federal rules. This makes states, cities, and counties interest groups as far as the federal government is concerned. Big cities and states usually maintain lobbyists to look after their special interests in Washington. There are also half a dozen general state and local government interest groups. Among the most important are the National Governors' Association, the National Conference of State Legislatures, the National Association of Counties, the U.S. Conference of Mayors, and the National League of Cities. Between them, these associations have thirty-four registered lobbyists and a budget approaching $6 million.

These groups recently formed an umbrella organization called the New Coalition. Sometimes the parts of the New Coalition work together smoothly. In 1976, for example, it helped keep revenue sharing alive. It was easy for the New Coalition to cooperate on revenue sharing because this issue offered something for every sort of government. But sometimes cooperation is not so easy. The states want highways; cities want more money for rapid transit. Thus, more specific issues often cause divisions between states and cities, or urban states and rural states, or old cities and new cities. These disputes are expressed in the formula for allocating funds under any particular grant program (of which there are more than a thousand). Consider the Emergency School Assistance Act, which authorizes hundreds of millions of dollars to local school districts to support desegregation by "reducing racial isolation." Should ESAA money be a reward for successful integration, an incentive for districts that have not been successful, or a temporary infusion to help cross the integration threshold? What if integrated schools slip back into desegregation? Is racial integration a bigger problem in big cities, and should smaller school districts be slighted? People of good will can differ about these issues, but the position a particular district takes will be determined by its own immediate situation.

State and local governments are politically powerful because their lobbying is built into the structure of Congress. Each member of Congress is an independent entrepreneur, building his or her own base within a constituency. A representative is often allied with state and local officials through the party organization; and many members of Congress are former local officials. One of the best ways members can look effective to their constituents is by bringing as much federal money as possible to their state or district. Therefore, the very nature of the national government enhances the political leverage of governmental interest groups.

network of alliances that link blacks to the labor movement, to organized religion, and to an assortment of liberal organizations. In other words, American blacks in the 1980s are a powerful interest group in every sense of the word. This is so even though the stable, solidly established organizations devoted exclusively to black interests are neither numerous nor very large.

By far the most important of these is the National Association for the Advancement of Colored People. The NAACP has been the spearhead of attempts for racial equality for more than half a century. Together with its legal fund, a separate but allied organization, the NAACP has symbolized black aspirations and has lobbied for them in Congress and the White House as well as through one of the most politically astute campaigns of litigation in the history of the American judiciary. Yet, although there are over 20 million American blacks, the NAACP has under a half million members, many of whom are white. Other black organizations, with the exception of the far less politically active Urban League, are much weaker in terms of membership, stability of leadership, and impact on national politics. Clearly, the political influence of blacks cannot be measured by the membership and budgets of black organizations. This leads to an important general observation: *The power of an interest cannot be measured by the size of its formal organizations.* Few politicians doubt the power of black voters, but none of them think that black power is contained in solely black organizations.

Although blacks recently have begun to pay some attention to American policy toward Africa, the focus of their political concerns is still largely on domestic policy. This contrasts sharply with the intense, long-standing involvement of American Jews in the conditions of overseas Jews and, in particular, U.S. policy toward Israel. Jews are exceptionally active as voters, campaign workers, and financial contributors, but they have little interest in domestic "Jewish issues." Their activity in behalf of Israel—which has received as much as half of all foreign aid in recent years—is coordinated by the American Israel Public Affairs Committee (AIPAC). This powerful but little-known organization is composed of representatives from over thirty different Jewish groups (AIPAC itself has about 15,000 members). When Congress considers action involving Israel, an informal network of legislative aides alerts AIPAC. That organization can mobilize activists around the country, each of whom in turn stimulates influential citizens to get in touch with their senators and representative.[17] One member of Congress observed: "If I cast a vote against Israel, every Jew in my district will know about it, and will be on my back."[18]

A major basis for Jewish influence is the fact that Jews are both prosperous and overwhelmingly Democratic. They are a far more important source of contributions to the Democratic party than might be thought from knowing their proportion of the population. A number of important Democratic politicians from areas with virtually no Jewish residents (such as Senator Henry Jackson of Washington) are active champions of Israel. Undoubtedly many of them are expressing their own political beliefs, but they are also aware that even in a state with few Jews, they may find Jews heavily represented among their financial backers.

Other ethnic groups are politically organized and influential in varying degree. Mexican-Americans, Puerto Ricans, and native Americans have followed the path of blacks in

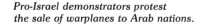

Pro-Israel demonstrators protest the sale of warplanes to Arab nations.

Wide World

[17] William J. Lanouette, "The Many Faces of the Jewish Lobby in America," *National Journal*, May 13, 1978, pp. 748–56.
[18] Quoted in Ornstein and Elder, *Interest Groups*, p. 49.

becoming more assertive and forming outspoken organizations. As each of these groups seeks to improve its members' circumstances, it may come into conflict with other groups. This may happen when the federal government officially designates certain ethnic groups as deserving of "affirmative action" — that is, various forms of special treatment. The usual political solution is to add more and more groups to the government's list of disadvantaged minorities.

The Women's Movement   The 1960s and 1970s were a period of consciousness-raising — a time when many categoric groups became self-conscious and politically aware. Women, of course, were the biggest such group. It is not that a belief in equality among the sexes was a new idea. In 1787, as John Adams was deliberating at the Constitutional Convention, his wife Abigail urged that he and the other Founding Fathers not

> put such unlimited power in the hands of the husbands. . . . If particular care and attention is not paid the ladies, we are determined to foment a rebellion, and will not hold ourselves bound by any laws in which we have no voice and representation.[19]

GAY LIBERATION

In many ways, the recent political emergence of homosexuals has paralleled that of women. Taboos against homosexuality traditionally have made it an underground phenomenon, with much shame, opportunities for blackmail, and interpersonal tension. As American society has become more tolerant of a wider range of sexual behavior, avowal of homosexuality — and even celebration of it — is increasingly common. This is particularly true in such cosmopolitan cities as San Francisco, where homosexuals are a formidable political interest group. Gay rights groups have had economic goals — for example, ending job discrimination. But the solidary aspects of gay liberation — the emphasis on taking pride in what once was a stigma (and still is in many parts of the country) — are even more evident. Organizations have sprung up with titles like Soul Sisters and Parents of Gays. There is also the beginning of an overall umbrella organization — the National Gay Task Force. At this level, among homosexuals as among so many of the groups we have considered, problems of internal conflict arise. Male and female homosexual groups have trouble cooperating, for example, partly because sexual attachment to members of one's own sex often is emotionally associated with antagonism to the opposite sex. The gay rights movement, like countless other types of interest group politics, has also been marked by a tendency for counterorganizations to spring up. The best-known symbol of this is the activities of the singer Anita Bryant.

---

[19] Quoted in Jo Freeman, *The Politics of Women's Liberation* (New York: David McKay, 1975).

Joel Gordon, DPI

Abigail Adams was ahead of her time. She expressed herself only in private to her husband. By the 1960s, women were displaying their feelings about what their status should be in best-selling books like Betty Friedan's *The Feminine Mystique*.[20] Ms. Friedan was not primarily concerned with economic discrimination against women; her concern was with redefining the meaning of being a woman — with establishing female pride and rejecting traditional deference to males. The development and expression of these beliefs were the basis of the women's movement, a powerful heightening of female reference-group identification and assertiveness. By 1966, a variety of smaller groups banded together in the National Organization for Women (NOW). NOW helped persuade Presi-Johnson to include bias against women in an executive order barring racial and religious discrimination in the federal government, and in forcing administrators to establish guidelines for enforcing that order. Along with other groups and millions of concerned individuals, NOW has been active in the campaign for the Equal Rights Amendment to the Constitution.

The new feminism did not appeal to all women. An opposing coalition of more traditionally inclined women's groups has formed on the other side of ERA and similar issues. These groups express concern that women might be deprived of such existing protections as alimony, exposed equally to the draft, and so on. Behind the specific objections lies an emotional revulsion at the thoroughgoing cultural and psychological changes that the women's movement embodies. Feminism has been almost entirely a middle-class movement, drawing primarily on the sorts of women who are already active in politics. Activists for the ERA are much younger, richer, better educated, and more politically experienced than their opponents.[21] For the latter, the fight against the ERA is a cause important enough to bring them out of their customary political inactivity.

PUBLIC INTEREST GROUPS

One thing that the Chamber of Commerce, the NAACP, and NOW have in common is their devotion to the interests of their members and constituents. Other groups do not claim to speak for a particular group or point of view. Instead, they claim to speak for "the public." In fact, these organizations do not always express the popular view, but they certainly do not appeal to economic self-interest in recruiting supporters and financial aid.[22] They rely instead on idealism and ideological commitment, and their members resemble the "purist" party activists described in

---

[20] Betty Friedan, *The Feminine Mystique* (New York: Norton, 1963).

[21] Kent L. Tedin et al., "Social Background and Political Differences between Pro- and Anti-ERA Activists," *American Politics Quarterly*, 5 (July 1977), pp. 395–408.

[22] Like other interest group officials, the leaders of these public interest organizations have a tangible stake in what they do — their jobs depend on maintaining the support of their members. Thus, they are motivated to stimulate public concern, if not outrage.

Chapter 9. For years, a variety of economically unselfish groups has operated in American politics. They represented inclinations from far left to far right, on issues ranging from prayer in the public schools to preservation of wilderness areas. Since the mid-1960s, a new kind of group has grown up, based on the power of publicity, direct mail fund-raising, and the use of litigation as a means of political action.

The Consumer Movement and Ralph Nader

The political power of consumers has risen dramatically since the 1960s, as the public career of Ralph Nader testifies. In 1965, Nader's book *Unsafe at Any Speed* created a sensation. In it, Nader attacked the Corvair, a compact car made by General Motors. Trying to discredit its annoying critic, General Motors hired a private detective to investigate him. Among other things, illegal efforts were made to pry into his private life and to trap him in a sexual adventure. The General Motors sleuthing was uncovered in the course of a congressional investigation into auto safety, and the president of General Motors apologized to Nader publicly. The resulting publicity aided the passage of the National Traffic and Motor Vehicle Safety Act and the Highway Safety Act, two major laws that brought federal control into the area of automobile design. Nader brought a multimillion dollar suit against General Motors for invasion of privacy and settled out of court for $280,000, which he promptly used to help develop an extensive program on consumer protection activities.

Nader has gone on to build a remarkable career as a political activist. A gifted writer and speaker, he earns hundreds of thousands of dollars annually in royalties and speaking fees. This income helps finance a "conglomerate" of organizations devoted to reforming various aspects of American life. Nader has also become a hero on college campuses. Together with his organizational talents, this reputation helps enlist thousands of recent college and law school graduates in his various organizations. Working at low salaries, or even as unpaid volunteers, people associated with Nader have investigated, exposed, and reported on a wide variety of corporations and government agencies, ranging from the nursing home industry to the Food and Drug Administration. At least fifteen organizations are associated directly or indirectly with Nader, including 75 full-time staff in Washington alone. This network is supported by Nader's book royalties and lecture fees, by grants from foundations, and by Public Citizen, Inc., a national organization that uses sophisticated direct mail techniques to raise over a million dollars a year.[23]

Nader's initial impact on government was the result of his extraordinary ability as a publicist. The projects he sponsored often succeeded because the magic of his name induced cooperation from officials who might otherwise have been reluctant to provide information. Nader's work has expanded beyond sensational exposés to litigation, lobbying on Capitol Hill, and testifying before regulatory commissions.

Common Cause

Low-paid or volunteer workers are one solution to the problem of financing public interest lobbies. The most important source of money for these organizations is direct mail advertising. (Along with some other

---

[23] Ornstein and Elder, *Interest Groups,* pp. 47–48.

interest groups, Common Cause benefits from a significant government subsidy. The bulk mail rate for nonprofit organizations is 3.1 cents per letter, quite a bargain compared to the regular third-class rate of 8.4 cents.) Common Cause, the best-known of all the public interest groups, depends entirely on direct mail membership drives and fund-raising campaigns. Founded in 1970, within four years it had 325,000 members, inspired in part by public outrage at the ethical shortcomings of the Nixon administration. With Watergate fading into history, Common Cause's membership has shrunk to about 215,000; but it is still the most influential organization of its kind, and a continuing force in Washington. Unlike other public interest groups, which are composed mostly of politically inexperienced young lawyers and scientists, Common Cause is staffed with seasoned veterans of the Washington scene. It has 80 full-time staff in its Washington office, supplemented by a corps of over 200 experienced volunteers, and chapters in almost every state. Its "Washington Connection," a telephone network connecting headquarters and members in hundreds of congressional districts, is used to pressure members of Congress. At peak effectiveness, the connection could mobilize as many as 3000 members. Common Cause regularly sends press releases to newspapers and radio and television stations and supplies a daily five-minute radio program to 125 stations.[24] Common Cause concentrates on Congress, where it finds many allies, as this observation points out:

> Much of the new power of "public-interest" lobbying groups stems directly from the intermediary role played by entrepreneurial [congressional] staffs. Young Democratic activists from the top Eastern law schools who work for a Congressional committee feel a basic kinship with their counterparts from the same schools who work for citizens' lobbying groups. Together, they form a network every bit as intimate as the one tying business lobbyists to Members of Congress on golf courses.[25]

Common Cause began by specializing in procedural issues like campaign financing and reform of the seniority system. It won so many of its battles that it is in some danger of running out of issues, so it is now becoming involved in substantive topics like tax policy. Like almost all public interest groups, Common Cause pushes liberal alternatives. Its allies include the unions and openly ideological organizations such as Americans for Democratic Action.

WHO GOVERNS INTEREST GROUPS?

The way a group is organized is determined largely by its purpose. If its main goal is nonpolitical — say the manufacture of automobiles — then it will be organized to achieve that purpose most efficiently. No one *expects* some of the groups that represent their interests in Washington, such as private businesses, to be democratically governed. But in fact even corporation executives are not always able to assert a position on an issue without some give-and-take within the organization. The various departments of a corporation may differ on how it should respond to a policy issue. For example, the export and domestic market divisions of a firm may disagree about whether it should support restrictions on foreign trade. Trade associations that represent groups of businesses are explicitly based on the consent and support of their members. The consent rarely, if ever, takes the form of detailed control of association officials by members. Rather, the staffs of trade associations are acutely sensitive to what association members want. Association officials have to touch base with so many members before they take action that their lobbying often is cumbersome and ineffective.

Most other sorts of organized interest groups have at least officially democratic organizations. Often, however, as in the case of labor unions, the surface differs from reality. As of 1979, the AFL and its successor, the AFL-CIO, had had only three presidents. In the late 1960s and 1970s there was an increase in contested elections in some unions, but usually union leaders stay in office for long periods of

---

[24] Ornstein and Elder, *Interest Groups,* p. 47; and Theodore Jacqueney, "Common Cause," *National Journal Reports,* September 1, 1973, pp. 1294–1304.

[25] Michael J. Malbin, "Congressional Committee Staffs: Who's in Charge Here?" *The Public Interest,* spring 1977, pp. 35–36.

time and have considerable leeway for independent action. Broadly speaking, in most associations most of the time, even if there is an official democratic structure, control of the group tends to be by the minority of members interested enough to be active. And most members are not sufficiently devoted to bother even to vote, much less to come to meetings and otherwise take part. This means that as long as the leadership does not go out of its way to take positions that will encourage a member uprising, they need only the support of the active minority to remain in power.

This applies even to groups that call themselves representatives of the public interest. Common Cause occasionally polls its members on issues and they elect its board, but only about 20 percent of them vote. In fact, policy is set by the leadership, with some concern for not exceeding the tolerance of the members and activists. Ralph Nader and his top lieutenants make the important decisions in his conglomerate of organizations. Nader, like Common Cause, acts "on behalf of" minority groups, consumers, the poor, and so on, but without sharing power with them. This situation led U.S. District Judge John J. Sirica to rule in 1979 that Nader's organizations had no right to bring lawsuits in behalf of the public. Sirica agreed that a democratic organization with elected officers could claim to represent the public. But since Nader's Public Citizen and Health Research Group had neither dues-paying members nor elected officers, Sirica said:

> Mr. Nader would hardly be in a position to seriously argue that his contributors or supporters exercise any substantial degree of even indirect control over such organizations. . . . Public Citizen (and in turn HRG) was founded by Ralph Nader and is operated by Mr. Nader, the board of directors he appoints and the employees hired by that board.[26]

If this decision is upheld, it will severely restrict the operations of public interest organizations.

It may seem puzzling that most members of interest groups prefer to contribute to "democracy" without themselves participating democratically in the organization they fund. But why *should* a member of the Teamsters Union or Common Cause care much about internal democracy as long as the organization provides what he or she wants from it? If a member of a union gets higher wages and better working conditions as a result of the leaders' activities, is it important to him or her that organization policies are not democratically made? Except for unions, these are voluntary associations. People who are dissatisfied with them can just not renew their membership. In the case of economic organizations and to a lesser extent solidary organizations, members may be reluctant to drop out because the organizations also fulfill nonpolitical needs. But many members of issue-oriented organizations exercise the freedom to drop out every year. Hence, such organizations must devote much effort to "cleaning" their mailing lists and otherwise working to renew their financial bases.

---

[26] Quoted in the *San Francisco Chronicle*, March 15, 1979, p. 7.

SELFISH INTERESTS OR
CONCERNED CITIZENS?

It is misleading to see politics as a contest between "selfish interests" and "the people." As individuals, we may sympathize more with one group than another, or with one policy than another, but that is quite different from saying that one group or policy is more "selfish." It is easy and comfortable to view a corporation seeking a favorable tax law as "selfish." But in what way are poor people less "selfish" for wanting more welfare, day care centers, and public housing? Are they any more or less selfish than people who want to buy saccharin, or the corporations that sell low-calorie drinks? Most people want what they can get from the government. One of the reasons why government exists, and one of the reasons why people consent to be governed, is because the government can provide its citizens with some of the things they want.

Any proposal is likely to be supported by a coalition of people with very different motivations, some of which may seem selfish and some of which may seem altruistic. Almost any government policy will bring economic benefits to particular individuals, so it is usually wrong to think that politics consists chiefly of conflict between good guys and bad guys. A few years ago, for example, a controversy arose over a canal that the Army Corps of Engineers was building across the width of Florida. Intense pressure by alarmed conservationists finally created so much public opposition that President Nixon ordered the engineers to stop. This was a victory for groups concerned about the quality of the environment and the protection of endangered species. But it was also a triumph for the railroad interests, whose business was threatened by the possibility of barge traffic across Florida. The railroads contributed generously to the conservation organizations that conducted the publicity campaign.

We tend to define selfishness in limited and material terms. If someone wants a law passed because it will raise his or her income, we consider that selfish. But there are many other motivations in politics, including power, self-righteousness, and other aspects of the murkier depths of the human psyche. Often the most intense political struggles involve intangible values, such as religious beliefs, racial prejudice, moral standards, and other things that have little to do with money. No current issue is more fiercely fought than abortion. The people on either side are motivated by emotion, not calculations of economic gain. The desire to fulfill these motivations may be just as deeply based in private, self-centered psychological needs as desires to have more money.

For all these reasons, it is important to realize that interest groups do not clearly divide between "selfish" vested interests and selfless paragons of virtue. Interest groups vary enormously in motivation. A group in favor of better health care for poor families is just as much an interest group as one seeking to

The fight about the Panama Canal Treaty in 1976–78 aroused patriotic emotions that had nothing to do with economic self-interest.

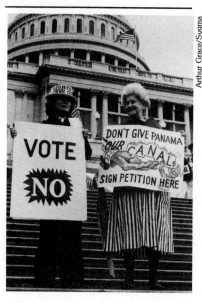

Arthur Grace/Sygma

have the government purchase silver. That one of these policies is an uneconomical use of public money for no useful purpose and the other will bring health and happiness to people deprived of basic human needs does not alter the fact that both groups are trying to influence economic conditions through government action.

INTEREST GROUP TACTICS

Unplanned Effects and
Anticipated Reactions

Sometimes an interest group can gain a major victory without any organized pressure at all. One striking example of this came during passage of the Civil Rights Act of 1964. Among other provisions, this law prohibits discrimination in employment on grounds of race or sex. The bill was aimed at discrimination against blacks. As originally drafted, it had nothing to say about women. Women's rights were not a conspicuous political issue in 1964. But when the measure was being debated in the House of Representatives, it was amended to cover discrimination on grounds of sex as well as race. This change was introduced by the leader of the opposition, who calculated that his "sex amendment" would muddy the waters, provoke stronger opposition to the bill, and dilute its eventual impact on racial equality by smothering the enforcement agency in complaints from women. As it turned out, he was right, but his stratagem did not affect the bill's passage.

After being passed by the House, the bill came before the Senate. Officials of the National Association of Manufacturers were alarmed at the sex amendment. They expressed their opposition to Everett Dirksen, the Republican leader of the Senate and a key figure in the bill's consideration there. Dirksen told the NAM that many of his fellow Republican senators shared its dislike of the sex amendment, but that not one of them would introduce an amendment to strike it from the bill. None of them wanted to chance the retribution from women that might result from publicly opposing a provision to outlaw sex discrimination. The result was the survival of the sex amendment, which has become the principal legal instrument against sex discrimination.[27]

One of the interesting features in the history of this law is the fact that there was no lobbying of consequence by women's groups in favor of the amendment. Indeed, in those years there were hardly any women's groups taking active political positions. The amendment was not a hard-won victory by advocates of women's rights, but the inadvertent outcome of an unsuccessful strategy to defeat the bill. Yet it stayed in the bill because politicians feared women's anger if attempts were made to remove it. Two conclusions, then, can be drawn from this episode.

1. Under certain circumstances, interest groups need not be organized or even politically conscious to be important in policymaking.

2. Interest groups often are influential not because of anything they do but because of what they are thought capable of doing. In other words, *anticipated*

---

[27] David B. Filvaroff and Raymond E. Wolfinger, *The Civil Rights Act of 1964* (forthcoming).

reactions can be as potent as direct pressure. As in poker, sometimes the cards you hold matter less than the cards the other players think you hold.

We are interested in groups as political actors, not passive beneficiaries. Among the ways that interest groups try to get what they want from government are campaign participation (discussed in Chapter 9), lobbying, litigation, and confrontation strategies.

Lobbying Lobbying is nothing more than trying to induce Congress to introduce, modify, pass, or kill legislation. A lobbyist is someone who spends much or all of his time in this pursuit. Some lobbyists are part-time or temporary Washington representatives for their employers or clients. Others represent several interests simultaneously or in succession. Lobbyists of this sort tend to be lawyers and public relations specialists. Most of them have worked on Capitol Hill or in the executive branch, and some are former members of Congress. The District of Columbia bar has its share of attorneys with conventional practices, but it also includes lawyers who specialize in government work, a type of practice that inevitably shades into lobbying. Many important national interest groups retain Washington law firms and also employ lobbyists who serve as long-term advocates for the organization or cause. The most influential lobbyists in this category are significant figures on the Washington scene, on a first-name basis with hundreds of politicians and reporters.

One of the lobbyist's important activities is providing members of Congress with information favorable to the lobbyist's clients. Although this is done primarily to alert congressional allies to a threat or an opportunity, it can benefit the members by supplying them with useful information. Of course, such information always must be weighed carefully, since it obviously does not come from a disinterested source. On the other hand, only the most short-sighted lobbyist would deliberately misinform a legislator in order to get support on a particular issue. One member of the House described the situation this way:

> It doesn't take very long to figure out which lobbyists are straightforward, and which ones are trying to snow you. The good ones will give you the weak points as well as the strong points of their case. If anyone ever gives me false or misleading information, that's it—I'll never see him again.[28]

Occasionally, a lobby scores a coup by being the only source of relevant information. When Congress convened in 1975, the seventy-five new Democratic representatives held the balance of power in the fight about maintaining the seniority system for appointing committee chairmen. Common Cause prepared a detailed "bill of particulars" that criticized several chairmen for violating party rules and other arbitrary behavior. This material was very influential with the new representa-

[28] Quoted in Ornstein and Elder, *Interest Groups,* p. 77.

tives, who had no personal experience with the chairmen and no other detailed sources of information about them.[29]

In addition to supplying members of Congress with information, lobbyists also keep their clients informed about developments in Congress that may affect their interests. Major lobbying campaigns rely mainly on constituent pressures. Rallying public support for a particular measure may involve stimulating mail and personal contact from constituents and inducing campaign contributors to call strategic legislators. Sometimes a lobbyist may bluntly remind a member of Congress of past favors or the possibility of future help or opposition. Tactics this crude are unusual and can easily backfire. Usually it is enough to speak the key phrase, "We're very interested in this bill." In political code, this gets the message across.

A third kind of lobbying uses publicity to make a public argument on the merits of a particular bill or simply to put direct pressure on Congress or the administration. When the Carter administration's efforts for an Israeli-Arab peace settlement seemed to American Jewish leaders to be hurting Israel, Jewish groups bought extensive advertising condemning the Carter proposals. Given the importance of Jews in the Democratic party, Carter went to great lengths to reassure Jewish groups. (At one point the tiny, electorally unimportant Arab lobby in Washington let it be known that it intended to place an advertisement in the *Washington Post* praising Carter's efforts. The White House discouraged this action.)

Regulation of Lobbying. The Federal Regulation of Lobbying Act, passed in 1946, requires lobbyists to register and report their expenses. There are more than 2000 registered lobbyists, with a total reported expenditure of over $10 million. These figures represent only a small fraction of the total lobbying effort. The reports are so inadequate because of the vague language in the original law and its subsequent interpretation by the Supreme Court. The gaps in the lobby registration law are obvious. But how they should be closed raises fundamental questions about whether lobbying can be effectively regulated without restraining free speech.

The 1946 law requires anyone to register and report if he or she obtains money "to be used *principally* to . . . influence, directly or indirectly, the passage or defeat of any legislation" (emphasis added). Eight years after the law went into effect, the Supreme Court used this "principal purpose" language to open a giant loophole in the law. The Court ruled that the law did not apply to organizations whose lobbying was *incidental* to their principal purpose, and that fund-raising for lobbying should be covered only where "a substantial part is to be used to influence legislation." Moreover, the Court defined lobbying as "*direct* communication with Members of Congress on pending or proposed federal legislation."[30]

The result of this interpretation was to exempt organizations whose main purpose is *not* direct lobbying—that is, most groups that lobby. It also excluded "grass-

---

[29] Michael J. Malbin, "House Upheaval," *National Journal Reports,* January 25, 1975, pp. 131–32.

[30] *United States* v. *Harriss,* 347 U.S. 612 (1954); emphasis added.

roots lobbying," attempts to sway members of Congress through their constituents, or by publicizing their voting records. Yet this is one of the principal techniques used to lobby Congress. In one year, for example, the National Association of Manufacturers spent over $2.5 million for activities related to grassroots lobbying, which it did not need to report.[31] Very few organizations disclose what they really spend on lobbying. Common Cause, because of its commitment to "open government," is one exception; it reports every penny spent—$1.6 million in one year alone. In contrast, the Chamber of Commerce of the United States reported less than $1000.[32] Since dozens of organizations do as much lobbying as Common Cause, hundreds more maintain full-time lobbyists, and many more have part-time legislative representatives, one can scarcely imagine how big the hidden part of the iceberg is.

The heightened concern for procedural reform that followed the Watergate scandals has focused attention on the failure of the 1946 act to achieve its purposes. A number of bills have been introduced in Congress to close the loopholes in the law. Among the proposals are the following:

1. Relax the "principal purpose" criterion to apply the law to all organizations that seek to influence legislation.

2. Require lobbyists to keep records of all officials whom they see and the specific measures they are trying to influence.

3. Expand the law to cover lobbying the executive branch as well as lobbying Congress, a form of group representation many political scientists consider more important than attempts to influence legislation.

4. Require members of the executive branch to keep logs of all contacts with private citizens. The idea here is to discourage secret meetings with people looking for favors.

None of these proposals was enacted by mid-1979, and their chances are not good. Common Cause is almost the only important group of any sort that favors "lobby reform." The opposition covers the entire lobby spectrum, from Nader and the Sierra Club to the Chamber of Commerce. One major complaint, particularly from smaller groups, is the bookkeeping cost that would be required. A more fundamental objection concerns the wisdom of trying to regulate contacts between the people and their government. If reports were required for anything more than an annual courtesy call on one's representative, the red tape would be enormous and people would be discouraged from the democratic practice of keeping in touch with their legislators. Presumably, everyone wants to encourage popular participation in government, citizen action, and so on. But there is no practical way to draw a hard and fast line between a "concerned citizen" and a "lobbyist." Each wants something from the government and will be better off (materially or psychologically) if he or she gets it. This is not an argument against amendments to the 1946 law. It *is* an

---

[31] *CQ Weekly Report*, July 27, 1974, p. 1949.

[32] Richard E. Cohen, "Lobbying Report," *National Journal Reports*, April 19, 1975, p. 573.

argument that one could easily cure one "abuse" by going so far in the other direction as to prevent direct access to the government and accountability of officials to their constituents. In the final analysis, interest groups are not something opposed to "the people." They *are* "the people," with all the selfishness, idealism, and diversity that exists in a country of 220 million individuals.

Litigation   The power to sue is a formidable political instrument. As many political observers have learned over the years, passing a law is only the first battle in a continuing struggle. It is something of a cliché among reformers that many problems do not need new laws; they could be solved if the laws already on the books were adequately enforced. Nader's organizations and other important public interest groups have turned to suing the government to compel it to enforce the law, or to suing private interests that may be violating the law.

For the private citizen, litigation is usually a prohibitively expensive way to get what one wants out of the government, because lawyers are expensive. But if a lawyer does not charge, or if she or he is employed by a public interest law firm, or even by a conventional firm that releases its members to work part-time in the public interest, then litigation changes from an expensive luxury into one of the cheapest forms of political action. This elementary fact, combined with the availability of hundreds of young law school graduates eager to use their training for idealistic purposes, has led to the development of nearly one hundred public interest law centers. The issues handled by these nonprofit, tax-exempt organizations include consumer problems, the environment, land use, occupational safety, health, "corporate responsibility," and racial equality. In the 1972–75 period alone, they received $130 million in contributions from various sources, including the federal government. These centers have a formidable list of accomplishments. However, they are very unevenly distributed around the country. Nearly two-thirds of them are in Boston, New York City, Washington, San Francisco, and Los Angeles.[33]

Although interest groups have greatly expanded their use of litigation, it is not a new technique. Groups traditionally turned to the courts to get what they could not obtain from Congress or the executive branch. When the NAACP found Congress, the president, the federal bureaucracy, and many state governments unwilling to work toward school desegregation, it tried lawsuits. The Supreme Court made it the official policy of the U.S. government to prohibit separate school systems for blacks and whites, and soon thereafter declared all forms of official segregation unconstitutional. Similarly, if the Interstate Commerce Commission were to refuse to give a trucking firm a license to haul freight to Des Moines, the firm might go to a federal district court to get the license. The Supreme Court itself has declared that litigation is a political right protected by the First Amendment.[34]

Individuals and groups can only "go to" courts in certain ways. Courts do not

---

[33] Council for Public Interest Law, *Balancing the Scales of Justice* (Washington: 1976), pp. 79–90.

[34] *NAACP v. Button,* 371 U.S. 415 (1963).

issue advisory opinions on general questions of public policy. They confine themselves to making statements of what the law or the Constitution require when there is an actual legal dispute between two parties. They only issue opinions to decide cases that are brought before them. If you want the courts to decide a dispute, you must become one of the two parties to a lawsuit. Moreover, anyone cannot litigate anything he or she wants to. Both parties must have a real and substantial legal interest in the outcome of a dispute before a court will accept a case for decision. Whether the court will hear the case is determined by very technical rules made in part by the courts themselves and in part set down in laws passed by Congress and state legislatures. For example, a taxpayer may not sue the federal government because he or she believes that its expenditures on an undeclared war are unconstitutional. The courts have held that a taxpayer does not have a sufficiently direct and specific interest in the spending of the tiny share of his or her tax dollars devoted to any particular government program.

Therefore, whether litigation is a useful form of political action depends on whether the Constitution, laws, administrative regulations, and previous court decisions provide good legal arguments for what an individual or group wants done. A person who wants to pursue a goal through litigating must have a plausible legal claim. Courts do make a lot of law, but not just any law they please. For example, a group that suddenly wants to seek federal protection for birdwatching may find that no legal provisions give it any claim to court attention. The NAACP has the equal protection clause of the Fourteenth Amendment. A trucking firm has a law passed by Congress that says that the Interstate Commerce Commission should issue trucking licenses to meet "public convenience and necessity." It will then argue in court that it would serve the "convenience and necessity" of the people of Des Moines to have another truck line serving their city.

Changes in the law may radically alter one's ability to litigate. Until the National Environmental Policy Act was passed in 1969, conservationists often could find no legal ground for challenging most federal construction projects, no matter how they would harm the environment. The new law, however, required an environmental impact statement (EIS) for each proposed project. Now conservationists can challenge proposed projects in court on the ground that no EIS has been filed, or that the statement is filed but inadequate, or that the federal agency involved is not paying enough attention to the statement. The Supreme Court's own actions may have similar effects. Its decision that advising and undergoing abortion were constitutionally protected in some cases led to a whole round of litigation testing the extent to which states could still restrict abortion.[35]

Of particular importance to the usefulness of litigation are changes in the legal rules about who can sue in particular cases — that is, who has standing. Congress and the Supreme Court have liberalized standing requirements to allow more and more people to challenge government policies in court. For example, at one time only a radio station had standing to challenge a denial of its application for a renewal of its license. Today not only the station, but local listeners have standing. People

---

[35] *Roe v. Wade,* 410 U.S. 113 (1974).

Some political activity by interest groups is financially supported by the federal government. We have already seen that nonprofit organizations pay only one-third of the regular cost for their bulk mailings. The most important and direct federal subsidies, however, come in the areas of litigation and testimony before regulatory commissions. In 1975 Congress authorized the Federal Trade Commission to pay attorneys' fees, expert witness fees, and other costs to anyone

> who has or represents an interest which would not be adequately represented . . . , and representation of which is necessary for a fair determination . . . and who is unable effectively to participate in such proceeding because such person cannot afford to pay costs of making oral presentations. . . .

This provision is a godsend to consumers groups. The FTC gave such organizations $285,000 to prepare testimony supporting a proposal to restrict television commercials aimed at children. The advertising and toy interests complained that it was unfair for the FTC to pay private lobbies to help it make its case against them. Other federal agencies now can reimburse interest groups for participating in their hearings.

These payments are small compared to spending on legal services, both for the poor and for groups claiming to speak in the name of the poor. In fact, the government is the biggest source of funds for public interest law centers. Part of the Johnson administration's poverty program, begun in the 1960s, paid for lawyers for people too poor to afford this help on their own. Many of the neighborhood legal groups funded by this program quickly evolved into sources of legal help for reformist and radical organizations. In this capacity, they won important victories—for example, removing California's residence requirement for welfare recipients. Criticism grew that many "poverty lawyers" spent more time on politically motivated lawsuits than on the legal problems of individuals. In the mid-1970s, responsibility for this program was given to a new, semi-independent public agency, the Legal Services Corporation. Congress also expressed the wish that emphasis be given to the original goal of providing legal aid to people who could not afford it. This has happened to some extent, and the LSC has been a political success story, with an annual budget over $300 million. It supports 335 programs that provide legal services to poor people in 900 branch offices throughout the country.

Sources: Council for Public Interest Law, *Balancing the Scales of Justice* (Washington: 1978), pp. 272–77; and *San Francisco Chronicle*, January 22, 1979, p. 4.

opposing a dam have standing if they can show that they have esthetic and conservationist values which might be damaged by the dam.[36]

Along with the expansion in standing has come increased judicial recognition of **class actions.** A class action is a suit brought by one person in the interest not only of himself but of other similarly situated persons. For example, an individual may feel that his electric bill is too high because of a possibly illegal state public utility commission decision to allow an increase in rates. He may sue the commission not only in his own behalf, but also in behalf of everyone paying the higher rate. If he wins, everyone else will get a rebate as well.

The growth of class actions has two major impacts on political participation. First, many unorganized people who have a common interest may participate in a single suit. The class action may win benefits for individuals who would not or could not expend the time and effort needed to organize successful lobbying in Congress or the bureaucracy. Second, class actions provide a financial incentive to sue. One person paying $2 too much every month for electricity would not be prepared to spend thousands of dollars on litigation. But if a lawyer brings a successful class action in behalf of 200,000 people, each of whom has been paying $2 too much, the electric company will have to pay back millions of dollars. The lawyer may be awarded several hundred thousand dollars in legal fees. Thus, the class action makes it worthwhile for lawyers to participate in what is frequently called **public interest litigation**—a suit designed to achieve the goals of a large set of people, each of whom has only a small interest in the particular goal.

Since the 1960s, there has been a tremendous increase in litigation. Some of this comes from the growth of the economy; more business leads to more disputes about contracts, patents, and so on. Related to this is the vast expansion of the government's role in everyone's life. Environmental, consumer, product safety, and civil rights legislation provide more bases for individual claims against the government and against private organizations. Third, and probably most important, is a greater willingness to litigate and more inclination on the part of judges to deal favorably with such litigation. Officials now assume that almost any major government step on construction, education, health, welfare, housing, mass transit, or natural resources will end up in the courts. Judges are more willing to make their own independent policy decisions on all sorts of problems. Political participation depends not only on individuals' desire and ability to act, but on whether their action is cooperatively received by its targets. Today we have many people anxious to litigate and many judges ready to give at least some of them what they want.

Confrontation Strategies   American politics has developed several forms of controlled, legal, ritualized confrontation: demonstrations, strikes, boycotts, and test cases. A test case arises when a group desiring change feels blocked by the prevailing interpretation of existing law. One response is to try to persuade

---

[36] Karen Orren, "Standing to Sue: Interest Group Conflict in the Federal Courts," *American Political Science Review,* 70 (September 1976), pp. 733–34.

legislatures to amend the law, or administrators to change their interpretation of it. If this approach fails, the group can try to get judges to change the law or their interpretation of it. But judges do not make decisions in hypothetical cases; to have a trial, there must be an alleged crime. People who want the judges' help must apparently break the law. Then, when they are prosecuted, they can argue against the constitutionality of the law, its consistency with more fundamental laws (e.g., with federal laws in the case of a state or local law), or against the current interpretation of it. Winners get the change they want; losers are declared lawbreakers.

Protest demonstrations, strikes, boycotts, and test cases are usually undertaken to achieve limited political objectives without bascially upsetting the normal functioning of government and society. These ritualized methods generally are recognized and protected by the law. Those who use them see themselves, and are seen by others, as acting legally. The protest march, or rally, is protected by the First Amendment. It occurs within a web of counterbalancing freedom of speech rights and valid police regulations for controlling traffic and maintaining order. Strikes are governed by federal and state regulations, court injunctions, and labor management contracts. Boycotts also are protected by law and subject to considerable legal regulation. The consumer boycott is firmly based on the legal right of the individual not to buy for any reason he or she pleases.

All these methods can be used to resist change as well as to initiate it. White parents have used the school boycott to resist integration of their schools just as black parents have used it to achieve integration. In both cases, boycotts are employed by those who have not found the normal processes of political persuasion effective.

Most of these methods require a fairly wide base of support and a high level of organization. Strikes and boycotts cannot be effective unless substantial numbers of persons refuse to work or to buy. Protest demonstrations attended by a few dozen people may be less effective than no demonstration at all. In contrast, the test case is a valuable technique precisely because it can be brought by a very small group surrounded by a large, hostile army of opponents. The test case takes matters out of the streets and the legislatures, where numbers are likely to count for a good deal, and puts them in a courtroom. There, in the case of *Smith* v. *Jones,* or even *Smith* v. *The United States,* each party counts for one, in terms of the time and attention it gets.

A particular advantage of the test case is that the appellate mechanism allows a minority badly outnumbered on the local scene to escape into the bigger world. The little band of Hare Krishna sectarians, jailed in Flower Patch for challenging an antinoise ordinance, may lose in the municipal court and even on appeal to the Alfalfa County Superior Court. But its appeal to the state supreme court may tap the more enlightened sentiments of the broader community. If the Hare Krishnas win their appeal, they will go back to Flower Patch flourishing their Supreme Court opinion along with their tambourines. They will depend on that opinion to stay out of jail.

The peaceful protest demonstration works in a rather different way. It is designed to show that a significant number of people feel very strongly about some social change, even though their voices have been ignored in the normal political process. It is a way of showing officials the extent and intensity of public sentiment so that they will respond through the normal governmental channels.

Small-scale Violence and Disobedience.   So far we have confined ourselves to the peaceful and legal forms of direct action and confrontation. Demonstrations, strikes, and boycotts may be mounted in the face of valid laws or court orders forbidding them. What is more, relatively high levels of social and physical coercion and violence may be mixed in with all these methods. We often read of fights breaking out between strikers and those who do not honor the picket line, of rock-throwing at demonstrations, of the occasional vandalism of businesses that refuse to stop selling boycotted goods. This sort of scattered violence often occurs in the context of massive movements aimed at bringing about change. When this happens, what began as a controlled, ritualized, and legalized confrontation escalates to a more intense level of direct action. And yet, there is no sharply defined legal or moral line separating the legal confrontation from the confrontation that is mixed with some degree of violence.

Many Americans try to draw a line between violent and nonviolent confrontation. The difficulty, of course, arises when we try to define what we mean by "nonviolent" physical coercion. Shouting a speaker down just as effectively deprives him of his right to speak as would shooting him, although it does him less physical harm. A barrier of massed bodies just as effectively deprives others of their right to come in and hear the speaker as would turning them away at bayonet point. If a group of strikers outside a factory indicate by their presence that they will not permit anyone to enter the factory, can their action be classed as nonviolent simply because no strikebreakers come forth to call their bluff? It certainly can be argued that the implicit *threat* of violence is itself a form of violence.

The purpose of most nonritualized, illegal, and actually or potentially violent conduct aimed at achieving change is *expressive* rather than directly instrumental. (In fact, even the scattered acts of violence by left- and right-wing "underground"

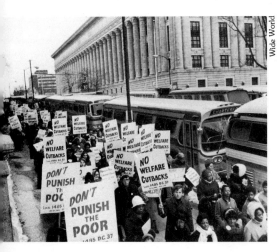
Wide World

protest groups of the past half-dozen years—e.g., the Ku Klux Klan and the Symbionese Liberation Army—were "propaganda of the deed" rather than specific attempts at concrete policy changes.) The "in system" forms of expressive confrontational politics have led to the routine politics of negotiation. It is in this context that civil disobedience as employed in the United States is to be understood. American practitioners of civil disobedience have rarely hoped to attain anything like what Gandhi hoped for in India. He aimed at generating such massive popular disobedience that the British imperial government would collapse because it simply would not have enough jails and police to deal with the offenders.

In this country, in contrast, civil disobedience has been a means for minorities to deal with a key fault in the electoral mechanism. Voting reflects only numbers. It cannot measure intensity of feeling. A minority that feels intensely may be overborne by an almost indifferent majority. By deliberately violating the law, such a minority can express the strength of its policy sentiment. This is why the classical (as opposed to the radical) theory of civil disobedience stresses the open, deliberate violation of the law and the willingness to be punished for the violation. Willingness to go to jail is important because it testifies to the intensity of the sentiment at issue and to the protester's desire to be protected by the rules of the political system rather than to wipe out the system itself.

The mass media's craving for sensational news often makes it a willing accomplice of groups causing expressive confrontations. This is particularly true of television, with its search for stories that will provide something interesting for audiences to see. The importance of "visual values" to television news provides an opportunity for any group "wretched or angry or clever enough to do what was needed to become photogenic."[37] Furthermore, no matter how confused or complex a story is, reporters try to find a theme or draw a moral. One of the best themes is good guys versus bad guys. Thus the needs of the media make them vulnerable to exploitation by clever political operators.

The forms of illegal political conduct that have drawn so much public attention in recent years seem to involve a subtle combination of expressive and coercive elements. The mass protest march may or may not turn into a riot. The occupation of a government building may or may not obstruct its normal functions. A thousand farmers driving tractors to Washington may or may not bring traffic to a halt by blocking intersections at rush hour. Thus, the expressive element is mixed with a coercive threat as the demonstrators seem to be saying, "Look, you can see how strongly we feel about these things, how much moral fervor and dedication we have. If you don't give us what we want, we may smash something."

Other elements in our political system further complicate the issue of the legality of various forms of direct action. As we saw in Chapter 3, our constitutional traditions encourage the belief that an unconstitutional law is not really a law; hence, violating such a law is not really illegal. Thus, whether a particular march or demonstration is ultimately legal or illegal depends upon court decisions that may occur months or even years after the event. Many of the activities of Martin Luther King, Jr., and other southern black leaders have fallen into this ambiguous category, as do all instances in which a person breaks the law in order to bring a test case to court. By breaking the local law of the moment, the demonstrators express the intensity of their needs and beliefs. By asserting that their actions are protected by the Constitution, they clothe their immediate lawbreaking in a higher legality and morality. And if the courts agree with their view of the law, they will escape punishment while showing their willingness to go to jail for their beliefs.

SUMMARY An interest group is a collection of people making claims on the government on the basis of one or more shared attitudes. Almost any trait by which humans can be classified may be the basis

---

[37] Michael J. Robinson, "Television and American Politics: 1956–1976," *The Public Interest,* summer 1977, p. 13.

for an interest group. Interest groups usually are represented by organizations (and often the group itself is an organization such as a corporation), but often only a few people belong to an organization that looks after the interests of millions of other group members. Everyone is not equally represented by interest groups, although most people's interests are looked after by a number of organizations.

The principal types of groups are based on economic, solidary, and issue incentives. Politics is one of many activities, and often only an incidental one, for economic organizations like corporations, trade associations, unions, and professional groups. Solidary groups draw on feelings of common identity based on a shared characteristic, such as race, age, or sex.

The most influential issue-incentive groups are such "public interest" organizations as Common Cause. Unlike the other two types, these organizations are not based on the self-interest of their members, although they usually form alliances with some economic and solidary groups on particular issues. Thus interest group politics is seldom a case of "special interests" versus the "public interest," because any controversy is likely to bring together allies with mixed motives.

Even groups with formally democratic constitutions are governed by small numbers of active members. Most members seem content to contribute to the group's goals by belonging.

Among the ways groups try to get what they want from government are campaign participation, lobbying, litigation, and confrontation. Lobbying is a traditional tactic; litigation (suing the government to get something) is a newer one. The opportunities for litigation have been greatly expanded by changes in the definition of *standing*—the legal rules about who can sue in particular cases, and increased recognition of *class actions*—suits brought by one person in behalf of himself and all those similarly situated. In American politics, confrontation strategies are usually controlled, legal, and ritualized: the demonstration, the strike, the boycott, and the test case are all undertaken to achieve limited objectives without greatly upsetting the normal functioning of government and society.

political parties

...tional parties that they employ... ...olitical campaigns drew the party membership... ...political campaigns drew the party and elections, and guide their... ...party, which... ...individuals to give parties... ...the party influence... ...the parties influence... ...of the party and the community...

CHAPTER 11

Here we will look at the parties as organizations, and we will see that "the Democratic party" and "the Republican party" are labels covering a wide variety of organizations and activities. We will consider how the parties select the presidential candidates from whom the voters make the final choice on election day. In doing so, we will examine the entire process of selecting the president, from nomination to campaign and election. Finally, we will analyze the dynamics of party competition — what makes the parties similar and what drives them apart.

Almost forty years ago, an influential political scientist wrote:

> . . . the political parties created democracy and . . . modern democracy is unthinkable save in terms of the parties. . . . The parties are not therefore merely appendages of modern government; they are in the center of it and play a determinative and creative role in it.[1]

Few contemporary political scientists disagree with this view — but no one else seems to like the parties as much as scholars do. From the Founding Fathers to the present, parties as institutions have been distasteful to most Americans. When asked, "Which part of the government has done the worst job in the past couple of years?" more Americans name the political parties than Congress, the Supreme Court, and the president combined. The parties are something of a stepchild, unloved but unavoidable.

Why are the parties so unpopular? In some parts of the country, one or both parties is represented by machines that take graft, collaborate with gangsters, and corrupt law enforcement. But parties are not more popular where local government is clean; in fact, sometimes they are less popular. The basic explanation is that most Americans believe the parties stir up political conflict. In the most detailed study of the parties' public image, almost two-thirds of those interviewed agreed that "The political parties more often than not create conflicts where none really exists"; and 53 percent thought that "Our system of government would work a lot more efficiently if we could get rid of conflicts between the parties altogether."[2]

In contrast to the broad public, which seems to want politics to be more placid, ideologues of both Left and Right believe that the parties betray the public interest by failing to generate *enough* conflict. These critics assert that the major parties confuse the voters by failing to present them with two clearly opposed alternative programs. To some extent, these criticisms refer to matters of degree and political preference. How much conflict is "enough"? How big must a difference be to become significant? This debate is not wholly a matter of taste, however; in the concluding section of this chapter we will explore the causes and dimensions of differences between the two parties. But first, let us examine some of the contributions the parties make to the operation of the political system.

---

[1] E. E. Schattschneider, *Party Government* (New York: Farrar & Rinehart, 1942), p. 1.

[2] Jack Dennis, "Support for the Party System by the Mass Public," *American Political Science Review*, 60 (September 1966), p. 605.

WHAT THE PARTIES DO:
THE TWO-PARTY SYSTEM

The Parties' Functions   The party system organizes political conflict by providing channels for competition for public office. This does not mean that all political conflict is partisan; all *issues* are not primarily conflicts between Republicans and Democrats. It does mean that competition for national elective offices occurs in the framework of the two parties. Indeed, a political party could be defined simply as an organized attempt to win electoral office. How do parties go about achieving this aim? The answer lies in the five principal functions they perform.

1. *Parties organize individual perceptions of the political world.* One aspect of this perceptual organization is party identification, which we discussed in Chapter 8. In addition, the parties provide a way to link events and candidates so the voters can fix responsibility. Party labels help the public identify officials and would-be officials. They make it possible for voters to blame one ticket for failure and/or to reward the other ticket for success. Although parties often cannot deliver what they promised, they are held responsible for what they appear to have done. No Republican member of Congress had any part in the Watergate scandal, President Ford's pardon of Nixon, or the combination of inflation and recession that plagued the country in 1974. But thirty-six of them were defeated in the 1974 election primarily because of what the public saw as Republican failures. Hubert Humphrey had no part in Lyndon Johnson's disastrous Vietnam policy, but the fact that both men were Democrats cost Humphrey the 1968 election. If a presidential candidate is very popular, he may carry into office other candidates on his party's ticket. In this case, we talk of the strength of his "coattails." Again, this is an example of the party as a perceptual link. People tend to see all candidates from the same party as a group. We will note the same phenomenon again in discussing relations between president and Congress. It can be summed up simply: What is good for one Republican or Democratic candidate is good for all of them, and vice versa. The party affiliation shared by all candidates on the same ticket is the only clue much of the electorate has about how to allocate blame and credit.

2. *The parties organize electoral competition.* They simplify the problem of choice for the voters by giving them two alternatives instead of an infinite variety of possible candidates.

3. Because of these two functions, *the parties are a major way of coordinating decisions both within and between the executive and legislative branches,* as we will see in Chapters 12 to 14.

4. *The parties select general election candidates through the nomination process.* We will examine presidential nominations later in this chapter and congressional nominations in Chapter 12.

5. *The parties restrain social conflict and unite people with different interests and characteristics.* Each party contains members from all races, social classes, regions, religions, occupations, and so on. Neither party can assemble a majority without appealing to a variety of groups. Both parties try to win votes from Catho-

lics, Protestants, Jews, farmers, city dwellers, rich, and poor. Although they have varying levels of success in these appeals, usually a party does not write off any major social group. When a group cannot vote, as was true of southern blacks until recently, politicians may feel free to attack it. But when blacks got the vote in the South, race-baiting by southern politicians faded away. Political observers differ on the desirability of the parties' tendency to muffle conflict. Some people think more conflict is needed, either to make better public policy or simply to abolish the ambiguity that characterizes the party struggle. They feel that firm lines should be drawn between the parties. Other commentators celebrate the way the American parties restrain direct confrontation; they feel that the horrors of civil war illustrate the penalty of unlimited political conflict.

Why Two Parties? The five party functions we have just described are not basic to all parties. Many countries have political parties which do not do some of these things. American parties work the way they do not just because they are parties, but because there are only two of them. If, for example, there were five significant parties, there would be much less incentive for any party to appeal to a broad constituency. As a result, the level of political conflict would rise. It is not difficult to imagine a multiparty system in a country as diverse as the United States. There might be a party of labor, of southern whites, of blacks, of western agriculture, and so on. The contrast between the complexity of American interest groups and the presence throughout our history of only two parties is striking. The parties have an extraordinary heritage. The Democrats descend from the party

THIRD PARTIES

There are two sorts of parties other than the Democrats and Republicans. One, by far the more common but less important, consists of sectarian groups founded to express a particular ideological, ethnic, or issue orientation. There are a surprising number of these in any election year, although it is rare for one of them to get enough votes to affect the result in any state. Some of these parties have a good deal of continuity; others are one-time affairs. These sectarian parties use the electoral process as a publicity device for airing their respective points of view. Table 11.1 lists the various parties on the ballot in the 1976 election, showing the variety of sectarian third parties and the fraction of the popular vote they won.

The other type of third party is a "breakaway movement" from one of the major parties. Such parties are a vehicle for the personal career of a leader whose ambitions have been frustrated in the major party. The possibility of a third-party candidacy is an important weapon in factional conflict within the Democratic and Republican parties. A popular figure like Ronald Reagan or George Wallace often can exert influence within his own party by threatening to run for president outside the party. Many McGovern delegates at the 1972 Democratic convention hinted that their man would take this route if he lost the nomination.

Table 11.2 shows the presidential votes won by all significant third parties in the twentieth century. Except for the Socialists in 1912, these were all breakaway movements.

Table 11.1

The Popular Vote in the 1976 Presidential Election

PARTY	CANDIDATE	NUMBER OF VOTES	PERCENTAGE OF VOTES
Democratic	Jimmy Carter	40,828,587	50.1%
Republican	Gerald R. Ford	39,147,613	48.0
None	Eugene J. McCarthy	751,728	0.9
Libertarian	Roger MacBride	172,750	0.2
American Independent	Lester G. Maddox	170,780	0.2
American	Thomas Anderson	160,600	0.2
Socialist Workers	Peter Camejo	91,226	0.1
Communist	Gus Hall	59,114	0.1
People's	Margaret Wright	49,024	0.1
U.S. Labor	Lyndon H. LaRouche	40,045	*
Prohibition	Benjamin C. Bubar	15,898	*
Socialist Labor	Jules Levin	9,590	*
Socialist	Frank P. Zeidler	6,022	*

*Less than $\frac{1}{10}$ of 1 percent of the total popular vote.

Source: Congressional Quarterly Weekly Report, December 18, 1976, p. 3332.

Thomas Jefferson founded for the election of 1800. The Republican party has its roots in the time of Abraham Lincoln.

Why they have survived is a matter of some dispute, but several reasons seem to be important. The first political battle after the Revolutionary War was fought over a simple and clear issue—whether or not to adopt the Constitution. Subsequent struggles between the Federalists and the Jeffersonian Democrats followed the same line. Debtors—usually farmers—were pitted against creditors—usually merchants, bankers, professional men, and shippers. Thus there were two main political groupings. There were no distractions from ethnic conflicts, an established church, or an aristocracy—all factors that shaped the political history of most democratic nations with more than two major parties. First experiences are very influential on later behavior. In the American case, the initial dualism of political conflict seems to have shaped later political struggles.

Table 11.2

Significant Third Parties in Presidential Elections in the Twentieth Century

PARTY	YEAR	PERCENTAGE OF TOTAL POPULAR VOTES	NUMBER OF ELECTORAL VOTES
Progressive	1912	27.4%	88
Socialist	1912	6.0	0
Progressive	1924	17.1	13
States' Rights	1948	2.4	39
Progressive	1948	2.4	0
American Independent	1968	13.5	46

The new nation's governmental institutions encouraged two-party politics. One key institutional feature was the single-member legislative district. In each district, only one individual was elected to the legislature. The candidate who got the most votes in the district won the legislative seat. This system discourages lasting third-party movements, because it gives nothing at all to anybody but the winner. Only a party that has a chance of getting the most votes has any reason for existence. To make their voices effective, potential third-party voters are apt to switch to one of the major parties.

Countries with more than two major parties usually use a system based on proportional representation. This is a method of allocating legislative seats to each party in accordance with its share of the total number of votes. Under proportional representation, a party that received only 10 percent of the vote would still get 10 percent of the seats. Under a single-member district system, a party that won 10 percent of the votes in each district would get no seats in the legislature. Proportional representation provides an incentive for splinter groups to persevere, whereas our system based on plurality voting and single-member districts does not.

The second major institutional incentive to a two-party system is the fact that the president in our system is a unitary executive elected in a winner-take-all contest. The presidency has the same effect on the number of parties as the single-member district. Since only one party can win the presidency in any given election, there is little point in voting for the presidential candidate of a party that has no chance of winning.

Thus, three factors set the United States on the road to two-party politics: the initial dualism of conflict dating from the nation's earliest days, the adoption of single-member districts, and the unitary executive. To this list a further factor should be added. Once a political system takes on a particular form, politicians have a vested interest in maintaining the existing ways of doing business. They pass laws and regulations designed to perpetuate those forms — the ease of third parties getting on the ballot, laws making it simpler for voters to back the entire slate of a party, and so forth. Similarly, once the two-party system is established, voters tend automatically to see political conflict as a matter of Republicans versus Democrats. The psychological habits of the people also serve to reinforce the existing pattern. We have already noted the extraordinary persistence and strength of party identification in the United States. This makes it difficult for contenders to challenge candidates running as Republicans or Democrats.

A more promising approach for dissenters is trying to win the Republican or Democratic nomination. The parties are vulnerable to takeovers by any candidate who can exploit an issue to appeal to primary voters. Until the early days of the twentieth century, both parties used conventions to nominate their candidates for state and congressional offices. When primary elections replaced this method, there was a sharp decline in the success of third-party candidates.[3] The reason was simple: primaries gave dissidents a much better opportunity to appeal for popular sup-

---

[3] Benjamin Ginsberg and Peter F. Galderisi, "Irresponsible Parties, Responsible Party Systems," paper presented at the 1977 annual meeting of the American Political Science Association.

port. Winning a major party's primary was a route to real power. As one observer puts it:

> . . . the two parties are not rigid or doctrinaire or terribly ideological. They are pretty much empty vessels, and because of the unique nature of our primary system, these . . . empty vessels can accept any color liquid you choose to put in them. . . .[4]

Finally, the two parties keep their monopoly by *ideological opportunism.* Both parties have been threatened from time to time by the prospect of defection by a substantial number of supporters. Usually, these efforts have been reactions against middle-of-the-road policies. The prospective defectors want something, such as old age pensions or an end to school busing, that their party has not strongly supported. The party threatened with such desertions usually tries to bring the bolters back into the fold by offering to incorporate some of what they want into the party's goals. The same thing occurs when a third party seems likely to attract a significant vote. Candidates from one or the other major party—and sometimes both—will steal its thunder.

PARTY MEMBERSHIP

We often hear it said that someone is "a member of the Republican (or Democratic) party." Yet generations of scholars, lawyers, judges, and politicians have been unable to agree on a satisfactory definition of what it means to be a "member" of a party in the United States. The question is far from academic, because presumably only "members" should participate in each party's principal organized activity— nominating candidates for office. Moreover, all the talk about making party conventions "representative" assumes it is possible to define just what it is they should be representative of.

Some possible meanings of membership can be dismissed fairly easily. Psychological membership—party identification—is one common definition of party membership. About 85 percent of the adult population of the country identifies to some extent with one party or the other. Although it is useful to social scientists, the concept of party identification has no legal meaning.

A second definition of membership depends on stricter standards, such as belonging to a formal organization that has a formal process for joining, dues, a roster of members, and so on. In Europe, for instance, many people are members of the Socialist or Christian Democratic party in the sense that they have formally applied for membership, have been accepted, pay dues, and carry a membership card. In the United States, less than 4 percent of the population belong to a party organization in this way. At its 1974 midterm conference, the Democratic party voted overwhelmingly against a proposal that might have been a start to formalizing membership in the party, with cards, written application, and the like.

A third possible definition of membership involves legal registration as a Democrat or Republican. State laws vary enormously in this field, however. In

[4] Ben J. Wattenberg, quoted in *National Journal,* May 31, 1975, p. 811.

some states there is no registration by party. Elsewhere, voters register in a party only if they wish to. And in some states, a party member is anyone who declares that he or she is a member when voting in that party's primary. This lack of uniformity makes registration useless as a criterion for party membership.

The main purpose of registration by party is to prevent adherents of one party from voting in the other party's primary. A party primary in which only party members are allowed to vote is called a **closed primary**. In contrast, an **open primary** is not restricted to adherents of any party.[5] The Supreme Court has weakened the ability of the states to limit access to primaries. In 1973 it struck down an Illinois law that prohibited a voter from participating in one party's primary within twenty-three months of voting in another party's primary. On the other hand, the Court did sustain a New York law that required a delay of eight to eleven months before switching.[6] Austin Ranney sums up the present political reality this way:

> You are a Democrat if you say you are; no one can effectively say you are not; and you can become a Republican any time the spirit moves you simply by saying that you have become one. You accept no obligations by such a declaration; you receive only a privilege—the privilege of taking an equal part in the making of the party's most important decision, the nomination of its candidates for public office.[7]

In short, one "joins" a party by engaging in its activities, with or without benefit of formal admission procedures. A party consists of all those people who participate in any of the following activities: running for office under its label, trying for its nomination, contributing money, working for a candidate, attending a caucus or other meeting, or voting in its primary.

Because American parties are such open institutions, they are vulnerable to invasions by activists who have never taken much interest in party affairs. People who have worked for a party often resent those who suddenly arrive in great numbers, trying to win a nomination for their favorite. This was a complaint of regular Republicans against both the liberal backers of Eisenhower in 1952 and the conservative supporters of Goldwater in 1964 and Reagan in 1976. Veteran Democrats successfully resisted the McCarthy newcomers in 1968 but were overwhelmed by McGovern's skillfully organized "outsider" campaign in 1972. In 1976, both the regulars and the McGovern-style liberals were beaten by Jimmy Carter, another kind of outsider.

Party Activists: Regulars, Purists, Hybrids Political observers commonly classify one sort of party activist as regulars They are sometimes called "professionals," although this is misleading, since they do not usually make their living at politics. On the other hand, there are the "purists," whose commitment is basically to a particular cause. There are important differences in how these two

---

[5] Beginning in 1980, delegates to the Democratic National Convention must be chosen in closed primaries.

[6] *Kusper* v. *Pontikes* 94 SC 303 (1973); and *Rosario* v. *Rockefeller,* 93 SC 1245 (1973).

[7] Austin Ranney, *Curing the Mischiefs of Faction* (Berkeley: University of California Press, 1975), p. 166.

types of activist regard the party in which they are working. To the regulars, the party itself is the most important consideration; its success has first claim on their loyalties and efforts. Purists, in contrast, see the party only as a means to the policy they favor. They do not look at things in the same long perspective as the professionals. They tend to be in a hurry, to think that this year's favored candidate is the country's last hope. These two opposed tendencies are nicely summarized in the following passages. The first is by Arthur Miller, the noted playwright and a purist delegate at the 1968 Democratic convention:

> The professionals . . . see politics as a sort of game in which you win sometimes and sometimes you lose. Issues are not something you feel, like morality, like good and evil, but something you succeed or fail to make use of. To these men an issue is a segment of public opinion which you either capitalize on or attempt to assuage according to the present interests of the party. To the amateurs . . . an issue is first of all moral, and embodies a vision of the country, even of man, and is not a counter in a game.[8]

The professional outlook is described by Ranney, a political scientist sympathetic to this viewpoint:

> The professionals are people who have a substantial commitment to the party itself. They have served it before the nomination contest and expect to serve it after the election. . . . The professionals seek a candidate whose style they think will appeal to the voters they need to win, not necessarily to party leaders. They judge a candidate by how well or badly he runs in the election and by how much he has helped or hurt the rest of the ticket. And they see negotiation, compromise, and accommodation not as hypocrisy or immorality but as the very essence of what keeps parties — and nations — from disintegrating.[9]

Few people are unreserved purists or professionals. Purists compromise to get what they want, and professionals are not amoral calculators. But purists whose motivations are centered in a cause or a hero are not likely to be concerned about the party's other candidates and long-term prospects. Professionals are likely to see issues as a means to the end of victory rather than as go-for-broke goals. Both parties always have both points of view represented in them. Candidates themselves generally try to exploit both approaches in order to attract enough support to win a nomination.

"Hybrids" combine traits of both purists and regulars. Like the purists, they are outsiders. But they do not base their political action on "a vision of the country, even of man." Their attitude toward issues resembles the regulars' feeling that issues are a means to an end. Hybrids are committed to a candidate. For some, he or she is their passport to power and fame. Most, however, are impressed by the candidate's personal qualities and think that "a good person" is what this country needs more than a lot of talk about issues.

[8] Arthur Miller, "The Battle of Chicago: From the Delegates' Side," *The New York Times Magazine*, September 15, 1968, p. 29.

[9] Ranney, *Curing the Mischiefs of Faction*, pp. 140–41.

This is, of course, a description of Jimmy Carter's campaign for the 1976 Democratic nomination. He was not an ideologue like Wallace or McGovern, nor an insider like Senator Henry Jackson. He attacked "Washington" for being insensitive, secretive, corrupt, and unworthy of the great American people. This line let him avoid taking positions on issues—unlike McGovern, who was undone by his issue stands. Like McGovern, Carter was supported by few regulars and prominent officials until he had the nomination sewed up. Again like McGovern (and Goldwater and Reagan), he showed how vulnerable the parties are to candidates who skillfully exploit their real or imagined lack of connection with "the establishment."

HOW THE PARTIES ARE ORGANIZED

One difficulty in understanding parties is the language we use to describe them. In talking about "the national Republican (or Democratic) organization," we are using a term that suggests much more coherence and discipline than exists. The same is true in most states and localities, where "the party organization" is a mixture of activities and officials, candidates' personal campaign apparatuses, and past and future participants. If the right candidate comes along, with the right combination of popularity, organizational ability, and probability of success, some of these elements can be mobilized in a network that actually works together for a common purpose. More often, though, the "party organization" is little more than a figure of speech. In a few states and localities, on the other hand, there really is a stable and ongoing party organization. We will look briefly at the most common patterns of organization at each level.

In doing so, two points should be remembered. The first is *decentralization*. As Schattschneider observed, "Decentralization is . . . the most important single characteristic of the American major party."[10] No common chain of command holds together the networks that make up our major parties. No one can give orders to the many localized centers of power in either party. In the party that occupies the White House, the president is nominally the party leader. But this does not prevent other party members, either in Congress or in the localities, from going their own way. The president simply does not have enough patronage and organizational strength to impose discipline on his party. The key to party discipline is centralized control over nominations. No such control exists in the United States. The president has very little influence over his party's nomination of congressional candidates, and none at all over state and local nominations. Thus, he cannot impose his will on lesser officials in his party if they defy or ignore him. The party that does not control the presidency has even less hierarchy. It is headless—or it has dozens of would-be leaders, which amounts to the same thing.

The second important point about party organization seems paradoxical. Side by side with the fact that the parties have almost no centralized organization we must set the fact that, *in terms of popular perceptions, the parties appear to be*

---

[10] Schattschneider, *Party Government*, p. 129. As we will see, the recent introduction of national guidelines for selecting delegates to the presidential nominating conventions has imposed a measure of centralized influence on one aspect of the parties' functions.

quite centralized indeed. Party identification is not a matter of local loyalties. It is a national phenomenon. No matter where they live, people see the party with which they identify as a national entity, not a state or local group. Something that is good for one of the parties in one part of the country is almost always good for it everywhere. Changes in voting patterns are related to shifting party images, which reflect the popularity of the presidential candidates and the public's assessment of the current administration's performance. These popular verdicts are reflected in the tendency for party fortunes in congressional elections to move generally in the same direction. The common observation that "1974 was a good year for the Democrats" or "1966 was a Republican year" captures this important truth about the parties. Their fortunes move in national tides. Thus, the parties are *national* without being *hierarchical.*

National Structures In theory, each party's presidential nominating convention is that party's highest governing body. The delegates at the conventions pass resolutions on the mechanics of future conventions and delegate selection. They also create committees, commissions, and task forces to meet during the inter-election period. These groups often are empowered to adopt and enforce rules that can have important consequences. But conventions cannot serve as stable sources of leadership. Massive, confused assemblages of several thousand strangers who meet for five days every four years to choose the party's presidential candidate can hardly be expected to give much serious attention to anything else.

The ongoing national party leadership rests formally in each party's national committees. These groups consist of varying numbers of people from each of the fifty states, plus the District of Columbia, Puerto Rico, the Virgin Islands, and, in the case of the Democrats, the Canal Zone. Normally, the national committee meets as a group two or three times a year. The best academic study of the national committees has a title that reveals its authors' conclusions about their topic: *Politics without Power.*[11]

One of the few important tasks of the national committees is the selection of the national party chairman. In the case of the party in the White House, this involves rubber-stamping the president's choice. In the opposition party, the choice falls to the presidential nominee, and then is automatically ratified by the committee. After the presidential election, however, the chairman of the party that lost usually resigns and the national committee than picks a new chairman. The defeated presidential candidate may have some influence, but he obviously is in no position to dictate a choice to the committee.

The chairmanship varies in significance. The head of the party in power has only as much influence as the president wishes to give him, because presidents traditionally have considered the national committee their private property. At best, the chairman is one of the president's political operatives. He may be a mouthpiece through which the president speaks on national party matters, and sometimes he is not even that. Some presidents, such as Nixon and Johnson, ran national party af-

[11] Cornelius P. Cotter and Bernard C. Hennessy, *Politics without Power* (New York: Atherton, 1964).

Become a Sustaining Member

You can play a special role in the Democratic Party by becoming a Sustaining Member of The President's Club. Sustaining Members are a special group who agree to contribute monthly to the Party. By pledging $10, $15 or even $20 a month, they provide the Party with the financial flexibility it needs. In return they receive special political reports prepared for mailing with their monthly statement.

☐ I would like to enroll as a Sustaining Member. Please send me a statement each month in the amount of:

☐ $10   ☐ $15   ☐ $20   ☐ $25.

My check for the first month is enclosed.

_____
Signature

This appeal is sponsored by the Democratic National Committee. A copy of our report is filed with the Federal Election Commission and is available for purchase from the Federal Election Commission, Washington, D.C.

---

fairs directly from the White House, further reducing the chairman's role. Carter began by keeping his distance from the Democratic National Committee, and then tightened his control and attention as the 1980 election approached. From the outset of his presidency he maintained his personal grassroots network around the country, and formed a separate organization for the 1980 election, thus further pushing the DNC into the shade.

In the party out of power the chairman usually is more important, simply because that party has no president to speak for it and control it. It is the party chairman who makes statements, appears on Sunday television public affairs programs, and generally "represents" his party. Yet he must do so without stealing the thunder from any of its potential presidential candidates. A national chairman also can exercise his political skills in raising funds, encouraging strong candidates to run for office, and healing hurt feelings. This is particularly important after an electoral disaster such as the Republicans suffered in 1964 or the Democrats in 1972. In both cases, able chairmen helped rebuild the party.

Under the leadership of its national chairman, each party maintains a national committee headquarters with substantial staffs and budgets. In a recent nonelection year, for example, the Republican National Committee had about 220 employees. These included researchers, writers, and specialists in polling, public relations, campaign organization, and fund-raising. They provide a variety of technical services to their party's primary and general election candidates, including position papers on issues and advice on campaign organization. Thirty people work on electing Republicans to state legislatures in time for the congressional redistricting that will follow the 1980 census. During Jimmy Carter's first years in office, the Democratic National Committee had about a third as big a staff and budget. This reflects both the "natural" consequence of controlling the White House and the Democrats' lower fund-raising capacity.

The two parties have campaign committees in each house of Congress. These organizations contribute to candidates and also spend money directly on such campaign services as research and registration drives. Republicans customarily are far more active and successful in this area. In either house, their campaign committees have much bigger staffs and budgets than their Democratic counterparts. The Republicans use direct mail to raise their money in small amounts from many contributors; the Democrats rely on $500-a-plate dinners. (An obscure amendment to a minor bill passed in the closing days of the 1978 congressional session gives state and national party committees the 3.1¢ bulk mail postage rate that nonprofit organizations enjoy.)

State and Local Parties   Variety is the hallmark of any comparative study of American parties below the national level. Generally speaking, parties are organized around elections and candidates — and around patronage, where it exists in quantity. Patronage consists of government jobs, contracts, and other benefits given by the party to those who work for it. If substantial patronage is available, there are likely to be party organizations that have some continuity between elections and are more than the personal creations of individual officeholders.

In some places, one can still find thriving specimens of political machines. A political machine is a close-knit hierarchy of politicians, beginning with the "captain" of the individual precinct (a precinct is the area covered by a single polling place) and ascending up to the city or county boss. The party structure includes leadership positions at every level — ward, assembly district, state senatorial district, city, and county. These official posts often carry a good deal of power over patronage and thus are eagerly sought after. Machines of this sort are fueled by patronage and therefore are focused on state and local politics. Where patronage is common, it usually provides the motivation for a corps of activists who pack nominating caucuses and conventions, get out the votes in the more obscure primaries, and maintain the organization in power. Contrary to popular belief, machine politics is not necessarily monolithic, with all power coming from one center. If patronage comes from more than one source — say, both city and county government — the result may be two competing machines. In some cities, such as New York, the machine leaders are more likely to be at each other's throats than each other's sides.

Although machine politicians are most interested in the local elections that provide them with the spoils of office, their command of those spoils often makes them the most influential figures in national party affairs in their areas. This is especially true in places where the local leaders speak with one voice. Chicago traditionally is a prime example because of the regular machine's control of thousands of government jobs and other benefits. In New York, on the other hand, a vigorous amateur reform movement contests primaries with the divided regular leaders.

A more common situation is found in places where patronage is not the main incentive. In such places there may be no stable political organizations with continuity of membership, substantial influence over nominations, and a chain of command. Official party positions may be unfilled or held by people who do nothing. In these cases, the most meaningful examples of party organization are the structures built by individual candidates for the purpose of winning their own

ADVANCING, RALLIES, AND MASS MEETINGS

INTRODUCTION
PLANNING
MUSIC, DECORATIONS AND SIGNS
PRESS
ADDITIONAL SUGGESTIONS
PLANNING A RALLY
TIPS FOR A SUCCESSFUL RALLY
RALLY CHECK LIST

INTRODUCTION

Advance work in a Congressional campaign, particularly for an incumbent, is a relatively simple routine if some basic rules are strictly followed by those working for the candidate.

Overall, good advance work is common sense. It is the type of work cut out for persons with a great deal of diplomacy and with great administrative abilities. There are many factors, such as the height of the microphone, proper seating at head tables and in motorcades, which might seem unimportant in the overall picture, but which have greatly contributed to winning or losing an election. It is the responsibility of the advance man to make sure that no one is inadvertently snubbed in the rush of the campaign. He must make it an unbroken rule never to speak unkindly of any person, even one who has tried his patience. To do so would reflect adversely on the candidate.

Since Congressional Districts vary in size, advance men are confronted with problems such as determining a tight airplane and helicopter schedule, as well as perhaps deciding which traffic-congested city streets should be avoided in order to move his candidate from place to place on time.

In most cases, particularly with an incumbent, the candidate will know almost everyone attending the rally. However, it is always a good idea to prepare 3x5 cards with the names of special people, and a line or two of briefing for the candidate.

For example, if a Congressman helped a constituent with a case involving a Federal agency, this could be noted on the card. It will give the candidate the opportunity to mention a few specifics, such as names and circumstances, to his constituent. This is always helpful.

An advance man is also responsible for all follow-up work after the candidate's appearance. A good advance man will obtain the names and addresses of persons who were particularly helpful and see that they are passed on to Headquarters. Many Congressmen purchase ashtrays with the Congressional Seal through the Stationery Room and send them to those who have made a particular contribution to the campaign. It is an impressive but relatively inexpensive gift, and the thoughtful gesture is always appreciated.

Names of individuals who were helpful in advancing should be sent back to Headquarters, where letters of appreciation from the candidate should be sent promptly.

PLANNING

1. In advancing a dinner or banquet appearance, it is wise to leave some extra room at the head table and have at least two extra chairs available in case someone has been overlooked or a dignitary unexpectedly arrives.

2. When in doubt as to the size of crowd to anticipate, it is best to select the smallest hall or auditorium available. Far better to have people standing in the aisles—or on the outside of a hall listening to a speech over an outside loudspeaker—than to have a large hall or auditorium half empty. The press invariably refers to the size of the crowd in terms of a "jam packed hall" or a "sparsely attended" rally.

3. The advance man should have extra copies of speeches and press releases available. While several members of the press may travel with a Congressional candidate, there are always local reporters who are covering only one stop. Copies of speeches and press releases should be available to them.

4. Bios and glossies (black and white) should be included with copies of the speech, particularly if the candidate is an incumbent.

5. Whenever possible, arrangements should be made for the candidate to stop in at the local newspaper office to meet with its executives.

Source: Democratic National Committee, *Democratic Campaign Manual* (Washington: Democratic National Committee, n.d.), p. 90.

personal nomination and election. We will examine this process as it concerns members of Congress in Chapter 12 and as it concerns presidential candidates in the next few pages.

First, though, let us sum up what we have said so far about national party politics. The Democratic and Republican parties consist of a diffuse, fluctuating, and loosely affiliated rank-and-file membership, weak national party organizations, and a variety of local organizations. These local organizations range from highly disciplined local machines exhibiting great continuity to sporadic, undisciplined amateur efforts that pop up only at election time. Most typically, the local party will consist of a number of elements. There may be several party leaders and regular organizations built around various sources of patronage. There will be separate campaign organizations built up by individual politicians to work for their own election or reelection. And there will be sporadic activities by reform movements or amateur clubs. These movements come into existence around election time because a particular candidate or issue is so important to some people at that moment that they will take time out to become temporarily active in politics.

This diffuse organization of American parties is both a cause and an effect of the scattered flow of campaign contributions. Only a small proportion of all political contributions is given to the national committees and the congressional campaign committees of the two parties. Candidates for most offices, both national and local, raise most of their own money. The national parties cannot discipline their candidates by giving or withholding money because the national parties have little money to give. Indeed, fund-raising by individual candidates may undercut national party efforts. Let us look next at how these collections of people and organizations manage to nominate presidential candidates every four years.

NOMINATING A PRESIDENTIAL CANDIDATE

Choosing a presidential candidate is the most important single action the parties perform. Nomination is a far greater part of the process of political choice than is the general election. In the election, the voters' choice is limited to two serious candidates. The nominating process reduces the alternatives to two by eliminating all other contenders, of whom there may be a dozen or more. In some years, the choice of nominees predetermines the outcome of the election, as with Goldwater in 1964 or McGovern in 1972; neither had much of a chance in the general election.

The Legal Framework   The parties nominate their presidential candidates in national conventions held in the summer of the election year. Whether the conventions are actual decision-making bodies or just occasions for crowning a winner is an issue we will take up later. Irrespective of the answer, the most important parts of the nominating cycle occur before the convention, in the long process of selecting convention delegates.

The number of delegates varies from one party to the other and has been trending upward. In 1980 the Republicans had around 2000 delegates and the Democrats had 3331. Both parties apportion delegates to states on a basis both of population and past support for the party. How these factors are weighted has consequences that do not fall evenly on all factions.

The method for choosing delegates traditionally was left up to the individual states. As long as the state parties did not violate their own rules or state law, their delegates were seated. Since the 1960s, the Democratic party has imposed national guidelines for delegate selection. This era began with a decision by the 1964 Democratic convention that in the future no delegates would be seated if they had been chosen by procedures that excluded any party members. This was aimed at the Mississippi Democratic party, which kept blacks out of delegate selection. After the 1968 election, the Democrats appointed a commission whose recommendations for overhauling selection procedures were largely accepted by the national committee. The party threatened to refuse to seat delegations that were not chosen in accordance with the new guidelines.[12] After the 1972 and 1976 elections, the Democrats made further adjustments in their rules. The Republicans adopted some, but not all, of the Democrats' "reforms," and sometimes approached the same goals by different methods, and allow their state parties much more leeway instead of imposing nationwide rules.

While these developments brought some measure of uniformity to presidential nominations, they did not eliminate most of the state-by-state differences. This diversity makes the nominating process exceptionally intricate. The most basic distinction is whether delegates are chosen in primaries or by the caucus-convention method. Because this is determined by each state's election laws, both parties in a state generally choose their delegates by the same method.

Presidential Primaries.   The United States is unique in entrusting the choice of candidates to voters in **primaries,** that is, elections to decide who will be each party's nominee in the general election. Elsewhere in the democratic world, party leaders pick candidates in order to get the most electoral appeal and the most effective and loyal legislators. In the United States, almost all congressional candidates are now nominated in primaries. Until recently, fewer than half the delegates to presidential nominating conventions were chosen this way. But by 1980, at least 33 states held presidential primaries and around three-quarters of the convention delegates were picked in or bound by primary elections.[13]

Primaries seem to be a more "democratic" way to pick candidates, since they involve far more people than the handful who participate in conventions and caucuses. In 1976, the rate of participation in presidential primaries was about ten times higher than that for caucuses. Yet primary voters are far from a simple cross section of the population. For one thing, turnout is only half as high as in the following general election.[14] Considerably older, richer, and better educated, primary voters are more politically aware and ideologically conscious than people who vote only in general elections. They are usually more intense about the issues and often take more extreme stands. Democrats who vote in their party's primary are more

---

[12] The Supreme Court has decided that in most areas national party rules are superior to state law. See *Cousins* v. *Wigoda*, 419 U.S. 477 (1975).

[13] *Congressional Quarterly Weekly Report*, August 4, 1979, p. 1609.

[14] Ranney, *Participation in American Presidential Nominations*, pp. 15–24.

liberal than the larger number of Democrats who vote in general elections. Voters in Republican primaries are more conservative than Republican voters as a whole.[15]

When several candidates run against each other in a presidential primary, various things can happen after the votes are counted:

1. All the state's delegates can be given to the candidate who received the most votes.

2. The delegates can be divided among the candidates in proportion to their statewide vote.

3. The delegates for each congressional district can be given to the winner in that district.

4. The delegates for each congressional district can be divided according to the candidates' votes in the district.

5. Each delegate can be elected in his own district.

At first glance, all five plans seem reasonable and "democratic." Each plan favors some candidates at the expense of others. As a general rule, incumbent presidents and other "dominant" candidates are favored by winner-take-all plans. Proportional arrangements benefit contenders with limited backing who are trying to establish themselves. Sometimes the same plan is not equally beneficial to a candidate in every state, since his pattern of support may vary from state to state. The ideal situation is winner-take-all where one is strong and proportional representation where one is weak.

New York Governor Thomas E. Dewey on a 1948 tour of Oregon to capture the votes of the state's delegates to the Republican convention.

Wide World

The Democratic party has outlawed winner-take-all arrangements at both the state and district levels. This had some effect on the Republicans, but there were still, in 1976, twelve states with winner-take-all Republican primaries. The Democrats now require that 75 percent of a state's delegates be chosen at the congressional district level. To win any delegates at all, a candidate must receive a minimum of 15 to 20 percent of the vote. The single-delegate district plan was not in force in any state in 1978, and was banned by the Democrats for their 1980 convention.

The Caucus-Convention Method. This begins with precinct **caucuses,** that is, meetings open to all party members who live in the precinct. At these caucuses delegates are chosen to a convention at the next level, usually the county. The county convention may pick delegates to the state convention, or there may be another level of meetings before the final state-

---

[15] James I. Lengle, "Representation and Presidential Primaries," unpublished doctoral dissertation, University of California, Berkeley, 1978; and Austin Ranney, "Turnout and Representation in Presidential Primary Elections," *American Political Science Review,* 66 (March 1972), pp. 21–37.

wide gathering, where delegates to the national convention are chosen.

The precinct caucus is the crucial one, for it is here that the basic political alignment of the delegates is set. Attending such meetings is relatively demanding, so they tend to be limited to people who are either strongly committed to a candidate or mobilized by a local political machine. As a result, this method favors the candidates with the best organization. Because few people other than party activists know when and where the precinct caucus is held, small numbers of party workers can — and do — pack the caucuses. Local caucuses are thus one reason for the continued power of "old-fashioned" political machines.

The caucus-convention equivalent of the winner-take-all primary is the **unit rule.** This binds all delegates chosen at a caucus to support the winning candidate, and so on up the line. The unit rule is a thing of the past in the Democratic party. Its new guidelines require that at every level the distribution of delegates be proportional to the candidate preferences at the gathering that chose them. As with the primary, there is a 15 to 20 percent minimum level of support, to guard against excessive splintering of the party.

Routes to the Nomination   The formal process of delegate selection begins in January of the presidential election year when the Iowa precinct caucuses meet. Several more caucus-convention states hold neighborhood caucuses before the New Hampshire primary in late February. The primary season ends fifteen weeks later, in early June. The last state conventions do not pick their delegates for another two or three weeks. The culmination is the national conventions, which are generally held in July or August. The entire process takes seven or eight months. (The candidates, of course, have been planning, organizing, and raising money for months or years before the first caucus.) It also consumes many millions of dollars, an extraordinary amount of human energy, and some political reputations. One political scientist summed up the situation this way:

> The United States must have the most elaborate, complex, and prolonged formal system of nominating candidates for chief executive in the world. The selection of delegates to the national party conventions is spread over approximately six months. The states decide when and how this is to be done. . . . The result is mind-blowing complexity and variety in delegate selection methods and the extent to which delegates are mandated to support specific presidential candidates at the convention. The winning candidates must somehow attract the votes of 50 percent plus one of these delegates, chosen under 50 different sets of laws and political arrangements.[16]

Complexity is reduced, of course, if one candidate has an overwhelming lead in the public opinion polls and consistently wins most of the delegates as the weeks roll by. Sometimes this happens in one party or the other. Political observers used

---

[16] Donald R. Matthews, "Presidential Nominations: Process and Outcomes," in James David Barber, ed., *Choosing the President* (Englewood Cliffs, N.J.: Prentice-Hall, 1974), p. 56.

to believe that renomination of an incumbent could be taken for granted—unless he was presiding over a policy disaster. This was the case with the Korean war for Truman in 1952 and Vietnam for Johnson sixteen years later. In the face of heavy opposition within the party and good showings by other candidates in the New Hampshire primary, both men quit. President Ford's position was a bit different because he had not won a presidential election. He came closest of any modern president to losing his party's nomination, but finally turned back Reagan's challenge. In mid-1979, President Carter was considered vulnerable to a challenge for the nomination from Senator Edward M. Kennedy or perhaps even a dark horse candidate. The reasons included Carter's failure to develop solid relationships with labor and other major constituencies, his rather boring television style, and such apparent policy failures as rising prices for everything in general and oil in particular. The lower the Gallup Poll ratings of Carter's performance, the greater his danger.

Sometimes a politician is so clearly the heir-apparent to his party's nomination that there is no point in resisting fate. This was the case with Nixon in 1960. As Eisenhower's vice-president, he moved almost inevitably to the top of the ticket when Ike had to step down after completing two terms. Again in 1968 Nixon met few reverses in his capture of the Republican nomination.

Much of the time, however, there is no clear popular favorite. Instead, there are a number of candidates, announced and unannounced. The chances are that none of the hopefuls will be known to most primary voters. Early in the campaign, popular ignorance, indecision, and apathy are widespread. At the beginning of 1976, for example, almost 70 percent of all Democrats said that they had not given the campaign much thought and had not decided what candidate they liked for the nomination. Half of those with a preference were for Hubert Humphrey or Edward Kennedy, who were not candidates. Of the active seekers after the nomination, only Wallace was familiar to half the population. Only 20 percent said they knew anything about Carter and less than 5 percent preferred him for the nomination. Six Democrats had substantially more support and four others had about the same amount of backing as Carter.[17] Four years earlier, McGovern was in a similar position.

Candidate's for their party's presidential nomination travel with a pack of journalists and hold news conferences for them and the local press at every stop in their travels.

Wide World

The Role of the Media. Faced with this situation, the candidates have to make themselves known and differentiate themselves from each other. The mass media are an essential part of the process. Journalists are perpetually starved for news, for something to write about and show on television. The race for the White House is one of the big continuing stories of the year. But it is too untidy for easy presentation, particularly in the early stages when there are many candidates. In such com-

[17] Our source for all data here on press coverage and candidate familiarity is Thomas E. Patterson, "Press Coverage and Candidate Success in Presidential Primaries: The 1976 Democratic Race," paper presented at the 1977 annual meeting of the American Political Science Association.

plex situations, journalists look for themes to dramatize and simplify reality. Nothing is more dramatic than conflict, and nothing about conflict seems simpler than labeling winners and losers. No matter how ambiguous and uncertain the reality, the picture presented by the media was clearer and more definite.

The Iowa caucuses were the first opportunity for the press to declare a winner in 1976. The largest number of delegates — 37 percent — were undecided. Twenty-seven percent favored Carter, more than double the proportion for the next candidate. To the press, this made him the winner, the "man to watch," and so on. The Iowa result represented the views of just 45,000 people, but it was the only result available. For the next few days, Carter got four to five times as much media attention as any of his rivals. This was hardly an accident, for Carter had spent considerable time in Iowa in the previous two years, and a substantial part of his organization had been devoted to the state.

The New Hampshire primary is the first blockbuster event of the campaign season. In the three months before the date, a third to a half of news stories about the campaign dealt with the New Hampshire contest. Carter won just 30 percent of the votes cast by 77,000 New Hampshire Democrats, but this was six percentage points ahead of the runner-up. That week, Carter enjoyed three times more media attention than any of his rivals. In the nine weeks between the New Hampshire and Pennsylvania primaries, he had almost as big an advantage. He was the subject of almost half the space given to the campaign in *Time* and *Newsweek,* the evening network TV news, and a sample of daily newspapers. In Pennsylvania, Carter eliminated Senator Henry Jackson, the last of his major opponents. After that, established as the leading candidate, he repelled last-minute challenges from Senator Frank Church and California's Governor Edmund G. Brown, Jr.

Political observers often say that the media are the "scorekeepers," the judges of who "really" won each primary. There is little evidence, however, that the public swallows these verdicts whole and accepts the media's winner as the real winner. Rather, the media are the most important consumers of their own scorekeeping, because their coverage of the campaign reflects their pronouncements about who has won the most recent contest:

> No matter how close the voting, the headlines and most of the coverage went to the winner, and he alone. Other candidates, even those losing by small margins, received only a few lines in the newspaper and a few seconds on the evening newscasts.[18]

When people knew only one candidate, that one was likely to be Carter. He had much more media coverage than anyone else, thanks to early victories that set him apart from a crowded field. Being known has a lot to do with getting votes; hardly anyone voted in a primary for someone about whom they knew nothing. About a fourth of all votes cast in Democratic primaries went to Carter from people who felt he was the only candidate they knew. In other nomination contests since the advent of polling, there has also been a strong relationship between being

---

[18] Patterson, "Press Coverage and Candidate Success," p. 1.

Wide World

Campaigning in Texas, President Ford hugs and kisses his way through the Tyler Junior College drill team.

known and being supported. The more people who say they are familiar with a candidate, the more support he is likely to get. Only rarely is there a candidate, like George Wallace, whose support is strikingly out of balance with the extent of public knowledge about him.[19]

Carter's campaign emphasized his position as an outsider free of any guilt by association with the evils of "Washington." This let him suggest that his Democratic rivals, most of whom were congressional veterans, were part of the problem. Carter depicted himself as an underdog challenger, which was a perfectly correct self-portrait. His emphasis on morality and efficiency also let him avoid taking positions on issues, which always carries the risk of making more enemies than friends. McGovern's nomination campaign illustrates this danger. Like Carter, McGovern was an underdog in a crowded field. And like Carter, he had a better organization and understanding of the rules than anyone else. But his ideological position was vastly different. His basic strategic problem was how to establish himself as the leading liberal candidate when other liberals were better known and had more support. His early primary victories brought him more press attention and higher name recognition. He attracted the support of liberal activists, who rallied to the candidate with the best chance of winning for their cause. He became the champion of one wing of the party, not merely one of several contenders for "peace money" and the backing of ideological activists.[20] Like Goldwater in 1964, McGovern could win only by differentiating himself from the pack and appealing to an existing ideological constituency. Yet this strategy, which was essential to capturing the nomination, contained the seeds of his defeat in the general election. By dramatizing his support for ultraliberal causes, McGovern won the nomination but lost the election.

A National Primary?   One alternative to the present complex and exhausting nomination process is a single nationwide primary in which each party would choose its candidate for the general election. If the first round did not produce a clear majority for any one candidate, a runoff primary would be held a short time later. In addition to its simplicity, this plan also has the virtue of removing the national conventions as a possible distortion of the popular will. Bills for a nation-

[19] The data for 1976 are from Patterson, "Press Coverage and Candidate Success." For earlier years, we used Gallup Poll data analyzed by Steven J. Rosenstone, who kindly made his findings available to us. Although Carter's campaign was skillfully planned to exploit the media's overemphasis of the early results, he also had a good deal of luck. He won at least one primary every week in which there were primaries, and so always had a victory to compensate for any defeats. Second, Carter did best against conservative opposition, and less well when opposed by candidates more liberal than he. But since there were several major liberal contenders, the liberal vote was always divided among them. See Warren E. Miller and Teresa E. Levitin, *Leadership and Change* (Cambridge: Winthrop, 1976), p. 197.

[20] William Cavala, "Changing the Rules Changes the Game," *American Political Science Review,* 68 (March 1974), pp. 34–35.

al primary have been introduced in Congress, and the idea is supported by over two-thirds of the public.[21]

The disadvantages of a national primary are clear and, in our opinion, overwhelming. This plan would favor the candidates with the greatest initial popularity and financial support. It would also exclude outsiders who can use the present system to work their way into public attention. The sequence of primaries strung out over several months favors underdogs and challengers. A candidate near the bottom of the polls has a chance to show his appeal in small states, where he does not need a huge budget. A good showing in these first attempts can help accumulate the backers, money, and attention that are needed in the bigger late primaries. In 1960, the protracted primaries let John Kennedy show that he could win elections in wholly Protestant states, thus convincing party leaders that his Catholicism was not an insuperable obstacle. We have already seen how Carter and McGovern used the present system to go from obscurity to their party's nomination (Figure 11.1 shows the dramatic increases in support that they and some other candidates

[21] Austin Ranney, *The Federalization of Presidential Primaries* (Washington: American Enterprise Institute, 1978).

Figure 11.1
Growth in Support for Presidential Nomination

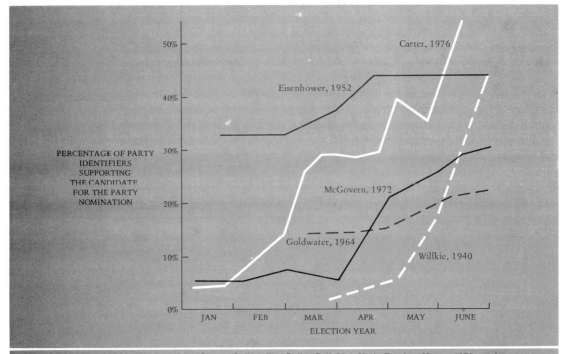

Source: Based on data from George Gallup, *The Gallup Poll* (New York: Random House, 1972); and from *Gallup Opinion Index.*

have achieved). The early primaries are also a way to push unpopular incumbent presidents aside. Truman in 1952 and Johnson in 1968 surely could have won national primaries against scattered opposition, but both men decided not to run again after their humiliating showings in the New Hampshire primary.

The National Convention

The conventions are the "supreme governing body" of their respective parties. They nominate candidates, make rules for the party, and write the platform. All this is done in five days by several thousand people, the vast majority of whom do not know each other, have never been at a convention before, and do not know the rules. The tasks that must be performed by the convention delegates are not as staggering as this might suggest, however. For one thing, the major criterion for all convention decisions is what will hurt or help one's own candidate. Since almost all important decisions are made with an eye on the candidate's chances, it is not difficult for the individual delegate to figure out what to do. He or she does what the candidate's representative tells him or her to. Moreover, in recent years the conventions have not really been where the actual choice of candidates was made. *In every national convention from 1956 through 1976, the presidential nomination was settled on the first ballot.* Even before the convention met, the leading candidate already had enough delegate votes to remove any doubts about the outcome. The convention was merely a ceremony to crown the candidate who had the nomination locked up, not a meeting at which a choice was to be made. In fact, in only three of the twenty conventions from 1940 through 1976 was more than one ballot needed to pick the nominee.

For a long time, then, all the talk about "smoke-filled rooms" and bosses manipulating conventions has been nonsense. This is not because conventions are necessarily purer than the cynics think, but because there was little for the "bosses" to manipulate. These misconceptions about the convention *may* be more plausible in the future, however. This prediction stems from the wave of reforms in the early 1970s. A main goal of these changes was making convention delegates more representative of the grassroots party faithful. The unit rule and winner-take-all primaries sacrificed representativeness for decisiveness. For example, McGovern won 25 percent of the votes cast in Democratic primaries in 1972, but he got 65 percent of the delegates chosen in those states.[22] Proportional representation increases the chance that several candidates will each have a substantial number of committed delegates. This is most likely when each candidate has a clear constituency and less likely when, as in 1976, a contender like Carter appeals successfully to all major elements in the party. Nevertheless, proportional representation is more congenial to a **brokered convention,** in which the nomination is decided in negotiations among a handful of leaders.

To understand how such negotiations work, one must realize that under most state laws, delegates who are pledged to a certain candidate need vote for him only on the first ballot at the convention. This rule is necessary or else a convention that started out deadlocked would remain deadlocked forever. If the first ballot does not produce a candidate with a majority of delegate support, there must be a second

[22] *Congressional Quarterly Weekly Report,* January 31, 1976, p. 226.

and then a third ballot, and so on until one candidate does receive a majority. As the balloting proceeds, therefore, the various candidates, their friends, and the delegates begin to bargain with one another. Eventually, as a result of these negotiations, enough delegates switch their votes from whomever they supported on the first ballot to give another candidate a majority on the second or tenth or hundredth ballot. The greater the probability that conventions will have real decisions to make, the more possibility of backroom wheeling and dealing.

One student of parties describes the delegate reforms as a triumph for people who think that the parties should be "expressive" of all points of view, rather than "effective" agencies for winning elections.[23] Another political scientist thinks that the reformers have created a serious dilemma:

> The contemporary convention problem is that recent demands for fairness and democracy in procedures may clash headlong with the convention's traditional objective of efficiency, legitimacy, reasonableness, and unity as a means to victory. For example, it may be difficult to reconcile fairness to every faction with the rapid choice of a nominee and approval of a platform and the rallying of a broad party consensus. And a party that bares its internal struggles to public scrutiny may find it difficult to win elections.[24]

The Delegates.   Up to this point we have talked about the convention delegates as if they had no will of their own. This ignores the fact that the kind of people chosen as delegates has been a subject of bitter controversy. The most famous measure in the Democratic "reforms" after the 1968 election was quotas requiring certain proportions of women, minorities, and people under 30 in each state delegation. At the 1972 convention, 15 percent of the delegates and alternates were minorities, 40 percent were women, and 22 percent were under 30. Mandatory quotas were discarded in 1974. The 1976 figures were a bit smaller in all three categories, but still far higher than before 1972.[25] The Republican experience is similar. In a sudden move in December 1978, President Carter proposed and the Democratic National Committee adopted a requirement that state delegations to the 1980 Democratic National Convention be equally divided between men and women. The national Republican party suggested the same goal and at least one prominent 1980 Republican presidential candidate said he would insist on it for his delegates.

One problem with these quotas is the moral difficulty stated by Ranney: "The party could provide for a fair fight or it could provide for a guaranteed result, . . . but it could not provide for both."[26] The second problem is that these three quotas had little effect on many other categories in which the delegates were not representative.

> The new rules, like the old, produced a convention whose members had much higher incomes, higher education, higher social status, and less religious

---

[23] Austin Ranney, "Changing the Rules of the Nominating Game," in Barber, *Choosing the President*, pp. 79–82.

[24] Judith H. Parris, *The Convention Problem* (Washington: The Brookings Institution, 1972), pp. 14–15.

[25] Democratic National Committee, *Report of the Commission on Presidential Nomination and Party Structure* (Washington, 1978), p. 19.

[26] Ranney, *Curing the Mischiefs of Faction*, p. 114.

commitment than regular Democratic voters, a convention in which some age and ethnic groups were clearly unrepresented. It also produced a convention whose majority did not reflect and was not responsive to the values, views, and policy preferences of most Democrats or most voters.[27]

The third problem gets us closer to the heart of the matter: the race, sex, and age of the delegates had no relationship to their political positions.

The opinions of women, youth, and blacks supporting McGovern in the convention were essentially like those of the white middle-aged males supporting McGovern. The views of women, youth, and even the black or two supporting Wallace were in basic respects like those of middle-aged white male Wallaceites, and so forth.[28]

In other words, the great debate over delegate quotas is more symbolic than real. Convention delegates are not important in themselves. They are not free

[27] Jeane Kirkpatrick, *The New Presidential Elite* (New York: Russell Sage Foundation and The Twentieth Century Fund, 1976), p. 328.
[28] Kirkpatrick, *The New Presidential Elite,* pp. 330 – 31.

The 1976 Democratic National Convention in New York's Madison Square Garden.

J. P. Laffont/Sygma

agents who can act as they please. As long as their candidate has a chance, they are largely inanimate symbols of his strength. If a convention becomes deadlocked and bargaining determines the result, we doubt that age, sex, or race will have much to do with the ways the delegates then vote. The most likely outcome is that the candidate to whom they are pledged will be able to deliver them as a bloc to whichever candidate he favors in the later ballots. This is only a guess, however, since deadlocked conventions are most uncommon.

Before the "reforms," delegates were thought to be mostly committed to their state party. They judged presidential nominations in terms of their impact on local party interests. In contrast, delegates nowadays are thought to be interested mostly in particular candidates or issues, without concern for the interests of the party as an organization. This distinction is said to reflect the declining role of local party organizations in presidential nominations. The nominee is not someone picked by party leaders, but the person who wins the most delegates by his own efforts.

Evaluating the Results At least three criteria can be used in evaluating the nominating procedures of the two parties. (1) Are they fair? (2) Do they pick the candidate most popular with party members? (3) Do they pick the strongest candidate for the general election? These are all apparently reasonable standards, but they are not necessarily consistent with each other.

The most difficult criterion is the first one. What is fairness? Does it mean giving every party member a chance to participate? If so, how is membership defined? Should the privilege of participating be limited to people who have assumed certain minimal responsibilities to their party, or should anyone who calls himself a party member be allowed to participate equally?

The second criterion is easier. The leading candidate in the public opinion polls has become his party's nominee at twenty-one of the twenty-two conventions held since the advent of polling. (The only exception was Adlai Stevenson in 1952.)[29] No system, however, can guarantee that the party's candidate will be the choice of a *majority* of party members. There may be no candidate on whom a majority agree. Twice in recent years the leading candidate received the nomination but had much less than a majority of grassroots support. In 1964, Goldwater was the choice of 22 percent of all Republicans, compared to the same proportion for Nixon, 21 percent for a third candidate, and 20 percent for a fourth. In 1972, McGovern led all other candidates but still had the support of only 30 percent of rank and file Democrats.

The third criterion poses a great problem for any nominating system. With the examples of Goldwater and McGovern before us, it is not difficult to see that the candidate who is most popular in his own party may not have the most appeal to Independents and members of the other party. What is more, Goldwater and McGovern are not the only such cases. In 1968, Humphrey, the preferred candidate of Democrats, was less attractive to Republicans and Independents than Eu-

---

[29] William R. Keech and Donald R. Matthews, *The Party's Choice* (Washington: The Brookings Institution, 1976), p. 215.

gene McCarthy, who was a poor third in his own party.[30] This, then, is the ultimate dilemma of the presidential nominating process: *If the party's goal is to win the election, increasing participation may be counterproductive.* The more the candidate reflects the rank and file preferences of his own party faithful, the less he may appeal to independent voters and those who identify with the other party. A candidate who must demonstrate in a very open nominating process that he is liberal or conservative enough to win his own party's nomination may be demonstrating simultaneously that he is too liberal or conservative to appeal to a majority of the electorate. And it is the majority of the electorate that decides who actually gets to be president. This is one reason why party leaders sometimes oppose openness and total democracy in the nominating process. They feel that if they can avoid excessive pressure from their own activists, they can come up with candidates who have a better chance of actually winning the election.

CAMPAIGNING FOR OFFICE

Once nominated, a presidential candidate must face the problem of uniting the party behind his campaign. One route to unity depends on lining up the active support of the candidates he defeated for the nomination. This support is not always easy to request or give, however. The wounds of recent combat may be too painful. The losing candidate may be willing to cooperate, but his key staff may find peacemaking more difficult. The problem is worse if the winner is an "outsider" who has won by overwhelming the regulars. This situation increases the normal tension between the candidate's own staff and activists whose loyalty is to the party. It is even more difficult when the candidate is someone like Carter or McGovern, who based their preconvention campaigns on criticism of party regulars. Relationships were so bad in 1972 that some major Democratic leaders would not talk to the McGovern campaign chairmen in their states.

Even when there is a history of bad feeling between a nominee and other influential members of his party, cooperation may still be possible. For example, Governor Nelson Rockefeller of New York scarcely lifted a finger to help Richard Nixon when Nixon ran for the presidency unsuccessfully in 1960 and successfully in 1968. But in 1972 Rockefeller's entire political apparatus was mobilized for Nixon. Rockefeller supplied Nixon with more than three hundred specialists on every aspect of campaigning. How did Nixon induce Rockefeller to cooperate? In essence, he offered a simple exchange: if

"The big guy in front is Joseph T. Cochrane. Call him Joe. You met him in Marysville three weeks ago. Talk about hunting. He goes after deer every fall. Man on left is Leo Brown. Sixteenth district in his pocket. Don't ask him about his wife. She's ditched him. Fellow with mustache is Jim Cronin. Watch your step with him. He's Cochrane's brother-in-law, and . . ."

Drawing by Peter Arno; © 1946, 1974 The New Yorker Magazine, Inc.

[30] Arthur C. Wolfe, "Challenge from the Right: The Basis of Voter Support for Wallace in 1968," paper presented at the 1969 annual meeting of the American Political Science Association, p. 15.

Rockefeller would help Nixon, Nixon would not have to create his own organization in New York, an organization that could threaten Rockefeller's control of Republican politics in that state.

In the broad sense, "the campaign" includes innumerable efforts ranging from registration campaigns aimed at voters likely to support a candidate to carefully planned symbolic actions addressed to key groups. This latter category includes face-to-face attempts to obtain endorsements from influential individuals, groups, and newspapers. (One ritual of every presidential campaign is a meeting between each major candidate and the editorial board of *The New York Times*.) A famous example of campaigning-by-deed was John Kennedy's 1960 telephone call to the wife of Reverend Martin Luther King, Jr. King had been jailed on a trumped-up charge and Kennedy's highly publicized gesture of support for him was widely considered a master stroke of publicity.

The oldest and most basic element of campaigning involved direct personal contacts with voters. To secure these contacts, the candidate traditionally relied on the memory of the precinct captain, who knew his neighbors intimately and could count on a reservoir of votes by mobilizing patronage jobholders and other citizens beholden to the party organization. Today the box of file cards and the computer have supplemented the precinct captain's memory, but the traditional techniques are still very much in use, especially by the ideologically motivated activists of the so-called new politics. The Democratic boss of Buffalo commented on this marriage of old and new:

> If the new politics teaches anything at all, it's that the old politics was pretty good. The McCarthy kids in New Hampshire rang doorbells, made telephone calls and made the personal contact that people associate with the old-style machines.[31]

In 1976, fully 29 percent of the public was contacted by a worker for one party or the other. A substantial fraction of them were reached by both parties.

Along with the survival of old-time personal politics has been the introduction of new techniques and technology. Commercials for radio and television typify the wholesale expansion of advertising techniques into the political arena. These commercials are designed, produced, packaged, and disseminated by teams of specialists on scenario writing, photography, media space buying, and television direction. Some people used to worry that the influence of television would lead to the rise of candidates who could offer the public nothing but personal glamor. After looking at such distinctly unglamorous figures as Gerald Ford, Richard Nixon, Lyndon Johnson, Jimmy Carter, and George McGovern, it is safe to conclude that the ranks of successful politicians include about the same proportion of movie star personalities as the general public.

---

[31] Quoted in Martin and Susan Tolchin, *To the Victor* . . . (New York: Random House, 1972), p. 23.

Strictly speaking, we do not vote for a presidential candidate, but for the electors pledged to the candidate we prefer. The candidate with the most popular votes in each state gets all the state's electoral votes—one for each senator and representative.[32] In each state, the electors pledged to the winning candidate gather to cast their ballots for him. The whole **electoral college,** that is, all the winning electors, never actually meets in one place.

This method was devised by the Framers of the Constitution because they wanted the president chosen by a body of distinguished people exercising their own judgment. The emergence of popular candidates and political parties immediately put an end to the electors' independence. In our history only 8 electors (out of more than 17,000) have failed to vote for the candidate to whom they were pledged.

If no candidate receives a majority of electoral votes, the House of Representatives chooses the president from among the top three candidates. Each state delegation has a single vote. This formula increases the chances that the House would pick someone who did not get the highest popular vote. Indeed, this happened in

THE FRANTIC PACE OF CAMPAIGNS

To the major participants in a campaign the pace is constant and frantic. Authority in a campaign tends to be fluid rather than rigid, based on persuasion rather than command, and enforced rather through a sense of legitimacy than through sanction. Because most activists are involved in a campaign at least as much for the pleasure they derive from the activity as for a concern with the hope of eventual gain, should victory be theirs, compliance with campaign decisions is best obtained primarily through discussion. The smallest decision may involve a campaign staff person in hours of such discussion. But to neglect this form of "involvement" often means making the campaign less enjoyable to the participant, thus diminishing one of the prime motives for his or her participation in the first place. Further, the need for money is infinite and the supply is always less than needed. Endless hours must be spent on fund-raising. Events must be planned. Contributors have a somewhat annoying wish to be talked with on matters other than money. "Leaders" of every group, no matter how small, must be courted courteously. All such activities take time—leaving precious little time for reflective thought. Moreover, the best minds of a campaign will usually be put to work on the most serious problems—which are always the most immediate problems.*

*William Cavala, "Changing the Rules Changes the Game," p. 33n.

---

[32] In Maine, electoral votes are given separately to the winner in each of the two congressional districts.

1824, the most recent election decided in the House, when John Quincy Adams was chosen. This problem could be corrected by a constitutional amendment that gave each member of the House one vote. Similarly, the remote threat of faithless electors could be removed by abolishing the job of elector but preserving this method of tallying votes. These two steps would "perfect" the electoral college.

These changes would not affect what some people consider its fundamental flaw: the winner-take-all feature on a state-by-state basis means that the most electoral votes can go to a candidate with fewer popular votes. This last happened in 1888, when the winner had 95,713 fewer popular votes. Innumerable imaginary outcomes seem more important to some people, however. For example, a difference of 9,245 votes in Hawaii and Ohio would have reelected Ford in 1976, although he got 1.7 million fewer votes than Carter. These hypothetical possibilities are often cited by proponents of direct popular election. Their goal is to ensure that the candidate with the most votes is the winner by abolishing the electoral college altogether.

Opponents of direct popular election think that its supporters overlook the more subtle effects of the electoral college. Its real significance is the way it structures the presidential campaign and the calculations of politicians. Because a candidate who gets a plurality of a state's popular votes wins all its electoral votes, there is no reason for him to pay much attention to states where he is sure to win or lose. One more popular vote for a Democratic candidate in a state that is already going Democratic (or Republican) by a two-to-one margin makes no difference. Thus the campaign efforts of both candidates are concentrated on the doubtful states. The most important voters are those in large states which are closely balanced between Democrats and Republicans. This encourages the candidates to compete for the same common ground, rather than maximizing votes by appealing to their supporters in the states they are sure of winning.

A more important effect of the electoral college is the way it discourages third parties. Since a plurality is enough to get all a state's electoral votes, only a party with a chance of winning has any motivation at all to run. There is little opportunity for third parties to play a spoiler role or to use this possibility to blackmail a major party into making concessions. The electoral college does not completely eliminate this threat, since a regionally based third-party candidate (like Wallace) can seek to throw the election into the House, but it does make the threat considerably less credible. Consequently, the two parties are the main arenas for political struggle. Only when a prospective third party is large enough to win a plurality of votes in a substantial number of states does a vote for that party really count, and then only in states where it has a chance to win. In short, the electoral college has two basic results: It helps preserve the stability of the two-party system, and it focuses the attention of presidential candidates on swing voters in close states rather than on piling up bigger and bigger leads in states already favorable to them.

Every close election revives interest in replacing the electoral college with direct popular election. The polls show a healthy popular majority against the electoral college—but they also show that few people really know what the controversy is all about. There is little public pressure behind direct election proposals. Most political scientists would agree that the public's indifference to these proposals is not a bad thing. The advantages of the electoral college are well understood and its hazards seem remote. Since the uncertainties of direct popular election are substantial, the status quo does not look so bad.

HOW DIFFERENT ARE THE PARTIES?

It is easy enough to provide reasons why the Republican and Democratic parties should be similar, or why they should be different. We will do just this shortly. But first let us explore some of the dimensions along which the gap between the two parties can be measured. Differences and similarities between Republicans and Democrats can be measured along any or all of the following lines:

1. *The parts of society from which they draw supporters.* As we saw in Chapter 8, Republicans and Democrats are not quite the same kind of people. The Democratic party includes more blacks, Jews, Catholics, poor people, and southerners. Except for blacks and Jews, however, the Democrats do not have anything even approaching an exclusive hold on any group, and the Republicans do not have a corner on millionaires.

2. *The opinions of rank and file members.* Here again, we saw in Chapter 8 some issues where there were distinct but moderate differences between the parties, and other issues where their followers had almost identical patterns of belief.

3. *The attitudes of activists and primary voters.* The partisan gap is considerably greater among convention delegates and participants in campaign activities than among rank and file voters. It is even wider among congressional candidates, as Table 11.3 shows.

4. *The behavior of officials.* As we will see in Chapter 13, party is the best predictor of voting patterns in the House and Senate.

Table 11.3

How Republican and Democratic Congressional Candidates Differ on Issues

	PERCENTAGE WHO AGREE	
ISSUE	*Democrats*	*Republicans*
"Defense spending should be substantially reduced and the funds diverted to domestic social needs."	73%	21%
"Would you favor a federally financed national health insurance plan covering all medical expenses?"	77	21
"Any licensed physician should be allowed to perform an abortion for any woman who wants one."	61	31
"Civil rights laws enacted in the past decade should be significantly expanded in the years ahead."	57	19

Source: Congressional Quarterly Weekly Report, October 16, 1970, pp. 2567–69.

5. *Party platforms.* It is generally believed that platforms are meaningless. Sometimes even the presidential candidate does not seem to care much about the platform on which he is to run. At other times, however, the platform is a subject of hot dispute. But even at the ideologically aware 1972 Democratic convention, few delegates had actually read the platform they fought about and finally approved. The authors of a study on the convention report their findings about delegate familiarity with the platform:

> When asked about the platform, one old-line leader from Connecticut replied with an incredulous stare and finally growled, "Have *you* ever read a platform?" (The questioner had not.) A veteran Missouri labor leader said, "It means nothing. There's only twelve people that read it. The candidate is the platform."[33]

One political scientist decided to test what "everyone knows" about party platforms by actually reading and comparing them for every election year from 1944 through 1964. He found that more than half the planks in the platform were specific enough to enable him to see if they had been carried out. *Fully 72 percent of the promises made in the party platforms had indeed been kept by 1966.* He also found that the platforms differed considerably, partly in emphasizing different issues, partly in making opposing promises. Over half the promises were made by one party only, a third were made by both, and the rest were in conflict.[34] It appears, then, that the platforms are not meaningless. They represent an accumulation of what each party has been pushing for in Congress and what its more issue-oriented activists would like to see enacted.

Perhaps the most fundamental source of disagreement between the parties does not come from real differences in policies but from the fact that their leaders feel there is a difference. Even when they favor the same policies, politicians see politics as an us-against-them business. What is good for Republicans must be bad for Democrats, and thus what Republicans propose should be opposed by Democrats on grounds of simple self-interest. Opposition to what the president does is expressed by members of the other party with presidential ambitions of their own, as well as by any other party figure looking for publicity and knowing it is available by criticizing the administration.

One long-standing belief about the American electorate is that it is composed of some extreme liberals, a lot of moderate liberals, a lot of moderate conservatives, and some extreme conservatives. Figure 11.2 shows this view of the electorate graphically. According to this view, if the Democratic party adopted a quite liberal stance, it would allow the Republican party to move over the hump and capture more than half the votes, as shown in Figure 11.3. Conversely, if the Republicans adopted a very conservative position, then the Democrats might get all the liberal votes plus most moderate votes. Thus the desire to capture the high ground where most of the voters are supposed to be pushes both parties toward the same intermediate policy positions.

---

[33] Denis G. Sullivan et al., *The Politics of Representation* (New York: St. Martin's, 1974), p. 73.

[34] Gerald Pomper, *Elections in America* (New York: Dodd, Mead, 1970), pp. 149–70.

Figure 11.2

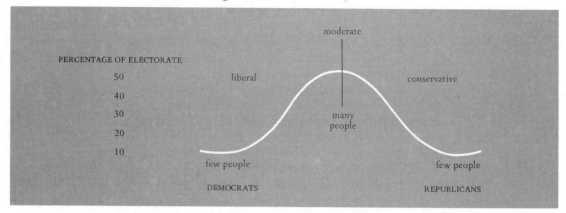

At times this may be a true picture, but there are also a number of major forces pushing the parties apart. First, public opinion on an issue often does not resemble this bell-shaped curve. On some individual issues there may be two humps. For instance, a substantial share of the population may be in favor of government aid to parochial schools while another substantial portion is opposed (see Figure 11.4). In such instances, each party could climb to the top of one of the humps without giving much advantage to the other. They would then have distinctly different positions.

Another factor keeping the parties apart is the fact that voters often split differently on different issues, as we saw in Chapter 7. They oppose school busing and favor government-subsidized medical care. The Republican party might seek to win votes by denouncing school busing while the Democrats concentrated on advocating socialized medicine. As long as we have only two parties, it is not possible for each to be ideologically distinct and coherent, because there is no corresponding ideological clarity and polarization among the population.

In short, our one-hump model with the two parties elbowing one another in the middle assumes that all Americans are arranged along a single all-encompassing liberal-to-conservative dimension. In reality, however, presidential elections involve many overlapping and conflicting issue dimensions with differing distribu-

Figure 11.3

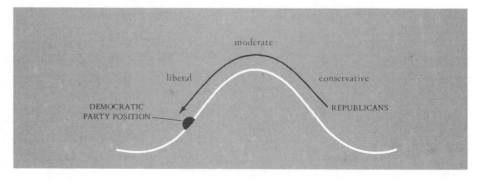

Figure 11.4

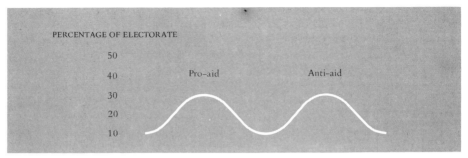

tions of voter attitudes. The two candidates may choose to emphasize different issues. Both parties can occupy several humps, each of which contains the majority opinion on one issue. In this way, the two parties may present different images to the public while both are taking individual issue positions that a majority of the voters want.

The parties also may be pushed apart by their leaders' differing estimates as to which issues will be most important to the voters. Not surprisingly, Republican politicians will tend to believe that their party's favored positions are more popular with the public, while Democratic leaders will justify their own preferences by rationalizing that these positions will enable them to win favor with more voters. (In point of fact, of course, politicians of all varieties are likely to overestimate the electorate's knowledge, interest, and decisiveness about issues. As we saw in Chapter 8, few voters base their decisions on the issues. Party identification and candidate image account for the vast bulk of voting decisions in any election.)

We have seen that Republican and Democratic activists have quite different attitudes. Moreover, the two parties traditionally have relied on somewhat different bases of support. The Democrats have been more popular with labor, blacks, city dwellers, and certain farm groups. The Republicans have had more support from business and other farm groups. These associations have been sources of votes, campaign workers, and campaign funds. Even if Democratic leaders believe that most people are opposed to school busing and that this issue will be important in the election, they will not rush toward the same antibusing positions Republicans may take. There are a number of reasons for this. First, the active members of the party may be strongly in favor of busing. Second, an antibusing position might lead to wholesale black defections. Similarly, the Republicans may not come out for government-subsidized medical care, even if most Americans want it, because a majority of Republican leaders and activists are opposed to it.

In short, a party may not move to a position occupied by the majority of voters on a particular issue because the party's more active members strongly support the minority position on the issue. Or the leadership may feel that adopting the most popular position on a given issue might cause terrible splits in the party that would reduce its chances of winning the election. Frequently, then, one party may not seek to get next to the other on an issue. Instead, it may take a less popular stand or no stand at all in order to avoid a split in the party or a policy stance some key supporters dislike.

The combination of different tactical notions, rival candidates, and opinion-ated activists introduces powerful dynamic elements into party competition. We have seen that sometimes the gap between the two presidential candidates is rela-tively narrow, as was the case in the 1950s. And sometimes the partisan gap is sub-stantial, as it was in 1964 and 1972. When this happens, the more moderate candi-date generally exploits the situation by holding out a hand of welcome to voters from the other party. The Democrats responded in this way to Goldwater's nomi-nation in 1964. In his convention speech accepting the Democratic vice-presiden-tial nomination, Hubert Humphrey said:

> Yes, yes my fellow Americans, it is a fact that the temporary Republican spokesman is not in the mainstream of his party, in fact he has not even touched the shore. . . . I say to those responsible and forward-looking Republicans — and there are thousands of them — we welcome you to the banner of Lyndon B. Johnson. . . .

When the winner is someone like Goldwater or McGovern, the party's con-gressional candidates hastily try to dissociate themselves from what they consider a symbol of disaster. The other party's campaigners, of course, gleefully try to hang the unpopular presidential nominee around the neck of every candidate running on his party's ticket. In 1972, the director of the Fair Campaign Practices Committee reported that the "one specific complaint received more than any other was from Democrats claiming they were unfairly identified with George McGovern."[35] Noth-ing could illustrate more clearly the fragmented character of American political par-ties.

The gap between the parties is like an accordion. Sometimes it is narrow as moderate candidates lead both parties in search of the golden mean. Then each party tries to appeal to the same body of popular opinion. But sometimes the par-ties diverge sharply, under the influence of leaders in pursuit of the ideal society, their own place in history, or the campaign contributions and workers they need to win. We will learn more about these motivations in the next three chapters, as we look directly at the political calculations of members of Congress and the president.

SUMMARY   Political parties select candidates and seek to influence people to vote for those candidates. They provide orderly channels for political competition among those seeking public office; they organize various political ideas and personalities into two large packages designed to compromise and coordinate the diverse political strivings that we find on the American scene.

A number of factors, including the debate over adoption of the Constitution, the initial duality of political conflict, the prevalence of single-member electoral districts, the winner-take-all presidency, and the tactics of the major parties themselves, created and maintain a two-party system in the United States.

[35] *San Francisco Sunday Examiner and Chronicle,* November 19, 1972, p. A28.

American political parties do not have specifically defined memberships. An American is a Democrat or a Republican if he says he is. Some activists are party regulars who work election after election irrespective of the candidates and the issues. Others only work for the party when they feel that the party can become the means of gaining victory for persons or policies that they consider as particularly good.

Basically, American parties are decentralized. Most workers and money are found and used by local organizations in behalf of individual candidates. Although the voters perceive the Democratic and Republican parties as national parties, there is little national organization. The President serves as national spokesman for his party but has little control over its state and local branches. State and local parties exist in a wide variety of forms, from disciplined patronage-based machines to informal working groups put together by a particular candidate for a particular election.

The greatest single task of each party is nominating a presidential candidate at its national convention held every four years. The delegates to these conventions are chosen either in state primary elections or in state caucuses and conventions. Both methods of delegate selection involve a number of complex problems that revolve about the issue of whether presidential nominations ought to be controlled by party regulars or by people who are more concerned with issues of the moment than with long-term party success.

Presidential nominating politics today is dominated by the long string of state primaries beginning in late winter and running into early June. In the last forty years the outcome of almost every national convention was determined before the convention went into session because one candidate already had captured enough delegates to win on the first ballot.

The national conventions almost always nominate the candidate who is most popular among rank-and-file party identifiers. However, this is not necessarily the person who would have the most appeal to Independents and members of the other party.

The question of who will be convention delegates has been bitterly argued. After 1968 the Democrats imposed quotas for women, some minorities, and people under 30 in each state delegation. But the age, sex, or race of delegates has little real significance, since none of these factors is related to delegates' candidate choice or issue positions.

Americans do not actually vote for a presidential candidate, but for electors pledged to one or the other candidate. The candidate with the most votes in a state wins all of that state's electoral votes. Changing this system is frequently proposed, but some of its advantages are often overlooked: It discourages third-party candidates and focuses the candidates' attention on swing voters in close states.

The two major parties are similar in some respects and different in others. The gap between them is like an accordion: Sometimes it is narrow; sometimes it widens because of a particular issue or because one candidate rather than another has won a presidential nomination.

national governmental institutions

PART THREE

how congress is elected and organized

Congress differs from other national legislatures in two important ways. (1) It is genuinely independent, not a mere appendage of the executive branch, as in Britain, France, Germany, and other democratic countries. Although members of Congress are in many ways responsive to the executive, they are not dominated by it. (2) Congress is also one of the very few effectively **bicameral legislatures,** which simply means it has two houses rather than one. The two houses are also rather different, both formally and informally.

CHAPTER 12

Congress is the most unpopular of the three branches of government. More people disapprove than approve of "the way the U.S. Congress is handling its job." The drastic congressional reforms of the early 1970s, which abolished most grievances about Congress, had no impact on its low public image. At the same time, Americans express satisfaction with their own representatives by a ratio of more than three to one.[1]

Congress is criticized for being unresponsive, dishonest, old-fashioned, and so on. It is denounced for not doing what "the people" want, for not doing what the president wants, for not doing what is obviously just and true. Congress does not do what the president wants because it is genuinely independent of the president, both by constitutional prescription and in political reality. It does not do what "the people" want because it is not a clear lens, reflecting public opinion directly into laws, but rather a series of distorting lenses resembling prescription eyeglasses. And Congress does not do what its critics think is obviously just and proper because its members have their own ideas about what is just and proper. We will explore the reasons for this behavior in this chapter and in Chapter 13. This chapter describes how members of Congress (a term that means both representatives and senators unless the context suggests otherwise) reach office and how Congress is organized. As we will see, these topics are intertwined. If the legislature were elected by different means, it would have a very different structure. Chapter 13 is about Congress in action: how the mechanism described in this chapter operates.

[1] *Gallup Opinion Index,* April 1977, pp. 4–6.

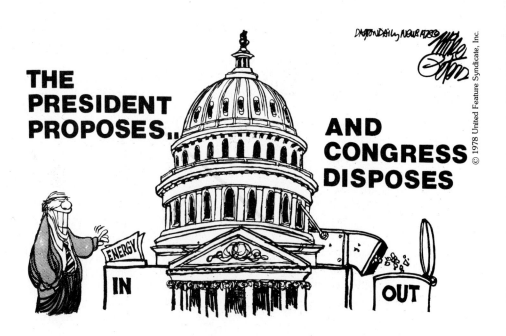

THE BASES OF REPRESENTATION

The Constitution   The division of Congress into two bodies came about because the Framers of the Constitution were faced with a dilemma. On the one hand, they believed that the legislature should reflect popular opinion through elected representatives. On the other hand, they feared "the people" were not capable of complete responsibility for self-government.[2] Because the House of Representatives was elected by popular vote, it was expected to be a direct expression of the people's will. The Senate, in contrast, was originally designed as a check on the popular will. For this reason, it was to be elected by a method that would prevent its being a direct expression of public opinion. For a century and a quarter, senators were chosen by state legislatures. It was thought that this would provide more distinguished, judicious, and deliberate legislators who would also be more sympathetic to the interests of the wealthy.

The Seventeenth Amendment to the Constitution, ratified in 1913, provided that senators would be elected by the people. This change, together with various other developments, produced a reversal of the original conception of the relationship between the House and the Senate. Now, rather than being the more conservative body, the Senate is generally the more liberal of the two houses.

Having decided on two branches, the Framers had next to decide how to apportion membership in the Senate. They easily agreed that the House, "the popular body," would be based on population; the more citizens each state had, the more representatives it would be allowed in the House. (In tabulating population each slave counted as three-fifths of a free person.) The small states, however, feared they would be dominated by the larger ones if Senate seats were apportioned the same way. They felt so strongly about this issue that the Constitutional Convention almost broke up. That disaster was avoided by the Great Compromise, which provided that each state would elect two senators. This decision has since come to be regarded as a basic principle of American political theory, rather than as the completely pragmatic compromise it was.

From that day to this, small states have been grossly overrepresented in Congress. An American citizen living in Nevada or Wyoming has forty times the Senate voting power that a Californian or New Yorker does. Fortunately, few issues have had small states on one side and large states on the other, so it is not clear that this imbalance has actually damaged the interests of California and helped those of Wyoming.

The constitutional differences between the House and the Senate are important but limited. The Senate ratifies treaties with other nations and confirms presidential nominees to the cabinet, the Supreme Court, ambassadorships, and certain regulatory commissions. Bills for taxation originate in the House. One other difference is generally irrelevant, but occasionally crucial: the House has the power to impeach the president or other high officials by majority vote. Impeachment is comparable to indictment. The impeached official is then tried by the Senate, where a two-thirds majority is required for conviction.

[2] Alexander Hamilton once remarked, "Your people, sir, is a great beast."

The size of the Senate is determined by the number of states and has never been an issue since the Constitution was adopted. Because House membership is based on population, however, the House grew in size during the nineteenth century. This trend began to pose a serious threat to efficiency as the country's population approached 100 million. In 1911, it was decided that the size of the House would be fixed at 435 members. It has remained at this level ever since, with temporary and unimportant exceptions. But the relative populations of the states have changed enormously since 1910, and this fact is the base of a continuing problem about representation. The number of House seats for each state is determined objectively after each census by the Bureau of the Census, using its statistics on population trends. This has meant gains for Texas, California, Florida, and the rest of the Sunbelt, at the expense of many northeastern and midwestern states.

Legislative Apportionment   Each state is responsible for drawing the district lines for the seats assigned to it. Unlike the objective allocation of the number of seats given to each state, districting has always been a political and subjective process. Two kinds of bias are possible in drawing congressional district lines. One is **malapportionment,** in which districts are of unequal population size so that voters in large districts have a smaller share of representation than those in small districts. Shortly after the 1960 census, for example, the twenty smallest House seats represented an average of 227,000 people each, while the twenty largest seats represented an average of 697,000. The small seats were usually in rural areas while the large ones were usually urban or suburban. The result of this practice was to reduce the political power of cities and suburbs and to increase that of farmers. This problem was ended by a series of Supreme Court decisions in the 1960s that established the principle of *one person — one vote* in all legislative districts. Congressional districts now are about the same size, averaging around 500,000 people each.

The second type of bias in districting is called **gerrymandering.** The guiding principle is to take political considerations into account in drawing the lines between districts, to achieve the largest number of legislative seats for one's own party and the smallest number for the opposition. This can be accomplished either by concentrating the opposition party's strength in a few seats or by scattering its voters through many districts. State legislatures continue to draw lines to the advantage of the majority party. District lines in some cities are drawn so carefully that they wiggle around individual apartment houses or residential blocks as a way of avoiding or including certain social classes or ethnic groups.

Gerrymandering may sound complex, but the basic idea is simple. For example, assume a city of 1,000,000 people, surrounded by suburbs with a million residents. Assume also that this metropolitan area elects five representatives to Congress and that the city is overwhelmingly Democratic while the suburbs are overwhelmingly Republican. Each party thus has just about equal support. If the Democrats were drawing the lines, they could draw them so that four of the five districts each consisted of 220,000 inner-city residents (Democratic) and 180,000 suburbanites (Republican). The fifth district would contain the remaining 120,000 inner-city voters and 280,000 suburban Republicans, giving the Democrats a margin of four seats to one. Or they might draw lines to put one district entirely in the suburbs.

This would concede a seat to the opposition but would mean that the remaining 600,000 suburban votes would be divided among the remaining four districts, again leaving the Republicans with only one seat. Of course, if the Republicans were doing the dividing, they could just as easily do it the other way around.

The problem of fair districting raises some fascinating and complex problems. How should district lines be drawn? Should districts be "compact and contiguous"? Should such natural areas as cities, geographic units, metropolitan areas, and so on be kept together, or should they be divided? Should districts be as socially and economically diverse as possible, or should they be homogeneous? It is difficult to give objective answers to these questions, for it really comes down to a question of which political interests one wants to help. The more diverse the district, the greater freedom its representative is likely to have because he or she will not be beholden to a particular interest. Yet making districts more diverse reduces the number of minority legislators, thus hurting groups like blacks and Chicanos who have few resources in politics other than their votes.

Should district lines be drawn to make a state's total number of representatives more or less proportionate to the total number of votes cast? If the statewide vote averages 55 percent Democratic, should the lines be drawn in order to give the Democrats 55 percent of the seats? Or should they be drawn so that each district contains 55 percent Democrats and 45 percent Republicans? If the latter procedure were followed, the Democrats would have a good chance of winning all the seats, but every election would be close. Politicians are no fonder of uncertainty than anyone else; they shy away from formulas that could produce great payoffs by taking a chance. They would rather have as many safe seats as possible and not take risks with close races, even if this means conceding some safe seats to the opposition.

After generations of Republican influence in congressional districting, the tables are now turned. In 1979 there were twenty states in which Democrats held the governorship and both houses of the legislature. Republicans held both in only three states. (Partisan control was divided in the remaining states. This situation usually produces districting to protect all incumbents.) Barring a remarkable Republican revival, the party will suffer from post-1980 census districting dominated by Democratic state legislatures and governors.

CONGRESSIONAL ELECTIONS

Popular images of Congress are weak and indistinct: Scarcely half the population knows or cares which party controls Congress, and fewer still know anything about the voting record of their representative. Twenty percent do not have an opinion about how well Congress is performing.[3]

[3] Unless otherwise indicated, findings reported in this section are from our own research or from Thomas E. Mann and Raymond E. Wolfinger, "Candidates and Parties in Congressional Elections," paper presented at the 1979 annual meeting of the American Political Science Association. The data source for our research is the 1978 National Election Study of the Center for Political Studies of the University of Michigan, obtained through the Inter-University Consortium for Political and Social Research. We computed the data and are solely responsible for the analysis.

Individual members of Congress are not very familiar to their constituents. In 1978, only 56 percent knew the names of their Senate candidates, and just 40 percent could recall who was running for the House in their district. Barely half remembered their representative's name and, as we might expect, challengers and candidates for open seats were known to far fewer people.

Similar findings have been familiar to political scientists for some years. This led us to underestimate the public's knowledge of their congressmen. As we all know from personal experience, it is far more difficult to recall someone's name without help than it is to recognize a name when we come across it. Recognition is the politically relevant test. After all, each candidate's name is on the ballot. The important thing, therefore, is what the experience of seeing the candidates' names means to the voter: how many find the names familiar? And how many have positive or negative impressions? Once again, it is not difficult to believe we could think well or ill of someone without being able to recall his or her name. The latest research confirms these notions.[4] Almost everyone who votes recognizes the name of the incumbent representative, but less than half as many find the challenger's name familiar. Moreover, most voters have some positive or negative reaction to them, and these personal images of the candidates affect many votes. The level of name recognition is higher in Senate races, particularly for candidates challenging incumbent senators (Table 12.1).

A minority of voters are in the dark about at least one candidate. Lacking any other guide to a decision, these voters fall back on their party identification. Sixty-nine percent of the votes cast in the 1978 House elections were by party identifiers voting for their party's candidate. Since senatorial candidates are better known, the figures are slightly lower for these races. Party-line voting is most common in races for open seats, where both candidates are less likely to be known.[5] The more a voter knows about a candidate, the greater the likelihood that he will learn something that will cause him to defect if the candidate belongs to the

Table 12.1

Voters' Knowledge of Congressional Candidates, 1978

	Percentage of Voters Who Recognized the Name of Candidates Who Were:	
	INCUMBENTS	CHALLENGERS*
House elections	93	44
Senate elections	96	86

*A challenger is the general election opponent of an incumbent running for reelection.

Source: Data from the 1978 National Election Study of the University of Michigan Center for Political Studies, analyzed by the authors.

[4] The first statement of these ideas and evidence for them is in Thomas E. Mann, *Unsafe at Any Margin* (Washington: American Enterprise Institute, 1978), Chap. 2.

[5] There were 56 open House seats in 1978 and 13 Senate races without an incumbent. Both figures are a bit higher than normal.

other party. Since incumbents are far better known than challengers, they are the greatest beneficiaries of defections. Over three-quarters of defecting votes go to incumbents.

The Advantages of Incumbency The importance and stability of party identification combine with incumbents' greater familiarity to produce a high probability that they will be reelected. Since 1956, the average success rate for sitting representatives has been well above 90 percent. Despite all the talk about hostility to politicians, only thirteen incumbents were beaten in 1976 and nineteen in 1978. Senators are less secure because of their challengers' greater visibility and the closer partisan balance in statewide races. Their reelection rate was only 64 percent in 1976 and 68 percent in 1978, compared to nearly 90 percent in the previous fifteen years.

Reflecting the growing advantages of incumbency, more and more House elections are being won by large margins. The more competitive races are those without an incumbent. In 1978, 69 percent of all House seats were won with at least 60 percent of the vote — a 20 percent margin between winner and loser. (In seventy House districts there was no major party competition at all; the winner had no opposition except from splinter candidates. Most of these uncontested seats were won by Democrats in the South.)

It would be a mistake to conclude that incumbents are invulnerable. At times,

Because public knowledge of nonincumbent congressional candidates is scanty, a well-known name is a great benefit to would-be congressmen. Here, John Glenn is shown as an astronaut in 1962 and as a senator from Ohio in 1975. (A second former astronaut was elected to the Senate in 1976.)

Wide World

members of one or the other party do find that being in office is no guarantee of resisting a strong tide against their party. In 1974, for example, 36 of the 163 Republican representatives were defeated for reelection (compared to 4 of 220 Democrats).[6] Some incumbents are no better known than their challengers. Some members do not exert themselves to develop constituent support; a few try but are not very good at it; and a few find that to be known is not necessarily to be admired. Adverse publicity can be very visible indeed. During the impeachment hearings of the House Jucidiary Committee in 1974, several Republican committee members were conspicuous defenders of President Nixon. They suffered severely in the elections that fall.[7] More commonly, negative public images have little to do with the content of policy. Citizens' impressions of their representatives feature their personal qualities or constituent service. While these are strongly positive on balance (to be known is usually to be known favorably), there are exceptions. One of the most dramatic was a Utah congressman convicted after two undercover policewomen claimed he had propositioned them. He was exceptionally well known to his constituents — and was one of two Democratic freshmen who were defeated in 1976.[8] Thus, the greater visibility of the incumbent can bring greater attention to his unattractive qualities. Incumbency is not an automatic advantage; the extent of its benefits depends on what the individual does with the opportunity.

Incumbents have these major advantages:

1. They have access to publicly supplied staffs and free or very cheap services, including postage, stationery, television and radio facilities.

2. As officeholders, they are in a position to do things for people, and this makes it easier to raise campaign funds.[9] Although incumbents need contributions less than challengers, they get more of them. And why not, given the odds? Who wants to contribute to a loser?

3. Much of what they say and do is genuinely newsworthy, often for nonpolitical reasons.

4. They are sought-after celebrities and can use this status to create networks of admiration, gratitude, trust, and agreement.[10]

[6] Walter Dean Burnham, "Insulation and Responsiveness in Congressional Elections," *Political Science Quarterly,* 90 (fall 1975), p. 416.

[7] Gerald C. Wright, Jr., "Constituency Response to Congressional Behavior: The Impact of the House Judiciary Committee Impeachment Votes," *The Western Political Quarterly,* 30 (September 1977), pp. 401 – 10.

[8] Mann, *Unsafe at Any Margin,* Chap. 4.

[9] One political scientist argues that members establish new federal programs which often require legislative intervention in order to help citizens get what they want. The grateful citizen becomes the legislator's political supporter, thus strengthening the power of incumbents. While both federal services and congressional interventions are increasing, the evidence for the other parts of the argument is still missing. See Morris P. Fiorina, *Congress: Keystone of the Washington Establishment* (New Haven, Conn: Yale University Press, 1977). Another ingenious book, explaining all congressional behavior as a product of a desire for reelection, is David R. Mayhew, *Congress: The Electoral Connection* (New Haven, Conn.: Yale University Press, 1974).

[10] This is what Richard F. Fenno, Jr., calls "home style." See his *Home Style: House Members in Their Districts* (Boston: Little, Brown, 1978).

Skillfully exploited, incumbency protects representatives from unwelcome political change, whether short-run party images or long-run partisan trends.[11] The most important illustrations of the insulating effect of incumbency come from recent House elections in the South. As we saw in Chapter 8, southerners are finally giving up their traditional loyalty to the Democratic party, but Republicans still have less than a third of the South's House seats. This is a vast improvement over the mere half dozen they used to have before the so-called Solid South crumbled, but it is far from what one would expect, given the dramatic changes in party loyalty in that part of the country. With rare exceptions, Republicans capture Democratic House seats only when the incumbent no longer runs for reelection. When a Democratic incumbent is the candidate, the Democrats still win 97 to 100 percent of all southern House elections. But when the seat is open, the victory levels for the Democratic party have fallen as low as 40 percent.[12]

The Fifth Congressional District in Mississippi dramatically illustrates the power of incumbency. For forty years the district was represented by William C. Colmer, an ultraconservative Democrat who usually was returned to the House without opposition. When Colmer announced his retirement in 1972, his young assistant switched parties and was elected to Colmer's seat as a Republican. He was reelected with 75 percent of the vote in 1974, which was not generally a good year for Republican congressional candidates.

***Party Images
and Presidential Coattails***   National changes in the fortunes of the two parties have an impact on the electoral chances of congressional candidates.

Party images are determined largely by the president and the candidates for the White House. Here as elsewhere, Congress is eclipsed by the president in public attention. Because most voters do not know which party controls Congress, they do not know what party can be held responsible for what Congress does. The president is the focus of public satisfaction and discontent. Party labels link public assessments of the president with voting choices in congressional contests.

Therefore congressional elections are in part referendums on the president and the presidential candidates. When a presidential candidate is popular, his candidacy helps everyone on his party's ticket. This is the **coattail effect,** so called because the lesser candidates are said to be carried into office on the president's coattails. When the presidential candidate is unpopular, he hurts the ticket—or, at the very least, does it little good. In 1976, Jimmy Carter ran behind 270 of the 292 Democrats elected to the House, and was ahead of only one Democratic senator.

In off-year elections, representatives who benefited from the coattail effect no longer have this source of added strength. Moreover, the president—and therefore his party—may lose some of the popularity that originally got him into the White

---

[11] Candice J. Nelson, "The Effect of Incumbency on Voting in Congressional Elections, 1964–1974," *Political Science Quarterly,* 93 (winter 1978), pp. 665-78.

[12] Raymond E. Wolfinger and Robert B. Arseneau, "Partisan Change in the South, 1952–1976," in Louis Maisel and Joseph Cooper, eds., *Political Parties: Development and Decay* (Beverly Hills: Sage Publications, 1978).

House. In fact, there is a general tendency for a president's popularity to decline as his years in office go by. The curve is very uneven, however. Two years after he was elected, a president may be popular or unpopular, successful or unsuccessful. Voting in midterm congressional elections is affected by the incumbent president's popularity and performance. Over the past forty years, a shift of 10 percentage points in the president's Gallup Poll rating produces a corresponding change of 1.3 percentage points in his party's vote in the midterm election. Changes in real income are also reflected in the midterm vote, which one political scientist calls "a referendum on the performance of the president and his administration's management of the economy."[13]

The 1974 midterm election provided a particularly dramatic illustration of how congressional candidates can suffer for their president's record. Nixon's resignation might have lifted the curse of Watergate from Republican campaigns that year. But President Ford's pardon of Nixon not only dropped his own popularity by 20 percentage points, it also hurt his party's campaigners. Together with the country's economic decline, the pardon dashed the hopes of Republican office-seekers. As a result, the Republicans lost forty-nine House seats while the Democrats lost only six. Of course, if a president is unpopular, his party's congressional candidates try to minimize their connection with him—although this is difficult to achieve completely. In the summer of 1978, with Jimmy Carter's public rating at a record low, he was shunned by Democratic candidates. But after Carter's spectacular Middle Eastern diplomatic summit at Camp David, he was besieged by Democrats asking him to campaign in their districts. Perhaps because the gain in Carter's popularity lasted through election day, the administration party's midterm losses were on the mild side in 1978. The Republicans picked up only eleven seats in the House, and three in the Senate.

Dynamic Factors in Congressional Elections Over the years, the performance of the two parties has been much more stable in congressional elections than in presidential voting. As Figure 12.1 shows, since 1952 the Democrats have had as much as 61.1 percent of the votes for president and as small a share as 37.5 percent, a gap of 23.6 percentage points. But their fortunes in congressional returns have been much stabler, from a low of 49.7 percent to a high of 57.6 percent. These nationwide findings average in many drastic shifts in individual states and districts, reflecting the ability of individual candidates to alter the partisan balance through personal popularity. Such candidates create seats that are safe for an individual, not a party. This source of change displays no coherent pattern, since it depends on individual political skill.

A second dynamic factor is short-term change in the national fortunes of one party or the other. These usually result from an unpopular presidential candidate (or an unusually popular one), or a war, depression, or other major disaster that affects widespread public images of the parties. When such a shift occurs, candidates belonging to the unlucky party are likely to suffer.

[13] Edward R. Tufte, *Political Control of the Economy* (Princeton, N.J.: Princeton University Press, 1978), p. 115.

Figure 12.1

Democratic Percentage of the Total Vote for President and for House Candidates, 1952–1978

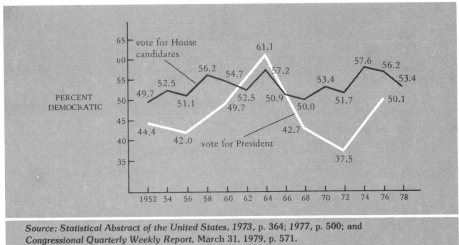

Source: *Statistical Abstract of the United States, 1973*, p. 364; *1977*, p. 500; and *Congressional Quarterly Weekly Report*, March 31, 1979, p. 571.

A third factor is perhaps the most important of all in the long run—population change in a district or state. This may be a shift from rural to urban, from middle class to working class, from white to black, or some combination of these. For instance, as the core cities of America have grown increasingly poor and increasingly black, they have become to a much larger degree safe bastions of the Democratic party. This accounts for the considerable growth in the number of safe northern Democratic seats, and also for the dramatic increase in the number of black representatives, from five in 1962 to sixteen in the 1970s.

A fourth source of change is a historic shift in party alignment—the only dynamic factor that actually means a lasting change in the political outlook of individual voters. The only important example at present is in the South, where the overwhelming loyalty of southerners to the Democratic party has eroded dramatically in recent years. This last case also reminds us that changes in voter attitudes and loyalties are muffled by the advantages of incumbency and the large electoral margins in most congressional elections. These considerations are among the reasons why elections are *not* a very sensitive measure of changing public moods. Congressional contests simply do not yield much of a mandate, except perhaps as a rough index of popular discontent with the president's performance.

Nominations   Because most general election contests are not competitive, nomination by the majority party often guarantees election. If incumbents are a fairly safe bet to win reelection in general elections, they are even more likely to win in primaries. Primary elections attract less attention and about

313

half the turnout of general elections. Moreover, the primary challenger lacks one great advantage that the general election opponent has—the party label. A primary challenger does not start out with an assured bloc of votes, for he or she belongs to the same party the incumbent does. Because voter discontent usually is expressed in party terms—voting for the candidates of the opposition party—the incumbents whose party image is unpopular will not suffer the consequences until the general election. Besides, if the incumbent is so much better known than his general election opponent, it seems reasonable to assume that people who challenge for renomination within the same party will have even less public visibility. Thus, despite a great deal of talk that Watergate would lead to widespread primary defeats for incumbents in 1974, Republican legislators did not have to fear being ousted by other Republican candidates at the primaries. The general elections were, of course, a different story.

In other words, renomination is a smaller hazard than reelection. Since World War II, less than 2 percent of incumbent representatives seeking reelection have lost primary elections. Most primary losers are either very old or are beaten by other incumbents when redistricting has thrown two representatives into the same district. In 1978, supposedly a year when politicians were especially unpopular, only five representatives and one elected senator lost their primaries. The same factors that make senators slightly more vulnerable in general elections also mean they tend to lose primaries a bit more often. Just 7 percent have lost their bids for renomination.

Clearly, the most crucial nomination contest is the first one, when the House or Senate seat is open. Nomination is a party process, the means by which the two parties select the candidates from whom the voters choose the winner. In discussing this process, we proceed on the assumption that what a legislator has to do to reach and hold office influences his behavior once in office. Thus, our main concerns are the nature and sources of the obligations that may govern a legislator's conduct. As we will see, there are great variations in sources of support and therefore in the obligations each member accumulates.

Sources of Support   In most democratic countries, each party's legislative candidates are picked by the national party organization. The ability to deny renomination to a legislator is the foundation of party discipline. This form of control is wholly lacking in the United States, where neither party has anything remotely resembling a national "machine." The closest approach is the influence the president exerts over his party. He is a national focus, his program is the "party line," he has certain resources that can be used to influence local figures, and he is somebody whom no politician in his party antagonizes lightly.

The president is the symbol of his party, but this is not a power that can be deployed selectively, to help loyal party members and punish disloyal ones. The president has little capacity to defeat candidates to whom he is opposed. Indeed, not since 1938 has a president openly intervened in his party's congressional primaries. In that year, Franklin Roosevelt attempted to deny renomination to several Democratic senators and representatives who had obstructed his legislative program. But his failure was so complete that presidents generally have resigned themselves to putting up with hostile members of their own party rather than attempting to prevent their renomination.

Although the president lacks life-and-death power over the campaigns of his party's congressional candidates, he does have some sources of leverage. Presidents can help by making personal appearances at campaign rallies or fund-raising affairs.

The more important national party organizations are the two national committees and the campaign committees in each house of Congress. Their financial and technical help is not negligible, particularly on the Republican side. By federal law, the most a candidate can receive from all party groups together is $30,000 in each election year. This is more than petty cash, but still not a big share of a serious campaign budget. As we saw in Chapter 9, less than 10 percent of congressional campaign budgets comes from all levels of the two parties. What is more, the congressional campaign committees do *not* use their limited financial power to enforce party discipline. Their help goes to candidates without regard to their support for party positions.

Private National Contributions. Incumbents have less need for campaign contributions, can raise money easily, and get less benefit from it. Challengers need money more, have more trouble raising it, and get more benefit from it when they are successful (see Chapter 9). In 1976, average spending by incumbents was $91,000, compared to $50,000 by challengers. *Successful* challengers spent an average of $290,000.[14]

Major interest groups give to members of committees that deal with their interests. The unions limit themselves to Democrats, but corporations and trade associations are remarkably evenhanded. They give to both sides to be sure of finding a welcome in the right place. Often their beneficiaries have little in common other than membership on a particular committee.

Some representatives and a good many senators have another kind of nationwide constituency. They are able to gain the support of people with special concerns and political orientations that make them delight in members of Congress who express and personify particular points of view. For example, two California congressmen, John Rousselot, a former member of the John Birch Society, and Ronald Dellums, a fiery black radical, each has a national constituency and hence financial support that extends throughout the country. Occasionally, this sort of support is so strong that a congressional campaign is dominated by out-of-state contributions. In the 1970 North Dakota Senate race, for example, it was estimated that almost 90 percent of the money spent by both sides came from outside the state.[15] But this seems to be an exception. In the vast majority of cases, the bulk of

---

[14] Congressional Quarterly, Inc., *Electing Congress* (Washington: Congressional Quarterly, Inc., 1978), p. 7; and Richard E. Cohen, "Incumbents in Congress—Are the Cards Stacked in Their Favor?" *National Journal*, September 23, 1978, p. 1510.

[15] Mayhew, *Congress: The Electoral Connection*, p. 39n.

aid comes from inside the constituency. Therefore, we now turn from national to local sources of campaign support.

Local Party Organizations. Are state and local parties any more important to members of Congress than the national organizations? Do they decide who is nominated in the first place? How helpful are they in campaigns?

As we saw in Chapter 11, there are enormous variations in the style and strength of party organizations across the country. Where an organization is strong and tightly held, House nominees may be chosen by a few leaders or even a single boss. In Illinois, Pennsylvania, and a few other states, there are still some seats whose incumbents were first picked by the local machine. (Organizations of this kind seldom have power that extends far enough to control a senatorial nomination completely.) But because members of Congress have little patronage power, seats in Congress are not as highly prized by machine politicians as local posts. Thus, even strong organizations usually are not greatly interested in controlling members of Congress. As one representative explained, "The sheriff in my county has seventy or eighty jobs to pass out, and everyone is interested in who is sheriff. No one cares about us." A political scientist who interviewed dozens of representatives repeatedly to discover who had tried to influence their votes found that less than one in ten was ever contacted by local party officials about pending legislation.[16]

More common than tightly controlled machines are situations where party power is fragmented or there is no organization to speak of. For the vast majority of members of Congress, then, the local party is no more relevant than to this member.

> The party is no damn good. . . . They can't organize and they can't raise money. . . . I don't have anything to do with the party organization. . . . They have their function. They give you a vehicle to run on.[17]

Since national party organizations cannot affect nominations and local ones are largely weak, uninterested, or both, there is only one solution for individual members: they must develop their own organizational support. Most candidates do not inherit their campaign workers, contributors, and precinct workers from the local party. Instead, they recruit their own. The most common type of campaign organization is centered on the individual candidate. He (or she) is the focus. It is *his* organization, *his* supporters, *his* contributors. Contributors like to give to an individual candidate rather than to the party as a whole. By doing so, they get credit directly with the beneficiary rather than diluting the obligation through the party as intermediary. In short, the nominating process does not lend itself to being a source of organized discipline over the representative. Once in office, this danger is fairly slight. The gravest threats to renomination are advanced age, population change, or an incumbent's failure to cultivate the district.

---

[16] Charles L. Clapp, *The Congressman: His Work as He Sees It* (Washington: The Brookings Institution, 1963), p. 344; and John W. Kingdon, *Congressmen's Voting Decisions* (New York: Harper & Row, 1973), p. 34.

[17] Quoted in Fenno, *Home Style*, p. 176.

Popular Accountability   Elections play a crucial role in democratic theory. Not only are they the method of choosing leaders, but they also provide the threat of defeat in the next election, which supposedly keeps leaders responsive to the public. At least this is the theory. But if incumbents are seldom defeated and if most elections are not even close, how can members of Congress be considered answerable to their constituents?

Although the odds favor incumbents, there still are upsets—and even occasional disasters, like 1964 and 1974 for Republicans and 1966 for Democrats. Furthermore, although narrow electoral margins may be the exception rather than the rule, the number of close races adds up to a fairly impressive total in the long run. In 1974, over half the members of the House and 70 percent of the Senate had won by less than 55 percent at least once in the course of their careers. Over three-fourths of the House and 86 percent of the Senate had gone below 60 percent on occasion.[18] Close calls remind members that the law of averages is cold comfort to someone who lost when the odds were in his favor. Although the *chances* of defeat may be slight, the *consequences* of defeat are enormous.

A member whose share of the vote is smaller than expected will worry that this may be a sign of vulnerability to potential rivals and to interest groups that have been resenting his positions quietly. One congressman described his situation this way:

> People can be mad at you, but if they don't see a chance of beating you, they will keep it inside. If I looked vulnerable, the right-to-life people would be on me like a hen on a June bug. And the gun control people, too.
>
> It's important for me to show strength to keep the young state representatives and city councilmen away. If they have the feeling that I'm invincible, they won't try [to run against me].[19]

In any state or district, there are few issues where a vote on the "wrong" side will get a member in serious trouble with the voters. Sometimes a vote either way will be infuriating to an intense minority—the abortion issue is a good example. With rare exceptions, a "wrong" vote will not be damaging unless it becomes an election issue. And herein lies the dilemma, as expressed by another member of the House: "You know your opponent will pick on one vote or two, but you don't know which one it will be."[20] For all these reasons, prudence and human nature lead representatives to run scared and thus to be "unrealistically" sensitive to constituent opinion. Richard Fenno, who traveled with eighteen House members in their districts, reports that they

> . . . see electoral uncertainty where outsiders would fail to unearth a single objective indicator of it. No matter how secure their electoral circumstances may seem, therefore, members of Congress can always find reasons to feel insecure.

[18] Mayhew, *Congress: The Electoral Connection*, p. 33.
[19] Quoted in Fenno, *Home Style*, p. 13.
[20] Quoted in Fenno, *Home Style*, pp. 142–43.

. . . House members will continue to be a lot more uncertain than the statistics of their last election would warrant.[21]

Members of Congress can be sure that some constituents may be more attentive to what they are doing in Washington: campaign activists, interest group leaders, journalists, local public officials, and other people whose political capacity goes beyond their own votes. Knowledge of politics is one factor in identifying the people to whom each member is responsive. Importance to the member is another factor. Representatives are particularly sensitive to the views of those people whose support is most significant to them. As we have already seen (Chapters 8 and 9), however, political support often has nothing to do with issues. The reasons constituents offer for liking (or disliking) their representatives are mostly concerned with personal qualities. They are admired for working hard, being available, seeming to care about their constituents, and so on. The same is often true of campaign contributors. Thus members' constituent relations are shaped more in their districts than on the floor of Congress.

We can summarize the important influences on congressional candidate selection as follows:

The nomination process is determined locally. Individual campaigns usually are financed and organized locally, although money from outside is sometimes available. The outcome of the general election is determined by the local division of party identification, modified on the one hand by skill at exploiting the advantages of incumbency and on the other by the prevailing tides of national party fortunes.

Representatives are seldom obligated to national or even local party organizations for nomination and election. The principal limits on them are predominant

[21] Fenno, *Home Style*, pp. 10–11, 14.

"Well, it's a new approach."

sentiment in their constituencies, modified by the individual coalitions they have built to gain nomination and election. As one political scientist wrote, "The constituency has a virtually unqualified power to hire and fire. If the member pleases it, no party leader can fatally hurt him; if he does not, no national party organ can save him."[22] Although members of Congress cannot ignore the sentiments of their constituents, constituency opinion is often confined to vigilant activists and interest groups. On most issues, members are *not* constrained by public opinion.

WHO IS ELECTED TO CONGRESS?

The demographic characteristics of representatives are far different from those of the population as a whole. Half of all members of Congress in 1979 were lawyers, 29 percent were businesspeople, and 12 percent were educators. Hardly any were in the working class, although many had held blue-collar jobs at earlier points in their careers. Most members are college graduates. They are also far wealthier than the average citizen. Sixteen women were elected to the House in 1978, and one to the Senate. There were 16 black representatives, and about a dozen Spanish-heritage and Asian-American members. The average age of senators was 53 and of representatives, 49. (In 1978 the average citizen of voting age was 41.) Thus, the age difference between the electorate and Congress is not enormous.[23]

It is easy to describe these obvious personal characteristics, but difficult to figure out what difference they make. As was true about convention delegates, the behavior of legislators does not seem to be related to race, age, sex, or income. For example, the voting records of the sixteen black representatives (all Democrats) are no different from those of all northern Democratic representatives. All ten members to whom the National Women's Political Caucus gave perfect voting scores in 1977 were men.[24] A senator need not be a woman or a black or a worker in order to understand the views and interests of women, blacks, or workers. It is no more necessary for a representative to resemble his constituents than it is necessary for a lawyer to have the same education, race, and sex as his clients in order to look after their interests effectively. The most important forces for effective advocacy are not parallel demographic categories but the desire of politicians to be reelected and their own sense of obligation to serve their constituents.

Whatever their "civilian" backgrounds, most representatives are dedicated to just one occupation. They are professional politicians. Few are elected without significant political experience at the state and local level, most commonly as state legislators or some kind of district attorney. Nearly half the members of the Senate have served either in the House or as governor of their states. Fifty members of Congress in 1979 had worked previously on Capitol Hill as aides to a member or a committee.

[22] Ralph K. Huitt, "Democratic Party Leadership in the Senate," in Ralph K. Huitt and Robert L. Peabody, *Congress: Two Decades of Analysis* (New York: Harper & Row, 1969), p. 140.

[23] Information on the characteristics of members of Congress is from *Congressional Quarterly Weekly Report,* January 27, 1979.

[24] Charles P. Henry, "Legitimizing Race in Congressional Politics," *American Politics Quarterly,* 5 (April 1977), p. 156; and *National Journal,* May 20, 1978, p. 818.

Incumbents' ability to be reelected makes for an experienced Congress. The main causes of membership turnover are not electoral defeat, but voluntary departure. Some representatives give up their seats for a run at the Senate or another post. Others quit because of age — and some elderly members keep going until they die. A few quit in anticipation of electoral defeat or because they do not feel up to the exertion required to avoid it. In the past decade, however, voluntary departures from the House have increased in every election year. In 1978, 31 representatives retired who did not run for another office. Some of these were old men who had come to the House as long ago as 1935; but 15 of the 31 retirees were under the age of 60. More and more members of Congress are finding the job unsatisfying. Partly this is because of the growing workload — far beyond what would be required in any other job. Many members feel they are so pressured to attend to the problems of constituents that they cannot concentrate on legislative solutions to serious national issues. Like politicians everywhere, some think that public concern for officials' morality subjects them to abusive criticism and unreasonable prying into their private lives. This increase in turnover means a great many members are relatively new to Capitol Hill. In 1979, over half the House and 48 percent of the Senate were first elected in 1974 or later. This influx of newcomers is a major cause of the waves of reform that swept Congress in the early and middle 1970s.

What Do They Want? In trying to explain the behavior of members of Congress, the future is more important than the past. The question, then, is not what they have done, but what they want, what they hope to get out of politics, what aspirations they have for their future careers. Many representatives want to be elected to the Senate and a few hope to be governor of their state. Whatever their other ambitions, most members want to succeed in the House, to become powerful and influential in that body, to leave their mark on legislation, and to earn the respect and prestige that come with recognition by their colleagues. There are many ways to attain this goal of power and recognition in the House. Senators who are not content can look to only one higher office — the presidency. The Senate has become the biggest single source of presidential candidates. Fully 10 percent of all the men and women who served in the Senate from 1936 through 1972 received appreciable popular support for a presidential nomination in the Gallup Polls.[25] Usually at least a dozen senators actively entertain thoughts of moving to the White House. Their behavior in the Senate is directed in part to this goal, principally by seeking publicity and identification with popular issues.

One may be fairly confident that almost all members of Congress have one ambition in common. They want to be reelected. Here again, there are several roads to success, but the constancy of this desire and the possibility of defeat serve as a fixed point of reference from which one can safely interpret their behavior.

If the future is more important than the past, and there are many ways by which future ambitions can be realized, we should turn to the context of these am-

---

[25] Donald R. Matthews, "Presidential Nominations: Process and Outcomes," in James David Barber, ed., *Choosing the President* (Englewood Cliffs, N.J.: Prentice-Hall, 1974), p. 45.

bitions. First, we will examine working conditions and resources on Capitol Hill. Then we will turn to the structures and procedures Congress has evolved to solve the problem of coherence and organization.

WORKING CONDITIONS

The grounds of the Capitol cover 155 acres on a low hill overlooking the Potomac River, northern Virginia, and the Washington Monument. A mile to the west, down Pennsylvania Avenue, lies the White House. In between, along Pennsylvania and Constitution Avenues, are the massive office buildings housing most of the principal executive departments. This is "downtown" — the common Capitol Hill expression for the executive branch.

The Capitol sits on the brow of the hill. Behind it, to the east, are the Supreme Court and the Library of Congress. On the south flank of the Capitol are the three huge House Office Buildings, each taking up a solid block. To the north are the two Senate Office Buildings, and the construction site of a third. Linking these six buildings is a maze of tunnels that house the innumerable service facilities required to keep this city-within-a-city operating.

The Capitol is jammed with statuary, portraits, and heroic canvases depicting stirring moments in American history. A popular tourist attraction, it draws as many as 25,000 visitors a day. Few tourists venture into the fascinating underground life of the Capitol, with its subway trains, tunnels, and offices. The Capitol complex includes a dozen restaurants and cafeterias, at least four barber shops, a beauty parlor, radio and television studios, several banks and credit unions, a travel agency, several post offices, a picture framing shop, and a facility where a man called "Father Time" repairs the Capitol's several thousand clocks. Many first-aid rooms, an

Capitol Hill

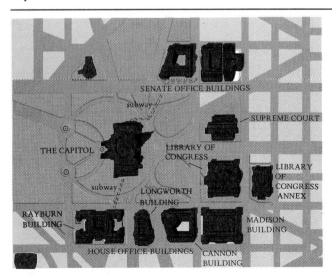

around-the-clock doctor, as well as x-ray, laboratory, pharmacy, and electrocardiographic services are available on the Hill. For members' more routine health needs there are two swimming pools, two gymnasiums, and an indoor paddle tennis court.

In addition to the separate chambers of the House and Senate, commonly referred to as *the floor*, the Capitol contains the offices of the leaders of both parties in both bodies, their staffs, a few committee rooms, and several dozen "hideaways" — rooms where senior members get away from workaday pressures. In the office buildings, each senator has a suite of five rooms and each representative, three. Staffs have doubled in the 1970s, with no compensating increase in space. Staff offices are very crowded, and the overflow is accommodated in nearby buildings.

Members of Congress spare few expenses in giving themselves a comfortable working environment. The total cost of running the legislative branch was $1.12 billion in the 1979 fiscal year. The current major construction project, the Hart Senate Office Building, will cost at least $142 million. If Congress lacks certain things, it is not because its members are unwilling to provide the money for themselves. The one exception is their salaries: Representatives and senators alike get $57,500 a year. This is a modest amount compared either to the responsibilities or to pay in business and the professions. Few members take a raise if they go to Congress from private employment, or a pay cut if they go the other way. Congressional salaries are a lightning rod for public resentment of government and are very difficult to increase. The cost of living rose almost 50 percent between significant pay raises, yet the current level, set in 1977, brought tremendous controversy, both across the country and in Congress. For a time the law provided for pay to be set by an impartial commission and to reflect rises in the cost of living. The idea was to get raises without publicly voting for them. But public hostility is so great that these devices do not insulate congressional salaries from politics. Whether out of politics or conviction, some members carry on about raising congressional pay "secretly." Thus, Congress voted in 1978 to forego a scheduled cost-of-living pay hike and is likely to continue doing so for a few years at least. Fringe benefits are more generous and extensive than the salary levels suggest and are comparable to those of big business executives.

Members of Congress work harder than people in almost any other occupation. While in Washington, representatives work about 60 hours a week. The average member of the House makes thirty-five round trips annually between Washington and his constituency and spends about a third of his time there. Most leave their families in Washington and stay with friends or rent rooms when they are in their districts.[26] Specific figures are unavailable for senators, but from all indications most of them work just as hard.

[26] Fenno, *Home Style*, pp. 39, 222. In 1978 representatives could make 33 trips to their constituencies at government expense, while senators were authorized 40 to 44 trips annually. Information on workloads, staff assignments, and similar topics is taken from the studies of the House Commission on Administrative Review, commonly called the "Obey Commission" after its chairman, Representative David Obey (D. – Wis.).

Perquisites of Office   Representatives can hire as many as eighteen assistants to help them in Washington and in their districts. They get $273,132 a year for this purpose. The average representative has a personal staff of sixteen, of whom about 60 percent work in Washington. Usually there will be three or four "professional" staff in Washington. The remainder are secretaries and "caseworkers" who handle constituents' problems with the government.

Senators get between $580,000 and $1,021,000 for staff, depending on the size of their state, and can hire as many people as they like with the money.[27] A senator's personal staff typically will have 6 to 12 professionals. One will be a press secretary, two or three will be experts on state and national politics, and the rest specialists on subject matter of particular concern to the senator. Many members in both houses also draw on the services of committee and subcommittee staff. Because often no real distinction is made between committee and personal staff, a senior senator can have as many as eighty aides.

Answering mail is the biggest single task in most members' offices; more than 100 million pieces of mail come to the House every year, and over 40 million to the Senate. Each California senator gets over 10,000 letters a week. Handling this flood takes over half the budget and the services of thirty people in each office.[28] Routine answers are produced by "robotypes" — machines that can turn out individually typed letters (minus the name and address) every 25 seconds, to be signed by another gadget called an "autopen."

The franking privilege allows members to send mail free and accounts for over 300 million pieces annually. Congress pays for each member to produce six newsletters a year to be sent to every "postal patron" in his or her constituency.[29] Members also have a variety of free government publications that are prized by many people. For example, each member can send free 3000 copies of the Department of Health, Education and Welfare's popular book, *Infant Care*. All in all, one million copies of this perennial favorite were mailed by members in 1976, along with 233,450 copies of *Gardening for Food and Fun* (392 pages), and 198,000 wall calendars.[30]

The list of free or subsidized goods and services available to members is almost endless. The congressional party offices will print, fold, and insert in envelopes a variety of newsletters, questionnaires, and similar items. Another office on Capitol Hill maintains computerized mailing lists for each member. Both parties also provide media consultants of all kinds to advise or provide brochures, billboards, slides, movies, television tapes, and so on. Congressional television and radio studios produce tapes at a fraction of their commercial cost.

---

[27] The figures for House and Senate staff-hire allowances doubtless will rise at least as fast as the cost of living. Senators may each receive as much as $143,100 more to hire aides to help with committee work.

[28] *The Washington Post*, January 29, 1978, p. A15.

[29] No franked mass mailings may be sent within 60 days of an election in which the member is a candidate.

[30] *The Washington Post*, December 23, 1977, p. A4.

Congress of the United States
House of Representatives

RONALD V. DELLUMS
8TH DISTRICT, CALIFORNIA

DISTRICT OF COLUMBIA COMMITTEE

CHAIRMAN, SUBCOMMITTEE ON FISCAL
AND GOVERNMENT AFFAIRS

ARMED SERVICES COMMITTEE

WASHINGTON OFFICE:
1417 LONGWORTH BUILDING
WASHINGTON, D.C. 20515
(202) 225-2661

DISTRICT OFFICES:
201 13TH STREET, ROOM 105
OAKLAND, CALIFORNIA 94604
(415) 763-0370

3557 MT. DIABLO BOULEVARD
LAFAYETTE, CALIFORNIA 94549
(415) 283-8125

2490 CHANNING WAY, ROOM 202
BERKELEY, CALIFORNIA 94704
(415) 548-7767

DONALD R. HOPKINS
DISTRICT ADMINISTRATOR

Dear Friends:

We all know how difficult rising food prices and other living expenses have made it for Bay Area residents to make ends meet. None of us can afford to take for granted the price and quality of the products we buy.

The Federal government has prepared a wide variety of pamphlets which provide factual information on numerous products, services and other matters of concern to consumers. I am happy to pass along to you this list of selected consumer publications that can help you get your money's worth when you shop.

Some of these publications are free, but there is a small charge for others. The prices are noted after each listing. Please use the order blank provided and send your order to:

CONSUMER INFORMATION CENTER
PUEBLO, COLORADO 81009

Do not send your order to my office, as this will only delay the processing of your order.

I hope you will find these publications useful.

Sincerely,

Ronald V. Dellums
Member of Congress

Social Life   National politicians are sometimes accused of losing touch with
            "the real America" as a result of living too long in the special
environment of Washington, a town whose one industry is politics. Capital society
does indeed run at a hectic pace. Most foreign embassies (there are around 130)
give two formal banquets a year, to which most or all members of Congress are invited. Innumerable organizations, ranging from trade associations to reform groups,
provide an unending round of cocktail parties and dinners. (If politics is Washington's leading industry, catering must be a close second.) As a result, members are
thoroughly immunized against the pettier forms of social influence. A lobbyist has
little hope of buying a senator with a free dinner when the senator has more dinner
invitations than he wants. Indeed, when a politician goes to the lobbyist's dinner, he
is doing the lobbyist a favor, not vice versa.

For much the same reason, no one need worry that congressmen can be
won over by women procured for them by vested interests. Although it was a
member of the executive branch who observed that "power is the ultimate aphro-
disiac," congressmen come to the same conclusion from the profusion of what
might be called Capitol Hill groupies. Barbara Howar, who speaks with authority in
such matters, has observed, "Political power, like wealth, gives an otherwise ordinary man the sexual attractiveness generally reserved for movie stars, athletes, and

Even when taking a postelection vacation in Florida,
Senator Edward Kennedy keeps himself in the public eye.
Here he is shown with Bee-Gees Barry (L) and Maurice (R) Gibb
while visiting their recording studio.

Wide World

playboys. . . . Power is the magic that turns tiny, portly, egocentric, albeit person-able, men into dashing, mysterious sex symbols.[31]

The line between social life for pleasure and for business is extraordinarily hard to draw in Washington. Most important politicians seem to work almost all the time, even when engaged in social activities. For this reason, determination and physical stamina are among the most important qualifications for a successful political career. The demands placed on a prominent congressman are well illustrated in the following comments on Massachusetts Senator Edward Kennedy:

> Successful modern politicians, for better or worse, have a special kind of intelligence — like an oil slick, broad, restless, and only deep enough to make sure everything is covered. . . . [Kennedy] is no scholar, and he is neither reflective nor imaginative — he has people to do all that for him — but on any day he can absorb two twenty-pound briefcases of memos and background papers, take a couple of dozen verbal briefings ranging from 30 seconds to an hour, handle a dozen confrontation situations with senators, reporters, or bureaucrats trying to trap him, juggle the egos of 50 staff members and ex-officio advisers, interrogate the presidents of four drug companies and their counsel about their business, debate . . . about handgun production in the South, read the newspapers, remember 500 faces and names, and be witty at dinner. You try it.[32]

Congressional Ethics Politics is a profession with many opportunities for unethical behavior, perplexing moral ambiguities, and chronic public mistrust. It is often difficult to draw a line between innocent and corrupt behavior. Many relationships are blameless or tawdry depending on the motivations of the participants. On the other hand, there are a few examples of outright corruption in congress.

Some states seem to have more than their share of dishonest legislators. Maryland had three in the early 1970s: a former senator convicted of accepting an "illegal gratuity"; a former representative jailed for his part in a savings and loan scandal; and an incumbent representative who committed suicide after testimony that he failed to report a $25,000 cash contribution. A former New Jersey congressman was jailed in 1973 for tax evasion. Two New Yorkers were convicted of bribery in 1974. At about the same time, a Texan went to jail for taking a $25,000 bribe to block an investigation of a home improvement firm. None of these cases involved major policy issues. They concerned such mundane issues as a Capitol garage, a clause in a bill regulating mail order houses, and similar particular measures of concern to a single person or firm. All told, twelve congressmen were indicted and five convicted of various crimes from 1976 through 1978.[33]

In addition to these cases, there were assorted examples of behavior that fell short of being criminal but was nevertheless highly unethical, and often broke con-

---

[31] Barbara Howar, *Laughing All the Way* (Greenwich, Conn.: Fawcett Publications, 1973), pp. 99, 231.

[32] Richard Reeves, "Teddy or Not," *New York,* April 22, 1974, p. 43.

[33] *CQ Weekly Report,* September 9, 1978, p. 2438.

gressional rules. With some exceptions, Congress as an institution was rather easy-going about these. So were the voters, again with some exceptions. Watergate changed public opinion about public morality and launched a wave of political reform across the country. Reform on Capitol Hill was given a boost in 1976 by a scandal involving Wayne Hays, chairman of the House Administration Committee. His mistress, Elizabeth Ray, served on his committee staff, despite her subsequent confession that "I can't type, I can't file, I can't even answer the phone." The Hays-Ray case spotlighted what many observers considered the heart of the ethics problem on Capitol Hill: not lawbreaking, but moral laxity. Worried about the post-Watergate mood in the coming election, House Democratic leaders pressured Hays to resign his chairmanship. Faced with investigations by the House Ethics Committee and the Department of Justice, he gave up his seat later in the summer.

By 1977, the House and Senate had both adopted new, far stronger codes of ethics. They required disclosure of most aspects of each member's financial life—sources and amounts of income, property, liabilities, and so on. Second, they prohibited or limited a variety of actions that are morally ambiguous or easy to abuse, such as "office accounts" (slush funds for surplus campaign contributions), and converting unused official allowances into cash for the member's pocket. Each body's ethics committee was charged with overseeing its members' conduct. It is too early to judge the full impact of these developments. A few members probably retired out of resentment at the invasions of their privacy. The first financial disclosures provided some interesting fallout: evidence that two senators had falsified their financial worth in recent divorce proceedings. This news contributed to the defeat of the senator who was up for reelection in 1978, Edward Brooke (R.–Mass.). One thing that is clear is the reluctance of the ethics committees to pass judgment on their colleagues. Evidently they will do so only when pressed either from inside or outside Congress. Still, the various prohibitions do eliminate much potentially questionable behavior, while the financial disclosure directs a strong publicity spotlight that may reduce temptations.[34]

Outside Income.   In 1977, twenty-four senators each earned at least $20,000 in fees for speeches and magazine articles.[35] Most of this money was speaking fees, which can easily be $2000 for a celebrity. Nevertheless, some of these transactions are disturbing. Senator Donald Riegle (D.–Mich.), a member of the Banking, Housing and Urban Affairs Committee, received $4000 for two

---

[34] The voters returned two of the three California Democrats who were reprimanded by the House Ethics Committee for failing to report gifts or campaign contributions from Tongsun Park, the prime figure in the Koreagate scandal. A fourth California Democrat, retired from the House, served a prison term for a greater degree of culpability in Koreagate, and a retired Democrat from Louisiana was acquitted in 1979. This may be all the American casualties of Koreagate. The long House investigation was hampered by Park's limited testimony and the complete unavailability of the former South Korean ambassador, who allegedly bribed a number of members. The known facts about Koreagate disappointed those people who were expecting a really sensational, widespread scandal that would rival Watergate in its political impact.

[35] Information about members' incomes and investments is from the first disclosure statements required by the new ethics codes, summarized in *CQ Weekly Report*, September 2, 1978, pp. 2311–66.

speeches in four months to the American Bankers Association. Sometimes "speeches" are more like cozy after-dinner talks to a few executives or union leaders. Some members of Congress retain an interest in law firms, insurance agencies, and other businesses from which they draw salaries or fees. Some of these concerns may have attracted clients because of their congressional connections.

Outside earned income raises eyebrows for two reasons. First, because it seems in conflict with the notion that members are full-time legislators. And second, a few of the relationships have not been above suspicion. The new ethics codes prohibited members from earning more than 15 percent of their salary ($8,625) in outside income. There was no limit on unearned income — that is, return from investments. The outside income limit took effect in 1979, but early in the year the Senate voted to delay this provision until 1983. Thus, the limit changed back to $25,000 for senators, but remained at $8,625 for representatives.

Conflicts of Interest.   Most successful professional and business people have investments, and members of Congress are no exception. So most members have an economic stake in a great many decisions made by Congress. It is difficult to see how this could be avoided, nor it is really the issue. The concern about conflicts of interest is the extent to which members use their power to advance their own economic ends. For example, a representative who owns Coca-Cola stock introduced legislation to delay the Food and Drug Administration's proposed prohibition of saccharin in soft drinks. But so did a number of members without Coca-Cola stock.

A better approach is to examine the relationships between members' investments and the committees on which they serve. Six members of the House Banking, Finance and Urban Affairs Committee own stock in banks and other financial institutions, but so do 102 representatives who are not on the committee. Thirty-one senators own oil or gas stock, including four (of eighteen) members of the Energy and Natural Resources Committee. We find similar patterns on other committees; there is no tendency for assignments to reflect investments.

Senator Russell Long is a millionaire from oil and gas holdings in his native Louisiana, the chairman of the Finance Committee, and a staunch defender of oil and gas interests. He explained himself this way: "If I didn't represent the oil and gas industry, I wouldn't represent the state of Louisiana."[36] One of Long's strongest opponents on these issues is Senator Kennedy, who himself has close to a million dollars in oil and gas investments. For every example of a member voting for personal financial interest, there is a counterexample of another member voting against. Students of Congress have been unable to find systematic relationships between members' investments and their behavior on Capitol Hill. The cynical explanation for this honesty is that they have political interests as well as economic ones. Not to be ignored is the possibility that Congress has about as many dishonest people as any other organization — but they operate in a much more public arena than anyone else.

[36] Quoted in *Newsweek*, June 14, 1976, p. 32.

THE COMMITTEE SYSTEM

The House consists of 435 highly diverse people; the Senate, of 100. Most of them are intelligent, ambitious, energetic, self-confident, strong-willed, and politically experienced. They represent diverse constituencies. Each is affected by various political, economic, and social interests. Although one interest or another, from dairy farming to rifle shooting, may touch many members, few are important to all. The United States Congress does not have distinct groups of communist, socialist, or Catholic members whose ideological and party identifications produce close-knit blocs of the kind found in many European legislatures. No one member, or even a majority of all members, can do much to help or hinder the electoral future of any other.

In short, organization and discipline for Congress do not emerge from the kinds of people who are elected, the process that elects them, the party structure, the ideological climate, or the character of interest group representation in Congress. Quite the contrary. The diversity of constituencies and personal ambitions, the absence of polarizing ideologies, and the weakness of the national political parties produce a lack of "natural" outside forces from which congressional organization could be devised. And yet Congress has a staggering workload:

1. Enacting new laws and amending existing ones to govern a complex and interdependent society of 220 million people: Over 15,000 bills were introduced in Congress in 1977.

2. Appropriating money to operate the federal government and, through the numerous grant-in-aid programs, much of state and local government. The annual federal budget exceeds $500 billion.

3. Overseeing how the laws are administered by almost 3 million federal employees.

4. Confirming presidential appointees to the courts and high executive posts.

The basic challenge to Congress, then, is how to organize its membership in order to get things done. One major response to the challenge is specialization. Each house is divided into standing committees according to subject matter. Each committee has a fairly stable membership and a fixed jurisdiction, such as taxes, agriculture, defense, or education. When a bill is introduced, it is referred to the relevant committee, which considers it, probably amends it, and reports on it to the entire membership (or fails to do so, thus killing the bill). The committees are the places where most of the work of Congress is done.

There are twenty-one standing legislative committees in the House and fifteen in the Senate.[37] Each representative serves on one or two of these, each senator on

[37] A standing committee has an indefinite life, generally assumed to be unlimited. Legislative committees report legislation as well as investigating problems and overseeing the executive branch. Each house also has several "select committees" with specific jurisdictions that generally do not report legislation. Occasionally a select or "special committee" is established to study and report on a particular problem. Such groups have a fixed life span and may or may not develop legislation. The committees on Watergate and on the assassinations of President Kennedy and Martin Luther King are examples. In addition, each party in each house has several committees concerned exclusively with party matters.

two or three. Once assigned to a committee, a member remains until he or she voluntarily moves to another committee or leaves office. The ratio of Democrats and Republicans on each committee is roughly proportionate to the ratio in the parent body as a whole. Three committees in the House — Appropriations, Rules, and Ways and Means — are *exclusive* committees; a member of one of them may not belong to any other committee, except the Budget Committee. Another group of House committees is *semi-exclusive;* no one may belong to more than one of them. Representatives may belong to two of the remaining committees. Senators are limited to membership on two "major" committees and one "minor" committee.

It is essential to understand the simple but often overlooked fact that committees differ in several important respects:[38]

1. Some, such as the Committees on Merchant Marine and Fisheries or Post Office and Civil Service, deal with relatively narrow areas. These committees are of little concern to most members. Other committees deal with matters that affect the political interests of all members — for example, the Appropriations Committees, the House Ways and Means and Senate Finance Committees (concerned with taxes, social security, foreign trade), the Public Works Committees.

2. Some committees have more prestige than others. The easiest way to discover a committee's appeal is to examine the ratio of voluntary departures to transfers. In the House, the three exclusive committees are clearly the most desirable. In a twenty-year period, no one left any of them, except to switch to another one of the three. On the other hand, the Post Office and Civil Service Committee had fifty-seven departures and only five voluntary transfers to it. Less than a third of the Democrats assigned to this committee served there more than one term.[39] Although Senate committees also vary considerably in prestige, the issue is less important for individual senators, each of whom serves on several committees.

3. The least prestigious committees nevertheless are much more important to some members than to others. The stepchild Committee on Post Office and Civil Service is attractive to members whose constituents include many government employees or companies that make heavy use of the mails. The members who remain on the Interior Committee are likely to be from western states where public lands, national parks, Indians, mining, and irrigation are major issues.

4. Because some committees affect all members and others touch the interests of only some, the first type tends to be representative of the membership of the body as a whole with respect to region and ideology. These committees usually enjoy a much higher level of trust than groups like the Agriculture Com-

---

[38] Although we differ in some respects, our discussion of variations among committees relies heavily on Richard F. Fenno's brilliant *Congressmen in Committees* (Boston: Little, Brown, 1973).

[39] Charles S. Bullock, III, "Committee Transfers in the United States House of Representatives," *Journal of Politics,* 35 (February 1973), pp. 85 – 120.

mittees, which are composed largely of legislators from farm areas, or the House Education and Labor Committee, whose members tend to be prolabor ideologues (if they are Democrats) or promanagement ideologues (if they are Republicans).

5. In some committees, decisions are made in subcommittee and the full committee meets only to ratify what its subcommittees have worked out. The Appropriations Committees can fulfill their mission of scrutinizing and adjusting the federal budget only by dividing into thirteen subcommittees, each of which specializes in a particular part of the government. The detailed budgets approved by each subcommittee are seldom altered in full committee. Other committees, particularly in the Senate, preserve considerably more responsibility in the full committee. There are over 120 standing subcommittees in the House and 100 in the Senate. There is some flexibility about the number and jurisdictions of subcommittees, particularly in the Senate. For example, the Senate Finance Committee has a Subcommittee on Tourism and Sugar, chaired by Spark Matsunaga, a new Democrat from Hawaii.

Committee Assignments   Republicans are assigned to committees by the Republican committee on committees in each chamber, and Democrats by similar bodies. Committee assignments are a separate matter for each party and are among the most important functions and sources of power for the congressional party organizations.

Once elected, the new member's committee assignments are his first concern. By custom, new senators are given at least one desirable committee. Thereafter Republican senators move to "better" committees on the basis of seniority; Democratic senators do so partly by seniority and partly through political maneuvering. Most new representatives get the assignments they request. In later years, some shifting occurs as vacancies open and interests change.[40]

A number of factors influence members' requests for committee assignments. Perhaps the most important is their desire to be where they can do something for their constituents. They want to be on a committee that concentrates on matters of particular interest to their constituents. They also want to serve on committees that handle the broadest central concerns of government— that is, the Appropriations and Ways and Means Committees. Because these committees concern themselves with the whole range of government taxing and spending, they are important to every constituency. Then too, much of what is done in Congress proceeds by exchanges of support between members. A member of any important committee can serve his own particular constituents by offering aid to other members in return for their support of projects for his constituency.[41] Thus a second consideration in

---

[40] Charles S. Bullock, III, "House Committee Assignments," in Leroy Rieselbach, ed., *The Congressional System,* 2d ed. (North Scituate, Mass.: Duxbury, 1978).

[41] Trading a vote on a matter of indifference in return for someone else's vote on a matter to which he or she is indifferent is called **logrolling.** Since most issues are important only to some members, logrolling is an inevitable method of building coalitions for the passage of all but the most important and controversial legislation.

committee assignments is accumulating power in the body as a whole through the ability to do favors for colleagues and build up obligations that can be parlayed into influence.

A third major motive in requesting committee assignment is being in a position to influence public policy. Some committees are attractive because they provide opportunities to play important roles in central areas of government decision-making, like education, regulation of the economy, and social welfare. This opportunity may be desired for its own sake, because helping write laws that deal with major problems is a rewarding experience. It also is valued as a way of getting publicity. The Senate is more open to individual policy initiatives that produce both mass media exposure and legislative results. Members of the more workaday House often grumble that "senators make speeches, we make laws."

The party leaders and committees who make committee assignments look at the subject from much the same point of view as the individual members. Each party wants all its legislators to be reelected and therefore tries to put them on committees that will let them serve their constituents' interests. Since 87 percent of Nevada is owned by the federal government, the single representative from that state is always on the Interior Committee, despite changes in party control of the seat. The "universal" committees, whose work affects every member, are of greatest concern to the party leaders. They want to be sure that the members appointed to these committees are competent, hard working, and reasonable — that is, able to compromise and to recognize the importance of considerations other than their own reelection. Faced with a choice, the nod goes to the member more loyal to his party.

The constituency-oriented committees often are geographically unbalanced. Other House committees are often so geographically balanced that their seats virtually "belong to" state delegations or groups of several states. Thus a new committee member usually will be from the same state or region as the person he replaces and is expected to look after the interests not only of his own constituency but of the entire state.

Until the early 1970s, House committee chairmen made subcommittee assignments. Many tried to accommodate their members' wishes, but some used this power politically. Occasionally a chairman removed from a subcommittee a member who had displeased him. On the Democratic side, this changed in 1973 with the "Subcommittee Bill of Rights," which created in each committee a caucus of its Democratic members. Among other things, this caucus assigns Democrats to subcommittees. Each member is guaranteed one subcommittee of his or her choice, in order of seniority on the full committee. There has not been much of a problem in the Senate, where there are more than enough subcommittees to go around.

House-Senate Differences In both houses, the committees are the place where all but a few members make their contributions to governing the country. They are where most legislative work is done. But the role played by committees in the careers of individual members differs considerably from one body to the other.

We can illustrate these differences by comparing the assignments of Representative Sidney R. Yates (D. – Ill.) and Senator Gaylord Nelson (D. – Wis.). Yates' current House service began in 1965. He chairs the Interior Appropriations Subcommittee and also serves on the Foreign Operations Appropriations Subcommittee. These are his only assignments. He can focus his attention on funding the Interior Department. He has more to say than any other representative about when Interior projects can begin. Senator Nelson, elected in 1962, has these committee assignments.

Finance, and these subcommittees of that committee:
Health
International Trade
Social Security (chairman)

Human Resources, and these subcommittees:
Employment, Poverty, and Migratory Labor (chairman)
Health and Scientific Research
Labor

Select Committee on Small Business (chairman), *and these subcommittees:*
Monopoly and Anticompetitive Activities (chairman)
Financing, Investment, and Taxation

The contrast between Yates and Nelson illustrates the different role of committees in the two bodies. The Senate has less than a fourth as many members as the House but almost as many committees and subcommittees. Legislation usually gets its most meticulous study in the House. Senators often cannot devote the necessary time because there are so many competing claims on their attention. Senators can be specialists — and many of them are — but only by neglecting some committee assignments in favor of concentrating on others.

Because each representative has only two or three subcommittees in which to make a mark on public policy, House committees usually consider legislation more thoroughly. Consequently, the House tends to defer to its committees' decisions more than the Senate does. Each representative expects that *his* committee's work will be respected and therefore is inclined to reciprocate when another committee reports a bill to the floor. Senators, whose committees usually are not so thorough, are more likely to amend legislation on the floor.

Because there are more than two committees and subcommittees for *every* Democratic senator, each of them chairs at least one subcommittee within two years. Nelson, with less seniority than eighteen other Senate Democrats, already headed two subcommittees and one full committee. As a result, he has access to additional staff, can schedule hearings, and can otherwise use these subcommittees to focus public opinion and help advance the chances of legislation he favors. Nearly every Republican senator is ranking minority member on one or more committees and subcommittees, which usually gives him control of the minority committee staff.[42] Although some senators have more important chairmanships

---

[42] The majority party has about 75 percent of all committee staff positions.

than others, power is widely distributed in the Senate. Almost everyone is the dominant senator in some policy area.

Power is more closely concentrated in the House, where scarcely half the Democrats head a committee or subcommittee. Unlike senators, who quickly gain control of *some* bit of jurisdiction, representatives must wait a few years. In 1971, House Democrats decided that no member could chair more than one subcommittee.[43] This important but little noticed reform dispersed power more widely in the House. Because of the shrinking number of senior conservative southern Democrats, it also increased liberal influence.

Many members seek careers as subject matter specialists. Long service on a committee or subcommittee makes them experts on atomic energy, civil aviation, school lunch programs, or whatever. Within their special areas they become highly influential, for their colleagues who know little about the subject defer to the person who does. This type of long-term, quiet expertise is found in both houses but is more typical of the House of Representatives. A different pattern is more evident in the Senate, where committee service can be a springboard to national prominence and even a chance at the presidency. This prominence often comes from use of a subcommittee or select committee to conduct eye-catching investigations of such sensational topics as hunger, crime, drug prices, Watergate, the CIA, and so on. Senators often exploit their committee and subcommittee positions to become national spokesmen for new policy proposals.

Committee Chairmen and the Seniority System   If he wanted to, a chairman once could have dominated almost every aspect of a committee's activity. The entire subcommittee structure was under his thumb. He could create and abolish subcommittees, pick their members, chairmen, and staff, and determine jurisdictions. He could refer bills to one or another subcommittee, or retain them for attention by the full committee. Some chairmen exploited these powers to the hilt; others did not. Technically, most of the chairman's actions were subject to the will of the committee's majority. Occasionally a committee did revolt against a chairman who was incompetent or who grasped too much power too often, but those with even moderate political skill rarely had this kind of trouble. No matter what, the chairman kept his post, which came to him automatically and remained his as long as he wanted it and was reelected. Although these conditions existed in both bodies, they were more severe in the House. The Senate, less hierarchical and more easygoing, offered a piece of the action to every member.

The Subcommittee Bill of Rights, adopted in 1973 as party policy by House Democrats, changed all this. Each committee was to have a minimum number of standing subcommittees with fixed jurisdictions. Most bills had to be referred to them within two weeks. Organizational decisions about the subcommittees would be made by the full committee's Democratic caucus. Their chairmen would be picked this way: The member with the longest continuous service on the full com-

---

[43] Each senator now is limited to three subcommittees on each committee and no senator can chair more than three subcommittees, or two subcommittees and one full committee.

mittee would announce to the Democratic Caucus which subcommittee he or she wanted to head. If ratified by the caucus, that person had the job for two years. If not, the next senior member would bid for it, and so on down the line until all the chairs were filled. Seniority is almost always observed, although there are occasional upsets. Majority staff for each subcommittee would be hired by its chairman and thus be loyal to him or her, not to the full committee chairman as in the past.

Committee chairmen suffered some loss of power from these developments, but they still retain considerable influence. The full committee must approve any proposed legislation from its subcommittees. The chairman hires and fires staff, calls and presides over committee meetings, sets the agenda, represents the committee in negotiations, and usually manages the more important bills on the floor. It is still difficult to pass a proposal that a chairman opposes or to defeat one he favors. But the chairman's freedom to make full use of his remaining powers has been modified by changes in the way the chairman is appointed — the seniority system.

No feature of Congress is more criticized and misunderstood than the **seniority system.** Seniority (length of service) in Congress is useful in many ways, including committee assignments and choice of offices. This is not what all the criticism is about, however. As an object of criticism and reform, the seniority system is the method by which chairmen of full committees are chosen, *and nothing else.* The member of the majority party with the longest continuous service *on a committee* is the chairman of that committee. Although not a formal rule, the seniority system was violated in picking a chairman only once between 1946, when the present committee system was devised, and 1975. It was seldom violated in the previous thirty years.[44]

Before seniority determined committee chairmen, it was the practice for party leaders to choose them. This was tolerable when most members served in Congress for relatively brief periods. But as more people stayed on Capitol Hill, they could not so easily accept having their careers subjected to the whims of a single person. A House vote in 1910 stripped the Speaker of his power to appoint chairmen. This was a victory for progressives over forces that had blocked many popular reforms. And seniority aided long legislative careers by providing a measure of security about the rewards of congressional service. Thus it helped develop a veteran Congress able to hold its own against the executive branch.

Changing Biases of the Seniority System Seniority has several systematic biases. Obviously, chairs go disproportionately to older members. In 1979, the average age of the twenty-one House chairmen was 61. Three were in their seventies, and four were 52 or younger. It is not clear that members in their sixties and seventies are necessarily either better or worse at governing than their younger colleagues. There is some loose talk about the "senility system," but there are really not many real-life examples. Nor is this the source of opposition to seniority.

[44] Nelson W. Polsby et al., "The Growth of the Seniority System in the U.S. House of Representatives," *American Political Science Review,* 63 (September 1969), pp. 787–807.

Wide World

Senator Carl Hayden on his
ninetieth birthday in 1967.
He stands before a portrait
of himself painted shortly before
he was elected to Congress in 1912.
He retired in 1969.

Another built-in bias of the seniority system gets us closer to the real issue. Chairs go to members from safe seats, for they are the ones who are returned to Congress year in and year out. With fewer worries about reelection, they are insulated from the tides of electoral change. Are they better chairmen because they need not worry so much about their own political survival and can concentrate on legislation and think about the national interest? Or are they worse, because they need not pay attention to public opinion for their own reelection?

The seniority system became so controversial because members with safe seats used to come mostly from rural areas and were more conservative than their party's congressional membership as a whole. Although this problem existed in the Republican party, it was far more severe and conspicuous among Democrats for two reasons. In the first place, except for 1947–48 and 1953–54, Democrats have controlled both houses of Congress since 1932. And in the second place, because of the pronounced conservatism of most southern Democratic members, the Democratic party is deeply split along ideological lines. From the late 1930s through 1965, most of the twenty-two senators and one hundred representatives from the South usually voted on the conservative side of controversial domestic issues. They were also unanimously conservative on civil rights. The corresponding split in the Republican party was relatively trivial, since only a handful of members voted for liberal positions with any consistency.

The southern Democrats, then, are the main reason for attacks on the seniority system by liberals. Because of historical Republican weakness in the one-party South, almost all southern members used to be reelected without significant opposition. But most Democrats in the North, where the bulk of the population lives, faced strong Republican competition. If the Democrats controlled Congress, it was because of their victories in the North. Yet the consequence in Congress of a nationwide Democratic victory was that southerners got most of the benefits. Being a majority among the senior Democrats, they headed most of the committees. Democratic presidents were frustrated by conservative opposition from the Democratic heads of the committees through which liberal legislation had to pass.

The conservative bias of the seniority system reflected an era that has passed into history: a time when the conservative South was solidly Democratic and the liberal North had few safe seats. In recent years, Republicans have won a fair number of southern seats. At the same time, the number of safe northern seats has increased sharply, particularly in the House. As American core cities become more working class, they also become safer for Democratic candidates. Growing black and brown urban populations have the same effect. This trend can be seen most clearly in the growing number of minority representatives, almost all of whom consistently win reelection by over 70 percent of the vote. Figure 12.2 shows the southern decline in the House from 1964 to 1979. In the earlier year, southerners comprised 38 percent of all Democratic representatives; by 1979, they had dwindled to

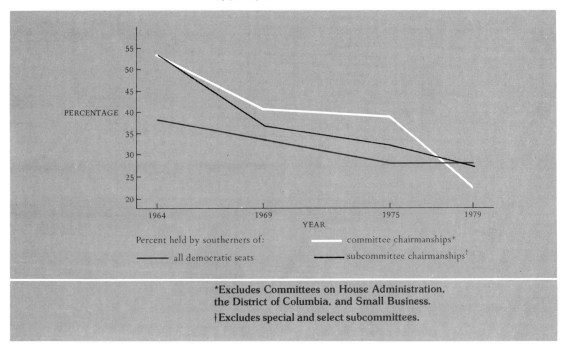

Figure 12.2
Declining Southern Power in the House,
1964–1975

PERCENTAGE

Percent held by southerners of:

committee chairmanships*

all democratic seats   subcommittee chairmanships†

*Excludes Committees on House Administration,
the District of Columbia, and Small Business.
†Excludes special and select subcommittees.

28 percent. Their share of committee chairs fell more dramatically, from 53 percent to 22 percent. The story is the same in the Senate, where only three of the fifteen committee chairmen in 1979 were from the South. In the forseeable future, southern Democrats will be lucky to have a share of committee power proportionate to their numbers. This is forecast in Figure 12.3, which shows the seniority of northern and southern Democratic senators. Nine northerners and three southerners have twenty or more years of seniority. Only two southerners and eleven northerners have ten to nineteen years of service. This second group contains the heirs-apparent to committee power, and some of them are chairmen already. In the House, the tables have turned even more: Southerners are outnumbered more than four to one in the most senior generation.

The Revolt against Seniority   Criticism of the seniority system had little practical consequence on Capitol Hill until the early 1970s. In 1971, House Republicans adopted a crucial modification of the seniority system. The Republican Conference (that is, all Republican representatives) would take an automatic secret vote on the ranking minority member on each committee. The House Democrats did the same two years later for the more important job of picking committee chairmen. (Senate Democrats followed suit in 1977.) In the House, nominations for

Figure 12.3

Seniority among Democratic Senators from the North and South, 1979

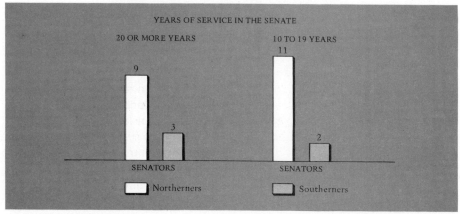

chairmen come from a new party body, the Democratic Steering and Policy Committee, which itself chooses nominees by secret ballot.

At the beginning of 1975, the Democratic Caucus stunned political observers by deposing three veteran chairmen, all from the South, and replacing them with younger northern liberals. This was widely acclaimed as the death knell of the seniority system. A closer look at the three cases suggests that the obituaries are premature.

One of the victims was the eighty-one-year-old Wright Patman, who had served in the House since 1929 and was the most senior member of Congress. Far from being a conservative obstructionist, Patman was an old-fashioned populist praised by Ralph Nader. But he had lost his ability to control his committee, which had been in a state of near-anarchy for years. The other two deposed chairmen stubbornly adhered to right-wing policies that were increasingly unpopular with the growing liberal majority among Democrats. Both were in their mid-seventies; one ran his committee in a highly arbitrary manner, and the other had a furious, abrasive speaking style. The caucus basically followed seniority in replacing the three. The two conservatives were succeeded by the next senior member of their committees without any question or controversy. Patman was replaced by the fourth-ranking Democrat on his committee, but this was only a slight violation of seniority. The next man in line to Patman was a seventy-eight-year-old machine politician widely known to possess only modest talent, energy, and ambition. The third-ranking member was already chairman of another committee. Since 1975, all House committee chairmen have been chosen by seniority. The Senate's experience also suggests that seniority still has a future. In 1977, the closest call for any committee chairman was a favorable vote of 42 to 6 in the Democratic Caucus.

As we have seen, committee seniority is also the usual guide for appointing House subcommittee chairmen, subject to two restrictions: Democratic members of the full committee must ratify each appointment, and no representative may chair more than one subcommittee. (In 1979, there were three cases where committee Democrats failed to appoint the most senior member to a subcommittee chair he wanted.) Moreover, the chairmen of the thirteen powerful and nearly autonomous House Appropriations subcommittees must be confirmed by the House Democratic Caucus. It did not fail to do so in 1975 and 1979, although some of those proposed were far to the right of the party's mainstream. In 1977, one of the more conservative chairmen was deposed by the caucus. There was an additional reason, however; he had been reprimanded by the House Ethics Committee for failing to disclose his financial interest in two concerns doing business with government agencies in his subcommittee's jurisdiction.

Although predictions are always risky, we will try one here. The "revolution" in 1975 did not overturn the seniority system but did apply some controls to it. In the future as in the past, the most senior member of each committee will be its chairman unless he is senile or persistently uses his power to flout the wishes of a strong majority of his party. The threat of being deposed will make chairmen more responsive to majority sentiment.[45] If this happens, reformers will have gotten the substance of their goals without changing the form. This result would be consistent with the merit most members see in the seniority system—its compatibility with and encouragement of long careers on Capitol Hill. Long careers and expertise contribute to the ability of Congress to maintain its independence of the executive branch and its capacity to deal with the president as an equal partner.

Seniority has another virtue that should not be overlooked; it protects mavericks from party discipline by guaranteeing them their slice of power. Black militants and white segregationists alike stand to benefit from a method of choosing chairmen that works without reference to their political opinions. As liberals inherit the fruits of the system, it will be interesting to see if they continue their attacks on it. Perhaps they will. On the other hand, it is useful to remember this observation:

> Representatives and senators start out their congressional careers resenting the seniority system. But after a while, as one of them once told me, "it sort of grows on you."[46]

PARTIES IN CONGRESS

Committees are the framework in which work is done. Parties are the second solution to the problem of congressional organization. They guide the decisions that are made about most issues. In the electorate, parties usually are weak as organizations

---

[45] Some observers fear that the modification of seniority, combined with the new autonomy of the subcommittees, has created a power vacuum in the House. In this view, chairmen may be too anxious about their security in office to impose coordination on their subcommittees, each of which is going its own way. Moreover, weakening the chairmen may have destroyed their ability to negotiate with the Senate and the executive branch. The result could be a House with so many weak power centers that decision is made more difficult. This gloomy forecast does not seem justified by the first years of experience with the new reforms.

[46] Nelson W. Polsby, "Seniority, What Is It?" in *Political Promises* (New York: Oxford University Press, 1974), p. 112.

House Speaker Thomas P. O'Neill (D.–Mass.) talks with Senate Majority Leader Robert C. Byrd (D.–W. Va.).

but strong as frames of reference for individual perceptions of the political world. The same things are true in Congress. Party membership is by far the most important determinant of how members vote; yet the organized parties in Congress have relatively little power to control the behavior of members.

When talking about individual voters, we used the notion of reference groups as a handy way to understand party identification. *Republican* and *Democrat* are important identities for most of the electorate. The same is true of members of Congress. Their constituencies, their committees, their areas of expertise, their personal political organizations, and various other factors may guide their behavior. But by far the most important aspect of their identity is party. With occasional insignificant exceptions, members of Congress are all elected as Democrats or Republicans. Their previous political careers have usually occurred in partisan politics. They have been nominated as the candidate of one party or the other. Together with their party's other nominees, they are the Democratic or Republican ticket. What is good for one of the party's candidates is likely to be good for all of them. Indeed, the extent of many voters' knowledge about them is the party label next to their names.

Many aspects of Congress reflect this fundamental division. In each chamber, the Republicans sit on one side of the center aisle and the Democrats on the other. They have separate cloakrooms and usually enter the floor through different doors.[47] The same segregation occurs on committees; Republicans sit on one side, Democrats on the other. Each party assigns its members to committees, and once there, elevation to a chairmanship depends on being a member of the majority party. Although it would be an exaggeration to say that social life also is organized along party lines, it is true that legislators are likely to find their friends among members of their own party. The same attitudes are mirrored in congressional aides, whose lunchtime companions, professional connections, and off-duty friends usually are in the same party.

Party Organization   Leadership.   Congress has its own party organs and leaders, distinct from the national party organizations and the presidency. Chosen by the party's members in each body, the party leadership reflects the interests and inclinations of the legislators who elected it. (In its special congressional sense, *the leadership* refers to a party's elected leaders in one or the other body (see Table 12.2). Each party's legislative leaders are among its principal national spokesmen.

The Speaker of the House of Representatives is elected by the majority party

---

[47] The cloakrooms are not places to check overcoats, but lounges where members can telephone, nap, hold strategy conferences, negotiate, make last-minute notes, and otherwise conduct business literally a step away from the floor.

Table 12.2

Congressional Party Organization, 1979

DEMOCRATS	REPUBLICANS
HOUSE OF REPRESENTATIVES	
Speaker	Minority Leader
Chairman of the Caucus	Chairman of the Conference*
Majority Leader	Minority Whip
Majority Whip	Regional Whips
Deputy and Assistant Whips	Committee on Committees
Steering and Policy Committee	Policy Committee
Democratic National Congres-	National Republican Congres-
sional Committee	sional Committee
Patronage Committee	
SENATE	
Majority Leader	Minority Leader
Majority Whip	Minority Whip
Chairman of the Conference*	Chairman of the Conference*
Policy Committee	Policy Committee
Steering Committee	Committee on Committees
Senatorial Campaign Committee	Senatorial Campaign Committee
	Personnel Committee

*The conference consists of all members of the respective party.

and in effect is the head of that party in the House. He is more than a party figure, however. He presides over the House and is next in line of presidential succession after the vice-president. The minority party in the House has no counterpart to the Speaker. Otherwise, the leadership organizations of the two parties are similar. Each party has a **floor leader,** a **whip** (or assistant leader), and a number of assistant whips in charge of floor business. The Speaker joins these officers on the majority side and is actually above the majority leader in scheduling legislation, acting as a party spokesman, and representing House Democrats (or Republicans) to the president and the public.

Party organization in the Senate takes a similar form. The vice-president is the Senate's presiding officer (technically, he is the "President of the Senate"). Otherwise he has little independent influence there except to cast the deciding vote in case of a tie and to issue an occasional parliamentary ruling. (In fact, the job of presiding over the Senate usually is done by junior Democratic members unless an important debate or vote brings the vice-president to the chair.) The Senate Democrats put all party organs under the control of their leader, while the Republicans use a system of plural leadership in which each party committee is headed by someone other than the floor leader.

Contrary to popular belief, neither the Speaker nor the other party leaders are chosen by seniority. Speaker Thomas P. O'Neill (Massachusetts) was tied for sixteenth most senior Democrat when his party first picked him in 1977. The Senate leader, Robert C. Byrd (West Virginia) was the twelfth most senior Democrat when he first gained office, also in 1977. The leaders have, of course, been around long enough to become widely known and helpful to their colleagues. The House Democrats, in particular, have a tradition of elevating the Speaker from a lesser party leadership position.

Leaders seldom are committed ideologically to any one wing of their party. Moreover, they recognize, as Byrd put it, that "The responsibilities of leadership require that one represent an over-all, middle-of-the-road philosophy." Their approach to politics is pragmatic. They are more interested in reaching agreement than in defending any position to the bitter end. One aide said of Byrd: "He usually doesn't give a damn about the bill but wants to make sure all people with an interest are represented [in deciding what to do]."[48] Senator Everett Dirksen, the Republican leader for ten years, once remarked: "I am a man of principle, and one of my basic principles is flexibility."[49]

The majority leadership in each house manages legislation after it comes out of committee. Scheduling the workload is an important power in itself because a bill's chances of passage or escaping major alteration are affected by how and when it comes before the entire membership. Much legislation is interesting to only a few members. The leaders can use their knowledge of members' travel schedules to schedule particular bills when concerned members are present—or absent. This control of the schedule is one reason prudent members try to stay on the good side of the leadership. This is not so hard to do as one might think, for the leadership traditionally prides itself on its broad tolerance and willingness to oblige.

Because the leaders handle all the scheduling, they are at the center of the web of information, adjustment, compromise, and negotiation about pending legislation. They must be consulted on every bill and kept informed of its progress. Thus, they have the power of brokers. They know more than their Senate or House colleagues about what is going on, what bargains are possible, and who needs to talk with whom. They can use this knowledge to facilitate members' pet projects. Their power over low-visibility bills gives leaders bargaining "chips" that can be exploited on major issues. Byrd put it this way:

> The Senate is a forest. There are ninety-nine animals. They're all lions. There's a waterhole in the forest. I'm the waterhole. They all have to come to the waterhole. I don't have power but I have knowledge of the rules. I have knowledge of the precedents. I have knowledge of the schedule. So I'm in a position to do things for others.[50]

The leadership also plays a role in committee assignments. The extent of its involvement varies over time and from party to party and house to house. At a minimum, party leaders are useful allies to a member looking for a spot on a desirable committee. The maximum amount of power here is illustrated by the new method

---

[48] These quotes are from *The New York Times,* March 27, 1977, p. 44; and Richard E. Cohen, "Byrd of West Virginia—A New Job, A New Image," *National Journal,* August 20, 1977, p. 1293.

[49] Quoted in Neil MacNeil, *Dirksen* (New York: World, 1970), p. 153.

[50] Quoted in Laurence Leamer, "Changing," *The Washingtonian,* May 1977, p. 127.

WHY THE SPEAKER IS POWERFUL

Speaker O'Neill talks about the sources of his influence:

> You know, you ask me what are my powers and my authority
> around here? The power to recognize on the floor; little odds and
> ends—like men get pride out of the prestige of handling the
> Committee of the Whole, being named the Speaker for the day;
> those little trips that come along—like those trips to China, trips to
> Russia, things of that nature; or other ad hoc committees or special
> committees, which I have assignments to; plus the fact that there is
> a certain aura and respect that goes with the Speaker's office. He
> does have the power to be able to pick up the telephone and call
> people. And Members often times like to bring their local political
> leaders or a couple of mayors. And often times they have problems
> from their area and they need aid and assistance, either
> legislativewise or administrativewise. We're happy to try to open the
> door for them, having been in the town for so many years and
> knowing so many people. We do know where a lot of bodies are and
> we do know how to advise people.
>
> And I have an open door policy. Rare is the occasion when a man
> has a personal fund-raiser or being personally honored that I don't
> show up at it. I've made more public appearances and visited areas
> if they believe I can help them. I'm always accessible. These are
> part of the duties and the obligations of the Speaker, and it shows
> the warm hand of friendship. . . .

In one half-hour period, the Speaker had these visitors to his office:

> • Rep. Harold L. Volkmer (D.–Mo.) stuck his head in the office to find
> out if there would be any votes on the following Friday because some
> constituents wanted him to deliver a speech that day in his district.
> • Rep. James H. Scheuer (D.–N.Y.) paged O'Neill from the House
> floor to have his picture taken with an Orthodox Jewish rabbi from
> Brooklyn. ("This man can make or break me," Scheuer told O'Neill.)
> • David Cohen and Fred Wertheimer of Common Cause stopped by to
> tell O'Neill about a letter they were sending all members backing his
> position on a congressional pay raise amendment to the budget resolu-
> tion.
> • Rep. Edward J. Patten (D.–N.J.) came in to talk about getting more
> money in the budget for World War I veterans.

Sources: Quoted in *National Journal*, June 18, 1977, pp. 942, 941.

of making Democratic appointments to the House Rules Committee. The Speaker makes these himself, to ensure that this crucial committee is responsive to him.

Party Caucuses.   This change was one of several new departures mandated by the House Democratic Caucus. The party caucuses (called "conferences" in the Senate and by House Republicans) have always been the ultimate authorities of the parties in Congress. The extent to which they actually assert themselves, or merely rubber-stamp the seniority system and the committee chairmen, has changed from one historical era to another. For the half-century after World War I, the caucuses were largely passive ratifiers of decisions made elsewhere. But beginning in the early 1970s, the House Democratic Caucus became the most important element in the wave of procedural reforms that swept the House. Almost all the changes in the committee system were its products.

The caucus also plays a limited role in the legislative process. It has exercised its power to permit consideration by the full House of provisions that might otherwise be killed in committee. In contrast to the early days of the century, no party caucus now tries to impose binding instructions on all party members to vote a certain way on pending legislation. The House Democrats, by far the most activist of the four caucuses, recently repealed the old rule that authorized such instructions. The outlook is that, at most, the caucuses will limit themselves to an occasional procedural instruction to all party members. And even this is plausible only in the House, always the more disciplined of the two bodies.

We can summarize the power of the party organizations this way: Although the leaders have a good deal of influence, they do *not* have the power to give orders to other lawmakers. They cannot tell their members how to vote and expect the members to follow orders. It should already be clear why congressional party leaders do not enjoy this sort of power. Party discipline is weak in Congress because it is weak in the nation at large. Party leaders cannot control who will get congressional nominations or even how much campaign help will go to individual candidates for the House and Senate. To be sure, they can provide some marginal assistance by giving members good committee assignments or helping push pet bills. But because they give only marginal aid in keeping their party members in office, and because they cannot keep them out, they exercise only marginal power over them.

Party Programs So far we have pointed out that the leadership uses its influence to encourage members to support the party position. But where does the party position come from? Who originates it? The party leaderships themselves certainly are not the people who develop substantive programs. They are specialists in the politics of getting policies adopted rather than in the policies themselves. Their job is to make majorities, not policy.

The answer is relatively simple with regard to the president's party. The president's position *is* his party's position. Once a piece of the president's program emerges from committee, his party's leadership is concerned with getting it passed. Relations between the president and "his" party leadership are not simple, however. The leaders are both the president's main channels to Congress and Congress' representatives to the White House. This double-facing position puts considerable strain on the legislators involved. They are elected by their colleagues and seldom lose sight of the fact that this is the source of their power. Yet the leaders are also *party* leaders and know that the popular perception of their party is determined largely by the president's popular standing.

Leaders who are too subservient to the wishes of the president will lose credibility with the members who elected them. This will undermine their effectiveness and ultimately cost them their jobs. On the other hand, leaders who are not willing to work for the president by putting pressure on colleagues will find that party unity is crumbling, with disastrous results for the president's—and the party's—programs. The leadership thus has a double job. In the first place, they want to reelect all their members and add to the seats their party already holds. This means getting members in line to ensure the success of the party's program. In the second place, they want to be sure of holding their party together in Congress, and this may mean being careful not to step on too many toes by pressuring members to support party programs they dislike. The president shares both these goals, so there is a sizable community of interest between the two elements.

The strength of the bonds between the president and his party in Congress can be illustrated by examining the behavior of Republican legislators during the last years of the Nixon administration, a period when extraordinary strains were placed on those bonds. Shortly after Nixon's landslide reelection in 1972, the Watergate scandal exploded and the president's popularity dropped to historic lows. Before his resignation in August 1974, Nixon was universally considered a tremendous electoral handicap to his party in the 1974 midterm campaign. In private, few Republican politicians had a good word for Nixon. But in public, the reverse was true. Until the final crisis, relatively few Republican members would criticize their president and *relatively few voted against his legislative positions.* They were particularly reluctant to override his vetoes.

The support given by members to their president's policies is partly a matter of substantive agreement and partly a reflection of the fact that they have a common identity as members of the same party. Normally, a president will not propose legislation unless he thinks he and his party will benefit politically from its passage. Some congressional members of his party may not share the president's political assessment; some may not agree with what he proposes; and some may agree but feel that a proposal is unpopular in their own state or district. There is still a strong presumption, however, that if the president gets what he wants from Congress, it will be good for his party because it is good for him. The president and his party will get the credit and, as an astute congressman remarked some years ago, "Politics is 80 percent getting credit."

The position of the opposition party is somewhat more complicated. If a Democratic president wants a bill passed because it would raise his popularity, then it would seem to follow that Republicans should try to defeat the bill and prevent their opponent from strengthening himself. What is good for the Democrats must be bad for the Republicans, and vice versa. During Democratic administrations, some Republican members of Congress argue that they need not offer legislative programs of their own because, in the words of one Republican leader, "The business of the opposition is to oppose." Other Republicans thought this unwise—bad for the country because it restricts ideas to only one party, and bad for their party because it gives it a negative image. They try to develop "constructive alternatives" to Democratic proposals.

The Republican position on an issue is essentially the stance taken by the

Republicans on the relevant committee. If necessary, the Republican leadership helps them reach agreement. The drawback to this approach is that the Democrats, being in the majority, can take Republican ideas as their own and get the credit. The Republican leader in the House, John J. Rhodes of Arizona, quoted O'Neill as follows: "If you Republicans think you are going to have anything to do with legislation, forget it."[51]

We can summarize our discussion of congressional parties with two generalizations. First, a Democratic (or Republican) president and the congressmen of his party are held together not as parts of a single disciplined organization, but because they share a common identity as Democrats. The voters think of them as Democrats and, for better or worse, they must think of themselves in the same way. Second, the two main modes of congressional organization — parties and committees — have contradictory influences. The committee system *decentralizes* Congress by delegating decision-making to specialized groups, each of which has a vested interest in maintaining its own power. The parties are a *centralizing* impulse that brings national forces to bear on decisions. The House reforms of the 1970s exaggerated these tendencies. The reforms were aimed at obstructive full committee chairmen, often more conservative than the Democratic mainstream. One prong of the attack on them was the freeing and strengthening of subcommittees. Of course, this further decentralized the House. The other attack came in steps to strengthen the party leadership and make the chairmen more accountable to the caucus. These actions created further centralizing powers to counteract the greater fragmentation of the subcommittees. We will examine this tension further in the next chapter, which focuses on the dynamics of the legislative process.

OTHER WAYS TO ORGANIZE

Although parties and committees are the two principal instruments for bringing order and coherence to congressional business, there are other types of organization, usually more evident in the House than the Senate. There are state delegations and ideological groups.

State Delegations   Delegations — all the members of one party from one state — are a response to the impersonal size of the House and the fragmentation that results from the committee system. Committee assignments are strongly affected by delegation influence. Members are much more likely to get the assignments they want with the backing of their delegation. Committee places are often "reserved" for particular states or regional blocs. It is generally understood that each member of a committee on committees acts on behalf of all the colleagues of his or her party and region. Committee assignments are important to the entire delegation, since wide representation on committees extends the delegation's ability to help its members. Covering all committees of interest

---

[51] *National Journal,* October 29, 1977, p. 1688.

to the delegation is more important than putting each member on the committee he individually is interested in, because someone else from the delegation will look after his special interests, just as he is expected to look after the special interests of other constituencies in the state. By representing the interests of all the districts in the state, it is possible to do a better job of looking after one's own district.[52] Thus, a cohesive state delegation helps members extend their influence beyond the jurisdiction of their own committees.

Although delegation cohesiveness clearly is beneficial, some delegations are a good deal less united than others. The New York Democrats, for example, are notoriously divided. Others, like the California or Texas Democrats, get together frequently to trade information and make plans on issues of statewide concern. For example, California has stringent laws on automobile exhaust pollution, and its representatives want to be sure federal exhaust emission rules do not interfere with state law. They refused to vote for a major air pollution measure some years ago until it was amended to protect their state's stricter approach.

Delegations can use their cohesion to enhance their negotiating position. A bloc of twenty votes is a potent bargaining counter. Sometimes a delegation may vote as a bloc on issues of no particular statewide concern in order to build up obligations that can be cashed in later. The Democrats from Chicago are well known for this practice. On other occasions, a delegation may trade its vote for a particular concession. When the Johnson administration's antipoverty legislation was being considered in the House in 1965, the North Carolina Democrats told the White House they would vote for the bill in return for a commitment from Johnson that Adam Yarmolinsky would have no connection with the war on poverty. Because Johnson needed their votes, he agreed to sacrifice Yarmolinsky, a lawyer who had played a prominent part in drafting the legislation and had become *persona non grata* to conservatives because of his liberal views.

Ideological Groups Both parties have liberal and conservative wings, each of which has some degree of organization, ranging from elaborate to casual. The conservative southern Democrats have long had an informal caucus, called by northerners the "Boll Weevils." The liberal Democrats have by far the most ambitious organization, the Democratic Study Group. The DSG was founded in 1959 to provide a counterweight to the deference then given by the party leadership to senior conservative southerners. Originally composed largely of junior members, the DSG now dominates the mainstream of the party, includes more than two-thirds of all House Democrats, and is a combination goad and partner to the speaker and majority leader. It has its own whip system, a staff of twelve, and a nationwide fund-raising campaign to help liberal congressional candidates. Despite its name, the DSG's goals are not to study problems, but to reform congressional procedures, enact progressive legislation, and elect liberal Democrats to the House. DSG staff drafted many of the committee reforms discussed earlier and its leaders

[52] Barbara Deckard Sinclair, "State Party Delegations in the United States House of Representatives—An Analysis of Group Action," *Polity*, 5 (spring 1973), pp. 323–24.

did the politicking that brought these steps to achievement. The DSG also prepares fact sheets on bills. At election time, it provides liberal candidates with campaign material as well as money.

Republican counterparts to the Boll Weevils and DSG were slower to get underway and are less important, perhaps because their party split is not so serious. The biggest is the Republican Study Committee, with eighty-five members and a staff of fourteen. It hopes to duplicate the success of the DSG from the opposite side of the spectrum. Two or three dozen liberal Republicans band together in the Wednesday Group. It has a small staff and issues occasional position papers, sometimes in conjunction with liberal Republican senators.

The seventy-five new Democrats elected in 1974 formed their own caucus immediately after the election to exert collective influence. Encouraged by their success in modifying the seniority system, they formalized this body, hired staff, and continue to exist. (Funds came from one or two prominent liberal benefactors.) What these members had in common was the year of their first election to Congress. This bond was weak compared to their diverse committee assignments, constituencies, and reelection problems. The latter considerations usually dominate individual perspectives, although they have occasionally made their collective weight felt, as in the Koreagate investigation, where they urged a vigorous pursuit of the leads.

Reflecting broader societal tendencies, there are several groups based on sex and ethnicity. The best organized is the Congressional Black Caucus, composed of the sixteen black representatives, all of whom are Democrats.[53] It develops positions and strategies on behalf of policies to help blacks. Its leaders say they follow the familiar slogan: "We have no permanent friends or permanent enemies, only permanent interests." Yet they can hardly escape the fact that they are all Democrats. Finally, there are organizations representing regional or specialized economic interests. Perhaps the most important of these looks after the older, energy-short industrial states of the Northeast and Midwest. All these groups function much like a cross between a state delegation and an external interest group.

SUMMARY The organization of Congress reflects the way its members are nominated and elected. Most influences on these processes are local. Because state and local party organizations usually are weak, Republican and Democratic candidates owe their nominations to their own efforts and alliances, not to a party machine. The main factors in the outcome of the general election are the division of party identification in the district or state, the advantages of incumbency, and the candidates' skill at establishing favorable public images. Congressional election outcomes are also affected by the prevailing tides of national party fortunes—which mostly comes down to the popularity of the president and the two presidential candidates.

---

[53] There is a seventeenth member—the delegate to the House from the District of Columbia. This person has an office, a staff, committee assignments, and access to the floor—but no vote on the floor.

This electoral environment does not impose much structure or discipline on Congress. Once they get to Capitol Hill, members must organize themselves to get things done without being merely a rubber stamp for the executive branch. One major solution to this problem is the committee system, which combines division of labor and delegation of responsibility. Congress maintains its independence as an institution by encouraging specialization. Decisions about all but the most important and controversial measures are made in the relevant committee and subcommittee.

The second major solution to congressional organization is the two-party system. The majority party's leaders in each house are in charge of scheduling the flow of business on the floor. Perhaps more important, a congressman's party often guides the way he thinks about issues, particularly when his constituents do not have a clear opinion. The parties counteract the fragmentation resulting from the committee system and aid the passage of legislation from the committee hearing rooms to the president's desk.

Thus the two main modes of congressional organization—committees and parties—have contradictory influences. The committees decentralize power by delegating decisions to specialized groups, and the parties impose a national perspective on decisions. The third major factor in congressional decision-making is the desire of each member to please his constituents in order to increase his chances of reelection—the first goal of almost all members of Congress.

congress in action

CHAPTER 13

that might destroy thousands of houses. Similar conditions in 1926 had produced a fire that devastated much of Berkeley.

Believing that the trees had to be cleared to avert a catastrophe, local interests began to look for a way to finance the clearance. As Americans often do, they thought of federal money, and to get it, they turned to their representatives in Congress. Ultimately the attempt to draw on the federal treasury failed. Berkeley's representative, Ronald V. Dellums, reported his efforts in a newsletter to his constituents. His description of his attempt to make eucalyptus clearance a federal project is a fascinating short account of the legislative process. It illustrates many of the motivations and relationships we describe in Chapter 12 and this chapter.

In early February, the East Bay Congressional Delegation, Congressmen Jerome Waldie, Pete Stark and I joined with Senator Alan Cranston, Governor Reagan and local officials in asking the Secretary of Agriculture to provide financial assistance to local governments and citizens to meet the fire threat. Projected costs were estimated to be in excess of $50 million.

In late February, the Department of Agriculture told us no money was available. At the same time, representatives of Governor Reagan and local officials met to develop joint local-state plans aimed at substantially reducing the fire danger. These plans emphasized fire suppression, and also included an appeal to President Nixon to declare threatened portions of the East Bay hills a disaster area.

Congressmen Stark and Waldie joined me in contacting the White House and urging action by the President. These appeals brought flowery responses — but no action.

Since it soon became apparent that effective and complete fire suppression efforts were beyond the capability of local governments, and since we had no offer of financial or other assistance from President Nixon, I met again with Senator Cranston and Congressmen Stark and Waldie, this time to develop a legislative response that would furnish predisaster assistance in accordance with the Disaster Relief Act of 1970. As a result of this meeting, we introduced identical bills in both houses of Congress.

We wrote these bills in such a way that the Senate version would be sent to the Small Business Subcommittee of the Senate Committee on Banking, Housing and Urban Affairs, a subcommittee chaired by Senator Cranston. An initial hearing was held on May 9, 1973 during which I testified along with the other East Bay legislators. Cranston's bill (S. 1697) was rapidly approved by his subcommittee, the full committee and finally by a voice vote of the Senate.

In the House, the measure was referred to the Forestry Subcommittee on Agriculture. I brought the issue before the California Democratic Delegation and secured unanimous support. I took this step essentially because the Delegation includes the influential House Majority Whip, John McFall of Manteca, and an important member of both the Agriculture Committee and the Rules Committee, Congressman Bernie Sisk of Fresno.

In response to significant Democratic Leadership support, the Forestry Committee held hearings in June and approved the bill. Unexpectedly, the measure gained the enthusiastic support of the Subcommittee Chairman, Representative John Rarick. "Judge" Rarick from Baton Rouge, Louisiana, is one of the strongest advocates of conservative causes in the Congress. He proved to be an appreciated exception to the many Congressmen, on both sides of the aisle, who oppose all legislation from political opposites. It turned out that Baton Rouge had greatly benefited from federal disaster aid after several Mississippi River floods. Congressman Rarick gave us strong and visible support as the measure moved forward. Also, Congressman Charles Teague, Republican of Santa Barbara, the Ranking Minority Member of the committee, actively entered the struggle for the bill.

Unfortunately, the Agriculture Authorization Bill—which authorizes every program in the Department of Agriculture from food stamps to crop subsidies—got to the full committee before the Eucalyptus Bill. All else stopped, as various agriculture interest groups fought over the main authorization bill.

Finally in July, after a delay of weeks, the full committee got around to consideration of our bill. The hearings were extensive. I, and the other East Bay Congressmen, testified along with representatives and experts from the state and local governments. As a result, the committee re-wrote parts of the bill. The final version authorized the President to make funds available for fire suppression and tree removal activities on both public and private lands in Alameda and Contra Costa counties. Federal aid was to be matched by state funds and the total federal grant was not to exceed $11 million.

Owners or operators of public and private lands could receive reimbursement of up to 75% of the removal expenses.

The House of Representatives has a peculiar legislative process. All bills that pass the committees which actually work on their relevant subject area must go before the Committee on Rules before actually reaching the floor for a vote. This is the Committee that, in earlier years, blocked many progressive measures such as civil rights legislation for a long time. Now, however, with a moderate Chairman and several new members, it is much more responsive to the House Leadership. The Rules Committee decides when and how a bill is scheduled for debate or action. Although more than 20,000 bills are submitted to the House, only some two to three hundred go through the committee process and are approved by the Rules Committee. By the time the Eucalyptus bill came before Rules, the Legislative Calendar was very full. Odds on a bill that benefited only three congressional districts being given favorable treatment were very long.

I contacted Speaker Carl Albert, Majority Leader "Tip" O'Neill and Congressman McFall. Their active support joined with support from Congressman Sisk, all the California Democrats, Representative Teague and Senator Cranston together secured a rule and placed the bill on the House Calendar for debate and a vote.

It was scheduled for just before the August recess. At this time, the House was meeting even on Saturdays and very late into the night. There were many controversial measures before the House being considered under time constraints. Tempers grew hot and careful reflection was not the watch-word. The narrow application of the bill caused it to become a lightning rod for chance frustrations of the moment. Rather than have it defeated on irrelevant emotion, the East Bay Delegation requested that the House Democratic Leadership pull the bill off the Calendar until after the recess. This was done.

During the recess, we worked very hard to contact each Member

"I want you to draft the bill with all your usual precision and flair. Explain its purposes, justify its expenditures, emphasize how it fits the broad aims of democratic progress. And one other thing: Can you make it sound like a tax cut?"

Drawing by Fisher; © 1979 The New Yorker Magazine, Inc.

and carefully explain the purpose of the bill and the nature of the fire danger problem in the East Bay.

At this point in late August, Governor Reagan announced a $800 million state budget surplus. The House naturally began to question why the state couldn't spend some of this money to solve the eucalyptus problem. All our efforts to actively engage the Governor to explain the background and intentions regarding the surplus or to involve him in lining up Republican votes were completely ignored.

When the House reconvened in September, the bill came to the floor with the albatross of Governor Reagan's statement and rebate tossed around its neck.

On September 11th, the House voted "NO" on the rule and refused even to debate the bill, despite solid and active support of the House Leadership and most Democrats.

This has not been a partisan effort. We received invaluable help from former Republican Senator Bill Knowland as well as Congressman Teague.[1]

This chapter describes the steps by which a bill becomes a law and analyzes the major features of this process. Then we consider minority rule, information, lobbying, representation, relations with the executive branch, and other general aspects of Congress as an institution. Our purpose is to explain Congress's place in the political system and give a realistic understanding of what it can reasonably be expected to do.

FROM BILL TO LAW: THE LEGISLATIVE PROCESS

Before becoming law, a bill passes through several stages and points of decision. First is the committee stage. Then the bill is brought to the floor and debated. Then comes the floor vote, which is affected by both party and ideological alignments. If both houses have passed versions of the same bill, it goes to a conference committee for the resolution of differences.

The Committee Stage Hearings. Once a bill is introduced, it is assigned to the committee having jurisdiction over its subject matter. The committee in turn usually refers the bill to a subcommittee. Most of the thousands of measures introduced each year are discarded simply because there is not enough time to consider them. Committees and subcommittees exercise great power by picking out a few hundred bills for consideration—as our example indicates. The first step in the process is **hearings:** formal meetings of the committee or subcommittee where witnesses present facts and arguments and answer questions. Dozens of hearings are held every day that Congress is in session. Witnesses who testify at hearings usually are invited by the committee staff. Their appearances are orchestrated to make a point—and, usually, to attract the attention of the mass media. If

---

[1] This narrative is taken from Dellums' December 1973 newsletter.

the issue is controversial, the witnesses will mostly repeat arguments that have been heard before. But most bills are not very controversial; designed to help specific interests, they have no strong opponents. Often, the only testimony will be from the potential beneficiaries. Only when a measure would clearly help some people at the expense of others is a real conflict likely.

Although hearings are rarely the occasion for searching pursuit of the truth, they are important for a number of reasons. First, they provide help in polishing the draft of the proposed legislation. Government officials who are experts on the subject and who will have to administer the proposed law are key witnesses. So are representatives of the private groups that will be affected. Often they can point out the practical consequences of using one wording in the bill rather than another, or of adding or subtracting a provision. They can help Congress get a clearer picture of what consequences will follow from various alternative proposals.

Hearings also help members assess the strength of support and opposition to a particular measure. This kind of information is important both to the sponsor (and opponents) of a measure and to those who are on the fence. The sponsors need to know their chances of success and what amendments they may have to accept to get a majority to support the bill. In other words, they must know how much they need to compromise in order to win. The uncommitted members want to know the political hazards of voting yes or no on the measure. This is important for political survival and because many members base their votes on the opinions of particular groups. Some vote with the oil industry, or the unions, or blacks, or bankers, or conservationists, and so on.

A third purpose of hearings is to provide time to mobilize additional support or opposition. A hearing brings a proposal to greater public attention, so that groups outside Congress with an interest in the bill are alerted, along with their members and allies. Sometimes hearings will provide the time and publicity necessary to build a coalition strong enough to push a bill through. Public opinion may be far more favorable (or hostile) than the attitudes of bureaucrats, lobbyists, and politicians. Usually the side that thinks it can get wider public backing will try to raise the level of attention in order to bring public pressure to bear on Congress.

The Markup Session.   After hearings, the subcommittee marks up the bill. The **markup session** is crucial for any bill. It is the point of final decision for all but the most controversial items. Members go over the bill line by line to fix its wording. Provisions may be struck out and new ones added, or features of various proposed bills combined. Opponents will offer amendments to delete or "gut" parts of the bill. Figure 13.1 shows some of the table of contents of a bill passed in 1975.

The marked-up bill is then reported by the subcommittee, along with a report that explains and defends the bill. Sometimes, particularly when there is ideological or partisan division, there is also a minority report attacking the legislation. The whole process of subcommittee consideration is then repeated in the full committee. If the issue is uncontroversial or highly technical, the full committee may just ratify the subcommittee's work without much fuss.

For most bills, the subcommittee or committee has almost complete power;

Figure 13.1
Part of the Table of Contents of a Single Bill
Passed by Congress
The entire act is 24 pages long.

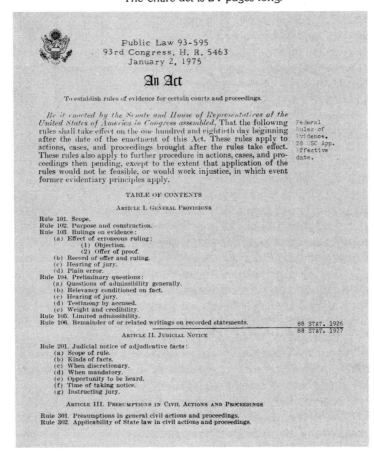

Public Law 93-595
93rd Congress, H. R. 5463
January 2, 1975

An Act

To establish rules of evidence for certain courts and proceedings.

Be it enacted by the Senate and House of Representatives of the United States of America in Congress assembled, That the following rules shall take effect on the one hundred and eightieth day beginning after the date of the enactment of this Act. These rules apply to actions, cases, and proceedings brought after the rules take effect. These rules also apply to further procedure in actions, cases, and proceedings then pending, except to the extent that application of the rules would not be feasible, or would work injustice, in which event former evidentiary principles apply.

Federal Rules of Evidence. 28 USC App. Effective date.

TABLE OF CONTENTS

ARTICLE I. GENERAL PROVISIONS

Rule 101. Scope.
Rule 102. Purpose and construction.
Rule 103. Rulings on evidence:
  (a) Effect of erroneous ruling:
    (1) Objection.
    (2) Offer of proof.
  (b) Record of offer and ruling.
  (c) Hearing of jury.
  (d) Plain error.
Rule 104. Preliminary questions:
  (a) Questions of admissibility generally.
  (b) Relevancy conditioned on fact.
  (c) Hearing of jury.
  (d) Testimony by accused.
  (e) Weight and credibility.
Rule 105. Limited admissibility.
Rule 106. Remainder of or related writings on recorded statements.

88 STAT. 1926
88 STAT. 1927

ARTICLE II. JUDICIAL NOTICE

Rule 201. Judicial notice of adjudicative facts:
  (a) Scope of rule.
  (b) Kinds of facts.
  (c) When discretionary.
  (d) When mandatory.
  (e) Opportunity to be heard.
  (f) Time of taking notice.
  (g) Instructing jury.

ARTICLE III. PRESUMPTIONS IN CIVIL ACTIONS AND PROCEEDINGS

Rule 301. Presumptions in general civil actions and proceedings.
Rule 302. Applicability of State law in civil actions and proceedings.

what it decides is what the chamber passes. When bills are controversial, partisan, or very conspicuous, however, the committee is only the first hurdle. The next stage — consideration on the floor of the House and Senate — is equally crucial.

Bringing the Bill to the Floor   Scheduling. Although the committees filter out most bills, they still turn out hundreds of important measures every year. Some are essential housekeeping bills, including those that appropriate money and continue the authorization of most major federal programs. Others represent major innovations. Scheduling is thus a delicate subject with major strategic implications.

In the Senate, scheduling legislation is formally the responsibility of the Democratic Policy Committee. As a practical matter, it is done by the majority leader. He works closely with the bill's floor manager, who is usually the chairman of the com-

Ralph Nader testifying before a congressional committee considering auto safety legislation.

mittee that considered it. The floor manager is the expert on substance; the majority leader specializes in tactics. It is the leader's responsibility to schedule the bill to accommodate any interested senator of his party. He also keeps the minority leader informed, for the Senate disapproves of springing scheduling surprises on the opposition. (The conduct of business in both houses is based on a general recognition that all the people concerned will be dealing with each other for decades. In these circumstances, it would be foolish to think only of the day's issue.) In the Senate, every member is given ample opportunity to have a say on any pending bill.

The House Rules Committee.   In the House, the path of major legislation is more complicated. Unless it is noncontroversial or falls into certain "privileged" categories, a bill must get a "rule" after being reported from the committee that considered it. A **rule** in this sense specifies the conditions under which the bill will be considered. Will amendments from the floor be permitted, or will there be a "closed rule" forcing the House to accept or reject the bill as it stands? Will the House be able to consider amendments that do not concern the substance of the bill? Will it be forced to adhere to its "germaneness rule" that forbids the introduction of irrelevant amendments? These are the sorts of technical but crucial decisions the Rules Committee makes on every major bill after it leaves the committee where it originated and before it reaches the floor. No significant measure, other than an appropriations bill, can be considered by the House without a rule. Thus, if the Rules Committee refuses to grant a rule to a bill, it can go no further.[2] At the end of each session, when there are more bills awaiting action that can possibly be considered, the Rules Committee decides which will reach the floor and which will die.

The first step in consideration of any bill by the whole House is a vote to approve the rule proposed by the Rules Committee. That is, the House debates the tailor-made procedure before getting to the substance of the bill itself. The proposed rule is generally approved. In the past, coalitions between the Republican and conservative southern Democratic members of the Rules Committee endangered many progressive bills backed by a majority of Democrats. By refusing to grant a rule at all, the committee prevented the House from taking up major measures. The committee's ideological make-up was altered by an increase in its size in 1961, and it is no longer a device to obstruct liberal majorities. As a result of the reforms of the 1970s, the Speaker

[2] A **discharge petition** signed by a majority of the House (218 members) can remove a bill from the control of the Rules Committee, or any other committee, for that matter. This maneuver however, is cumbersome and used irregularly. It has worked only two or three times in the past generation. Other ways to get around the Rules Committee are even less commonly successful.

THE NEW RULES COMMITTEE

In 1977 some Democrats on the House Rules Committee opposed parts of a measure wanted by Speaker O'Neill. They changed their minds after the Speaker went into action:

> O'Neill invited the Rules Committee Democrats to breakfast, at which he pounded the table, demanding their cooperation. They were not convinced. Next day, O'Neill got tougher. They were all his personal friends, O'Neill said, but by God they would find themselves on the District of Columbia Committee next year if they failed him on this one.

Source: *The Washington Post,* March 8, 1977, p. A1; quoted in Walter J. Oleszek, *Congressional Procedures and the Policy Process* (Washington: Congressional Quarterly Press, 1978), p. 95.

now appoints the Democratic members of the Rules Committee, subject to confirmation by the Democratic Caucus. The committee Democrats are, in O'Neill's words, "a strong right arm to the leadership."[3] Furthermore, the House Democratic Caucus occasionally instructs the Rules Committee Democrats on procedural matters. But all these changes have not made the committee a rubber stamp. Neither the Speaker nor the caucus can look over the Rules Committee's shoulder all the time. So it remains an important part of the legislative process, particularly on routine measures.

Debate and the Filibuster   A bill's supporters worry not only about getting the bill passed but also about turning back amendments that may delete or water down major provisions. If a sure majority for passage is not in sight, the floor manager may agree to amendments in order to win votes or to attract the support of members with particular interests. In order to avoid giving away more than is necessary, this requires a reliable headcount of those for, opposed, and undecided. Headcounts are one of the leadership's most important activities. (They are also made by the White House and lobbyists.)

It would take over thirty-six hours for each member of the House to speak for five minutes on a single bill. In view of the complexity of many bills and the need to consider amendments, controlling time in floor debate is crucial. Floor action is therefore tightly and precisely scheduled. Half the time is controlled by the bill's floor manager, the other half by his or her counterpart for the opposition. They parcel the time out in chunks of several minutes, which go mainly to members who know something about the issue at hand. In contrast to the Senate, which may debate a bill off and on for weeks or months, the House disposes of even the most important legislation in a day or two, or a week at most.

---

[3] Quoted in *National Journal,* June 18, 1977, p. 942.

The floor stage takes longer in the Senate and generally changes the bill more. This leisurely approach is encouraged by the Senate's rules, which permit unlimited debate. This makes it possible also for a small group of determined opponents to filibuster—to prevent a bill's passage by refusing to stop talking and permit a vote. A filibuster can be stopped by a procedure called **cloture,** which requires the votes of sixty senators. By raising the threshold of success from a simple majority to three-fifths, the filibuster increases the bargaining power of the senators whose votes are needed for passage. It gives a minority the power to win compromises as the price of support.

A filibuster used to be the last resort of outnumbered senators on very important, emotional issues. It was particularly associated with southern opposition to civil rights measures.[4] In the past few years, filibusters have become increasingly common; half of all the cloture votes in the history of the Senate have occurred since 1973.[5] Both liberals and conservatives are using unlimited debate on a wide variety of legislation. In addition to being more common and general, filibusters are also less invincible. But they are still a formidable weapon. They are most effective toward the end of the year, when there is a big backlog of pending bills, and delay means death.

Senators contemplating a filibuster are restrained by the fear that overuse will produce a backlash—a change in the rules that will make this tactic more difficult, or even outlaw it altogether. The more frequent use of filibusters has already brought one such change, a reduction in 1975 from 67 to 60 votes as the minimum required to impose cloture on all bills that do not change the Senate's rules.

Conference Committees   A bill supported by the administration or any major interest group is sure to be introduced in both houses of Congress. The process of working out its provisions involves negotiations between the legislative sponsors and other interested parties: lobbyists, bureaucrats, and often the White House. This bargaining generally occurs in one house. The version of the bill passed by the first house to consider it thus reflects a compromise between most of the relevant political figures.[6] But a bill must be passed by both houses (and signed by the president) to become law. The second house to take up the bill will probably produce a somewhat different version,[7] in part because representatives and senators are jealous of their own house's autonomy.

---

[4] In fact, only one major civil rights bill supported by a majority in both houses was killed by unlimited debate. See Raymond E. Wolfinger, "Filibusters," in Raymond E. Wolfinger, ed., *Readings on Congress* (Englewood Cliffs, N.J.: Prentice-Hall, 1971), pp. 286–305.

[5] *Congressional Quarterly Weekly Report,* October 1, 1977, p. 2066.

[6] Gerald S. Strom and Barry S. Rundquist, "A Revised Theory of Winning in House-Senate Conferences," *American Political Science Review,* 71 (June 1977), pp. 448–53.

[7] There are two fairly persistent differences between bills passed by the House and the Senate: (1) The Senate usually provides more money in appropriations bills. (2) The Senate usually is more liberal on domestic legislation. See Richard F. Fenno, Jr., *The Power of the Purse* (Boston: Little, Brown, 1966); and Sam Kernell, "Is the Senate More Liberal Than the House?" *Journal of Politics,* 35(May 1973), pp. 332–63.

Table 13.1

The Legislative Process

HOUSE	SENATE
1. Bill is introduced by one or more members and referred to committee. *	1. The same.
2. Committee phase:	2. The same.
a. Bill may be referred to a subcommittee or considered in the full committee.	
b. Hearings scheduled:	
(1) This is the highest hurdle; the vast majority of bills do not get hearings.	
(2) Staff does research, requests information, invites witnesses.	
c. Hearings: testimony and publicity; transcript of hearings is eventually printed.	
d. The bill is "marked up": subcommittee goes through the bill line by line, voting on amendments proposed by members.	
e. The bill is reported, accompanied by the subcommittee report—the arguments for the bill.	
f. The process is repeated in the full committee, although hearings may be omitted and the mark-up session may be perfunctory.	
3. Rules Committee:	3. No equivalent committee. The leadership usually negotiates a unanimous consent agreement governing the length of floor debate.
a. Holds hearings.	
b. Grants a rule.	
4. Leadership schedules the bill for floor debate.	4. The same.
5. Floor debate:	5. Floor debate:
a. Vote on rule.	a. Amendments considered.
b. Amendments considered.	b. Vote on final passage.
c. Motion to recommit the bill; this is offered by the opposition and effectively kills the bill if it passes.	
d. Vote on final passage.	
6. Members of a conference committee are appointed if the bill is different from Senate version. †	6. The same.
7. Conference committee works out a compromise version of the bill.	
8. Vote to accept the report of the conferees.	8. The same.
9. Bill goes to the president. If he signs it, it becomes law. If he vetoes it, it goes back to Congress. ††	
10. Vote to override veto, which requires a two-thirds majority.	10. The same.

*Identical or similar bills may be introduced in one or both houses, except for tax and appropriations bills, which originate in the House. Bills may be considered simultaneously or in sequence. Each house may amend bills that come to it from the other body. A bill does not last after the end of the two-year Congress in which it was introduced. If not passed, it must be introduced again in the next Congress.

†The House and Senate may pass identical bills or one body may vote to accept the other's version, but either of these possibilities is rare on controversial bills.

††There is no "item veto"; the President must take the whole bill or veto it.

The differences usually are resolved by a conference committee composed of the senior Democrats and Republicans on the relevant committee in each house and appointed just for a given bill. Its members work out a compromise between the two versions. A majority of both House and Senate conferees must agree to all committee decisions. The conference committee report is then voted on by each body. Rejection of a conference committee report is rare, because the members, having passed the measure once, know there is little reason to expect the conference committee will do a better job the second time around. As at every stage of the legislative process, there is a presumption in favor of those legislators who have done the work.

Party Voting   Despite the weakness of party discipline, there is a remarkable degree of party voting in Congress. Democrats vote together not because they are compelled to, but because they are likely to share certain opinions about policy, because they rely for support on certain elements in their constituencies (labor, blacks, liberals), and because they have a common orientation to the president (either he is theirs or he is the opposition's). The same factors are likely to make the Republicans coalesce around another position. If none of these factors operates—if the president has not taken a stand, for example—then the issue is less likely to see the two parties pitted against each other. Voting coalitions may form on some basis other than party.

Even when an issue is not openly partisan, however, voting alignments still follow party lines to some extent. The reason is simple. Members often do not have opinions on the issues on which they must vote; and even if they do have some inclinations, they need the advice of trusted specialists. What better sources of advice than other members? Among all their colleagues, the most trusted sources are members of their own party, who share the same basic orientations, interests, and sources of support.[8]

For all these reasons, party is the best predictor of voting patterns. If you know what party a member belongs to, you can predict his or her vote more accurately than with any other characteristic. The extent of party-line voting is shown in Figure 13.2, which is based on the most thorough scholarly analysis of congressional voting patterns.[9] This graph also demonstrates that party voting is much stronger on some issues than others. It is quite weak on civil rights, for example, because few southern Democratic representatives voted for civil rights measures and few northern Democrats voted against them. It is relatively weak on foreign policy, because the two parties tend to lack fixed positions on most international questions. But it is quite high on the issue of government intervention in the economy.

The skill of congressional party leaders is shown in their ability to take advantage of the natural tendencies of members of the same party to vote together, to add whatever incentives and persuasive power they have, and to make good use of

---

[8] John W. Kingdon, *Congressmen's Voting Decisions* (New York: Harper & Row, 1973), Chap. 3.

[9] Aage R. Clausen, *How Congressmen Decide* (New York: St. Martin's Press, 1973).

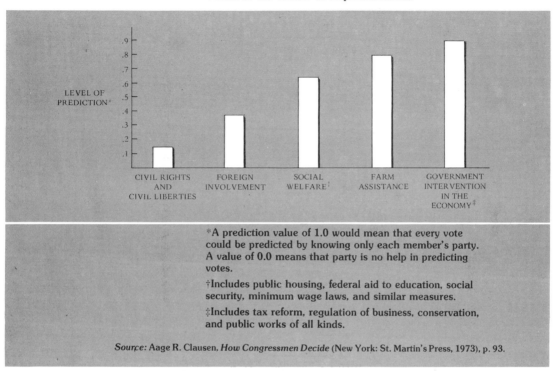

Figure 13.2

Party as a Predictor of Voting on Five Policy
Areas in the House of Representatives

LEVEL OF
PREDICTION*

CIVIL RIGHTS
AND
CIVIL LIBERTIES

FOREIGN
INVOLVEMENT

SOCIAL
WELFARE†

FARM
ASSISTANCE

GOVERNMENT
INTERVENTION
IN THE
ECONOMY‡

*A prediction value of 1.0 would mean that every vote
could be predicted by knowing only each member's party.
A value of 0.0 means that party is no help in predicting
votes.

†Includes public housing, federal aid to education, social
security, minimum wage laws, and similar measures.

‡Includes tax reform, regulation of business, conservation,
and public works of all kinds.

Source: Aage R. Clausen, *How Congressmen Decide* (New York: St. Martin's Press, 1973), p. 93.

their scheduling and informational role. The result is more party-line voting then
would occur from natural tendencies alone. Party leaders are more effective when
they can rely on the help of the president, whose techniques for influencing Congress
include not only most of those available to the leaders, but also others that
only a president can muster, such as the ability to command public attention.

The Conservative Coalition   The Democrats have controlled Congress since 1932, except
for 1947–48 and 1953–54. This does not mean, however,
that policies supported by most Democrats have always been successful on Capitol
Hill. The reason is the lack of party discipline in general and the major deviation of
the southern Democrats in particular. The northern "mainstream" Democrats have
never had a majority in Congress since World War II. Table 13.2 shows the Republican,
northern Democratic, and southern Democratic strength in every Congress
from 1963 through 1980. Southerners have always held the balance of power.
A few southern congressmen are fully as liberal as any nothern Democrat;
others favor particular progressive measures or could be induced to vote for them

Table 13.2

Party Strength in Congress, 1963–1980*

	1963–64	1965–66	1967–68	1969–70	1971–72	1973–74	1975–76	1977–78	1979–80
House of Representatives									
Republicans	176	140	187	192	180	193	144	143	158
Southern Democrats	95	89	83	79	79	74	81	81	77
Northern Democrats	163	206	165	164	177	168	210	211	200
Senate									
Republicans	32	33	36	42	45	43	38	38	41
Southern Democrats	21	20	19	18	17	15	16	17	16
Northern Democrats	47	47	45	40	38	42	46	45	43

*At the beginning of each Congress. Minor changes occur subsequently as a result of retirement and deaths.

on grounds of party loyalty or as part of a bargain. The majority of southerners in both houses, however, are conservatives. In any other part of the country, most of them would be Republicans.

This is why Democratic presidents have so much trouble with Congresses that have a Democratic majority. The *real* majority much of the time has been the **conservative coalition,** an alliance of Republicans and most southern Democrats. Indeed, Republican party leaders confer frequently with leading southern members. The conservative coalition is "an informal, bipartisan bloc of conservatives with leaders who jointly discuss strategy and line up votes."[10]

While the coalition is often evident in committee, the easiest way to measure it is in floor voting when a majority of southern Democrats vote with a majority of Republicans against a majority of northern Democrats. By this criterion, the coalition was at work on 21 percent of the votes in both houses in 1978, and won half of those votes.[11]

The conservative coalition often seems "irrational" to observers of American politics, who ask why the two parties do not realign themselves on the basis of ideology — conservatives in one party and liberals in another. Like many such prescriptions for reform, this one overlooks the interests of the politicians involved. Until very recently, few southern conservatives could be elected as Republicans. If they wanted to win, they had to be on the Democratic ticket. Nor could the northern Democrats afford to kick the conservative southerners out of the party. Although they make up a majority of the party nationwide and control its presidential nominations, they would have been a consistent minority in Congress without the southerners.

The coalition does not seem to have a bright future. Democrats newly elected to Congress from the South are more liberal than their senior colleagues. As southern voters desert the Democratic party in growing numbers, conservative candidates who want to win will not be restricted to the Democratic ticket. As northern liberals become an ever-larger group in the congressional Democratic party, they

[10] John F. Manley, "The Conservative Coalition in Congress," *American Behavioral Scientist,* 17 (November–December 1973), p. 235.

[11] *CQ Weekly Report,* December 16, 1978, pp. 3441–42.

will have less need of the southerners to reach a majority. Thus, the processes of political change are producing a gradual realignment in the strongest bastion of the old Solid South — Congress.

Veto Politics   We will discuss the president's use of his veto powers more fully in the next chapter. Here we will consider the veto from the congressional viewpoint. Unlike the governors of many states, the president does not have an item veto. He cannot veto a specific provision he dislikes in a bill he finds otherwise satisfactory. The president must accept or reject the entire bill. Congress sometimes attaches provisions the president dislikes to bills he either must sign in order to keep the government going (such as appropriations bills), or cannot afford to veto for political reasons. For example, when the dimensions of the depression that began in late 1974 first became evident, there was general agreement that taxes had to be cut to stimulate the economy. President Ford quickly submitted such legislation to Congress. The legislature took advantage of this opportunity by attaching to the bill various provisions to reform the tax laws in ways that had nothing to do with the original goal of providing a quick stimulus to the economy. Ford would have vetoed some of these proposals if they had come across his desk as separate pieces of legislation. But because he felt a tax cut was urgent, he had to swallow the amendments.

The lack of an item veto often leads to a game of "chicken" between president and Congress. He vows to veto crucial legislation if Congress attaches certain provisions to it. Are such threats genuine? Sometimes Congress backs down, and sometimes it calls his bluff. Calling the bluff may produce a presidential retreat, or a nasty shock for Congress.

Congress can override a veto by a two-thirds vote of each body. The difference between the simple majority required to pass a bill in the first place and the two-thirds needed to override a veto is great enough to make the veto a potent presidential weapon. The ability to veto legislation gives the president considerable leverage in bargaining with Congress.

Overview: A Bias   The slowness and openness of congressional proceedings
against Action?   make Congress a good public educator. Hearings and floor debate bring issues out in the open and leave them there long enough for special interests to make their views known, and for at least part of the general public to learn what the issues are and to express its preferences. (The distinction between special interest and the general public is very often nonexistent. Here we mean by the general public those people who learn about a particular issue and respond to it without direct contact with an organized group.) Public access to the lawmaking process is guaranteed by the requirement that the president, the bureaucracy, and interest groups submit their legislative proposals to the publicity and delays of congressional procedures.

The impediments to fast action are apparent from Table 13.1, which summarizes the steps in the lawmaking process. The long series of decision points is a bias not only against speed, but also in favor of the status quo. The proponents of any measure must win all along the line to get what they want. They must assemble a majority at every stage from subcommittee markup to final passage. Opponents can get their way by winning only once.

Table 13.1 describes the path a bill *normally* takes. Both houses have rules that permit quick action to avoid many of the potential bottlenecks in this long, tortuous road. For example, discharge petitions or other devices can remove a bill from a committee's control or keep it from going to committee in the first place. But Congress is generally unwilling to clear bottlenecks even for bills desired by a majority. Why? Because what look like bottlenecks to outsiders may look like flood control projects to members. Every year Congress is deluged with thousands of bills, each with supporters who think their bill is the most urgent business before Congress. The typical member has seen so many "must" bills come and go that he or she develops considerable skepticism about whether the country will collapse if something—or anything—is not done. Most members are content to let normal procedures work, convinced that occasional abuses are less important than disruption of time-tested ways of doing business. They trust the committees to get rid of most bills and pass the best ones on for floor consideration.

The easiest power to wield in Congress is the power to say no. Getting things done is not too hard if a member is strategically placed and what he or she wants has no apparent victims, only beneficiaries. But as proposals become more controversial or promise to help some people at an apparent cost to other interests, they become more and more difficult to achieve. The hurdles a bill must cross grow higher if the measure is conspicuous enough to attract public attention, controversial enough to attract enemies, and important enough to inspire those enemies to exert themselves. These are important qualifications to the simple belief that the cards are stacked against action. (As we saw, Dellums' bill to tap the federal treasury for the benefit of Berkeley homeowners moved to the House floor rather easily.) A great deal of legislation is inconspicuous, uncontroversial, or seems to have specific beneficiaries and diffuse costs. The sum total of congressional action in these areas is a substantial proportion of the laws passed each year.

Thus, it is a little too glib to say simply that congressional procedures are biased in favor of the status quo. Because the committee system means that Congress delegates so much of its authority to quasi-autonomous bodies, it is almost more accurate to speak of Congress as "they" rather than "it." We will turn now to this crucially important feature of Congress—its variability.

MINORITY RULE

Organizing congressional business by committees results in a great decentralization of power. Careful attention to most issues can be sustained only at the committee or subcommittee level. The result is that single members acquire great power over particular aspects of public policy. They are powerful because they are the only ones who have done the work and because their colleagues defer to their knowledge. The other side of the coin, of course, is that every member has a bit of turf that he or she hopes will be equally respected.

The direction of federal policy on all but the most important and conspicuous issues depends in large measure on the interests, attitudes, and abilities of individual members in strategic positions. For any particular policy area—air safety, higher education, national parks, soil conservation—the House and Senate each has a legislative subcommittee and an appropriations subcommittee. The chairmen and perhaps the ranking minority members of these tiny panels are the effective legislative decision-makers. We can illustrate how this division of labor works by describing the political environment of the public health field.

For many years, congressional action concerning public health and medical research was determined by two legislators who were sympathetic to expanding federal activity in these areas. The key figure was Senator Lister Hill of Alabama. Raised in a doctor's family and named after Sir Joseph Lister, a famous figure in nineteenth-century medicine, Hill was chairman of three key groups: the Senate Committee on Labor and Public Welfare,[12] its Subcommittee on Health, and the Appropriations subcommittee on health. Hill's major ally in the House was John Fogarty of Rhode Island, chairman from 1949 to 1967 of the corresponding Appropriations subcommittee, and equally favorable to more and bigger federal health programs. The year after Hill assumed his Appropriations post, funds for the Public Health Service increased 56 percent. Within ten years, they had multiplied eight times, and spending for the National Institutes of Health had gone up more than twelvefold. In contrast to most Appropriations subcommittees, which try to trim the president's budget requests, both Hill and Fogarty would actually increase administration requests for health programs.[13]

The committee system gives great weight to the interests of legislators who occupy strategic positions. There was no reason inherent in their constituencies or their committee positions for Hill or Fogarty to be so openhanded about spending on medical research. It was purely a matter of chance that for almost twenty years the congressmen concerned with health programs were unusually sympathetic to this area of public policy. This point is illustrated by how drastically the situation changed when Hill and Fogarty left office. A former HEW official who dealt with Congress described the shift this way to one of us:

> They [Hill and Fogarty] criticized John Gardner [Secretary of HEW] for not asking enough, and would add half a billion on top. You didn't even have to go up to the Capitol, you'd just write them a note asking for what you wanted, and they'd add half a billion on top.
>
> Then those fellows retired and their places were taken by very different kinds of men, and it was a whole new ball game. It was like facing Murderers' Row when you sent health legislation up to the Hill.

Limits on Minority Rule   When policies are of concern principally to restricted groups—cherry growers, say, or cancer researchers—a committee's decisions are accepted by Congress almost automatically. The vast majority of members will follow the lead of those who do know and care—the members of the

---

[12] Now called the Committee on Human Resources.

[13] Our discussion of Hill, Fogarty, and the National Institutes of Health is taken from David E. Price, *Who Makes the Laws?* (Cambridge, Mass.: Schenkman, 1972), pp. 216–21.

committee. With controversial bills, however, the situation changes. The more attention and partisan conflict a bill attracts, the less the likelihood that the final decision will rest with the committee. This is because controversial issues motivate members not on the committee to examine the issues in the light of their own opinions and political situations. Even in the most publicized and partisan situations, however, the committee shapes the alternatives and defines the conflicts that will occur when the bill is considered by the whole House or Senate.

A congressional committee is powerful in proportion to the confidence the members of the entire body have in it. Yet, as we saw in Chapter 12, assignment to some committees is attractive primarily to members with certain constituent interests. Members from farm states, for example, want to be on the Agriculture Committee. This seems reasonable, given the nature of the committee system. Big-city representatives seldom can do much for their constituents there. The result, however, reminds us of the fable about the fox guarding the chicken coop. A committee with this image is likely to have its bills roughly handled on the floor:

> In recent years, as redistricting made the membership of the House more urban, the [Agriculture] committee remained overwhelmingly rural. When it took legislation to the floor, it was perceived increasingly as a single-interest committee that treated agriculture as a client to defend rather than an institution to regulate.[14]

The House Education and Labor Committee is another notoriously mistrusted committee. The reasons begin with the assignment process. The committee is so important to the unions that the leading labor lobbyist, Andrew Biemiller of the AFL-CIO, used to pick most of the Democrats who were appointed to it. Southern Democrats, who usually do not represent districts with much labor influence, are reluctant to serve on the committee. In 1979–80, only two southern Democrats were members. For its part, the Republican leadership wants only supporters of conservative economic doctrine on the committee.[15]

Because of these pressures, moderates of both parties are scarce. The committee thus becomes a cockpit of zealots who seem never to have heard the old proverb that "half a loaf is better than none." As Fenno puts it, "they will prefer a live political issue to a passed compromise."[16] The result is that education and labor bills are likely to be defeated or amended beyond recognition on the floor of the House. Over a twelve-year period, only 59 percent of its bills passed the House. In contrast, the Ways and Means Committee, dealing with equally important, partisan, and controversial legislation, had a 94 percent success rate in the same period.[17] In large part this is because the two parties do not assign such inflexible legislators to Ways and Means.

The reasons for the high success rate of Ways and Means help us understand the power of the committee system in Congress:

[14] *CQ Weekly Report*, February 22, 1975, p. 381.
[15] Richard F. Fenno, Jr., *Congressmen in Committees* (Boston: Little, Brown, 1973), p. 34.
[16] Fenno, *Congressmen in Committees*, p. 234.
[17] Fenno, *Congressmen in Committees*, p. 235.

1. Tax law is extremely technical. Most legislators feel that members who are not on the committee should not participate because they do not really understand what they are doing.

2. Various tax provisions are related to one another in complex ways. Before a bill reaches the floor, the committee has constructed an elaborate package of compromises and adjustments. Interventions by individual members might upset the whole applecart.

3. Many members are under pressure from constituents and supporters to obtain special tax treatment. If tax bills could be changed on the floor, they would be "amended out of shape" by special interest provisions. Each member might vote for every other's amendments on a you-scratch-my-back-and-I'll-scratch-yours basis. In the Senate, tax bills are so amended on the floor that they are called "Christmas tree bills" because of the way they are decorated with special provisions.

4. The House trusts the Ways and Means Committee to do the job because its members are broadly representative of the House as a whole. Its membership is respected in a way that some other committees are not.

Subgovernments   Deference to specialization cannot be understood in a purely congressional context. Because the Agriculture Committees deal with farm problems day after day, they are constantly seeing and talking to farm groups and Department of Agriculture officials. Each committee is embedded in a circle of lobbyists, interest groups, and bureaucrats, all of whom specialize in the same set of problems. Ideas for new legislation and suggestions for changes in existing legislation usually come from bureaucrats and lobbyists, who are also the major witnesses at committee hearings. Government officials typically provide the bulk of data about the real world that serves as the background for committee decisions. They and the lobbyists shuttle between House committees and their Senate counterparts, seeking to keep the two together. In many issue areas, lawmaking is dominated by clusters of committees, bureaus, and interest groups, each expert in its own field. Not inaccurately, they have been described as *subgovernments*.

The generous health appropriations in the Hill-Fogarty era were the product of just such a net of informal relationships. The heads of the National Institutes of Health were doctors chosen for their ability and achievements, not on political grounds. Each institute had an independent advisory council of eminent medical and scientific figures. Some of these were famous "doctor-politicians," whose pictures were on the covers of national magazines and who were skilled at using their medical achievements to advance public causes. Working through their advisory councils and sympathetic foundations, the National Institutes of Health could communicate their budgetary needs to Congress, thus frustrating the desire for lower spending of the Department of HEW, the Office of Management and Budget, and the White House.

Subgovernments tend to be limited to issues on which the two parties are not divided sharply and on which the president does not want to take the initiative.

With bills involving controversial issues of interest to masses of people and important in building party positions for the next election, Congress generally does not delegate as much authority to its specialists.

The Appropriations Process   One form of minority rule deserves special attention. This is the process by which Congress provides the money needed to run the government. Let us suppose that Congress has enacted and the president has signed a law to control gypsy moths. The law is an authorization to the Department of Agriculture to set up a spray program. *But an authorization is not an appropriation.* The Department of Agriculture cannot actually spend money to spray bugs until money has been appropriated for this purpose. So it asks for such an appropriation.

This request does *not* go to the Agriculture Committees. It goes, as one item in a massive annual Department of Agriculture appropriation bill, to the Subcommittee on Agriculture and Related Agencies of the House Appropriations Committee. This is one of thirteen subcommittees on the House Appropriations Committee (HAC). Each HAC subcommittee has its counterpart on the Senate Appropriations Committee. Effective control of the budgetary process in the House is centered in the HAC subcommittees. The full Appropriations Committee often does not pay detailed attention to the reports of its subcommittees. The HAC subcommittee chairmen are widely considered more powerful than the chairmen of most full committees, and the House Democratic Caucus now confirms them as it does committee chairmen.

The president's annual budget request comes to Congress as a series of appropriation bills, each for a different administrative agency. Each bill is assigned to a HAC subcommittee. After preliminary spadework by its staff, the subcommittee holds hearings at which the administrative agency defends its requests and justifies its conduct of affairs over the past year. Other witnesses contribute their testimony. Usually, these are clientele groups asking for more money for particular activities that benefit them. For example, the Student Lobby may ask for a higher funding level for scholarships, or the Navy League will argue the case for another nuclear-powered aircraft carrier.

After hearings, the subcommittee goes over the bill item by item in markup sessions. Each subcommittee's membership is stable from year to year — often from decade to decade. The subcommittees have a good deal of accumulated expertise about the operations of the agencies under their jurisdiction. Even so, the limited staff and time as well as the sheer size and diversity of any agency's activities restrict the subcommittee's deliberations. As a general rule, most attention goes to changes from the previous year's budget, on the assumption that the past establishes an acceptable precedent.

Unlike other committees, which often have the option of deciding not to take any action for the time being, the Appropriations Committees *must* report their annual crop of bills. Moreover, appropriations decisions are not choices between grand alternatives. It is not a question of either accepting or rejecting proposed bills. By their very nature, appropriations bills are amenable to adjustment and compromise. These considerations encourage a nonpartisan, consensual attitude on the Appropriations Committees, particularly on the House side. HAC members are convinced that only the HAC stands in the way of a perpetual wild spending spree by the executive branch, aided and abetted by the extravagant Senate. They are genuinely committed to the ideal of governmental economy. Moreover, if the HAC did not exercise a good deal of independent judgment about the federal budget, it would not be one of the most desirable committee assignments in the House. Therefore, HAC subcommittees cut most budget requests.[18]

It is also true that each subcommittee (and especially its chairman) is likely to look after the interests of its own favorite projects, agencies, and constituencies. The general inclination to cut budget requests is modified by the fact that some agencies have more political influence than others. Generally speaking, agencies with strong domestic clienteles fare better than those with no supporting interests. The contrasting experiences of the State Department and the FBI illustrate this point. Both agencies are under the jurisdiction of the HAC Subcommittee on State, Justice, Commerce, and the Judiciary. Except for two years of Republican control, this subcommittee's chairman for a quarter of a century was John J. Rooney, a conservative machine politician from Brooklyn. Rooney was an enthusiastic supporter of the FBI. His subcommittee always gave the FBI at least as much money as it requested. On the other hand, he was deeply suspicious of the State Department and regularly cut its budget to the bone. The State Department's inability to purchase modern communications equipment for most of its foreign posts forced it to rely on the Central Intelligence Agency's ultramodern facilities. The result, of course, was to make ambassadors dependent on their subordinates in the CIA.[19]

There is a good reason for lodging so much power in the hands of the Appropriations Committee. Each appropriations bill is a bundle of temptations to the membership of the full House, since each contains innumerable opportunities for the individual member to seek higher federal spending in his or her district. The HAC must maintain a solid front in order to defend its bills against floor amendments. Its power is based on its ability to make spending decisions in committee, and this ability depends on unity in the face of "outside" challenges. In order to be able to monopolize decisions about the budget in the House, the HAC must make sure the bills it reports are invulnerable to amendment. Each subcommittee exercises minority rule in the policy areas covered by its jurisdiction. Like other forms of minority rule in Congress, this is usually accepted by the majority, although appropriations bills are sometimes amended on the floor of the House.

After the House passes each appropriation bill, the bill goes to the relevant Senate Appropriations subcommittee. Senate attention is typically less detailed. Unlike members of the House Appropriations Committee, the Senate subcommittee members have many other assignments and cannot devote much time to scrutiny of budget requests. There is no feeling in the Senate corresponding to the special pride the HAC takes in budget cutting. Moreover, because senators have

---

[18] Our discussion of the appropriations process is based largely on Fenno, *The Power of the Purse.*

[19] John Franklin Campbell, *The Foreign Affairs Fudge Factory* (New York: Basic Books, 1971), pp. 157–58.

multiple committee assignments, Senate Appropriations subcommittees usually include members from the corresponding legislative committees. They naturally tend to identify with the programs whose budgets are being considered, and their sympathy is translated into higher budgets. For all these reasons, the Senate is likely to be more generous than the HAC. In effect, it serves as an "appeals court" to which agencies that have been roughly treated in the House can come for a second chance. Differences between the House and Senate versions of each bill are resolved by a conference committee.

COORDINATING LEGISLATION

The committee system strengthens Congress because it produces subject matter specialists with continuous concern for limited areas of public policy. Congress can be something more than a sounding board and rubber stamp for the executive branch because it counters the expertise of the bureaucracy with its own expertise. A legislature that just considered new proposals in general session or in committees without stable membership, staff, and jurisdiction could not really perform an independent policymaking role.[20] There are so many bills on so many topics that, if there were no committees, most of the time a legislator could form an intelligent opinion only by relying on the executive branch. The strength of the committee system is not that it provides specialized knowledge as such, but that it provides *specialists within its own membership* whom other members can trust.

The committee system heightens reciprocity among legislators. Many of the bills in which any particular member is interested will not fall within the jurisdiction of his or her committees. Every representative and senator will often need help from colleagues. The most natural mode of seeking help is to be willing to give help in return. Although the committee system works on the principle of minority rule, the fragmentation inherent in this situation is somewhat corrected by the ties of reciprocity and trust among members.

Committee jurisdictions overlap a good deal. Responsibility for broad policy areas like energy, transportation, and welfare is scattered among several committees. While this increases the number of approaches to problems, it also leads to waste motion and piecemeal solutions.[21] Because each committee is supreme in its own bailiwick, it is difficult for Congress to gather up a bunch of related bills, compare them with one another, and decide how to devise a coordinated program on the basis of priorities. These drawbacks have been especially evident when it comes to spending money.

The tax laws are written by the Ways and Means Committee in the House and the Finance Committee in the Senate. Spending is the jurisdiction of the two

---

[20] The British House of Commons refers important legislative proposals to ad hoc committees. Lacking continuity, staff, or expertise, such committees are little more than microcosms of the whole House. They do nothing to give Parliament any independence from the Cabinet, to which it is totally subservient.

[21] Bills that cover several committees' jurisdictions can now be considered in the House by ad hoc committees appointed for that purpose by the Speaker. This was done twice in 1977–78, to consider President Carter's energy bill and again on proposals for development of the outer continental shelf. The technique seemed successful on these two issues.

Appropriations Committees. The committees that decided on spending levels took little notice of the taxing committees' work, and vice versa. It would seem that the budget-making process would provide Congress with a chance to weigh priorities. It might consider questions like this: Since there are only X billion dollars to spend, how much should we give to program A — killing gypsy moths in the forests — and how much to program B — killing rats in the slums? But gypsy moth control is done by the Department of Agriculture and is part of its budget, which is reviewed by the Agriculture and Related Agencies Appropriations Subcommittee. And rat eradication comes under the Department of Housing and Urban Development and is part of its budget, considered by the Appropriations Subcommittee on Housing and Urban Development — Independent Agencies. Because the Appropriations subcommittees in each body are very nearly autonomous, the budget passed by Congress consisted of a bundle of different appropriations bills coordinated neither with each other nor with the tax outlook.

Tax policy also lacked internal and external harmony. Tax exemptions ("loopholes" to opponents) are decisions not to tax certain forms of income. Each exemption is justified by the argument that it will provide an incentive for some form of desirable activity, such as hiring handicapped workers, home buying, or charitable contributions. In 1975, tax exemptions totaled about $78 billion.[22] This income was lost to the government, and represented a federal subsidy of staggering proportions. Despite the cumulative impact of tax exemptions, they are enacted piecemeal. Once in the law, they are not reexamined each year.

The New Congressional   By failing to adjust spending to income, Congress was surren-
Budget Process   dering control of fiscal policy to the president. Presidents filled this vacuum by **impounding** — refusing to spend — billions of dollars of appropriated funds. As in so many other areas, President Nixon carried past practices to new extremes. The annual rate of impoundments under Presidents Eisenhower, Kennedy, and Johnson had been between $6 and $8 billion.[23] As Nixon's impoundments rose toward $11 billion a year, Congress responded with a new approach to fiscal policy designed to restore its slipping grip on the power of the purse. The 1974 Congressional Budget and Impoundment Control Act established a Congressional Budget Office and a Budget Committee in each house.[24] Its goal is to coordinate spending and revenues, rather than having them emerge as a by-product of separate legislative decisions. Each spring, Congress passes a resolution setting spending targets for each of eighteen broad areas of government activity for the coming fiscal year (which now begins on October 1). The budget resolution also sets a revenue target. The gap between it and the overall spending target is the projected deficit (or surplus). This "first budget resolution" provides guidelines to the appropriations and revenue committees. Equally important, these ceilings apply to all committees shaping legislation during the year. In the fall, when work has been completed on appropriations and revenue bills, the Budget Committees review the outcome and prepare the "second budget resolution" for consideration

[22] *CQ Weekly Report,* April 20, 1974, pp. 971 – 75.
[23] Andrew J. Glass, "Budget Battle," *National Journal,* April 14, 1973, p. 527.
[24] It also forbade the president to impound funds without congressional approval.

by their parent bodies and adoption by Congress. If the spring's goals have not been met, the Budget Committees can recommend any combination of raising taxes, reducing spending, or revising the original targets.

Each of the two Budget Committees has a staff of several dozen professionals. They receive help from the new Congressional Budget Office (CBO), which has a staff of more than 200. The CBO is the counterpart of the president's Office of Management and Budget (see Chapter 14). It gives five-year economic forecasts, estimates of the five-year costs of every authorization, and policy analysis on economic issues. Generally, it enables Congress to examine the fiscal implications of its decisions without depending on the executive branch.

This new budget process is the latest in a string of congressional attempts to achieve fiscal coordination. The earlier efforts were all defeated by the fierce jurisdictional pride of the committee system. It is still too early to tell if this latest effort will succeed. So far, the Budget Committees have always backed away from a confrontation when drawing up their second resolution in the fall. They have always found that the fiscal policy embodied in the year's legislative output was the correct one. So, instead of proposing changes in taxes or spending levels to bring that output into line with their first resolution, they have gracefully revised their original targets. On the other hand, the Budget Committees are a continuing source of pressure as Congress does its business during the year. They analyze pending bills to see how they will affect the figures in their first resolution, and they often persuade Congress to amend proposals that would violate the resolution's guidelines.[25]

GATHERING INFORMATION

Any policymaking organization must have ways of gathering information. Without knowing what constituents and the public want, legislators cannot fulfill their duties as representatives. Without information about problems in the real world and their possible solutions, Congress cannot enact policies that work. We will begin with the second sort of information and then consider how congressmen learn about public opinion.

Members of Congress have heavy reading loads, ranging from *The New York Times* to research reports, books, and magazines. They also learn a lot by listening, and by skimming the written record of what has been said by and to other members. The *Congressional Record* is an almost verbatim record of floor debate.[26]

---

[25] Joel Havemann, "A Good Year for the Congressional Budget Process," *National Journal,* September 23, 1978, pp. 1501–3.

[26] We say "almost" because members and their aides can look over the stenographers' rough transcripts of floor debate and add, remove, or alter material before the day's issue goes to press. Apart from this minor tidying up, members insert material in the *Record* to support their positions, do someone a favor, or make a good impression. They also insert "speeches for the record" that were never delivered on the floor but represent what they would have said if they had. The *Record* Appendix is devoted to reprinted newspaper and magazine articles, speeches made elsewhere, and miscellaneous other material. The *Record,* averaging 200 pages in length, is delivered to every member's office at 6 A.M. after each day Congress is in session. This remarkable feat helps explain why the 1979 budget for congressional printing is $74 million. Almost 50,000 copies of the *Record* are mailed daily to libraries, the mass media, scholars, and citizens who ask their congressmen for a subscription.

Members either read it themselves or assign this task to an assistant. Hearings and committee reports are quickly printed and distributed. Members also hear a great deal in their daily rounds—on the floor, in committee meetings, the cloakrooms, over lunch, riding home together, and so on.

Government agencies are the most important source of information for Congress. In addition to testifying at hearings and providing official reports, the executive branch responds to thousands of requests for information from committees and individual members. Much of this material comes from nonpolitical experts who try to be objective, but of course this is not always the case. Some subjects are amenable to precise reporting. For example, infant mortality can be described by exact and universally accepted measures. In other areas, the facts may be more elusive, or expertise may be a matter of professional judgment. Members may accept without question material from the Bureau of Labor Statistics but be deeply suspicious of a report from the State Department about the condition of our relations with Panama. Much information given to Congress comes from agencies reporting on their own past performance and asking for new programs and more money for the old programs. Few people would be surprised if they did not slant the story in their own behalf.

Legislators are far from helpless victims of whatever the executive branch tells them. For one thing, outright lies or blatant distortions are rare. The officials involved have to deal with Congress for years, and getting a reputation for lying is not helpful to a bureaucrat who must keep coming back to Capitol Hill for appropriations requests. Keeping things secret in Washington is difficult. Congress gets a constant stream of information leaked by officials on the losing side in factional struggles, employees shocked at their superiors' behavior, and other dissidents. If the president has imposed a policy on an agency against the wishes of its professional heads, they will find a way to let Congress know their side of the story despite injunctions to be loyal to the elected leadership in the White House.

Information Sources GAO and CRS. Congress maintains several information-gathering services of its own. The General Accounting Office (GAO) has a budget of $186 million for studying how appropriated funds are spent. Originally conceived as a kind of legislative auditor, the GAO has become a major watchdog of the executive branch. It also provides staff assistance to individual members or committees.

The Library of Congress is, among other things, the largest and most complete general library in the United States. Its Congressional Research Service has over 800 specialists to do research for members of Congress. This service is nonpartisan, and the CRS staff is not supposed to recommend policies. The CRS is not as important a resource as might be thought, however. One problem is its workload. Over 300,000 inquiries a year are made by congressional offices. Most of these are simply questions asked of members by constituents and forwarded for answers to the CRS. It is widely believed on Capitol Hill that many students write to their congressman for help on term papers—and get it in the form of a report from the CRS. The CRS staff includes able scholars in many fields. But the organization as a whole is not a major provider of the information members use in resolving major issues. Individual CRS staff members sometimes have contributed in important ways to the work of Congress, more through their informal work with committee staff than through official CRS studies. The requirement of political neutrality tends to produce CRS papers that are bland collections of general information rather than pointed, incisive analyses that bring new light to a problem or point the way to solutions. Above-the-battle objectivity has drawbacks in the politicized Washington environment. The heart of the congressional information problem is getting advice from experts whose loyalties are not doubted by the recipient.

For the same reasons, the Congressional Budget Office, while performing valuable services, has severe limitations. The same is true of the newer Office of Technology Assessment, which is the CBO's counterpart in the area of science policy. One political scientist explains the situation this way:

> In each case, an organization with responsibility for objective policy analysis is responsible to an institution primarily engaged in subjective policy analysis. For many congressmen, the purpose of policy analysis is to provide evidence for what their political judgment tells them is correct.[27]

Committee and Personal Staffs. For these reasons, the main information sources in Congress are the staffs of committees and, to a lesser extent, the staffs of individual members. Congressional staffs more than doubled in size during the 1970s. One reason was the rising volume of mail. Another was the growing number of issues Congress considered. The most important reason, however, was the sudden prominence of subcommittees, each of which could hire its own staff rather than having to rely on aides controlled by the full committee chairman. The Senate Judiciary Committee, with about 200 people, has the largest single staff. Most other committees have about half this many. House committees have about the same number, except Appropriations and Ways and Means, with about 100 each. Because the majority party has absolute control over how many aides will be allocated to each party, the question of minority staffing is always a sore point with Republicans. Currently, Democrats allow Republicans about one-quarter of the committee staff. Combining personal and committee staffs, there are about 6,700 Senate aides and 11,000 on the House side. Perhaps 5,000 of these are professionals, and the rest are clerical employees. Salaries are generous—up to $52,500 a year.

About half of the committee aides are lawyers. The other half are mostly subject matter experts in areas relevant to each committee's work, such as irrigation or fisheries. Many are former employees of executive agencies. Some staffs are highly professionalized and almost nonpartisan. Others are equally competent but work only for the chairman or ranking minority member. Some are little more than political operatives for senior committee members.

Congressional staffs are supposed to provide advice and check on the material provided by outside sources. Although they do increase congressional indepen-

---

[27] Charles O. Jones, "Why Congress Can't Do Policy Analysis," *Policy Analysis,* 2 (spring 1976), p. 259.

dence enormously, they do not solve the problem of providing Congress with enough information to do its various jobs. Compared to the huge staffs available to the executive agencies and major private interest groups, congressional aides are a tiny handful. They do not provide real experts on all the issues that Congress decides. No staff member of either Agriculture Committee (or either Agriculture Appropriations Subcommittee) knows half as much about the gypsy moth as the Department of Agriculture entomologists with whom they deal, and yet Congress must pass legislation dealing with gypsy moth control. Some help comes informally from lobbyists, sympathetic bureaucrats, journalists, and policy-oriented members of the academic community.

Most of the information capability Congress has belongs to committee and subcommittee chairmen and is not available equally to all members. For example, the House Armed Services Committee staff has access to military information and skill at interpreting that information. They are hired by and loyal to the committee chairman. Some junior members of the committee, who are rather hostile to the Pentagon, often complain that Congress lacks the technical experts to stand up to the administration on defense policy. Strictly speaking, this may not be true. Certainly these junior committee members lack the staff that could help them pursue *their* policy goals. Adequate staff is in fact available to Congress. It is simply unavailable to *them*.

This situation brings home the point that "information" and "experts" are not neutral. If only one side in a dispute can call on specialists for technical advice, it clearly has an enormous advantage over adversaries who lack such resources. The fact that most useful information comes from the executive branch is no hardship to the administration's allies in Congress. The same is true for congressional allies of particular bureaucratic interests. The Air Force, Soil Conservation Service, Office of Education, National Institute of Mental Health—these and hundreds of other agencies have their friends on the Hill whom they supply (openly or covertly) with information and technical advice. The forces in Congress that are at a disadvantage when it comes to expertise are those that cannot call on the White House or the bureaucracy for help and are not senior enough to command the staff resources that come with subcommittee chairmanships.

As we have observed, experts are not useful unless congressmen can count on their political loyalty. This means that Congress needs not a body of expert advice, but a number of bodies, to match the variety of political orientations issue by issue. Why, then, does Congress not hire such help? One reason, of course, is that plenty of members have enough already, either through staffs under their command or with the help of allies in the executive branch and private interest groups of all kinds. We think Congress is unenthusiastic about further expansion of its own staff for fear of losing control of them, much as the president loses control of his huge bureaucracy. In fact, most members do not hire as many aides as they are entitled to. If the staffs get much larger, there is always the danger that they will not so much serve congressmen as capture them. They may become yet another group who want certain things and provide loaded information to help get them. There are scattered indications that this is already happening. Thus, one price members of Congress pay to become more of a match for the executive branch is

THE HAZARDS IN EXPANDING STAFFS

Staffs influence the legislative process at every stage. They not only frame the legislative options for their bosses' consideration—they also schedule the committee hearings, select the witnesses, and orchestrate the efforts of lobbyists in support of, or opposition to, the legislation. When a vote is near, staffs will often act as brokers for their principals in hammering out legislative compromises.

After the committee has voted, it is the staff that writes the report as well as the speeches for the floor managers who will debate the bills. These reports, which are seldom read by members, become bibles for the agencies that administer the legislation and for the courts that must eventually interpret the intent of Congress. Throughout this process, staffs, who are the primary news sources for reporters, shape the news media's perceptions of what is taking place and why. . . .

A classic example [of staff influence] was the report of the House Agriculture Committee on the Food Stamp Act of 1977. It was in effect an enormously detailed directive of 862 pages to the Department of Agriculture, laying down what the committee—that is, the staff—wanted the legislation to accomplish. (Included were thirty-four pages of instructions on how to use food-stamp purchases to prepare such low-cost dishes as chili con carne and fried apple rings.) . . .

All those new subcommittees and their staffs are not easing members' work loads, but are now increasing them, by generating more bills, more hearings, and more reports. Those hordes of bright young men on personal staffs also keep dreaming up new ideas for legislation.

Source: Juan Cameron, "The Shadow Congress the Public Doesn't Know," *Fortune,* January 15, 1979, pp. 38–39, 42.

greater dependence on staff. The second price is an increase in the punishing congressional workload.

Lobbyists. Lobbyists are essential to legislators. They provide them with useful information about the merits of proposed legislation. More important, they also provide a political reaction. It is the lobbyist's job to know when the crucial decisions on a bill are being made. With this information, he or she can organize pressure when it will do the most good—before the politicians have made their deals and formed coalitions among themselves. Important bills are carefully constructed compromise packages designed to give satisfaction to each part of the coalition. Once such a package has been assembled, legislators are reluctant to disturb it. Each provision is related to the others. Changing one of them may alienate a key faction that has given its consent only because it was given this particular provision in return.

Those lobbyists who are not well informed about the progress of a bill may miss their chance to influence it. In 1963, the Kennedy administration introduced a major bill that became the landmark Civil Rights Act of 1964. When this bill was being considered in the House Judiciary Committee, pressure from labor and civil rights lobbyists resulted in adding a provision that would, for the first time, establish federal procedures prohibiting racial discrimination in employment. This provision was accepted by both the Kennedy administration and leading Republicans on the Judiciary Committee and was one keystone of the bill's bipartisan majority. The leading business lobbies, the National Association of Manufacturers and the Chamber of Commerce, had always opposed such provisions in the past and had not thought that they had to worry about them in 1963. They did not know about this bipartisan deal until after the bill had been reported out of committee. By then it was too late to oppose this provision, since both parties had accepted it.

In addition to bill-watching, lobbyists sometimes get involved in what might be called "bill management." There are many bills about which no congressman cares very much. In these cases, lobbyists often supply the energy to keep the bill moving. They do a great deal of running back and forth at various points in the legislative process, making sure that everyone involved knows what the relevant others are doing. In this way they supplement the efforts of the party leaderships and the executive branch to keep the process moving.

The most effective lobbying approach is through a member's constituents, rather than directly from a Washington office. The reason this is so was perfectly expressed by a representative who asked, "If it doesn't come from my district, why should I care?"[28] When individuals and groups want the government to do something, it is only natural for them to turn to their own representatives and senators. Hence it is often difficult to distinguish between "lobbyists" and "interested citizens," or between representing one's constituents and giving in to lobbyists.

REPRESENTATION

To a legislator, the most important kind of information often concerns not the substance of public policy, but what people think—specifically, what constituents think. Legislators want to know what their constituents are thinking both because they want to be reelected and because they want to represent them. This seems obvious enough, but the apparently simple notion of representation turns out, on close examination, to be one of the knottiest problems in political thought.[29]

For present purposes we can distinguish three different types of representative. Each of these definitions states an ideal, and each ideal is in conflict with the other two. But all three ideals also are at odds with what we know about the real political world. We will not try to resolve these conflicts or to state our own conception of proper representation, but we do want to focus attention on the conflicts.

[28] Quoted in Kingdon, *Congressmen's Voting Decisions*, p. 144.
[29] The complications are discussed in Hanna F. Pitkin, *The Concept of Representation* (Berkeley: University of California Press, 1967).

1. The *instructed delegate* does in the legislature what constituents want him to.

    a. In this view, does good representation consist of voting and talking so as to reflect the whole constituency's views? Or to reflect the views of the majority who voted for the congressman? What if most voters do not have an opinion on an issue? Should he express the preferences of those who do have opinions? But if he does this, won't he often be representing "special interests" rather than "the people"? Who has an opinion about depletion allowances for oyster beds except oyster farmers?

2. The *trustee* does what he thinks best for his constituents, or for the country as a whole, without concern for public opinion. If the voters dislike the performance, they can always vote him out of office.

    a. If a legislator is reelected, can we take this as evidence that he is doing a good job of representing constituents on all issues? Or on those issues of greatest concern to them? Since members usually *are* reelected, shall we conclude therefore that Congress does a wonderful job of representing the people?

3. The *responsible party legislator* votes for the party's legislative program because he campaigned on the basis of the party's position. This legislator represents the people in the sense that those who voted for him were really choosing the party and thus the party's policies.

    a. People who vote for a candidate on the basis of party (that is, most voters) do not even *know* the party position on many issues, much less agree with it. Does the legislator really represent those who voted for him or her to the extent that he votes with the party? If so, why do members often vote *against* their party's position because of local considerations?[30]

These views of representation all assume that the voters know a great deal about their congressmen and that congressmen know a great deal about their constituents. The first set of assumptions is largely unrealistic. What about the second set? How accurately do legislators perceive what is going on in the minds of their constituents? How do they find out? What difference does it make?

Systematic research on this subject is exceptionally difficult to do, and only one such study has been attempted.[31] Its authors report that representatives try hard to learn what their constituents think about issues confronting Congress. The results of their efforts are mixed, however. They have more accurate impressions of their constituents' opinions on some issues than on others. Voting in Congress was closely related to constituent opinion on civil rights, but only slightly so on foreign policy. Legislators were more likely to vote the way their constituents felt about economic issues than they were to perceive those views correctly.

---

[30] Warren E. Miller and Donald E. Stokes, "Constituency Influence in Congress," in Angus Campbell et al., *Elections and the Political Order* (New York: Wiley, 1966), pp. 351–72.

[31] Miller and Stokes, "Constituency Influence in Congress." See also Christopher H. Achen, "Measuring Representation," *American Journal of Political Science,* 22 (August 1978), pp. 475–510.

The study also revealed that legislators overestimate their own visibility to the voters. That is, they are far less widely known and observed by the general public than they think they are. Members of Congress exaggerate their position in the public eye for two reasons. One is the perfectly natural tendency of all human beings to have inflated impressions of their own importance to others. The second reason is more political. Although legislators are largely "invisible" to *most* voters, they are, nevertheless, on the receiving end of a substantial amount of communication from *some* constituents. And the constituents they hear from tend to be more articulate and informed.

How Members of Congress Learn What Constituents Want

Most legislators try to balance the hothouse quality of Washington life by touching base frequently with their constituencies.

The average representative makes thirty-five trips home every year and spends a third of his or her time there.[32] All members maintain one or more "home offices," which feed them information. Every member reads the local newspapers religiously.

Many members conduct "polls" by mailing questionnaires to some or all of their constituents. The results are inserted in the *Congressional Record* and are always good for a press release to the local news media. This is probably the most suspect kind of survey research imaginable. The questions are often slanted, it is impossible to calculate what kinds of people respond, and some members have been known to doctor the answers. In any event, few observers take these polls seriously and their chief purpose is propaganda. Professionally conducted surveys are usually bought for help in campaigning, not legislating.

Mail is an important source of information about what the folks back home are thinking. Dealing with the mail is an important task and takes about half the time of members' personal staffs. At the very least, all letters from the state or district are answered. No matter how critical or abusive the letter, the general rule is not to argue back. The basic reply thanks the writer, expresses the member's intention to keep his or her views in mind, and invites further expressions of opinion. The reply may also include information about the issue, but this is secondary to making the writer feel good. The style of much congressional mail is illustrated by the specimen reproduced on page 380.

Few members personally read very much of their mail, but they are keenly interested in what it reveals of public opinion. Many offices prepare weekly summaries to give the member an idea of what issues are agitating the public and what the predominant sentiment is. Very often "the issues around which mass opinion is mobilized are not the crucial ones in the minds of those who frame legislative policy." When this is the case, "the net effect of communication [is] to heighten attention to an issue, rather than to convey specific content about it.[33] At the very least, then, mail alerts the member to what the politically aware fraction of a constituency

[32] Richard F. Fenno, Jr., *Home Style: House Members in Their Districts* (Boston: Little, Brown, 1978), pp. 39, 222.

[33] Both quotations are from Lewis Anthony Dexter, "The Job of the Congressman," in Wolfinger, ed. *Readings on Congress*, pp. 76, 79.

July 2, 1962

Dear Friend:

I have received the petition you recently signed as an expression of your support of efforts to set aside the Week of July 15 to 21 as National Drum Corps Week.

Thank you for giving me the opportunity to know of your interest in this matter. I sincerely regret the necessity to answer you in this form, for I would much rather write you a personal letter. I am sure you will understand, however, that time prohibits a personal answer to each of you.

I would like to assure you that I am in complete agreement with your position on this and shall do everything I can to bring Congressional approval of this recognition.

I long have been an admirer of such organizations as yours and feel that you are more than deserving of this honor.

Again, thank you for signing this petition. Should you have any additional comments or questions on this or any other matter before Congress, I sincerely hope you will not hesitate to communicate directly with me.

Sincerely yours,

is thinking. This is true even when the member is on the receiving end of organized letter-writing campaigns. In this case it is not the individual messages that count, but the fact that some interest group has the capacity to generate hundreds or thousands of letters, and may have the same ability to mobilize workers at the next election.

Members are more likely to hear from and to pay attention to certain types of constituents — people who are active in local politics, people who speak for major social and economic forces, friends and supporters, or any combination of these. The tendency to listen to politically active rather than rank-and-file constituents is

REPRESENTATION VS. STATESMANSHIP

Many of the struggles I witnessed in the Senate involved conflict between statesmanship and representation. For many senators there was an almost constant effort to reconcile their own opinions with demands that emerged from the Senate itself—obligations to other senators, due bills for past favors, the need to establish future preference by a present vote—and with the views embodied in letters and phone calls from home. Where public opinion was rigidly fixed and overwhelming, they seldom resisted it. Where it was more evenly balanced, or where it was inchoate and amorphous, their freedom to be independent was correspondingly enhanced.

Source: Harry McPherson, *A Political Education* (Boston: Little, Brown, 1972), p. 63.

reinforced by the fact that members have committee constituencies as well as electoral ones. The committee constituencies will be even more completely composed of interest groups and political activists than the perceived home constituency. Rank-and-file voters rarely present their views to committees in person. If their views are expressed, it is through an organized group of some kind.

In short, sometimes members know what their constituents are thinking and sometimes they do not. Sometimes they follow this opinion and sometimes they do not. Generally, they guide themselves by the opinions of the outspoken and organized members of their constituency—and by the opinions of constituents who know and support them. As Fenno puts it, "They feel more accountable to some constituents than to others because the support of some constituents is more important to them than the support of others."[34] Because they overestimate the visibility of their behavior on Capitol Hill, members often play it safe, anticipating more constituent reactions than in fact exist. But even though they are responsive to public opinion, the "public" to which they are responsive is not a microcosm of their constituency. Instead, it includes a disproportionate number of the organized and articulate—the squeaky wheels who get the grease of congressional response.

What Americans Want from It would be a mistake to think that for most people represen-
Their Representatives tation is only a matter of issues, legislation, and votes on the floor. Most Americans do not put such weighty matters first when thinking about their representatives. Only a fraction of the mail to Capitol Hill concerns pending legislation; the rest is mainly requests for help or information. When asked their opinions of their representatives, most people ignore issues and votes to talk about personal qualities, casework, and what he or she has done for

[34] Fenno, *Home Style,* p. 234.

the district. Asked what is important for a representative to do, over 80 percent of members mention legislation and 41 percent mention oversight. Less than 60 percent of the public think legislation important, and a bare 1 percent value oversight. Instead, ordinary citizens want their legislators to help constituents, keep in touch, and "represent the people."[35]

Faced with this conflict, members subordinate their own preferences to those of their constituents. One representative explained the choice this way:

> Legislation . . . can be neglected without any immediate adverse impact on a congressman. He can miss a committee hearing, not be on the floor, neglect material necessary for an informed decision, and who's ever gonna know? But he cannot avoid . . . responding to constituent requests. So constituent requests take a priority over legislation. You have a turning upside down of what the priorities ought to be.

Members' assessments of Congress reflect this situation. Most of them think a good job is done at representation and ombudsman, a fair job at legislation, and a poor one at oversight.

In short, there is a gap between what members think they should do and what their constituents value in a representative. Much of the responsibility for this state of affairs rests with the members who complain about it. Working on legislation or oversight has less political payoff. Taking stands on issues always runs the risk of pleasing one voter at the cost of offending another. Morris Fiorina puts the choice this way:

> While less exciting, casework and pork barreling are both safe and profitable. For a reelection-oriented congressman the choice is obvious. . . . . He would rather be reelected as an errand boy than not be reelected at all.[36]

Members of Congress vs. Congress

As we saw in Chapter 12, many Americans like their congressman but hate Congress. The individual member is most commonly admired for nonlegislative reasons, while policy dissatisfaction seems to underlie popular assessments of the institution. This distinction is encouraged by the ways members present themselves to their constituents:

> Nothing, however, had prepared me to discover that each member of Congress polishes his or her individual reputation at the expense of the institutional reputation of Congress. In explaining what he was doing in Washington, every one

---

[35] The findings in this paragraph and the next one, and the long quotation, are from a series of studies conducted for the House of Representatives Commission on Administrative Review, reported in Thomas E. Cavanagh, "The Two Arenas of Congress: Electoral and Institutional Incentives for Performance," paper presented at the 1978 annual meeting of the American Political Science Association.

[36] Morris P. Fiorina, *Congress: Keystone of the Washington Establishment* (New Haven, Conn.: Yale University Press, 1977), pp. 46, 37.

of the eighteen House members took the opportunity to picture himself as different from, and better than, most of his fellow members of Congress.

. . . .

> The performance of Congress is collective; but the responsibility for congressional performance is not. Responsibility is assessed member by member, district by district. It is easy for each congressman to explain to his own supporters why he cannot be blamed for the performance of the collectivity. It is doubly easy to do so because the internal diversity and decentralization of the institution provide such a diversity of collegial villains to flay before one's supporters at home. . . . The beauty of the strategy is that everybody can use it and nobody will be called to account by those under attack.[37]

In short, a desire to take no chances with their political survival leads members to "run *for* Congress by running *against* Congress."[38] To many people, the institution is much less than the sum of its parts. Whether the split image retards American government, or is merely a harmless political myth, is anybody's guess.

LEGISLATIVE CONTROL OF THE EXECUTIVE BRANCH

As the old-fashioned civics textbooks saw American government, "Congress makes the laws; the president enforces them." In the real world, of course, there is often no clear line between making a law and enforcing it, between "politics" and "administration." Richard Neustadt provides a more realistic picture of relations between the executive and legislative branches:

> The constitutional convention of 1787 is supposed to have created a government of "separated powers." It did nothing of the sort. Rather, it created a government of separated institutions *sharing* powers. "I am part of the legislative process," Eisenhower often said in 1959 as a reminder of his veto. Congress, the dispenser of authority and funds, is no less part of the administrative process.[39]

Congressional *capacity* to intervene in what the executive branch does is considerable, although the number of such interventions is limited by the size of congressional staffs. Congressional *willingness* to do so is quite another matter. Considering these two issues, we will look at three major types of congressional power over the executive—legislative oversight, reorganization and confirmation, and then the special case of foreign policy.

[37] Fenno, *Home Style,* pp. 164, 167.
[38] Fenno, *Home Style,* p. 168.
[39] Richard E. Neustadt, *Presidential Power* (New York: Wiley, 1960), p. 33.

Legislative Oversight   Implicit in the power to make laws is the need to see how the executive branch is administering them. The same is true about the power of the purse. The twenty-six Appropriations subcommittees assess this year's budget requests by trying to find out how agencies are spending the money they got last year. Congress includes a number of specialists on various topics who devote part of their time to examining administrative efficiency. Usually they operate from a committee or subcommittee chairmanship that legitimates their interest, gives them a forum and staff, and, through hearings, provides occasions for questioning executive officials.

Congressional investigating committees traditionally have been a means of uncovering shady, unconstitutional, or incompetent behavior in the executive branch. The two Governmental Affairs Committees provide platforms for such inquiry. The Investigations Subcommittee of the Senate Governmental Affairs Committee has a staff of forty. It can be an important congressional watchdog, although it tends to be a vehicle for the ambitions of its chairman, who can use it to occupy the spotlight on whatever issue is most interesting to the public. The General Accounting Office reports to Congress on the legality and efficiency of the administration's spending practices. It has been one of the few outside forces to penetrate the Defense Department's screen of secrecy and publish useful information on cost overruns, delivery delays, irregular contracting arrangements, and other deplorable news.

For obvious reasons, presidents and bureaucrats are not fond of legislative oversight. They have two reasons for wanting to frustrate it. In the first place, some governmental activities should be kept secret. This is true of many aspects of military, diplomatic, and intelligence work. And in the second place, oversight embarrasses the administration and provides ammunition to its political opponents, particularly when Congress is controlled by the other party. The problem, of course, is that the first reason, which is a worthy one, is often used to justify coverups of incompetence and crimes. The Watergate scandal is the most striking example. President Nixon tried to abort investigations into the crimes of his lieutenants by claiming that further inquiry would jeopardize national security. Revelation of the tape recording of his discussions on this topic was the event that forced him to resign.

Sensational revelations of unsavory operations by the Central Intelligence Agency led to demands for greater congressional supervision. Some critics charged that Congress lacked the will to do a vigorous job of oversight. This accusation is close to the truth. The CIA oversight committees, for example, regarded that agency much the same way that the Agriculture Subcommittee on Cotton looked at cotton growers — as a constituency to be protected. The CIA is hardly a new issue for Congress. Between 1949 and 1971, almost two hundred bills to make it more accountable were introduced. Only two were reported from committee, and neither came close to passing.[40] It is difficult to escape the conclusion that Congress did not keep its eye on the CIA for the simple reason that most members were not too dissatisfied with the CIA. Those who complained about the lack of energetic oversight were a minority. More important, *they were not on the committees that approve*

[40] *CQ Weekly Report,* August 28, 1971, p. 1840.

Testifying in favor of strict limits on covert operations
before the Senate Select Committee on Intelligence were,
from left, Cyrus Vance, soon to be Secretary of State in
the Carter administration; Clark Clifford, Lyndon Johnson's
last Secretary of Defense; David Phillips, a career CIA official;
and Morton Halperin, a civil liberties activist and former Pentagon official.

the CIA's budget. When Congress finally did look into the CIA, it was by creating select committees in each body, not by investigations by any of the existing committees and subcommittees. The impact of these congressional investigations on the CIA — and American capacity in foreign affairs — was enormous. We think many examples of feeble oversight have the same explanation. When Congress fails to call the executive branch to account, the relevant committees may not be displeased with what the executive has been doing.

The most fundamental limitation on oversight is the shortage of time. There are only twenty-four hours in a day, and the average legislator already works eleven of them. Although many members think oversight is an important congressional function, virtually no one else does. In fact, only 1 percent of the public think oversight is something Congress should be doing. It should not be surprising that oversight takes a back seat to other things members could be doing with their time.

The Legislative Veto. Oversight ordinarily is enforced through public exposure, an adverse decision on next year's budget, or even remedial legislation. A more drastic sanction is the **legislative veto,** which gives Congress the power to overrule administrative actions. Over 400 laws contain provisions authorizing Congress to veto executive actions in particular fields. For example, a law passed in 1976 empowers Congress to block arms sales to foreign countries. Doing so requires a resolution of disapproval by both houses within thirty days of official notice from the president. This provides the leverage for congressional involvement in what had been the business of the executive branch. The newest development with the legislative veto is applying it to an entire agency, so that Congress claims the power to overrule any action taken by that agency.

The legislative veto poses two problems, one of them constitutional. It may be an excessive intrusion of Congress into the executive realm and therefore a violation of the doctrine of separation of powers. The Supreme Court has not ruled on this point, which has been made by President Carter in objecting to the veto. The second concern is more practical: Does Congress have either the time or the staff to maintain such scrutiny of the administrative branch? For the reasons we have examined, a major addition of staff is neither likely nor desirable. Thus, the legislative veto seems destined to be, at most, an occasional weapon in the continuing struggle between Congress and the executive.

Reorganization   Constitutionally, it is Congress, not the president, that has the authority to fix the organization of the executive branch. Organization can be a powerful weapon of policy control. Abolishing an agency or redefining its mission or jurisdiction is the ultimate weapon of administrative infighting. This is particularly true because in the United States Civil Service, rank goes with the job, not the person. By transferring a program and abolishing an agency, the policy survives but the bureaucrat may be among the unemployed.

Congress has given much of this power to the president, subject to congressional veto. Within certain limits, the president can propose new arrangements of administrative agencies. Such a proposal goes into effect unless Congress votes to disapprove the new organization. By putting the burden on Congress to veto what the president has undertaken, this legislation shifts some power away from Capitol Hill. Congress, though, has not surrendered all control over organization. Ambitious changes in organizational structure, such as the creation, abolition, or merger of existing departments, still require legislation.

Although Congress has not exercised the power, it can drastically rearrange the administrative structure of the government to achieve certain ends. If it wanted to, it could, for example, shift responsibility for military aid from the Pentagon to the Agency for International Development. Some politicians have argued that by using this power of organization more vigorously, the legislative branch could exert much more influence over the conduct of policy. We think its failure to do so reflects the vested interest in preserving existing agency-congressional committee relationships.

Confirmation   Cabinet officers, ambassadors, federal judges, and thousands of miscellaneous other officials appointed by the president must be confirmed by the Senate before they can take office. The number of such

*Theodore C. Sorensen sits
in the witness chair
at a hearing of the Senate
Intelligence Committee in 1977.
He had just told the committee
he no longer wanted to be considered
for confirmation as director of the CIA.*

appointments is really quite staggering. In 1977 the Senate confirmed 65,631 people. Almost all are approved routinely. A few appointments really originate in Congress. (This is particularly true of federal district judges, whose appointment is described in Chapter 16.)

Confirmation is not always automatic, however. Once in a while a presidential nominee is offensive to some groups, or some senators. This may be for reasons of policy, competence, or character. Often doubts on personal or policy grounds will masquerade as assaults on the nominee's character or competence. Theodore C. Sorensen, whom Carter proposed as his first Director of the CIA, encountered such senatorial hostility on all these fronts that he withdrew his name from consideration. Although such events are rare, the possibility means that presidents cannot ignore the likely Senate response when considering political appointments.

In extraordinary circumstances, the Senate may exact concessions from Cabinet nominees before agreeing to their appointment. When this happens, it means that the president's ability to be master in his own house is limited. In 1973, early revelations in the Watergate case made the Senate Judiciary Committee suspicious of the Justice Department's commitment to unearthing the truth. As a condition of confirming President Nixon's nominee as attorney general, the committee insisted on the appointment of a special prosecutor. This official would be appointed from outside the government and given a large staff and wide latitude to conduct an independent investigation of Watergate. Two special prosecutors, first Archibald Cox and then Leon Jaworski, subpoenaed tape recordings of Nixon's secret conferences about how to deal with the break-in at the Democratic headquarters in the Watergate complex. Nixon resisted the subpoena and the case went to the Supreme Court. Nixon argued, among other things, that as a member of the executive branch, Jaworski was his subordinate and therefore had no basis for demanding the tapes. The Court held, however, that the preconfirmation agreements about Jaworski's independence meant that Nixon had waived his right to give Jaworski orders. It was these tapes that revealed Nixon's plan to use "national security" as an excuse for covering up Watergate. His resignation followed.

This case shows how the confirmation power can be used to extract from Cabinet members concessions that could cripple the president's authority within the executive branch. But the extreme rarity of the Senate's use of this power demonstrates an even more important feature of American politics—the extent to which each of the major elements in the system respects the boundaries of the other branches. There is a good deal of guerilla warfare along the borders, to be sure. But both Congress and the president shrink from confrontations and blatant usurpations of the other's power.

Foreign Policy   Congress cannot conduct policies that require fast, secret decisions because its style and organization do not allow for secrecy, speed, or decisiveness. Foreign policy requires discriminating application, not general rules. This severely limits the potential for congressional influence in foreign and defense matters. But although Congress cannot easily participate in ongoing operational decisions, it does provide the resources used in foreign policy, ranging from economic aid to naval task forces. Thus Congress shapes the options available to the executive trying to decide how to deal with a particular situation. Certain policies may be limited or out altogether because the means to carry them out are lacking. Congressional responses to presidential requests for defense spending are the most obvious and important example of this opportunity to influence foreign policy. One student of this subject has written:

> Just as struggles within the executive branch over the content and direction of defense policy are manifest as conflicts over weapons systems, Congress may believe that decisions relating to present and future weapons systems, reflected in . . . budget actions, are at the very heart of national security policy, and constitute that part of the budget on which Congressional efforts to influence national security policy are most economically expended. As Charles Hitch, former Pentagon Comptroller, has observed: "These [weapons systems] choices have become the key decisions around which much else of the defense program revolves."[41]

The Vietnam war illustrates the limits of this sort of congressional control. During the first years of the war, Congress seldom dealt harshly with presidential budget requests for defense. As disenchantment with the war mounted, so did congressional willingness to take a hard look at Pentagon spending proposals. This scrutiny was focused on the most strategic point, requests for new weapons systems. Congress began to reduce these significantly by 1970, in some cases deleting all funds for a particular project. Explaining one such deletion, the chairman of the Senate Appropriations Committee said, "If we build anything like this, we are just going to be handed more and more of this business of fighting everybody's wars everywhere."[42]

By the mid 1970s, its willingness to exercise the power of the purse made Congress a significant source of restraint on the executive branch's foreign and military policy. In 1973, Congress forbade use of appropriated funds for bombing Cambodia. In 1975, it refused military aid to Cambodia, thus guaranteeing the defeat of the anti-Communist government we had sponsored for five years. In the same year, congressional distaste for further military expenditures in Vietnam hastened the doom of the Saigon regime, for whose survival we had spent so much blood and money. A few months before that, Congress had refused all aid to Turkey until its troops pulled back from their invasion of Cyprus. The president and his secretary of state called this a subversion of American efforts to solve the Cyprus crisis through diplomacy. Other observers felt that the cutoff strengthened our hand

---

[41] Arnold Kanter, "Congress and the Defense Budget: 1960–1970," *American Political Science Review,* 66 (March 1972), p. 135.

[42] Quoted in Kanter, "Congress and the Defense Budget," p. 137.

in this respect. Whoever was right, one thing seemed certain: Congress was having an impact on foreign policy.[43]

Treaties.   Making foreign and defense policy rarely is a matter of passing laws. Occasionally, however, the national interest seems to require the sort of formal relationship that is embodied in a treaty with one or more other countries. An example is the new legal status of the Panama Canal negotiated in the 1970s. The Senate plays a crucial role on such occasions because of its constitutional power to ratify treaties. Presidents have been forced to change treaties already negotiated in order to win the support of two-thirds of the Senate, and the Senate can effectively amend a treaty by attaching reservations to its ratification. Although making treaties is his responsibility, a wise president anticipates the need for Senate approval. The American position in the recurring Strategic Arms Limitation Treaty (SALT) talks with the Soviet Union is shaped by the views of influential senators whose help will be needed to ratify whatever agreement is reached.

SUMMARY   The lawmaking process begins with the introduction of a bill and its assignment to a committee and then a subcommittee. Most bills are ignored; a few hundred every year cross the first hurdle and are the subject of hearings held by the subcommittee. After hearings, the subcommittee will markup and report the bill if a majority of members favor doing so. The same process occurs in the full committee. The majority party leadership decides in what order the bills reported from committee will come to the floor. The floor debate stage involves trying to win enough votes for final passage and fighting off amendments that may cripple or seriously alter the bill. Both House and Senate must go through all these stages. If their versions differ, a conference committee is formed to bring in a single compromise version.

Despite the weakness of formal party discipline, there is a remarkable amount of party voting. It is stronger on some issues than others, and is often modified by the coalition between conservative southern Democrats and Republicans. This conservative coalition often defeats proposals supported by most Democrats, the party that has controlled Congress almost all of the past 45 years.

Because there is so much business to be done, and so many bills that most members do not know or care about, congressmen respect the established procedures and resist the available short cuts.

Committees are powerful in proportion to the confidence that the entire membership of the body has in their expertise and their willingness to work together. Responsibility in most policy areas is in the hands of a committee or subcommittee that is largely independent of other committees.

The process of appropriating money for the government to spend is separate from creating the programs on which the money is to be spent, that is, it is done by different committees. Moreover, providing the money through

---

[43] In 1978 the Carter administration persuaded Congress to lift the ban on aid to Turkey.

taxation is also handled by a separate pair of committees. Because each committee is dominant in its own jurisdiction, it is difficult for Congress as a whole to compare related bills, devise priorities, and match income and spending. Coordinating fiscal decisions is the goal of the new congressional budget process. The heart of this process is a budget resolution setting spending limits in each category of federal expenditures.

In order to know what bills to pass, Congress must know what the problems are and what people want done about them. The most important source of information is government agencies. In addition, Congress maintains its own information-gathering services—the General Accounting Office, the Congressional Research Service of the Library of Congress, and committee and personal staffs. Lobbyists are another source, one that provides both information and some idea of the likely political reaction by interested groups. The most important information is often not facts but what people, especially constituents, think. Most members spend about a third of their time in their districts and maintain elaborate mail-answering services. They do this because to most Americans, what is important is not how a representative generally votes, but what he or she does for individuals and the district.

Congressional control of the executive branch, a controversial issue in recent years, can be accomplished through several devices: legislative oversight, the power (seldom exercised) to fix the organization of the executive branch, Senate confirmation of high officials and of treaties, and the provision or denial of money.

the presidency

The "modern" presidency has powers the Founding Fathers could never have imagined. More people now work in the Executive Office of the President than in the entire civilian executive branch of the government in the early years of the Republic. Statutes, court rulings, and unofficial precedents enable presidents to issue a wide range of executive orders which are published in *The Federal Register* and which have the same legal force as laws passed by Congress. Most unthinkable is the president's control of a nuclear weapons system which could exterminate much of the human race.

CHAPTER 14

Yet if the Founding Fathers were able to examine the contemporary presidency, they also would see it subject to the restraints they wrote into the Constitution. Executive, legislative, and judiciary share power and check one another. In the last decade and a half, one president, Lyndon Johnson, encountered such bitter opposition that he chose not to seek reelection. The next president, Richard Nixon, resigned rather than be impeached and convicted in connection with the Watergate affair. Nixon's successor, Gerald Ford, faced a Congress that passed numerous laws he vetoed and was unsympathetic to his own policy proposals, as well as an electorate that voted him out of office. And Jimmy Carter quickly found that many of the programs he considered most important were substantially altered or blocked on Capitol Hill.

What, then, can we say of presidential power in the United States? Is there a dangerously uncontrolled presidency, just as many critics of Johnson and Nixon said? Or is the presidency a potentially vital source of national leadership, which is crippled by a Congress without national vision, an uncooperative civil service, and sniping by interest groups and the mass media? It would be surprising if such sweeping questions could be sensibly answered by a simple yes or no. First of all, questions about presidential power raise two different distinct issues: (1) What in fact *are* presidents able to accomplish? (2) What *should* presidents be able to accomplish? That is, what do we believe ought to be the powers of the president? Moreover, answers to each question need two qualifications. First, views of the "is" and the "should" of presidential power change over the years as the presidency evolves, and as presidential actions shift from administration to administration. Second, views differ about the "is" and the "should" of power in different spheres of presidential activity. One might conclude, for example, that presidents' economic powers are weak but their war powers are great, and one might approve or disapprove of the degree of presidential power in either sphere. This book deliberately focuses on "is" questions, providing information readers can use to make their own judgments of "should" questions. Nevertheless, in analyzing the workings of the presidency or any other aspect of politics, one important part of the factual record is the value judgments of those who take part in politics, including political activists, political commentators, and members of the public.

One of the realities of the American presidency has been the changing reputation of the institution and shifting views of what presidential powers are legitimate. As early as the Washington administration, two leading defenders of the Constitution, James Madison and Alexander Hamilton, published opposing views of whether the first president was exceeding his constitutional powers in foreign affairs. In the final decades of the twentieth century, debate about what is legitimate presidential power has not stopped. And in all periods, political commentators' positions on what powers should belong to presidents are very much affected by whether they approve of what the president is doing with those powers. A striking recent example of the effect of what the president is doing on views of how the presidency ought to operate is the about-face of many liberals who had defended sweeping exercises of independent presidential action by Presidents Franklin Roosevelt, Truman, and Kennedy. When Presidents Johnson and Nixon followed policies they disliked, many of the same liberals suddenly discovered that the presidency had become

THE PRESIDENT AND FOREIGN POLICY

George Washington's proclamation of American neutrality in the war between Britain and France (1793) led to a debate over presidential power by two authors of the Constitution, Alexander Hamilton and James Madison. Hamilton, who was Washington's secretary of the treasury, argued that declarations of neutrality—and by extension much of the conduct of foreign policy—"must . . . of necessity belong to the executive department." He noted that the judiciary had the power only to "decide litigation in particular cases" and hence could interpret treaties but not directly conduct foreign relations. And, he continued, the legislature ratified treaties but "is charged neither with making nor with enforcing" them. Hence Congress is "not the organ of intercourse between the United States and foreign nations."

In reply, Madison said: "Although the executive may be a convenient organ of preliminary communications with foreign governments," Congress, because of its powers to declare war and confirm treaties, was the "essential agency which gives validity to such determinations." Hamilton won on the immediate issue, but the general question of the extent of the president's foreign *and* domestic powers continues to be a matter of debate in the late twentieth century.

dangerously strong. Not surprisingly, some conservatives who had been critics of presidential autonomy defended broad presidential war powers during the Vietnam conflict.

The reality of what a president actually can accomplish fluctuates, depending on his political support, his skill, whether he is acting in an area that requires ratification by others, and prevailing views of what presidential powers should be. From President Roosevelt's second term in office, and especially from the midterm 1938 congressional election through President Johnson's overwhelming 1964 election victory, presidents typically had to deal with Congresses controlled by conservative coalitions that resisted many liberal policy initiatives. Lyndon Johnson was elected with a large enough Democratic majority to achieve a sweeping liberal program of domestic legislation. During the passage of Johnson's Great Society program, liberals still defended a strong presidency. In foreign affairs, Johnson from 1965 to 1968 increasingly expanded American troop commitments in Vietnam in the face of swelling congressional and public opposition. Liberal approval of presidential activism diminished and continued to do so during the Nixon years. Nixon used presidential military powers with a degree of independence that aroused congressional criticism and public protest. He impounded funds appropriated by Congress in a way that enabled him to make policies Congress would not have supported. During the first few months after his landslide 1972 reelection, Nixon consistently worked to enhance the power of the presidency. But during his two-year rear-guard action against the Watergate inquiries, he became much less assertive. Meanwhile, both unofficially and through president-curbing laws, Congress chipped away at what had come to be accepted executive powers.

Nixon's two successors, Carter and Ford, went out of their way to convey images of openness and informality. Both men, however, had definite policy goals, and in each case, partly because of backlash against "imperial presidencies" and partly because of forces that have always placed checks on presidents, their successes were few and hard-won. Less was heard of presidential imperialism after Nixon's resignation, and there were more references to the alleged failures of Ford and Carter to exercise the leadership required of presidents. We begin our examination of this complex institution by looking at the foundation—the Constitution. Then we will look at the role of the president in American life; the impact of the presidential personality; the president as politician, executive, and head of government; and the executive branch.

CONSTITUTIONAL POWERS

Although the Constitution is far from a precise guide to how the government works, let us begin by discussing the description of the presidency in Article II. The Founding Fathers were torn between worry about overbearing executives like the British king and desire for a government with more power of decision than the existing legislature-centered system. They thought the presidency should have modest and restrained powers. In their confidence that George Washington would be the first president and would exercise his powers in a responsible fashion, they described the duties of the office so vaguely that later presidents could make their own interpretations.[1]

For example, the president is "Commander in Chief of the Army and Navy of the United States." This is subject to congressional power to "raise and support armies," declare war, appropriate funds, and make rules for the armed forces. In practice, however, the president is given wide latitude in decisions affecting the equipment, organization, leadership, mission, and deployment of the armed forces. He can send soldiers to Arkansas to enforce a Supreme Court decision to desegregate a high school. He can send warships anywhere in the world to influence, by force or by threat, the behavior of other countries. He must decide whether to use nuclear weapons. Recent presidents have exercised their powers as commander-in-chief in very different ways. During World War II, Franklin D. Roosevelt decided only on the most general strategies, picked his generals and admirals, and then left the war to

President Nixon used the symbolic impact of his visit to China in 1972 to dramatize his reopening of diplomatic relations with that country. Here he and Chinese Premier Chou En-lai appear at a state banquet.

Wide World

---

[1] The classic discussion of the constitutional basis of the presidency is Edward S. Corwin, *The President: Office and Powers,* 4th ed. (New York: New York University Press, 1957). For a more up-to-date discussion, see Louis Fisher, *The Constitution Between Friends: Congress, the President, and the Law* (New York: St. Martin's, 1978).

them. Lyndon Johnson, on the other hand, went so far as personally to choose individual bombing targets in Vietnam.

Article II also authorizes the president to make treaties with other countries, subject to approval by two-thirds of the Senate. Presidents, however, can make **executive agreements** with foreign powers which are not subject to Senate approval. Under modern presidents, use of the executive agreement has increased to the point where this type of arrangement is now far more common than Senate-approved treaties. Article II also directs that the president will "receive Ambassadors." This is another way of saying that he will conduct relations with other countries. The power to receive ambassadors also quickly came to be the power to recognize foreign governments, as in the recognition of the People's Republic of China by President Carter. Moreover, in recognizing the PRC, Carter ended long-standing diplomatic relations with the Nationalist Chinese government in Taiwan, even terminating a treaty with "the other China." Although he does not have the power to declare war, the president is authorized to engage in relations with other nations that may in fact lead to war.

Taken together, the commander-in-chief and foreign affairs powers of the president have traditionally made him the main force in determining foreign policy. The power of one-third of the Senate to defeat a treaty was fatal to Woodrow Wilson's desire to bring the United States into the League of Nations after World War I. Jimmy Carter's desire to obtain a treaty that would gradually yield American sovereignty over the Panama Canal triggered intense organized pressures that came close to defeating the treaty. Increasingly, global economic complexity reduces the distinction between foreign and domestic politics. Energy policy is a case in point: it is cross-cut by domestic interest group politics and relations with foreign countries such as the oil-producing nations. The more domestic politics converges with foreign politics, the weaker is the president's traditional leadership in foreign policy-making. In the sphere of mixed foreign and domestic policy, as in most other spheres, he continues to be the single most important actor in the political system. But the frequency with which he can get what he wants, and the degree to which he must compromise, rises and falls with circumstances. Roosevelt, for example, was severely limited in foreign affairs during the isolationist 1930s, but had almost unlimited discretion after the United States entered World War II in 1941.

The Constitution also directs that the president "shall take care that the laws be faithfully executed." On the face of it, this may appear to be a restriction on the president, reminding him to obey the law. This requirement no doubt was in the minds of members of Congress when virtually all of them said they would vote to impeach and convict President Nixon after the release of tape recordings showing that he had lied about his involvement in obstructing the investigation of the Watergate burglary. Ordinarily, however, the "take care clause" has been used as justification for *extensions* of presidential power, because in administering legislation, the president must interpret it. Moreover, he may have to decide which of several seemingly contradictory laws applies to a decision, or even whether a law is consistent with the Constitution. Thus, the president is also a lawmaker.

Another presidential power, that of making appointments, is a major source of influence. The Supreme Court has held that this power carried with it the power to fire appointees, other than those holding judicial or quasi-judicial offices.

Finally, we should note the sentence with which Article II begins. Sometimes called the "wild card" in the deck of presidential powers, it declares: "The executive Power shall be vested in a President of the United States of America." The meaning of "the executive Power" is vague, vast, and constantly subject to expansion and redefinition. On many occasions this phrase has been used to justify striking acts of presidential autonomy. The Constitution provides for removal of the president by the Congress through impeachment (indictment) by the House of Representatives and a Senate trial requiring a two-thirds vote for conviction. Impeachment proceedings against Abraham Lincoln's successor, Andrew Johnson, led to a Senate trial that ended in acquittal—by one vote. Impeachment was then thought to be a dead letter, until the Watergate scandal.

But whether the president has too much power, as many Americans have argued, not enough, as others believe, or too much of some kinds of power and too little of others, he unquestionably has vastly more power than the Founding Fathers anticipated. This is due, in part, to his performance of roles not formally recognized in the Constitution. In part, too, it is a result of the inevitable impact on the public perceptions of the president generated by the central place he occupies in the real and the symbolic political world. And in part it is simply a product of aspects of twentieth-century national and international politics that have strengthened executives everywhere in the world.

WHAT THE PRESIDENT MEANS TO AMERICANS

We can begin to understand the president's complex and contradictory role today by examining his place in public opinion. He is the first public official children recognize and often the only one. Even among adults, he is the only political figure all Americans can identify. Less than a quarter of the public can name the Speaker of the House, the secretary of defense, or the secretary of the treasury. An occasional political celebrity may share this level of visibility. Normally, however, the president nearly monopolizes public perceptions of national politics.

The Symbolic President   Everything about the president is a source of fascination to the public and the mass media—what time he starts his day, his favorite entertainments, even the private lives of his family members. This extremely high visibility reflects the fact that two roles are combined in his office. He is both *head of government* and *symbolic leader of the country*. Moreover, except for the vice-president, he is the only nationally elected leader. The United States differs from parliamentary nations that give the prime minister and cabinet political power while the symbolic power of personifying the nation is embodied in royalty or a weak figurehead president. In England, for example, the queen symbolizes the

San Francisco Chronicle 9
★ Mon., May 23, 1977

Amy Carter's Nursemaid Baptized

Washington

Mary Fitzpatrick, Amy Carter's nursemaid and companion, was baptized yesterday at the First Baptist Church of Washington, with President Carter watching the ceremony.

Fitzpatrick was serving a murder sentence in a Georgia prison when the Carters asked that she be released so she could join the White House staff, February 4.

She had served as a nursemaid for Amy when the president was governor of Georgia as part of a work release program for inmates.

United Press

country; it is her food habits and clothes that attract public attention. The most admired man in England, according to a survey conducted some years ago, was Prince Philip, the queen's husband. That nation's real political leader, the prime minister, was in third place.

In his symbolic capacity, the president heads not just his party, but all the people. He is the personal embodiment of the United States of America. When he is photographed every year with a crippled child to publicize the fund-raising campaign for muscular dystrophy, he is above politics, just as when he lights the White House Christmas tree or pins medals on heroes. To be sure, he does benefit politically from ceremonial functions—but they can also make him politically vulnerable. As the embodiment of lofty aspirations, he is likely to be held to such high standards that the compromises taken for granted when made by other politicians lead to disillusionment if the president makes them. What is more, the president's high visibility and his role as symbolic head of the country mean that he will be held to account when things go wrong, regardless of his actual responsibility for them. Herbert Hoover was one president who became a scapegoat for national ills. Having taken office in March 1929, he could hardly be blamed for the depression that began that October. Nevertheless, the global economic collapse became "Hoover's Depression" for many Americans. In the same way, Carter has suffered for the energy crisis he inherited. The president so dominates public perceptions of the political world that it does him little good to protest that America is not all-powerful in the world, that the government has limited control of the economy, and that he is unable to control Congress, the Supreme Court, mayors, governors, and other political figures whose decisions have a great deal to do with public policy. If there is trouble, he is likely to be blamed. This vulnerability, as well as the impulse to win approval, is a powerful motive for presidents to take action, whether symbolic or real, to respond to every public misfortune.

Symbolizing the country itself, as well as his own political program and party, the president occupies a crucial place in the emotions of the public. This is revealed most dramatically when death or illness comes to the president. When news of President Eisenhower's heart attack reached Wall Street in 1955, the stock market fell to its lowest point since the 1929 crash. The widespread mourning into which the country plunged after John Kennedy's assassination resembled bereavement for the death of a loved one. Indeed, psychiatrists reported that patients displayed symptoms similar to those that accompany the death of a father or mother. Many Americans responded to news of Kennedy's death with psychosomatic symptoms—headaches, insomnia, loss of appetite, and dizziness. When Presidents Roosevelt and Harding died in office, similar mass sorrow took place. Since such dis-

Wide World

Here are two examples of presidents in the role of chief of state. President Ford dances with Queen Elizabeth II after a state dinner in the White House; President Kennedy throws the first ball to open the 1963 baseball season. (Notice the secret serviceman with a fielder's glove, in case a foul ball threatens the president.)

plays do not occur when an ex-president dies, the mourning seems to be for the loss of the leader and whatever is symbolized by his role, not simply for the death of a revered person.[2]

Aware of their position as symbolic guardians of the national destiny, presidents may go to great lengths to present what they consider "appropriate" images. Kennedy, Johnson, and Nixon all discouraged photographers from taking pictures while they were wearing glasses. Photographs of Franklin Roosevelt were taken above the waist; most people did not know he could not walk because his legs were withered from polio. Ford hired a photographer who specialized in snapshots of the president in informal, relaxed, "nonimperial" activities. Carter and his aides debated at some length about how he should appear in his first television address. Taking the post-Watergate approach of informality, he wore a cardigan sweater.

Presidents are not always able to control how they are portrayed, however. When Richard Nixon was forced to reveal the recordings of his conversations with aides about Watergate, the country was swept by a wave of revulsion at his obscene vocabulary. It is hard to believe that many of the people who were shocked by Nixon's language never talk that way themselves. Since this moral outrage was expressed by Republicans as well as Democrats, it was not mere political hypocrisy. Instead, it reveals how the president is held up to idealized standards of purity out of a desire to feel that the public's fate is in worthy hands.

Presidential Popularity No matter how narrow the electoral margin which brought them to the White House, presidents take office in a glow of popular approval. This was true of presidents like Richard Nixon, who did not even pull a majority of the popular vote, and of Jimmy Carter, who got barely more than half the votes cast in 1976. It was true in the first Gallup Poll ratings of Truman, Johnson, and Ford, who succeeded to office via the vice-presidency. The first flush of popularity invariably fades somewhat as the "honeymoon period" ends. Popular support for the president then goes up and down in response to the pressure of events, but every modern president except Eisenhower has experienced a long-term decline in popularity. Judging from Carter's generally low ratings in the Gallup Polls and the failure of Johnson, Nixon, and Ford to be two-term presidents, presidential vulnerability is increasing.

Is the presidency an increasingly fragile institution? Many political observers believe so. They argue that as the problems of government get greater, presidents make increasingly unrealistic promises and people hold them to higher standards.

[2] See Fred I. Greenstein, "What the President Means to Americans: Presidential 'Choice' Between Elections," in James David Barber, ed. *Choosing the President* (Englewood Cliffs, N.J.: Prentice-Hall, 1974).

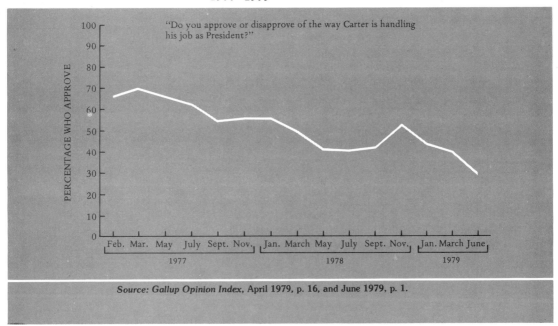

Figure 14.1
Public Approval of President Carter,
1977–1979

"Do you approve or disapprove of the way Carter is handling his job as President?"

PERCENTAGE WHO APPROVE

Feb. Mar. May July Sept. Nov.

1977

Jan. March May July Sept. Nov.

1978

Jan. March June

1979

Source: *Gallup Opinion Index*, April 1979, p. 16, and June 1979, p. 1.

This would seem to be a sure recipe for failure. One reason to understand the presidency better is to compare the actual institution with the expectations people have of it. That will be our task in the rest of the chapter: we will look at the president in all his roles — symbol, leader, politician, administrator.

THE MAN AND THE OFFICE

Who Are the Presidents? The Constitution states only two qualifications for the presidency. The president must be at least 35 years old and a natural-born American citizen. Political reality and American society impose some other qualifications that are almost as ironclad as these formal provisions.

Until Kennedy, no president had been a Catholic, and it was widely believed that Catholicism was too big a handicap for any candidate. Kennedy's religion was the most important issue in the 1960 election, but the country's ability to survive a Catholic president made this issue vanish without a trace. No one considered Senator Muskie's Catholic faith an issue in his quest for the Democratic nomination in 1972 or a factor in his failure to win the nomination.

Table 14.1 lists twentieth-century American presidents, the terms they served, their ages at inauguration, their occupations, and the offices they held before entering the White House. As can be seen, most presidents were in their fifties when they

Table 14.1

Twentieth-Century American Presidents

PRESIDENT	TERM IN OFFICE	AGE AT INAUGURATION	OCCUPATION	PREVIOUS PUBLIC OFFICES
William McKinley	1897–1901	54	Lawyer	U.S. representative Governor

Theodore Roosevelt	1901–05
	1905–09
		42	Writer	State assemblyman
				U.S. Civil Service
				  Commissioner
				President, New York
				  Police Board
				Assistant secretary
				  of the Navy
				Governor
				Vice-president

William Howard Taft	1909–13	52	Lawyer	Prosecuting attorney Superior court judge U.S. solicitor general Federal circuit judge Governor of Philippines Secretary of war
Woodrow Wilson	1913–17 1917–21	56	Professor College president	Governor
Warren G. Harding	1921–23	55	Newspaper owner	State senator Lieutenant governor U.S. senator
Calvin Coolidge	1923–25 1925–29	51	Lawyer	City councilman City solicitor State representative Mayor State senator Lieutenant governor Governor Vice-president

took office. Three of the five exceptions—Theodore Roosevelt, 42, and Truman and Ford, 60 and 61, respectively—succeeded as vice-presidents.

The occupations shown are a bit misleading, because modern presidents are almost always professional politicians, with decades of seasoning in public life before entering the White House. Ford spent scarcely three years in civilian life between his graduation from Yale Law School in 1941 and his election to Congress in 1948. Virtually his entire adult career was in the House of Representatives. Nixon was first elected to Congress in 1946 at the age of 33. He spent all his time in politics, including his years out of office, from then until his election to the presidency

Table 14.1 – continued

Twentieth-Century American Presidents

PRESIDENT	TERM IN OFFICE	AGE AT INAUGURATION	OCCUPATION	PREVIOUS PUBLIC OFFICES
Herbert Hoover	1929–33	54	Engineer Businessman	War relief administrator Secretary of commerce
Franklin Delano Roosevelt	1933–37 1937–41 1941–45 1945–45	51	Lawyer (briefly)	State senator Assistant secretary of the Navy Governor
Harry S. Truman	1945–49 1949–53	60	Farmer Clerk Haberdasher (briefly)	County administrator U.S. senator Vice-president
Dwight D. Eisenhower	1953–57 1957–61	62	General College president	Supreme Allied Commander, World War II NATO commander
John F. Kennedy	1961–63	43	Journalist (very briefly)	U.S. representative U.S. senator
Lyndon B. Johnson	1963–65 1965–69	55	Teacher (briefly) Congressional aide	U.S. representative U.S. senator Vice-president
Richard M. Nixon	1969–73 1973–74	56	Lawyer	U.S. representative U.S. senator Vice-president
Gerald R. Ford	1974–77	61	Lawyer (briefly)	U.S. representative Vice-president
Jimmy Carter	1977–	53	Naval officer Farmer-businessman	State senator Governor

twenty-two years later.[3] Johnson was elected to the House at the age of 28 and had been exposed to or involved in professional politics since childhood. He served in the House and Senate until be became vice-president and, as a result of Kennedy's assassination, president. John Kennedy was elected to Congress at the age of 29 and remained there until he reached the White House. With the exceptions of

[3] Nixon practiced law in New York City for six years, but most of his energies were devoted to presidential politics. See Jules Witcover, *The Resurrection of Richard Nixon* (New York: Putnam's, 1970), Chaps. 2–9.

Wilson, Eisenhower, and Carter, every president elected in the twentieth century has had at least a dozen years of prior full-time political experience.

There is little in the family backgrounds of the various presidents to provide obvious clues about the direction their policies will take.[4] Nixon, a conservative, was the son of an unsuccessful grocer; Kennedy, who advocated liberal policies, was a multimillionaire's son. Herbert Hoover, although a self-made millionaire at the time of taking office, was the orphan child of a blacksmith, passed from one relative to the next. Franklin Roosevelt came from an aristocratic family with roots deep in American history. Yet Hoover was a conservative, unable to bring himself to provide direct aid to the poor during the depths of the Depression, whereas Roosevelt molded a major political realignment by championing the poor and underprivileged.

In short, there are too many complications to explain presidents' behavior on the basis of their socioeconomic backgrounds. Anyone who reaches the White House is far too unusual an individual to be classified according to his outward social and economic characteristics.

The Presidential Role   Every president must carry out several major tasks. Many political scientists have found it helpful to describe these as *roles*. This term is borrowed from sociologists, who in turn have borrowed it from the theater. In essence, a role is simply a part a person plays whenever he or she behaves more or less in conformity with certain social expectations. In everyday life, each person plays many roles. You are simultaneously a student, a classmate, a co-worker, an employee, a brother or sister, and so on. Each of these roles presupposes different behavior patterns in the way you relate to situations and to the other people involved in your role performance. In a sense, roles are the "scripts" we follow in going about our business. But as any theatergoer knows, even a well-established role like Hamlet will be performed differently by different actors. The same is true in everyday life and in the performance of presidential roles. The president has to function as chief of state, as party leader, as chief legislator, as chief executive, chief economist, and as commander-in-chief of the armed forces. Each of these roles will demand different types of behavior. What is more, each president will play each of the roles with his own unique style, which is determined largely by his personality and political beliefs. The role provides only a rough script. To understand the performance, we must understand the actor himself. Here are some of the constant aspects of the script around which various presidents improvise.

Primacy.   The recurrence of the word "chief" in listing presidential roles is no accident. Whatever he does, the president gets top billing. This is

For an attempt to find some of the roots of presidential behavior in the presidents' psychological background, see James David Barber, *The Presidential Character*, 2nd ed. (Englewood Cliffs, N. J.: Prentice-Hall, 1977). For scholarly debate about Barber's position, see Alexander L. George, "Assessing Presidential Character," *World Politics*, 26 (1974), pp. 234–82; Erwin C. Hargrove, "Presidential Personality and Revisionist Views of the Presidency," *American Journal of Political Science*, 18 (1973), pp. 819–35; and Barber's "Strategies for Understanding Politicians," *American Journal of Political Science*, 19 (1974), pp. 443–67.

true even in summit conferences with the heads of other major nations, except when he is dealing with one of the other superpowers. George E. Reedy, a veteran aide to President Johnson, describes one of the dangers of this aspect of the modern president's position:

> A President moves through his days surrounded by literally hundreds of people whose relationship to him is that of a doting mother to a spoiled child. Whatever he wants is brought to him immediately — food, drink, helicopters, airplanes, people, in fact, everything but relief from his political problems.[5]

Ford and Carter went to great lengths to avoid flaunting the trappings of office. Great publicity was given to Ford's toasting his own English muffins for breakfast. On the campaign trail, Carter made a point of carrying his own luggage. After his inauguration, he walked back to the White House instead of riding through the crowds in a limousine as other presidents had done. Both men could afford these symbolic displays of humility, for they also had at their disposal almost any conceivable service, including virtually unlimited communications and travel facilities.

Goals.   Each president has different goals and may choose different means to achieve them. Nevertheless, a few general points apply to all presidents. Most important, every first-term president wants to be popular enough to be reelected, if only because his proposals will receive less support if it is known he plans to retire or is sure of defeat. Any president also wants to avoid depressions, riots, war, loss of natural resources, and the decline of American world power. Beyond this, any president will want to improve the condition of Americans at home and of American power abroad, out of commitment to national values and to his place in future history books. As one of President Kennedy's closest aides noted, obviously reflecting Kennedy's own view: "A President knows that his name will be the label for a whole era. Textbooks yet unwritten and schoolchildren yet unborn will hold him responsible for all that happens."[6]

A Different Time Perspective.   The president may be the most visible figure on the Washington scene, but he also is the most transient major political actor. We have already discussed the long tenure in office of contemporary members of Congress. Civil servants, judges, and such informal leaders as interest group representatives and journalists are usually around Washington for many years more than the president, who is limited by the Constitution to two terms. This creates a divergence in outlook between the president and his appointees on the one hand, and these other leaders. The president is, to paraphrase Shakespeare, but a poor player with a brief time on the stage before exiting. Modern presidents are in a hurry; none of Washington's other major actors need be. Little wonder that before President Carter was in office long, he found it in his interest to try to estab-

---

[5] George E. Reedy, *The Twilight of the Presidency* (New York: World, 1970), p. 24.
[6] Theodore C. Sorensen, *Decision-Making in the White House* (New York: Columbia University Press, 1963), p. 83.

President Carter's first television address
to the nation from the White House.
His cardigan sweater was picked
after careful deliberation to convey
a note of casual formality,
and also to demonstrate one technique
for saving energy.

lish friendly relations with and take political advice from such long-time Washington veterans as the Speaker of the House.

The Need to Persuade. This difference in time perspective complicates the president's central challenge. If he is to make his mark in history, or even to survive politically, he must win the cooperation of members of Congress, bureaucrats, and judges whom he did not choose and cannot get rid of. He can fire high administrative officials if he is willing to bear the political consequences, but as a practical matter no president can afford to discharge too many of his own appointees, whether they are political appointments or career officials. Purging his own appointees can make the president look bad and cause organizational uncertainty until the replacements settle into their jobs and pick their subordinates. Because of his limited coercive power, the president must *persuade* other people if he is to do his job. He must arrange circumstances so that other political actors find it in their interest to do what the president wants them to do. In doing this, whether or not he likes it, he must learn to bargain and compromise.[7]

Personalization. One of the most enduring features of the presidency is its openness to change. Since the 1930s, the modern presidency has in some ways become a separate branch of government, comparable to the 535 members of Congress and their staff aides. Yet no other "branch" of government undergoes as complete a change in personnel as the president's. The stability of incumbents makes for a high degree of continuity in Congress. There is lifetime tenure in the judiciary and civil service protection in the bureaucracy. But the president and his chief advisers on the White House staff can change completely on inauguration day. The presidential office responds dramatically to the personal needs and political style of its incumbent.

This personal quality of the presidency is enhanced by our "entrepreneurial" method of presidential selection, in contrast to the "apprenticeship" system typical of parliamentary systems.[8] The president takes office at the head of *his* political coalition that *he* has built and led in order to gain *his* nomination and election. He is more like the sole owner of a company than the head of a corporation with a board of directors. There is no permanent party framework to provide continuity from one administration of the same party to the next, as there is, for example, in Great Britain. In most democratic countries, if one knows that the head of government belongs to a certain party, one can readily predict the names of most of the cabinet officers. This is not the case in the United States. If Hubert Humphrey rather than

[7] Richard M. Neustadt, *Presidential Power,* 2nd ed. (New York: Wiley, 1976).

[8] Hugh Heclo, "Presidential and Prime Ministerial Selection," in Donald R. Matthews, ed., *Perspectives on Presidential Selection* (Washington: The Brookings Institution, 1973), pp. 28–29.

Jimmy Carter had been elected president on the Democratic ticket in 1976, the cabinet would have been almost wholly different.

Long Hours. Calvin Coolidge often slept eleven hours a night, finished his official day by noon, and napped after lunch. But Coolidge was the last president to take it easy in the White House. His successor, Herbert Hoover, seemed unresponsive to the Depression, yet he drove himself from early morning to late at night, rarely sleeping more than four hours. Since then, the presidential day has resembled Hoover's more than Coolidge's. President Eisenhower was generally thought to avoid working too hard in the White House, but this impression was a result of his preference for keeping much of his schedule off the record. In fact, Eisenhower generally had read several newspapers before his first appointments began at seven in the morning, and did not leave his office until 6 p.m. Jimmy Carter begins work before six and keeps at it until lunch, which he generally eats alone. After a mid-afternoon break for exericse, Carter works until dinner, and then again until he goes to bed around eleven.[9] In addition to their long schedules, modern presidents can never escape the pressure of knowing they are always on duty. Woodrow Wilson, disabled by a stroke brought on by the strains of office, made this comment about the job's demands:

> Men of ordinary physique and discretion cannot be presidents and live. . . . We shall be obliged always to be picking our chief magistrates from among wise and prudent athletes—a small class.

The Impact of Personality Because the presidency is such an individual office, it is important to consider some of the ways in which the president's personal needs and capacities have an impact on public policy. Presidents seem to differ enormously in their ability to maintain informal give-and-take with their advisers, weigh competing points of view, and tolerate disagreement. Ability to "take the heat" seems to be more a matter of personality than of intellect. Woodrow Wilson probably understood as well as any president the importance of good press relations, and at times he held frequent press conferences. But he failed in dealing with the press because he could not tolerate skepticism, inconvenient questions, or signs of opposition to his policies. When he talked to reporters, they considered him resentful, lofty, and often angry. Wilson was a striking contrast to Theodore Roosevelt, who began the official practice of making room for the press in the White House. Roosevelt cheerfully held forth to reporters while sitting in the barber's chair for his afternoon shave!

Differences in personal style from one president to another are visible in even the smallest details of the way they run their offices. The president has enormous flexibility in the way he organizes both his time and his staff. He can arrange matters

---

[9] Fred I. Greenstein, "Presidential Activism Eisenhower Style: A Reassessment Based on Archival Evidence," paper presented at the 1979 annual meeting of the Midwestern Political Science Association; and Dom Bonafede, "How the White House Helps Carter Make Up His Mind," *National Journal*, April 15, 1978, p. 584.

*As the outside world becomes more threatening, the need
to protect the president grows and his privacy and sense of
freedom shrink. In 1947, President Truman could still walk
on the streets of Washington. Here, he crosses
Pennsylvania Avenue, flanked by secret servicemen. On
the left, President Johnson rides in a 1964 motorcade,
guarded by agents with automatic rifles.*

to suit his own capacities and habits. The ways he chooses to do this can have vast
consequences for public policy outcomes. Nixon and Eisenhower liked a neat, hierarchial staff arrangement in which aides generally reported to a chief of staff, who in
turn supervised the flow of both paper and advice from assistants to the president.
On the other hand, Kennedy and Truman were more like the hub of a wheel. Kennedy often saw his major assistants one at a time, and even assigned the same task
to more than one individual. He used this method to avoid the isolation and restriction of information that might occur if a single person stood between him and the
outside world. Kennedy liked to hear opposing points of view argued out in front of
him by members of his administration. He also liked informal contacts with reporters—often in order to influence them. Although criticism annoyed him, he was able
to avoid the kind of suspicious "bunker mentality" that plagued Johnson and Nixon when they encountered heavy criticism.

    In marked contrast to this approach was Nixon's preference for pondering
decisions in solitude and excluding the normal give-and-take of contending view-

points. He wanted options for choice, but these had to be provided in writing. His staff controlled access to him and thus had enormous power both of decision and of information. Nixon disliked reading the newspapers and instead had an aide prepare an elaborately detailed press summary, including television broadcasts. One of his first rearrangements of the Oval Office was to remove the multiple television screens Johnson had controlled from a console on his desk.

Carter returned to a more president-centered staff system with a number of aides reporting directly to him. Before deciding on a policy, he would read long papers that ended with "decision boxes" (yes, no, etc.) that he could check to indicate his final judgment. But because he solicited the views of all his senior staff and made personal decisions when they disagreed, Carter often was involved in details. For example, when two groups of presidential aides could not agree on proposed changes in federal employee pay, Carter made the decisions on highly technical issues such as geographic wage differentials. One experienced aide commented: "Ten years ago, this would not have been sent to any president. We would have worked it out and made these decisions, and then someone would have taken 15 minutes of the president's time to explain it to him."[10] Perhaps because this system did not work well, Carter decided in 1979 to have a chief of staff, who would control access to him and direct his other aides.

There are arguments in favor of both the hierarchical and the more informal styles. The first is often thought to preserve the president from being flooded with details, but to insulate him from a rich array of alternative possibilities. But the president-centered approach has the opposite strengths and weaknesses. In the final analysis, a president gets the advisory system he thinks best fits his personal needs and preferences. He cannot be forced to use a system that clashes with his own work style. His ability to use advice and staff effectively will be affected not only by the organization of the system, but also by such leadership qualities as his own capacity to set priorities and ask the right questions. The combination of staff organization and presidential style of seeking information in turn has a major impact on how policy is made and what policies emerge from the political system.

THE PRESIDENT AS PARTY LEADER

The president is traditionally thought of as the leader of his political party, and it is very much in his interest to make this unofficial but widely recognized role a reality. To the degree that he is backed by other party leaders in and out of government as well as party identifiers in the public, his chances of achieving his goals are greater. Yet party leadership poses two major problems for a president. First, Americans have great respect for the presidency but they do not trust political parties and "politicians." In pursuing his partisan role, a president is especially likely to encounter the disillusionment noted earlier in connection with the president's role as national symbol. Second, and far more important, the real organizational strength of the two

---

[10] Timothy B. Clark, "The Power Vacuum Outside the Oval Office," *National Journal,* February 24, 1979, p. 297.

parties—such as it is—is at the state and local levels. Even here there are many weak or nonexistent party organizations. The other major figures in the president's party— members of Congress, mayors, and governors—typically are not part of his administration. Nominated and elected by local voters as a result of their own efforts, they are not dependent on the president. He cannot order them to support his program because he cannot control their nomination.[11]

This does not mean that members of the president's party will be indifferent to his proposals. Although the president does not command a disciplined party organization, he does symbolize his party to the mass electorate. His party's current image is determined primarily by his popularity. What people think of the president shapes what they think of his party. If Jimmy Carter is an unpopular president, his lack of voter appeal rubs off on other Democratic candidates. Moreover, the president and other of his party's elected officials tend to have broadly similar outlooks on political issues. They also are likely to depend on the same interest groups— business in the case of Republicans and labor in that of the Democrats. Finally, the president controls a fair amount of patronage, not so much jobs as contracts and regulatory decisions that can be adjusted to help or hurt dissident members of his party. For example, many people suspected that the Carter administration deliberately manipulated gasoline allocations in 1979 to cause shortages in California and thus make trouble for its governor, Jerry Brown, considered a rival of Carter's for the 1980 Democratic presidential nomination.

Although the two parties' national committees are far from nationwide party organizations, they do have some influence. The committee of the president's party usually is a political arm of the White House. For example, the Democratic National Committee (DNC) contributed about $40,000 a month to pay for political activities of President Carter's that could not properly be charged to the taxpayers. The DNC chairman attended weekly meetings with the president's political aide Hamilton Jordan, and the DNC's polls and regional political soundings were made available to the White House.

THE PRESIDENT AND CONGRESS

Half the time between 1957 and 1981, Republicans held the White House, but both houses of Congress were controlled by Democrats. The rest of the time, Presidents Kennedy, Johnson, and Carter found that large Democratic margins in both houses of Congress were no guarantee that their legislative programs would be approved, because the combined forces of the Republicans and the southern Democrats formed an effective opposition coalition.

Congress is a genuinely independent body, unlike most legislatures elsewhere in the world. As we saw in Chapter 12, members of Congress are nominated and

---

[11] Presidents do not openly seek to influence congressional nominations in order to bring into office more cooperative legislators. The major attempt to do this was by Franklin D. Roosevelt in the 1938 primaries. FDR's efforts, with one exception, were unsuccessful. Since the result was more rather than less congressional opposition, later presidents have avoided overt involvement in congressional primaries.

elected by their own efforts, not by national party organizations. Each house of Congress, moreover, controls its own organization and procedures. Decisions about such matters as who is to lead the party in each house are based on calculations in which the wishes of the president are not very important.

This is not to say that Congress and the president are always at odds. What is unusual about the American political system, however, is that, unlike virtually every other democratic government in the world, the executive leadership and the legislature do not *necessarily* work together. Many textbooks recite long lists of reasons for conflict between Congress and the president. Boiled down, these lists simply say that conflict occurs because the policy views and political interests of the people in these two interdependent institutions are frequently not identical. Needless to say, these interests do coincide in individual cases; or at least they can be made to coincide after careful negotiation. Otherwise, the United States Code, the countless laws passed by both houses of Congress and signed by the president, would not exist.

The President as Chief Legislator

The framers of the Consitution did not anticipate that the president would become the major source of the legislative agenda.

Traditionally, it was Congress that proposed laws and the president who disposed of them by signing or vetoing the bills sent to him. It was thought that a president who played too big a role in proposing legislation would be acting in an unseemly manner. From time to time during the nineteenth century, even modest presidential exercise of the constitutional privilege of "recommending measures" to Congress would be met with cries of "tyranny" and "Caesarism." As a result, what legislative strength nineteenth-century presidents had was largely negative. Andrew Jackson first used the veto as a way of asserting the theory that the president, as the country's single nationally elected official, should have a major voice in legislative policy. Presidents did occasionally propose legislation, but usually through friendly congressmen. These people carried the burden of influencing public opinion and negotiating the winning legislative coalition. But things began to change in the twentieth century. Theodore Roosevelt and Woodrow Wilson made suggestions for legislation and played a public role in winning passage. Wilson was especially active and hard-driving in this respect. But Wilson's three successors once again left legislation largely to the legislators.

When Franklin Roosevelt took office in 1933, the depths of the Depression, the country was desperate for governmental remedies to a series of crises. Congress *wanted* Roosevelt to tell it what to do. Banks were failing daily. One out of every four members of the labor force was unemployed, with virtually no welfare programs in force. While Congress rushed through FDR's emergency banking bill in March 1933, the Republican leader of the House urged congressional approval with the famous statement that "The house is burning down, and the President of the United States says this is the way to put out the fire."[12] In the whirlwind "Hundred Days" that began his first administration, Roosevelt submitted and Con-

---

[12] Quoted in Pendleton Herring, *Presidential Leadership* (New York: Farrar and Rinehart, 1940), pp. 57–58.

gress quickly approved an impressive list of major laws designed to deal with the Depression. When the immediate emergency was over, Roosevelt continued to propose legislation and urge Congress to pass it. He even made personal radio appeals to rally public opinion in support of his policies.

With the advent of the Truman administration in 1945, the presidential practice of submitting legislation to Congress became firmly institutionalized. It soon became customary for the State of the Union message, which in the nineteenth century was not even personally delivered by the president, to be accompanied by an official presidential legislative program—including draft bills. Members of the executive branch cannot officially introduce bills, but it is standard practice for senior congressional members of the president's party to introduce items in his legislative program. The growth of the presidential role in the legislative process suffered a temporary setback when Eisenhower took office in 1953. Disapproving of presidential legislative initiative, Eisenhower presented no program during his first year in office. This led to substantial congressional confusion, however, for the complexity of national life and government policy had become too great to permit the government to rely on whatever bills just happened to be introduced by various members of Congress. In his second year in office, Eisenhower submitted a legislative package, and all later presidents have done the same.

The sheer bulk of technical knowhow about diverse problems of almost 3 million executive branch employees has contributed to the tendency to think of the president as the country's chief legislator. Every year executive agencies come forth with new proposals for legislation, both to improve the handling of existing programs and to innovate with new ones. Although the president himself cannot possibly examine all these proposals personally, a presidential legislative program is hammered out of these agency proposals by the Office of Management and Budget. This agency processes budget requests from the other federal agencies. Since the 1930s it also has had the job of clearing and coordinating executive branch legislative proposals.

Occasionally, when a federal agency finds its proposals for legislation rejected by the president, it will attempt an end run to its friends on Capitol Hill. Agencies like the Army Corps of Engineers, which devotes itself to public works which legislators want for their districts, are particularly good at this technique. Such agencies are governed by their horizontal links to key committees or subcommittees of Congress, as well as by their nominal superior, the president. Most agencies, however, are under firmer presidential control. Nevertheless, there are informal ways of getting around the need for presidential clearance of agency proposals. This can occur because the bureaucrats in the agencies have congressional allies with whom they worked before the incumbent entered the White House and with whom they will continue to work long after he has departed to write his memoirs.

The President's Policy Stance and Initiative

For a number of years it was thought that presidents tend to be liberal because they must appeal to voters in large industrial states in order to get elected and because, once in office, the fact that they have a national constituency gives them the perspective to see national problems. Congress, on the other hand, seemed to be more conservative because of the rural overrepresentation that existed for many years and because each individual member represents only "parochial" local interests. But if we look systematically at the period from 1953 to 1977, a different picture emerges. During most of the Eisenhower administration, all of Nixon's tenure, and the Ford administration, Congress was *less* conservative than the president with respect to almost any particular piece of major legislation.

Thus, one of the main arguments for casting the president in the role of chief legislator — that he wants to innovate whereas Congress wants to stand still — does not hold water. Even during the New Deal, Congress was responsible for major innovative legislation. During the two Democratic administrations of the 1960s, Congress took the lead in pioneering legislation in consumer protection, conservation, and automobile safety. In these and other areas, important bills were supported by presidents only after they were prodded into action by enterprising members of Congress. It was the legislators who identified problems, proposed solutions, refined those solutions through consultation with interested groups, and stimulated public opinion to a greater awareness of both the problems and the possible solutions. Of course, once the president decides to support a proposal, it is in his interest to put his own brand on it so that the credit will go to him rather than to the legislator who may have done much of the early work in identifying the problem and building support for the proposed solution.

A bill controlling the drug industry, signed into law by Kennedy in 1962, illustrates all these tendencies — the congressional function of identifying problems, the presidential tendency to steal congressional thunder, and the weakness of the argument that Congress is conservative while Democratic presidents are liberal. During the last days of the Eisenhower administration, a subcommittee of the Senate Judiciary Committee chaired by Senator Estes Kefauver began hearings on pricing, advertising, patent policy, and other aspects of safety and competition in the drug industry. Stretching over several years, Kefauver's sensational hearings demonstrated that the drug industry was making enormous profits and was spending far more on advertising than on research.

Kefauver drafted a bill to deal with the worst of these abuses but found the opposition so strong that he could not even get his bill considered by the full Judiciary Committee. He sought support from the White House, but reforming the drug industry was not one of Kennedy's priorities. Wary of alienating members of Congress whose help he wanted for matters of greater importance to him, Kennedy decided not to support Kefauver's bill. Instead, he sent his own drug message and draft legislation to Congress. It fell far short of what Kefauver had proposed. Without consulting Kefauver, members of the administration met with the conservative Senator Eastland, chairman of the Judiciary Committee, to work out a compromise that drastically reduced Kefauver's bill. At this point, the thalidomide scandal broke. A worldwide uproar resulted when it was revealed that thalidomide caused pregnant women to give birth to tragically deformed babies. His hand forced by this publicity, Kennedy made a television speech in favor of a stronger drug bill. Pressed hard by Kefauver, the Kennedy-Eastland coalition strengthened its bill somewhat, although the result still fell short of what Kefauver had originally drafted.[13]

[13] Richard Harris, *The Real Voice* (New York: Macmillan, 1964).

Once he decided to play a legislative advocacy role, Kennedy did his best to gain credit for drug legislation himself and tended to bypass Kefauver both in public recognition and in private decision-making. His intervention made the drug bill a party issue and thus rallied to its support many Democratic senators and representatives who were not fervent believers in the cause but who were loyal Democrats prepared to support their president. Although the president did not initiate the ideas and specific proposals in this major legislation, his support was necessary to make passage of the bill a realistic possibility. As a Kefauver proposal it was doomed, but as a Kennedy proposal it became law.

Often, the question of where ideas originally come from is almost impossible to sort out. Many bureaucrats, members of Congress, and lobbyists have pet ideas for dealing with problems that are not generally recognized or arouse no political interest. To the president, Congress is something like a cafeteria—he usually can find what he likes among the innumerable bills that have been introduced by various members. When the time seems ripe, such ideas become more publicized. If their advocates are lucky, the president will seize upon them and lend them his prestige and support. Thus, the president's distinctive contributions to legislation include *focus, leverage,* and *party image.* If he does not provide all the major items on the legislative agenda, his proposals at least establish its broad outlines.

Legislative Liaison: The Presidential Lobby

How does the president get Congress to do what he wants? By far the most important source of presidential influence is the fact that *his program is the program of his party in Congress.* This is not to say, of course, that all members of his party automatically vote for what he proposes, but only that his program provides a focus for his party's congressional membership.

Once the president advocates a legislative measure, he is assured the strong support of those members of both parties who already were enthusiastic about it. He is unlikely to win over out-and-out opponents from either party, especially if the measure contradicts deeply felt views of theirs or seems not to be in the interest of their districts. But at least some members of the president's party who would otherwise be reluctant to support the bill will do so when the magic words are spoken: "The President is very interested in this bill and really would like to have your help." Presidents, even relatively unpopular ones, have both an aura of importance and a wide array of rewards and punishments to dish out. This is not to say, however, that popularity is irrelevant in a president's dealing with Congress. The more public support a president has, the stronger the incentive for members of Congress to go along, and the greater the political risks of defying him.

As presidents have come to play an increasingly active legislative role, the need has become recognized for specialists in the White House who can deal with Capitol Hill on the president's behalf. This was done on an ad hoc basis by Roosevelt and Truman. During the relatively undemanding administration of Eisenhower, a formal legislative liaison staff was organized in the White House. Kennedy, who had both a slim majority in Congress and ambitious legislative plans, gave responsibility for dealing with Capitol Hill to Lawrence O'Brien, one of his most trusted aides. O'Brien's operation, which continued through the Johnson presidency, occupied a central place in the White House, and since then legislative liaison has been one of the major activities of the president's staff. When Carter took office, one of his former aides in the Georgia state house, Frank Moore, became head of the White House lobbying team. Moore, who had no Washington experience, was briefed by O'Brien. His initial relations with Congress were uneven, partly because Carter did not always give him advance warning of presidential decisions that affected the interests of key congressmen.

As a general rule, attempts to build support for the president's program are directed at members of his party whose position on particular bills is uncertain. The techniques and perspectives of the White House liaison people resemble those of the congressional party leadership. Like the congressional leaders, the White House aides are less concerned with the substance of policies than with getting them passed or blocking them. Liaison aides devote a good deal of time to headcounting, trying to find out who will support a particular measure, who is certain to be against it, who is on the fence, and how many votes can be swayed by particular changes in the bill or other influences. They work in cooperation with the congressional leadership of the president's party.

In attempting to exercise influence over Congress, the president makes use of the following sources of leverage:

Patronage. Although there are fewer patronage jobs in the federal government than in many cities, counties, and states, it is nevertheless true that the available federal appointive jobs are highly desirable. Members of Congress are interested in gaining these appointments for their own political supporters. Presidents normally make these appointments with some care in order to get the most political mileage out of them.

Pork Barrel. Every year the federal government makes tens of thousands of decisions to spend money on particular projects. These include dams, reclamation programs, small boat marinas, community development projects, urban renewal projects, highways, airports, hospitals, and college dormitories. Politics plays a greater role in deciding where and when to build a dam than a cancer research facility. Different presidents have different attitudes about the extent to which political considerations should dictate decisions about local federal expeditures. Nevertheless, presidents normally recognize that funding for some categories of projects can be allocated in accordance with political considerations. Because members of Congress are always eager to obtain federal projects for their consituents, the White House can use this power—which in some cases is at the sole discretion of the executive branch—to get favorable votes in Congress. In fact, pork barrel procedures come to be so taken for granted that the president who does not follow them is likely to lose credit on Capitol Hill. When President Carter took office, he cancelled a number of water resources projects. Both the cancellations and his failure to give advance warning to members of Congress whose districts were affected led to a predictable storm and restoration of some of the projects.

The President's Presence.   The president is so obviously the most important person in the country that any sort of connection with him is highly prized. Members of Congress value help from the president in fund-raising or other campaign activities. One member of Carter's staff said of his boss:

> He may not be popular in all parts of the country, but he sure can get the fellows in the $300 suits to fund-raising events. If people on the Hill don't cooperate with us, we're not likely to help them out with fund-raising.

So simple a thing as a hometown newspaper photograph of a congressman in the president's presence or a presidential appearance in the congressman's district goes a long way toward enhancing the legislator's image as an important person. Any suggestions of access to or influence with the president are considered great boons in Washington and at home. Even such apparently trivial tokens as matchbooks with the White House seal are prized as symbols of presidential intimacy. Members of Congress who offend the president may not be able to send their important constituents on uncrowded VIP tours of the White House.

Influential Constituents.   The federal government affects the fortunes of a large number of people who do business with it, are regulated by it, or have ambitions that can be frustrated or satisfied by it. In many cases, people dependent on presidentially controlled agency decisions are important congressional

PROVIDING A PERSONALIZED PRESENCE

The president's presence is often prized by the mass media and therefore can be a means of getting his views across. Major White House announcements, including press conferences, are carried by all television networks. Journalists are almost invariably willing to report exclusive interviews with the president at great length. A means of providing a widespread yet "personalized" presidential presence to radio stations was introduced by President Carter's staff in 1979. The White House began to provide, free of charge, taped "radio spots" to about 600 radio stations around the country. These stations were able to phone the White House on a toll-free number. A radio announcer was hired to introduce these tapes. On phoning the White House, the radio station would receive an audio tone, a 3-2-1 countdown and a statement by the announcer ("This is Rich Nelson at the White House . . . President Carter on Friday announced . . .") followed by a recorded statement by the president himself. "We are leaving it up to the radio stations to identify the source of the tapes," a White House press office official explained. He described the tapes as a way of reaching "the small radio stations around the country that do not have access to the network services and obviously cannot afford their own man at the White House."

Source: The New York Times, December 2, 1978.

constituents and therefore can be mobilized to help the president's lobbying. Recent presidents have exploited these opportunities to win support from reluctant members of Congress.

The President's "Vote" in
Congress: The Veto Power

The president has a final part to play in the legislative process. After a bill has been passed by Congress, he has ten days to sign it into law or veto it. (Or he may leave it unsigned, in which case it automatically becomes law.) The president's veto kills the bill unless it is overridden by a two-thirds vote of each house of Congress. If the president does not sign a bill and Congress adjourns before the ten days are up, this is called a pocket veto. This is more potent, since Congress has no chance to override.

More than 2000 bills have been vetoed in American history, and less than 100 of these vetoes were overridden by Congress. Thus the threat of a veto is an important lever of presidential influence in Congress. The effectiveness of the veto leads to a paradox: A president who does not want political change often *looks* more powerful than a president who does. Eisenhower faced Democratic majorities in both houses of Congress for six of his eight years in office and vetoed 181 bills. The difference between one-half and two-thirds is so great that only two of these vetoes were overridden. Kennedy and Johnson, who had more ambitious legislative programs than Eisenhower, vetoed less than a third as many bills. Nixon had relatively modest legislative goals and was confronted by Democratic Congresses with far greater ambitions. His ability to veto legislation made him look far stronger than he actually was, because his goals were negative rather than positive. The same was true of Ford, who used the veto power frequently. Carter, seeking congressional approval of numerous comprehensive programs, did not exercise his veto power until he had been in office for nine months (see Table 14.2).

THE PRESIDENT
AND THE EXECUTIVE BRANCH

According to the Constitution, the president is the official in whom "the executive Power shall be vested." We often call him the "chief executive" because he is in charge of the immense administrative machinery of the federal government. Yet there are only so many hours in the president's day, and therefore only so many things he can supervise directly. Other people must do most of the work of running the government. The president appoints cabinet members and their deputies and assistants to direct the executive departments. Theoretically, they are the bosses of the career civil servants; in fact, their control over the bureaucrats is often in doubt, as we shall see.

Presidential Appointments

The permanent civil service of the federal government consists of almost 3 million civilians, plus nearly 2 million uniformed servicemen. To supervise this multitude of bureaucrats, the president has available

Table 14.2

Vetoes by Twentieth-Century Presidents

PRESIDENT	BILLS VETOED	VETOES OVERRIDDEN
McKinley	42	0
T. Roosevelt	82	1
Taft	39	1
Wilson	44	6
Harding	6	0
Coolidge	50	4
Hoover	37	3
F. D. Roosevelt	635	9
Truman	250	12
Eisenhower	181	2
Kennedy	21	0
Johnson	30	0
Nixon	43	5
Ford	66	12
Carter	19*	0

*Through May 10, 1979.

Source: Congressional Quarterly Weekly Report, December 7, 1974, p. 3281; and November 11, 1978, p. 3325.

less than 2700 appointive positions.[14] These are "the president's people," the officials through whom he imposes his policies on the vast body of the permanent government. Since he has so few people to help him direct the behavior of so many others, the president must pay a great deal of attention to filling this handful of positions. Judicious use of the appointing power is one of the most pressing tasks facing any newly elected president if he is to establish mastery of his own branch.

Days after their election and months before taking office, presidents-elect form personnel selection teams that generate long lists of prospects for presidential appointments. Names come mainly from congressional and party recommendations, interest groups, and campaign workers. Presidents lean toward one of two patterns of appointment. In one, the president is involved in all levels of political appointment, while each cabinet member negotiates with the president's team about appointments in his or her own department. This was Kennedy's approach. It was designed both to reward people who helped elect him and to let subcabinet appointees know that they owed their jobs to the president rather than to their own department secretary. The other approach is for the president to pick his cabinet and then let department secretaries choose their own subordinates, subject to White House clearance. This was Nixon's first approach. He later regretted it, and

[14] A study by the House Post Office and Civil Service Committee lists 2677 jobs that can be filled by the president or his appointees. (*National Journal,* November 20, 1976, p. 1652.) In addition, political considerations sometimes enter into appointments to higher career civil service posts. This is most commonly a form of political clearance, but sometimes outright political choices are made. See Hugh Heclo, *A Government of Strangers* (Washington: The Brookings Institution, 1977), pp. 51–55.

after his reelection went to extraordinary lengths to substitute Nixon loyalists for many of his first-term appointees. Despite a widely publicized nationwide talent search that was largely a smokescreen, Carter also delegated lesser appointments to the people he chose for his cabinet. (Some cabinet members, however, found that a few subordinates had already been appointed before they themselves were selected.) Within a couple of years, Carter also began to regret giving away so much power and increased White House participation in departmental appointments. Four factors govern the recruitment of the new presidential appointees: expertise, political considerations, loyalty, and availability.

Expertise.   Each new administration looks hard for truly qualified individuals. Typically, they are in short supply. Most administrations find themselves with far fewer options than they would like. The problem is often finding someone of sufficient competence who will take the job rather than choosing among applicants. The skills prized in high presidential appointees are not familiarity with particular issue areas, but more general ability to administer large organizations in political situations. In a career of less than five years in the Nixon administration, Elliot Richardson, a highly respected administrator, served as undersecretary of state, secretary of health, education and welfare, secretary of defense, and attorney general. President Ford appointed Richardson ambassador to England and in late 1975 made him secretary of commerce. President Carter appointed him ambassador-at-large to a United Nations Law of the Seas conference. The repeated stints of government and government-related service of Carter cabinet members are striking, as Table 14.3 shows.

Political Considerations.   Party workers are pushed for appointment by those around the president and in Congress who want to reward faithful service. A second sort of political consideration applies to those agencies strongly oriented to specific clienteles. With departments such as labor, agriculture, HEW, and transportation, the relevant interest groups want appointments for people who reflect their own points of view. These groups can sometimes exercise a veto on appointments in "their" area of concern. Sometimes more than one major interest is part of a department's clientele and conflicts occur over top appointments. President Carter's first thought for secretary of labor was John Dunlop, who had held the same job in the Ford administration after a long career at Harvard as a specialist in labor matters. This was agreeable to the labor unions who traditionally were the labor department's main clients, but not to blacks and women's groups, who attacked Dunlop for insensitivity to their problems. The unions lost the fight when Carter passed over Dunlop, but were not unhappy about the eventual choice, Ray Marshall.

Although presidential willingness to respond to such pressure groups is sometimes denounced as a "sellout to the interests," in practical terms it is necessary and serves a useful purpose. Officials in these agencies have to work with the people in the private sector who make up these clientele groups. Making a faith healer assistant secretary for health in HEW would not do much to bring government and the medical profession into partnership, nor would it make sense to appoint a

Table 14.3

Career Patterns of Selected Members of Carter's First Cabinet

CABINET MEMBER	ACADEMIA	GOVERNMENT	CORPORATE BUSINESS/LAW	ELECTIVE POLITICS
Michael Blumenthal (Treasury)	Ph.D. Economics teacher 1953–57	Deputy assistant secretary 1961–63 U.S. trade representative 1964–67	Manager 1957–59 Vice president 1959–61 Executive 1967–72 President and chairman 1973–76	
Harold Brown (Defense)	Ph.D. Physics teacher 1947–49 Research scientist 1949–52 Laboratory manager 1952–60 University president 1969–77	Consultant 1956–61 Director of research office 1961–65 Secretary of the air force 1965–69		
Joseph Califano (Health, Education, and Welfare)	LL.B.	Judge Advocate General's Office 1955–58 Special assistant 1961–63 General counsel 1963–64 Deputy secretary 1964–65 Presidential assistant 1965–68	Law practice 1958–61 Law practice 1969–71 Law firm partner 1971–76	

pacifist as secretary of the army or a professional strikebreaker as secretary of labor. In some fields there are two clienteles, fiercely opposed to each other. This is the case on environmental matters, where conservationists oppose natural resource producers. In such situations, most of the people with expertise have taken sides, and it is difficult to pick officials who can work with all the relevant private citizens and groups.

Loyalty.   A third consideration is that appointees should be supporters of the president's policy positions and of the president himself. Presi-

Table 14.3 – continued

Career Patterns of Selected Members of Carter's First Cabinet

CABINET MEMBER	ACADEMIA	GOVERNMENT	CORPORATE BUSINESS/LAW	ELECTIVE POLITICS
Bob Bergland (Agriculture)		Regional official 1961–62 Regional director 1963–68	Farmer Farmer 1968–70	Congressman 1971–76
Juanita Kreps (Commerce)	Instructor 1942–43 Instructor 1945–46 Ph.D. 1948 Lecturer 1952–55 Associate professor 1963–68 Dean 1969–72 Vice president 1973–76	Economist 1943–44 Various advisory positions 1963–76		
Patricia Harris (Housing and Urban Development)	LL.B. Associate dean 1962–65 Dean 1967	Attorney 1960–61 Ambassador 1965–67	Law firm partner 1967–76	Various part-time party positions 1960–76

Source: Hugh Heclo, "Issue Networks and the Executive Establishment," in Anthony King, ed., *The New American Political System* (Washington: American Enterprise Institute, 1978), pp. 109–11.

dents want loyalty not out of vanity, but because they want to increase their ability to control the government. Knowing that permanent civil servants have their own ideas about policy, presidents need to maximize their chances of imposing their imprint on Washington. Obviously, in many instances these considerations run at cross purposes, particularly when the appointment power is delegated downward from the White House. In that case, satisfying interest groups is likely to become more important than personal loyalty to the president. When the president plays an active role in the appointment process, he is liable to weigh loyalty to himself most heavily and also to reward campaign workers. Presidents make sure that at least one personally loyal person is in the cabinet. The favorite post for this purpose is that of attorney general, the official who heads the department of justice—the federal law enforcement agency. Kennedy made his brother attorney general; Nixon picked John Mitchell, his law partner; and Carter gave the job to Griffin Bell, an old friend and supporter from Georgia.

Availability. Most people likely to be considered for a presidential appointment would face a major financial loss if they were to accept the post. Federal executive salaries may seem high compared to average income levels, but they are far lower than those available to top executives and professionals in the private sector (see Table 14.4). One exception is people appointed from non-profit organizations, such as the low-paying public interest groups that provided many sub-cabinet appointments in the Carter administration. These officials generally got large pay increases by joining the government. What is more, conflict of interest laws often require newly appointed public officials to give up investments. In extreme cases, such losses have amounted to millions of dollars. Although young executives have fewer assets than their older colleagues and therefore face this problem in less acute form, they are often reluctant to go into government service because they are on career ladders and may find their rivals gaining on them if they take time out in Washington. In the past this has been somewhat compensated for by the increased experience in dealing with the government that comes from federal service. But this in turn has led to complaints about so-called revolving door public-private service. President Carter asked appointees to sign a pledge that they would not officially or unofficially act to influence the government within a year after leaving public service, a requirement that deterred some potential appointees from joining his administration.[15] For all these reasons, the appointment process

Table 14.4

Salaries of Federal Officials in 1979

OFFICE	SALARY
President	$200,000
Vice-president	75,000
Speaker of the House of Representatives	75,000
Chief Justice, Supreme Court	75,000
Associate Justice, Supreme Court	72,000
Cabinet member	66,000
Member of Congress	57,500
Court of appeals judge	57,500
Undersecretary	57,500
District court judge	54,500
Assistant department secretary	52,500
Bureau chief	50,000

Source: Commission on Executive, Legislative and Judicial
Salaries published in *Congressional Quarterly Weekly Report,*
February 12, 1977, p. 268.

[15] W. J. Lanouette, "The Revolving Door—It's Tricky to Try to Stop It," *National Journal,* October 19, 1977, pp. 1796–1803. A desire to prevent "revolving door" conflicts of interest produced a law prohibiting former high officials from: (1) any contact with their old agency for one year after leaving office; and (2) for two years after leaving, helping anyone else in dealing with their old agency on any matter in which the former official had been "personally and substantially involved." Although motivated by high ethical standards, this law would have made it almost impossible for some officials to return to their old private jobs. (A university official, for example, cannot help dealing with the government.) Faced with a mass exodus from government before the law went into effect in mid-1979, Congress took hasty action to repeal its worst excesses.

can turn into a long search. It took the Nixon administration a year to fill the political posts available. Carter was in the same situation a year after taking office.

Before the Carter administration, the annual turnover rate of presidential appointees was 25 percent. Trying to build an administration with more experience, Carter asked prospective appointees for a written letter promising to serve for "[your] entire first term or as long as you wish me to serve."[16] While this may have been a further impediment to recruiting, it seems to have cut the turnover rate.

What sorts of people does the president appoint? A few cabinet members have been elective politicians, but increasingly presidents have been choosing for their cabinets "generalist executives" with a mix of private and public experience.[17] Of Carter's seventeen cabinet-level appointments in 1977, five were lawyers and seven held Ph.Ds. Two were black and two were women. Three were U. S. representatives and one had been governor of Idaho. Only six were known to the president before he took office, and only a few of these had been involved in his campaign. Appointments to the cabinet after the beginning of an administration often go to people already serving in lower-ranking political positions. The vast majority of the subcabinet appointees also had no part in Carter's election. Strong orders from the White House produced big increases in the numbers of blacks and women in these posts. About 11 percent were black and 13 percent were women, with smaller percentages for other minorities.[18] Many political appointees could not easily be distinguished from people at the top of the civil service. Indeed, many were appointed from the ranks of career bureaucrats.[19]

The Cabinet The work of the federal government is done by about a dozen departments and a host of nondepartmental agencies. Each department is headed by a secretary, who is appointed by the president and confirmed by the Senate. Together with the vice-president and several other major officials, the secretaries comprise the **cabinet.** As an organization in its own right, the cabinet is not particularly important. The very term cabinet is not mentioned in the Constitution and any comparisons with the British cabinet, which plays the major leadership role in British political life, would be totally misleading. The American cabinet is *not* an executive council of the government, a forum for discussion of large questions, or a source of advice to a president pondering major decisions. Cabinet meetings are infrequent, superficial, and brief. Kennedy observed that they were "simply useless." A former member of his cabinet wrote:

> Decisions on major matters were not made—or even influenced at cabinet sessions and . . . discussion there was a waste of time . . . . When members spoke up to suggest or to discuss major administration policy, the President would listen with

[16] Quoted in *CQ Weekly Report,* March 5, 1977, p. 397.
[17] Nelson W. Polsby, "Presidential Cabinet Making: Lessons for the Political System," *Political Science Quarterly,* 93 (spring 1978), pp. 15–25.
[18] *Washington Post,* June 19, 1977, p. A4.
[19] Heclo, *A Government of Strangers,* pp. 49, 67–68.

thinly disguised impatience and then postpone or otherwise bypass the question. . . .[20]

It is customary for each incoming president to announce that his cabinet will play a major role in his administration. Then, like Kennedy, he usually ignores it. The occasional president (FDR, Eisenhower, and Ford) who calls frequent cabinet meetings uses them as a general morale-building device rather than a vehicle for making important decisions.

The reasons for the weakness of the cabinet illuminate why presidents have so much trouble maintaining control over the executive branch. Traditionally, only one or two members of the president's cabinet have been close to him politically in his struggle to gain the White House. For the most part, the cabinet is made up of people the president may not even have known before being elected. They are chosen partly to satisfy the claims of various major interests to which the president feels bound to be responsive, and partly to satisfy different factions in his party.

Although cabinet members are appointed by the president and owe their primary allegiance to him, they also must develop good relations with the departments they head. These departments are composed of career civil servants who remain at their posts from one administration to the next. Quite understandably, they have interests which may be different from those of the president. Often they are fiercely dedicated to the programs they administer. They expect that the secretary who heads their department will be as committed to representing their interests to the president as he is to representing the president's interests to them. The secretary cannot hope to control a department without the loyalty of its career bureaucrats. He cannot win that loyalty without defending the department and speaking up for it when it is attacked. The secretary's need for loyalty from his staff gives him commitments and perspectives different from those of the president. The secretary's tendency to be somewhat at cross-purposes with the White House is strengthened by the fact that he is responsible only for part of the government and thus lacks the president's need to balance a wider range of interests. The secretary must build alliances in Congress and among clientele groups if he is to get the job done, for a secretary cannot go running to the White House for help every time there is political trouble. But then these allies become a source of pressure on the secretary, often pushing him in a "parochial" direction inconsistent with the president's overall goals.

President Carter's first cabinet meeting.

Wide World

Moreover, much legislation specifically orders a particular department head to carry out certain programs. All secretaries are especially accountable to the congressional committees that authorize their programs, appropriate funds for their departments, and oversee their operations. The "iron triangle" of career bureaucrats, congressional committee members, and constituency groups can be a formidable obstacle to the president trying to see that "the laws shall be faithfully executed."

[20] Quoted in *National Journal Reports,* October 6, 1973, p. 1473.

Presidents, of course, are not without ways to deal with the centrifugal tendencies of the cabinet. One technique is to "colonize" a department by putting a presidential agent in it. Nixon was notorious for this practice, but was often disappointed by the yield. Commenting on the poor results, Nixon's aide John Erlichman said that, after such officials had been appointed and had their picture taken with the president, "We only see them at the White House Christmas party. They go off and marry the natives."[21] This happened because the president's agents could not do their jobs without the support of their bureaucratic subordinates, and to get this they had to abandon their presidential perspective.

Despite such strategems, all modern presidents have complained about their difficulties in getting the executive departments to do what they want. In many accounts of recent administrations, it seems that the principal villains are not Russians or members of the other party, but the permanent civil service.[22] The ploys just described have not been enough to give the president close control of the administrative branch. A major way to enhance his administrative powers is the institutionalized presidency.

THE INSTITUTIONALIZED PRESIDENCY

When the telephone rang in the McKinley White House, the president himself often answered. Woodrow Wilson typed his own speeches and even some of his own correspondence. Hoover was the first president to have a telephone on his desk. In those more leisurely days, the White House staff consisted largely of gardeners and cooks. For help with governmental affairs, the president needed only a handful of stenographers and clerks and a couple of personal assistants. By Franklin Roosevelt's time, the president's official household had expanded somewhat. But FDR's highly publicized and dedicated aides—the so-called Brain Trust of college professors who helped him early in his first term with legislation drafting—were not listed on the payroll as presidential aides. Neither was Harry Hopkins, Roosevelt's key wartime lieutenant who lived in the White House. To secure their services, Roosevelt had to employ the mild subterfuge of giving them jobs without duties in other executive agencies. It was not until 1939, after several years of political give-and-take, that legislation was passed creating the Executive Office of the President (EOP). The Executive Office of the President now has a staff of almost 2000 officially budgeted personnel, along with many others who are officially on departmental payrolls but work full- or part-time to manage the presidency. President Carter, who during his first year in office brought about a publicized reduction in EOP size, had to borrow more than the usual amount of agency

[21] Quoted in Richard P. Nathan, *The Plot That Failed* (New York: Wiley, 1975), p. 40.

[22] This is a constant theme in the innumerable books written by participants in the Watergate episode, and is equally striking in the accounts of the Kennedy administration written by his former assistants. *See* especially Theodore C. Sorensen, *Kennedy* (New York: Harper & Row, 1965); and Arthur C. Schlesinger, Jr., *A Thousand Days* (Boston: Houghton Mifflin, 1965). Also see Rowland Evans, Jr., and Robert D. Novak, *Nixon in the White House: The Frustration of Power* (New York: Random House, 1972); and Thomas E. Cronin, " 'Everybody Believes in Democracy Until He Gets to the White House . . .': An Examination of White House–Departmental Relations." *Law and Contemporary Problems,* 35 (summer 1970), pp. 573–625.

personnel. For example, he had to borrow people to answer the letters that poured in after he urged citizens to tell him their views. (One hundred and seventy people work in the White House mailroom.)

The White House itself is flanked by buildings housing staff offices. The building immediately to the west, once occupied by several departments, became first "the Executive Office Building," and then "the Old Executive Office Building." The "New Executive Office Building," a high-rise red brick structure north of the White House, is set beyond a facade of renovated early nineteenth-century buildings facing Lafayette Park, most of which house EOP offices. The widely photographed Oval Office of the president faces south to the White House gardens and the Washington Monument.

The White House Staff

Within the Executive Office of the President, the White House Office has about 350 employees charged to it, a reduction of about 100 achieved in 1977 largely by moving some White House jobs elsewhere in the EOP, some EOP jobs elsewhere in the executive branch, and increasing the use of employees detailed from outside the EOP. Although Carter denounced big White House staffs as a symptom of the "imperial presidency," by 1979 he had more aides than Nixon or Ford. Even his wife has a staff of seventeen people. Like Nixon and other presidents before him, Carter gradually came to rely more on his White House staff, and less on his cabinet appointees.

Unlike the department secretaries, White House aides have no need to develop loyalties or commitments to anyone but the president himself. Usually young and unknown before going to the White House, they are not chosen to please party factions or constituent interest groups and are not subject to confirmation by the Senate. Because their careers depend exclusively on the president, they are undistracted by outside loyalties. Their organization and assignment of tasks can be changed at will by the president. A great many White House aides usually share the president's political background. Most major offices in Carter's White House were headed by people from Georgia, of whom there were more than fifty on the White House payroll. Like the president, they work long hours and have at their disposal the White House's many support facilities, including a switchboard of telephone operators famous for being able to reach almost anyone in a brief period of time. In the last thirty years, these presidential aides have occupied an increasingly important place in the center of the national government. As the complexity and size of the bureaucracy increase the challenges to presidential control, his staff inevitably grows more influential. A former presidential assistant confided to an interviewer: "I had more power over national affairs in a few years in the White House than I could if I spent the rest of my life in the Senate."[23]

The White House Complex

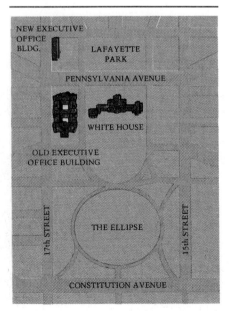

[23] Quoted in Patrick Anderson, *The President's Men* (Garden City, N.Y.: Doubleday, 1969) p. 1.

One major function of the White House staff is to protect and advance the president's political interests. This includes legislative liaison, press relations, speech writing, and control of the president's schedule, travel, and relations with major interest groups and party figures. Every president also has to have assistants who perform such inevitable but disagreeable tasks as refusing access, discharging officials, and denying requests for special consideration. Such aides do what the president wants; their function is to give the boss the results without the blame. The need for this service is explained in Patrick Anderson's description of Sherman Adams, Eisenhower's chief of staff:

> Eisenhower remained beloved, even by those who were fired or turned away; it was always Adams who was hated. Eisenhower was the most beloved man of his time. . . . The people's affection for him was his strength, and he hoarded it like a miser. On the national scale he saw it as his mission to unite the nation, and on a personal scale it pained him, more than most men, to say "no." . . .[24]

Another group of staff are "policy people," those concerned with developing new programs, identifying problems and opportunities, defining issues, reconciling proposals from agencies and interest groups, and overseeing execution of major programs. The Office of Management and Budget (OMB) coordinates policy proposals flowing upward from the cabinet departments. The president's own assistants, more alert to politics than the OMB, also work out many policy programs. In the field of domestic policy, since the Johnson years much coordination and background policy research have been done by the domestic policy staff. It is involved in issues on which the administration wants to place a distinctly presidential stamp. About fifty people work on the domestic policy staff and its director is probably the most important administration figure on most domestic policy matters.

White House aides typically have something of an adversary relationship with career civil servants. The president's men are preoccupied with speed and the presidential perspective, which inevitably grates on bureaucrats accustomed to a specialized and long-term perspective. Anderson described the Kennedy staff's attitude toward the civil service:

> It astounded the New Frontiersmen that the civil servants were disinclined to work until ten at night and all day Saturday, that they were somehow immune to the magic of the moment.[25]

Often there is also tension between the president's aides and some of his cabinet. On any issue, the relevant department secretary will compete for the president's support with one or two people on his staff. Theoretically this sort of give-and-take is healthy, but sometimes the competition gets out of hand and feuds develop that interfere with good government and good politics. The White House staff are closer to the president politically and physically, and are not distracted by a need to win the support of departmental bureaucrats, as the cabinet members are. Thus the staff are more likely to win such internal struggles. The

[24] Anderson, *The President's Men*, p. 184.
[25] Anderson, *The President's Men*, p. 242.

AN EXAMPLE OF PRESIDENTIAL STAFF WORK

During the campaign, . . . we indicated our support for legislation to make it illegal for U.S. companies to enter into an agreement which stipulated as a condition for doing business with an Arab country that they discriminate against any U.S. citizen on the basis of his religion, race or national origin; it would further make it illegal to signify their intention not to do business with the State of Israel as a condition of doing business with the Arab countries. . . .

Unfortunately, some elements contained in the various anti-boycott legislative proposals go beyond what is necessary and could hamper the efforts of the new Administration to bring about a just and lasting peace in the Middle East. In addition, these measures would place American industry at a serious competitive disadvantage in this area and make it impossible for many multinational companies to conform to the laws of the host countries within which they operate and threaten the already fragile U.S. energy supply. . . .

Several weeks ago, I began to work with the State and Commerce Departments on the Arab boycott bill to develop a coordinated Administrative position. The position that was developed and agreed to . . . fell between the positions taken by the Jewish community (represented by the Anti-Defamation League) and the business community (the Business Roundtable). . . .

Our position was to support strongly the pending anti-boycott bills but to seek certain exceptions in order to permit Arab-American diplomatic relations to remain reasonably sound. That position was not, of course, totally acceptable to either the Jewish community or the business community.

Title II of the bill (HR 5840) contains anti-boycott legislation which is in substantial conformity with the agreement between the Jewish service organizations and the Business Roundtable which you announced and endorsed in your statement of May 3. Title II would prohibit any U.S. person from taking or knowingly agreeing to take certain actions with the intent to comply with any boycott against a country friendly to the U.S.

Source: These are selections from memos to President Carter from Stuart E. Eizenstat, assistant to the president for domestic affairs and policy, quoted in *National Journal*, April 15, 1978, p. 588.

most spectacular example of this process in recent years was Carter's 1979 purge of four cabinet members, all of whom had bad relations with his "Georgia mafia" assistants.

The counterpart to the domestic policy staff is the National Security Council, which plays an important role in planning and coordinating foreign policy. The president, vice-president, secretary of state, and other senior officials are members of the NSC. Its key figure is the executive director, who is also assistant to the president for national security affairs. He directs a staff of about seventy people. The NSC helps the president decide among the conflicting positions advocated by different agencies concerned with foreign policy. Under Henry Kissinger in the Nixon and Ford administrations, the NSC had a larger staff and more direct policy role than under Carter's assistant, Zbigniew Brzezinski. Some observers have criticized the growth in size and influence of the NSC because they believe it has weakened the morale and influence of the state department's professional diplomats. Nevertheless, the development of some kind of a shadow state department in the White House is an inevitable result of the increase in scope and complexity of government, the need to synthesize a presidential foreign policy out of the competing recommendations of the foreign affairs agencies, and the increasing convergence of foreign and domestic policies. Notice, however, that the problem of preventing American businesses from complicity in the Arab boycott of Israel was handled by Carter's domestic policy staff. Doubtless this issue was judged to be more a matter of reconciling American Jews and business interests than of diplomatic relations in the Middle East.

The development of the National Security Council is the most dramatic, but by no means the only, example of the emergence in recent years of presidential agencies largely independent of the bureaucratic departments. These include the Office of Management and Budget, the Council of Economic Advisers, and other EOP agencies contributing to the institutionalization of the presidency. The expansion of these agencies reflects not just a need for coordination and advice, but the president's desire for officials loyal to his goals, not to the interests of the career bureaucracies. As the tasks of government have become more diverse and specialized, the permanent civil servants themselves become increasingly specialized. This trend challenges the president's ability to impose his own direction on government.

Advising the President   It is important to distinguish between those who *act for* the president and those who *advise* him. Advice from members of his official family comes from people who are dependent on him for their jobs and are tempted to tell him what they think he wants to hear. In addition, as one close observer of such matters put it, "the aura of reverence that surrounds the President when he is in the Mansion is so universal that the slightest hint of criticism automatically labels a man as a colossal lout."[26] In order to free himself from this combination of self-interested caution and overprotectiveness, a president may choose aides with diverse views and give them overlapping assignments. He may also turn for advice to members of Congress, Washington lawyers, journalists, retired elder statesmen, and others who are not dependent on him and are likely to provide more disinterested counsel. Such advisers may not be more "loyal" to the president than White House aides, but they are less dependent on him for jobs and status than his staff. Only a man without further ambition could speak as frankly to a president as former Secretary of State Dean Acheson, who, when asked by Lyndon

[26] Reedy, *The Twilight of the Presidency*, p. 80.

Johnson, "Why don't people like me?" replied, "Because, Mr. President, you are not a very likable man."[27]

Presidents generally are aware of their advisers' reluctance to express unwelcome opinions. Eisenhower tried to cope with this problem by keeping silent or noncommittal in meetings until everyone else had spoken, knowing that if he expressed his opinion he would inhibit others from speaking frankly. Similarly, Kennedy sometimes left the room during crisis discussions to avoid stifling dissent. Recognizing the chilling effect of the president's prestige, Johnson made use of it in the opposite way, to protect himself from after-the-fact criticism of his policies. He would announce a decision at a meeting, and then ask each person in the room if he agreed with the decision. There were seldom any open dissenters. Johnson then could use this coerced agreement to "lock in" people to his policy and keep them loyal to it. This gained him support, but the cost was high. He was kept insulated from advice that might have convinced him to stop the bloody and politically damaging war in Asia.

One sometimes hears about a president: "It's not his fault, he just had bad advice." Indeed, supporters of certain candidates have argued that their lack of substantial mental ability was not crucial, because what is really important is the president's advisers. These arguments have a number of flaws. In the first place, the president picks his advisers, so the nation is dependent upon his ability to choose capable ones. Second, the president organizes his advisers and chooses how he will use them. And finally, advisers often present opposing views. It is the president alone who must finally choose among them or reconcile them.

THE UPS AND DOWNS OF PRESIDENTIAL POWER

The American political system is based on the assumption that power will be shared among the three branches of government. Each branch will be dominant in certain areas, while in other areas decisions can be made only if there is some sort of coordination or cooperation. In any event, the three branches are supposed to be in a rough kind of equilibrium. This system of checks and balances was designed to avoid undue concentration of power and to provide multiple points of citizen influence over government.

At various times in American political history, each of the three branches has been accused of seeking and exercising too much power—of disturbing a presumably ideal balance of power among the three institutions. In the mid-1930s, the Supreme Court was widely accused of "judicial tyranny" because it struck down as unconstitutional many major pieces of New Deal legislation that had been passed by overwhelming congressional majorities and signed into law by a popular president. At the same time, another set of critics believed that Roosevelt had so far exceeded traditional presidential powers as to pose the threat of a dictatorship. As with the shifts in views of the presidency summarized at the beginning of the chap-

[27] Quoted in Barber, *The Presidential Character*, p. 93.

ter, the Court critics were largely supporters of the policies it declared unconstitutional, while those who feared that Roosevelt would become a tyrant were largely
opponents of his policies. Most political observers at the end of the 1970s feel,
whatever their views of the ideal level of presidential power, that Presidents Ford
and Carter have been far more limited in their ability to get their way than were
Presidents Johnson and Nixon. Moreover, apart from the political failures that
ended each of these assertive presidencies, a backlash against Johnson and Nixon
practices has led to a range of legislation designed to "restore the balance" among
the branches of government.

Even more important than specific president-limiting measures is a general
climate of skepticism about many of the powers asserted by presidents. The inability of Ford and Carter to get things done also was caused by the former's lack of a
congressional majority and the latter's combination of big ambitions and inexperi-
ence. Nevertheless, the legal restraints on presidents of recent years may in the long
run prove to be of major consequence in and of themselves. A summary of them
also provides a way of considering other areas of past and continuing presidential
policy discretion.

The Power to Use Throughout American history there have been numerous in-
Military Force stances in which American troops were used abroad or in the
United States without congressional authorization. There is lit-
tle controversy (at least legally) about brief exercises of military force in response either to minor disturbances or to events that unfold too rapidly for congressional action. During the period of sustained military confrontation with the Soviet Union
and other Communist nations that followed World War II, a pair of major undeclared wars were fought. United States participation (under United Nations aus-
pices) in the Korean conflict was deliberately conducted without a congressional
authorization because of President Truman's expansive view of the war powers of
the commander-in-chief. Congress tacitly supported Truman by voting military
appropriations, but he suffered politically from accusations that he had not followed
constitutional practice. When President Johnson ordered successive increases in
troop commitments to the Vietnam conflict, he used a legal justification, the Gulf of
Tonkin Resolution voted in 1964 in response to reported North Vietnamese attacks
on American ships in international waters. Johnson, like Truman, received implicit
congressional war support via military appropriations, but there was a crescendo of
criticism of the overall military commitment in Indochina. The Gulf of Tonkin Resolution came to be viewed as a ruse by which Johnson had tricked Congress into
legalizing an undeclared war.

Anticipating future situations in which the president might exploit his power as
commander-in-chief to precipitate military confrontations abroad, Congress adopted the War Powers Resolution in 1973. Passed over President Nixon's veto, this
measure set a sixty-day limit on presidential commitment of American troops
abroad, unless Congress specifically authorized their deployment. A thirty-day extension also was authorized, if necessary, in order to extricate troops safely. In addition, Congress could end such assignments before the sixty-day deadline by pass-

ing a concurrent resolution, which does not require presidential consent. Only time will tell if this measure will trim the president's power in foreign affairs. In situations in which the War Powers Resolution might be applied, the tendency to rally around the president in foreign affairs may provide widespread support for his action. Certainly this was true early in the Ford administration when the president took immediate military action to recover an American merchant ship (the *Mayaguez*) and its crew when they were seized by Cambodian Communist forces. Although the view of some professional observers was that Ford had acted too hastily, much approval and virtually no criticism was heard on Capitol Hill. And Ford's Gallup Poll popularity score rose sharply, if temporarily.

Although presidential dominance in foreign affairs undoubtedly will continue, congressional power to influence foreign policy seems to be increasing—for example in such areas as foreign military aid, economic policy, arms sales abroad, and arms control negotiations. When the president wants to do something that requires the creation of new institutions or formal alliances, congressional assent is crucial. In the period after World War II, the Truman administration had to gain congressional support for the North Atlantic Treaty Organization (NATO), a binding agreement that keeps an American army in Europe; and the Marshall Plan, a scheme to finance postwar economic recovery in Europe. Such recent steps toward peace as the Test Ban Treaty and the Strategic Arms Limitation Talks (SALT) Treaty were modified in response to Senate pressure and continue to be closely scrutinized by Congress.

The most important source of congressional power in foreign affairs comes from the fact that money cannot be spent for any purpose unless Congress appropriates it. Congress continued to fund the war in Southeast Asia until the summer of 1973, when all American troops had been withdrawn from Vietnam. Then it passed an appropriation bill forbidding the bombing of Cambodia after August 15, 1973. And it refused Ford's requests for grants of funds to the collapsing South Vietnam government. Finally, Congress provides those who disagree with the president's foreign policy opportunities for criticism and publicity. During the war in Vietnam, this opportunity was often exploited by opponents of the war. This is important because in foreign affairs the president usually needs or wants to present a united face to the world. The ability to disturb this public posture by threatening open criticism is often a source of congressional influence on foreign policy that is exercised behind the scenes.

Executive Privilege   Nixon's presidency brought two further developments that led to cries of excessive presidential power—his extensive impoundment of funds and claims of executive privilege. In neither case were his actions unprecedented. Presidents throughout our history have argued successfully that the separation of powers entitles the chief executive to receive privileged advice—that is, advice without congressional inquiry into the character of that advice. Consequently, members of the White House staff traditionally have refused to testify before Congress on the grounds that doing so would violate the constitutional prerogative of the president to receive counsel without congressional scrutiny. This claim, although occasionally challenged, has nevertheless been respected. On the other hand, cabinet officers, their subordinates, and officials of the regulatory agencies have always been answerable to Congress. But as the powers of the White House staff have grown in recent years, key decisions have increasingly been made in the White House, not in the executive agencies. Congressional ability to question cabinet officers has been of decreasing utility, while congressional inability to question White House personnel has been an increasing source of frustration.

The Nixon administration's attempts to claim total executive privilege for all members of the Executive Office of the President foundered on the rock of possible criminal acts committed by members of the EOP. Public opinion and Congress alike were intolerant of the argument that no one on the president's staff could be required to testify about *anything,* including criminal matters, on grounds that it might be a breach of executive privilege. The president was forced to retreat from his blanket claim of executive privilege. The most striking instance of this retreat came when the Supreme Court denied the president's claim to executive privilege over subpoenaed tapes of conversations in his office in the landmark case of *United States* v. *Nixon.*[28] But the decision also seemed implicitly to grant that under some circumstances executive communications can properly be kept from Congress. Moreover, congressional attempts to legislate against executive privilege have not succeeded.

Impoundment   Just as Congress can refuse to appropriate funds for activities of which it disapproves, so the president can refuse to spend money Congress has appropriated. This process is known as **impoundment,** and it has been used by many presidents. One of the most famous examples was Truman's refusal to build an air force as big as Congress wanted. In this case, and in others during the Kennedy administration, impoundment was based in part on the president's powers as commander-in-chief of the armed forces. As it did in so many areas, the Nixon administration carried an established practice to unacceptable lengths. Nixon's impoundments were concentrated in areas of domestic spending where Congress provided more money than the president wanted. At one point, more than $10 billion in appropriated funds was impounded and whole programs were in danger of termination because the president did not agree with their objectives.

In a series of decisions beginning in 1973, the courts ordered the president to spend impounded funds. Congress echoed this view with legislation in 1974 that forbade impoundment except with its permission and set up congressional budget committees as a counterweight to the president's OMB. As the courts saw it, both the bills authorizing the programs and the appropriations measures were laws. The courts also have held that the president cannot plead general budgetary considerations as a legitimate ground for impoundment. But the courts have not always struck down impoundment. Once again, the ultimate resolution of this question is in doubt.[29] In fact, ultimate resolutions of such issues are few and far between in

---

[28] *United States* v. *Nixon,* 418 U.S. 683 (1974).

[29] On impoundment and a variety of more subtle ways presidents get around congressional intent in allocating funds, see Louis Fisher, *Presidential Spending Power* (Princeton, N.J.: Princeton University Press, 1975).

American politics. As we saw with Congress, attempts to carry an advantage too far bring a severe reaction. The end result of Nixon's enthusiastic use of impoundment was a net loss in the president's power to withhold appropriated funds.

THE VICE-PRESIDENCY

The Constitution says that "the Vice President of the United States shall be President of the Senate, but shall have no Vote, unless they be equally divided." His principal duty is to be available to take office in the event of the president's death, resignation, or removal from office. In this century alone, one president has resigned, two have been assassinated, and two more have died of natural cases. Five of the fourteen twentieth-century presidents first reached the White House by succeeding a man who died in office. Yet the post itself provides no formal powers of any consequence besides that of resolving a tie vote in Congress.

How Vice-Presidents Are Chosen

Presidential nominees almost always personally choose their running mates. Occasionally, the vice-presidential nomination is a bargaining counter needed to clinch the presidential nomination. This was the case in 1932, when Franklin D. Roosevelt had to promise the nomination to John N. Garner, a prominent conservative Democratic congressman, in order to win the support of the Texas and California delegations for himself. Usually, the nominee chooses a running mate who will contribute strength where the presidential candidate considers himself vulnerable, someone with complementary ideological, regional, or ethnic qualities. In 1960, John F. Kennedy, knowing that his Catholicism would be particularly costly in the South, chose as his running mate the leading southern politician, Lyndon Johnson of Texas. Although this decision was unpopular with many northern liberals, it was a master stroke, Johnson concentrated his campaigning south of the Mason-Dixon line, where he was most appreciated and effective.

Not only are vice-presidential candidates picked for reasons other than their suitability as presidents, but very often the decision is not carefully considered. In 1972, McGovern assigned very little staff time to investigating possible running mates. He chose Senator Thomas Eagleton of Missouri, who was forced to withdraw a few weeks later when the press revealed that he had been hospitalized three times due to psychological problems. Similarly, in 1968, Nixon seems not to have looked very deeply into Spiro Agnew's background in Maryland politics when he chose him as a running mate. Five years later, the Nixon administration, already reeling under the Watergate crisis, suffered yet another blow when Agnew (who had nothing to do with Watergate) became implicated in

Lyndon Johnson is sworn in as president aboard Air Force One in Dallas on November 22, 1963.

Wide World

a federal investigation of corruption in Maryland. While serving as a county of-ficial and then as governor, Agnew had required county and state contractors to pay him illegal kickbacks, some of which he still received after he became vice-president. Agnew resigned in October 1973 as part of an agreement that let him escape a prison term by pleading no contest to a single charge of income tax evasion.

The Eagleton and Agnew fiascos prompted the two parties to consider (but not adopt) more rational methods of nominating vice-presidential candidates. The most likely improvement is to give the presidential nominee the option of post-poning the decision for several weeks. Then the nomination would be made for-mally by the party's national committee, which doubtless would pick whomever the presidential candidate desired. Carter chose Walter Mondale as his vice-presidential running mate, after extensive background investigation of a number of possible choices. He could afford the time because his own nomination was as-sured. Pondering his choice of a running mate, Carter considered his own position as a moderate southerner with few Washington connections about whom many liberals and union leaders were uncertain. Mondale had ten years' experience as a senator from Minnesota, strong liberal credentials, and friendly relations with the labor movement.

With the ratification of the Twenty-fifth Amendment in 1967, a new method of choosing a vice-president was added to the constitutional system. It operates only when the office is vacant. The president nominates an individual who takes of-fice when confirmed by a majority vote of each house of Congress. This procedure was followed in 1973–74 when Nixon picked Ford to replace Agnew, and again in 1974 when Ford, having succeeded Nixon as president, named Nelson Rockefeller as his vice-president. In striking contrast to the hasty convention method, this new procedure results in a painstaking scrutiny of the nominee by House and Senate committees. The FBI investigation preceding Ford's confirmation included more than a thousand interviews. Congressional testimony on Ford covered everything "from his voting record on civil rights to how much paint his family's paint and var-nish company had sold to a Michigan furniture maker; from his experience in for-eign affairs to how he financed his vacation home in Colorado."[30]

What the Vice-President Does The vice-president's duties as president of the Senate are not very time-consuming. Unless the legislative situation calls for an important parliamentary ruling, he actually spends little time presiding over the Senate. Mondale spent only eighteen days at this task during his first year in office. Nor does the office carry much congressional influence. When the Senate majority leader formally presented Vice-President Ford to the Senate, he warned him, "Here, presiding officers are to be seen and not heard, unlike the House where the Speaker's gavel is like a thunderclap."[31]

---

[30] *CQ Weekly Report,* January 12, 1974, p. 48.

[31] Quoted in Dom Bonafede, "Ford and Staff Tend to Business . . . and Wait," *National Journal Reports,* August 10, 1974, p. 1181.

One of the staple items of political commentary is the suggestion that the vice-president's status be raised so that full use can be made of his talents. Incoming presidents always promise to do this and then make a great show of doing so. In fact, though, they rarely do anything to upgrade the vice-presidency. After the campaign, the vice-president's usefulness to the president is limited. Whatever he does (except presiding over the Senate) is on the president's sufferance. As former Vice-President Humphrey observed of the post, "the only authority he has is what the President gives him. He who giveth can taketh away."[32]

Mondale seems to be an exception — he is a vice-president who really has an important, active role in government. A frequent, close, and valued adviser to Carter, he is also the president's agent on delicate negotiations with high officials. In addition, he chairs a White House executive management committee that assigns priorities to each proposal in the president's legislative program. The goal is to allocate the limited resources available to influence Congress, to be sure that the president is not lavishing too much effort on unimportant bills while neglecting crucial measures. Mondale's position depends entirely on his excellent relationship with Carter and therefore could end any time the two men have a falling out. No one knows whether this new importance for the office of vice-president is an exception or the beginning of a trend.

Vice-presidents usually perform ceremonial and rhetorical tasks such as good will tours abroad, political advocacy at home (not always in the spirit of good will), standing in for the president as head of state, and so forth. They often become administration apologists to their particular political constituencies. As Johnson escalated the war in Vietnam, he assigned Humphrey to defend administration policies to the liberals who had been the basis of Humphrey's following. Nixon used Agnew as a spokesman to conservative Republicans to whom Agnew had extraordinary appeal. Thanks to the power of the mass media, vice-presidents now have a visibility that was lacking before the television era. As a result, since the 1950s vice-presidents have been serious contenders for the presidency.

The vice-president's main responsibility, however, is to wait — which is not much of a job for an energetic, intelligent person accustomed to activity and influence. Yet who else would be desirable in the post but an experienced, energetic, intelligent, and ambitious person? This is the paradox of the office.

One political scientist summed up the situation this way:

> There seems, in short, to be no way for a Vice President to avoid the dilemmas built into the office: unless he is scrupulously loyal to the President, he cannot get the access to the President that he needs to discharge his constitutional function; when he is loyal to the President, he is saddled, at least in the short run, with whatever characteristics of the President or his program the President's enemies or his own care to fasten on him. He sits there in the limelight, visible, vulnerable, and for the most part, powerless.[33]

---

[32] Quoted in the *San Francisco Chronicle,* December 17, 1973, p. 24.

[33] Nelson W. Polsby, "Dilemmas of the Vice Presidency," in *Political Promises* (New York: Oxford University Press, 1974), p. 159.

SUMMARY   One of the realities of the American presidency is the institution's changing reputation and shifting views of what the president's legitimate powers are. Questions about presidential power raise two distinct points: (1) What in fact are presidents able to do? (2) What should they be able to do? Most observers' views on these questions reflect their political judgments of what the current president is doing; liberals and conservatives may shift position on these issues from one administration to the next.

The Consititution checks and balances the president's powers with those of other national governmental institutions. He is commander-in-chief of the armed forces, but needs Congress to appropriate funds; he makes treaties, but needs them approved by two-thirds of the Senate; he executes the laws, but Congress must make them and provide the money to carry them out.

The president is both head of the government and "chief of state," that is, the nation's symbolic leader. His influence on public opinion is great and he is held responsible for almost anything that happens. The presidency as an institution is shaped by the popularity, personality, and political problems of each individual president. Nevertheless, each president develops his conception of the office around some constant features: primacy; reelection; improving conditions at home and strengthening American power abroad; limited time to accomplish goals; the need to bargain and compromise; and the need to administer a huge permanent civil service.

In the twentieth century, the president has been party leader, chief legislator, and administrator of the executive branch. The president's ultimate weapon with Congress is the veto power, since vetoes are seldom overridden. This is only a negative weapon, however; the president's affirmative powers with Congress come from his position as focus of his party, his command of public attention, and the resources of the executive branch. These provide both information and ways to get the support of some congressmen.

The president appoints department secretaries and their deputies and assistants to run the government, that is, to give orders to the permanent civil servants. But in order to do a good job of running a department, its politically appointed officials usually have to gain the support of that department's bureaucrats and clientele. This requirement often leads them to have loyalties other than to the president — to become "parochial."

This development, which occurs in every administration, contributes to the importance of the White House staff. These presidential aides work in or near the White House, are loyal only to the president, and represent his political and policy interests. Together with specialized agencies in the Executive Office of the President, they plan and coordinate government policy for the president. They are one way the president imposes his direction on government, and are often in a state of tension with the regular administrative departments.

The vice-president takes over if the president dies, resigns, or becomes disabled. He may contribute some voter appeal to the president's ticket. Otherwise, the vice-president has few duties unless the president decides to give him something to do. The usual pattern has been for vice-presidents to perform only ceremonial tasks, and wait.

435

the politics
of administration

One of President Carter's first major difficulties in the
White House was his failure to keep his old friend, Bert Lance. Lance had been
accused of handling money in unethical and criminal
ways when he had headed a Georgia bank. He was forced out even though
Lance was indicted for bank fraud and various other crimes. Most Americans probably thought it would be risky to have someone who had handled money in
ney unusually handling the government's money. They also probably could not
understand why Carter wanted Lance as badly. In fact, Bert Lance had been

CHAPTER 15

not handle any government money, the secretary of the treasury does that. As we shall see, what the budget director handles is the bureaucracy. The struggle between the president and the bureaucracy can be a fierce one, which is why every president wants a budget director who is loyal to him and a fighter for what he wants. What was important to President Carter was not Lance's professional competence as a banker, but his long record of friendship and loyalty. In this chapter, it will become clear why the president needs so much help in trying to bring the executive branch under his control.

The federal government takes about a fifth of our national income in taxes and spends the money on a staggering variety of goods and services. The government is the country's biggest buyer of almost everything, and the biggest source of many services. It delivers the mail, patrols the coasts, the high seas and their subterranean depths, and outer space. It operates ferry boats, hospitals, nuclear submarines, museums, and parks. It helps farmers grow better strains of food, pays them not to grow crops, and provides food stamps to 20 million people. It pays people money when they are out of work and when they retire. It finances research into the causes of war and heart disease, the consequences of malnutrition and lovesickness, the mating calls of fruitflies and undergraduates. It stockpiles corn and hydrogen bombs.

The people who do all these things are often called "civil servants" if one feels sympathetic to them, and "bureaucrats" if one does not. In this chapter we use the terms "bureaucrats" and "the bureaucracy" simply to refer to all the people and agencies who administer the programs of the federal government, whether we think they are doing a good job or not. We do not mean any criticism by the words themselves, although we will point out that bureaucracy creates a lot of problems for democratic politics.[1]

Because the federal government is a large organization, we would expect it to have many things in common with other large organizations like corporations, universities, cooperatives, and labor unions. Any big organization has certain characteristics that seem to be universal:

1. *Specialization, or division of labor.* Each individual does a few special tasks rather than everyone trying to do everything. One transportation bureaucrat regulates railroads, another works on highways.

2. *Hierarchy, or fixed lines of command and communication.* Each worker knows who the boss "above" him is and who the subordinates "under" him are. Decisions from the top flow to the people below who carry them out. Information about what is happening lower down flows up to the people at the top so they know what orders to give. The private tells the sergeant: "The enemy are shooting at us." The sergeant tells the captain. The captain tells the sergeant: "Shoot back." The sergeant orders the private to shoot.

---

[1] Good general surveys of the bureaucracy are Alan Altshuler and Norman Thomas, *Politics of the Federal Bureaucracy* (New York: Harper & Row, 1977); and Francis E. Rourke, *Bureaucracy, Politics and Public Policy,* 2nd ed. (Boston: Little, Brown, 1976).

3. *Incentives to attract people to the organization and to be loyal to its purposes.* The biggest incentive is money—organizations pay salaries. But the most important incentive for loyalty is usually job security. The organization worker is told: "If you do the job satisfactorily, you keep the job." That is why nearly any large organization is staffed mostly by permanent employees who continue on despite the comings and goings of the people at the top.

Large organizations usually share some other characteristics. One is the concept of "office" as separate from the person holding it. Ms. Smith holds the "office" of security guard. Her job is to guard the organization's front door. But she only does that during working hours when she is on the job; when she goes home she cooks for her family and raises her children. We do not want her to move her family into the lobby and stir the soup with one hand and guard the door with the other. People who hold office in organizations are expected to behave in a certain way on the job—a way defined by the work rules of the organization. What they do off the job is their own business and should be kept separate. If Ms. Smith is replaced in her guard job by Ms. Jones, who spends her free time flying airplanes, we do not expect that the door will be guarded any differently than it was before. "Office" makes bureaucracies seem "impersonal." But most of us would not want to be handled nicely by one guard because we remind her of her son and roughly by another because we remind her of her copilot.[2]

A steam power generating plant of the Tennessee Valley Authority, an agency of the federal government. The "bureaucrats" who run the TVA plant are not very different from workers in the privately-owned plants that generate most of the country's electric power.

Wide World

Another way of putting this is that people who work for large organizations are expected to behave according to the organization's rules rather than their personal values. And most organizations have many rules designed to make sure that all the guards and all the meat inspectors and all the purchasing agents of the organization act roughly alike. Then they and the people using the organization will know what to expect from one another. Continuity is important in organizations, because without it people would not know what to expect. The rule that you must put "last name first" on all the forms of a certain organization ensures that a person reading the form will always know exactly where to look for your last name. Otherwise he or she would have to stop to figure out which name was which, which would waste time and lead to mistakes. Rules also protect individuals from arbitrary treatment. For instance, let us look at a rule that anyone who has lost the use of one arm is 25 percent disabled. It means that one disability counselor cannot tell such a person "You can do enough with your other arm to earn a living so you're not disabled at all," while another gives a similar person an 85 percent disability rating. In order to ensure continuity and prevent arbitrariness, organizations not only make rules but keep records of what they have done in

[2] Victor A. Thompson, *Without Sympathy or Enthusiasm: The Problem of Administrative Compassion* (University, Ala.: University of Alabama Press, 1975).

the past. Each past decision by an organization can be used as a **precedent,** that is, a guide in making future decisions. If the organization meets a new problem just like one it has solved successfully in the past, then it should try the same solution on the new problem. Organizations use precedents even more than courts, and for the same reasons. If an organization follows the precedents shown in its records, its members do not have to spend a lot of time deciding over again what has already been decided. And its users can predict how the organization will treat them in the future from how it has treated others in the past.

It is for these reasons that people complain about red tape and curse at "bureaucracy." The individual naturally wants to be treated like an individual. But he is often told by an organization that it cannot help him because he has not followed the rules or filled out the right form or his records cannot be found. The organization's answer to many complaints is, "Well that's the way we've always done it around here." So the impartiality, uniformity, continuity, and predictability that we want from organizations can have its bad side in impersonality, red tape, excessive paperwork, and inflexibility. Both sides are frequently seen in our government. Although all large organizations are somewhat "bureaucratic" in the bad sense, Americans seem to complain more about government bureaucracy than other kinds. This is not because government workers are inherently more objectionable, but because certain features of American government make public administration a more difficult challenge than ordinary administration. Thus, to understand how and why the executive branch is as it is, we must understand the traits common to all large organizations. Then we must realize that government organizations operate in a very special environment which affects their behavior in a number of important ways.

What makes the United States government different from, say, the United States Steel Corporation? The most obvious point is that some governmental functions are exclusively public, notably diplomatic and military affairs. Beyond this, the most important factor is that the government operates under the Constitution. It requires that many things about government must be different. The president of this organization is elected and serves a term considerably shorter than that of most other important officials with whom he must work. Many governmental decisions are reviewed by the courts. Congress must be looked to as a source of the laws and money that empower the organization to do things. Federal employees have a much higher degree of job security than workers in the private sector. The president of US Steel can fire or reassign his subordinates much more easily than can the president of the United States. Beyond all this is publicity. It is legitimate to pry into government affairs far beyond what is tolerated (or legal) in private business. There is far more public curiosity about government activities. Finally, of course, there is partisan politics. There are no parallels in US Steel to Democrats and Republicans, who routinely criticize the administration of the other. Federal civil servants are very conscious of public accountability and of the need to justify what they do. Federal administrators are legally accountable both to their superiors in the executive branch and to Congress. The possibility of lawsuits often makes them answerable to the courts as well. And they also are accountable, informally but realistically, to the private organizations with which they deal and to the general public.

THE ORGANIZATION
OF THE ADMINISTRATIVE BRANCH

The Line Agencies The oldest, most conventional government organizations are the cabinet-level *line departments*. The line departments, composed of agencies and bureaus, are responsible directly to the president through the cabinet secretaries who head them. They are the work-horses of the federal administrative establishment. The basic working segments of most departments have a variety of names, such as those shown in Figure 15.1 which depicts the department of the interior's table of organization. These component parts typically are referred to as *bureaus*. The people who work in the bureaus are almost exclusively civil servants who stay on over the years. In contrast, the political executives above them come and go with each changing administration.

It is instructive to see when the line departments were established and how they have grown and evolved. A core set of these agencies performs tasks that must be done by some agency in any political system. Others have grown up over the years in response to the evolving needs of the government itself and the people it serves. In 1802 there were less than 10,000 government employees, of whom roughly 3000 were nonmilitary. The fighting establishment consisted of the war (army) and navy departments until after World War II. The other departments were concerned with managing the government's money (the treasury department) and foreign relations (the state department). The presidential staff consisted of a single clerk. Certain other functions were carried out but did not yet have cabinet status. The attorney general had no staff and operated out of his own home. There were roughly a thousand revenue collectors and a thousand postmasters. Revenue collection was not officially part of the Treasury, and the Post Office had not received cabinet status.[3] (Recently the Post Office has become a government-controlled corporation, rather than a cabinet department.) The march of agencies to cabinet status, plus the growth of sizable agencies outside the cabinet, continued throughout the nineteenth century. By noting the dates that cabinet status was acquired, we get some sense of when groups became recognized as quasi-official partners in the process of governing. We also get a notion of when the increasing complexities of American society made new agencies necessary.

In the next few pages we will take a brief look at the various federal departments (leaving aside the Post Office and the basic departments already in existence by 1802). The major agencies of the federal government, together with the number of employees each had in 1978, are listed in Table 15.1.

Interior. The department of the interior was established in 1849. At first it was concerned with the expansion of population into the western states. Even today, it is primarily involved with the special requirements of land, water, and natural resource development in those states. The congressional committees that oversee and fund this agency are dominated by westerners.

---

[3] James S. Young, *The Washington Community: 1800–1828* (New York: Columbia University Press, 1966), p. 29.

Figure 15.1
The Department of the Interior

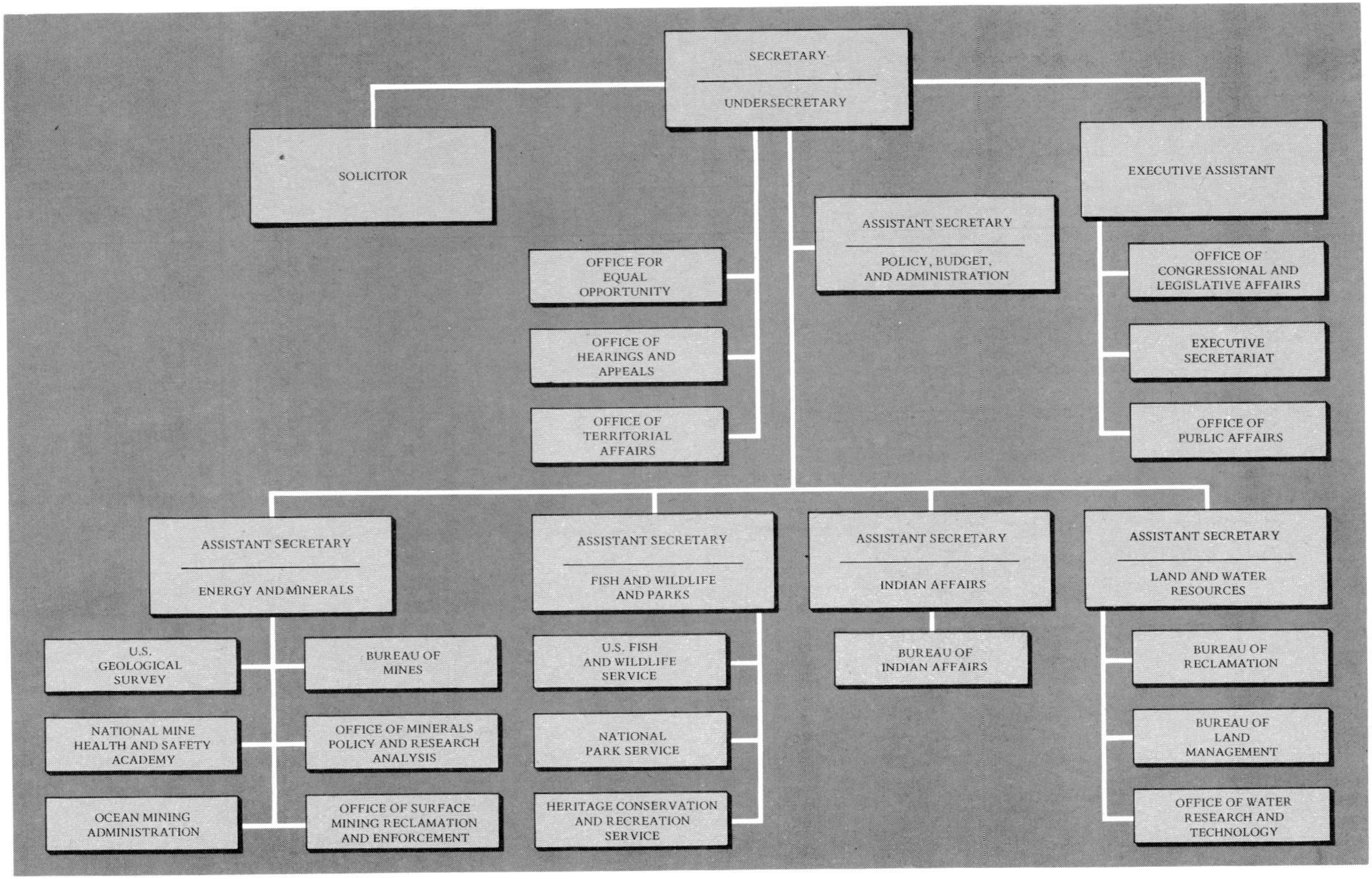

Table 15.1

Agencies of the Federal Government

AGENCY	NUMBER OF CIVILIAN EMPLOYEES
All Agencies	2,838,806
Legislative branch	39,148
Judicial branch	12,785
Executive branch	2,786,873
Executive Office of the President	
White House Office	379
Office of Management and Budget	621
Council of Economic Advisers	34
Executive Mansion and Grounds	87
National Security Council	65
All other	530
Executive Departments	
Agriculture	114,099
Commerce	38,645
Defense	982,198
Department of the Army	350,130
Department of the Navy	311,108
Department of the Air Force	243,643
Other defense activities	77,317
Energy,	19,743
Health, Education and Welfare	158,364
Housing and Urban Development	17,575
Interior	75,937
Justice	52,962
Labor	17,271
State	30,092
Agency for International Development	5,977
Transportation	74,445
Treasury	132,393
Independent Agencies	
ACTION	2,031
American Battle Monuments Commission	385
Arms Control and Disarmament Agency	218
Board of Governors, Federal Reserve System	1,462
Canal Zone Government	3,292

Agriculture.   The department of agriculture was established in 1862, at a time when the secession of the slave states made the small northern farmers key constituents of the ruling Republican party.

Commerce and Labor.   A department of commerce and labor, established in 1903, provided federal recognition of the decades of massive industrial expansion and the rise of labor union organization that followed the Civil

Table 15.1 – continued
Agencies of the Federal Government

AGENCY	NUMBER OF CIVILIAN EMPLOYEES
Civil Aeronautics Board	797
Civil Service Commission	8,794
Commission on Civil Rights	329
Community Services Administration	1,065
Consumer Product Safety Commission	991
Environmental Protection Agency	12,423
Equal Employment Opportunity Commission	2,368
Export-Import Bank, U.S.	432
Farm Credit Administration	259
Federal Communications Commission	2,118
Federal Deposit Insurance Corporation	3,578
Federal Home Loan Bank Board	1,467
Federal Maritime Commission	302
Federal Mediation and Conciliation Service	575
Federal Trade Commission	1,777
General Services Administration	37,624
International Communications Agency	8,348
Interstate Commerce Commission	2,115
National Aeronautics and Space Administration	24,191
National Credit Union Administration	584
National Foundation on the Arts and Humanities	893
National Labor Relations Board	2,906
National Mediation Board	101
National Science Foundation	1,360
Nuclear Regulatory Commission	2,902
Panama Canal Company	11,409
Railroad Retirement Board	1,939
Renegotiation Board	176
Securities and Exchange Commission	1,967
Selective Service System	70
Small Business Administration	5,700
Smithsonian Institution	3,961
Soldiers' and Airmen's Home	1,030
Tennessee Valley Authority	40,121
U.S. Postal Service	648,419
Veterans' Administration	227,903
All other	2,665

Source: Statistical Abstract of the United States 1978.

War. In 1913, labor lost its stepchild status with the formation of separate labor and commerce departments.

Health, Education and Welfare. In 1953 President Eisenhower brought the Republicans back to power after twenty years of vast expansion in federal welfare programs under the Democrats. The agencies administering these programs were consolidated and given cabinet status as the department of health,

These Treasury employees help burn around $31 million of wornout money every day.

education and welfare (HEW). The new department has been little more than a loose holding company of bureaus, each with its own strong ties to constituency groups and congressional committees and subcommittees.

Housing and Urban Development. One of the first of Lyndon Johnson's Great Society acts, following his 1964 election, was the founding of a department of housing and urban development (HUD). It brought together a number of independent agencies concerned with housing, urban renewal, and related issues. As the Great Society produced new programs — such as Model Cities — to deal with urban problems, these were added to HUD's jurisdiction.

Transportation. Another of Johnson's Great Society actions was the establishment in 1966 of a department of transportation to coordinate the many overlapping jurisdictions of agencies concerned with land, sea, and air transport. This coincided with increasing public awareness of grave problems of transportation management, such as the decline of passenger railroads.

Energy. This department was created in 1977 in response to the energy crisis. Prior to its formation, dozens of agencies in several departments handled energy problems.

Other Agencies. In addition to the cabinet-level departments, numerous other agencies conduct important programs. Among the most prominent are the Veterans' Administration, the National Science Foundation, and the Central Intelligence Agency. Some of these are as large and do as important work as cabinet departments.

Sometimes the responsibility for major new programs is not assigned to an established department, but is given instead to a new agency not placed under the jurisdiction of a line department. This is done to increase the chances that the new tasks will be attacked in new ways rather than by officials who are already set in their ways. Thus Johnson's "war on poverty" was conducted largely by the independent Office of Economic Opportunity rather than by HEW or HUD. (OEO was abolished during the Nixon administration, along with some of its programs. The more popular or successful programs were assigned to established departments or the newly created Community Services Administration and Legal Services Corporation.) When public concern with environmental issues grew in the early 1970s, the new Environmental Protection Agency was given independent status.

Independent Regulatory Commissions The independent regulatory commission is another major component of the executive branch. This type of agency was invented because Americans believed in free enterprise but also believed that some businesses would not be fair to the public unless the government supervised them. Most regulatory bodies deal with industries that are natural monopolies (such as electric power) or with business activities in which wholly unrestrained competition seems undesirable. For example, without some controls, unfair trade practices such as false advertising might harm consumers. Government regulation rather than government ownership seemed the best substitute for competition where competition did not seem to work.

For similar reasons, it was generally felt that such regulation should be kept free of "politics." The commissions were intended to make general policies in the public interest. Because most of their actions would necessarily be an interference with the private property rights of the business they regulated, the commission form was chosen. These agencies include the Interstate Commerce Commission, the Federal Communications Commission, the Federal Power Commission, the Federal Trade Commission, the Securities and Exchange Commission, and the National Labor Relations Board. Each is headed by a board numbering between three and eleven members appointed by the president for staggered terms of from three to fourteen years. At any given time, therefore, these boards consist of appointees of two or three presidents who may have had very different views on the kind of regulation desirable. What is more, they lack unified direction because authority is dispersed among a number of individuals rather than concentrated in one.[4]

The commissions are independent because, unlike the line departments, they are not in the chain of command leading to the president. He cannot dismiss the commissioners at will, as he can cabinet members. They are *quasi-legislative* in the sense that they typically operate under very general congressional statutes that empower them to make many supplementary laws of their own. They are *quasi-judicial* in the sense that they must follow courtlike "hearing" procedures in making decisions affecting the interests of individual firms or entire categories of economic interests. Their decisions have the force of law although they often can be appealed to the federal courts.

Another set of devices for government intervention in the economy includes the government-owned corporation, the mixed corporation in which both government and private persons hold stock, the corporation established by statute to pursue specified government policies whose stock is nevertheless privately owned, and agencies that ensure or guarantee or provide loans underwriting various business transactions. Table 15.2 illustrates the diversity of forms and purposes of these governmental corporations.

INDIRECT FEDERAL ADMINISTRATION

A conventional treatment of the executive branch of government would end here and would leave out some of the most significant developments in the years since the New Deal. As we will see, major developments have taken place outside the official organization chart of the central government.

[4] Marver H. Bernstein, *Regulating Business by Independent Commission* (Princeton, N.J.: Princeton University Press, 1955); and Paul W. MacAvoy, ed., *The Crisis of Regulatory Commissions* (New York: Norton, 1970).

Table 15.2

Government Corporations

Wholly-Owned Under Executive Departments
St. Lawrence Seaway Development Corporation
Commodity Credit Corporation
Federal Crop Insurance Corporation
Federal Prison Industries, Inc.
Federal Savings and Loan Insurance Corporation
Panama Canal Company

Wholly-Owned Independent Corporations
Federal Deposit Insurance Corporation
Export-Import Bank of Washington
Tennessee Valley Authority

Mixed-Ownerhsip Government Corporations
Central Bank for Cooperatives
Regional Banks for Cooperatives
Federal Intermediate Credit Banks
AMTRAK
CONRAIL

Quasi-Official Corporations
Legal Services Corporation
Smithsonian Institution

Independent Not-For-Profit Corporations*
Aerospace Corporation
Institute for Defense Analysis
Logistics Management Institute
Institute for Urban Studies
Rand Corporation

University-Affiliated Research Centers*
Applied Physics Laboratory
Human Relations Research Organization
Brookhaven Laboratory
Lincoln Laboratory
Los Alamos National Laboratory

Research Centers Operated by Private Industry*
Oak Ridge National Laboratory

*Private institutions organized and initially financed by the federal government to provide contractual services to government.

For example, as we saw in Chapter 5, there has been an enormous growth of federal **grants-in-aid**— that is, payments of federal funds to state and local governments. These grants, distributed and supervised from Washington, account for much of the activity of the departments of health, education and welfare, housing and urban development, and transportation. The size of the grant programs means that many state, county, and city agencies are now supported largely by federal funds and devote much of their time to administering federal programs. In effect, thousands of local government agencies serve as part of the federal administration. The level of federal supervision of these programs varies from careful to nonexistent. Many *national* programs are carried out largely by state and local agencies that operate under their own political officials, with their own budgeting, personnel, and policy directives.

An even more innovative administrative device was introduced with the war on poverty under Presidents Kennedy and Johnson. Many new federal programs provide for grants directly to any local organization, governmental *or private,* that submits a suitable plan. In many cases, local governments were not eager to participate in some of these programs. As a result, the bulk of funds under the Economic Opportunity Program (EOP) was spent by nongovernmental community action groups organized specifically for the purpose.[5] Self-appointed representatives of the poor and minority groups are very active in these bodies, which frequently become potent political forces in their communities. Subsequently, funding of this kind was largely replaced by community development grants that usually go to regular units of local government. Substantial sums of federal money are spent today by administrators who are not in any traditional sense federal bureaucrats, or in some instances even civil servants or government employees.

Outside Contractors The Distant Early Warning (DEW) Line is a sophisticated complex of radar and communications facilities to detect aircraft and missiles approaching the United States from the north—the likely route of a Soviet attack. In other words, the DEW Line is a fundamental part of our air defense system. It is not operated by the air force, however, but by a private corporation, on a contract with the government.

This is an example of contracting out—hiring private individuals to do a job the government might do directly. Such jobs range from running the DEW Line to cleaning government buildings or managing government property. An increasing amount of the federal government's work is done this way, and a great many other activities—less clearly federal jobs—are financed from Washington. These two sorts of "indirect employment" explain why the number of federal employees has remained constant in recent years while the amount of government acitivity has grown: the federal government is hiring other people to do much of its work. It is estimated that fully 8 million people are not on the federal payroll but receive their pay from the federal treasury. This is only a guess, however, because many agencies literally do not know how many people they employ indirectly.[6]

Military Contracting. For years, the armed services operated their own arsenals and shipyards. They also bought substantial quantities of supplies—including food, clothing, and weapons—from civilian firms. Often, these

[5] Daniel P. Moynihan, "What Is Community Action?" *Public Interest* (1966); and John C. Donovan, *The Politics of Poverty* (Indianapolis: Pegasus, 1967).

[6] Barbara Blumenthal, "Uncle Sam's Army of Invisible Employees," *National Journal,* May 5, 1979, pp. 730–33.

*Instead of using the Air Force, the Army chartered
planes from a private airline when it withdrew
form Korea.*

purchases were made by contracts that specified quality, design, price, and delivery
date. The contracts were let after sealed bidding between competing firms and went
to the firm providing the best merchandise at the lowest price. These transactions
were not substantially different from those between, say, a department store and a
pants manufacturer. Indeed, most of the firms involved produced roughly the same
goods for the civilian market; they devoted only a small part of their production to
military supplies. The government was simply one customer among many, and a
clear line could be drawn between the government and its suppliers. The combination of World War II and the sudden demand for aerospace equipment in the postwar years produced a new system of defense production. It has since been extended by the increasing reliance on extremely expensive, incredibly elaborate weapons
systems such as intercontinental missiles and supersonic aircraft. These systems are
useless for any but military purposes. They usually require technological innovations that will only occur in the actual course of developing the weapon.

The acquisition of these new weapons systems follows a typical course.[7] One
of the armed services indicates its desire for a new weapon to fulfill a particular mission. If such a system seems worthwhile to the defense department, it will authorize
a design competition. A number of firms then will be given government contracts to
create designs. This operation typically involves several million dollars and the work
of hundreds of engineers and scientists. If none of the designs seems entirely satisfactory, a second and perhaps a third stage of design competition will be financed.
The government retains the power to choose among the completed designs, but it
is the private firms and their employees that make the thousands of decisions which
go into the two or three packages from which the government makes its choice.
Thus, most of the design decisions on which the nation's security rests are made by
private companies. When the defense department finally selects a design, it awards
a contract for "development" — that is, doing the actual construction of the first pro-

[7] J. Ronald Fox, *Arming America: How the U.S. Buys Weapons* (Cambridge, Mass.: Harvard University Press, 1974); and Edmund Beard, *Developing the ICBM* (New York: Columbia University
Press, 1976).

totype. If the prototype is successful, contracts for quantity production will be awarded.

The design stage does not involve competitive bidding. The successful firm almost always has such an obvious advantage over other firms in knowhow and experience about its own design that it normally will get the subsequent contracts. These usually guarantee the contractor the cost plus some profit. Frequently, the government supplies the contractor with a great deal of production equipment and facilities. Moreover, major weapons systems contracts often are handled by firms that do most of their business with the government. When they get into financial trouble, they request assistance from the government. In this situation, it is not at all clear where government leaves off and private industry begins.

Government and Science.   Behind the design and development of new weapons lie the major scientific advances that are the basis for technological advance. Recognizing this, the defense department has financed a great deal of basic scientific research for many years in the expectation of eventual payoffs. But the government's science business is not confined to defense; many federal agencies finance scientific research. Some of this is done "in house" — that is, by scientists directly employed by the government and working in government facilities. Most of it, however, is accomplished by grants to outside scientists. Basic science is very difficult to manage. There is usually no way to tell in advance which leads will pay off in terms of "practical" knowledge. Research for which there seemed to be no practical application has proved to be the foundation for technological breakthroughs a few years later. Nor is it clear that the government *should* finance only research that has a practical payoff. "Pure" science is likely to be neglected by private corporations engaged in scientific research. As a result, the purer the research in which scientists are interested, the more they rely on federal grants.

From the government's standpoint, it is sensible to invite scientists to submit research proposals and then to finance as many as possible. Of course, there is never enough money for everything. So the proposals must be evaluated and the best ones supported. But as long as the government has no science policy goals, "best" can only mean most interesting from a scientific point of view. The best judges of this are the best scientists. The best scientists are interested in doing science, not in working for the government. Most government science agencies have small staffs who delegate decisions about what projects to support to advisory panels of distinguished nongovernment scientists who devote a few days or weeks a year to government service. The grant system accounts for so much of the financing of university science departments and medical schools that today we get the same tangle in science and education that we have in weapons development. The "private" units become heavily dependent on the federal government. At the same time, it is scientists employed by universities and research firms who make most of the "advisory" decisions about who should get money. So it is not clear where the government begins or ends.

Delegating Administrative Responsibility.   The federal government provides 90 percent of the money for the National Direct Student Loan

(NDSL) program, which makes it possible for millions of Americans to attend college. In 1977, over 700,000 people who had received such loans failed to repay them. The U.S. Office of Education stepped up its efforts to reduce these debts. The result was that a year later the number of defaults had risen to 800,000, and the total amount of bad loans was $700 million. There was little more the U.S. Office of Education could do, however, because actual administration of the NDSL program was in the hands of the nation's colleges and universities. Schools process NDSL application forms, approve loans, disburse the money, and receive the repayments. The schools are much more effective at giving money away than at getting it back. Furthermore, they are not even willing to turn the tough cases over to the government for collection. In 1977–78, only 500 bad loans were referred for further action. This is typical of many federal programs: The money and the broad guidelines come from Washington, but the government relies on other people to run the program.[8]

It should be obvious by now that it is misleading to speak of civil servants or bureaucrats as if they were a closed and distinct group. The design engineer at General Dynamics and the systems analyst at the Rand Corporation do the work of the national government. So does the assistant secretary of state for Near Eastern Affairs. So does the financial aid office at the University of Delaware. On the other hand, even within the national government, conceived in the narrowest sense, thousands of secretaries, shipping clerks, and auto mechanics are doing work that differs not at all from what their counterparts employed by private companies are doing.

ACCESS TO GOVERNMENT EMPLOYMENT

The Civil Service The patronage system, in which federal jobs were given as rewards for service to one of the political parties, was replaced with the passage of the Civil Service Act of 1883 by a merit system supervised by the U.S. Civil Service Commission.[9] A job description and an appropriate examination are created for each job in the classified system, and individuals seek out jobs by taking the scheduled examinations.

The Civil Service Commission allowed the departments considerable discretion in hiring and promotion, particularly at management levels. Commission supervision was aimed at preventing arbitrary and unfair decisions and at equalizing promotion and pay policies among the departments. The commission also recruited young management talent. Yet there were still many complaints that commission red tape hampered dynamic personnel management in the departments and that the federal government failed to compete successfully for professional and executive talent.

---

[8] *Higher Education and National Affairs,* February 2, 1979, pp. 1–2.

[9] President Carter's civil service reform bill, passed by Congress in 1978, authorized him to divide the Civil Service Commission into two new agencies. The Office of Personnel Management continues the CSC's work of classifying jobs, while the Merit Systems Protection Board carries on the function of protecting the rights of federal employees.

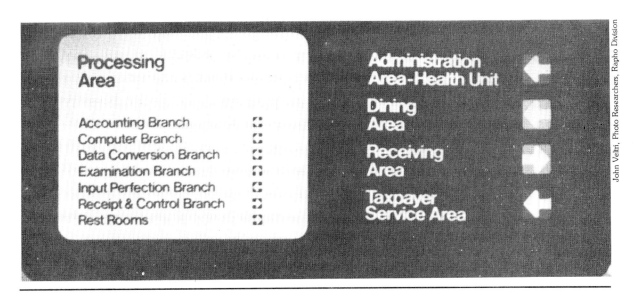

The Internal Revenue Service is the government agency whose work and policies are best known by Americans. This sign helps citizens find their way around one big IRS facility.

One reason for the lack of appeal to top talent is the ceiling on civil service salaries. The highest possible pay in 1978 was $47,500 for a GS-18, the highest career rank. Like the salaries paid members of Congress, this looks high until one realizes that top executives and professionals in private jobs often make twice as much. The newest attempt to deal with this problem was the creation, in Carter's reform bill, of the Senior Executive Service. Eligible to join the SES, at their own option, are the 8000 top-ranking career bureaucrats, those in grades GS-16 to GS-18. Through bonuses and special awards, members of the SES can make as much as a cabinet secretary ($66,000 in 1979). They can also be shifted from job to job in order to assemble teams of executives who work well together. By encouraging transfers from one bureau to another, the SES breaks down the tight compartments in which civil servants now work. The disadvantages of the SES are the obverse of its benefits: its members give up much of their security from being fired or demoted. In the first few months of its existence, the SES attracted almost all eligible officials. The coming years will reveal the success of this attempt to increase both the risks and the rewards of reaching the top of the civil service.

The civil service system has generated other snags from the management side. In most modern organizations, personnel management is an important executive tool in establishing policies and ensuring their implementation. Experts on management understand that there is no clear line between policy and administration: even "lower level" administrators influence what policies are adopted and how they really turn out. Consequently, government officials are often frustrated by the merit system, which protects civil servants against arbitrary firing and demotion so thoroughly that they are often free to thwart or change the policies of their superiors. For instance, a president who decides that we really ought to spend much less on highways cannot fire the highway engineers of the department of transportation. They have spent their whole careers urging and planning bigger and better and more highways. They will continue to press for "better" roads—and for them "better" means "more," even if the president wants "less." Moreover, if a particular federal highway engineer turns out to be incompetent, cumbersome procedures make it extraordinarily difficult to fire him. Thus, the virtual impossibility of firing civil servants protects them not only from political interference, but also from their immediate supervisors.

Although most federal workers do jobs that are in no way distinctively governmental, they are linked by common concerns. The growth of interest in federal employee unions is a reflection of that concern. This movement had gone quite far in the Postal Service even before its reorganization, and presumably will go further now. Many other federal employees belong to unions or professional associations that have many features of unions, including a major role in the political process. Nevertheless, normal union-management relations are difficult to introduce into the federal government for three reasons. In the first place, it is not easy to see just how the right to strike can be incorporated into government service or what substitute for it can be invented. Second, although "management" for some purposes consists of the executive heads of the federal agencies, it is Congress that sets wages and the outlines of the hiring, firing, and promotion system. It is not easy to see how to bargain collectively with Congress. Third, the movement toward unionism is dis-

BEING CIVIL TO THE CIVIL SERVICE

Like other presidents, Jimmy Carter felt that executives—both political and in the career civil service—should have more control over their subordinates. He proposed legislation that would change civil service rules so that it would be easier to fire those who did poor work. By the time Congress had finished with the legislation, it contained a whole new set of elaborate procedures designed to protect the government employee against arbitrary dismissal. The final statute recognized the principle that inefficient civil servants should be fired. But it appeared to most observers that it would take almost as much time and trouble to fire a civil servant under the new rules as the old.

We certainly do not want civil servants fired just because they disagree with their political superiors or because their superiors dislike them. It would be possible for political executives to destroy the civil service by charging career people with inefficiency. So there must be procedures such as hearings and reports to ensure that the executive really has legitimate reasons for firing someone. On the other hand, the more rules and procedures we introduce to protect the good civil servant, the harder it is to get rid of the bad. The government executive who knows that the only way to fire an inefficient subordinate is by filing a fifty-page report and testifying at hours and hours of hearings and appeals is likely to just shrug and forget the whole thing. It is not his money being wasted, but the taxpayer's.

couraged because of a fear that unions might attempt to influence questions of public policy, trying to assume powers that belong to the president and Congress.

Government Executives   **The Political Executives.**   An incoming president can appoint about 2700 people to help him impose his will on government: secretaries, undersecretaries, assistant secretaries, agency heads, and special assistants to these officials. About two-thirds of presidential appointees have had some previous federal administrative service.[10] As an administration goes on, most of the president's subsequent appointments will be promotions from the ranks of his first appointees. Thus, the political executives are not wholly inexperienced; they are not the governmental innocents some reports claim. More than general governmental experience, what they lack is familiarity with a given job: About two-thirds of them have held their particular post less than two years.[11]

These executives are supposed to be the key link in ensuring presidential control of the government and the bureaucracy. They are the ones who reach deep into each department to be sure that what is going on is in line with the president's policies. But to a considerable extent, they are "substantially on their own and vulnerable to bureaucratic power."[12] Before coming to Washington, they probably did not know the other appointees with whom they must work, nor the president, nor the cabinet secretary of their department. And, of course, they are unlikely to know many of the career civil servants who work for and with them.

President Eisenhower, who took office after twenty years of Democratic administration, faced a career bureaucracy built up over these years of New Deal rule. By executive order he created a new type of government appointment called Schedule C. Schedule C appointees hold regular civil service pay grades and are covered by most civil service rules, but are chosen by the president or department secretary for their particular job. There are about 600 Schedule C appointees. In addition, there are now about 600 government posts called noncareer executive assignments (NEAs). Like Schedule Cs, these are filled by political appointment. Schedule Cs and NEAs are supergrades. That is, they are in the three highest pay categories of the civil service, GS 16–18. Schedule C and NEA are often used to pick people who have reached the top levels of the career service and boost them up a rung to more important posts. Schedule C appointees come largely from the career service, and so have the knowledge and staying power to get the job done. About half the NEAs are also drawn from the career service. Those career bureaucrats who show them-

Shirley Temple Black held political appointments in the Nixon and Ford administrations. She is shown here as ambassador to Ghana.

Wide World

[10] David T. Stanley et al., *Men Who Govern* (Washington: The Brookings Institution, 1967), p. 137.

[11] Arch Patton, "Government's Revolving Door," *Business Week,* September 22, 1973, p. 12.

[12] Hugh Heclo, *A Government of Strangers* (Washington: The Brookings Institution, 1977), p. 112.

selves most in sympathy with the president's programs can be promoted to Schedule C and NEA. Some presidents have thought this important enough to order that no promotions to such positions be made without their direct approval. Schedule C and NEA have increased the president's power over the bureaucracy by increasing the number of "his" executives in government.

The Career Executives.   The entire federal bureaucracy is broadly representative of American society in education, income, and parental social status. The higher reaches of the bureaucracy—the career executives—are a bit less representative, particularly because they include relatively few women and racial minorities. However, these background characteristics do not have much to do with the actual outlook and behavior of career executives.[13] The typical executive is at least 40 years of age, with a college degree and perhaps some graduate training. If the bureau's activities are concentrated in particular parts of the country, he or she is likely to come from one of those regions. For example, someone in the Bureau of Land Management probably comes from the West; someone in the Bureau of Family Services probably comes from a city. A bureaucrat's college degree probably matches his or her bureau. The BLM employee may well have majored in forestry or conservation, and the Bureau of Family Services has more than its share of people with master's degrees in social work.

As we might suspect from these patterns, bureaucrats' political views differ depending on the kind of agency they serve in. There are three Democrats for every Republican among high-level bureaucrats, and the ratio is even higher for officials in social service agencies like HEW and HUD. What is more, these social service bureaucrats are strongly in favor of expanding government services.[14] This helps explain why mistrust between political appointees and bureaucrats might be greater when a Republican is president. Mutual suspicion between civil servants and the White House, for example, was notorious during the Nixon administration.

If an executive had significant work experience in the private sector, it was long ago. He or she has served in no more than two government agencies, and has been in the one where he or she reached executive status for at least twenty years. The executive probably joined that bureau early in adult life and worked up from a low-level position to top management. Most departments have an extensive network of field offices. Many executives spend their entire careers outside Washington (only 13 percent of all federal employees work in the capital). He or she is unlikely to move to another bureau. Dedicated to a particular slice of the government's business, the executive probably knows more about it than anyone else. Talking about a "typical bureaucrat" conceals the crucial fact that executives identify with their particular agency, not with the government service as a whole. One distinguished bureaucrat captured this important perspective:

---

[13] *Ibid.*, pp. 113–19.

[14] Joel D. Aberbach and Bert A. Rockman, "Clashing Beliefs Within the Executive Branch: The Nixon Administration Bureaucracy," *American Political Science Review,* 70 (June 1976), pp. 456–69.

I've never thought of myself as a career civil servant. . . . Ask a civil servant who he is and you'll probably find he'll say he is an economist who works for the Treasury Department, a manager for the Housing Department and so on. What he's *not* likely to say first is that he's a civil servant.[15]

It is easy enough to see the drawbacks of this personnel system: (1) The absence of an elite career track discourages the brightest young people. It is not so much that *everyone* starts at (or near) the bottom, but that for people of great promise there is no recognized special route to the top that begins at the bottom. (2) There is little opportunity for lateral entry into the highest ranks by outsiders who have not worked their way up, no matter how qualified they may be. (3) In practice, qualifications for high-level posts are defined in limited technical terms corresponding to the bureau's special mission, rather than in more general terms that would emphasize broad administrative skills. The result is that top-level civil servants know and care a lot about the bureau in which they have "grown up" but know little about the rest of government. Thus, they are likely to have narrow perspectives. The man or woman who has spent most of a career knowing more and more about timber management may find it hard to understand that many things are more important to the fate of the nation than whether the pine trees are growing well this year.

The Officer Corps.   There are two major "officer corps" in the government. They have their own personnel systems rather than falling under the Civil Service Commission, and their numbers are relatively small. Admission to the corps is not easy, occurs only at the junior level, and is assumed to be the first step on a ladder to high position. Thus, all members of the corps share an identity as a self-conscious elite. There is no lateral entry except in unusual circumstances, such as a major war.

The best known of the officer corps is, of course, the military one. Military officers do not have a distinctly different philosophy or set of values from the rest of us.[16] Like all professionals, they probably overemphasize the importance of their own responsibilities. But unfortunately, their responsibilities have in fact been almost impossible to overemphasize in recent times. If "the military mind" creates any problems for American politics, they come from the fact that there is not one mind but three. The separate personnel systems and the separate loyalties that go with each of the three services have done more than anything else to hamper true unification of our military system.[17] As a general rule, the leaders of any administrative agency are committed to their agency as an institution and to what they consider its traditional missions. The closer the missions of different agencies, the greater the potential for conflict between them. Thus, the departments of the interior and

[15] Quoted in Heclo, *A Government of Strangers,* p. 116.

[16] Morris Janowitz, *The Professional Soldier* (New York: Free Press, 1961).

[17] Ernest J. King and Walter M. Whitehill, *Fleet Admiral King: A Naval Record* (New York: Norton, 1952), p. 635.

agriculture have squabbled for seventy years about where the Forest Service should be located and which department should be in charge of soil conservation. Since all three military services have overlapping missions, they are often rivals.

The other major officer corps is the Foreign Service. The Foreign Service is designed to be an elite corps. Entrance is by a difficult examination favoring first-class liberal arts students. Traditionally, most entrants were drawn from a dozen prestigious colleges and universities, including some major state universities. Foreign Service officers gradually work up in rank, just as military officers do, on the basis of seniority and written evaluations submitted every year by their superiors. Officers usually alternate between a job in the state department in Washington and in an embassy or consulate abroad. Nearly all important jobs in the state department except at the very highest levels are held by Foreign Service officers.

The aim of an officer corps is to provide each officer with a career-long chain of work and education to fit him or her for one of the top jobs, whether it be general, admiral, or ambassador. Their careers must be managed so that they develop whatever quality the corps uses to symbolize the capacity to do the top job. In the military services it is called "leadership"; in the state department, it is known as "diplomacy." These qualities, it is widely felt, can best be generated by exposing an officer to a wide range of the jobs done by the corps and by protecting him or her from the narrowing influence of specialization. Both the Foreign Service and the military rotate all officers from place to place and job to job every three or four years. Although an officer's experience usually is concentrated somewhat in particular fields and regions of the world, someone who specializes excessively is doomed to end his or her career short of the top. As a result, most officers are jacks-of-all-trades and masters of none; the commander of a navy yard may know nothing in particular about ship repair, although he has served on lots of ships. Or the ambassador to Peru may never before have worked in Peru although he has served previously in Brazil and Panama. This places officer corps at a disadvantage in dealing with the rest of the government, where special expertise is considered essential. The state department in particular has paid dearly for its lack of expertise in such specialized fields as economics; it has lost much of its influence in such areas to other agencies.

A second weakness of the officer corps is the preoccupation of such people with their career prospects rather than with the job at hand. Since they are transferred frequently, naturally they worry a good deal about getting a good assignment next. Both the military and the Foreign Service have a "selection out" or "up or out" policy. Officers who do not perform well enough to merit promotion are "separated" — that is, fired. Firing and promotion decisions are based largely on written evaluations of each officer made frequently by direct superiors. This system weeds out incompetents; it also may weed out those with original minds or independent dispositions who do not devote sufficient attention to pleasing superiors. In the military, this tendency is somewhat offset by the high premium placed on independence and aggressiveness as qualities of the good combat leader. In the Foreign Service, it is further aggravated by the emphasis on "diplomatic" qualities.

Members of the Professions   The Foreign Service and the military illustrate the more general
as Civil Servants   problem of professionalism in government service. The diplomatic and military professions, of course, encompass a vari-
ety of more specific skills, and are limited to single departments. The only way to be
an ambassador or the commander of an armored division is in government service.
The other professionals used by the federal government are different. Their special-
ties cut across departmental lines and are practiced largely outside government;
and their training and sources of identity and achievement are also largely nongovernmental. Professionals are loyal to the ethics, values, standards, and personnel of
the profession itself, as well as to those of the government agency where they work.
Thus a physicist in the Bureau of Standards thinks of himself as a physicist first, and
a member of the Bureau of Standards second. Circumstances may arise in which
the primary loyalty to the profession may run counter to the demands of public policy and political leaders. Someone with a doctorate in education working for HEW
may resist or even refuse as "unprofessional" the task of creating a particular kind
of audiovisual teaching program. The secretary of HEW may favor the new program, but the professional may feel it violates the basic rules she learned in her
graduate courses on audiovisual techniques.

On the positive side is the fact that professional ties outside government provide an important check on certain aspects of government power. Loyalty to
professional standards may lead civil servants to resist political pressure. The government chemist is unlikely to falsify experimental findings on the safety of food
additives to satisfy a political superior or even her own policy preferences. Nor is
she likely to conceal what she is doing from other chemists, who are the peer group
to which she looks for professional approval. Thus, professionalism encourages a
certain openness in government. Government professionals outraged by political
decisions that contradict their professional judgments are a major source of leaks to
the press and Congress. We should be quite clear, however, that the price of this
openness is insubordination by bureaucrats to the country's elected leaders. What
looks like "political pressure" to the government specialist on birth control may
look like the voice of the people to the elected official who overrules the specialist.

CLIENTELISM

Clientele Agencies   There is a twilight zone where government overlaps the private
sector. Among the inhabitants of this twilight zone are the agen-
cies frequently described as clientele-oriented, or, for short, "clientele agencies." A
clientele agency generally acts as if its contributions to the public interest consist of
taking care of its clientele. The Women's Bureau in the labor department cares primarily about women's rights; the Equal Employment Opportunity Commission
looks after complaints of job discrimination, not the interests of employers; and the
Maritime Administration helps American shippers without worrying about other
ways to move goods. In other words, clientele agencies seem to place a higher
priority on certain special interests than on the general public interest. But it is difficult to condemn this, to insist that all officials look beyond their clients to a concern

for the public interest. The public interest cannot easily be defined and in any event is too vast a concept to be a useful guide for most policymakers. But the interests of, say, wheat farmers are not so vague, and certainly deserve protection by the government. The departments of agriculture, labor, and commerce were established to be the voices of farmers, workers, and business in the inner circle of the cabinet.

To be sure, none of the great departments serves exclusively as a benevolent friend of its clients. For the very federal programs its clients wanted and the department now administers invariably contain controls and limitations on the clients. Clients do not necessarily want all the rules the department enforces, but they have to face the fact that government help and money are never unlimited. Congress generally demands some level of accountability from the recipients. At the very minimum, departments often must choose which clients get more and which less. For example, the educational policymakers in HEW could never hope to make both their academic and vocational education clienteles totally happy, because they are in direct competition for the available funds.

One cause of this phenomenon is the fact that specialization merges so readily with clientelism. The typical official at the Soil Conservation Service has spent many years dealing with farm problems. His whole career revolves around farming and erosion. Most of the people he talks to outside government are in agriculture. If and when he leaves the SCS, he probably will become a farmer himself, teach in an agriculture school, or work for a farm organization. The official who eats, breathes, and sleeps soil erosion — or job discrimination, or the stock market — would have a heart of stone if he did not develop some special sympathy for "his" industry or field and the problems of the people in it.

Clientelism in the Regulatory Commissions.   Special factors have the potential of creating especially high levels of clientelism in the regulatory commissions. Chief among these is the ambiguity of the concept of regulation. One of the responsibilities written into the statutes creating each commission is the duty to preserve the health of the industries regulated. This means, in effect, protecting their profits. The regulator thus walks down both sides of the street. The industry side of the street is thick with executives who are skilled exponents of their industry's point of view. Sometimes the public side is not as well defended. Thus, the amount and direction of regulation depends on the regulators themselves. It has sometimes seemed that one or another of these agencies had been captured by the industry it was supposed to police. Some observers generalized from these examples to blanket statements that all regulatory bodies were nothing more than fronts for private business. A favorite charge was that the commissioners themselves were recruited from the regulated firms. A congressional study of seven commissions shows that this particular idea is wrong. Only 11 percent of agency members were from the regulated industry, and another 26 percent were attorneys who had practiced before the commission to which they were appointed. Nearly half of all commissioners had been government officials before their appointments.[18]

[18] Reported in *National Journal,* November 27, 1976, p. 1690.

Developments in the 1970s shifted the balance of power away from the regulated industries, at least for the time being. The dramatic growth of consumer, environmental, and other groups claiming to speak for the public created a new force in regulation. These new groups are just as much clients of the regulatory agencies as the industries whose behavior they watch. Through a combination of publicity and litigation to compel the commissions to enforce the law (and often to expand the dimensions of the law), these groups have forced the regulatory commissions to pay attention to a wider range of interests. Partly for this reason, and partly because commissioners and their administrators are increasingly aggressive, these agencies now are anything but pushovers. In fact, they sometimes seem to go overboard, as in the crusade by the Federal Trade Commission against the slogan "Everybody needs milk."[19] The most notoriously excessive regulatory agency may be the Occupational Safety and Health Administration (OSHA), which for a time seemed to be controlled by impractical zealots. OSHA once prepared a farm safety booklet warning that manure is slippery and could cause a bad fall if stepped in. Among its more famous rules is this:

> Every water closet shall have a hinged seat made of substantial material having a nonabsorbent finish. Seats installed or replaced after June 4, 1973, shall be of the open-front type.

Along with more than 1100 other nit-picking regulations, the open-front rule was scheduled for revocation.[20]

Regulatory commissions traditionally provided private firms with services they would otherwise have had to provide for themselves — such as compiling rates for shipments on two or more railroads. They also do things private industry could not do for itself without violating the antitrust laws — for example, allocating the limited number of broadcasting frequencies to individual radio and television stations. In some industries these regulatory allocations diminished competition instead of maintaining it. For example, the Civil Aeronautics Board used to assign domestic routes to airline companies and approve all interstate air fares. The CAB worked on the theory that if many airlines competed for passengers on a given route, the result would be "cutthroat" competition that would ruin profits and perhaps safety as well. But the result of CAB regulation was higher prices and crippled competition. A move to deregulate airline fares and routes began in the Ford administration and was finally achieved in 1978. Many airlines opposed this attempt at ending "government interference." The result of deregulation is more choice of airlines and lower fares. When one airline controlled the route from Miami to San Juan, Puerto

---

[19] A federal judge forbade the chairman of the FTC to have anything to do with the FTC's attempt to limit advertising on children's television programs because he "had conclusively prejudged factual items which will be disputed in the rule-making proceedings." One of the other four FTC commissioners withdrew from any involvement in this case because he had been associated before his appointment with a public interest group trying to get the FTC to ban all ads aimed at children. Linda E. Demkovich, "Can Regulators Be Fair?" *National Journal*, November 18, 1978, p. 1866.

[20] Timothy B. Clark, "What's All the Uproar Over OSHA's 'Nit-picking' Rules?" *National Journal*, October 7, 1978, pp. 1594–95.

DOES EVERYBODY NEED MILK?
DOES EVERYBODY NEED THE FTC?

In the early 1970s a TV commercial told Americans that "Everybody needs milk." It was paid for by the California Milk Advisory Board. One of the jobs of the Federal Trade Commission is to protect the public against false, misleading, and deceptive advertising. It issued a complaint against the Milk Board. The FTC argued that everybody doesn't need milk; some people are allergic to milk, and some have trouble digesting it. The Milk Board replied that if you pick any healthy and nutritious food, you can find someone who is allergic to it or can not readily digest it. All their slogan meant was that milk was good for you, which it is. People who had previously broken out in hives or stomachaches after drinking milk would not be persuaded by the commercial to start drinking it again, so no one was misled or deceived.

After a first round of inconclusive hearings and court cases that went all the way to the Supreme Court, the FTC held new hearings in San Francisco in 1979. There were dozens and dozens of huge boxes of documents, so many that the lawyers appearing against the FTC kept a secretary and a clerk in the hearing room just to keep track of the papers. Two lawyers for the FTC were in constant attendance; two others came and went. The administrative law judge conducting the hearing was, of course, on the government payroll. Because the Milk Board was partly an agency of the State of California, a lawyer from the California attorney general's office was also present helping the two private attorneys representing the Milk Board. The hearing ran on week after week. Thousands of dollars of taxpayers' money were spent each day as lawyers and witnesses quarreled over just how many people had how many stomachaches. No one knows just how much the whole thing will cost, but clearly it is going to be well over a million dollars. Everybody literally does not need milk, so it may be worth something to stop the Milk Board claiming that they do. But the Milk Board had stopped using that slogan years before the 1979 hearings and promised not to use it again.

Why did the FTC go on spending huge amounts of government money on a proceeding that eventually may require the Milk Board to stop saying what it had already stopped saying? Even more important, given all the really terrible junk food sold to Americans, why does a government agency use its limited resources to attack milk? Why did these hearings, which cost both sides so much, continue so long? The answer seems to lie in one of the complexities of federalism discussed in Chapter 5. The Milk Board is composed of representatives of private dairy farmers, but it is set up under a state law that regulates milk production and sales. So the Milk Board is not quite private and not quite a state agency. The FTC may regulate private businesses but not state agencies. This whole set of hearings was not really about milk at all. It was about whether the FTC has legal authority over organizations like the Milk Board that fall on the boundary between state government and private business. In order to solve this legal problem of federalism, hundreds of thousands of pages of evidence about milk drinking have to be accumulated. For eventually a court must decide the question of the FTC's authority to regulate the Milk Board. And, for reasons that will become clear in the next chapter, a court will do so only after the FTC has completed its milk hearings and ordered the Milk Board to stop doing what it actually did stop doing long ago.

Rico, a one-way ticket cost about $80. After deregulation, four lines compete on this run, and a ticket cost $49.[21]

Interest Groups and Administration One of the reasons organized interest groups are able to exert influence in Congress is because they can supply the staff work and special expertise Congress may lack. This source of influence is, of course, sharply reduced in dealing with the bureaucracy, which knows as much about a subject as does the lobbyist. Nevertheless, there is a great deal of formal lobbying of bureaucrats. Interest group representatives make the views and goals of their clients known to the relevant agency. In many instances, they actually bring to light some facts or at least interpretations of the facts that are new to the agency. If an interest group is not satisfied with the response it gets from an agency, it can direct its appeals to Congress, the White House, or the department head. When agency officials cannot satisfy the interest groups that come to them, it is often not because they are unwilling to do so, but because their hands are tied by policies and regulations coming from higher up. In such cases, officials may welcome the assistance of lobbyists who can rove across the government and elsewhere in society lining up support.

The major access of the "interests" to the bureaucracy does not come through contact by lobbyists or organized groups. It comes through day-to-day routine business government officials do with recipients of government services. The Bureau of Land Management officials who run the grazing program find themselves out on the range talking with cattlemen about cows, grass, water, and beef prices. The U.S. Office of Education people who supervise federal grants for elementary education find themselves corresponding regularly with the reading curriculum supervisor of the Omaha Public Schools over details of her proposal for a grant to cover the costs of a remedial reading project. Reinforcing this constant routine contact is the high degree of similarity between the bureaucrat and his or her counterpart in the private sector or in local government. Chances are that the government man on the range himself grew up in the West and has a degree in animal husbandry from a state university. The U.S. Office of Education executive probably has an advanced degree from the same kind of university as her Omaha counterpart, and they both probably share whatever professional ideas the schools of education have been teaching.

[21] *San Francisco Chronicle,* May 12, 1979, p. 32.

461

This convergence not only makes routine contact easier and more harmonious, it also reduces the need for actual lobbying as a means of bringing outside views into the bureaucracy. There is a great deal of "virtual representation" in Washington and the field offices. The bureaus tend to be staffed by people who look at things in much the same way as those with whom they deal. Thus, it should not be assumed that because the bureaucracy is not an elected branch of government, it is necessarily an alien force that must be prodded by a democratic, elected Congress. Various elements in the bureaucracy *do* represent various interests in the world at large. Whether the pattern of bureaucratic representation adequately reflects the pattern of needs in the society as a whole is about as open a question as whether the congressional pattern does.

ADMINISTRATORS AND GOVERNMENTAL DECISION-MAKING

In the last decade or so, political scientists have overemphasized the impact of clienteles and interest groups on government. The result has been a picture of the government official as frantically balancing and compromising conflicting political demands. Although this phenomenon is real and the pressure is felt by most high-ranking bureaucrats, the bureaucrats are not just mediators. Most of their time is spent dealing with what they see as the problems of the "real" as opposed to the "political" world. How can minority children be brought to reading grade level most economically? Which line of research is most likely to yield a cure for cancer? Can we get a nuclear reactor design that will produce power at competitive cost without excessive pollution? Which cutting practices will produce maximum long-term timber yield? How can we organize a local poverty office to coordinate the thirty-seven antipoverty programs Congress has enacted?

Bureaucrats are devoted to finding technically correct answers, rational and efficient administrative arrangements, and the best solutions to real human problems. It is for this reason that we have placed so much emphasis on the professional training and specialized expertise to be found in the bureaucracy. Bureaucrats usually define what is technically correct, efficient, and rational not by the political demands made on them, but by the standards and procedures resulting from their professional training and identity. The highway engineer in the department of transportation does not consult the wishes of the president, the steel industry, or the American Automobile Association in determining whether the right girders have been specified for a bridge. He consults a stress table in an engineering text. For most bureaucrats, the outside world consists primarily of problems to be solved, and only secondarily of political conflicts to be resolved. It is precisely this ordering of priorities that makes the bureaucracy such a potent political force.

Unfortunately, the strengths of the bureaucracy are also its weaknesses. The most important of these arise from the division of labor that is inherent in any bureaucracy. The single-minded concern of many bureaucrats with their own specialized fields leads to problems of internal control and coordination in the bureaucracy as a whole. Each group of specialists tends to develop particular perspectives in which the value of its own programs and policies naturally tends to be exaggerated. This distortion is aggravated by the fact that each segment of the bureaucracy deals almost exclusively with its own clientele, who naturally think the government services they get are particularly important. As a result, bureaucrats often find it difficult, if not impossible, to see the programs they administer as only a small part of the big picture.

Limitations on Hierarchical Control

Presidents, cabinet members, and the other political executives face major limitations in controlling the bureaucracy. The first is that the politicians do not have policy preferences on most of the specific decisions that must be made. They do not enter office convinced of how much money should be spent on the school lunch program or whether the army should have one or two airmobile divisions. By the time policy decisions reach the secretary, the bureaucracy has defined the problem, narrowed the alternative solutions, and gathered the factual data to support its recommendations.

This brings us to the second major limitation on political control of bureaucrats. It is almost impossible for political executives to reclaim data or alternatives discarded early in the policymaking process. They will never know of the memorandum to an official in the Food and Nutrition Service of the department of agriculture citing experiments conducted under a federal grant at the University of Kansas showing that school breakfasts would be both cheaper and more beneficial to students than school lunches. Nor are they likely to discover that if the army reorganization of three years ago had given more artillery to the first airmobile division, it would have been strong enough to do the job the army now says two divisions are needed to do. We cannot expect that the president or the relevant department secretary will know enough about childhood metabolism or artillery support plans even to ask the right questions at the right time. The people who do know enough, of course, are the bureaucrats—nutritionists in the department of agriculture and career officers in the army. (Both of these examples are imaginary.)

The president and his appointees' third major limitation is their limited follow-up capacity. A president may make policy decisions, but it is difficult for him (and his cabinet appointees) to ensure that the decision is really carried out after it is passed to the bureaucracy for execution. The president may choose school lunches because he wants to improve learning conditions for poor children. Two years later, he may find that his purpose has been totally defeated. The department of agriculture may have supplied food to every school district that qualified for aid by submitting a complicated application. The department's officials may not have known or cared that most poor school districts were not applying and that most wealthier ones were. So most of the food might have gone not to the poor, but to the middle class.

There are, of course, various organizational devices that a president and his cabinet members can use to deal with these three problems, as we saw in Chapter 14. We should not conclude that political officials are helpless before the bureaucrats. But we also should remember that there are less than 3000 political appointees and almost 3 million civil servants.

Agency Overlap and Many government programs overlap any single bureau or
Competition other subunit of the government. For example, the Office of
Contract Compliance in the department of labor, the Civil
Rights Division of the department of justice, the Office of Civil Rights in HEW, and
the Equal Employment Opportunity Commission, which is independent of any department, are all concerned with the problem of sex and race discrimination in
universities. Sometimes a university can painstakingly work out an affirmative
action program after years of negotiation with one agency, only to find that the
agreement does not satisfy another one. This happened in 1978 to the University
of California's Berkeley campus, when the department of labor refused to approve
an agreement hammered out with HEW.

Because problems overlap, but federal agencies and personnel do not, interagency coordination is a challenge for the executive branch. A number of devices
are available to attack this problem. The most obvious and common is the hierarchical pattern of organization. Bureaus operating in similar areas and thus likely to
encounter overlaps are grouped together under an assistant secretary who presumably can coordinate their activities from above. In turn, the assistant secretaries are
grouped under a secretary who also undertakes coordination. Coordination between agencies of two different departments can be achieved through the two secretaries concerned. And if the secretaries cannot coordinate their departments, the
White House staff can. Subordinate agencies that come into conflict are highly motivated to solve the problem themselves in order to avoid the imposition of solutions
from above. As a result, the hierarchical system is responsible, both directly and indirectly, for a great deal of coordination. Indeed, if the hierarchical system did *not*
work, it is unlikely that the government could be run at all.

But if hierarchy worked perfectly, Washington would be far different. Career
officials sometimes appeal the unfavorable decisions of their political superiors by
making end runs to Congress with the backing of friendly interest groups. This is a
risky strategy, but it is not uncommon or unsuccessful when done with skill and
subtlety. Moreover, hierarchy is unsuitable when coordination must be attained
between two or more equal and independent agencies, like the departments of
defense and state. In such circumstances, two methods of lateral coordination are
widely used to supplement hierarchical methods. The first is the much-denounced
but quite unavoidable committee system. Hundreds of committees composed of
officials of roughly equal status from different agencies meet constantly to work out
differences and make mutual plans. For instance, an interdepartmental committee
on recreation might have an assistant secretary of agriculture because agriculture
runs the national forests, an assistant secretary of interior because interior runs the
national parks, and an assistant secretary of housing and urban development because HUD is concerned with recreation in urban areas.

The membership and jurisdiction of some of these committees are established
by statute. Most are temporary arrangements that come and go as new problems
arise and are settled. Generally, an assistant secretary in one department who encounters overlapping concerns with an assistant secretary in another will avoid re-
ferring her coordination needs upward to her own secretary. Instead, she will discuss the problem with her fellow assistant secretary in a committee where they both

To do business with a certain Middle Eastern government, an American company is told it must hire a local businessman to serve as its agent—a common practice in many parts of the world.

In the past, local agents have routinely passed along part of their commissions to government officials to obtain business. The company explains that, under a new U.S. law, this practice is now illegal.

The company finally chooses a local agent who, it believes, will be unlikely to operate in the old way. The firm gets the business, the agent gets his commission—and later it is learned that he bribed a government official.

Under the Foreign Corrupt Practices Act, . . . it is quite likely that the American company as well as some of its employees would be criminally liable for the conduct of its foreign agent in this hypothetical but not implausible example. This kind of possibility—which could arise because those who have "reason to know" that a bribe may be paid to obtain business are criminally liable—is prompting some companies and attorneys to press the government to clarify the new law.

. . .

The Justice and Commerce Departments are trying to develop the government's position.

Justice, unwilling to tell companies how far they can go without risking prosecution, is inclined to offer a minimum amount of guidance. On the other hand, Commerce, eager to further the cause of American business abroad, would like to do whatever the business community seems to prefer—whether that turns out to be clarifying the law in detail or not providing such guidance.

Justice holds the upper hand. While Commerce is charged with implementing the government's export policy, Justice enforces the criminal parts of the new law and will issue whatever guidance will be furnished on the anti-bribery provisions.

. . .

The greatest uncertainty under the anti-bribery law, according to a number of attorneys, concerns what one lawyer called the "runaway agent"—the local agent who disobeys instructions not to pay bribes to retain or obtain business.

Attorneys said companies need to know how much they have to find out about the agents they employ. And they need to know what steps they must take to ensure that they and their employees are not criminally liable if the agents pay bribes.

. . .

While the law is full of uncertainties, the Justice Department does not appear ready to do much to clarify it. Instead, American companies may just have to hope that their local agents keep their commissions to themselves.

Source: James W. Singer, "Businesses Seek Guidance on Foreign Bribery Law," *National Journal,* November 18, 1978, pp. 1864–65.

sit as equals. Committees are often criticized for reaching "lowest common denominator" solutions. Differences between agencies are compromised; unresolved conflicts are papered over by vague generalizations. A false front of harmony is established behind which each agency continues to go its own way. To some extent, this criticism is valid. Committees of equals can hardly be expected to resolve basic agency quarrels. Fortunately however, the areas of mutual concern with which committees must deal rarely involve such quarrels. Most interagency committees operate as arenas for the exchange of information. They allow officials who are concerned with similar or overlapping problems but who are not normally in face-to-face contact with one another to share views. More often than not, these officials can find common, mutually beneficial courses of action.

A second and similar lateral coordination mechanism is the clearance system. A report, evaluation, or policy recommendation drawn up by one agency must be "cleared" by other agencies involved in the same area before being sent on to higher authority. Clearance does not usually involve a veto power, but it does give the agency receiving the report an opportunity to file a dissent. Agencies do not want their reports passed on with dissenting opinions attached, so the first agency usually is willing to modify its proposals or at least its language to meet the objections of others. Thus, clearance provides the same opportunity for cooperation, and the same risks of delay and papering over differences, as the committee device. The clearance system is most widely used in international affairs. There it is obviously important that whatever the United States says, it speaks with one voice.

The most general complaint about lateral coordination is its discouraging effect on new programs. An agency with a new idea immediately finds itself confronted by half a dozen other agencies anxious to preserve the old way of doing things. New ideas can be compromised to death. Bureaucrats may be less concerned with changing the real world than with getting the fourteen necessary signatures. The state department's Italian Desk officer must get the clearance of state's Bureau of Near Eastern and South Asian Affairs, the commerce department's Bureau of International Commerce, that of the assistant secretary of the treasury for international affairs, and that of an assistant secretary of defense for a proposal to encourage a particular program of Italian technical aid to Lebanon. By that time the Lebanese may not want the aid any more. Despite these drawbacks, however, lateral coordination seems to be necessary; totally independent agency initiatives would have the government charging off in all directions at once.

THE POLITICS OF ADMINISTRATIVE REORGANIZATION

It is often felt that many of the problems of both hierarchical and lateral coordination could be eased or eliminated if only the government were correctly organized. Since the 1930s, the United States government has been subjected to a series of reorganization studies, proposals, and actions, all designed to improve "management," which for the most part meant improved coordination of government programs. The would-be reorganizers argued that if all the similar activities of government could be put in the same organizational box, or at least in neighboring boxes, it would be easier to coordinate them. Presidents Eisenhower, Nixon, and Carter made government reorganization a major theme of their election campaigns.

In fact, however, a closer look at many reorganization proposals reveals that they are more often concerned with bringing certain policies to the fore and suppressing others than with coordination.[22] Although occasional bureaucratic overlaps and other irrationalities can be organized out of existence, most reorganization schemes merely substitute one coordination problem for another. For instance, when the Office of Education had a Division of Vocational Education, a Mental Retardation Branch, and a Technical Education Branch, all three were concerned with elementary schools, secondary schools, and higher education. Interbureau coordination of their programs was required for each level. When the Office of Education was reorganized into elementary, secondary, and higher education bureaus, each bureau had vocational, technical, and remedial programs that had to be coordinated with similar programs in other two bureaus.

Nevertheless, because hierarchy is an important tool of coordination, government reorganizations are important sometimes. The creation of a department of energy does not solve the energy crisis, but it does put in one place and under one head dozens of previously scattered federal agencies that have energy responsibilities. The new organization does make it easier to arrive at coordinated policy proposals. But it does not ensure that they will be good proposals or that Congress will accept them. Congress has now delegated much of its reorganization power to the president. He can use it to create new and more hospitable organizational settings for programs that might not appeal to the agencies to which they normally would have been assigned. President Carter sought to do this and to achieve greater coordination when he proposed the new department of energy to Congress. Or the president can create new positions in old agencies that can be filled with new people dedicated to the program while agency deadwood is shunted aside. Nevertheless, as President Nixon learned when he attempted a major consolidation of departments, the politics of administrative reorganization is sticky and complex. Interest groups and Capitol Hill allies of the agencies involved frequently are able to block efforts at reorganization.

A Case Study in Government Reorganization: A Separate Department of Education

Traditionally state governments looked after the health and education of their citizens and the welfare of their poor. By the 1950s the federal government had dozens of programs in these areas, administered by a variety of separate bureaus. Many programs that did not really fit into any of the old departments were gathered together into a new U.S. Department of Health, Education and Welfare. At the time, the new department was criticized as combining apples and oranges. Specialists in elementary school reading had little in common with cancer researchers or social security experts.

President Nixon wanted to create four "superdepartments" to do most of the government's work. The idea was to group two or three departments under a "su-

---

[22] Harold Seidman, *Politics, Position, and Power,* 2nd ed. (New York: Oxford University Press, 1975).

per secretary" so that their work could be better coordinated. Such an officer would be well placed to establish priorities among departments by comparing their programs and giving more money to the best ones. If you think along these lines, HEW was well organized because it already put one department head in a position to coordinate and set priorities for a large number of different programs.

Watergate killed the superdepartment idea, and President Carter took the opposite approach by proposing a separate U.S. Department of Education. One of his arguments was that federal education activities were too complex and important to be administered efficiently in the same department with health and welfare. Moreover, Carter pointed out that many education programs are outside HEW: schools for children on Indian reservations in the department of the interior; schools for children of overseas servicemen in the department of defense; the school lunch program in the department of agriculture; basic science research funded by the National Science Foundation. All told, over forty major educational programs are outside HEW. Putting everything into HEW would increase that department's chronic fragmentation and its secretary's inability to keep track of what is going on. Decisions that have to clear through several layers of the education bureaucracy also must go through an extra level of approval, that of the secretary of HEW. This creates delays and extra costs and also keeps education issues too far away from the White House. In contrast, putting education into one department would give educators their own secretary, their own budget, and their own direct access to the president. With these advantages, they could hope to get more attention and money than they do now.

The idea of a separate department of education had been around for many years. The first real push was a consequence of the 1976 election. In May of that year, candidate Jimmy Carter promised the National Education Association that he would work for the creation of a separate department. The big teachers' organization was so pleased at this support for a long-cherished goal that it endorsed Carter for president, the first such action in its history. This was a major coup for Carter, because the NEA's 2 million members and bulging treasury made it a potent campaign ally.

Once in the White House, Carter honored his commitment and backed the necessary legislation. The education community was deeply split. The elements that felt comfortable with the NEA and state school superintendents favored the new department. The NEA's bitter rival, the American Federation of Teachers, feared the department would be dominated by the NEA and school administrators. Most of higher education was wary, and many important organizations and individual universities ultimately declared their opposition. They feared being swamped in the new department by the more politically influential elementary and secondary sectors. For many interests, the crucial issue was preventing agencies of particular concern to themselves from being included. Scientists opposed including the National Science Foundation and doctors liked the independent status of the National Institutes of Health. All the major federal sources of financial support for research were left out: the NSF, NIH, National Endowments for the Arts and Humanities, as well as the research-funding activities of the regular line departments.

Bureaucratic interests were just as divided. The secretary of HEW naturally was unhappy about losing part of a sprawling empire. Many education agencies were perfectly satisfied with the existing arrangements. The bargaining on this subject was so fierce that the first congressional hearing on the administration's bill was delayed half an hour while the president and his OMB director decided just which agencies would be in the department. They included the Head Start program, which gives preschool education to children from poor families. Angered at this prospect, Head Start officials mobilized their students' parents in a grassroots lobbying campaign that convinced the Senate to leave Head Start where it was. Two years after the president first presented his proposal to Congress, the issue was finally settled when Congress narrowly passed the bill creating the new department.

THE BUDGET: KEY TOOL OF POLICY
COORDINATION

Today, perhaps the most important tool of coordination is the budget. The budget provides the president with a method of controlling the bureaucracy. Presidential leadership is largely a matter of setting priorities, and the best measure of priorities is money. The budget is the government's instrument for allocating money. The budgetary process and the format of the budget are rather complex. Figure 15.2, which shows the timing of the budgetary process in the executive branch, should help you grasp this process more easily.

The president's overall budget target is a crucial aspect of presidential control over the bureaucracy. In May and June, at the start of the budget planning cycle, the president sets ceilings for each department for the following year. By setting these target figures, the president tells each agency roughly what it can expect and what is reasonable to ask for. Of course, within each department, bureau heads routinely put in requests whose totals exceed the department ceiling. Nevertheless, their general budgetary ambitions, their own receptiveness to new programs, and their bargaining power are deeply affected by the reactions they anticipate from "above." Whether the presidential target figure looks tight or generous determines much of their anticipations.[23]

Each department's own internal budget examination is potentially an instrument for the secretary to control the bureaucracy. The budget requests submitted to the department by its various bureaus always exceed any realistic hopes about what the department will be able to get. It is clear to all bureaucratic subordinates that the secretary will have to make some choices between bureaus. Whether or not those choices become tools for ensuring that the bureaucracy responds to the policy desires of the administration varies widely from department to department. In some departments, for example, subunits operate popular programs which enjoy strong support from public and congressional constituencies. The secretary may not feel in a position to shift budgetary favor from them to other subunits. What the secretary takes away, Congress might well restore in the appropriations process. The

[23] Aaron Wildavsky, *The Politics of the Budgetary Process,* 3rd ed. (Boston: Little Brown, 1979).

Figure 15.2
The Budget-Making Process
in the Executive Branch

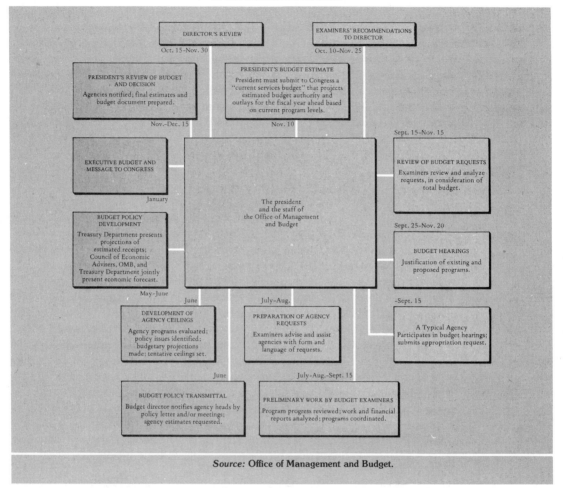

Source: **Office of Management and Budget.**

more popular a subunit's programs, the more friends that agency will have on Capitol Hill. In addition, there are always some cases in which the secretary simply does not know enough about the affairs of the department to apply the budgetary carrot and stick as a means of determining policy. If the secretary cannot penetrate subordinates' budget figures to grasp the relative merits of various programs, the theoretical power to alter those figures will be of no use. In many instances, however, the department secretary can use the budget to give more money to the bureaus that are doing what he or she wants and less money to those that are not.

The Office of Management and Budget performs a critical coordinating function in connecting the president with the numerous agencies of the administrative branch. The core of the OMB is a group of less than 100 budget examiners. Most examiners work on the budgets of the same set of bureaus for a number of years. Although they are familiar with the programs and history of the organizations they cover, the examiners are spread very thin. For example, there are only seven examiners for the $20 billion budget of the U.S. Department of Agriculture. Viewed from the standpoint of presidential control, the basic purpose of the Office of Management and Budget is to get one group of career government experts—the examiners—to watch another group—the department bureaucrats. The risk is, of course, that the experts who have been set to watch the experts will have policy views of their own which differ from those of the president. The OMB staff has had a very good record of loyalty to the president—at least when they could discern what the president wanted.

The style adopted in most budget negotiations is often called **incrementalism.** Most government programs go on from year to year. An official makes next year's proposed budget by taking this year's figures as a base.[24] He or she then asks for a little more—an incremental addition—for some programs, the same for others, and a little less for others, depending on current experience with each. With such an approach, it is natural for the department budget officer and later the budget examiners to focus on the changes proposed for next year. Under such a system, most programs pass through a rather similar life cycle. First, a small sum is requested for research and/or preliminary planning for a new program. It is not easy for a department to get a new "line" put in its budget. Usually a recent congressional authorization for a new program serves as the justification. Once the new line is born, it is carefully nurtured each year by a request for somewhat larger funding. A pilot program is usually the next step after research and planning have been completed. This is followed by an attempt at nationwide application of the successful pilot. Most programs thus continue from year to year at a gradually rising budgetary level once they have been accepted as a routine part of government.

Perhaps the chief reason for the widespread use of the incremental approach is simple necessity. In the first place, the budget contains an extremely large number of lines. It would be impossible to start from scratch and reexamine the validity of each line or program each year. Focusing only on the changes saves the most precious of all governmental commodities, decision-making time. Second, of necessity budgets must be based on predictions about future needs and demands that cannot be known with certainty. In such circumstances, it seems more reasonable to take small steps out from current experience than great leaps into the unknown. Third, ongoing government programs generate large-scale human expectations among government workers, political leaders, and segments of the public (that is, interest groups). Many government programs—for instance, farm subsidies and weapons development—involve massive, complex, and long-term arrangements of people and resources. Rapid changes in such programs would lead to confusion and demoralization in government, and to severe hardship in the private sector. The price in pain and confusion of abrupt change is greater than we are usually will-

---

[24] Otto A. Davis et al., "A Theory of the Budgetary Process," *American Political Science Review,* 60 (September 1966), pp. 529–47; Wildavsky, *The Politics of the Budgetary Process.*

"Relax. Rome wasn't fully funded and operational in a day."

ing to pay. Even relatively small decisions may result in closing down a defense installation that provided most of the jobs for a small town or a community mental health clinic that provided the only psychiatric help available for thousands of people.

As necessary as incrementalism is, however, it does have a major drawback; it robs the budgetary process of much of its value to political leadership as a mode of bureaucratic control. Even with the Office of Management and Budget and the secretaries working hard to move the government in the directions the president wants it to go, the budget has a sticky, molasses-like quality. It is difficult to redirect funds rapidly from some programs to others or to make radical changes in overall levels of expenditure. The incremental technique is not well suited to asking questions such as these: Why do we have this program at all? Does it work at cross purposes to other programs we have funded? Would some other program do more for less money? It is for this reason that presidential candidate Carter talked a good deal about **zero-base budgeting.** Zero-base budgets look at every government program afresh each year. The budget examiners would not ask an agency just to defend changes from last year in appropriations requests; instead, the agency would have to start from scratch and show each year that all its programs were worth having. It would have to justify not only new expenditure levels, but the continuation of the old ones.

Looking at every one of the thousands of government programs from scratch each year, however, would require spending an enormous amount of money and time on the budgetary process itself—probably hundreds of times as much as we do now. Perhaps this is why President Carter has talked much less about zero-base budgeting than did candidate Carter. Nevertheless, the president's budget is a way to enforce the principle that a proposed expenditure which looks all-important from one perspective is merely one rival among thousands for limited public funds (Figure 15.3). (In fact, some programs are cut substantially or eliminated entirely after surviving only a few annual budget cycles. On the other hand, most agencies manage to achieve growth in the size of their total budgets even though a few programs are killed off.)

After requests have passed through the departments and the Office of Management and Budget, the president has one more round in which to invoke his will. In the final budget meetings held in November and December each year, the president, with an eye to his fiscal and monetary policies, is likely to take a strong line on the gross budget figures. For many a bureaucrat, these final sessions determine whether he or she will live in pleasure or pain over the next year. Of course, this power of the president is largely of the meat-ax rather than the scalpel variety. He can do much more about the total figures than about which programs go ahead and which slow down. The president's role in the budget is not finished when he delivers his budget message, but at this point the main arena shifts to Congress. The power of Congress to raise or lower any figure in the president's budget allows bureaucrats who are dissatisfied with what they got from the president to appeal to

Figure 15.3
The Government of the United States
as Reflected in the Federal Budget

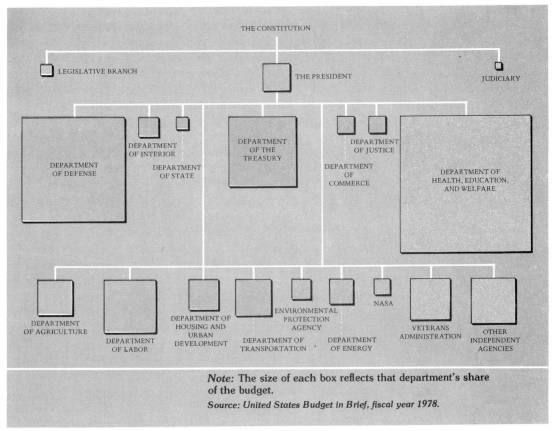

THE CONSTITUTION

LEGISLATIVE BRANCH

THE PRESIDENT

JUDICIARY

DEPARTMENT
OF DEFENSE

DEPARTMENT
OF INTERIOR

DEPARTMENT
OF STATE

DEPARTMENT
OF THE
TREASURY

DEPARTMENT
OF JUSTICE

DEPARTMENT
OF
COMMERCE

DEPARTMENT OF
HEALTH, EDUCATION,
AND WELFARE

DEPARTMENT
OF AGRICULTURE

DEPARTMENT
OF LABOR

DEPARTMENT OF
HOUSING AND
URBAN
DEVELOPMENT

ENVIRONMENTAL
PROTECTION
AGENCY

DEPARTMENT OF
TRANSPORTATION

NASA

DEPARTMENT
OF ENERGY

VETERANS
ADMINISTRATION

OTHER
INDEPENDENT
AGENCIES

Note: The size of each box reflects that department's share
of the budget.
Source: United States Budget in Brief, fiscal year 1978.

their friends on Capitol Hill. (The budgetary process in Congress is described in Chapter 13.)

AN OVERVIEW OF ADMINISTRATION AND POLICY

The bureaucracy is clearly a major participant in policymaking. It might be convenient briefly to summarize here the various facets of bureaucratic policymaking we have already encountered. First, the bureaucracy (or, more correctly, the many and often competing groups and individuals in the executive branch) is probably the major initiator of public policy. Most proposals for new legislation come from the bureaucracy, which thus helps set the agenda of alternatives for other policymakers. The initiative for the most important new legislation does come from the president and Congress, but even here the bureaucracy usually provides the alternatives and much of the background information and analysis.

The bureaucracy also provides a significant share of the continuity and flow of information necessary to pass legislation. Agencies join forces with pressure groups, presidential staff, and congressional leaders to shepherd bills through Congress. It is a bureaucrat from HEW who will appear six times before six House and Senate subcommittees in six successive years. He will keep telling them why they should pass the new vocational education bill until they finally do. Some of the agencies' congressional work is done by political appointees, but a great deal is done by bureau chiefs and other career people. And much of what the political appointees say to Congress has been composed by their career staffs. The bureaucracy also does an enormous amount of supplementary lawmaking after statutes are passed. In many instances, Congress deliberately delegates broad discretion to agencies. But even when it does not intend such delegation, Congress necessarily writes legislation in relatively general language. It is the bureaucracy that "interprets" this language in each specific instance. For example, Congress may pass a law calling for "maximum feasible participation" by the poor in poverty programs. But when HEW turns down the grant application of Dry Forks, Wyoming, because its community council plan does not provide for separate representation for Indians and Mexican-Americans, it is HEW, not Congress, that has made the policy of ethnic representation for the poor. Similarly, if the antitrust division of the justice department decides not to fight mergers in industries threatened by foreign competition, the division has made a major antitrust policy. The pattern of its decisions will have precisely the same effect as if Congress had passed a bill granting an exemption from the antitrust laws to industries threatened by foreign competition.

Closely related to this factor is another that also derives from the bureaucracy's responsibility for the thousands of routine decisions that make up the day-to-day business of government. The federal government is a large buyer of goods and services. In some cases it is the largest buyer, or the only one. It is a major builder and an even more important building inspector. Most dam, flood control, harbor, bridge, highway, school, home, military, and ship construction is done either by or for the federal government or under federally approved codes and standards. For instance, Federal Housing Administration standards have been the most important single determinant of the style and quality of the homes owned by most Americans. It is FHA standards that determine how many windows of what size most of us have in our bedrooms. The millions of decisions about what the government will or will not buy, or provide its money for, are made by career civil servants subject to very general supervision and guidelines. But the collective impact of these decisions *is* the government's policy.

The less important or salient or controversial a policy decision, the larger the part the bureaucracy is likely to play in it. The president and Congress play greater roles in what appear to be the major decisions. But many decisions that seem small at the time can be seen in retrospect as the first step either up to the heights or down the slippery slope. What is more, the sum of many small decisions may have an impact rivaling that of the few big ones. It is for these reasons that some of the grander problems of bureaucracy continue to trouble us. These problems can be shaped into three overlapping paradoxes. The first involves client orientation versus problem-solving. There are real problems in the real world. Most people believe that some solutions to these problems are better than others, and that scientific and technical knowledge rather than self-interest is a sound basis for deciding which are best. Therefore, most of us would want an expert, independent bureaucracy that seeks the best solutions to such problems as smog and high infant mortality. Something strikes us as wrong with a Food and Drug Administration that is too intimate with the drug industry or an air pollution agency too closely associated with the auto industry. On the other hand, an independent and isolated bureaucracy may develop a high level of inertia and indifference to pressing human needs. When they intervene in private affairs, most of us fear that bureaucrats may be arbitrary and high-handed. We want a responsive and sensitive bureaucracy that really understands our problems and treats us like individuals. But how can a bureaucracy be both sensitive and responsive on the one hand, and on the other stay sufficiently uninvolved with special interests that it can make right decisions rather than the ones they want?

The second paradox involves generalization versus specialization. Our society solves its problems by specialization. We practice division of labor among experts, each trained and interested in a specific set of problems. We want a bureaucracy that can solve problems. Thus, we want a specialized bureaucracy. But we also want a bureaucracy that pursues the public interest. We want one that has some sense of perspective and priorities We want one that realizes government is there to achieve the general good. Experts and specialists are notorious for lacking perspective and pursuing their own particular problems and solutions at the expense of others. Thus, we also want a generalist bureaucracy that sees the big picture. There may be a few people who combine a specialist's skill with a generalist's perspectives, but only a few. And of those few, fewer still choose to work for the government.

The third paradox involves representativeness versus elitism. Both the British and French have developed elite corps of civil servants drawn from the best graduates of the best universities. The government is assured some share of the best young brains in the country. The prestige, sense of mission, and social status of these elites help keep them in government in spite of low pay. But such an elite corps may become highly unrepresentative of the people it is supposed to serve. Eventually it may come to feel that *it* is the government, that it knows best, and that it is responsible for giving the bumbling politicians and the ignorant masses what is good for them, not what they want. But without such an elite corps, are we not in danger of being governed by leftovers and people who cannot succeed in the private sector?

Because "the bureaucracy" is so vast and complex, and because the term covers so many phenomena, it is difficult to make any authoritative closing remarks on the subject. Certainly citizens are unwarranted in their easy use of the term "bureaucrat" as a negative stereotype. They *are* warranted in their desire to evaluate the public service and to have it be efficient, competent, and responsible.

SUMMARY   The federal bureaucracy is sufficiently large and independent of presidential control to constitute a fourth branch of government. Its basic units are the cabinet-level departments, each of which is subdivided into bureaus. In addition, there are many important noncabinet agencies, such as the Veterans Administration and the independent regulatory commissions. And much federal administration is done indirectly through grants and contracts. Thus, federal administration involves not only the federal bureaucracy itself, but millions of state and local administrators and employees of private firms.

The civil service system has replaced the previous patronage method of filling federal jobs. That system has the disadvantage of making the career bureaucracy less responsive to its superiors, most of whom serve only for a short time. Career executives come from a wide range of backgrounds, but most have spent their adult lives working for one or two agencies of the federal government. The Foreign Service and military officer corps are separate sets of federal executives with special characteristics and problems, as are the members of various professions who work for the government.

Federal agencies develop special ties with the particular segments of society they assist and regulate. Interest groups lobby the administrative branch as well as Congress, and administrators themselves become representatives of various segments of public opinion. Nevertheless, bureaucrats basically see themselves as seeking to provide workable solutions to real world problems rather than as simply reflecting the political desires of others.

Because agencies are highly specialized but operate overlapping programs, the federal government employs both hierarchical and lateral methods of coordination. Although most reorganization proposals are supposed to be aimed at solving coordination problems, in reality they may be more concerned with encouraging or suppressing specific programs or policies. The budget is a key tool of policy coordination because it presents a relatively clear picture of all government programs in relation to one another. The incremental style of budgeting, however, makes it difficult to raise fundamental questions about which government programs are most worthwhile and which might be dropped altogether.

The bureaucracy is a major participant in policymaking and makes a major contribution to the lawmaking process. The bureaucracy presents three overlapping paradoxes: (1) client orientation versus problem-solving; (2) generalization versus specialization; and (3) representativeness versus elitism. On the whole, the American bureaucracy tends to be clientele-oriented, specialized, and representative.

the courts

In 1795, a group of land speculators bribed the Georgia legislature to give them a large part of what later became Alabama. The Supreme Court eventually ordered them to give it back. President Andrew Jackson reportedly said, "John Marshall [the Chief Justice] has made his order. Now let him enforce it."[1]

[1] C. Peter McGrath, *Yazoo* (Providence: Brown University Press, 1966).

CHAPTER 16

• In 1960, the Internal Revenue Service asked the Supreme Court to state a set of rules that would define a "gift" as opposed to "income" for tax purposes. The Court refused.

• In 1964, the Court told the Interstate Commerce Commission what factors to consider before allowing a railroad to abandon passenger service. The Court also decided that the Santa Fe Railroad could run a truck line between Fresno and Los Angeles.

• In 1952, the U.S. Patent Office was so fed up with the Court's refusal to acknowledge the validity of the patents it issued that it pushed a new patent law through Congress. Few members of Congress realized that the law was intended to force the Court to agree with the Patent Office. Fourteen years later, the Court said the law really had been intended to force the Patent Office to agree with the Court. The Patent Office continues to issue thousands of patents knowing that they would be invalidated if they ever got to the Court. They seldom do.[2]

• In 1849, a major Supreme Court decision held that the Court should not decide political questions. In 1963, the Court held that litigation (that is, suing someone in court) was a form of political activity protected by the First Amendment.[3]

In order to see a pattern in this diversity, let us briefly outline the general powers and impact of the Supreme Court. First, the Supreme Court wields the power of **judicial review.** In the American context, judicial review is the power to declare that statutes and the actions of administrative officers are unconstitutional and thus legally null and void. The power of review extends over local, state, and federal governments. Besides the special American meaning of judicial review, the term more generally refers to the power of courts to examine the actions of administrative officers to see if they are in accord with the statutes governing those officers. The Supreme Court does this to federal administrative officers. Second, the Court has **appellate jurisdiction.** This is the power of a higher court to correct legal errors made by a lower court. The Supreme Court has appellate jurisdiction over lower federal courts on all matters of law and over state courts on legal issues arising under the federal Constitution.

In exercising judicial review and appellate jurisdiction, the Supreme Court has had a major impact on American life. In recent years, its decisions have been at the center of the rapid and not always peaceful changes in race relations. They have led to a major national controversy over the practice of busing children to achieve school integration. They have radically changed the composition of state legislatures forced to equalize the populations of the districts from which their members were elected. Other decisions have overturned state laws against birth control and

---

[2] Martin Shapiro, *The Supreme Court and Administrative Agencies* (New York: Free Press, 1968), Chap. 3.

[3] *Luther v. Borden,* 7 How. 1 (1849); *NAACP v. Button,* U.S. 415 (1963).

The Supreme Court's decisions prohibiting school prayer have not succeeded in removing religious observations in public schools. Here, a Massachusetts teacher reads aloud from the Bible, in obedience to a local school board's order.

Wide World

abortion. Still others have fundamentally changed the system of criminal justice by providing lawyers for poor defendants and forbidding police misconduct. Its obscenity decisions now permit explicit sexual expression in books, magazines, films, and on the stage that was undreamed of twenty-five years ago. And Court decisions have blocked numerous proposals to provide state aid to parochial schools, one of the most fundamental bread-and-butter issues in many communities.

Yet this very list indicates the limits of the Court's political power. All its actions combined have not succeeded in bringing blacks full educational equality in many parts of the country and have not integrated the schools. In thousands of communities, police and courts have made no appreciable changes in their methods despite the long string of Court decisions designed to ensure better treatment of suspects. Perhaps most important, there are large areas of government activity about which the Court has virtually no say. It has always been extremely timid in challenging the war and foreign affairs powers of the presidency. It has no direct way of dictating priorities to legislatures, of forcing them to spend more on hospitals and less on highways. It can intervene sporadically to ensure that the bureaucracy has followed proper procedures or obeyed specific statutory commands. Most of the planning and operation of federal programs, however, remain beyond its reach. In short, the Court can alter the real world in some areas, but in many others it is powerless.

The web of relationships between the Supreme Court and the rest of American government and politics is extremely complex. The central fact, however, and the one that needs the most explanation, is that we accept this Court as a central part of our political process.

Few nations have a supreme court as politically active as ours. In this chapter we will examine the basic nature of courts in general and then that of our Supreme Court in particular. We will look at whether the Supreme Court ought to be very active politically and describe what kinds of people the justices are and how they are appointed. After that we trace the relations between the Supreme Court and other federal courts and the way the Supreme Court gets and decides its cases. Finally, we will look at the various roles the Supreme Court plays in American politics.

THE SUPREME COURT AS COURT

The Supreme Court is, like any court, the "third person" in disputes between two parties. It is also lawmaker, instrument of government, and the nation's highest court.

479

The Third Person When two people quarrel, it is so logical for them to find a third person to help them resolve their dispute that nearly every society uses some form of this third-person device. The universal appeal of the third person explains the social magic of courts, the special something that earns them popular favor and support. The judge is an official chosen to serve as a third person to settle quarrels according to law. The judge is also an officer of the government. The laws the judge applies are passed by the government, and they reflect the general interests present in the society. When the two disputants come to court, they do not face a third person whose sole concern is their particular interests, but a person who is concerned with the interests of each of them *plus* a third set of interests— those of the government and the society. To an extent, the solutions the court imposes seem to reflect the interests of the government rather than a simple compromise between the interests of the disputants. Thus, courts lose some of their appeal to disputants. All modern courts suffer from this loss of social magic. The Supreme Court has suffered more than most because it often seems to represent the interests of a central government very far away and very unsympathetic to the interests of the disputants.

Lawmaker Legislators have neither the time nor the imagination to write laws that dictate the solution to every quarrel that might arise in a society. They therefore write more or less general statutes in broad language. A statute forbidding "assault" is an example. Such general statutes must be interpreted to provide solutions to specific quarrels. The job of bringing the general words of the law down to specific cases falls to the courts. If the courts decide that "assault" includes hitting a man with a cleaver but not with wet spaghetti, they have made the law mean that hurting a man's body is forbidden, but not hurting his dignity. If they decide that assault does include spaghetti, then they have made the assult law protect dignity as well as body. Either way, they have made part of the law of assault. In interpreting the meaning of law, the courts inevitably and inescapably *make* law. Their statutory interpretations are like those made by administrators. Courts, like administrators, *make* public policy.

Two factors push some courts very far into lawmaking. Courts that apply the most generally and vaguely worded laws must fill in more meaning than courts that apply relatively specific, detailed, and precise laws. As we will see shortly, one of the laws the Supreme Court applies is the Constitution, our most generally and vaguely worded law.

Besides the vagueness or specificity of the law, a second factor moves some courts deeper than others into lawmaking. Consider what would happen if one trial court decided that spaghetti-hurling is assault and another court decided that it is not. We do not want the law to mean one thing in one courtroom and something different in another. For this reason, we have a system of **appeals courts.** They review trial court decisions and make sure that all courts are interpreting the laws in the same way. An appeals court does this by taking a specific appeal in a specific case from one of its trial courts. In the course of deciding the specific appeal, it announces the one single correct interpretation of the law that all its trial courts must follow in the future.

In such cases, the main energies of the appellate court are likely to be devoted to providing a legal interpretation — that is, making a law — that will work well for all its trial courts. It is less concerned with satisfying the interests of the two parties and more concerned with making a law that will best serve the interest of society in the future. As the highest appellate court in the nation, the Supreme Court spends more of its energies making legal interpretations for the guidance of lower courts and less on the settlement of specific quarrels than any other American court.

Instrument of Government   We use courts in disputes not only between two individuals, but also between individual and government. Court cases often read not *Smith* v. *Jones* but *United States* v. *Jones* or *Connecticut* v. *Jones*. The judge is a government official. The laws he or she applies were made by government. The government is also one of the litigants. We have a situation that looks more like two-against-one than one-against-one with an independent third person deciding between them. To guard against this impression of unfairness, we have taken steps to ensure the relative neutrality and impartiality of judges when their own government is one of the parties before them. For example, federal judges hold office for life, so the government cannot fire them if they decide against it. Nevertheless, a person who loses a case to the government is likely to have some suspicions about the impartiality of the judge. A high proportion of the Supreme Court's cases involve the federal government as one of the parties. So here again, the Supreme Court looks less like an impartial third person than most other courts.

Right-wing opposition to many liberal Supreme Court decisions in the 1960s led to a conspicuous but futile campaign to impeach the Chief Justice.

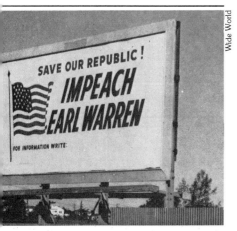

Wide World

Highest Court   The existence of the Supreme Court is commanded by Article III of the Constitution: "The judicial power of the United States shall be vested in one Supreme Court. . . ." More important than these few words, however, has been the intimate link between the Court and the Constitution. As we have seen (Chapter 3), our intellectual tradition identifies the Constitution both with the notion of "higher law" and with the notion of a "contract of government." Considered as a legally binding contract, the Constitution contains five basic kinds of provisions:

1. Specification of the structure of the central government and boundaries between the various parts of that structure.

2. Limited grants of power to the central government, authorizing it to do certain specific things.

3. Open-ended clauses giving the central government those powers "necessary and proper" for carrying out its specific

duties and making it "supreme" over the states in the exercise of the powers granted to it.

4. Specific prohibitions against certain activities by the central government.

5. Specific prohibitions against certain activities by the states.

Our belief that constitutional provisions are legally binding made it seem normal and natural that a court should decide disputes over their meaning. John Marshall, the first great Chief Justice, took advantage of what seemed "natural," and established the Court's role as the arbiter of constitutional quarrels in a series of historic decisions.

In *Marbury* v. *Madison* (1803), the Court held unconstitutional a congressional law giving additional powers to the Supreme Court itself, arguing that those powers belonged to another part of the government—the lower federal courts.[4] In denying *itself* these additional powers, the Court asserted its general authority to police the boundary lines between the various branches of the central government. The Constitution did not specifically confer the power of judicial review on the Court. It was Marshall who reasoned that since the Constitution was law, and judges interpret the law, it followed that judges should be the ones to interpret the Constitution. Americans always have tended to restate their political quarrels as constitutional quarrels. From the time of the Marshall Court, they became accustomed to restating their constitutional quarrels as legal quarrels to be settled by the Supreme Court.

The Era of "Judicial Supremacy."   The decisions of the Marshall Court went a long way toward confirming the natural association of Court and Constitution. In subsequent periods, the Supreme Court built on this foundation with varying degrees of success. A rather simple-minded historical view pictures the great heyday of the Supreme Court as roughly the period from 1890 to 1930. It is to these four decades that the label "judicial supremacy" has often been applied.[5] The Justices, it is charged, used the Constitution to strike down government actions regulating business and aiding the poor that were not in harmony with their conservative economic and social outlook.

The actual historical pattern is not so cut and dried. It is not really clear that the Justices differed very much from others in government in their political sentiments. Their decisions went both ways; there was a strong preference for free enterprise, but there were also occasional bows toward governmental intervention to correct the malfunctions in what they saw as a fundamentally sound system. About the same mixture is to be found in the legislative and executive branches. For every liberal statute "vetoed"—that is, declared unconstitutional—by the Supreme Court, state governors and presidents vetoed dozens.

Despite complaints about "judicial supremacy" and "judicial tyranny," the history of the Court does not show a single instance in which the Court succeeded

---

[4] 1 Cr. 137 (1803).

[5] Charles G. Haines, *The American Doctrine of Judicial Supremacy,* 2nd ed. (Berkeley: University of California Press, 1959).

over time in preventing a determined people from doing what it wanted to do. Even its defense of free enterprise during the 1890–1930 period reflected rather than opposed the general political sentiment of the day. The Court was, as it always is, one source of political influence and point of access for interest groups. From the 1890s to the late 1930s, it was often most hospitable to business and its sympathizers. Its weight was cast, more often than not, on the conservative side of the struggle over economic regulation. The Court may have delayed, modified, and occasionally deflected social policies, but this was no more than what other government agencies had done. In short, the Court did not stand alone between "the people" and what they allegedly wanted. This is not to say that the Court played no major role in shaping public policy; it is simply an acknowledgement that there is little evidence to show that the Court subverted government by the people.

The Court as One of the Three Branches of Government. The tendency to exaggerate the supremacy of the Court is in large part due to our traditional constitutional belief that the federal government is divided into three great and presumably equal branches. The standard view is that Congress makes the laws, the executive administers them, and the Supreme Court decides individual cases arising under them. The problem is that the standard view is incorrect in a number of fundamental ways.

First of all, as earlier chapters have shown, the American lawmaking process is complex. It involves many different participants from each of the branches and many others from outside government. The mix and the relative contributions of the participants vary from statute to statute. If we began from the reality of the lawmaking process instead of the frozen vision of three great branches, we would quickly see that the Supreme Court participates either very little or not at all in the making of most laws and very much in the making of some.[6]

One brief example will show how small a part the Supreme Court often plays even when it makes a major constitutional pronouncement. Welfare programs had for many years been almost exclusively the business of the states. State legislatures had passed thousands of laws on relief, aid to dependent children, and so on. Beginning in the 1930s, the federal government entered the field, setting standards, making grants to the states, and establishing social security programs. Congress passed dozens of detailed laws. By the 1960s there were increasing demands that the whole welfare program be federalized, with a single, national minimum income guaranteed to every family.

In 170 years of welfare legislation, the Supreme Court had intervened significantly only once. This was in 1937, when it upheld the constitutionality of the Social Security Act. Then, in 1969, the Court struck down state residency requirements for welfare.[7] This was a sweeping decision, which in effect declared that portions of the welfare laws of nearly every state were unconstitutional. It was just the sort of decision that evokes cries of judicial supremacy. The practical effect was to hasten the movement toward uniform national standards. But the Court decision

---

[6] Martin Shapiro, *Law and Politics in the Supreme Court* (New York: Free Press, 1964).

[7] *Shapiro* v. *Thompson,* 394 U.S. 618 (1969).

came only after the movement for national standards was well under way. The Court did not and could not determine what kind of welfare program we should have, how much each family should get, which old programs should be phased out, or how new programs should be financed. A major constitutional intervention by the Supreme Court thus becomes a minor event in the history of welfare law-making. The decision may mean much less to the future shape of welfare programs than a key vote in a House committee or a few paragraphs in a presidential message.

Later in this chapter, we will see that the Supreme Court does exercise more power in some areas than it does in the welfare area. But the problem is always one of discovering how much the Court does in each area. We cannot make blanket statements about *the* power of the Supreme Court.

The temptation often arises to think of the Court as one of those three large and equal squares on the organization chart of American government. This temptation should be met by remembering that the Court's square contains nine men with a few dozen assistants making a few thousand decisions a year, while the other two squares, those of Congress and the president, contain thousands or millions of people making hundreds of thousands of decisions. If the proverbial man from Mars were to descend on Washington and wander around looking at what goes on in the federal government, it might be weeks before he stumbled upon the Supreme Court. The Supreme Court can play a major and even occasionally decisive role in American politics. But nothing about our political system requires or ensures that it ever will play such a role, let alone play it continuously and across all fields of public policy.

SHOULD THE SUPREME COURT ACT?

The Court and Democracy   It has been necessary to say many general things about the nature of the Supreme Court, because the central fact of its political existence has been the debate over whether the Court ought to do anything at all. One side in this debate has been labeled **judicial activism,** the other **judicial self-restraint** or **judicial modesty.**[8] The arguments for and against judicial activism rest largely on the nature of American democracy. The Supreme Court consists of nine persons appointed by the president, confirmed by the Senate, and serving for life. As Table 16.1 shows, Supreme Court Justices do indeed serve for long terms, well beyond the tenure of the presidents who appoint them. The average justice sits on the Court for fifteen years. Their decisions are not subject to formal veto or change by anyone else, with two major exceptions: (1) If the Court rules an action unconstitutional, the Constitution may be amended to change the basis of the deci-

---

[8] The debate over judicial activism and judicial self-restraint is summarized in Alexander M. Bickel, *The Least Dangerous Branch: The Supreme Court at the Bar of Politics* (Indianapolis: Bobbs-Merrill, 1962); Wallace Mendelson, *Justices Black and Frankfurter: Conflict in the Court* (Chicago: University of Chicago Press, 1961); and Martin Shapiro, *Freedom of Speech: The Supreme Court and Judicial Review* (Englewood Cliffs, N.J.: Prentice-Hall, 1966), Chap. 1.

Table 16.1

Years of Service of Supreme Court Justices

Number of Years on the Court	Number of Justices	Percentage of Justices
Less than 4	7	7%
4–8	25	26
9–16	27	28
17–24	18	19
25+	18	19
Total	95	99%

Source: Congressional Quarterly Service, *Congress and the Nation,* Vol. I–III.

sion. For example, the Court's ruling that income taxes were unconstitutional was offset by the Sixteenth Amendment, which specifically permitted taxes on incomes. (2) Likewise, if the Court decides that a particular action is contrary to a law, Congress may change the law to make that action legal. In order to preserve their virtues as third persons, the justices must remain isolated from the normal play of political pressures that make other parts of government responsible and responsive to the people. In other words, the very qualities that establish the Court's independence from "political pressure" also make it "undemocratic."

The crux of the argument against judicial review is that it permits nonelected justices to frustrate democratic government by overruling elected officials. As we have seen in earlier chapters, however, it is unrealistic to believe that elected officials necessarily do what the majority of the public wants, or that they are undemocratic if they do not. We have also seen that many nonelected officials in the executive branch make policy. So the contrast between a democratic, elected Congress and president and a nondemocratic, nonelected Supreme Court is a bit simpleminded.

The standard response of those favoring Supreme Court activism has been that "we the people" who established the Constitution and continue to support it never wanted pure democratic government. They insist that the Constitution itself and the role of the Court in its enforcement are beneficial, popularly approved checks on majorities who might otherwise destroy individual rights and freedoms.

The whole argument about the democracy or nondemocracy of the Court can be put in a clearer perspective by looking at the cases in which the Court has invalidated laws passed by Congress and signed by the president. As we saw earlier, the Court has seldom frustrated a determined majority in the other branches of government. When it did, it rarely was at odds with them for very long. The Court changed its position, the other branches changed theirs, or they accepted what the Court had done. Some of the confrontations have involved a Court whose members were appointed by past presidents and reflected political doctrines that were no longer accepted by contemporary elected officials. Time supplies an inevitable corrective to this sort of conflict. The chances are about five out of six that a president will get an opportunity to make at least one Supreme Court appointment during his first four-year term. Given the fact that the Court decides most controversial questions by five-to-four or six-to-three votes, it does not take long for the Court to react to at least those changes in public sentiment reflected in the outcome of presidential elections. Table 16.2 illustrates this point by depicting the interval between individual appointments to the Supreme Court. It is unusual for more than two years to go by without the president having an opportunity to fill a vacancy on the Court. Nixon, for example, appointed four Justices (who were confirmed by the Senate) in less than three years. Ford named his first Justice after eighteen months in office, while Carter went at least thirty months without appointing anyone to the Court.

The table also shows that occasionally a long period goes by when the membership of the Court is "frozen" and the president has no chance to make his imprint on it. Franklin Roosevelt had to wait four years before he could make his first appointment. In this period there was a crisis in which the Court struck down laws the president wanted and the president threatened the Court. Then a series of retirements, beginning in 1937, gave Roosevelt chance to alter the balance on the Court.

In another sense, too, the Supreme Court does seem to follow the election returns. The Justices depend upon the cooperation of others to have their decisions enforced. The Court's major weapon is the fact that most Americans have a firm commitment to the rule of law. An official who will not obey an order of the Court may be considered a lawbreaker. Of course, other public sentiments may balance or even overwhelm the long-term commitment to the rule of law at various times. After the Court's ban on prayers in public schools, for example, some school systems went right on praying. This illustrates an important fact of life for the Court. The more unpopular the policy embodied in the Court's command, the less the Court can hope to get its policy enforced. The Justices rarely have been willing to invite massive resistance by pressing policies opposed by the public.

Table 16.2

The Interval between Appointments
to the Supreme Court, 1789−1975

Interval in Years	Number of Appointments	Percentage of Total	Cumulative Percentage
Less than 1 year	40	41%	41%
1	23	23	64
2	12	12	76
3	10	10	86
4	6	6	92
5	7	7	99
12	1	1	100
Total	99	100%	100%

The table excludes six Justices appointed in 1789. It includes only Justices who were appointed and confirmed and served on the Court.
Source: Robert A. Dahl, *Pluralist Democracy in the United States* (Chicago: Rand McNally, 1967), p. 157; and Congressional Quarterly Service, *Congress and the Nation*, Vol. I−III.

The Court must call on the executive branch to force compliance with its orders. If, however, those orders encounter nationwide opposition or even indifference, the executive may not cooperate. So at the crucial point of enforcement, the Court is linked to the mainstream of democratic politics.

The Finality of Court Decisions There has been much confusion about the finality of Court decisions because of a failure to distinguish between the Court's role as resolver of disputes between two litigants and its role as a policymaking branch of the government. Let us consider a hypothetical antitrust suit brought by the Baxter Button Company against Superglomerate, Inc. Baxter, a little firm, is trying to force the big corporation to sell a button company that it has recently bought in order to gain 90 percent of the button market. A Supreme Court decision that Superglomerate has violated the antitrust laws and must divest itself of the Bikini Button Company is final and binding on Superglomerate. No other agency of government may block it, change it, or reverse it. As a resolution of the dispute between the two litigants, the Court's decision absolutely and forever determines that Baxter won and Superglomerate lost.

Behind the Court's decision, however, lies a set of policy preferences held by the justices. Let us say that in this instance, they prefer an economy in which there are many small producers and no single giant. The decision does *not* fix this preference for small firms as the final policy of the government. It may encourage some other small firms to sue conglomerates, but that is about all. If other branches of the government do not share the Court's economic preference, the Court can do almost nothing to bring about the type of economy it desires. The Justice Department may be reluctant to prosecute giant firms for antitrust violations, and the Defense Department may actually favor industrial giants in its procurement policies.

The point is not only that the Supreme Court is not so supreme as it sometimes looks. Just as important is the fact that, in order to achieve policy goals, the Justices may need to enlist the cooperation of the whole machinery of politics. They themselves are one cog rather than the final governor of that machinery. Thus, at the very point at which the Court seems to threaten the democratic political process, it becomes most subordinated to that process. Even in the highest constitutional spheres, it is difficult to discover any Supreme Court pronouncement so final that its goals can be obtained without a great deal of cooperation by other political actors. Those actors have the power to withhold that cooperation. They can blunt or redirect the thrust of the Court's policy when it does not enjoy sufficient popular support. This is a decisive democratic check on the Court's activity.

In the next few pages we will show what kinds of people the Justices are and how they are appointed. Then we will describe the work of the Supreme Court and the lower federal courts, the way cases flow up to the Supreme Court, how the Court handles its cases, and what its opinions are like. The last part of the chapter will describe the various roles the Supreme Court plays in the policymaking process.

THE JUSTICES

So far, we have dealt with the Court as if it were a unit. It is time now to recall that it is composed of nine human beings. Detailed examination of the personal characteristics of the Justices who have served in the past half-century reveals little that is surprising. As one might expect, some substantial differences can be seen between the backgrounds of the Justices and those of other political actors, particularly bureaucrats. The Justices are drawn from a wealthier, better educated, more socially prominent level of society than most other officials. Most distinguished lawyers are likely to have had high incomes before reaching the Court. Justices Brandeis, Goldberg, and Marshall, for instance, were themselves members of minority groups. Each had been engaged in legal battles against corporate wealth and governmental power before his elevation to the bench. Yet all were well off.

Only about a quarter of all appointees to the Court had much judicial experience before being named. Almost all had held some kind of political position. They were not necessarily "professional politicians," but it is clear that practice at being a judge counts for far less than exposure to the world of practical politics. The actual work of the Court is so far removed from that of other judges that this lack of judicial experience means little. Few of the Court's most distinguished members were judges of any kind before their appointments.

Considerable ingenuity has been spent attempting to relate the Justices' back-

The Supreme Court in 1979. From left: Associate Justices John Paul Stevens (1975); Lewis F. Powell, Jr. (1971); Harry A. Blackmun (1970); William H. Rehnquist (1971); Thurgood Marshall (1967); and William J. Brennan, Jr. (1957); Chief Justice Warren E. Burger (1969); Associate Justices Potter Stewart (1959); and Byron R. White (1962). The date after each Justice's name is the year in which he took his seat on the court.

grounds to their behavior on the bench. About all that has emerged so far is the obvious — but very important — fact of the shared educational and professional experiences of the Justices. This shared experience leaves them with a common language, allegiance to certain ways of doing business, and some sense of community with other lawyers and judges. We do not know the relative weight of these professional norms compared to their individual political, social, and economic views.[9]

Judicial Attitudes. Most of the Justices have well-developed political outlooks which are expressed in their decisions.[10] These attitudes seem to be arranged along two dimensions. The first concerns the issue of individual freedom versus the power of government. When cases involve a conflict between the two, some Justices seem to side fairly consistently with the government, others with the individual. The second dimension concerns the issues of business versus government and business versus labor. Some Justices are consistently pro-business and some consistently anti-business. In general, the Justices stay well within the limits set by the American ideologies described in Chapter 6 and exhibit about the same mixtures of liberalism and conservatism.

Appointment. Supreme Court Justices are appointed by the president with the advice and consent of the Senate. Most presidents have viewed this as one of their major prerogatives. When a vacancy is created on the Court through death, retirement, or resignation, the president will be flooded with suggestions from other politicians. Normally, the president will delegate to members of the White House staff and/or the attorney general the initial chore of making up a list of candidates. They will conduct a further search for names and then begin to shorten the list. Prospective candidates will be investigated by the FBI and evaluations will be solicited from many sources. At this stage, almost any prominent individual, political organization, or interest group that is not absolutely out of favor with the president may participate. The American Bar Association has sought to assert a right to rate prospective candidates as "qualified" or "not qualified" before their names are submitted to the Senate. Since the Eisenhower administration, however, presidents have been careful to reject such a right, although Justice Department officials may consult the Bar Association informally.[11]

Among the characteristics that may mark a particular lawyer as "eligible" for a Supreme Court appointment are distinguished prior judicial service, high status in the legal profession, personal friendship with the president or special service to him, or identification with a politically powerful interest group. Traditionally, some effort has been made to achieve geographic and religious balance on the Court. Typically, there has been some western, southern, Catholic, and Jewish representation. President Nixon explicitly rejected this tradition, however, and it remains to be seen whether it will be revived. As of this writing, for example, there is no Jewish mem-

---

[9] John R. Schmidhauser, *The Supreme Court* (New York: Holt, Rinehart & Winston, 1960).

[10] Glendon Schubert, *The Judicial Mind: Attitudes and Ideologies of Supreme Court Justices* (Evanston, Ill.: Northwestern University Press, 1965).

[11] Joel Grossman, *Lawyers and Judges: The ABA and the Politics of Judicial Selection* (New York: Wiley, 1965).

ber of the Court. There is, however, one black on the Court and increasing pressure to appoint a woman.

No generalization can be made about the degree of presidential involvement in the final selection. Some presidents have personally selected their nominees; others have delegated virtually the whole appointment power to the attorney general or other aides.[12] President Nixon and many of his predecessors sought quite deliberately to choose Justices whose political values matched their own in the hope of shaping the future policies of the Court.

When the president has determined who his official nominee will be, the name is sent to the Senate Judiciary Committee for hearings. Then there is a general debate on the floor of the Senate and a vote. The Judiciary Committee hearing usually provides a public forum for those opposing an appointment. At this stage, the American Bar Association and other interest groups present their evaluation of the appointee. In general, the Senate has taken the position that the president is entitled to appoint whomever he pleases. However, the Senate did reject two of President Nixon's nominees.

By his appointments a president may shift the direction of the Supreme Court's policies. Yet his power is severely limited by a number of factors. First, it is not easy to predict from past behavior how a person will act as a Supreme Court Justice. Many a "safe" Justice has turned his vote against the policies of the president responsible for his appointment. Second, it is difficult for a president to find acceptable condidates who agree with all his policy views. A Justice appointed because he agrees with the president on "law and order" may differ from the president on race questions or abortion. Third, and perhaps most important, the Court's policies are determined by the interaction of judicial attitudes and existing legal doctrine, not by attitudes alone. The president cannot expect a new appointee rapidly to change legal positions firmly established by his predecessors.

Earl Warren,
Chief Justice from 1954 to 1969.

Wide World

A president's Supreme Court appointments are also likely to have unpredictable consequences. Earl Warren, who gave his name and leadership to the most activist Court in memory (from 1954 to 1969), was the first appointment of President Eisenhower, an advocate of political tranquility. President Nixon campaigned against abortions, yet his appointees joined the Court's seven-to-two majority in striking down state antiabortion laws. Nixon appointed four men to the Court from 1969 through 1971. By 1978, these four Justices were not much of a united bloc on the Court; they voted together in just 36 percent of the cases decided that year.[13] In short, it is wrong to assume that a president's appointees to the Court will reflect his views when deciding cases.

[12] A revealing case study of the appointment of one Justice is presented in David Danelski, *A Supreme Court Justice Is Appointed* (New York: Random House, 1964). A systematic treatment of the whole subject is to be found in Henry J. Abraham, *Justices and Presidents* (New York: Oxford University Press, 1974).

[13] *Newsweek,* October 9, 1978, p. 54.

We have treated the Supreme Court almost as if it lived all alone in its marble palace quite apart from other courts. It is important, however, to have some general understanding of the place of the Supreme Court in the American judicial system (see Figure 16.2).

The bulk of criminal prosecutions and lawsuits between individuals take place in state courts. Only those few that involve a federal constitutional question can move along the line from state supreme court to United States Supreme Court. When a case arises under a federal statute, it will begin in the lower federal courts. And when residents of different states become involved in a legal conflict, they may take their case to a federal district court rather than to the courts of either of their states. The Supreme Court has appellate jurisdiction over all cases, including military courts-martial, that first arise in lower federal courts. Congress, however, has the authority to create or abolish the lower federal courts and to determine what classes of appeals from them the Supreme Court may or may not hear. In short, subject to congressional limitations, the Supreme Court supervises all the work of the federal courts, but only those state court decisions that involve national constitutional issues.

The Lower Federal Courts   The ninety-four district courts are the basic trial courts of the federal judicial system. Each state has at least one district, and some larger states are divided into as many as four. There are from one to twenty-four judges in a district, each of whom usually holds court alone. In 1979, after a major expansion of the federal judiciary, there were 517 federal district judges.

Above the district courts in the judicial hierarchy are the eleven courts of appeals. Each of them hears appeals from the district courts within its circuit. The geography of the eleven circuits is shown in Figure 16.1. (The individual appeals courts are often referred to by their number: the Fifth Circuit, the Ninth Circuit, and so on.) There are 132 circuit court judges, of whom thirty-five were appointed to newly created posts in 1979. Court of appeals decisions normally are rendered by three-judge panels named by the chief judge of the circuit. Cases of unusual importance, however, may be decided by all the judges of a given circuit sitting together (sitting *en banc*). District court cases normally reach the Supreme Court only after having been reviewed by a court of appeals. Another major job of these courts is to hear appeals from the legal decisions of federal administrative agencies and regulatory commissions.

The Supreme Court supervises the lower federal courts in a number of ways, apart from its powers of constitutional interpretation. Its most important supervisory function derives from the fact that the Supreme Court is ultimately responsible for national uniformity in interpreting federal law. In the course of deciding thousands of cases each year, the lower federal courts must declare what many different federal statutes mean — that is, how their relatively general words relate to specific cases. The courts of appeal try to eliminate conflicts among their own district courts, but some courts of appeal will interpret a given statute one way and others another. The Supreme Court must settle these differences, to be sure that a federal law

Figure 16.1
Judicial Circuits of the United States Courts
of Appeals

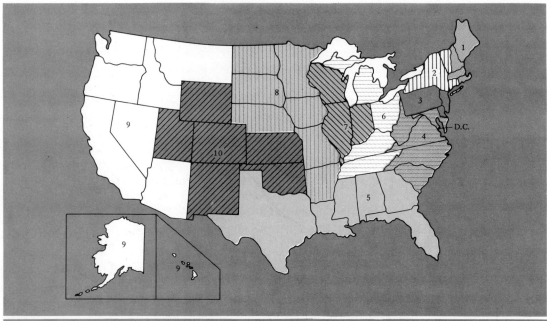

See Richard E. Cohen, "Picking the U.S. Attorneys—Patronage or Perfection?" *National Journal,* July 2, 1977, p. 1038.

means the same thing in Seattle that it does in Miami. As a result, much of the Supreme Court's own lawmaking is done in the process of settling conflicts between lower federal courts regarding the meaning of a particular statute.

Appointment of Federal Judges. In Chapter 15 we saw that department heads rarely have much say in choosing most of their subordinates. The Supreme Court is in the same position with its judicial subordinates. Appointments to the lower federal courts are made for life by the president, with the advice and consent of the Senate. When one or both senators from the state where a district court appointment is to be made are of the same party as the president, they will submit a short list of prospective candidates to the Justice Department. At the same time, the Justice Department may make its own list of candidates, although it knows it has little hope of gaining Senate confirmation of its choice if the senator involved is opposed. The final presidential nomination usually goes to that one of the candidates suggested by the senator whom the Justice Department likes best. When neither senator from the state belongs to the president's party, the recommendations come from members of the House or other state politicians, usually those with good White House relationships. The administration usually has more to

FEDERAL PROSECUTORS

The job of prosecuting cases in the district courts is done by the United States attorney for each district, assisted by a staff of lawyers. U.S. attorney is a patronage post that reflects the political sensitivity of many law enforcement decisions. Attorneys are appointed to four-year terms by the president, with the advice and consent of the Senate. Because Senate confirmation is required, a president usually names the person recommended by the senator from his party, or makes the appointment from a list provided by the senator. During the 1976 campaign, candidate Jimmy Carter said, "All federal judges and prosecutors should be appointed strictly on the basis of merit, without any consideration of political aspects or influence." After Carter was elected, however, many U.S. attorneys appointed by Ford or Nixon were asked to resign, or fired if they refused. Defending this process, the Attorney General, Griffin B. Bell, said: "We had an election last November and the Democrats won." This observation captures more of the reality than Carter's campaign rhetoric.

say about appointments to the circuit courts, each of which covers at least three states.

The overwhelming majority of federal judges come from the president's party, as Table 16.3 shows. About half of district judges, and a higher proportion of circuit judges, usually have rendered important services to their parties as candidates, campaign managers, and the like, before appointment. Attorney General Bell, who was named to a federal court in 1961, explained his appointment this way:

> For me, becoming a federal judge wasn't very difficult. I managed John F. Kennedy's presidential campaign in Georgia. Two of my oldest and closest friends were the two Senators from Georgia. And I was campaign manager and special, unpaid counsel for the governor. It doesn't hurt to be a good lawyer either.[14]

The tendency of presidents to appoint only members of their own party probably has some effect on the collective policy decisions of the federal courts. It does not mean, however, that the judges are the servants of the president or the party that appointed them. John Sirica, the judge whose determined prodding of the Watergate burglars finally resulted in the resignation of President Nixon, was named to the bench by President Eisenhower, a Republican. The federal judge in New York who refused to halt publication of the Pentagon Papers as demanded by the Nixon administration had been named to his post by President Nixon only a few days earlier.

The importance of political considerations in naming federal judges naturally led to demands that the process be based solely on "merit." By the late 1970s a

---

[14] Quoted in Richard E. Cohen, "Choosing Federal Judges — The Senate Keeps Control," *National Journal,* March 3, 1979, p. 355.

Table 16.3

Characteristics of Appointees to Federal Judgeships, 1963–1978

	District Courts				Appeals Courts			
	CARTER NOMINEES*	FORD APPOINTEES	NIXON APPOINTEES	JOHNSON APPOINTEES	CARTER NOMINEES*	FORD APPOINTEES	NIXON APPOINTEES	JOHNSON APPOINTEES
Occupation								
Politics/gov't	4.4%	21.2%	10.7%	21.3%	–	8.3%	4.4%	10.0%
Judiciary	42.2	34.6	28.5	31.1	41.7%	75.0	53.3	57.5
Large law firm	40.0	34.6	39.7	21.3	25.0	16.7	24.4	20.0
Moderate size firm	2.2	5.8	11.7	4.9	16.7	–	6.7	2.5
Solo or small firm	8.9	3.9	6.7	18.0	–	–	2.2	7.5
Other	2.2	–	2.8	3.3	16.7	–	8.9	2.5
Experience								
Judicial	46.7	42.3	35.1	34.3	58.3	75.0	57.8	65.0
Prosecutorial	33.3	50.0	41.9	45.8	41.7	25.0	46.7	47.5
Neither	33.3	30.8	36.3	33.6	25.0	25.0	17.8	20.0
Party								
Democrat	95.6	21.2	7.8	94.8	91.7	8.3	6.7	95.0
Republican	4.4	78.8	92.2	5.2	–	91.7	93.3	5.0
None	–	–	–	–	8.3	–	–	–
Party activism	53.3	50.0	48.6	48.4	75.0	58.3	60.0	57.5
Race								
White	91.1	90.4	97.2	96.7	66.7	100.0	97.8	95.0
Black	8.9	5.8	2.8	3.3	25.0	–	–	5.0
Asian-American	–	3.9	–	–	8.3	–	2.2	–
Sex								
Male	86.7	98.1	99.4	98.4	100.0	100.0	100.0	97.5
Female	13.3	1.9	0.6	1.6	–	–	–	2.5
Total number of nominees or appointees	45	52	179	122	12	12	45	40

*Through August 27, 1978.

Source: Judicature magazine, reprinted in National Journal, November 25, 1978, p. 1918.

handful of senators were experimenting with citizen nominating commissions that would recommend the "best" candidates without regard to politics. As we have seen, candidate Jimmy Carter had come out strongly for "merit" and against "politics." But once he got to the White House, he met the brute fact that the Senate dominates the appointment process for district judges. What is more, if a Democratic senator from the state of a prospective district judge dislikes the president's nominee, the Senate Judiciary Committee will not recommend confirmation. Carter decided not to consider anyone for a district judgeship who was not recommended by the relevant senator (or senators) or by a nominating commission appointed by the senator(s).[15] Carter publicly urged senators to appoint nominating commissions. With the president's strong encouragement, this technique became far more popular. About half the 117 district judgeships created in 1978 will be filled with the help of nominating commissions.[16]

Reflecting political changes in the 1970s, another consideration besides judicial merit came to public attention: How many minority and women judges would be appointed? It turned out that this goal often clashed with merit selection. A number of controversies erupted when nominating commissions produced lists of white males. Indeed, "politics" often seemed a better route to affirmative action than "merit." In the first few months of filling the new judgeships, almost half the female and minority nominees came from two states whose senators had kept the recommending power in their own hands rather than appoint nominating commissions.[17] The end result was more women and minority judges than before, but fewer than organizations representing these groups would like.

Senators have less to do with appointing circuit judges. Carter appointed a nominating commission for each of the eleven circuits, with heavy minority and female membership. It seemed likely that thirteen to fifteen of the thirty-five new circuit judges would be women or members of racial minorities. This was quite a change from the two blacks and one woman on the circuit court bench when Carter took office.[18]

Policymaking in the District and Circuit Courts   Of all federal courts, the Supreme Court is far and away the most important. Yet, particularly in recent years, the district and circuit courts have become increasingly important policymakers. After announcing its school desegregation policy in 1954, the Supreme Court took very few school desegregation cases. It has been the district and circuit courts that have determined the pace of desegregation and have worked out each city's specific desegregation plan. Relations between the courts and the executive branch agencies and regulatory commissions are governed by a set of congressional and court-made rules called **administrative law.** Since 1970, most of the basic changes in administrative law have been made by the circuit courts; the Supreme Court has

---

[15] Cohen, "Choosing Federal Judges," p. 356.

[16] *Congressional Quarterly Weekly Report,* November 11, 1978, p. 3313.

[17] *CQ Weekly Report,* February 3, 1979, p. 189.

[18] Richard E. Cohen, "A Step in the Right Direction," *National Journal,* May.5, 1979, p. 747.

chosen to say little. Decisions of the Warren Court greatly expanded the habeas corpus jurisdiction of the federal courts. (Habeas corpus is explained in Chapter 4.) As a result, federal district courts have been hearing many more cases that normally would be tried wholly in state courts and then moved from state supreme court to the Supreme Court. The Burger Court has been cutting back on the tendency of the Warren Court to make federal courts available earlier and more often to individuals in conflict with their states.[19]

One of the most important increases in the policymaking of the lower federal courts has occurred because Congress has been passing more laws creating federal statutory rights enforceable in federal courts.[20] The various civil rights statutes forbidding discrimination against racial and linguistic minorities, women, the aged, and the handicapped have created a whole new federal legal world. Almost any American who is denied housing, fired, not hired, or denied a government benefit can now sue somebody for discrimination in a federal court. The Environmental Protection Act and other environmental and consumer protection statutes also give many people access to the federal courts to push their policy preferences. Many interest groups make frequent use of these statutes to block or slow down all sorts of government and private projects they do not like by going to court and seeking **injunctions** against them (an injunction is a court order forbidding someone to do something). Both government agencies and large businesses now assume that almost any major piece of construction or any major change in operation will be the subject of lawsuits in the federal courts.

In the long run, the policymaking powers of the lower federal courts in these statutory areas will probably decline. Remember that if a law is vague or very generally worded, those who administer it exercise much policymaking power as they fill in its specific meaning. That has been what the lower federal courts have been doing with many new federal statutes for the last dozen years. As statutes are around longer, their meaning becomes more settled: Congress amends them to make them more precise. The Supreme Court issues decisions interpreting them. The lower courts themselves build up a body of past decisions saying what they mean. The more the meaning of the statutes is filled in by amendment and administrative and judicial interpretation, the less leeway a court has to put in new meanings in new decisions. Urged on by the litigation of interest groups, the federal district and circuit courts have been very busy in the past twenty years making policy by giving specific meaning to many new statutes. (See the discussion of litigation as an interest group tactic in Chapter 10.)

Routes to the Supreme Court The Supreme Court does not issue general or advisory opinions. It acts only where a genuine legal case or controversy exists. Because some kinds of public policy simply cannot be made into issues for

---

[19] Periods of the Court's history are often referred to by the name of the Chief Justice. Chief Justice Warren was followed by Chief Justice Burger in 1969.

[20] A federal *statutory* right is one created by a law (statute) passed by Congress. Blind persons, for instance, have a statutory right to a federal check each month because Congress has enacted a law providing for assistance to the blind. A *constitutional* right is one created by the Constitution itself. The right to freedom of speech is a consitutional right created by the First Amendment.

Figure 16.2
Routes to the Supreme Court

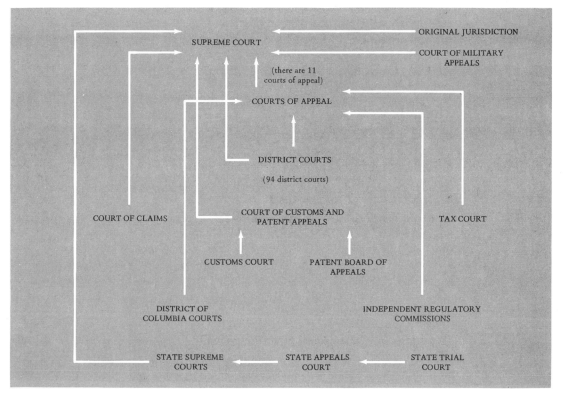

litigation, there are areas in which the Supreme Court is not a suitable forum for settling the issues. For instance, opponents of the war in Vietnam never managed to wrap the issue up in a case that the Court would have to decide.

There are two basic routes to the Supreme Court. The first involves cases that arise under federal statutes. As we have seen, where violation of a federal statute is alleged, the trial will take place in a federal district court. If the district court's decision is appealed, the appeal will usually go to a court of appeal. If the decision of a court of appeals or of a three-judge district court is appealed, the appeal goes to the Supreme Court. Such appeals may be on the ground that the lower federal court has misinterpreted the federal statute; that the federal statute was unconstitutional; or that the trial court proceedings themselves violated the Constitution or federal rules of procedure.

The second route is through the state courts. Where a violation of state law is alleged, the trial will be in a state court. One of the parties at that trial may allege that the state law in question violates the U.S. Constitution or that something about the state trial itself violates the U.S. Constitution. After an issue of violation of the Constitution has been raised in a state trial court, that court will decide on it. If the state trial court's judgment on the U.S. constitutional issue is appealed, then state appeals courts will redecide it. If the *state* supreme court decides an issue of the violation of the U.S. Constitution, then that decision may be appealed to the U.S. Supreme Court in Washington.[21] Either a decision of a state supreme court upholding the constitutionality of a state law under the U.S. Constitution, or one striking down the state law as a violation of the U.S. Constitution, may be appealed to the U.S. Supreme Court. Where a case involves only *state* law and *state* constitution, it stays entirely in *state* courts. Only if a violation of the *U.S.* Constitution is alleged in a state proceeding may the case move from the state supreme court to the U.S. Supreme Court.

We have consistently used the word "appeal" here. Technically there is a distinction between cases that come to the Supreme Court on appeal and those that come on *certiorari*. In theory, the Supreme Court must hear appeals, but has discretion to hear or refuse to hear cases brought on certiorari. It is not worth explaining the technicalities here, however, because in fact the Court exercises just about as much discretion in deciding whether to hear appeals as it does in deciding whether to hear certiorari cases. If the Court refuses to hear a case, the decision of the last court to decide it before it reached the Supreme Court stands.

The Constitution also gives the Supreme Court **original jurisdiction**—that is, makes it the trial rather than an appeals court in a few classes of cases. Of these, suits between two states or between a state and the United States are about the only important ones.

The Workload of the Court

The Court's time is scarce. We have already seen this problem in dealing with Congress and the president. We have seen how elaborate practices have been developed in these parts of government to reduce the claims for attention to a number small enough to be handled by the human beings involved. The Judiciary Act of 1925 provides the Court with an opportunity for similar selection of cases. The act, in effect, provides that the Justices may choose the cases they wish to hear and the ones on which they wish to take no action.

Despite this discretionary control of their own time, the workload of the Justices is enormous, as Table 16.4 reveals. The data on petitions dismissed or denied clearly shows that just deciding which cases to decide would absorb most of the Justices' time if they did not adopt further time-saving measures. The Court currently has an administrative staff barely large enough to keep its paperwork straight. It has no research staff, no enforcement personnel, and no one to whom it may assign any of its formal tasks of judging. Each Justice does have from one to three law clerks, who are recent law school graduates. Customarily, as student editors of their school's law review, they have experience in legal research and writing. The clerks play a major role in selecting from the thousands of petitions those the Court will

---

[21] Those who do not promptly seek to appeal their state convictions to state supreme courts may later appeal by filing writs of habeas corpus in federal district courts. Such writs may allege that a prisoner is being illegally held because his state conviction violated the U.S. Constitution. Many cases involving the rights of accused persons reach the Supreme Court on appeal from district court decisions on these habeas corpus proceedings rather than along the normal route from state trial court to state supreme court to U.S. Supreme Court.

Table 16.4

Final Disposition of Cases by the Supreme Court

	1969 Term	1971 Term	1973 Term	1975 Term	1977 Term
By written opinion or per curiam decision	220	449	527	356	278
By dismissal, denial, or withdrawal, of appeals, petitions for certiori, or other application	3137	3196	3349	3716	3576
Total disposed	3357	3645	3876	4072	3854
Remaining on docket for disposal in the next term	793	888	1203	955	850

Source: Harvard Law Review.

finally consider. The Court has developed a set of "cues" for rapidly sorting out which cases it wants to hear. For instance, the Court will almost always hear a case in which a court of appeals has reversed the decision of a regulatory commission.[22]

Even after the selection process is completed, the workload is large. The Court does have a number of major labor-saving devices, however. The most important is the adversary proceeding itself. Each of the lawyers for the two litigants submits a written brief, and each makes oral arguments summarizing the factual and legal arguments for his side and rebutting those of the other. The Court also frequently permits *amicus curiae* (friend of the court) briefs to be filed by other interested groups or government agencies that are not actually litigants. Instead of doing research itself, the Court forces the litigants to finance extensive research out of their own pockets as each competes with the other to make a better case for its position and then to present the results in a form readily comprehensible by the Justices. (The word *brief*, however, is misleading. Such briefs, with their supporting appendices, frequently run into hundreds of pages.)

The Court's decisions take the form of an order to a lower court or a government agency to carry out the mandate of the Court. If any follow-up work has to be done, such as preparing detailed plans in school desegregation suits or spelling out the detailed rules to be followed for the registration of stock certificates, one of the Court's "subordinates" becomes responsible for it.

In view of all this, it is not clear that the Court actually is any more seriously overburdened than Congress or the president. Proposals to create subinstitutions to

[22] Joseph Tanenhaus et al., "The Supreme Court's Certiorari Jurisdiction: Cue Theory," in Glendon Schubert, ed., *Judicial Decision Making* (New York: Free Press, 1963).

take over part of the load have been made for the Court, but nothing has come of them yet. And a number of the Justices have denied that the workload has gotten beyond them.

The Decision-Making Process If any four Justices wish to accept a case, it is placed on the calendar for oral argument. After their written briefs have been submitted, the attorneys in each case present the main points of their arguments orally to the Court. Sitting together on the bench, the Justices listen to these arguments and often interrupt with questions. Each Friday they customarily discuss the cases they have heard that week. As each case is taken up, each Justice speaks in turn, the Chief Justice first and then the others in order of seniority. Here the Chief Justice can exercise leadership through his opening remarks, which can set the tone for the discussion that follows. After voting is completed, if the Chief Justice is in the majority, he assigns the writing of a draft "opinion of the court" to one of the majority. If the Chief Justice is in the minority, the senior Justice of the majority assigns the opinion.

These opinions are then circulated among all the Justices, who make suggestions for changes and improvements. Justices use this device to indicate what they object to, what is most important, and what will have to be modified in order to gain their votes. Although these marginal notes are kept confidential, we know enough about them to conclude that this procedure for circulating opinions is a vehicle for internal bargaining on the Court. The extent to which the final opinion reflects the comments of the other Justices depends partly on their rational power—and partly on the internal politics of the Court on that case. A final opinion of the Court usually carries the signatures of five or more Justices. As a result it may be less a tightly reasoned statement of policy than the kind of vague, internally contradictory compromise that so often emerges from committees. We have repeatedly seen bargaining in connection with parties, Congress, and the executive branch. It is hardly surprising to find it on the Court, where the same policy issues are presented and many of the same attitudes, values, and ideologies are involved.

Since the 1950s, few of the major constitutional decisions of the Supreme Court have been unanimous or even nearly so. The Justices are clearly not working very hard at internal bargaining. Or at least they do not go much beyond the level of bargaining necessary to get a simple majority behind one outcome or the other. Yet there are a few instances in which the Justices clearly do put up a united front. From 1954, when *Brown* v. *Board of Education* was decided, until 1970, all of the Court's school desegregation decisions were unanimous. The Court was also unanimous in *United States* v. *Nixon* (1974). Nixon's own appointee, Chief Justice Burger, wrote the opinion ordering the president to turn over the Watergate

Warren E. Burger, appointed Chief Justice in 1969.

Wide World

tapes to a federal district court. The release of the tapes then provided such damning evidence of presidential involvement in the Watergate coverup that Mr. Nixon was forced to resign.

SUPREME COURT OPINIONS

All the behavior of the Supreme Court is verbal behavior. About the only visible traces of the Court's activities are its opinions, printed in the official and commercial reports.[23] Other political actors interact with the Court by reading and interpreting those opinions and trying to get the Court to change them. Opinions must be written *to* somebody; they are messages, not simply the embalmed record which scholars later resurrect for study of what the Court did. To whom are these messages sent? We can distinguish seven distinct audiences for the Court's opinions.

1. *The two litigants.* An opinion is an explanation and justification of why the Court decided for one and not the other.

2. *Other similarly situated persons and their lawyers.* By explaining why the Court decided as it did in a particular case, the opinion is supposed to help others predict how it would decide similar cases in the future. Then they can conduct their future affairs legally — that is, in such a way as to avoid losing in future litigation.

3. *Lower courts and administrators.* The opinion gives directions to those officials supervised by the Court as to how they are to decide similar matters in the future.

4. *Law teachers and other Court watchers.* The opinion is supposed to demonstrate that the Court has followed the canons of legal craftsmanship taught in the law schools, thus preserving legal standards.

5. *The other participants in the lawmaking process.* The opinion registers the Court's policy position and seeks to recruit support and to disarm opposition.

6. *The publics.* We deliberately use the plural "publics" because all the data we have on public reaction to the Supreme Court suggests that it is confronted with a number of separate special issue publics rather than a single body of public opinion. For example, the law teachers and court watchers mentioned above constitute one issue public, concerned with the issue of the Court's craftsmanship — with whether it makes good legal arguments. Other publics focus on specific policy issues. There is a patent public, a labor relations public, a criminal justice public, and so on, composed both of lawyers who specialize in those areas and ordinary people whose interests are immediately

---

[23] The reports are published in three forms: *United States Reports,* which is the official version from the Government Printing Office; and *The Supreme Court Reporter* and *United States Supreme Court, Lawyers' Edition,* both from commercial publishers. *United States Law Week* and the *Supreme Court Bulletin* print the opinions in a looseleaf format a week or so after they have been issued by the Court.

concerned. Yet most lawyers do not read the Court's opinions at all, and even the most concerned citizens hear about them from their lawyers rather than reading them themselves. As is the case with most other political actors, the Court reaches the more general levels of the public through a series of intermediaries, including the press. Thus, the general level of public response seems to be determined less by the Court's specific words and deeds than by the general evolution of events and states of the world with which the Court is identified.

7. *The Justices themselves.* As we have seen, the drafting and redrafting of opinions is a vehicle for reaching agreement on the Court. In this sense, the various paragraphs of many opinions are quite literally written for one Justice or another in order to gain a vote.

Once the multiple audience to which opinions are necessarily directed is understood, it is easier to see why the Court's opinions are criticized so frequently even by those who admire it as an institution. In theory, at least, it would seem best in addressing audiences 1 through 4 to write very clear, precise, complete opinions that define and take a firm stand on the legal issues. The loser (in audience 1) will then be satisfied that the law—not the Court's partiality—made him lose. Other potential litigants (audience 2) will be able to predict the Court's future decisions. Clear and precise commands give bureaucratic subordinates less room to evade and maneuver. Therefore, to the extent that lower courts and administrators (audience 3) are subordinate to the Supreme Court, clear opinions mean better discipline. The law professors and other Court watchers (audience 4) will give the Court high grades for professionalism.

For audiences 5, 6, and 7, however, vaguely worded, incomplete opinions that fall short of deciding all the issues will frequently be desirable. The need to gain the cooperation, or at least the neutrality, of others frequently makes it desirable for American politicians to avoid premature commitments, dramatic confrontations, and rigid insistence on all-or-nothing positions. For this reason, the Supreme Court frequently must avoid issuing opinions that unnecessarily antagonize other lawmakers (audience 5).[24] Like other political actors, the Court often wants to keep its options open, and this frequently requires opinions that do not neatly answer all the questions raised by the case. Much the same can be said for the Court's relations with the publics (audience 6). Like any other political actor faced with multiple publics, the Court must seek to issue messages that appeal to more than one public. As a result, it often gets accused, sometimes rightly, of resorting to double talk. For instance, it may seek to placate churchgoers by declaring that ours is a religious nation, while appealing to the libertarian by saying that school prayers violate the Constitution. Finally, the Court's vagueness often results from demands placed on it by audience 7—itself. The bargaining process used to reach a decision sometimes means that only an equivocal compromise decision is possible.

It is no wonder, then, that along with the endless debate about how much the

---

[24] On this and other problems of judicial strategy, see Walter Murphy, *Elements of Judicial Strategy* (Chicago: University of Chicago Press, 1973).

Court should do, there has been continuous complaining about the quality of the Court's opinions. Those opinions cannot possibly satisfy all the contradictory demands made on them.

THE ROLES OF THE SUPREME COURT

Chapter 4 dealt with civil rights and liberties and the Court's role in maintaining and protecting them. At that point we noted that such rights and liberties were also part of the policy output of American politics. It is no more possible to catalog all the Supreme Court's contributions to this public policy output than it is to catalog the contributions of Congress or the president in the space available to us here. Nor do we have space to survey the nonconstitutional business of the Court in which it interprets statutes involving every area of policy in which the federal government is active. In the discussion that follows, each area of the Court's constitutional concern will be briefly indicated and a specific example or two offered. The examples are chosen not only to illustrate the substance of the Court's work, but to indicate the wide variety of political contexts in which the Court acts and the various weights its acts may have in the political process.

Maintaining Constitutional Boundaries   Even those who are most reluctant to have the Court do anything have usually conceded its authority to police the boundaries between the central government and the states, and between president, Congress, and Supreme Court. In a way this is odd, because it is precisely in these areas that the Court is likely to arrive at the most dramatic face-to-face confrontations with other major political actors. The potential for head-on conflict can be seen in the steel seizure case. During the Korean war, President Truman seized control of a steel mill whose workers were on strike. After examining the president's constitutional powers as commander-in-chief and those granted to him by congressional statute, the Court held the seizure invalid. The president chose to obey the Court, but it is not at all clear what would have happened if he had refused to do so.

Defender of Civil Liberties   The Court is now so identified with the defense of various personal liberties that one has to stop and remind oneself that it really did not get into that business in a major way until the 1930s.[25] The freedoms of speech and religion and the right to privacy that are described in Chapter 4 have largely been shaped by the Supreme Court.

The story is not, however, an entirely positive one. In the first place the Court is not always obeyed, particularly when its decisions are controversial. Undoubtedly its greatest problems in this area have involved the question of religion in the public

[25] Henry J. Abraham, *Freedom and the Court* (New York: Oxford University Press, 1967); and Samuel Krislov, *The Supreme Court and Political Freedom* (New York: Free Press, 1968).

schools. We have a clear, well-documented record of the impact of Supreme Court decisions in this field.[26] Detailed investigations of the patterns of compliance to these decisions indicate the following:

1. Relatively few of the local officials involved, including lawyers, actually read the opinions.

2. Disobedience, however, was not the result of ignorance of the Court's decisions. Noncompliers knew at least as much about the decision as compliers did.

3. The attitudes and policy goals of individual school officials, teachers, and the attorneys counseling them were an important factor influencing compliance.

4. Compliance was greatest in those sections of the country where religious instruction was a traditional requirement embodied in old state statutes. It was weakest in areas, particularly in the Midwest, where such programs were optional to the local districts.

In other words, the Court was most successful where its ruling swept away a practice that had been preserved simply by the existence of an old law rather than by active community interest. It seems safe to conclude that the Court's opinions did not operate as overwhelming orders. They were simply an additional element injected into the community scene that altered the balance of pro- and anti-religion forces without necessarily being decisive in its own right.

In many instances the Court itself severely limits the reach of civil liberties. In freedom of speech cases, for instance, it uses a "balancing" approach. Under this approach, laws that limit freedom of speech are held to be constitutional if they serve a public interest strong enough to outweigh the interest in freedom of speech. Thus, the Court upheld the Smith Act, which makes it a crime to advocate the overthrow of the government by force, on the grounds that our interest in national security outweighed the speech interests of those who advocated overthrow.

The Court and Rights of the Accused Closely related to other individual freedoms are the rights associated with the criminal law process. This area is particularly appropriate for examining the Court's ability to maneuver and to start positive governmental programs.

From the 1880s until well into the 1960s, the Court enforced the most rigorous standards on its own federal subordinates, but took no responsibility for the states. This tactic allowed the Supreme Court to institute a pilot program of federal reform. Such a program was protected from the storm of resistance it would have encountered had the Justices attempted to impose their standards on state criminal law procedures. Because most criminal law enforcement is handled by the states,

---

[26] See Theodore L. Becker and Malcolm M. Feeley, eds., *The Impact of Supreme Court Decisions,* 2nd ed. (New York: Oxford University Press, 1973); and Stephen L. Wasby, *The Impact of the United States Supreme Court* (Homewood, Ill.: Dorsey Press, 1970).

even people most opposed to "coddling criminals" could not get too excited about experiments conducted only in the federal arena.

Confining itself to the federal sphere, the Court slowly progressed. It introduced such "revolutionary" reforms as guaranteeing defense counsel to those who could not afford it, refusing to admit illegally seized evidence at trial, and insisting that prisoners be promptly arraigned rather than held secretly for days and even weeks by the police. It seems to have hoped to influence state courts by its example—which in fact it did. By the late 1930s, many state criminal law systems were substantially reformed. As a result, great differences existed between the way accused persons were treated by the federal courts and the most advanced state courts on the one hand, and the worst state courts on the other. Quite naturally, this situation led to the feeling that something unconstitutional must be going on somewhere.

In the early 1940s, the Court sought to combine this feeling with its strategic decision to avoid the massive reform of state practices. It invented something called the **fair trial rule.** That rule declared that although the Court would not impose detailed regulations on the states, it would invalidate state convictions resulting from trials that violated "our fundamental concepts of ordered liberties." The fair trial rule kept the Court out of most state business, and at the same time gave it latitude to nudge and nibble at state injustices. The idea was to avoid imposing rules on the states while educating them into cleaning up their own problems.

Unfortunately, a large number of the states refused to learn. By the 1950s, the disparities between the federal system and the worst state practices were still very great. In response to this problem, the Court slowly shifted from the fair trial rule to the much stronger doctrine of **selective incorporation.** As early as 1925, the Court had suggested that although the freedom of speech provisions of the First Amendment did not apply directly to the states, they might be "incorporated" into the due process clause of the Fourteenth Amendment. If so, they would be binding on the states. Now, one after another, the Court incorporated most of the criminal law guarantees of the Bill of Rights. In this way, the Supreme Court federalized the state criminal law process. So we have here not only an example of the Court's role in protecting liberties, but also of its role in adjusting federal relationships. In this instance it greatly increased federal control by increasing its own control over state courts.

This is a good example of the Court using its negative powers to initiate positive programs. By invalidating all convictions in which poor defendants were not offered legal counsel, the Court forced many communities to finance public defender offices. The alternative was to let go everyone who could not afford a lawyer. The Court really acted as positively as a state legislature that passed a statute requiring the establishment of such offices. Nevertheless, as with most other programs, it is clear that the Court cannot do the whole job. The thorough reform of the criminal law process the Justices desire can be obtained only through a wide range of initiatives, from better police training through more efficient criminal court procedures to vastly improved correctional programs. Only a fraction of these reforms can be made directly by the Supreme Court.

The Court and Elections   Enough has been said about elections to make clear our belief that there is no single, ideal electoral mechanism, and that every alteration in the mechanism may favor some interests and harm others. In a series of cases in the 1960s, the Court came to grips with the electoral process and imposed a constitutional requirement that legislative districts be of equal population.

Several points are dramatically illustrated by the reapportionment cases. First, the Court is deeply involved in politics. The reapportionment decisions did shift political power from people living in rural areas to those in suburbs and central cities. Second, the Court is in a position to do things that the popularly elected branches are incapable of doing. It was absurd to expect state legislators, who owed their own seats to malapportionment, to reform themselves out of office. But the Court could act in this area. Although its reapportionment decisions raised a storm of political protest, the Court met the protest effectively under the banner of "one person–one vote." The opposition to the Court eventually was silenced because most Americans saw one person–one vote as an obviously correct principle of democratic government.

Race Relations   The Court's activities in behalf of black Americans are surely the central phenomena of its post-World War II existence. The decision in the famous case of *Brown* v. *Board of Education,* which prohibited separate schools for blacks and whites, raises a number of key problems in evaluating the work of the Court.[27] The major issue we examine here revolves around what Charles Black calls the *legitimating role* of the Court.[28] Too many discussions of the Supreme Court focus on its power to declare laws *un*constitutional. The Court rarely exercises that power. Most of the time it finds that the laws before it *are* constitutional. This is not simply a neutral act, but the addition of some margin of legitimacy to the law at issue. It is a kind of constitutional blessing added to the legitimacy the statute has already acquired in its passage through Congress.

This legitimating role was particularly important in the school segregation case. The Supreme Court did not invent the southern practice of legally enforced segregation. It had given it constitutional legitimacy in 1896 when it declared that "separate but equal" facilities met the equal protection requirements of the Fourteenth Amendment.[29] Thus, if the Court had sidestepped the issue in the *Brown* case, it would have been continuing to legitimate most segregation. Those who have criticized the boldness of the *Brown* decision rarely face up to the problem of just how the Justices could have legitimated segregation in 1954 and still lived with their consciences as judges and as political leaders.

In the last analysis, the crucial issue may be political leadership. By 1954, the majority of Americans were opposed in principle to legally enforced segregation. But this sentiment was not focused in ways that would move Congress or the presi-

---

[27] 347 U.S. 483 (1954).

[28] Charles L. Black, Jr., *The People and the Court* (New York: Macmillan, 1960).

[29] *Plessey* v. *Ferguson,* 163 U.S. 537 (1896).

The most dramatic dismantling of a dual school system came in Little Rock, Arkansas, where federal troops were used to place black children in a previously segregated school.

dent. The Court could and did focus it. Perhaps even more important, the *Brown* decision gave tremendous impetus to the process through which racial minorities trained themselves to make the kinds of self-conscious, specific demands that lead to legislative and executive action. It was only in the aftermath of *Brown* that Congress finally began to pass significant civil rights legislation and the executive began to take major steps toward the goal of racial equality.

This is a good point to note the Court's special relation not only to racial equality but also to equality in a much more general sense. Equality has always been a part of the American ideology. In the past it has been balanced by other important American values, but in recent years Americans seem to have become particularly sensitive to issues involving equality. The Supreme Court has been a principal promoter for this sentiment. In the three major areas in which it has intervened — legislative apportionment, equal criminal justice, and desegregation — it has done so under the banner of equality. The Court also has moved against racial discrimination in voting, jury selection, and other important areas of government activity.

The Court and   The standard historical cliché about the Court is that it served
Economic Rights   as the principal protector of the interests of business against
government from the 1890s until 1937, when it finally ap-
proved New Deal legislation to regulate business.[80] Earlier in this chapter, we saw
that this cliché is partly wrong. It is true, however, that after 1937, many Justices
and commentators argued that the Court should not defend economic rights. Instead it should concentrate on civil rights and liberties. But the Court did not stop
protecting economic rights after 1937; what it did was stop protecting some people's economic rights and start protecting those of others. It greatly reduced its protection of private property rights and particularly the economic rights of business. It
began protecting economic rights that take the form of receiving government benefits. The old Court said a person could not be deprived of property rights or profits
without due process of law. The new Court increasingly says a person may not be
deprived of a government job or welfare check, or other things he or she has a right
to expect from government, without due process of law. The Court may pretend
that its cases somehow involve individual liberties rather than economic rights, but
there is no more economic right than the right to receive a salary or a government
check that pays the grocery bills.

THE COURT TODAY: AN OVERVIEW

During the early 1970s, the federal courts, and the Supreme Court in particular,
became dramatically visible to the American people in new ways. Almost every
time a new bridge or dam or public building is proposed, an old house torn down, a
woman fired, a television station's license renewed or a new town incorporated,
someone may sue.[31] As a result, the federal courts find themselves looking into
thousands and thousands of routine governmental and private decisions about investments, hiring, construction, advertising, pricing, procurement, personnel management, education, and school admissions that would have seemed totally outside
their jurisdiction a few years ago. The number of cases in U.S. district courts increased 50 percent from 1970 to 1978. (The number of lawyers rose at the same
rate in this period.)[32] So far, much of this activity has occurred in the lower federal
courts. But as appeals build up, the Supreme Court is entering the new areas. Within the last few years, it has handled cases involving admissions to professional
schools, job qualifications for factory workers, the routing of highways through
parks, and the location of hiking trails.

Quite apart from this explosion of judicial activity in the environment and job
equality fields, the Supreme Court recently has become involved in a number of
major public controversies. Supreme Court decisions led the way to great changes

---

[30] See Arthur Selwyn Miller, *The Supreme Court and American Capitalism* (New York: Free Press, 1968).

[31] See, for instance, Frederick R. Anderson, *The National Environment Protection Act in the Courts* (Washington, D.C.: Resources for the Future, 1973).

[32] Linda E. Demkovich, "The Clogged Federal Courts—Who Are the Culprits?" *National Journal*, February 11, 1978, pp. 223–25.

in the abortion and death penalty laws in most states. In the Pentagon Papers incident, in which the Nixon administration sought to prevent the publication of classified information about the Vietnam war, and then in the Watergate case, the Court made historic decisions about the extent of presidential powers. And it continues to be embroiled in the school busing controversy. Under Chief Justice Burger, the Court has pretty clearly been trying to avoid the extreme integrationist position. It has stressed that exact mathematical integration in which each school has the same proportion of majority to minority students is not required. It has hinted that one-race schools caused by residential patterns rather than by conscious government policy are not unconstitutional. It has cautioned that the means chosen for desegregation should not be so costly and disruptive as to undermine the quality of education. It has blocked lower court attempts to create huge new school districts in which suburban white students would be made available for integration with central city blacks. Yet the Court has not abandoned its basic commitment to the dismantling of school segregation. The Burger Court has shown some tendency to cut back on the most extreme of the Warren Court's criminal justice and obscenity holdings. It has often refused to go further along paths of social reform down which the Warren Court had started.[33] Here, as in so many other areas of public policy, the Supreme Court seems to be in the same boat as most other political actors. Questions of racial integration and equality of access undoubtedly will continue to trouble not only the Court but the president, Congress, the political parties, and many state and local governments.

SUMMARY   The Supreme Court makes many large and small policy decisions over a wide range of issues. It wields two powers of judicial review: the power to declare acts of government unconstitutional and the power to review the legality of administrative and lower court decisions. Courts derive their basic legitimacy from their position as a neutral third person resolving conflicts between two opponents. But courts also act as lawmakers and instruments of government. The lawmaking and governing aspects of the Supreme Court's work tend to overshadow its basic legitimacy as a conflict-resolving agency. The Supreme Court is supreme in the sense of its close ties to the Constitution, but it is only one agency among the many that govern the country. How much or how little the Supreme Court ought to engage in policymaking in a democracy has long been a subject of debate. In evaluating that debate, it must be remembered that Supreme Court decisions are rarely final, that interest groups have considerable access to the Court, and that by his appointments, a president may materially shift the direction of Supreme Court policies.

Each state has its own judicial hierarchy that handles most cases. Only a limited variety of cases can enter the federal hierarchy headed by the Supreme

---

[33] Richard Funston, *Constitutional Counter-Revolution: The Warren Court and the Burger Court* (Cambridge, Mass.: Schenkman, 1977); Stephen Wasby, *Continuity and Change: From the Warren Court to the Burger Court* (Pacific Palisades, Calif.: Goodyear, 1976).

Court. The Supreme Court does not issue general or advisory opinions; it acts only where a legal case or controversy exists. Even though the routes to the Supreme Court are few, its caseload is heavy.

The Court's decision-making process allows each Justice to reach an independent decision or act with colleagues to reach collective decisions. Its written opinions are the mode by which the Court issues policy messages to various audiences.

The Court has many roles. It seeks to set constitutional boundaries, defend personal liberties, regulate race relations, and deal with economic problems. In its role of announcing uniform national interpretations of federal statutes, it participates in the lawmaking process in nearly every area of national policymaking from labor relations to home financing. During the last three decades, the federal courts have become increasingly visible to most Americans as they have become more actively involved in a wider range of public policymaking.

the policy process

PART FOUR

public policymaking

Before, during, and after the presidential election of 1976 there was a lot of talk about energy policy. Was President Ford's energy policy any good? Did President Carter have an energy policy? The creation of a new cabinet-level Department of Energy did not end this debate. No one assumed that just because we had a department we necessarily had a policy—let alone a good one. This book is largely about the way government works, not what it produces. The student must begin somewhere, and how the government works seems to be a good place to start. In the longer run, however, people care more about what the government

CHAPTER 17

Energy is one policy area where the consequences of government action often are obvious to everyone, as illustrated by this line of cars waiting for gasoline.

actually does — that is, its policies. We do not have the space to describe farm policy and foreign policy and environmental policy and transportation policy and so on. What we can do is outline some of the factors that go into policymaking — into deciding what the government does.

In Part Three we examined the major government institutions one by one. We saw how each of them makes decisions and how they interact with each other. Each of these institutions — Congress, the presidency, the bureaucracy, and the courts — has its own way of doing things. Nevertheless, certain common features of policymaking are found in all our national institutions. These common features are what we will discuss in this chapter, as we examine American politics from the standpoint of how issues are decided rather than who makes the decisions.

Many aspects of policy formation discussed in previous chapters should be assumed here, including these features of the American political process: patronage; the multiplicity of interest groups; specialized interests among both officials and lobbyists; the president's desire to create a public record of accomplishment; the importance of judicial review; the possibility that the same result can be achieved by legislative, judicial, or executive action; the difference between symbolic and tangible results; and the dispersion of power among different institutions.

GOALS AND PRIORITIES

Policy is about getting somewhere — accomplishing something that someone or everyone wants. Political goals are almost unlimited, but since resources are scarce, only some can be realized. At any given moment, policymakers face demands far greater than what they can achieve. Which of the many good things we want should be pursued first and which should be left for later? An individual acting alone might be able to choose which goals had first claim on how many of his or her own resources. Even if a single official had the power to decide, he or she still would want to take into account the preferences of other people. But policy is not made this way. In the real world, decisions are seldom in the power of a single person, and therefore we face the problem of many people with many different goals trying to decide what to do first.

One of the greatest problems in policy formation is comparing utilities, the use or benefit people get from various objects or activities. It may be a practical benefit, such as the nutrition provided by a meal of apples, soybeans, alfalfa sprouts, and yogurt. Or it might be a sensual benefit provided by a meal in a three-star restaurant. There is no correct way of comparing one person's utilities with those of another. We cannot say that the satisfaction one person gets from plums is worth more or less than the pleasure another derives from strawberries. Counting noses is generally no help. We cannot say that the more people a policy benefits, the better the policy. Spending $100,000 on a kidney machine that keeps ten people alive may be a better use of public funds than a fresh-air program that sends 200 city children to a summer camp for two weeks.

Goals and priorities are one aspect of the problem of policy formation; approaches to making decisions are another. What is decided often depends on the decision-making process itself.

DECISION-MAKING STYLES

The Synoptic Approach   The *synoptic* approach to making policy proceeds rationally in clear stages. Values are defined and specific goals identified. Available resources are surveyed. Alternative ways of reaching goals are explored: Both the probability that each alternative will achieve the stated goal and the cost of doing it that way rather than taking another route are calculated. Finally, a set of priorities that reflects both the desirability of the goal and the cost and feasibility of ways to reach it is established.

The synoptic model is a beautiful dream, not a description of reality. It requires that officials not only be saints, but possess superhuman capacity for learning and processing information. In the real world, policymakers have neither the time nor the capacity to learn everything. Indeed, much of the information the synoptic model demands often just cannot be obtained. Perhaps most important, synoptic policymaking assumes that everyone involved has the same interest, sees the world the same way, and will define success similarly.[1] The model, however, continues to crop up in political rhetoric. President Carter, for example, talked a great deal about his dedication to "scientific administration" during the 1976 campaign. Once in office, he tried to put his ideas into practice. In the summer of 1977, the Office of Management and Budget gave each executive department a dollar ceiling for its share of the 1979 budget. This was the customary procedure, to be followed a few months later by submission to the OMB of the department's detailed budget request. But the OMB also said each department should rank *every* program in its request. This was a step in Carter's attempt to get the bureaucracy to follow more "rational" procedures.

The OMB request puzzled the departments. For example, how could the Agriculture Department compare the value of food stamps and farm price supports? Why should it bother, knowing that Congress would continue both programs? The possibilities for playing games with the ranking system were considerable. An anonymous official of the Treasury Department observed: "Suppose we ranked interest on the [national] debt last. We'd still have to pay it."[2] Most departments found it so difficult or awkward to set priorities that they failed to obey. The Department of

---

[1] Charles E. Lindblom, "The Science of 'Muddling Through'," *Public Administration Review,* 19 (1959), pp. 79–88; Richard M. Cyert and James G. March, *A Behavioral Theory of the Firm* (Englewood Cliffs, N.J.: Prentice-Hall, 1963); and John D. Steinbrunner, *The Cybernetic Theory of Decision* (Princeton, N.J.: Princeton University Press, 1974).

[2] Quoted in *National Journal,* January 28, 1978, p. 132. Most of our information about recent budgets and budget-making is from that issue.

A SYNOPTIC APPROACH TO BUYING A FAMILY CAR

I. State all family goals and specify how important each is in relation to every other. In the light of all family goals, decide whether you want a new car now more than you want anything else.

II. List in order of collective family preference all the values or goals all members of the family want from a new car.

A. For example, here is an *incomplete* list of values. See if you can put them in order for your family.

1. acceleration
2. maneuverability
3. style
4. safety
5. initial cost
6. cost of repair
7. gas mileage
8. comfort
9. availability of service
10. number of people carried
11. trunk space

B. Now see if you can not only list them from most to least important, but specify exactly how much more or less important each is than every other. (For example, exactly how much would your family be willing to give up in comfort in order to have a car that would accelerate 10 percent faster?)

III. Get all the information on all the factors listed above for all the models of all makes of all American and foreign cars from all dealers.

IV. Survey all family resources, including cash, property, and available time for work. (For example, carefully consider selling your house in order to get money for a new car, and the possibility of your mother and father taking on second jobs to earn more money.)

V. Considering all eleven values for all 200 or so makes and models, decide exactly which one from which dealer most exactly matches the mix of the eleven values.

Does anyone buy a car this way? Could anyone buy a car this way? If you tried to buy a car this way, how long would it take?

Health, Education and Welfare, for example, ranked programs worth $5.5 billion out of a total budget request of over $185 billion. The failure to obey the OMB request reflected the departments' reluctance to be completely candid about their preferences. It was also a measure of the difficulty of ranking priorities. In later years, the OMB did succeed in getting departments to group their budget requests in four categories. One category is for absolutely essential activities. The fourth category is for new proposals that would "enhance" the agency's contributions. In between fall funding requests for programs that may already be in operation, but are judged less crucial by the agency proposing them.

THE VIRTUE OF AMBIGUITY

We have a political process precisely because people have multiple goals that somehow must be reconciled into a single course of governmental action. This resultant course of action may be called a "policy," but that term is misleading if it is regarded as implying one mind, one will, and one theory. Legislation requires ambiguity in the statement of goals so that coalitions can be formed in support of it, and each group can believe that the legislation serves its own special purposes. As Charles Schultze [Chairman of the Council of Economic Advisers] has explained, "The first rule of a successful political process is, 'don't force a specification of goals or ends' . . . necessary agreement on particular policies can often be secured among the individuals or groups who hold quite divergent ends." Insisting that the government's purposes be clear may reduce the scope of legislation and thus limit government involvement in social programs.

Source: Martin Rein and Sheldon H. White, "Can Policy Research Help Policy?" *The Public Interest,* fall 1977, p. 123.

The Incremental Approach   Incrementalism refers both to the way policy actually is made and to a belief that this method is superior to the synoptic method. Policymakers do not in fact constantly search for the best or ideal policy; instead, they stick to what they have been doing until it becomes obvious that old policies are not adequate. Even then, they are content to identify what has gone wrong and try to move away from it; they do not begin a searching examination of the whole field. They will examine a few alternatives that are only a little different from what they have been doing. Instead of long-range planning, they do estimates of the immediate consequences of the alternatives that seem most interesting. These rather modest things are not done all at once. The work is spread over a period of time, with a series of small decisions that are constantly revised. Instead of picking the alternative that will best achieve an ultimate goal, policymakers may adjust the goal to match what they think is the best alternative they can actually achieve.

One reason for the prevalence of incrementalism is the limited time and intellectual capacity of human beings. Aaron Wildavsky puts the case this way:

> Organizations would find life unbearable if they treated each stimulus requiring action as something new. Every situation would then require an agreed definition of the situation, a frame of reference for interpreting events, a specification of the mixture of values involved, a thorough search for policy alternatives, and much more. In order to avoid the enormous effort and intellectual capacities required to accomplish these tasks, organizations ordinarily cut their decision costs and their burden of calculation by developing set patterns of responses to frequently encountered stimuli.[3]

[3] Aaron Wildavsky, "The Analysis of Issue Contexts in the Study of Decision-Making," *Journal of Politics,* 24 (November 1962), p. 718.

AN INCREMENTAL APPROACH TO BUYING A FAMILY CAR

I. Keep driving the car you have until something goes wrong with it.

II. Then get it repaired.

III. When too many things go wrong, talk about buying a new car, but do not try to settle on exactly who wants what how much.

IV. Look at some cars and then decide, in the light of what you have seen, which make and model you like best. (This often involves settling for less of a car because you find you really cannot afford what you first thought you wanted.)

V. Look at a few more cars to make sure.

VI. Shop at three or four dealers for the best price on the make and model you have chosen. Then buy from the dealer who gives you the best deal.

If you look a lot longer and studied more cars more carefully, you would get a car you liked a little better for a little less money.

A second argument for incrementalism is the simple fact that policy decisions almost always are made by a number of officials, not by a single person. With the synoptic approach, all the decision-makers must agree on objectives, facts, probabilities, interests. Such agreement is rare in the real world. Incrementalism allows for different views of the problem. It generally involves: (1) searching for an alternative that satisfies each of the decision-makers, although no one believes it is the ideal solution; (2) accepting the first proposal to which no one strongly objects; and (3) avoiding pressing the search for basic values so far as to threaten cohesion and alliances. Incrementalism assumes that people can embrace the same proposal for very different reasons, so exposing "ultimate goals" is likely to get in the way of agreeing what to do. In reaching decisions, incrementalism considers the smooth working of the organization and cooperation with other agencies.

"Rational" Policymaking   We have drawn this contrast between synoptic and incremental approaches to help readers understand the policymaking process as it really works. Many people believe that synoptic decision-making is rational and incrementalism sloppy or corrupt. But incremental decision-makers are not behaving irrationally. Instead, they are recognizing that certainty is itself a scarce commodity. If government decision-makers were (1) certain of all the facts they needed to know, (2) certain they could know all the possible alternatives, (3) certain they could predict the outcome of each alternative, and (4) certain of what values to pursue, then they would act synoptically. Because they are uncertain, they act incrementally. Much — not all, but much — of what appears to be irrational, stupid, lazy, or selfish about policymaking is the result of uncertainty and of the scarcity of time to be certain.

Let us take crime as an example. Politicians call for a national policy to deal with rising crime rates. In order to get one, we should know what causes crime, but in fact, we do not. There are many theories that poverty, discrimination, and broken families cause crime. Yet only a few poor children from broken homes become criminals, and some rich children from unbroken homes do. Years of massive, intense, and expensive research might not give us the answers. We need to deal with crime now. So we try a variety of tactics, ranging from aid to police forces to financial aid to victims.

Even if we had all the facts about crime, we would not be certain what all the alternative ways of combatting it were or which would work best. Will better street lighting or more police patrols be a bigger deterrent to street crime? Or should we have everyone carry a big stick? Until we try, we will not know. We must choose some of these alternatives *before* we know which one will work, or whether one we have not thought of would work even better. If we were certain more street lights would work, we might spend a lot of money now to light up the whole town. Because we are not certain, we will spend a little money to light up some streets and see if crime goes down there.

Perhaps none of the alternatives currently available to us will significantly reduce crime. But what if we had strong reason to believe that making everyone carry a pocket device which signaled his or her location to a government computer every fifteen minutes would really deter crime? What are our values? Do we want to end crime enough to sacrifice that much of the freedom and privacy we value? Some people will; others will have the opposite values. For instance, some American cities forbid police to use helicopters and police dogs even if they would help reduce crime and protect both citizens and police. They do so because they place a high value on individual freedom from police intervention. Other cities spend money on the same items because they place a higher value on catching criminals.

A Bias toward the Status Quo?   A common objection to incrementalism is that it is an excuse for never doing anything. Indeed, some incrementalists add to this impression by remarks like this one: "If you want to predict what next year's budget will be, take a look at this year's budget." There is a powerful element of truth in this, of course, because no one is immune to the common human tendency to start planning for the future by looking at the present. But just because the future begins with the present is no reason to think that nothing ever changes. One obvious source of shifting government activities is changes in the outside environment. For example, the energy crisis produced a sharp increase in federal spending in this field. In 1973, the year the world awakened to oil shortages, the federal government spent $1.2 billion on energy. Four years later, the figure had escalated to $4.2 billion, and President Carter's budget called for expenditures of $9.6 billion by 1979. These later increases reflect both the objective conditions of oil shortages and high prices and decisions about how to respond by two presidents with different views of the urgency of the problem. Defense spending has declined since the end of the Vietnam war, from 30 percent of the budget in 1973 to 23 percent in 1978. (It may increase slightly at the end of the 1970s because of the continued growth in Soviet arms spending and the aging of weapons slighted during our preoccupation with Vietnam.)

Other shifts in government activity are a product of administrative decisions and political responses to citizen demands. For example, the share of the budget going to the Department of Health, Education and Welfare doubled from 1964 to 1979 and now accounts for 36 percent of all federal spending. This does not reflect a single decision to increase the federal role in health, education, and welfare. Nor is it an ideological commitment to the welfare state; most of the increase occurred during the Ford and Nixon administrations. This growth in spending on human resources came from literally thousands of programs. We can see this more easily by focusing on federal financial aid to college students. Spending for this purpose went from about half a billion dollars in 1967 to $9.1 billion in 1978.[4] Much of this increase was from new programs, but a substantial part reflects higher appropriations for existing programs. All told, the federal government puts money in students' pockets through dozens of separately authorized and administered programs intended for a variety of purposes. Every year, funding levels for each program are examined. A few are cut, most are increased, and a rare program is killed. Every year the executive branch and Congress consider new programs. Occasionally they start one, and thus create a new opportunity for interest groups and bureaucrats to request more federal spending. Figure 17.1 shows how the budgets for seven student aid programs have varied over the years.

In short, incrementalism is quite consistent with sweeping changes in federal activities. These shifts usually do not occur as a result of a single comprehensive decision, but instead reflect a series of decisions that culminate as major policy departures, even if they were never planned that way.

Uncontrolled Spending The federal budget grows at a rapid pace — it went from under $100 billion in 1965 to over $500 billion in 1979. Taken by itself, this looks like an alarming sign that we are all in danger of being bankrupted. We often forget that both productivity and inflation have also increased. If we take these into consideration, the situation looks less alarming. In fact, as a share of gross national product, federal spending has stayed around 20 to 22 percent for a generation. It is not much more important now than it was in the Eisenhower administration of the mid-1950s.

Nevertheless, the continued increase in government spending bothers a lot of people. Perhaps for this reason, President Carter made a big thing of zero-base budgeting as a cure for an inflated federal budget. Zero-base budgeting (ZBB) is the latest in a long line of devices to control public spending. It is based on the correct notion that, in making up next year's budget request, a bureaucrat starts with this year's spending level and uses that as the base for his calculations. Since any energetic official will have new ideas about how to serve the public interest, this means that the new ideas will be added to the base of present spending. So the budget inevitably increases. Supposedly the way to break this vicious cycle is to make the

---

[4] *National Journal,* April 1, 1978, p. 514.

Figure 17.1

Federal Student Aid and How It Grew
(in millions of dollars)

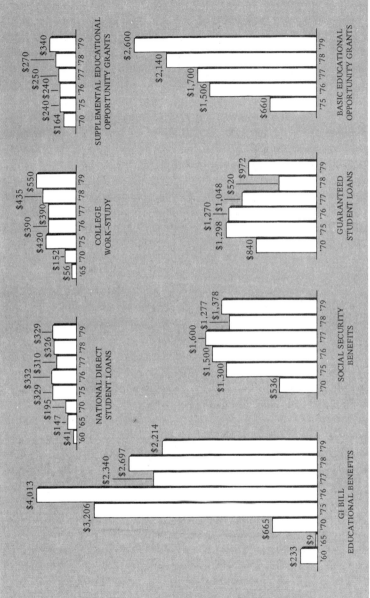

Source: For 1978 and 1979, *Higher Education and National Affairs,* January 26, 1979, p. 3: for other years, *The Chronicle of Higher Education,* October 11, 1977, p. 5.

base zero— to start from scratch. That is, instead of assuming that he will be able to spend at least as much on the program next year as he did last year, the administrator must start all over. He must justify any expenditure, not just any increase. No program will be taken for granted; everything will be reexamined every year. The old will be compared with the new. ZBB is a close cousin of ranking priorities. In Carter's first budget-making cycle, it had an equally sad end.[5]

In the first place, three-quarters of the federal budget represents *uncontrollable spending,* money the government must spend because of previous commitments. By far the biggest share of this amount, almost half the total budget, is payments to individuals guaranteed by the government and authorized into the indefinite future. These include social security, federal employees' pensions, unemployment and welfare benefits, medicare and medicaid, and veterans' benefits. Individual entitlements of this sort are often tied to the cost of living and go up automatically. Eighty-nine percent of HEW's 1979 budget, for example, was uncontrollable. As long as eligible people apply for benefits, HEW must pay. A second kind of inescapable federal commitment comes from contracts signed in previous years. For example, the government may sign a contract in 1979 to pay $200 million a year during the next three years for a submarine that takes three years to build. A third ironclad claim on the treasury is for interest on the national debt— $55.4 billion in 1979.

Quite apart from uncontrolled spending, ZBB was a flop for much the same reasons as the order to rank priorities: People just cannot reopen all the old, settled controversies and bargains every year to take a fresh look. ZBB survives as the four-level ranking of programs described on page 516. This is a far cry from the annual reevaluation of every program that was first proposed.

DISTRIBUTIVE AND REDISTRIBUTIVE POLICIES

One factor that affects the balance between incremental and synoptic decision-making is whether the policy being considered is distributive or redistributive.[6]

Distributive Policy   Many government programs *distribute* services and goods to specific segments of the population. Farm subsidies are an obvious example of a policy that transfers money from the national treasury to a select group of people. Far more typical, however, are college student grants, irrigation projects, flood control, or grants for community development. Here the government gives something to students or farmers or towns along a river or slum residents. The gains from such distributive policies are specific and the costs are diffuse. The people who receive benefits can see that they are better off. The bene-

---

[5] *National Journal,* January 28, 1978, p. 129.

[6] Theodore J. Lowi, "American Business, Public Policy, Case Studies, and Political Theory," *World Politics,* 16 (July 1964), pp. 677–715.

The Works Progress Administration (WPA), a New Deal program that provided jobs for over 2½ million Americans, was a large scale government distributive policy. Over $10 billion in federal funds flowed through the WPA and into the national economy.

fits cost every taxpayer a little bit because the money spent is tax money. But no particular taxpayer or group of taxpayers especially feels the pinch. Thus, such policies create winners but no identifiable losers. If a million dollars is spent on flood control in West Virginia, construction workers get jobs, building material suppliers get contracts, and businesses in the area prosper. But less than a penny of any individual taxpayer's money is spent. The key point is that distributive policies usually have specific friends but no specific enemies, because each project is only a tiny part of the entire tax bill.

Distributive policymaking often works on a "take turns" principle with regard to particular programs. Public works legislation is a perfect example. Every year, Congress passes on hundreds of projects for dam-building, harbor-dredging, and the like. Los Angeles gets a new flood control channel; Yazoo County, Mississippi, gets a new levee. This is generally called **pork barrel legislation** because every place in the country gets its chance to dip into the barrel and pull out a piece of pork. Representatives from Los Angeles and Yazoo County do not fight each other for money. In fact, the representative from Yazoo County will vote for the Los Angeles channel although it does not do his constituents a bit of good. But he knows that soon votes will be needed for the levee. There is not enough money for everyone to have every conceivable federal project. But there is enough so that everyone will get some projects — and the congressmen on the relevant subcommittees will get considerably more than their share.[7]

Meanwhile, there are few opponents to the public works bill. Few congressional constituents are hurt by the bill. Only those institutions, like the Office of Management and Budget and the appropriations committees, which are generally concerned with keeping a lid on spending, are likely to be opposed. And they will be concerned more with keeping the total figure down than fighting any particular project. Just after taking office, President Carter issued a list of dam-building projects that he wanted to cancel because the anticipated benefits did not match the costs. He did this both on the merits and to show that he was against waste in government. His proposal was strenuously resisted by those members of Congress whose districts would benefit from the projects on the list, as well as by other members who worried about what would happen when their turn came. The president eventually backed down on many of the projects because the cost to him of so much congressional hostility was not worth the benefit to the budget.

Zero-Sum or Redistributive Policies

A **zero-sum game** is one in which whatever one player or team wins, the other player or team clearly loses. Poker is such a game — the sum of winnings equals the sum of the losses. In politics, sometimes what the government does for one group is achieved by a

---

[7] John A. Ferejohn, *Pork Barrel Politics* (Stanford, Calif.: Stanford University Press, 1974).

proportionate loss to someone else. The crucial point is whether giving the benefit to some winners involves an identifiable set of losers who are worse off only because of that particular program and who would not lose anything if that program did not exist. The Yazoo County levee does not have costs of that kind; if it is built, no one in particular will be noticeably worse off. Now consider a bill to extend the federal minimum wage to agriculture laborers. There will be identifiable winners— the fruit pickers and grapevine pruners. But this provision would also impose considerable costs directly on an identifiable group of losers—the farmers who hire these laborers. They can be counted on to oppose the bill intensely, because they can calculate their own loss.

Government actions in the field of labor-management relations are often seen as zero-sum. It often seems that if management gains something, labor must lose, and vice versa. Any policies perceived as zero-sum are likely to be highly controversial. This is why, for example, the House Education and Labor Committee is so deeply divided along ideological lines.

Politicians' Preference for Distributive Policies

Much of the art of politics consists of avoiding the appearance of redistribution. Policymakers usually try to treat their choices as if they were distributive rather than posing "us or them" dilemmas. A number of features of policymaking flow from avoiding confrontation. Perhaps the most obvious is a refusal to treat the available money as fixed in amount. If there were only so much money available every year to fund federal programs, every new proposal would be a threat to every existing program. A new idea could be funded only by taking something away from people already enjoying federal benefits. Grants to make school buildings accessible to the disabled could be paid for only by cutting the amount of money for work-study jobs. Solar energy research would take money away from national parks.

But the amount of available money in fact is not so strictly limited. Government expansion is financed not by dividing up the pot all over again with every new program, but by making the total size of the budget bigger this year than last year. Then there is enough money to continue the old benefits and add some new ones. This is, among other things, a major reason for the huge ($30 to $60 billion) deficits in the federal budget. A second device is to conceal the costs of a new program. This is generally done by starting at a modest level, developing a market for the program, and then using this constituency to pressure for future expansion.

The budget process usually asks, "should we spend a little more or a little less on this program next year?" It does not ask, "In view of all the other claims on the Treasury, should we have this program at all?" This kind of zero-sum question is the most difficult for policymakers to handle. The reasons are not wholly political. Would *you* like to have to choose between kidney machines and sickle cell anemia research?

All policy, of course, is redistributive in the sense that the money has to come from somewhere. Combining the federal tax structure with the pattern of government benefits hypothetically might let an analyst compute the cost-benefit ratio of

HOW LITTLE PROGRAMS GROW

In 1954 Congress amended the Social Security Act to provide that if workers could not contribute to social security because they had been disabled, their ultimate retirement benefits would not suffer as a consequence. This did not give benefits to anyone; it merely protected existing benefits from being lowered because of disability. The following years, however, brought a series of expansions to this modest beginning. Payments were authorized to disabled workers before retirement; the definition of disability was loosened considerably; medicare eligibility was granted to the disabled; and the monthly payments grew rapidly.

By 1978, the average payment for disabled workers with families was nearly $800 a month—tax free. The cost of the program had quadrupled in seven years, and the number of workers receiving benefits had doubled to 2.8 million. Over 1.2 million workers filed disability claims in 1977 alone. These claims are initially heard by more than 10,000 state employees (who are organized into the National Association of Disability Examiners). Claims rejected by the states can be appealed to a series of federal tribunals. In 1978, over 80,000 cases were pending before 650 administrative law judges. These judges, who also handle other social security cases, nearly outnumber all other judges in the federal judicial system.

Congress originally intended to link the disability provisions to state vocational rehabilitation programs. However, only about 2 percent of those receiving disability benefits ever return to work as a result of state rehabilitation. The original modest step in 1954 has resulted in a major redistribution of income that provides handsome benefits for those disabled by accidents, disease, or mental disorders. As one Secretary of HEW put it, "This program has drifted into crisis."

Source: James W. Singer, "It Isn't Easy to Cure the Ailments of the Disability Insurance Program," *National Journal,* May 6, 1978, pp. 715–19.

all public policy.[8] Using this as a base, one could then calculate how any particular proposal would alter this balance. In fact, "redistributive" policies are more common in the minds of social scientists than officials. For one thing, most officials are concerned with only one side of the revenue-spending combination; they work either at spending the money or at getting it, but not at both. And even the few who are in a position to combine the two usually treat taxation and benefits separately and as problems in distribution. They talk about a fair distribution of the tax burden and treat the poor as one among many groups to whom government benefits should be distributed.

[8] This assumes that we could put a dollar value on the benefit each person gets from common goods like clean air, national defense, public health, and the like.

American politicians are most responsive to groups that can point to a specific need, a limited remedy, and no particular opponents. This style puts more emphasis on benefits than costs. After all, any single program is not all that big a slice of the budget. This is particularly so because many measures start out small and then grow. There is, then, a tendency to slight the cost when considering proposals aimed at distributing benefits to some segment of the population. The intended beneficiaries are surely deserving; why not do something to help them? So politicians try to conceal costs and emphasize benefits, to treat every measure as a distributive policy. (The opponents of any proposal, of course, may try to make it look like a redistributive issue, hoping to build a coalition against it.) The effect of this process is a growth of federal spending beyond what would result from a comprehensive and comparative look at costs and benefits together. The gap between federal income and spending reflects in part politicians' preferences for short-term responses at the cost of long-term budget balancing.

The lawmaking process in the United States depends on demands being broken up into small enough bits to allow easy bargaining. Our examination of the American people, including interest groups and parties, shows the potential for such division of demands. But the extent to which demands are fragmented so that bargaining is possible depends on how the demands are perceived. For example, suppose every policy proposal aimed at distributing government services to the poor, unemployed, and uneducated was defined as a redistribution of wealth from whites to blacks. Once every issue was defined in this way, bargaining might become impossible. Why should the white majority give anything away to the black minority? In such a situation, violence or the threat of violence might be the only bargaining tactic available to blacks.

Another way of putting the point, then, is to say that a major function of the political process is to hide rather than expose clashes between majorities and minorities. As long as social demands are broken up into little pieces, each identified with a relatively small part of the population, bargaining over distribution is relatively easy. Everyone can be given a little something and no one appears to lose much. The more sharply issues are defined as majority versus minority, the more apt the majority will be to stop bargaining and simply do what it wants. Indeed, one of the greatest challenges facing our political system in the years ahead will be whether or not the demands of black citizens can be broken up into small, piecemeal interests that permit the kind of bargaining our policymaking process is accustomed to handling. If this happens, we will be more able to satisfy enough of these demands to prevent the sort of polarization in which there is a black position and an opposite white one on every policy question.

For all these reasons, the legislative process is more incremental than synoptic. It tends to be a bit messy. Politicians usually try for acceptable solutions to medium-run problems rather than ultimate goals. They recognize that uncertainty, scarcity of time, multiple and conflicting values, and the risk of unanticipated consequences make perfectly rational policymaking impossible. So the system accepts and works with personal and organizational limitations.

The Role of the Political **Because the lawmaking process does not run very smoothly, it**
Entrepreneur usually takes a lot of individual will and energy to make it produce major innovations. Someone or some group must believe
strongly in a policy and continue to push it along from one hurdle to the next. This
calls for political entrepreneurs who, like their counterparts in the business world,
start a new firm, nurse it along through the days when no one has heard of it, keep
trying to attract new customers, and work hard to make it a success. One of the
most important functions of the presidency is to encourage the invention of new
policy proposals. The president then chooses some of them as his own and seeks
popular and congressional support for them. Bureaucrats also are the entrepreneurs of many new measures, usually those with less popular appeal and partisan
possibilities.

Members of Congress, particularly senators, often seek this role. The National
Highway Safety Act, for example, emerged from well-publicized hearings as "Senator (Robert) Kennedy's bill" and went on to become law. Of course, not all entrepreneurs are successful. Politics, however, often provides rewards to those who fail
with a new enterprise. At the very least, there is the publicity. A well-known piece of
Washington folklore is the losers' cynical remark, "We may not have the bill, but
we do have the issue" (to use in the next election campaign). Moreover, years of
effort and failure may be needed to "educate the public" and lay the groundwork
for an ultimately successful action.

INFORMATION AND POLICYMAKING

An accurate picture of a problem does not guarantee a satisfactory solution. Nevertheless, it is difficult to argue that ignorance is an advantage. Here we describe several types of ignorance or limited information that make successful policymaking
more difficult.

Popular Ignorance **First is what might be called "popular ignorance." It is general-**
ly accepted that Americans consume too many scarce and
expensive fossil fuels — oil, coal, and natural gas. Congress and the president,
deadlocked by conflicts among interest groups, have been wrestling with the problem for years. Two presidents have tried and failed to rally public opinion behind
their definition of the public interest. At bottom is a fundamental fact: half the
American public still does not know that we import almost half the oil we consume.

Some kinds of ignorance have a decidedly self-interested character. One of
the hot political issues of 1978 was the tuition tax credit — reducing individuals' tax
payments by a proportion of the money they spent for college (or even elementary
and secondary) tuition. The strong popular appeal of this measure (defeated in
1978 but sure to come back again) grew out of widespread horror at the rising cost
of college. College costs have indeed been rising sharply — but not quite as fast as

Wide World

There is no easy way to calculate who benefits most from clean air.

median income. Therefore, the proportion of family income spent on college actually *declined* between 1967 and 1976.[9] Politicians and college administrators, however, had a strong interest in exaggerating the cost of college. For the politicians, the claim had the virtue of providing them with an enormously appealing remedy—the tuition tax credit.

Another widespread American delusion is that people of low and moderate income bear the lion's share of the tax burden, which the rich escape through mysterious "loopholes." In fact, the poorest 11 percent of taxpayers in 1975 contributed a mere 0.5 percent of federal income tax payments, while families in the over $50,000 bracket (2 percent of all taxpayers) kicked in 23.7 percent of all income taxes paid.[10] As long as the myth persists, politicians can make hay by further reductions in the tax liabilities of the more numerous voters in the lower tax brackets.

Technical Ignorance Popular ignorance is a political problem. In other fields, there are important facts that nobody knows, because they are difficult to discover, either for technical reasons or because nobody has bothered to do the research. As we saw in Chapter 2, illegal aliens have become an important component of the population, but just how important they are is a mystery. By the very nature of the situation, the number of illegal aliens is not known even to the nearest million. Whether the aliens are a serious, moderate, or trivial problem depends on other considerations that at present are largely a matter of guesswork. Are they a major drain on hard-pressed public services? Do they pay their share of taxes? Do they take jobs away from Americans or do work no citizen would touch? On the answers to these questions depend not only our assessment of the seriousness of the problem, but also an estimate of what to do about it. As long as the dimensions of the situation are unknown, it is difficult to find either urgency or solutions.

Unanticipated Consequences Another sort of ignorance among policymakers concerns consequences. The actual results of some policies occasionally are surprising to advocates and enemies alike. Sometimes these unanticipated consequences overshadow the expected results. The environmental impact statement (EIS) is a particularly striking example of this tendency. The National Environmental Policy Act of 1970 required that plans for "major federal action" include on EIS. The intent was to monitor what seemed to be our heedless destruction of the

[9] *San Francisco Chronicle,* May 3, 1978, p. 26.
[10] *Congressional Quarterly Weekly Report,* April 8, 1978, p. 830. Also see Table 18.3.

environment by taking a closer look at what the federal government was doing to land, air, and water.

It is not at all clear that the EIS requirement has done much for the environment, but its dampening effect on federal programs is all too apparent. A whole new industry has sprung up to prepare EIS and now consumes many millions of dollars. Many courts have been quite willing to issue injunctions halting construction until an EIS was filed, and almost as ready to find the EIS inadequate. The EIS has become a major weapon to delay, change, and kill projects. Initially exploited by environmental groups, it has become an all-purpose obstructive device. As two students of the subject comment: "Any local interest that wants to oppose a development project, for any reason whatsoever, finds it convenient to dress itself in environmental clothing."[11] The EIS requirement, for example, was used by large landowners to halt a court order that the Department of the Interior develop new rules to limit the size of farms receiving federal water. The judge ruled that the government had to show the environmental consequences of breaking big farms up into smaller farms. A representative of the landowners claimed that the decision "points out that the Environmental Protection Act applies to human environment as well as the physical environment."[12]

POLICY IMPLEMENTATION

So far in this chapter we have talked about the early stages of the policymaking process, in which the government decides what to do. In a sense, though, there are no "early" and "late" stages of the process, but only an endless loop. The government decides what to do and tries to do it. Then it sees how well the policy is working. On the basis of its experience in administering the current policy, it makes new decisions about what it ought to do next. Most new policy decisions come out of the experience gained in running the old policies. And the new policies in turn generate new experience out of which further policies grow. Thus, the stage of policy implementation is important both for its own sake and because it is the basis for the next round of policymaking. By policy implementation we simply mean making the policy work. If the government decides on a policy of cancer research, it is the cancer researchers who are the implementers.

Overload and Implementation   One factor that adds to the importance of the implementation stage is the workload of high officials. Top policymakers — the president, members of Congress, Supreme Court justices, and cabinet members — have to make many decisions about things they know little about. As a result, they delegate a great deal of policymaking to the bureaucracy. Congress often writes a

---

[11] Eugene Bardach and Lucian Pugliaresi, "The Environmental-Impact Statement vs. the Real World," *The Public Interest,* fall 1977, p. 36.

[12] Quoted in *San Francisco Chronicle,* December 8, 1977, p. 23.

general statute, leaving it to the administrators to fill in the details. If a law authorizes the licensing of "safe" nuclear power plants, but does not spell out what "safe" means, it is the civil servants enforcing the law who really make safety policy. They decide what kind of construction is safe by their decisions about which plants they license.

Because American government involves so many problems of such complexity and technical detail, most policymaking is necessarily done by officials other than those who are responsible to the electorate. This means that top policymakers have to take a lot on trust from their subordinates, and that there are many policymakers speaking with a variety of voices.

Ease of Administration   A key factor in deciding on any policy is whether implementation will be easy or difficult. Let us imagine that we find unauthorized entry into the United States could be cut in half by the expenditure of an additional $100 million a year for policing the Mexican border. This would drastically curtail the ease of movement across the border that Americans and Mexicans have customarily enjoyed. It would therefore deal a severe blow to the complementary economies of such adjoining cities as San Diego and Tijuana, or El Paso and Ciudad Juarez. If it were also established that millions of jobs were taken away from citizens by foreigners willing to work for substandard wages, the government might put some teeth in the present unenforceable laws against hiring illegal aliens. The laws' current weakness is employers' ability to plead ignorance about the status of those whom they hire. An owner whose factory is operated by illegal aliens can plead there is no way to know that they are not all American citizens or legal immigrants. The obvious solution is to require a government identity card as proof of citizenship or legal immigrant status. Do Americans consider illegal aliens a sufficient problem to accept a national identity card, something traditionally regarded as a step toward a police state? In other words, how high a price are we willing to pay for effective implementation of an alien worker policy?

Of course, not every significant public policy requires elaborate administrative mechanisms. A good example of a measure that is almost self-enforcing is the earned-income credit. This important provision was added to the tax laws in 1975. It works this way: People earning up to $4000 a year are given a credit on their taxes equal to 10 percent of their earnings. Families making this little seldom owe any taxes, and so there is nothing to offset against the credit. The government therefore pays the family the difference between its credit and the taxes owed, if any. The credit reaches its peak at $400 for an earned income of $4000. As earnings grow beyond that point, the credit declines at a rate of $100 for every $1000 increase. At the $8000 mark, the credit vanishes.

Depending on how one looks at it, the earned-income credit is a tax loophole for the poor, a negative income tax, or a method of redistributing income. For our purposes, the interesting thing is that it is easy to administer. Anyone filing a tax return has to make the computations anyway. Poor people who would not ordinarily have to file a return now have an important incentive for doing so. The Internal

The Rehabilitation Act of 1973 was passed by Congress and signed into law by President Nixon. Section 504 of that act provides that "no otherwise qualified handicapped individual . . . shall . . . be excluded from participation in . . . any program or activity receiving federal financial assistance." No committee hearings or debate provided any clue about what Congress intended in Section 504. Groups representing the handicapped saw Section 504 as a mandate that any facility built with federal money include features to make it as convenient as possible for handicapped people to use. In the next few years, each federal department issued its own rules for implementing Section 504. The Transportation Department's guidelines on every conceivable aspect of public transportation, from restrooms to pedestrian overpasses, filled fifty-one pages in the *Federal Register*. The results can already be seen in the nation's newest subway system, the Washington, D.C., Metro:

> For people in wheelchairs who cannot use stairs or escalators, the futuristic stations in Washington's subway system have elevators. Along the tracks, lights flash on and off to warn the deaf of approaching trains. The lights are set into 18-inch-wide strips of granite, whose rough surface warns blind people that they are too close to the tracks.
>
> These features . . . make Washington's Metro the nation's most accessible subway system for the handicapped. They also cost money — an estimated $72 million when the 100-mile system is complete.

The same impact of Section 504 can be found in other areas. The Department of HEW estimates that its regulations to implement Section 504 will require $400 million in expenditures to provide easier access to the handicapped, largely in schools. All this has been done because of a single sentence in a law, added without much thought about its meaning and implementation. The sponsor of Section 504 later conceded: "We never had any concept that it would involve such tremendous costs." Another representative admitted: "When Congress passed this statute, it failed to consider that vague and innocent-sounding words in federal law give rise to an endless variety of controversies." Even if Congress had been aware of the implications of Section 504, the basic point remains: Bureaucrats, not legislators, would have spelled out the specific provisions required to implement the law. Should there be a teletype-telephone for the deaf wherever there is a regular telephone in a train station? This is the sort of question answered by career civil servants, not politicians.

Source: Timothy B. Clark, "Access for the Handicapped — A Test of Carter's War on Inflation," *National Journal,* October 21, 1978, pp. 1672–73.

Revenue Service processes tax returns just as it always does, and within a few weeks the check arrives in the mail.

One of the reasons the earned-income credit is so easy to administer is the absence of any room for official discretion. All that is required is the proper numbers on the income tax return; the check is programmed on a computer. Contrast with this another major federal policy, the national speed limit enacted after the 1973 oil embargo. As a fuel-saving device, Congress ordered that any state receiving federal highway funds had to adopt a maximum speed limit of 55 miles per hour. Since most drivers were accustomed to higher speeds, the new limit required the cooperation of a wide assortment of people: ordinary motorists, truck drivers, and fifty state police forces. Truckers complained that such low speeds were less efficient for their rigs and wasted valuable time. Some of their interest groups announced they would not obey the law. Individual drivers announce the presence of police cars over their citizen band radios, thus combining maximum speed with minimum risk of arrest. As anyone who has been on a highway knows, the fast lane is no place for someone who wants to observe the national speed limit. With the exception of a few crackdowns, the police seldom enforce the new limit very strictly. The task is too great; there are other demands on their time; and perhaps many of them do not really believe that 55 is the proper maximum on a straight, clear road. Although the congressional command has lowered the average speed on the nation's highways by a bit, it has not achieved its stated goal.

Administrators may also simply refuse to do the implementation job they are asked to do. During the Nixon presidency, the FBI and the CIA often refused to carry out the domestic spying policies desired by the president. They recognized that if implicated in such illegal actions, their agencies could suffer punishment from Congress. Or a policy may inspire such massive resistance and evasion as to be unworkable. Prohibition of the production and consumption of alcoholic beverages in the 1920s was a classic example of a policy that simply could not be administered effectively.

THE EFFECTIVENESS OF POLICY

We have seen how important it is to carry out, administer, or implement a policy decision once it is made. In discussing incrementalism, we noted how past experience in implementing a policy paves the way for changes in that policy. So a major part of policymaking is looking at the policy once it has been implemented to see how well it has worked. Some of the ways in which this is done are auditing and analysis.

Auditing   Government agencies devote considerable attention to monitoring their own performance. They also worry about evaluations of that performance conducted by outside agencies. The simplest form of auditing is checking the books to see that money is spent properly. This conjures up images of accountants in green eyeshades poring over ledgers (or computer printouts), alert for signs of fraud or sloppy arithmetic. Each administrative agency has its own auditors, and the OMB does some of the same sort of checking on behalf of the president.

Congress's interest in ensuring that funds are legally spent for the designated purpose is served by the General Accounting Office. The GAO is the biggest auditing agency in government, with a budget well over $100 million. More than 1200 GAO professionals work on the Department of Defense alone.[13] The GAO's services are available both to congressional committees and to individual members.

Policy Analysis   In recent years auditing has expanded far beyond simple scrutiny of bookkeeping to include much broader ideas of what the government should do to assess its performance. The term for this more comprehensive type of auditing is **policy analysis.** The focus is not on fiscal efficiency, but on more fundamental questions of program evaluation: How well are the program's objectives being accomplished? Could those goals be better achieved by a different policy or different organizational structure? This is one of the fastest-growing areas in government; almost half of the new professionals hired at GAO are not accountants. Both GAO and OMB make liberal use of private firms and individuals as consultants in program evaluation.[14] Outside these two agencies, there was, from 1969 to 1974, a 500 percent increase in federal policy research,[15] most of it done by independent consultants, not public employees.

Sometimes policy analysis reveals failures to administer the laws as Congress intended. The basic federal statute for aid to education was the Elementary and Secondary Education Act (ESEA) of 1965. Its Title I was intended to provide substantial aid to schools serving the poor. But much of the money authorized under Title I went to school districts with few pupils from poor families. This information came to the attention of civil rights organizations (perhaps leaked by sympathetic bureaucrats), and the interest groups sued successfully to compel adherence to the law.[16] This sort of auditing does not, of course, require much sophisticated analysis. Despite the growing interest in evaluation, federal officials often have a sense of frustration about the usefulness of analysis in making policy: "Some programs are simply hard to evaluate, either because their objectives are not well specified or because their stipulated objectives are difficult to translate into research questions."[17] In other words, before we can evaluate a policy, there must be agreement on what the goal is. And as we have seen, often politicians can agree on the need for a particular policy without agreeing on why they want that policy.

This difficulty can be observed in the fate of program budgeting, an attempt in the Johnson administration to rationalize budgetary decisions. Programs were to be defined in terms of goals, not activities. For example, the domestic activities of the Army Corps of Engineers were to be defined not as, say, building dams; instead, the activities were stated in terms of goals: flood

---

[13] Ira Sharkansky, "The Politics of Auditing," in Bruce L. R. Smith, ed., *The New Political Economy: The Public Use of the Private Sector* (New York: Wiley, 1975), p. 302.

[14] Sharkansky, "The Politics of Auditing," p. 314.

[15] Martin Rein and Sheldon H. White, "Can Policy Research Help Policy?" *The Public Interest*, fall 1977, p. 119.

[16] Ibid., p. 128.

[17] Ibid., p. 122.

"Gentlemen, the fact that all my horses and all my men couldn't put Humpty together again simply proves to me that I must have more horses and more men."

control, electric power, irrigation, recreation. The costs and benefits of each program were to be calculated in *dollar terms.* The programs with the most favorable cost-benefit ratios were to be funded.

There has been a continuing debate over the effectiveness of program budgeting. Most of its procedures did not survive the Johnson administration. One problem was predicting costs and deciding which costs went with which program. For instance, the government builds a dam that provides flood control, electric power, and recreation on the new lake behind it. How much of the cost of the dam should be charged to flood control, how much to power, and how much to recreation? Imagine that the amortized construction cost, together with the operating cost, comes to a million dollars a year. Then suppose that the dam produces $300,000 worth of electricity each year. If the costs are split evenly between flood control, power, and recreation, then the power program has a poor cost-benefit ratio; $333,333 in costs and only $300,000 in benefits. On the other hand, if 90 percent of the costs are charged to flood control and recreation, then the power program looks good: $100,000 in costs and $300,000 in benefits.

There is obviously a lot of room for fiddling around with this sort of calculation.[18] Although one way to fiddle is in the allocation of costs, the biggest problem is on the benefit side. Costs and benefits cannot be compared unless the benefits are expressed in dollars. But in many cases there is no convincing way to assess benefits in monetary terms. How can the virtues of fresh air and family picnics be given a dollar figure? The fact is that it is impossible to provide money values for many government programs. How much benefit in dollars and cents does society get from giving a hungry child breakfast or desegregating a school or exploring space? Because many governmental outputs are not bought and sold in stores, it is impossible to determine their worth in dollars.

Under the impact of the environmental movement, this problem came to be important even on the cost side of program budgeting. We know exactly how many dollars in wages and materials it took to build the dam. But suppose it is built through an area that was previously wilderness. The loss of the wilderness is a "cost" of building the dam. How do we put a dollar amount on that loss? There are not only public benefits but public costs. Economists call them "externalities" — that is, costs borne by persons other than those directly involved. Government programs often involve large externalities, the exact dollar costs of which are hard to calculate.

By the early 1970s, only remnants of program budgeting remained in most Washington agencies. From these remnants, and from greater awareness of the need to look at indirect and unanticipated costs and benefits, came the newer style

---

[18] The Army Engineers, who build most federal dams, seem to exploit the possibilities, in part to build support in Congress. See Ferejohn, *Pork Barrel Politics.* The Engineers' use of cost-benefit ratios began before the program budgeting movement and survived its decline.

WHAT IS A HUMAN LIFE WORTH?

For almost all of us, the highest value is preserving life. Most people like to think that human life is literally priceless—that no amount of money would justify exposing another person to lethal danger. This belief underlies the movement for stringent control of hazardous consumer products, air and water pollution, and dangerous conditions in the workplace. Since the mid-1960s a number of laws and administrative regulations have left their mark on many areas of everyday life. The cars we drive are safer and emit fewer noxious gases. The water we drink is often purer. Many products are safer. Workers are protected from hazards that in the past crippled and killed thousands.

This is progress, but it has a literal cost: Safety and emission control devices add many hundreds of dollars to automobile prices. Safety measures in factories often cost millions and push up the prices of products. Industry objections about the costs of safety used to be brushed aside as selfish pleading. But now scholars and government officials are pointing out that in many cases steps to reduce occupational risks will impose astronomical costs on consumers. For example, the federal Regulatory Analysis Review Group calculated that setting higher standards for one industrial chemical would increase safety, but at a cost of almost $170 million per life saved. Dwelling on the problem of limited resources, the group concluded: "At this cost, there may well be more effective uses for these resources." The same approach was taken by a federal judge hearing a proposal by the Occupational Safety and Health Administration (OSHA) to set a higher standard for control of benzene in oil refineries. OSHA did not challenge an industry estimate that the new standard would prevent one case of leukemia every three years at a cost of $300 million. The judge ruled against OSHA, criticizing the notion of "creat[ing] absolutely risk-free workplaces regardless of cost."

Estimating the costs of safety measures is sometimes called risk-benefit analysis. It depends on assumptions and calculations that often are very uncertain. One labor official criticized risk-benefit analysis because ". . . the worker fares poorly; he is selected for unnecessary and unwarranted risks; he is cannibilized." There *is* something cold-blooded about deciding to sacrifice an unknown worker so that millions can continue to enjoy a product at lower prices. The alternative, however, may be inflationary costs. Despite our common belief that human life is priceless, we have a government that cannot avoid making decisions that set a price on life, a price that sometimes is judged too high to pay.

Source: Dick Kirschten, "Can Government Place a Value on Saving a Human Life?" *National Journal,* February 17, 1979.

in policy analysis. What program budgeting proved unable to do on a large scale can nevertheless often be done on a smaller scale. Careful research into costs and benefits can be done. We may not be able to assign an exact dollar amount to the benefits of giving a hungry child breakfast. But if we discover that it costs the government $2 to give a child a meal that could have been gotten at the local diner for 75 cents, we know we have a problem. We also have a problem if the government spends $2 million on a new reading program for the child's school and the child then does not read any better than do similar children in similar schools that have not had the program.

FOREIGN AND DEFENSE POLICY

The legislative process is at the heart of domestic policymaking. In defense and foreign policy, however, legislation plays only a limited—although occasionally crucial—role. Foreign policy is made primarily by executive decision within the specialized bureaucracies: the Foreign Service, the military, and the intelligence community. Or it is made by the president acting with the aid of a few advisers. It is necessary, therefore, to sketch briefly a separate analysis of the policymaking process for foreign affairs and defense.

Intelligence   The high stakes of foreign policy and other nations' natural efforts to mislead and conceal vital facts produce a great need for information. It is widely felt that we should know every fact relevant to our security about every nation on earth. These considerations led, after World War II, to the creation of an immense apparatus for gathering information about other countries—the "intelligence community." More than 200,000 government employees presently work in the foreign intelligence field. The major organizations here are the Central Intelligence Agency, the Defense Intelligence Agency (coordinating the individual armed services' intelligence activities), the National Security Agency, and the Department of State.

Recent suspicions of the CIA have not changed this basic pattern. The raw material is information acquired in millions of specific factual bits, much of it from newspapers, magazines, and books. A phenomenal amount of raw data comes from monitoring radio transmissions and radar signals (the work of the NSA). Together with photographs and sensings from space satellites, these electronic readings are perhaps the major sources of defense intelligence. Technological advances have reduced but not eliminated the need for old-fashioned espionage. The more difficult part of intelligence-gathering is interpretation. This means both determining the reliability of each report and interpreting information to make it useful to policymakers. "What does it mean?" is as crucial a question as "Is it true?" One culmination of the process is the National Intelligence Estimate that is handed daily to the president.

Like nations everywhere, we have done much better at collection than evaluation, particularly in the realm of political intelligence. We usually know the names and positions of all the players in some struggling new or old nation. But we may be unable to figure out in advance whether the game they are going to play is waiting or revolution. Even more important, we often do not know who is going to win—the old government, the new generals, or the Communists. More often than not, this is because there is *too much information,* much of it contradictory or ambiguous.[19] Somebody on our side "knew" that the generals were going to try a coup on March 16th. But somebody else "knew" equally well that they weren't. Confronted with this phenomenon, the crucial analytical question is not what data exist somewhere in the intelligence net, but whether policymakers have a clear idea of what is going on.

Continuity and Crisis: In examining the invention of alternatives, let us separate de-
Inventing Alternatives fense from foreign policy. The Defense Department and its research and development contractors have been fertile in the invention of new weapons systems. After a period of relying primarily on our advantage in atomic bombs and strategic bombers, the Defense Department has shifted to a constant and aggressive search for new and better systems of many different kinds. An incredible number and variety of science fiction weapons has been considered, selected, and discarded. Yet the armed services tend to cling to traditional weapons such as the bomber and the aircraft carrier when such weapons are viewed as essential to maintaining their independent missions.

Turning from military planning to foreign policy, we can see that just after World War II there was a period of enormous innovation. We took the lead in creating the United Nations, gave generous economic aid to war-ravaged Europe, and for the first time pledged to defend nations that were attacked. These were all major efforts of political creativity—the inventing of new policies. *Containment* was the overarching policy of this period. It became the policy of the United States to intervene actively throughout the world to "contain" the expansion of Soviet power by military, diplomatic, and other methods. In the three decades since the end of World War II, our economic and military aid and our troop commitments abroad have changed with events overseas and with our domestic political situation. But only in the aftermath of Vietnam have fundamental questions been raised about the policy. Containment was based on a vision of the world in which only two nations counted, the U.S. and the U.S.S.R. The world is now a much more complicated place, and we are seeking to evolve new policies to deal with it.

Many outsiders and a number of presidents have voiced the complaint that the State Department never has any new ideas. The department's response has been to insist that diplomacy thrives on continuity and coordination. Certainly the department has not been a major generator of new policy alternatives; many new ideas have come from the White House and from the Pentagon. When new foreign policy has been made, it is often a response to a crisis rather than a result of an ongoing effort to generate alternatives and choose the best of them. This is

[19] The classic study of the complex interaction between information and readiness is Roberta Wohlstetter, *Pearl Harbor: Warning and Decision* (Stanford, Calif.: Stanford University Press, 1962).

Wide World

Foreign policy decisions often are made in informal meetings like this one on Middle Eastern peace negotiations. From left, Secretary of State Cyrus Vance, President Carter, Zbigniew Brzezinski, assistant to the President for national security affairs, and three aides.

so largely because in foreign affairs, cost-benefit studies are in fact attempts to predict what other nations will do in the future. Such predictions are very hard to make and often prove wrong. So there is a tendency to proceed one step at a time, pausing after each move to see how the other side reacts.

For this reason, foreign policymaking has a peculiar pattern. The State Department devotes most of its energies to keeping abreast of developments, essentially a matter of gathering intelligence and maintaining diplomatic contacts with foreign leaders. Much of the time, our foreign policy relating to most of the countries of the world consists of treading water. Officials are content to keep doing whatever they have been doing as long as things are tolerably quiet. When things are not tolerably quiet, the whole picture changes. In a crisis, choices must be made even if the policymakers cannot predict the eventual outcome with great confidence. This is why the period immediately after World War II was so rich in initiatives. The traditional international system had collapsed, and crises existed everywhere. As the world has gradually stabilized itself, the pace of new American policymaking has slowed. We interpreted Fidel Castro's triumph in Cuba as a crisis that stimulated a new round of policymaking toward Latin America. This slowed down as we saw that Castro could not duplicate his success elsewhere. Vietnam similarly inspired a reassessment of our Asian policies and some effort to readjust our relations with China and Japan. The Middle Eastern crisis and the energy crisis have left us in the mood for policy innovations.

When decisions are made during crises, the center of policymaking tends to shift from the bureaucracy to the White House. International crises are, after all, the president's responsibility. This leads to one of the strange contradictions of American politics. Presidents complain that they are nearly powerless to control the State Department or even to inspire it to new initiatives. At the same time, Foreign Service officers constantly claim that no one ever listens to them and that policy is made by the White House.[20] In noncrisis periods, the president can do little more than talk about the need for dynamic policy while the State Department goes on with its daily routine. In times of crisis, the president moves in. Naturally, he relies on people whom he trusts the most, and these are generally not career State Department officials.

The real question here is how much conscious priority-setting actually gets done by the president in times of crisis. In one sense a crisis is, almost by definition, a setting of priorities. Some particular problem or situation—Russian missiles to Cuba, a fall in the international price of the dollar, a Mideast war—is seen as far more important than anything else at the moment and requiring immediate attention. But in another sense a crisis may simply mean that in one particular area

---

[20] I. M. Destler, *Presidents, Bureaucrats and Foreign Policy* (Princeton, N.J.: Princeton University Press, 1974); and Graham Allison and Peter Szanton, *Remaking Foreign Policy: The Organizational Connection* (New York: Basic Books, 1976).

something terrible is happening at the moment or will happen soon unless we act quickly. In other words, a crisis may command attention not because this particular matter is especially important in comparison with all other problems facing the United States, but only because it is something to which we must respond immediately if we are to respond at all. There is always the danger that the president and his advisers, shifting from one crisis of this sort to the next, will never get time to shape policy for our most important long-term problems.

Secrecy   Making foreign policy involves a paradox created by the intersection of three factors. First, because of great uncertainties and high stakes, the president needs the frankest advice he can get from those he trusts. But if the advice given him were made public, his advisers could not speak frankly. Other countries, which lack our tradition of open government, would be reluctant to talk seriously to us if they knew the conversation would end up in the newspapers. Second, given the world as it exists today, many of the decisions made in foreign policy, the reasons behind them, and the information on which they were based must be kept secret. It would hardly do to have *The New York Times* announce that we have begun secret talks with China that we do not want the Russians to know about. Much foreign policy is conducted in a situation in which we do not want to tell the other side what we are doing. Therefore, we cannot tell our own side either, because there is no way of telling one without telling the other. The third factor is that the United States has long traditions of popular involvement in government and the public's "right to know" what its leaders are doing. But by its very nature, foreign policy must be made in secret by a small and closed circle. How can this be squared with the desire for "open government?"

A partial answer is that the two are somewhat inconsistent. Foreign policy cannot be made in a goldfish bowl, any more than generals could plan battles on television. This is not, by our definition, undemocratic. As we saw in Part One, democracy is best thought of as a method of choosing leaders rather than a method of making decisions about specific policy alternatives. There are, however, elements that make the American foreign and defense policymaking process the most open—and often confused—in the world. On those matters, chiefly treaties and appropriations, where Congress must approve the president's proposals, public discussion is assured. Congressional oversight often gives opportunities for leaks, hearings, and conflicts among different foreign policymakers in the executive branch. Second, the mass media provide a fair amount of information about major events on the world scene and American reactions to them.[21] The lack of realistic penalties for disclosing official information gives journalists good sources among unhappy factions in the various bureaucracies dealing with foreign policy. Third, there are many relatively independent and knowledgeable experts who can and do criticize the president's policies on television and in print. As a result, citizens can use public debate and presidential elections to punish or reward the president and his party for his foreign policy performance. This is not a very precise or sophisticat-

[21] See Martin Shapiro, *The Pentagon Papers and the Courts* (San Francisco: Chandler, 1971).

ed weapon, but it does make presidents take public opinion into account more than leaders in other countries.

Coordination   The principal mode of coordination in foreign policy is organizational. The three armed services are in a Department of Defense headed by a civilian secretary of defense and the Joint Chiefs of Staff. They are supposed to coordinate the three services. The State Department is organized geographically. Each group of country directors is supervised by a regional assistant secretary (see Figure 17.2), and the assistant secretaries report to the secretary. Both defense and state also make an attempt to coordinate in the field. Defense is organized into regional field commands coordinating all army, navy, and air force units in a particular area. The State Department uses "country teams" under the leadership of the ambassador. These teams coordinate the work of all American government representatives in each country.

The most important foreign policy coordination is done by the president, with the aid of the National Security Council staff. Most presidents have used formal and informal advisory groups on important foreign policy issues. These groups have various names, but in every instance they consist of a small cluster of presidential assistants and cabinet and subcabinet members. They meet, usually weekly, to advise the president, and to make sure that the various parts of the foreign and defense policy establishment are pulling together and moving in the direction desired by the president. In the last analysis, the major foreign policy decisions of the United States are made by the president in consultation with a handful of personal advisors who meet with him both singly and in small groups. Because these groups typically draw their members from a number of different agencies, they function as coordinating bodies even if they were not particularly designed for that purpose.

Foreign and Domestic Policy   The foreign policy process is different in a number of ways from domestic policymaking. It is more presidency-centered, more secret, more crisis-oriented, and less a matter of distributive policies. It is more anxious to achieve synopticism: to know everything and arrive at perfectly coordinated policies. Nevertheless, it operates within the same general context of parties, interest groups, public opinion, and government institutions as domestic policymaking.

Probably the most crucial factor in bringing domestic and foreign policymaking back together is that the president is heavily engaged in both. If Congress and the public are unhappy with his foreign policy, they may block his domestic policies. And the president may use his powers as commander in chief and chief diplomat to improve his domestic political image, as President Carter did through his Middle East policies. So even when we are aware of the differences between domestic and foreign policymaking, it should be remembered that both take place within the more general dynamics of the American political process.

Figure 17.2
Department of State Organization Chart

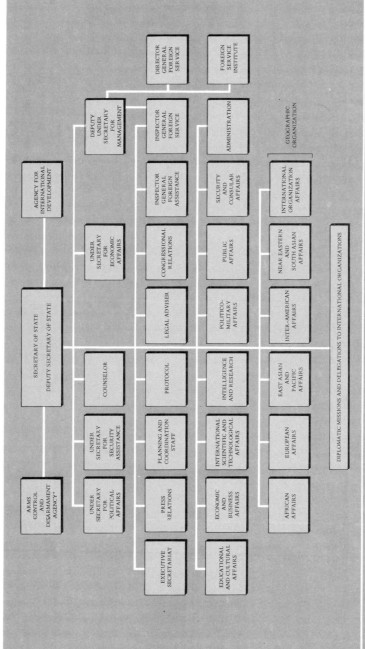

*A separate agency with the director reporting directly to the secretary and serving as principal adviser to the secretary and the president on arms control and disarmament.

SUMMARY   The output of the political system depends as much on how issues are decided as upon who makes the decisions. The synoptic style of decision-making is the popular ideal. It requires that the policymakers specify their goals, identify every alternative policy, and consider the probability that each alternative will achieve each goal. The synoptic style can never be more than a dream, because time and information are scarce and policymakers have different goals. Because it often is difficult to reconcile conflicting goals, one solution is to seek agreement about what to do without worrying about everyone's ultimate purposes. In the real world, policy is made incrementally: A policy is continued until it no longer works. Then the deficient policy is changed to the most similar alternative that seems likely to be successful. Incrementalism allows politicians with conflicting interests to accept solutions that do not threaten cohesion. Incrementalism is more consistent with the common need to act before adequate information is available.

The kind of policy to be made also effects the way policy is decided. Distributive policies, which have clear beneficiaries and no identifiable losers, are easier to adopt and carry out than redistributive policies, in which the costs are clearly borne by one group. Politicians therefore try to treat policies as distributive, to conceal or disperse costs, and to emphasize benefits.

Top policymakers, including elected officials, have too little time and expertise to decide most specific provisions in any area of government. Therefore the actual application of general laws to concrete cases is done by bureaucrats—often rather low in rank—to whom the job of implementation has been delegated.

Congress is less important in foreign and defense policy. In these areas, decision-making is more secret and less a matter of making general rules. Speed and decisiveness are more important, and information is even more difficult to gather, since it is usually in the interest of other governments to conceal their intentions.

evaluating the american political system

Our purpose in this book has been to describe and analyze the national political system. In explaining how the system works, we have tried to avoid judgments about its "goodness" or "badness." We leave that to you. But reasoned, well-informed political evaluation is not easy or straightforward. What features of a system make it "good" or "bad"? By what standards does one judge the system? These are questions to which there is more than one answer. And they are questions that must be understood and answered before any individual can

CHAPTER 18

begin to evaluate a political system. In this concluding chapter, we will look at some factors to consider in evaluating the American system of government.

LOOKING AT POLITICS FROM INSIDE

It is possible to lump all of American politics together and view the whole thing "from the outside." We could then ask "Is the American political system good or bad?" in a total, black-or-white sense. This style of analysis is either too simple or too difficult. Any sort of reasoned answer depends on basic questions of political philosophy and world history that are far beyond the scope of this book. An alternative approach is to establish a critical viewpoint from within the society. We can accept as given the society's general values and institutions. Such a perspective does not accept everything in the society as good. But instead of praising or condemning the whole system as "capitalistic," "elitist," "socialistic," or whatever, this approach examines how separate aspects of the society work in the context of other aspects that we accept as given. Using this style of evaluation, we would not conclude that "A society that tolerates poverty is unjust." Instead, we would ask: "How well does the food stamp program work in meeting the nutritional needs of poor people?" We would not ask: "Is Congress the champion of democracy and freedom?" Rather, we would ask: "Does the House Rules Committee block liberal legislation favored by congressional majorities?"

People who look at politics this way use a number of criteria. Here we consider a few, saving until later in the chapter a look at two of the most important, equality and freedom.

Efficiency is a widely approved performance criterion in the United States. Very few people of any political persuasion are likely to be pleased at paying taxes to support uneconomical programs, Whatever the purpose of a program, we would like it to achieve that purpose at the least cost in public funds.

Feasibility is another standard frequently used to evaluate political policies and procedures. Is a proposed policy politically practical? Will it arouse so much opposition that it cannot be adopted or, if adopted, cannot be effectively implemented? The nationwide 55-mile-per-hour speed limit is an example of the latter. President Carter's proposal to impose an extra tax on "gas-guzzling" cars is one that was too unpopular to be adopted by Congress.

Conflict resolution is a criterion often applied to political institutions. Political systems vary in their capacity to channel conflict constrictively. Without conflict resolution, political stability is difficult. Some minimum level of stability is valued from almost every perspective except that of the revolutionary who wants to destroy the existing political system. High and continuous levels of instability affect most people adversely. Few

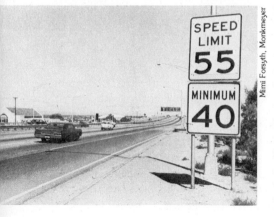

Lower speeds save gasoline, but the national speed limit is not a feasible policy, since state police are reluctant to enforce it.

Mimi Forsyth, Monkmeyer

of us live from day to day. It is difficult to plan if one does not know what laws and rulers will be in force from one month to the next. Why should a farmer plant more crops than his family needs if any surplus will be stolen by marauders? It is hard to be a great painter if one's studio is shelled by the government today and bombed by rebels tomorrow.

Well-being is a fundamental criterion that is easy to recognize but almost impossible to define. Government attempts to specify the good life for individuals meet a major obstacle: different people want different things out of life; one person's bliss is another's boredom. Moreover, yesterday's luxuries are today's necessities. Nevertheless, we expect more from government than that it keep us alive and from killing one another. We often seek to use government as a tool for improving the way we live.

WHAT'S GOOD FOR THE PEOPLE VS. WHAT THE PEOPLE WANT: THE ROLE OF THE EXPERT

Should policies be judged on the basis of whether "the people" like them? Or should they be evaluated on the basis of what experts think best? At first glance, it might seem that if one were committed to a democratic ideology, the answer would be that what the people want is the alternative that should be selected. However, even for the purest democrat, this answer is not always satisfactory. Certainly every one of us has felt at some time that a policy which does not enjoy popular support now could be of such great benefit that people would certainly approve of it once it was in effect. Much talk about creative democratic leadership is a polite way of saying that people must be pulled and hauled into things that they do not really want now but will like once they get them.

Consider the following example. If we know that contour plowing will reduce erosion and increase production, and if the farmer resists contour plowing out of sheer backwardness and suspicion, we may choose to "educate" and "provide incentives" to the farmer to contour-plow. In short, we may push him into what is "really" good for him rather than letting him go on doing what he wants. We can justify our action in terms of democratic values by saying that, deep down, what he truly wants is to live better and we are helping him do that. Or we may say that his current desires are a product of ignorance; once he is properly educated, he will want the better policy. Or we may say that the nation's need to conserve its natural resources is so great that it overrides the farmer's right to treat his own property as he wishes.

This type of problem is dealt with regularly in American politics. The survey data reported earlier in this book show that in day-to-day politics "the people" usually do not have any firm view of what they want (see Chapter 7). Even the most committed democratic leader must make decisions on the basis of what he or she thinks people would want if they were aware of and understood the alternatives. The people can always vote that leader out of office. We may agree that the people are not the best judge of their own interests without also agreeing that they should be deprived of the right to choose their leaders, because democracy includes the right to be wrong.

At one time, people were confident that rule by scientific experts promised a correct, impartial, scientific substitute for politics. Why should politicians bargain, struggle, and negotiate about what should be done, when experts could settle the matter in the best way for all concerned? Today, however, most observers are no longer so willing to hand over policy evaluation and decision-making to the "experts." In part, we are suspicious of experts because of our belief in majority rule. Rule by experts means rule by the few over the many. Our suspicion of experts also arises from awareness of the possibility that their recommendations are translations of the expert's own personal political preferences into scientific language. This is one reason why one expert is often contradicted by another. But even in the natural sciences specialists often disagree for reasons that have nothing to do with politics. And as one progresses from, say, physics to biology to economics to sociology, the range of issues that can be resolved by expertise shrinks dramatically. The unhappy truth is that expert knowledge is insufficient to deal with many of our worst problems because, with all the good will in the world, the experts often cannot offer more than educated guesses. A sensible politician would rely more on experts when deciding about bridge building than when worrying about slums. Construction engineers know how to build bridges, whereas sociologists have not yet demonstrated much skill in dealing with slums.

Frequently, conflicts in evaluation are conflicts over *which* set of experts should make the decisions rather than over *whether* experts or "the people" should make the decision. This conflict usually rests on the belief that one set of experts will make good decisions and another will make bad ones. For instance, someone may criticize current defense budgeting practices on the ground that too much power is given to the civilian budget experts in the office of the secretary of defense. This critic probably is saying two things: First, he is saying that the military experts representing the fighting branches are more qualified to make correct defense decisions than are the civilians. Second, he is saying that the military experts are likely to want higher expenditures, which he sees as a desirable policy. To offer another example, what a forest will look like ten years from now will be significantly different depending on whether control of the forest is left to an expert on timber management or an expert on wildlife preservation.

In sum, whether to use experts for making policy evaluations really raises two questions. First, should the decision be made by experts at all, or should it be made by "the people"? And second, if experts are to make the decision, *which* set of experts should be chosen to deal with the particular policy?

WHAT GOVERNMENT CAN AND SHOULD DO

So far we have assumed that there are no bounds to government action. We have assumed that government can and should do anything and everything that seems to contribute to achieving a particular set of goals. Yet this assumption itself must be evaluated.

Governmental Responsibility Are there limits to what the government is responsible for? Should political officials or the system itself be blamed for everything that is wrong, from unhealthy coal mines to unsatisfactory sex lives? If so, should the government also get the credit for pleasant parks and happy marriages? It is easy to believe that Americans of all political persuasions are more likely to give blame than praise. If something is wrong, it is the government's fault, but a success story does not earn points on the credit side of the ledger. This apparent inconsistency can be illustrated by considering the recent history of two racial minorities, blacks and Japanese-Americans.

Since World War II, Americans of Japanese descent have achieved remarkable levels of schooling, prosperity, and civic participation. In a generation, they have become better educated and richer than whites. The only governmental contribution to this success story was the repeal of laws that denied Asian-Americans rights enjoyed by other people. Do we think this is a triumph for enlightened public policy, or "merely" evidence of the openness of American society? In the same period, the unequal condition of blacks has been the nation's most important domestic political issue. Uncounted billions of dollars and great amounts of effort, sacrifice, and good will have been expended to achieve racial equality. Progress has been made, but blacks are still worse off than whites in almost every measure of the good life. This racial gap is considered by many to be the greatest single failing of American society.

Why do we pay more attention to failure than success? One reason, of course, is that bad news is more newsworthy. Another is that any society always has some people who pounce on bad news as evidence for their ideas. The most important reason, however, is that almost all Americans are still deeply influenced by the notions of laissez-faire we discussed in Chapter 6. We tend to think that limited government is best, that the government should stay out of people's lives. Fear of too much government power is widespread in the United States. But Americans also look to the government for help when something goes wrong—a damaging flood, the impending bankruptcy of New York City or Chrysler, rising college tuition. To be sure, liberals are likely to support bailing out New York City and to oppose similar guarantees for Chrysler, while conservatives take the opposite position. But this inconsistency in applying "pure principle" should not mislead us from the larger consistency: Americans think that the government is a source of help when the going is rough, not a constant presence in all aspects of their lives, rain or shine.[1]

Governmental Capacity Quite apart from what the government *should* do is the question of what it *can* do. Even if we believed the government should make everyone happy, few of us would believe it could. In recent years, many social critics have come to think that we ask the government to attempt tasks

---

[1] Even so, there are many problems most Americans consider beyond the proper concern of government. Only 28 percent of a national sample believe that the government is responsible for dealing with whatever personal problem worries them the most. See Paul M. Sniderman and Richard A. Brody, "Coping: The Ethic of Self-Reliance," *American Journal of Political Science, 21* (August 1977), pp. 501–22.

beyond its capacity. One result of such overoptimistic expectations may be growing cynicism about the whole political system. Another result of excessive demands is to shift the emphasis from the impossible to the attainable. For example, nothing seems effective in reducing the crime rate. Officials turn their attention, therefore, to criminal justice goals that are more modest and more attainable: treating prisoners equally, providing equal access to attorneys, compensating victims of crime, and the like. Such policies, no matter how worthwhile they are, do not actually reduce the number of criminal acts. This process is called **goal substitution:** turning from a goal that cannot be achieved to lesser goals that are feasible.

The government's immense expenditures on medical care do not achieve an ultimate goal—equal health. But they are a major stride toward a substitute goal—equal access to medical care. Medicare and Medicaid may not make everyone healthier, but they already have come close to providing equality between rich and poor in the number of visits to doctors. Thus, another consequence of the government's inability to solve some problems is to substitute effort for achievement. Instead of judging Medicaid by how it improves health, it is evaluated by the amount of money spent to pay for trips to doctors and hospitals. The real goal is not an equal number of doctor's appointments for everybody, but that may be the best we can expect.

Limiting Conflict   In addition to limits on the government's responsibility and capacity, a third factor tends to restrict the scope of government further. One of the principal tasks of government is resolution, moderation, and/or channeling of conflict. Even when a governmental solution to a social problem seems possible, it may generate so much conflict that it cannot be undertaken. It is in this sense that politics is sometimes defined as "the art of the possible." One of the first things that surprises novice social and political reformers is how often their "obviously right" solutions appear to be "obviously wrong" to others who will fight against them.

The laws against smoking marijuana are seldom enforced any more because even people opposed to marijuana are unwilling to go very far to suppress its use.

Mimi Forsyth, Monkmeyer

Whether conflict over policies arises from the clash of selfish interests or from genuine differences of opinion over what would best serve the public interest, the presence of conflict itself becomes a limiting factor. It is not enough to demonstrate that a problem exists and that a workable government solution is available. It is also necessary to achieve at least some minimum level of consent for the solution. This need for consent is not only one of the pragmatic needs of our particular processes—the need to get votes in Congress—it is also a response to a broader social need to minimize political conflict. If "good" policies threaten to create so much social conflict that the society may break apart in ways that would drastically diminish the quality of day-to-day life, then only an unusually intense ideologue would believe those policies worth having, no matter how well they solve some particular social problem.

In an open society like ours, such imposed solutions are not even likely to accomplish the purpose for which they were intended. Prohibition of alcoholic beverages is the best-known example of a policy that failed because it could not be enforced short of a police state. The more recent collapse of efforts to enforce the laws against marijuana makes the same point. Too many people did not share the majority view that marijuana use should be prohibited. And many of the antimarijuana majority did not approve the drastic and expensive police effort required to enforce the laws. Despite their disapproval, they did not think the cost of stamping out marijuana was justified.

POLITICS AS A CORRECTIVE IN POLITICAL EVALUATION

As the account throughout this book of how the American political system expresses and channels political conflict shows, individual political evaluation does not occur in a vacuum or take place from a pedestal. Nor is the information on which it is based available only through formal evaluation. We are well supplied with free evaluative reasoning and information, much of it from "interested parties." Many proposed policies will adversely affect the interests of some groups, who will demand modification or compensation. A policy issue that may appear to be simple in a news release or in a magazine article becomes much more complicated as it is subjected to genuine differences of opinion about specific details and the bargaining that is necessary to deal with those differences of opinion.

The promoters of great plans are often willing to give government practically unlimited powers in one field, although such powers in another field would terrify them. For example, people who condemn the "military-industrial complex" or see signs of police repression everywhere often propose ecological policies that would give bureaucrats enormous power to control how individuals can use air, land, and water. Naturally, they feel that environmental bureaucrats will be good bureaucrats, as opposed to the bad bureaucrats in the Defense Department. Others who are not so concerned with saving every last tree — for instance, people who earn a living as loggers — may have their doubts about the benevolence of the environmental bureaucrats. The simple and obvious solution to many problems often is to give the government vast powers to "fix things" immediately. Yet an evaluation of any new program that stops with the "plan" is hopelessly incomplete. Very often a sweeping solution may look good on paper, but its implementation may raise so many problems of conflict, power, and capacity that it is not really a good solution. Sometimes we may conclude that political considerations prevent a good policy from being implemented. But just as frequently we will discover that a proposal which cannot survive the give-and-take of politics is not such a good proposal after all. For politics often consists of bringing many evaluations from many different viewpoints together and asking just how the grand plan will work out on a day-to-day basis for the people involved. This kind of detailed evaluation by those directly concerned may prove to be a better evaluation than that of whoever first proposed a new policy.

COMPARATIVE ANALYSIS

One aid to the evaluation of the relative merits of various policies and procedures is comparative analysis. For example, some light is shed on the comparative value of capitalism and communism by comparing the United States and the Soviet Union. Similarly, we can learn something about the level of welfare and economic regulation that is compatible with a basically capitalistic system by comparing the United States and Sweden. Such evaluations run well beyond the scope of this book, but they are instructive ways of gaining some general perspective on the American political system.

In recent years, for example, some people have concluded that the United States is a "sick society." In an attempt to understand this evaluation, Benjamin F. Wright raises the following comparative questions:

> Is today's society less well — or sicker — than that of 40 years ago, when unemployment was far beyond anything this generation has known? Or sick as compared with 140 years ago, when slavery existed in about a third of the country, when labor unions were conspiracies in the eyes of the law, when men, women, and children worked 14 hour days in mills and factories — until laid off or discarded? Where would one find a well country? In the Communist bloc? In Africa, the Middle East, or South America? Even the small homogeneous countries of Western Europe have critical problems.[2]

The more specific a comparison is, the more immediate value it has. For instance, students of government health policy frequently compare the government programs that guarantee medical care to everyone in most European nations with the traditional American reliance on private enterprise. Whereas some nations had guaranteed medical care as long ago as the nineteenth century, it was not until the 1940s that serious attempts were made in the United States to introduce health programs that were not dependent on the individual's ability to pay. Intense lobbying by organized medicine defeated all such efforts for a generation. Eventually the overwhelmingly Democratic Congress swept into office in the landslide 1964 election passed Medicare legislation. But even this major step only provided government funding for the care of retired people on social security, plus people receiving public assistance.

One consequence of our failure to achieve government-guaranteed universal medical care is higher infant mortality than other advanced countries (Table 18.1). On the other hand, the United States invests heavily in education — as shown, for example, by substantially higher school enrollments. Comparison, then, allows us to look at various priority and distribution mixes. Other nations mix more medicine with less education. We do the opposite. The comparison, of course, does not tell us which mix is better, but it does permit the individual to make a more informed evaluation of the performance of our political system.

Comparative evaluation can also serve as a check on unrealistic standards.

---

[2] Benjamin F. Wright, review of *The Idea of Fraternity in America,* by Wilson Carey McWilliams, *Journal of Politics,* 36 (August 1974), pp. 824–25.

Table 18.1
**Infant Mortality and Proportion of Children in School,
Selected Industrial Nations**

Nation	Infant Mortality Rate*	Percentage of 15- to 18-Year-Olds in School Full Time
United States	18.5	87%
Sweden	10.8	68
France	13.3	55
Japan	11.7	69

*Number of deaths per thousand per year of infants under the age of one.

Source: *Social Indicators 1976* (Washington: U.S. Department of Commerce, 1977).

Before we conclude that any feature of American politics is good or bad, it is useful to see if any other nation has been doing better or worse, and at what costs. For instance, the often heard call for a more ideologically coherent and disciplined two-party system that will give American voters a real choice between alternative policies may be tested against the British experience of strongly disciplined parties. It is clear that this British party discipline has reduced the independent lawmaking power of Parliament nearly to zero. It is not clear, however, that it has given British voters any greater control over their own destinies than American voters have had. Nor is it clear that it has contributed to effective leadership geared to solving Britain's social and economic problems.[3]

In another example, we note that some people have proposed a multilingual American society in which Mexican-American and Puerto Rican citizens would be encouraged to continue speaking Spanish. These proposals must be checked against the failure of similar systems in other countries that have tried to maintain two or more national languages. Even such stable, prosperous, and democratic nations as Canada and Belgium continue to be wracked by language conflicts. Around the world, official minority languages seem to be highly correlated with low economic status and political discontent. Only in Switzerland has the linguistic problem been solved with relative satisfaction. But the situation in Switzerland is so historically and geographically peculiar that it can hardly be used as a model for the United States.

This last point raises the greatest difficulty of comparative evaluation. Nations are, of course, very different from one another. Each is so much a product of its own peculiar history and culture that we can never be certain if a procedure or policy which is successful in one country will work in another.

Because we have a federal system in which many local governments enjoy some degree of autonomy, comparison need not be confined to foreign countries. We may conclude that the state of Oregon manages its forests better than the U.S. Forest Service manages its forests. This conclusion can be tested by comparing two forests in Oregon, one run by the federal government and the other by the state

[3] Kenneth N. Waltz, *Foreign Policy and Democratic Politics* (Boston: Little, Brown, 1967).

government. The overlapping and parallelism of federal and state activities often provide fertile ground for comparative evaluations. Many federal programs have been modeled on earlier state or local experience, and vice versa. If we notice that the city of Omaha collects garbage once a week at a cost of 75 cents per house per week, while Kansas City provides the same service at a cost of $3.50, our critical senses are likely to perk up. An an evaluative tool, comparative analysis is ideologically even-handed. Comparison sometimes reveals that everyone has about the same problem (for example, air pollution) and that no one seems to be doing much better at solving it than we are. Or if they are solving the problem, it may be because they are paying more attention to its solution, while giving less attention to some other important problems on which we are doing better. Comparison can also be a dynamic technique that fuels demands for change and provides information about how to do a better job. If a British small businessman is not driven into bankruptcy by his hospital bills, why should an American be? If the courts in Minneapolis are trying cases within six months, why should people have to wait two-and-a-half years in Memphis? Why shouldn't the infant mortality rate in the United States be lower than that of any other country? Comparison frequently will reveal that something actually *can* be done because someone else has done it.

AMERICANS' EVALUATION OF THEIR POLITICAL SYSTEM

In principle anyone can judge a political system without caring what other people think of it. Nevertheless, a system that satisfies its citizens is more likely to merit our approval than one that does not. This might be a judgment for its own sake, or it might be based on a belief that citizen satisfaction fosters political stability, willingness to obey the laws, and simple patriotism. The most superficial approach measures individuals' political disaffection as expressed in answers to specific questions about governmental performance. In the twelve years from 1964 to 1976, many

Table 18.2
Trends in Political Disaffection

	Percentage Agreeing	
	1964	1976
Quite a few political leaders are crooked.	29%	43%
The government wastes a lot of money.	46	74
The government is run by a few big interests.	29	65
People running government don't seem to know what they are doing.	27	49
The government can be trusted to do what is right only some of the time.	22	62

Source: National Election Studies of the University of Michigan Center for Political Studies, obtained through the Inter-University Consortium for Political and Social Research and computed by the authors.

Most Americans were pleased to see the end of U.S. commitment in Southeast Asia.

more Americans said they distrusted the government and considered its leaders dishonest, incompetent, wasteful, and working for the benefit of a few big interests. These findings are summarized in Table 18.2.

Several specific sources of increased disaffection can be identified. One is the war in Vietnam. Those who favored either withdrawal or escalation were more cynical than those who liked the policy being pursued at the time — limited military operations combined with negotiations for a settlement. Race relations are a second source of alienation. As with the Vietnam war, those at the two extremes in their policy preferences were the most disaffected, whereas people who favored moderate policies were the least. Both those who wanted much more government help for minority groups and those who said minorities should look out for themselves were far more hostile to government and politicians. Similarly, people who thought the civil rights movement was pushing too fast and those who thought it was not going fast enough were more cynical than those who thought that the movement's pace was about right.[4]

Another explanation for rising disaffection seems to be an increase in expectations. Americans want more from government than they used to. New needs and standards of comfort have developed. The more new social policies the government enacts, the more social policies people expect. This explains why, as Aaron Wildavsky puts it, "We are all, in fact, doing better and feeling worse." The reason, he argues, is that we have generated "policy demands that impose burdens on government which no government can meet."[5] Those Americans who look to the government for solutions to their problems are more cynical than those who doubt that the cures for all society's ills lie in government action.[6]

How politically significant is the increasing disposition of Americans to speak cynically of their government and its leaders? To a remarkable degree, cynical attitudes do not seem to affect individual behavior. Cynics are neither more nor less likely to vote than noncynics. Nor are their voting patterns different. In fact, it is difficult to find *any* way in which the alienated differ from people who are not disaffected.[7] The consequences of the growing cynicism probably are limited to greater emphasis on the character of political candidates and to the popular demand for such recent procedural innovations as campaign finance reform.

[4] Arthur H. Miller, "Political Issues and Trust in Government: 1964–1970," *American Political Science Review,* 68 (September 1974), pp. 951–72.

[5] Aaron Wildavsky, "Government and the People," *Commentary,* August 1973, p. 25. Most Americans think that the federal government is "too big and bureaucratic" and should return more tax money to the states. They also think that the federal government should care for the poor, feed the hungry, regulate business, avoid inflation and depression, and so on. Hugh Heclo, *A Government of Strangers* (Washington: The Brookings Institution, 1977), p. 113.

[6] Sniderman and Brody, "Coping."

[7] Jack Citrin, "The Alienated Voter," *Taxing and Spending,* 1 (October–November 1978), pp. 6–11.

PERSONAL EXPERIENCE VS. STEREOTYPES

A great many Americans have personal encounters with bureaucrats when they seek help from government agencies. These are not usually cheerful occasions. People who need a job, workmen's compensation, welfare, medical care, or retirement benefits generally are not on top of the world. What do they think of their treatment by the civil servant on the other side of the desk?

Research on citizen responses to these "bureaucratic encounters" yields a happy surprise: more than two-thirds said they were completely satisfied with the way their problem was handled. With minor variations, people in different racial and income groups agreed on the fairness, efficiency, and helpfulness of the bureaucrats with whom they dealt.

The picture changed drastically when these people were asked not about their personal experiences, but about "most government offices." The same people who professed satisfaction with their own bureaucratic contacts nevertheless had negative views of the bureaucracy in general. For example, 80 percent of the people in the study said they themselves were treated fairly, but only 42 percent said that "government offices" gave people fair treatment. Stereotypes about insolent, inconsiderate, inefficient bureaucrats are so strong that they persist despite experiences with pleasant, considerate, efficient bureaucrats.

Source: Daniel Katz et al., *Bureaucratic Encounters* (Ann Arbor: University of Michigan Social Research, 1975).

In fact, attitudes about "the system" are far from wholly negative. Americans indicate a general sense of satisfaction with their nation and its institutions that scarcely suggests a population sunk in despair about its governance. In 1976, when asked whether the United States needed a change in its form of government, the most common response (45 percent) was "leave it as it is." Most of the people who said they wanted a change had no specific suggestions to make, and the single most common response was a wish for less financial waste. Only about one percent wanted a different form of government or a form practiced elsewhere in the world, such as a parliamentary or a communist system.

Asked explicitly whether they were proud of the American form of government, three-quarters said Yes, one-fifth said No, and the others were undecided. Most agreed that the problem with government was the caliber of people in office rather than the nature of the system.

Other evidence reveals broad satisfaction with life in America, both in general and with respect to the specific major aspects of personal experience. In 1974, only 4 percent of the

"My confidence in the system is restored. I really was guilty."

Drawing by Joseph Farris; © 1975 The New Yorker Magazine, Inc.

American adult population gave the United States an unfavorable rating. In 1973, 71 percent said they were satisfied with their standard of living, 61 percent were satisfied with their children's education, and 74 percent were satisfied with their housing situation. Among those who worked, 90 percent were satisfied with their jobs. This general acceptance of American life is also reflected in the fact that only 11 percent of the adult population said that if they were free to do so, they would like to settle in another country. And of these 11 percent, most would settle in Australia, Canada and Great Britain—countries with political systems very similar to that of the United States. Americans were more satisfied than people in other countries.[8]

MANAGING CONFLICT

In evaluating what a political system has done to solve society's problems, we must ask whether it has held conflict to tolerable levels. Has the ideal solution to some problem been avoided out of sheer stupidity and selfishness, or because the contemplated change would generate intolerably high levels of conflict? It would be a mistake, however, to assume that the society exhibiting the least conflict necessarily has the best government. Disagreement is inherent in human nature; it arises from individual differences in occupation, wealth, religion, ability, taste, temperament, race, opinion, and other human characteristics. Moreover, a certain level of dynamism, creativity, and change is beneficial, and when a society is changing there is bound to be conflict. Indeed, we may suspect that a society with a very low level of conflict is suffering from stagnation or oppression.

The crucial point, then, is the system's record in accommodating disagreements without stifling them. Does it facilitate the resolution of conflict? Does it impose a lockstep conformity or fan the flames of violence and hatred? The world has seen many societies torn apart by relentless conflict between factions that could not find peaceful means of resolving their differences. And we have had all too many political systems where every aspect of personal life is organized in government-controlled groups, where disputes are defined as sabotage or treason, and the secret police make sure that conflict never surfaces.

The final complication involves the question of how much and what kinds of conflict should be handled through political channels. In different areas we want conflict politicized to different degrees. For example, the National Labor Relations Board was created as a governmental means of resolving labor-management conflicts. The NLRB is an independent regulatory commission, partially insulated from day-to-day political influence. It presides over labor-management bargaining without imposing agreements on the bargainers. In this way, labor-management disputes are brought part way, but not all the way, into governmental channels. On the other hand, there are some areas where it seems best not to handle conflict politically. Religion is one. The "no establishment clause" of the Constitution was in

---

[8] *Gallup Opinion Index*, February 1974, pp. 11–13; *The Gallup Poll* release, December 6, 1973; Graham L. Staines et al., "Is Worker Discontent Rising?" *Economic Outlook U.S.A.*, 1 (summer 1974), p. 11; and David Gergen, "A Report from the Editors on the 'Crisis of Confidence,'" *Public Opinion*, August/September 1979.

part intended as a guarantee of religious freedom. More important, it reflected the Founding Fathers' desire to avoid the politicization of religious conflict that led to the bloody religious wars of seventeenth-century Europe. Recent experiences in Ireland, the Middle East, and the Indian subcontinent show that religion and politics continue to be a dangerous mixture.

Parochial schools in America are in desperate need of money. If the 7 percent of American children who attend parochial schools were transferred into the public schools, enormous new burdens on public education would result. Obviously, it is not in the national interest for the quality of schools handling a substantial portion of our children to deteriorate further. From the problem-solving perspective, the best solution would be federal aid to parochial schools. From the point of view of conflict resolution, however, it is not so easy to endorse general federal aid to parochial schools. There has been little explicit conflict between Catholics and Protestants in this country, because the religious issues that divide Catholics and Protestants have been rare and indirect. Unrestricted government aid to parochial schools would bring these conflicts into the open, and into the electoral arena. Catholic versus Protestant confrontations are a sight most of us wish to avoid. Thus, while recognizing the plight of Catholic schools, many political leaders—Protestant and Catholic alike—have sought to sidetrack parochial school aid proposals or to package them with other aid provisions (such as proposals to provide more science labs to all schools). In this way, the religious question is camouflaged in order to prevent the politicization of religious conflict.

In sum, any thorough evaluation of political performance must take into account how well the political system works in softening or resolving social conflict. Such an evaluation should analyze the society's potential for disunity, including an examination of its social, ethnic, and economic diversity. To what extent are disputes among different blocs contained and controlled? Are different socioeconomic groups at each others' throats? Are societal conflicts settled peacefully, or by violence?

EQUALITY

As we saw in Chapter 6, there is significant ideological disagreement over the meaning of equality. At one extreme are those for whom equality means that people with the same amounts of talent, property, or wisdom should be treated equally. This definition carries with it the recognition that these qualities are not equally distributed among the population as a whole. At the other extreme are the absolute egalitarians who believe that each person should have exactly what the next person has. In between is an infinite number of intermediate ideological positions. Some wave the banner of "equality of opportunity"; others emphasize the difference between equality in different areas of life. Some people taking this tack think that if one form of equality is assured—say, economic equality—the other forms of equality naturally will follow. Others argue that the only form of equality that should be guaranteed is political rights like voting and free speech. The rest, they argue, should be left to individual ability, initiative, and taste. The government's role

*What kinds of equality—political, economic, social—
should government attempt to ensure?*

should be limited to providing an absolute minimum level of subsistence to people who literally cannot care for themselves and their children.

Probably the greatest ideological split with regard to equality concerns the relationship between diversity and equality. Even the most extreme egalitarian does not call for a world in which every person is the same as every other in thought, action, appearance, and feelings. The egalitarian tends to believe that people can be equal and still be spontaneous, creative, and thus different from one another. Those who are suspicious of equality are likely to believe that it can be attained only by imposing a flat uniformity on all individuals. They argue that whatever the biological or social causes, inequalities of talent, taste, skill, ambition, and energy are

TWO KINDS OF EQUALITY

Equal access to public facilities sometimes requires spending large amounts of money for the benefit of very few people. Does the principle of equality mean that everyone should have equal access, or that every American should receive the benefit of equal amounts of government money? What if it takes much more money to give some people services that the majority take for granted? This has become a real issue as the handicapped rights movement has influenced the federal government to require that any public facility receiving federal funds be made accessible to the handicapped. For example, the new subway in Washington has many features to make it easier for use by disabled people, at a cost of $72 million. At present, only twelve people in wheelchairs use the system daily; when it is finished, as many as 200 more may do so. It would be cheaper to provide a "dial-a-ride" service to take each disabled person to and from his individual destination. Leaders of organizations for the handicapped reject this type of solution, arguing that access to the regular mass transit system is a basic right that should be available to everyone, irrespective of handicap. One federal official says that the costs of equal access are not the point, because a basic issue of civil rights is at stake: "Someone's rights do not depend upon someone else's ability to pay. It is a matter of the right to participate in American society."

Source: Rochelle L. Stanfield, "Bringing the World to the Disabled — The Feds Start to Get Tough," *National Journal,* February 18, 1978, pp. 273–76; and Timothy B. Clark, "Access for the Handicapped — A Test of Carter's War on Inflation," *National Journal,* October 21, 1978, p. 1672.

so deeply embedded in *all* societies that meaningful levels of equality could be achieved only by the repressive leveling of all individuals to a lowest common denominator. The anti-egalitarian is likely to feel that equality and mediocrity go hand in hand.

The anti-egalitarian might also point out that superior technical, economic, and cultural attainments can be achieved only through the division of labor, and that such a division necessarily means inequality. Some people can specialize in brain surgery only if others specialize in mopping up the operating room. Inequalities of all sorts inevitably will arise between the surgeon and the orderly. To all this, the egalitarian might reply that we are too much the prisoners of past social structures. Why should the surgeon make more money than the orderly? Like most creative people, the surgeon undoubtedly finds the work challenging, exciting, and intrinsically rewarding. The best surgeons would probably want to be surgeons even if they did not get paid for it, just as many artists now struggle at their craft through their whole lives without ever making a living at it. But the orderly probably does not get this kind of intrinsic reward from work. Perhaps he or she should be compensated for the drudgery of the work by getting *more* money.

In evaluating any existing political system, the result will necessarily depend in part on where the evaluator falls along this ideological spectrum. What is "equal enough" or "as equal as can be expected" to one person may appear grossly unequal to another. Even strictly in terms of political equality, the American picture is mixed. We have achieved equality in voting. But money, energy, and commitment still play extremely important roles in politics. Sometimes movements toward greater equality in one area may undercut equality in another. For example, the growth of presidential primaries has increased the influence of rank-and-file voters on presidential nominations. Primary campaigns require additional contributions, however. Prospective candidates can rarely throw their hats in the primary ring unless they have first found some financial backing. Attempts to reduce the influence of such backers by limiting campaign contributions help well-known incumbent candidates at the expense of new and unknown rivals.

Over and above all other pressures toward inequality in American politics is the division of political labor. As long as some people are willing to spend hours a day on politics while most are unwilling to devote minutes a month, the system is bound to produce great inequalities in political power. Whether a sufficient number of factors have been built into the political system to reduce this inequality to acceptable levels is a central question.

At this point many critics would argue that the separation we have been making between political and socioeconomic equality is naive. Depending on the individual's circumstances, equality can be close to meaningless. As the great French author Anatole France observed, "The Law in its majestic equality forbids the rich as well as the poor to sleep under bridges, to beg in the streets, and to steal bread." Such critics would also insist that any society with great disparities of wealth inevitably will see those disparities reflected in the distribution of political power. This may be true, but it is of little consequence unless political cleavages resemble the lines between rich and poor.

The mainstream of American thought has always insisted that democratic politics can exist side by side with disparities in wealth. Indeed, many would maintain that it is precisely because we have economic inequality that we need political equality to protect the majority from the abuse of the wealthy. (This is a highly abstract argument, of course. As we have seen in Chapters 7–9, rich people are no more united on political issues than anyone else, and their campaign contributions are given to candidates of all political persuasions.) The combination of democracy, capitalism, industrialism, socialism, and welfare that is America's current working ideology is certainly built on this view. We seek to preserve individual freedom and creativity by limiting the intervention of government in the economy and society. At the same time, the abuse of power that might arise from differences in wealth is to be countered by a relatively egalitarian political system. Antitrust laws, regulatory commissions, and free public education are examples of governmental policies designed to curb economic power and help equalize opportunity.

Table 18.3 tells us something about the level of income equality in the United States. These figures are based on joint income tax returns and therefore present an optimistic picture for two reasons: (1) The very poor tend not to file returns because they do not make enough money to owe taxes. (2) Families with two parents are much better off than single individuals and one-parent families, who are not included in the table. Even so, we can see how unevenly income is distributed.

Table 18.3

Distribution of Income and of the Federal
Income Tax Burden, 1975*

Annual Income Level	Percentage of All Tax Returns	Percentage of Income	Percentage of Income Taxes
Under $5,000	11.0%	1.3%	0.5%
$5,000 – $10,000	20.0	9.0	3.0
$10,000 – $15,000	23.0	18.0	12.0
$15,000 – $25,000	32.0	38.0	34.0
$25,000 – $50,000	12.0	23.0	28.0
Over $50,000	2.0	11.0	24.0

*For people filing joint federal income tax returns.

Source: Internal Revenue Service, Preliminary Statistics of Income
1975; as reprinted in Congressional Quarterly Weekly Report, April 8,
1978, p. 830.

Almost a third of all families—those making under $10,000 a year—took in less than 11 percent of all the income received in 1975. This is about the same amount received by the top 2 percent of American families, those making over $50,000. The sheer inequality of this picture is reduced—but surely not eliminated—by two factors. First, these figures report only income. They do not include the kinds of public aid that are so important to poorer people: unemployment benefits, welfare, food stamps, Medicare and Medicaid, and social security. Second, as Table 18.3 shows, the federal tax structure redistributes income considerably. The wealthiest 2 percent had income equal to the bottom 31 percent, but they also paid almost seven times as much in taxes. In fact, 52 percent of all individual income taxes were paid by the 14 percent of families at the top of the money tree.

We can also look at equality among different social groups. Figure 18.1 does this by comparing the salaries of black and white men and women over the past twenty years. This chart confirms the familiar picture of female and black inequality, but it also has some more interesting and encouraging aspects. In 1974, the income earned by black men averaged 74 percent of white male income. This evidence of racial disadvantage takes on a new meaning, however, when we note that as recently as 1966 black men made just 64 percent of white male salaries. What do we focus on—the racial gap, or the trend toward closing the gap? Optimism about the trend might well be tempered by the fact that at the present rate of improvement, it will be thirty to forty years before black men catch up. White women, on the other hand, are slightly worse off compared to white men than they were ten and twenty years ago. Black women have gained remarkably in the past generation. They now are almost as well off as white women, but still a long way behind men of either race.[9]

[9] See Social Indicators 1976, p. 459; and a more recent study reported in San Francisco Chronicle, May 8, 1978, p. 1.

Figure 18.1

Median Wage or Salary Income of Year-Round,
Full-Time Workers 14 Years Old and Over,
by Race and Sex, 1955–1974

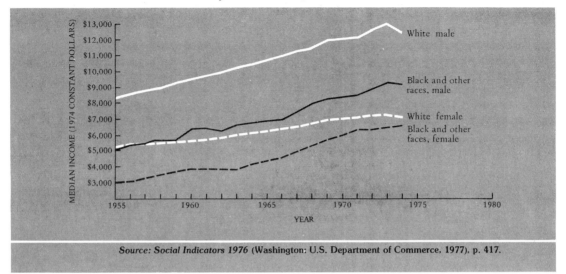

Source: Social Indicators 1976 (Washington: U.S. Department of Commerce, 1977), p. 417.

Evaluations of economic equality depend on whether we focus on present conditions or rates of change. Trends may be more or less encouraging than the picture at a single moment. Even so, reaching conclusions about the level of economic equality is not the final step. The question remains: Has the political system intervened to achieve the *right degree* of limitation on inequality? What should the government do to ensure that the poor get richer and the rich get poorer? Or do we care how much the rich have as long as the poorest people have an adequate standard of living? But what is "adequate"? Who is to decide if that means a color TV or only black and white? Our ideas of "minimal" standards of living change according to technology, fashion, cultural standards, and the total availability of good things. We can define minimal standards in nutrition, clothing, housing, medical care, and so on. But we already know that plenty of well-off people have dreadful diets, poor health habits, and the like. Is the government to ensure not only more equal incomes, but also minimal adequate diets and health practices? If we are to value equality as a goal, what about the things that are inherently limited, such as rewarding jobs and beach houses? These are things whose possession by some people means that others cannot have them. What amount of unequal rewards is necessary to motivate people to maximum efficiency?[10]

---

[10] No countries in the modern world have managed to achieve anything like equality, no matter how much devotion to the principle they may claim. In Communist nations, for example, income disparities are great among different occupations and also among the same jobs in different regions. Most such countries also imitate the Soviet Union, which provides special stores, housing, vacation facilities, and medical care to political leaders and those in privileged occupations.

THE TENSION BETWEEN FREEDOM
AND EQUALITY

Our discussion of political evaluation has focused on a wide range of ideas and factors to be considered. For many people, however, individual freedom is the most important guidepost for political evaluation. As we saw in Chapter 6, freedom is a tricky concept. If we define freedom by saying that the free person is the one who has a fair say in making the laws, then we can see that freedom and equality are closely related. On the other hand, we can define freedom simply as individual autonomy. In this case, freedom means being free from coercion and having the chance to develop one's own personality and destiny without outside interference. From this point of view, how closely freedom and equality are related is an open question. Different answers are supplied by different schools of political thought.

For those of us who remain roughly within the lines of traditional American ideology, the potential clash between equality and freedom from governmental coercion presents a difficult problem of political evaluation. As we noted earlier, our society is marked by considerable economic inequalities. Many actual and proposed government policies are aimed at reducing these inequalities, and a large proportion of these policies involve some form of coercion. They reduce freedom in an effort to increase equality. Should doctors and patients be forced to use only those medicines on a government prescription list in order to achieve greater equal-

"I guess we should count our blessings."

ity in medical care? Should an employer be forced to discriminate against whites now because the firm used to discriminate against blacks? Many governmental programs involve increasing the coercive power of government over individuals in order to correct social and economic inequalities.

Here we encounter the final difficulty in employing freedom as an evaluative criterion. In Chapter 6 we distinguished between the positive sense of freedom as freedom to participate in government and the negative sense of freedom as freedom from government interference. With this distinction in mind, one may argue that people who are sick, hungry, ignorant, or poor are not free to develop their own personalities. To say that an illiterate sharecropper with a family of six and a cash income of $1000 a year is free because the government leaves him alone is a rather odd view of the human condition or an extremely narrow use of the word freedom. A government program that compels each of us, through taxation, to help buy that man a farm and then regulates in detail how he must farm it increases the level of government power over individuals. But while it decreases freedom from governmental coercion, it can easily be argued that it increases the former sharecropper's freedom to develop as a human being. Put another way, governmental coercion may be used as a counterbalance to private social and economic coercion. On the whole, this may result in an increase in overall freedom. Yet the government program puts our individual freedoms more and more at the mercy of government.

Anyone seeking to evaluate American politics will have to calculate for himself or herself the tradeoffs between freedom and equality. Indeed, every one of us does exactly this, even if unconsciously, each time we say we are for or against some proposed policy or action. In this sense, evaluation is a continuous part of the dynamics of the American political system which this book has attempted to describe.

SUMMARY Political diagnosis is very different from medical diagnosis. Almost everyone agrees on what physical health is, but there is widespread disagreement about what to consider when evaluating a political system. Should it be political procedures, such as how the nations's rulers are chosen and what civil liberties the people enjoy? Or should we ignore the procedures and concentrate on the results? Does this mean that the level of popular satisfaction determines the system's success? Or should we consider objective conditions, like infant mortality rates, the distribution of income, and the availability of creature comforts? If so, which measures of performance are most important? Is every aspect of a society's existence a valid measure of its government's performance?

Asking these questions raises the problem of what areas of life governments *should* regulate. This is related to the growing problem of governmental capacity: how much *can* a democratic government do successfully?

Public acceptance or legitimacy is a basic evaluative dimension. Here there are findings to suit any preconception about public approval of the political system. A second fundamental dimension is the extent to which potentially severe conflicts in society are peacefully resolved or managed. Our political system seems to do fairly well on this score. A third dimension is equality. The problem is widespread disagreement about the areas of life in which equality should be guaranteed, and also about how to define "equal enough." Moreover, it is difficult to provide equality without limiting freedom. How much of one should be sacrificed in order to achieve how much of the other?

Clearly, how people answer these dilemmas depends in large measure on their own ideological preferences. Experts sometimes may be able to foretell the consequences of alternative policies, but they cannot provide answers to the question of how much each alternative should be valued. That is a problem for individual judgment, for the lifetime of each reader of this book.

the constitution of the united states

We the People of the United States, In Order to form a more perfect Union, establish Justice, insure domestic Tranquility, provide for the common defence, promote the general Welfare, and secure the Blessings of Liberty to ourselves and our Posterity, do ordain and establish this Constitution for the United States of America.

Article I

Section 1. All legislative Powers herein granted shall be vested in a Congress of the United States, which shall consist of a Senate and House of Representatives.

Section 2. The House of Representatives shall be composed of members chosen every second Year by the People of the several States, and the Electors in each State shall have the Qualifications requisite for Electors of the most numerous Branch of the State Legislature.

No Person shall be a Representative who shall not have attained to the Age of twenty five Years, and been seven Years a Citizen of the United States, and who shall not, when elected, be an Inhabitant of that State in which he shall be chosen.

Representatives and direct Taxes shall be apportioned among the several States which may be included within this union, according to their respective Numbers, which shall be determined by adding to the whole Number of free Persons, including those bound to Service for a Term of Years, and excluding Indians not taxed, three fifths of all other Persons. The actual Enumeration shall be made within three Years after the first Meeting of the Congress of the United States, and within every subsequent Term of ten Years, in such Manner as they shall by Law direct. The Number of Representatives shall not exceed one for every thirty Thousand, but each State shall have at Least one Representative; and until such enumeration shall be made, the State of New Hampshire shall be entitled to chuse three, Massachusetts eight, Rhode-Island and Providence Plantations one, Connecticut five, New-York six, New Jersey four, Pennsylvania eight, Delaware one, Maryland six, Virginia ten, North Carolina five, South Carolina five, and Georgia three.

When vacancies happen in the Representation from any State, the Executive Authority thereof shall issue Writs of Election to fill such Vacancies.

The House of Representatives shall chuse their speaker and other Officers; and shall have the sole Power of Impeachment.

Section 3. The Senate of the United States shall be composed of two Senators from each State, chosen by the Legislature thereof, for six Years; and each Senator shall have one Vote.

Immediately after they shall be assembled in Consequence of the first Election, they shall be divided as equally as may be into three Classes. The Seats of the Senators of the first Class shall be vacated at the Expiration of the second Year, of the second Class at the Expiration of the fourth Year, and of the third Class at the Expiration of the sixth Year, so that one third may be chosen every second Year; and if Vacancies happen by Resignation, or otherwise, during the Recess of the Legislature of any State, the Executive thereof may make temporary Appointments until the next Meeting of the Legislature, which shall then fill such Vacancies.

No Person shall be a Senator who shall not have attained to the Age of thirty Years, and been nine Years a Citizen of the United States, and who shall not, when elected, be an Inhabitant of that State for which he shall be chosen.

The Vice President of the United States shall be President of the Senate, but shall have no Vote, unless they be equally divided.

The Senate shall chuse their other Officers, and also a President pro tempore, in the Absence of the Vice President, or when he shall exercise the Office of the President of the United States.

The Senate shall have the sole Power to try all Impeachments. When sitting for that Purpose, they shall be on Oath or Affirmation. When the President of the United States is tried, the Chief Justice shall preside: And no Person shall be convicted without the Concurrence of two thirds of the Members present.

Judgment in Cases of Impeachment shall not extend further than to removal from Office, and disqualification to hold and enjoy any Office of honor, Trust or Profit under the United States: but the Party convicted shall nevertheless be liable and subject to Indictment, Trial, Judgment and Punishment, according to law.

Section 4. The Times, Places and Manner of holding Elections for Senators and Representatives, shall be prescribed in each State by the Legislature thereof; but the Congress may at any time by Law make or alter such Regulations, except as to the Places of chusing Senators.

The Congress shall assemble at least once in every Year, and such Meeting shall be on the first Monday in December, unless they shall by Law appoint a different Day.

Section 5. Each House shall be the Judge of the Elections, Returns and Qualifications of its own Members, and a Majority of each shall constitute a Quorum to do Business; but a smaller Number may adjourn from day to day, and may be authorized to compel the Attendance of absent Members, in such Manner, and under such Penalties as each House may provide.

Each House may determine the Rules of its Proceedings, punish its Members for disorderly Behaviour, and, with the Concurrence of two thirds, expel a Member.

Each House shall keep a Journal of its Proceedings, and from time to time publish the same, excepting such Parts as may in their Judgment require Secrecy; and the Yeas and Nays of the Members of either House on any question shall, at the Desire of one fifth of those Present, be entered on the Journal.

Neither House, during the Session of Congress, shall, without the Consent of the other, adjourn for more than three days, nor to any other Place than that in which the two Houses shall be sitting.

Section 6. The Senators and Representatives shall receive a Compensation for their Services, to be ascertained by Law, and paid out of the Treasury of the United States. They shall in all Cases, except Treason, Felony and Breach of the Peace, be privileged from Arrest during their Attendance at the Session of their respective Houses, and in going to and returning from the same; and for any Speech or Debate in either House, they shall not be questioned in any other Place.

No Senator or Representative shall, during the Time

for which he was elected, be appointed to any civil Office under the Authority of the United States, which shall have been created, or the Emoluments whereof shall have been encreased during such time; and no Person holding any Office under the United States, shall be a Member of either House during his Continuance in Office.

Section 7. All Bills for raising Revenue shall originate in the House of Representatives; but the Senate may propose or concur with Amendments as on other Bills.

Every Bill which shall have passed the House of Representatives and the Senate, shall, before it become a Law, be presented to the President of the United States; If he approve he shall sign it, but if not he shall return it, with his Objections to that House in which it shall have originated, who shall enter the Objections at large on their Journal, and proceed to reconsider it. If after such Reconsideration two thirds of that House shall agree to pass the Bill, it shall be sent, together with the Objections, to the other House, by which it shall likewise be reconsidered, and if approved by two thirds of that House, it shall become a Law. But in all such Cases the Votes of both Houses shall be determined by Yeas and Nays, and the Names of the Persons voting for and against the Bill shall be entered on the Journal of each House respectively. If any Bill shall not be returned by the President within ten Days (Sundays excepted) after it shall have been presented to him, the Same shall be a Law, in like Manner as if he had signed it, unless the Congress by their Adjournment prevent its Return, in which Case it shall not be a Law.

Every Order, Resolution, or Vote to which the Concurrence of the Senate and House of Representatives may be necessary (except on a question of Adjournment) shall be presented to the President of the United States; and before the Same shall take Effect, shall be approved by him, or being disapproved by him, shall be repassed by two thirds of the Senate and House of Representatives, according to the Rules and Limitations prescribed in the Case of a Bill.

Section 8. The Congress shall have Power To lay and collect Taxes, Duties, Imposts and Excises, to pay the Debts and provide for the common Defence and general Welfare of the United States; but all Duties, Imposts and Excises shall be uniform throughout the United States;

To borrow Money on the credit of the United States;

To regulate Commerce with foreign Nations, and among the several States, and with the Indian Tribes;

To establish a uniform Rule of Naturalization, and uniform Laws on the subject of Bankruptcies throughout the United States;

To coin Money, regulate the Value thereof, and of foreign Coin, and fix the Standard of Weights and Measures;

To provide for the Punishment of counterfeiting the Securities and current Coin of the United States;

To establish Post Offices and post Roads;

To promote the Progress of Science and useful Arts, by securing for limited Times to Authors and Inventors the exclusive Right to their respective Writings and Discoveries;

To constitute Tribunals inferior to the supreme Court;

To define and punish Piracies and Felonies committed on the high Seas, and Offences against the Law of Nations;

To declare War, grant Letters of Marque and Reprisal, and make Rules concerning Captures on Land and Water;

To raise and support Armies, but no Appropriation of Money to that Use shall be for a longer Term than two Years;

To provide and maintain a Navy;

To make Rules for the Government and Regulation of the land and naval Forces;

To provide for calling forth the Militia to execute the Laws of the Union, suppress Insurrections and repel Invasions;

To provide for organizing, arming, and disciplining, the Militia, and for governing such Part of them as may be employed in the Service of the United States, reserving to the States respectively, the Appointment of the Officers, and the Authority of training the Militia according to the discipline prescribed by Congress;

To exercise exclusive Legislation in all Cases whatsoever, over such District (not exceeding ten Miles square) as may, by Cession of particular States, and the Acceptance of Congress, become the Seat of the Government of the United States, and to exercise like Authority over all Places purchased by the Consent of the Legislature of the State in which the Same shall be for the Erection of Forts, Magazines, Arsenals, dock-Yards, and other needful Buildings;-And

To make all Laws which shall be necessary and proper for carrying into Execution the foregoing Powers, and all other Powers vested by this Constitution in the Government of the United States, or in any Department or Officer thereof.

Section 9. The Migration or Importation of such Persons as any of the States now existing shall think proper to admit, shall not be prohibited by the Congress prior to the Year one thousand eight hundred and eight, but a Tax or duty may be imposed on such Importation, not exceeding ten dollars for each Person.

The Privilege of the Writ of Habeas Corpus shall not be suspended, unless when in Cases of Rebellion or Invasion the public Safety may require it.

No Bill of Attainder or ex post facto Law shall be passed.

No Capitation, or other direct, Tax shall be laid, unless in Proportion to the Census or Enumeration herein before directed to be taken.

No Tax or Duty shall be laid on Articles exported from any State.

No Preference shall be given by any Regulation of Commerce or Revenue to the Ports of one State over those of another: nor shall Vessels bound to, or from, one State be obliged to enter, clear, or pay Duties in another.

No Money shall be drawn from the Treasury, but in Consequence of Appropriations made by Law; and a regular Statement and Account of the Receipts and Expenditures of all public Money shall be published from time to time.

No Title of Nobility shall be granted by the United States: And no Person holding any office of Profit or Trust under them, shall, without the Consent of the Congress, accept of any present, Emolument, Office, or Title, of any kind whatever from any King, Prince, or foreign States.

Section 10. No State shall enter into any Treaty, Alliance, or Confederation; grant Letters of Marque and Reprisal; coin Money; emit Bills of Credit; make any Thing but gold and silver Coin a Tender in Payment of Debts; pass any Bill of Attainder, ex post facto Law, or Law impairing the Obligation of Contracts, or grant any Title of Nobility.

No State shall, without the Consent of the Congress, lay any Imposts or Duties on Imports or Exports, except what may be absolutely necessary for executing its inspection Laws: and the net Produce of all Duties and Imposts, laid by any State on Imports or Exports, shall be for the Use of the Treasury of the United States; and all such Laws shall be subject to the Revision and Controul of the Congress.

No State shall, without the Consent of Congress, lay any Duty of Tonnage, keep Troops, or Ships of War in time of Peace, enter into any Agreement or Compact with another State, or with a foreign Power, or engage in War, unless actually invaded, or in such imminent Danger as will not admit of delay.

Article II

Section 1. The executive Power shall be vested in a President of the United States of America. He shall hold his Office during the Term of four Years, and, together with the Vice President, chosen for the same term, be elected, as follows

Each State shall appoint, in such Manner as the Legislature thereof may direct, a Number of Electors, equal to the whole Number of Senators and Representatives to which the State may be entitled in the Congress: but no Senator or Representative, or Person holding an office of Trust or Profit under the United States, shall be appointed an Elector.

The Electors shall meet in their respective States, and vote by Ballot for two Persons, of whom one at least shall not be an Inhabitant of the same State with themselves. And they shall make a List of all the Persons voted for, and of the Number of Votes for each; which List they shall sign and certify, and transmit sealed to the Seat of the Government of the United States, directed to the President of the Senate. The President of the Senate shall, in the Presence of the Senate and House of Representatives, open all the Certificates, and the Votes shall then be counted. The Person having the greatest Number of Votes shall be the President, if such Number be a Majority of the whole Number of Electors ap-

pointed; and if there be more than one who have such Majority, and have an equal Number of Votes, then the House of Representatives shall immediately chuse by Ballot one of them for President: and if no Person have a Majority, then from the five highest on the List the said House shall in like Manner chuse the President. But in chusing the President, the Votes shall be taken by States, the Representation from each State having one Vote; A quorum for this Purpose shall consist of a Member or Members from two thirds of the States, and a Majority of all the States shall be necessary to a Choice. In every Case, after the Choice of the President, the Person having the greatest Number of Votes of the Electors shall be the Vice President. But if there should remain two or more who have equal Votes, the Senate shall chuse from them by Ballot the Vice President.

The Congress may determine the Time of chusing the Electors and the Day on which they shall give their Votes; which Day shall be the same throughout the United States.

No Person except a natural born Citizen, or a Citizen of the United States, at the time of the Adoption of this Constitution, shall be eligible to the Office of President; neither shall any Person be eligible to that Office who shall not have attained to the Age of thirty five Years, and been fourteen Years a Resident within the United States.

In Case of the Removal of the President from Office, or of his Death, Resignation, or Inability to discharge the Powers and Duties of the said Office, the Same shall devolve on the Vice President, and the Congress may by Law provide for the Case of Removal, Death, Resignation or Inability, both of the President and Vice President, declaring what Officer shall then act as President, and such Officer shall act accordingly, until the Disability be removed, or a President shall be elected.

The President shall, at stated Times, receive for his Services a Compensation, which shall neither be increased nor diminished during the Period for which he shall have been elected, and he shall not receive within that Period any other Emolument from the United States, or any of them.

Before he enter on the Execution of his Office, he shall take the following Oath or Affirmation:- "I do solemnly swear (or affirm) that I will faithfully execute the Office of President of the United States, and will to the best of my Ability, preserve, protect and defend the Constitution of the United States."

Section 2. The President shall be Commander in Chief of the Army and Navy of the United States, and of the Militia of the several States, when called into the actual Service of the United States; he may require the Opinion, in writing, of the principal Officer in each of the executive Departments, upon any Subject relating to the Duties of their respective Offices, and he shall have power to grant Reprieves and Pardons for Offences against the United States, except in Cases of Impeachment.

He shall have Power, by and with the Advice and

Consent of the Senate, to make Treaties, provided two thirds of the Senators present concur; and he shall nominate, and by and with the Advice and Consent of the Senate, shall appoint Ambassadors, other public Ministers and Consuls, Judges of the supreme Court, and all other Officers of the United States, whose Appointments are not herein otherwise provided for, and which shall be established by Law; but the Congress may by Law vest the Appointment of such inferior Officers, as they think proper, in the President alone, in the Courts of Law, or in the Heads of Departments.

The President shall have Power to fill up all Vacancies that may happen during the Recess of the Senate, by granting Commissions which shall expire at the End of their next Session.

Section 3.   He shall from time to time give to the Congress Information of the State of the Union, and recommend to their Consideration such Measures as he shall judge necessary and expedient; he may, on extraordinary Occasions, convene both Houses, or either of them, and in Case of Disagreement between them, with Respect to the Time of Adjournment, he may adjourn them to such Time as he shall think proper; he shall receive Ambassadors and other public Ministers; he shall take Care that the Laws be faithfully executed, and shall Commission all the officers of the United States.

Section 4.   The President, Vice President and all civil Officers of the United States, shall be removed from Office on Impeachment for, and Conviction of, Treason, Bribery, or other High Crimes and Misdemeanors.

Article III

Section 1.   The judicial Power of the United States, shall be vested in one supreme Court, and in such inferior Courts as the Congress may from time to time ordain and establish. The Judges, both of the supreme and inferior Courts, shall hold their Offices during good Behaviour, and shall, at stated Times, receive for their Services, a Compensation, which shall not be diminished during their Continuance in Office.

Section 2.   The judicial Power shall extend to all Cases, in Law and Equity, arising under this Constitution, the Laws of the United States, and Treaties made, or which shall be made, under their Authority;-to all Cases affecting Ambassadors, other public Ministers and Consuls;-to all Cases of admiralty and maritime Jurisdiction;-to Controversies to which the United States shall be a Party;-to Controversies between two or more States; between a State and Citizens of another State;-between Citizens of different States;-between Citizens of the same State claiming Lands under Grants of different States, and between a State, or the Citizens thereof, and foreign States, Citizens or Subjects.

In all Cases affecting Ambassadors, other public Ministers and Consuls, and those in which a State shall be Party,

the supreme Court shall have original Jurisdiction. In all the other Cases before mentioned, the supreme Court shall have appellate Jurisdiction, both as to Law and Fact, with such Exceptions, and under such Regulations as the Congress shall make.

The Trial of all Crimes, except in Cases of Impeachment, shall be by Jury; and such Trial shall be held in the State where the said Crimes shall have been committed; but when not committed within any State, the Trial shall be at such Place or Places as the Congress may by Law have directed.

Section 3.   Treason against the United States, shall consist only in levying War against them, or in adhering to their Enemies, giving them Aid and Comfort. No Person shall be convicted of Treason unless on the Testimony of two Witnesses to the same overt Act, or on Confession in open Court.

The Congress shall have Power to declare the Punishment of Treason, but no Attainder of Treason shall work Corruption of Blood, or Forfeiture except during the Life of the Person attainted.

Article IV

Section 1.   Full Faith and Credit shall be given in each State to the public Acts, Records, and judicial Proceedings of every other State. And the Congress may by general Laws prescribe the Manner in which such Acts, Records and Proceedings shall be proved, and the Effect thereof.

Section 2.   The Citizens of each State shall be entitled to all Privileges and Immunities of Citizens in the several States.

A person charged in any State with Treason, Felony, or other Crime, who shall flee from Justice, and be found in another State, shall on Demand of the executive Authority of the State from which he fled, be delivered up, to be removed to the State having Jurisdiction of the Crime.

No Person held to Service or Labour in one State, under the Laws thereof, escaping into another, shall, in Consequence of any Law or Regulation therein, be discharged from such Service or Labour, but shall be delivered up on Claim of the Party to whom such Service or Labour may be due.

Section 3.   New States may be admitted by the Congress into this Union; but no new State shall be formed or erected within the Jurisdiction of any other State; nor any State be formed by the Junction of two or more States, or Parts of States, without the Consent of the Legislatures of the States concerned as well as of the Congress.

The Congress shall have Power to dispose of and make all needful Rules and Regulations respecting the Territory or other Property belonging to the United States; and nothing in this Constitution shall be so construed as to Prejudice any Claims of the United States, or of any particular State.

Section 4. The United States shall guarantee to every State in this Union a Republican Form of Government, and shall protect each of them against Invasion; and on Application of the Legislature, or of the Executive (when the Legislature cannot be convened) against domestic Violence.

Article V

The Congress, whenever two thirds of both Houses shall deem it necessary, shall propose Amendments to this Constitution, or, on the Application of the Legislatures of two thirds of the several States, shall call a Convention for proposing Amendments, which, in either Case, shall be valid to all Intents and Purposes, as Part of this Constitution, when ratified by the Legislatures of three fourths of the several States, or by Conventions in three fourths thereof, as the one or the other Mode of Ratification may be proposed by the Congress; Provided that no Amendment which may be made prior to the Year One thousand eight hundred and eight shall in any Manner affect the first and fourth Clauses in the Ninth Section of the first Article; and that no State, without its Consent, shall be deprived of its equal Suffrage in the Senate.

Article VI

All Debts contracted and Engagements entered into, before the Adoption of this Constitution, shall be as valid against the United States under this Constitution, as under the Confederation.

This Constitution, and the Laws of the United States which shall be made in Pursuance thereof; and all Treaties made, or which shall be made, under the Authority of the United States, shall be the supreme Law of the Land; and the Judges in every State shall be bound thereby, any Thing in the Constitution or Laws of any State to the Contrary notwithstanding.

The Senators and Representatives before mentioned, and the Members of the several State Legislatures, and all executive and judicial Officers, both of the United States and of the several States, shall be bound by Oath or Affirmation, to support this Constitution; but no religious Test shall ever be required as a Qualification to any Office or public Trust under the United States.

Article VII

The Ratification of the Conventions of nine States, shall be sufficient for the Establishment of this Constitution between the States so ratifying the Same.

Done in Convention by the Unanimous Consent of the States present the Seventeenth Day of September in the Year of our Lord one thousand seven hundred and Eighty

seven and of the Independence of the United States of America the Twelfth. In witness whereof We have hereunto subscribed our Names.

[The first 10 Amendments were ratified December 15, 1791, and form what is known as the Bill of Rights]

Amendment 1

Congress shall make no law respecting an establishment of religion, or prohibiting the free exercise thereof; or abridging the freedom of speech, or of the press; or the right of the people peaceably to assemble, and to petition the Government for a redress of grievances.

Amendment 2

A well regulated Militia, being necessary to the security of a free State, the right of the people to keep and bear Arms, shall not be infringed.

Amendment 3

No Soldier shall, in time of peace be quartered in any house, without the consent of the Owner, nor in time of war, but in a manner to be prescribed by law.

Amendment 4

The right of the people to be secure in their persons, houses, papers, and effects, against unreasonable searches and seizures, shall not be violated, and no Warrants shall issue, but upon probable cause, supported by Oath or affirmation, and particularly describing the place to be searched and the persons or things to be seized.

Amendment 5

No person shall be held to answer for a capital, or otherwise infamous crime, unless on a presentment or indictment of a Grand Jury, except in cases arising in the land or naval forces, or in the Militia, when in actual service in time of War or public danger; nor shall any person be subject for the same offence to be twice put in jeopardy of life or limb; nor shall be compelled in any criminal case to be a witness against himself, nor be deprived of life, liberty, or property, without due process of law; nor shall private property be taken for public use, without just compensation.

Amendment 6

In all criminal prosecutions, the accused shall enjoy the right to a speedy and public trial, by an impartial jury of the State and district wherein the crime shall have been committed, which district shall have been previously ascertained by law, and to be informed of the nature and cause of the accusation; to be confronted with the witnesses against him; to have compulsory process for obtaining witnesses in his favor, and to have the Assistance of Counsel for his defence.

Amendment 7

In Suits at common law, where the value in controversy shall exceed twenty dollars, the right of trial by jury shall be preserved, and no fact tried by a jury, shall be otherwise reexamined in any Court of the United States, than according to the rules of the common law.

Amendment 8

Excessive bail shall not be required, nor excessive fines imposed, nor cruel and unusual punishments inflicted.

Amendment 9

The enumeration in the Constitution, of certain rights, shall not be construed to deny or disparage others retained by the people.

Amendment 10

The powers not delegated to the United States by the Constitution, nor prohibited by it to the States, are reserved to the States respectively, or to the people.

Amendment 11

[Ratified February 7, 1795]

The Judicial power of the United States shall not be construed to extend to any suit in law or equity, commenced or prosecuted against one of the United States by Citizens of another State, or by Citizens or Subjects of any Foreign State.

Amendment 12

[Ratified July 27, 1804]

The Electors shall meet in their respective states and vote by ballot for President and Vice-President, one of whom, at least, shall not be an inhabitant of the same state with themselves; they shall name in their ballots the person voted for as President, and in distinct ballots the person voted for as Vice-President, and they shall make distinct lists of all persons voted for as President, and of all persons voted for as Vice-President, and of the number of votes for each, which lists they shall sign and certify, and transmit sealed to the seat of the government of the United States, directed to the President of the Senate;-The President of the Senate shall, in the presence of the Senate and House of Representatives, open all the certificates and the votes shall then be counted;-The person having the greatest number of votes for President, shall be the President, if such number be a majority of the whole number of Electors appointed; and if no person have such majority, then from the persons having the highest numbers not exceeding three on the list of those voted for as President, the House of Representatives shall choose immediately, by ballot, the President. But in choosing the President, the votes shall be taken by states, the representation from each state having one vote; a quorum for this purpose shall consist of a member or members from two-thirds of the states, and a majority of all the states shall be necessary to a choice. And if the House of Representatives shall not choose a President whenever the right of choice shall devolve upon them, before the fourth day of March next following, then the Vice-President shall act as President, as in the case of the death or other constitutional disability of the President.-The person having the greatest number of votes as Vice-President, shall be the the Vice-President, if such number be a majority of the whole number of Electors appointed, and if no person have a majority, then from the two highest numbers on the list, the Senate shall choose the Vice-President; a quorum for the purpose shall consist of two-thirds of the whole number of Senators, and a majority of the whole number shall be necessary to a choice. But no person constitutionally ineligible to the office of President shall be eligible to that of Vice-President of the United States.

Amendment 13

[Ratified December 6, 1865]

Section 1. Neither slavery nor involuntary servitude, except as a punishment for crime whereof the party shall have been duly convicted, shall exist within the United States, or any place subject to their jurisdiction.

Section 2. Congress shall have power to enforce this article by appropriate legislation.

Amendment 14

[Ratified July 9, 1868]

Section 1. All persons born or naturalized in the United States, and subject to the jurisdiction thereof, are citizens of the United States and of the State wherein they reside. No State shall make or enforce any law which shall abridge the privileges or immunities of citizens of the United States; nor shall any State deprive any person of life, liberty, or property, without due process of law; nor deny to any person within its jurisdiction the equal protection of the laws.

Section 2. Representatives shall be apportioned among the several States according to their respective numbers, counting the whole number of persons in each State, excluding Indians not taxed. But when the right to vote at any election for the choice of electors for President and Vice

President of the United States, Representatives in Congress, the Executive and Judicial Officers of a State, or the members of the Legislature thereof, is denied to any of the male inhabitants of such State, being twenty-one years of age, and citizens of the United States, or in any way abridged, except for participation in rebellion, or other crime, the basis of representation therein shall be reduced in the proportion which the number of such male citizens shall bear to the whole number of male citizens twenty-one years of age in such State.

Section 3. No person shall be a Senator or Representative in Congress, or elector of President and Vice President, or hold any office, civil or military, under the United States, or under any State, who, having previously taken an oath, as a member of Congress, or as an officer of the United States, or as a member of any State legislature, or as an executive or judicial officer of any State, to support the Constitution of the United States, shall have engaged in insurrection or rebellion against the same, or given aid or comfort to the enemies thereof. But Congress may by a vote of two-thirds of each House, remove such disability.

Section 4. The validity of the public debt of the United States, authorized by law, including debts incurred for payment of pensions and bounties for services in suppressing insurrection or rebellion, shall not be questioned. But neither the United States nor any State shall assume or pay any debt or obligation incurred in aid of insurrection or rebellion against the United States, or any claim for the loss or emancipation of any slave; but all such debts, obligations and claims shall be held illegal and void.

Section 5. The Congress shall have power to enforce, by appropriate legislation, the provisions of this article.

Amendment 15

[Ratified February 3, 1870]

Section 1. The right of citizens of the United States to vote shall not be denied or abridged by the United States or by any State on account of race, color, or previous condition of servitude.

Section 2. The Congress shall have power to enforce this article by appropriate legislation.

Amendment 16

[Ratified February 3, 1913]

The Congress shall have power to lay and collect taxes on incomes, from whatever source derived, without apportionment among the several States, and without regard to any census or enumeration.

Amendment 17

[Ratified April 8, 1913]

The Senate of the United States shall be composed of two Senators from each State, elected by the people thereof for six years; and each Senator shall have one vote. The electors in each State shall have the qualifications requisite for electors of the most numerous branch of the State legislatures.

When vacancies happen in the representation of any State in the Senate, the executive authority of such State shall issue writs of election to fill such vacancies: *Provided,* That the legislature of any State may empower the executive thereof to make temporary appointments until the people fill the vacancies by election as the legislature may direct.

This amendment shall not be so construed as to affect the election or term of any Senator chosen before it becomes valid as part of the Constitution.

Amendment 18

[Ratified January 16, 1919]

Section 1. After one year from the ratification of this article the manufacture, sale, or transportation of intoxicating liquors within, the importation thereof into, or the exportation thereof from the United States and all territory subject to the jurisdiction thereof for beverage purposes is hereby prohibited.

Section 2. The Congress and the several States shall have concurrent power to enforce this article by appropriate legislation.

Section 3. This article shall be inoperative unless it shall have been ratified as an amendment to the Constitution by the legislatures of the several States, as provided in the Constitution, within seven years from the date of the submission hereof to the States by the Congress.

Amendment 19

[Ratified August 18, 1920]

The right of citizens of the United States to vote shall not be denied or abridged by the United States or by any State on account of sex. Congress shall have power to enforce this article by appropriate legislation.

Amendment 20

[Ratified January 23, 1933]

Section 1. The terms of the President and Vice President shall end at noon on the 20th day of January, and the terms of Senators and Representatives at noon on the 3d day of January, of the years in which such terms would have ended if this article had not been ratified; and the terms of their successors shall then begin.

Section 2. The Congress shall assemble at least once in every year, and such meeting shall begin at noon on the 3d day of January, unless they shall by law appoint a different day.

Section 3. If, at the time fixed for the beginning of the term of the President, the President elect shall have died, the Vice President elect shall become President. If a President shall not have been chosen before the time fixed for the beginning of his term, or if the President elect shall have failed to qualify, then the Vice President elect shall act as President until a President shall have qualified; and the Congress may by law provide for the case wherein neither a President elect nor a Vice President elect shall have qualified, declaring who shall then act as President, or the manner in which one who is to act shall be selected, and such person shall act accordingly until a President or Vice President shall have qualified.

Section 4. The Congress may by law provide for the case of the death of any of the persons from whom the House of Representatives may choose a President whenever the right of choice shall have devolved upon them, and for the case of the death of any of the persons from whom the Senate may choose a Vice President whenever the right of choice shall have devolved upon them.

Section 5. Sections 1 and 2 shall take effect on the 15th day of October following the ratification of this article.

Section 6. This article shall be inoperative unless it shall have been ratified as an amendment to the Constitution by the legislatures of three-fourths of the several States within seven years from the date of its submission.

Amendment 21

[Ratified December 5, 1933]

Section 1. The eighteenth article of amendment to the Constitution of the United States is hereby repealed.

Section 2. The transportation or importation into any State, Territory, or possession of the United States for delivery or use therein of intoxicating liquors, in violation of the laws thereof, is hereby prohibited.

Section 3. This article shall be inoperative unless it shall have been ratified as an amendment to the Constitution by conventions in the several States, as provided in the Constitution, within seven years from the date of the submission hereof to the States by the Congress.

Amendment 22

[Ratified February 27, 1951]

Section 1. No person shall be elected to the office of the President more than twice, and no person who has held the office of President, or acted as President, for more than two years of a term to which some other person was elected President shall be elected to the office of the President more than once. But this Article shall not apply to any person holding the office of President when this Article was proposed by the Congress, and shall not prevent any person who may be holding the office of President, or acting as President, during the term within which this Article becomes operative from holding the office of President or acting as President during the remainder of such term.

Section 2. This article shall be inoperative unless it shall have been ratified as an amendment to the Constitution by the legislatures of three-fourths of the several States within seven years from the date of its submission to the States by the Congress.

Amendment 23

[Ratified March 29, 1961]

Section 1. The District constituting the seat of Government of the United States shall appoint in such manner as the Congress may direct:

A number of electors of President and Vice President equal to the whole number of Senators and Representatives in Congress to which the District would be entitled if it were a State, but in no event more than the least populous State; they shall be in addition to those appointed by the States, but they shall be considered, for the purposes of the election of President and Vice President, to be electors appointed by a State; and they shall meet in the District and perform such duties as provided by the twelfth article of amendment.

Section 2. The Congress shall have power to enforce this article by appropriate legislation.

Amendment 24

[Ratified January 23, 1964]

Section 1. The right of citizens of the United States to vote in any primary or other election for President or Vice President, for electors for President or Vice President, or for Senator or Representative in Congress, shall not be denied or abridged by the United States or any State by reason of failure to pay any poll tax or other tax.

Section 2. The Congress shall have power to enforce this article by appropriate legislation.

Amendment 25

[Ratified February 10, 1967]

Section 1. In case of the removal of the President from office or of his death or resignation, the Vice President shall become President.

Section 2. Whenever there is a vacancy in the office of the Vice President, the President shall nominate a Vice President who shall take office upon confirmation by a majority vote of both Houses of Congress.

Section 3. Whenever the President transmits to the President pro tempore of the Senate and the Speaker of the House of Representatives his written declaration that he is unable to discharge the powers and duties of his office, and until he transmits to them a written declaration to the contrary, such powers and duties shall be discharged by the Vice President as Acting President.

Section 4. Whenever the Vice President and a majority of either the principal officers of the executive departments or of such other body as Congress may by law provide, transmit to the President pro tempore of the Senate and the Speaker of the House of Representatives their written declaration that the President is unable to discharge the powers and duties of his office, the Vice President shall immediately assume the powers and duties of the office as Acting President.

Thereafter, when the President transmits to the President pro tempore of the Senate and the Speaker of the House of Representatives his written declaration that no inability exists, he shall resume the powers and duties of his office unless the Vice President and a majority of either the principal officers of the executive department or of such other body as Congress may by law provide, transmit within four days to the President pro tempore of the Senate and the Speaker of the House of Representatives their written declaration that the President is unable to discharge the powers and duties of his office. Thereupon Congress shall decide the issue, assembling within forty-eight hours for that pupose if not in session. If the Congress, within twenty-one days after receipt of the latter written declaration, or, if Congress is not in session, within twenty-one days after Congress is required to assemble, determines by two-thirds vote of both Houses that the President is unable to discharge the powers and duties of his office, the Vice President shall continue to discharge the same as Acting President; otherwise, the President shall resume the powers and duties of his office.

Amendment 26

[Ratified June 30, 1971]

Section 1. The right of citizens of the United States, who are eighteen years of age or older, to vote shall not be denied or abridged by the United States or by any State on account of age.

Section 2. The Congress shall have the power to enforce this article by appropriate legislation.

Proposed Amendment 27

[Proposed March 22, 1972]

Section 1. Equality of rights under the law shall not be denied or abridged by th United States or by any State on account of sex.

Section 2. The Congress shall have power to enforce, by appropriate legislation, the provisions of this article.

Section 3. This amendment shall take effect two years after date of ratification.

glossary

administrative law The body of legal rules governing the internal procedures of administrative agencies and judicial review of those procedures.

affirmative action Steps taken to increase the proportion of educational opportunities and jobs held by women and minorities. Such steps may range from providing more information about the availability of opportunities to requiring that a certain percentage of promotions or admissions be reserved for women and minorities.

appeals court A court that reviews trial court decisions to be sure all the courts over which it has jurisdiction interpret the law in the same way; appellate court decisions are precedents all trial courts must follow in the future.

appellate jurisdiction The power of a higher court to correct legal errors made by a lower court; the power to review a trial court decision.

balancing test Test applied by the Supreme Court to balance the interest in freedom of speech against the interest a law seeks to protect; the justification for upholding a law that abridges freedom of speech but protects the nation against serious evil.

bicameral legislature A legislature made up of two houses; the U.S. Congress is a bicameral legislature, as are all but one state legislature.

575

bill of attainder Law that singles out a particular individual and that individual's family for punishment.

brokered convention A national party convention in which no presidential candidate begins with a majority of delegates and the presidential nomination is decided in negotiations among a handful of leaders.

cabinet An executive branch body composed of the secretaries of the departments of the government, appointed by the president and confirmed by the Senate, plus the vice-president and several other major officials.

categoric group All the people who share a particular characteristic, regardless of their recognition of that characteristic or its political relevance. Blacks are a categoric group, as are farmers, fat people, and so on.

caucus A meeting open to all party members who live in a precinct, form a state delegation, or hold office in one house of a legislature to select leaders and make decisions about party policy.

checks and balances The system of shared functions and powers among the branches of the federal government which makes it difficult for a dominant majority to use the government for its own purposes.

civil liberties The constitutional guarantees of individual rights, except those relating to racial discrimination; *see also* civil rights.

civil rights The constitutional rules about racial discrimination; *see also* civil liberties.

civil service system A merit system for selecting and promoting career public officials, in contrast to using political standards; *see also* patronage.

class action A suit brought by one person in the interest not only of himself but of other similarly situated persons; *see also* public interest litigation.

class consciousness Awareness of belonging to a particular social class and the belief that this "membership" is important.

closed primary Election to nominate party candidates in which only members of the party are allowed to vote; *see also* open primary.

cloture A procedure to stop a filibuster (unlimited debate) in the U.S. Senate; it requires the vote of three-fifths of the senators; *see also* filibuster.

coattail effect The boost given by a popular presidential candidate to the votes received by other candidates of his party, who may be carried into office on the strength of the presidential candidate's popularity.

common law The portion of English and American law to be found in the past decisions of courts rather than in the statutes enacted by legislatures.

conference committee When each house of Congress passes a different version of the same bill, a conference committee is appointed to adjust the differences; it is composed of the senior Democrats and Republicans on the relevant committee of each house.

consciousness-raising Increase of awareness and sense of one's own stake in a group membership; the women's movement is an example.

conservative Refers to ideological position favoring the freedom of individuals to pursue their own economic interests, but likely to favor limits on personal expression; *see also* liberal.

conservative coalition The alliance of Republicans and southern Democrats in Congress.

cross-cutting social cleavage Situation in which lines of ethnicity, religion, and social class cross each other and do not build into a series of cumulative divisions; for example, Catholics would be both rich and poor, instead of the Catholics all being poor and the Protestants all rich.

de facto segregation Segregation in actual fact, not required by law. *See also* de jure segregation.

de jure segregation Separation of the races required by law or caused by other deliberate government action. *See also* de facto segregation; Jim Crow laws.

delegation All the members of one party from one state within a chamber of the legislature or at a convention.

desegregation The undoing of segregation laws or other government acts requiring separation of blacks and whites.

deviating election Election whose results are a temporary departure from ordinary party alignments rather than the beginning of a new alignment.

direct democracy Direct popular participation in governmental decisions, as in a referendum on an issue; *see also* representative democracy.

discharge petition A petition in the House of Representatives to remove a bill from the control of any committee and bring it directly to the floor for consideration by all members; requires a majority of the House membership.

double jeopardy Fifth Amendment provision which states that no person shall be tried twice for the same offense.

due process clause Provisions of the Fifth and Fourteenth Amendments forbidding the federal and state governments from depriving any person of life, liberty, or property without due process of law; used by the Supreme Court to protect all sorts of rights and liberties.

electoral college Refers to the electors chosen in each state whose votes actually determine the winner of the presidential election. Each state has one elector (and one vote) for each senator and representative. The presidential candidate who wins the most popular votes in a state gets all its electoral votes.

equal protection clause Provision of the Fourteenth Amendment that no state "shall . . . deny to any person within its jurisdiction the equal protection of the laws" and used by the Supreme Court against racial and other discrimination; the basis for the 1954 *Brown* v. *Board of Education* decision.

exclusionary rule   Rule of the Supreme Court requiring that trial courts refuse to consider evidence and confessions that have been obtained by unconstitutional means.

executive agreement   Agreement made by a president with a foreign power that needs no Senate approval, unlike a treaty.

ex post facto law   Law making an act a crime after it has been committed.

fair trial rule   A Surpeme Court policy of the 1940s and 1950s that would invalidate only those state convictions obtained in trials that violated "fundamental concepts of ordered liberties"; *see also* selective incorporation.

federalism   Division of political power among a number of governments sharing the same territory; one central government with jurisdiction over the whole territory of the nation shares power with other governments that each control some part of that territory.

filibuster   In the U.S. Senate, an attempt to prevent passage of a bill by refusing to stop talking and permit a vote; *see also* cloture.

floor leader   Congressional party leader whose job it is to manage floor business, to schedule the workload after a bill comes out of committee, and to manage the floor debate.

gerrymandering   Drawing congressional district lines to achieve the largest number of legislative seats for one's own party and the smallest number for the opposition.

goal substitution   Turning from a goal that cannot be achieved to lesser goals that can be; characteristic of many social programs.

grant-in-aid   A grant of federal funds to a state or local government for some specific purpose, the funds to be administered and used according to the law and federal regulations and guidelines; *see also* revenue sharing.

gross national product (GNP)   The total value of goods and services produced in a country in a given year.

habeas corpus   Constitutional guarantee of the right of an accused person to be brought before a judge who will then determine whether or not the imprisonment of that person is legal.

hearing   In each house of Congress, a formal meeting of a committee or subcommittee at which witnesses present facts and arguments and answer questions; part of the legislative process.

ideologue   Someone who has a general political philosophy on which his attitudes about issues or candidates are based; a person whose opinion on one issue will predict his opinion on other issues.

ideology   An internally consistent pattern of general beliefs that lead to specific attitudes about political issues.

impoundment   A president's refusal to spend funds already appropriated by Congress.

incrementalism   Style of decision-making in which decisions are made piecemeal and new policies are based on adjustments from the status quo.

injunction   A court order forbidding someone to do something.

integration   Blacks and whites using facilities such as schools, buses, and trains equally and together;

interest   Anything people want or value, from freedom of speech to a new house.

interest group   A collection of people making claims on the government on the basis of one or more shared attitudes or desires.

item veto   Executive power to veto a specific provision or provisions while approving the rest of a bill; not a power of the president of the United States.

Jim Crow laws   Laws passed in the South that segregated blacks and whites; another name for segregation laws.

judicial activism   Position in the debate over the Supreme Court's role that advocates an active role for the Court in the enforcement of the Constitution and the use of judicial review.

judicial modesty   *See* judicial self-restraint.

judicial review   Authority of the Supreme Court to declare that statutes and actions of administrative officers are unconstitutional and thus legally null and void; an authority derived not from the Constitution but from the Court's interpretations of it.

judicial self-restraint   The position that the Supreme Court should not declare laws unconstitutional.

laissez-faire doctrine   The principle that government should interfere as little as possible with the workings of society; that government should allow free competition in the open market.

legislative veto   Provision in a law giving Congress power to overrule administrative decisions or executive actions in a particular field; a form of legislative oversight.

liberal   Refers to an ideological position in which the emphasis is on freedom of personal expression, government regulation of economic activity, and government provision of a minimum standard of living, health, and employment; *see also* conservative.

lobbying   Trying to persuade officials to introduce, modify, pass, or kill proposals; an interest group tactic.

logrolling   Trading a vote on a matter of indifference in return for someone else's vote on a matter to which he or she is indifferent; a method of building coalitions for the passage of legislation.

machine politics   System in which every government decision is treated not as a matter of routine or rule but as a favor that will be repaid by a contribution of money or work; *see also* political machine.

majority of the moment   A combination of a number of factions or groups that find themselves in momentary agreement on a specific issue, unite to form a voting majority in Congress, and then dissolve to form new combinations on new issues.

malapportionment   Drawing congressional district lines so that districts are unequal in population and voters in large districts have a smaller share of representation than those in small districts.

markup session   Committee or subcommittee meeting after hearings at which a bill is gone over line by line and put into final form to be reported out of the subcommittee or full committee; part of the legislative process.

median family income   Figure that reflects the midpoint in the distribution of income; half of all families have more than this amount and half have less.

merit system   *See* civil service system.

mixed government   Government in which power is divided among a number of institutions and in which both the masses and the wealthier and better educated have a say.

natural law   A "higher law," inherent in nature and above human law, ultimately derived from God.

open primary   An election to choose a party's candidates in which those allowed to vote are not restricted to the members of that party.

original jurisdiction   The authority of a court to conduct a trial. *See also* appellate jurisdiction.

party regular   A type of party activist to whom the long-term success of the party itself is the most important consideration, rather than particular issues or candidates.

patronage   Giving government jobs and contracts to people who have helped the party in power; patronage is the major incentive to participate in political machines; *see also* machine politics.

pocket veto   A lawmaking power of the president; a bill neither signed nor vetoed by the president within ten days after its passage does not become law if Congress adjourns within those ten days.

policy analysis   A comprehensive type of auditing in which government programs are not only monitored for fiscal efficiency, but evaluated for how well goals are being accomplished.

political machine   A close-knit and stable hierarchy of party officials in a city, county, or state, generally motivated by patronage; *see also* machine politics.

political socialization   The processes through which children learn about politics and how to be citizens in a particular society.

populism   Post-Civil War political movement aimed at preserving the interests of the small farmer, businessman, and worker by government interference to protect individuals from the threat to those interests posed by large and powerful economic enterprises.

pork barrel legislation   Legislation for public works projects that are constructed in a particular locality.

precedent   A past decision used as a guide in making future decisions.

primary   An election to decide who will be a party's nominees in the general election; a unique feature of the American political process.

principled abstention   Refusal to vote in an election because all candidates are distasteful or because there seem to be no meaningful differences between them.

probability sampling   A technique of choosing the sample for a public opinion poll in which every person in the population being studied has a known chance of being chosen; *see also* sampling error.

proportional representation   Allocating legislative seats to parties in accordance with their share of the total number of votes; in contrast to the American single-member district system.

public interest litigation   A lawsuit designed to achieve the goals of a large set of people not simply those of a particular person; *see also* class action.

public opinion poll   A study of the opinions or behavior of a large population by interviewing a sample—a small number of people who are representative of the entire population.

real income   The actual purchasing power of money, taking inflation into account.

reference group   Any collectivity with which people identify that is a basis for self-definition: Jews, Democrats, students, Americans, etc. People usually have several reference groups, each of which is important in some circumstances.

representative democracy   Governmental system in which elected representatives participate directly in decision-making; popular participation is indirect, through voting, lobbying, campaigning. *See also* direct democracy.

respondent   Interviewee in a poll or survey; the person surveyed or polled.

revenue sharing   Federal grants of funds to states and cities over and above grants tied to specific programs, to be spent at the discretion of the recipient.

reverse discrimination   Discrimination against whites or men in the name of fair treatment for minorities or women.

rule   In the House of Representatives, the conditions under which a bill will be considered on the floor; part of the legislative process.

sampling error   The extent to which a poll or survey sample differs from the entire population.

selective incorporation   Supreme Court practice of "incorporating" most of the guarantees of the Bill of Rights under the due process clause of the Fourteenth Amendment.

seniority system   Giving the chairmanship of a congressional committee to the member of the majority party with the longest uninterrupted service on that committee.

single-member legislative district system   Each legislative district is represented by a single legislator, the candidate who received the most votes; *see also* proportional representation.

situational factors   Factors other than personal characteristics that affect who votes in an election, such as voting laws and the kind of election.

solidary group   An interest group based on a sense of kinship because of some shared characteristic, such as race, sex, service in the military, etc.

spoils system   The idea that administrative offices should be rotated at each election, and filled by supporters of the winning party, so that there will be no body of officials separate from the people and immune to party politics and election outcomes; the opposite of civil service.

standard metropolitan statistical area (SMSA)   A central city and its surrounding suburbs; U.S. Bureau of the Census classification for urban population distribution.

standing   The right to sue. Generally a person may not file a lawsuit challenging a government action unless he can show that he has been injured by that government action

survey research   Another term for public opinion polling.

unit rule   Rule that binds *all* delegates chosen at a precinct, county, or state caucus to support the candidate with the most votes.

unitary executive   A single executive elected in a winner-take-all contest, such as the president. The opposite is a cabinet system of government in which power is shared among a group of ministers.

voter turnout   The act of voting itself, as distinguished from how the voters decide which candidates to vote for.

whip   Assistant floor leader for a party in each house of the legislature, whose job is to persuade the rank and file members to vote for the party position.

zero-base budgeting   Method of budget-making in which every item in the budget is justified anew each year instead of assuming that what was approved last year should be the base for this year's decisions.

zero-sum game   Whatever one player or team wins, the other player or team clearly loses; the sum of the winnings equals the sum of the losses.

select
bibliography

The purpose of this bibliography is *not* to provide a complete compilation of all the relevant books and articles. Rather, we have identified those sources that we think are the important readings in each area of study. In addition, we have described where to find information on American government. General resources that are useful in all areas of study are discussed in the beginning of the bibliography, and more specific sources are discussed under the appropriate chapter headings.

Much of what is written on American politics and government is published in periodicals. The *Reader's Guide to Periodical Literature* indexes mass circulation magazines such as *Time* or *Newsweek*. The *Public Affairs Information Service* covers many scholarly journals (e.g., *The American Political Science Review*), selected books, government publications, and certain important background articles (such as *Wall Street Journal* feature stories). The *Index to Legal Periodicals* contains references to many law journals that cannot be found elsewhere. The *New York Times Index* is an excellent place to find out when something happened and the basic facts of the event. For each year it is organized by topic and then chronologically. In addition to the citation, a short synopsis of the article is given in the index itself. *Facts on File* is also useful in this respect.

All major political science journals in the world are indexed in the *International Political Science Abstracts. ABC Poli Sci, Advanced Bibliography of Contents: Political Science and Government* is a monthly publication of contents from periodicals in political science.

The leading scholarly journals in the field of political science also have their own indexes. These are: *The American Political Science Review; Public Opinion Quarterly; Journal of Politics; American Journal of Political Science;* and *Polity.*

Biographical information can be found in the *Dictionary of National Biography* and the *Dictionary of American Biography.* More recent biographies are found in *Current Biography,* and the very recent biographies not yet in *Current Biography* can be found in *Biography Index.* Other biographical sources include *Who's Who in American Politics; Who's Who in Government; Who's Who in America;* and regional publications of *Who's Who* (e.g., *Who's Who in The West*). Also useful in this context is the *Facts On File* series, *Political Profiles* (1978).

United States government publications are described in L. F. Schmeckebier and R. B. Eastin, *Government Publications and Their Use,* 2nd rev. ed. (1969). Therein you can learn of the various catalogues that list government publications from 1774 to the present. Most useful is the *United States Government Publications Monthly Catalogue,* which covers 1940 to the present. A useful unofficial source covering more than government publications is John Brown Mason, *Research Resources: Annotated Guide to the Social Sciences,* vol. 2.

The American Statistics Index is a complete index of all statistical publications in the United States government. The best place to begin, however, is with the *Statistical Abstract of the United States,* published annually. Other statistical compilations include *Historical Statistics of the United States; City and County Data Book;* and *Social Indicators: Selected Data on Social Conditions in the United States* (1976).

General review articles on specific topics in political science can be found in the *International Encyclopedia of the Social Sciences* (1968), edited by David L. Sills; and *The Handbook of Political Science* (1975), edited by Fred I. Greenstein and Nelson W. Polsby. *The Handbook* contains eight volumes of articles summarizing nearly every field of political science. The articles particularly relevant to American politics and government are cited in this bibliography.

The most valuable sources for following current American politics are the *Washington Post,* the *New York Times, Congressional Quarterly Weekly Report,* and the *National Journal.* The *New York Times Index* appears every two weeks, and *CQ Weekly Report* and *National Journal* publish quarterly indexes.

CHAPTER 1 *Introduction*

DAHL, ROBERT A., *Modern Political Analysis,* 3rd ed. (1976). An introductory discussion of basic concepts in the study of politics and how they may be put to use in political analysis.

EVERSON, DAVID H., and JOANN PAINE, *An Introduction to Systematic Political Science* (1973). An overview of some of the ways in which political scientists ask and answer questions about politics.

CHAPTER 2 *The Social Context of American Politics*

The *Statistical Abstract of the United States* is the best place to begin looking for basic economic, social, and governmental data. It is published annually and its footnotes will lead you to more specialized and current sources of information. Historical data can be found in back issues of the *Statistical Abstract* and in *Historical Statistics of the United States, Colonial Times to 1957.*

BRYCE, JAMES B., *The American Commonwealth,* 2 vols. (1888). An Englishman's view in the 1880s of the institutions of government, the political party system, and American politics. Still valuable particularly for Bryce's insights into the roots of American institutions.

DE TOCQUEVILLE, ALEXIS, *Democracy in America,* 2 vols. (1835). The most famous, enduring, and influential portrait of American society by a foreign visitor. A comprehensive overview of the political, social, and economic culture.

GREELEY, ANDREW M., *Why Can't They Be More Like Us? America's White Ethnic Groups* (1975).

LIPSET, SEYMOUR MARTIN, *The First New Nation* (1963). A discussion of the social conditions that made a stable democracy possible in the United States.

WATTENBERG, BEN J., *The Real America: A Surprising Examination of the State of the Union*, rev. ed. (1976). Demographic analysis of American society with emphasis on the changes that took place between 1960 and 1970.

WILLIAMS, ROBIN W., *American Society* (1970). A systematic sociological analysis of the many dimensions of American society.

WOLFINGER, RAYMOND E., *The Politics of Progress* (1974), "Ethnic Politics," chapter 3.

CHAPTER 3 *The Constitutional Context of American Politics*

CHAPTER 4 *Civil Rights and Liberties*

A useful reference published by the Library of Congress is *The Constitution of the United States: Analysis and Interpretation,* an extensively annotated (over 1500 pages) presentation of the Constitution with references to cases decided by the Supreme Court through June 1964. The most recent edition of the work was published in 1972.

ABRAHAM, HENRY, *Freedom and the Court: Civil Rights and Liberties in the United States,* 3rd ed. (1977).

BEARD, CHARLES A., *The Supreme Court and the Constitution* (1972). A classic work on the development of constitutional law.

CORWIN, EDWARD S., *The Constitution and What It Means Today* (1974). A periodically revised guide to current interpretations of the Constitution.

———, ed., *The Constitution of the United States of America: Analysis and Interpretation* (1953). The most exhaustive and authoritative commentary on the Constitution.

EMERSON, THOMAS I., DAVID HABER, and NORMAN DORSEN, *Political and Civil Rights in the United States,* 2 vols. The most complete collection of cases, materials, and comments on civil rights and liberties. It is revised every few years and the newest editions are likely to be found most easily in card catalogues under Dorsen's name.

FARRAND, MAX, *The Framing of the Constitution of the United States* (1965). Based on the journals of the Constitutional Convention.

FELLMAN, DAVID, *Defendant's Rights Today* (1976).

HAND, LEARNED, *The Bill of Rights* (1958).

KLUGER, RICHARD, *Simple Justice: The History of Brown* v. *Board of Education* (1975). The story of the school desegregation movement.

POLLACK, LOUIS, *The Constitution and the Supreme Court: A Documentary History,* 2 vols. (1966).

POUND, ROSCOE, *The Development of Constitutional Guarantees of Liberty* (1957).

ROSSITER, CLINTON, *1787: The Grand Convention* (1966). Description and analysis of the decisions made at the Constitutional Convention.

SHAPIRO, MARTIN, and ROCCO TRESOLINI, *American Constitutional Law,* 5th ed. (1979). An overview of materials on the political aspects of the Constitution and constitutional law, with extensive materials on civil rights and liberties.

SUTHERLAND, ARTHUR, *Constitutionalism in America* (1965).

TRIBE, LAWRENCE, *American Constitutional Law* (1978). A complete treatise on constitutional law and civil rights and liberties.

THOREAU, HENRY DAVID, *Civil Disobedience* (1854). The classic work from which most modern theories of civil disobedience are drawn.

WHEELER, HARVEY, "Constitutionalism," in *The Handbook of Political Science,* vol. 5, eds. Fred I. Greenstein and Nelson W. Polsby (1975).

CHAPTER 5   *Federalism*

BREAK, GEORGE F., *Intergovernmental Fiscal Relations in the United States* (1967).

DERTHICK, MARTHA, *The Influence of Federal Grants* (1970). How the policy decisions of state and local governments are constrained by Washington.

ELAZAR, DANIEL J., *American Federalism: A View from the States,* 2nd ed. (1972).

EPSTEIN, LEON, "The Old States in a New System," in *The New American Political System,* ed. Anthony King (1978).

GRODZINS, MORTON, and DANIEL J. ELAZAR, eds., *The American System* (1966). Analysis of federal-state-local relations in some detail.

NATHAN, RICHARD P., and CHARLES F. ADAMS, *Revenue Sharing: The Second Round* (1977). Evaluation of the largest program of federal financial assistance to state and local governments.

Publius is a scholarly journal devoted to federalism.

RIKER, WILLIAM, "Federalism," in *The Handbook of Political Science,* vol. 5, eds. Fred I. Greenstein and Nelson W. Polsby (1975).

SUNDQUIST, JAMES L. and DAVID DAVIS, *Making Federalism Work* (1969). Analysis of a number of federal grant-in-aid programs.

CHAPTER 6   *The Intellectual Context of American Politics*

An extensive bibliographical volume (approximately 1200 pages) also published by the Library of Congress is *A Guide to the Study of the United States of America: Representative Books Reflecting the Development of American Life and Thought* (1960). Also quite useful in this context is the *Harvard Guide to American History* in two volumes (1974) by Frank Freidel.

BAILYN, BERNARD, *The Ideological Origins of the American Revolution* (1967). Shows the roots of American revolutionary thought in 18th-century English political philosophy.

BEER, SAMUEL, "In Search of a New Public Philosophy," in *The New American Political System,* ed. Anthony King (1978).

CHAFFEE, ZECHARIAH, *Free Speech in the United States* (1954). The history of American ideas about freedom of speech.

COMMAGER, HENRY STEELE, *The American Mind* (1959). A standard work in American intellectual history.

DAHL, ROBERT A., *A Preface to Democratic Theory* (1956). Analysis of the meaning of democracy in light of the reality of behavior by citizens and politicians.

GABRIEL, RALPH, *The Course of American Democratic Thought* (1956). A history of American ideas about politics.

HAMILTON, ALEXANDER, JOHN JAY, and JAMES MADISON, *The Federalist* (1788). Originally published as newspaper columns in support of ratifying the Constitution, these papers are a source of insights into the ideas of the men who wrote the Constitution.

HARTZ, LOUIS, *The Liberal Tradition in America* (1955). Traces the origins of the dominant American political ideology.

HOFSTADTER, RICHARD, *The American Political Tradition and the Men Who Made It* (1954).

PITKIN, HANNA, *The Concept of Representation* (1967).

SABINE, GEORGE, *A History of Political Theory* (1973). A survey of the history of political ideas.

THOREAU, HENRY DAVID, *Civil Disobedience* (1854). The classic work from which most modern theories of civil disobedience are drawn.

CHAPTER 7   *Public Opinion*

CHAPTER 8   *Voting*

Data on public opinion and voting behavior can be found in a number of sources. *The Gallup Poll* (1972) is a three-volume compendium of *all* the American Institute of Public Opinion poll findings from 1935 to 1971. In 1978 two additional volumes were published, bringing the collected statistics through the end of 1975. Polls on everything from attitudes toward new fashions to presidential popularity are included. More recent polls can be found in *The Gallup Opinion Index,* published monthly. The bi-monthly magazine *Public Opinion* contains articles on the state of public opinion and recent poll findings.

Historical election data are in S. Peterson, *A Statistical History of American Presidential Elections* and in Congressional Quarterly Service, *Presidential Elections Since 1789.* Data on election results for the last twenty years are found in the *America Votes* series edited by Richard Scammon. These are published every two years and contain election results for all major races and the presidential primaries.

CAMPBELL, ANGUS, ET AL., *The American Voter* (1960). The first comprehensive national study of the American electorate using survey research. Although somewhat dated (the data are primarily from 1952 and 1956), many of the core theories of voting behavior are found here.

————, *Elections and the Political Order* (1966). A set of key essays on public opinion, voting behavior, and elections in America.

CONVERSE, PHILIP E., "The Nature of Belief Systems in Mass Publics," in *Ideology and Discontent,* ed. David Apter (1964). Landmark essay on the ideological capacity of the American public.

————, "Public Opinion and Voting Behavior," in *The Handbook of Political Science,* vol. 4, eds. Fred I. Greenstein and Nelson W. Polsby (1975).

JENNINGS, M. KENT, and RICHARD G. NIEMI, *The Political Character of Adolescence* (1974). A study of the development of political perspectives from high school through young adulthood, and of parental influence on children's political views.

KEITH, BRUCE E., ET AL., *The Myth of the Independent Voter* (1980). Compares the attitudes and behavior of Democrats, Republicans, and Independents from 1952 through 1976.

KEY, V. O., JR., *Public Opinion and American Democracy* (1961).

LIPSET, SEYMOUR MARTIN, "The Wavering Polls," *The Public Interest,* (Spring 1976). Many aspects of public opinion are revealed in this warning about some of the limitations of polls.

MILLER, WARREN E., "The Cross-National Use of Party Identification as a Stimulus to Political Inquiry," in *Party Identification and Beyond,* eds. Ian Budge et al. (1976). Brief analytic description of party identification.

MILLER, WARREN E., and TERESA E. LEVITIN, *Leadership and Change—Presidential Elections from 1952 to 1976* (1977). Traces changes in political attitudes and their relationship to voting patterns.

MUELLER, JOHN E., *War, Presidents and Public Opinion* (1973). Dissects public views of the Korean and Vietnam wars.

PAGE, BENJAMIN I., *Choices and Echoes in Presidential Elections* (1978). Comprehensive analysis of the role of issues in presidential campaigns.

SEARS, DAVID O., "Political Socialization," in *The Handbook of Political Science,* vol. 2, eds. Fred I. Greenstein and Nelson W. Polsby (1975).

STOKES, DONALD E., "Some Dynamic Elements of Contests for the Presidency," *American Political Science Review* (March 1966).

WOLFINGER, RAYMOND E., and STEVEN J. ROSENSTONE, *Who Votes?* (1980). A theory of why people vote based on analysis of the turnout of different social and economic groups.

CHAPTER 9 *Political Participation*

Contemporary description and end-of-campaign reports are available in both *Congressional Quarterly Weekly Report* and *National Journal*. The raw material comes from the reports of the Federal Election Commission, public documents that are available in most libraries and directly from the FEC.

ALEXANDER, HERBERT E., *Financing Politics* (1976). Describes the situation after the reform legislation of the 1970s.

KIRKPATRICK, JEANE, *The New Presidential Elite* (1976). Describes national nominating convention delegates and contrasts them with the rank-and-file members of their respective parties. Also compares male and female delegates.

REEVES, RICHARD, *Convention* (1977). Gossip about the 1976 Democratic National Convention that reveals a great deal about the ambitions of the famous and obscure.

TOLCHIN, MARTIN, and SUSAN TOLCHIN, *To the Victor . . . Political Patronage from the Clubhouse to the White House* (1971).

VERBA, SIDNEY, and NORMAN H. NIE, *Participation in America* (1972).

WILSON, JAMES Q., *The Amateur Democrat* (1962). Landmark study of ideologically motivated party activists.

WOLFINGER, RAYMOND E., *The Politics of Progress* (1974), "Machine Politics," chapter 4.

CHAPTER 10 *Interest Groups*

By far the most up-to-date, detailed, and sophisticated accounts of Washington-based interest groups are the background articles on individual groups that appear from time to time in the weekly periodical *The National Journal*.

BAUER, RAYMOND A., ITHIEL DE SOLA POOL, and LEWIS A. DEXTER, *American Business and Public Policy: The Politics of Foreign Trade*, 2nd ed. (1972). A detailed study of the process by which foreign trade legislation was written and passed between 1953 and 1962, with emphasis on the role of American business in the legislative process.

BERRY, JEFFREY M., *Lobbying for the People* (1977). A study of the new "public interest" groups.

Congressional Quarterly Service, *The Washington Lobby*, 2nd ed. (1974). Includes current federal lobby laws and proposed reforms, descriptions of various lobbies, and a number of case studies.

DEXTER, LEWIS A., *How Organizations Are Represented in Washington* (1969).

GREENSTONE, J. DAVID, *Labor in American Politics* (1970).

OLSON, MANCUR, JR., *The Logic of Collective Action: Public Goods and the Theory of Groups* (1965). A critical examination, using economic theory, of individual motivations touching on the formation, membership, influence, and tactics of interest groups.

ORNSTEIN, NORMAN, and SHIRLEY ELDER, *Interest Groups, Lobbying and Policymaking* (1978).

SALISBURY, ROBERT H., ed., *Interest Group Politics in America* (1970).

———, "Interest Groups," in *The Handbook of Political Science*, vol. 4, eds. Fred I. Greenstein, and Nelson W. Polsby (1975).

SCHATTSCHNEIDER, E. E., *The Semi-Sovereign People* (1960). A statement of the relationships between the scope of political conflict and the influence of interest groups on policy decisions.

TRUMAN, DAVID B., *The Governmental Process: Political Interests and Public Opinion* (1951). A basic text with many illustrations of how interest groups participate in the formation of government policy.

WILSON, JAMES Q., *Political Organizations* (1973). An examination of forces leading to the survival, growth, tactics, and appeal of private organizations that engage in political activity.

CHAPTER 11 *Political Parties*

The complete *Proceedings* — platforms, votes, reports, debates, etc. — of all major and many minor United States party conventions from 1832 to 1972 are published on microfilm by Micro Publications, Inc., Wilton, Conn. A summary of the major parties' conventions as well as a compendium of voting records can be found in Richard C. Bain and Judith H. Parris, *Convention Decisions and Voting Records* (1973). The text of party platforms can also be found in Kirk H. Porter and Donald B. Johnson, *National Party Platforms, 1840 – 1964* (1966).

Current party politics can be followed in the *New York Times*, the *Washington Post*, and *Congressional Quarterly Weekly Report*.

BARBER, JAMES DAVID, ed., *Race for the Presidency: The Media and the Nominating Process* (1978).

CHAMBERS, WILLIAM N., and WALTER DEAN BURNHAM, eds., *The American Party Systems: Stages of Political Development*, 2nd ed. (1975).

DOWNS, ANTHONY, *An Economic Theory of Democracy* (1957). A formal economic model of the role of parties and elections in democracies with emphasis on the "inevitable" character of party competition resulting from the existence of only two parties.

EPSTEIN, LEON D., "Political Parties," in *The Handbook of Political Science*, vol. 4, eds. Fred I. Greenstein and Nelson W. Polsby (1975).

HERRING, PENDLETON, *The Politics of Democracy: American Parties in Action* (1968). Emphasizes consensus and stability as political goals and argues that the American party system serves to maintain unity among a diverse population.

KEY, V. O., JR., *Politics, Parties and Pressure Groups*, 5th ed. (1964).

LADD, EVERETT CARLL, JR., *Where Have All the Voters Gone?* (1978). Analysis of growing confusion in the two-party system.

PARRIS, JUDITH H., *The Convention Problem: Issues in Reform of Presidential Nominating Procedures* (1972).

POLSBY, NELSON W., and AARON B. WILDAVSKY, *Presidential Elections*, 5th ed. (1980).

RANNEY, AUSTIN, *Curing the Mischiefs of Faction: Party Reform in America* (1975).

———, "The Political Parties: Reform and Decline," in *The New American Political System*, ed. Anthony King (1978).

SCHATTSCHNEIDER, E. E., *Party Government* (1942). A critical examination of the American party system calling for stronger and more centralized political parties.

SORAUF, FRANK J., *Party Politics in America*, 3rd ed. (1976).

SUNDQUIST, JAMES L., *Dynamics of the Party System: Alignment and Realignment of Political Parties in the United States* (1973).

WITCOVER, JULES, *Marathon: The Pursuit of the Presidency 1972 – 1976* (1977).

CHAPTER 12 *How Congress Is Elected and Organized*

CHAPTER 13 *Congress in Action*

The most useful source on Congress is *Congressional Quarterly Weekly Report*. Its quarterly and annual indexes are the best starting point for anyone looking for information about Congress. The *Congressional Quarterly Almanac* is an annual publication summarizing the major legislative action of each session. The *Congressional Record* is published each day that either the House or the Senate is in session. In addition to containing a transcript of the previous day's action on the floor of both houses, additional articles and remarks submitted by members of Congress are published in the *Record*. At the end of

587

each session, the *Record* is bound and indexed. In addition to the *Record*, a *Daily Digest* is published which summarizes the events that took place the previous day on the floor of both houses and in committees. Current information on members of Congress, committee assignments, and on some congressional staff is in the *Congressional Directory*, published annually. The *Almanac of American Politics* contains thumbnail sketches of every member. Election returns and information on congressional districts are in the *Almanac of American Politics*, the *Congressional District Data Book*, and in a volume published by the Congressional Quarterly Service entitled *Congressional Districts in the 1970s*, 2nd ed. Committee reports and hearings are published by the Government Printing Office and are found in over 1,100 government depository libraries.

Historical information on Congress can be found in back issues of the *Congressional Record*. The *Congress and the Nation* series published by Congressional Quarterly Service covers the period from 1945 to the present.

CLAUSEN, AAGE R., *How Congressmen Decide* (1973). The most thorough analysis of congressional voting patterns.

DODD, LAWRENCE C., and BRUCE I. OPPENHEIMER, eds., *Congress Reconsidered* (1977). A collection of useful articles on the workings of the House and Senate.

FENNO, RICHARD F., JR., *Congressmen in Committees* (1973). A study of six House committees, their relationship to the House, their goals, and the needs they serve for their members.

———, *Home Style: House Members in Their Districts* (1978).

———, *The Power of the Purse: Appropriations Politics in Congress* (1966).

FEREJOHN, JOHN A., *Pork Barrel Politics: Rivers and Harbors Legislation, 1947–68* (1974).

FIORINA, MORRIS P., JR., *Congress: Keystone of the Washington Establishment* (1977). An argument that congressmen build support by passing programs whose administration is influenced by congressional intervention on behalf of constituents.

HAVEMANN, JOEL, *Congress and the Budget* (1978). An account of the first years of the new congressional budget process.

HUITT, RALPH K., and ROBERT L. PEABODY, *Congress: Two Decades of Analysis* (1969). Five influential articles on the Senate by Huitt and a bibliographic essay by Peabody.

KINGDON, JOHN W., *Congressmen's Voting Decisions* (1973). Study based on interviews with representatives about the factors influencing how they voted.

MANN, THOMAS E., *Unsafe at Any Margin: Interpreting Congressional Elections* (1978). A study of voting patterns in congressional elections that attributes importance to individual candidate image.

MAYHEW, DAVID R., *Congress: The Electoral Connection* (1974). An analysis of how congressmen's activities in the House further their goal of reelection.

MILLER, CLEM, *Member of the House*, ed. John W. Baker (1962). A congressman's letters to his constituents about how Congress works.

OLESZEK, WALTER J., *Congressional Procedures and the Policy Process* (1978). Description of the path a bill takes to become a law.

ORNSTEIN, NORMAN J., ed., *Congress in Change* (1975). A collection on changes in congressional organization and procedures.

PEABODY, ROBERT L., and NELSON W. POLSBY, eds., *New Perspectives on the House of Representatives*, 3rd ed. (1977). A collection treating both continuity and change in the House.

REDMAN, ERIC, *The Dance of Legislation* (1973). A personal account by a 22-year-old student intern of one bill's route to passage.

RIESELBACH, LEROY, ed., *The Congressional System*, 2nd ed. (1978). Another collection of basic articles about Congress.

WOLFINGER, RAYMOND E., ed., *Readings on Congress* (1971).

CHAPTER 14 *The Presidency*

An extensive bibliography compiled by the Library of Congress entitled *The Presidents of the United States: 1789–1962* is a rich compendium of sources on the presidency. Published annually are the *Public Papers of the President*. Current public addresses, executive orders, and other documents are published in the *Weekly Compilation of Presidential Documents* and in the *Federal Register*. Fred I. Greenstein et. al., *Evolution of the Modern Presidency* (1977), is a compilation of both governmental and secondary sources on the presidency since 1933.

ANDERSON, PATRICK, *The Presidents' Men: White House Assistants of Franklin D. Roosevelt, Harry S. Truman, Dwight D. Eisenhower, John F. Kennedy and Lyndon Johnson* (1968).

BARBER, JAMES DAVID, *The Presidential Character: Predicting Performance in the White House*, 2nd ed. (1977). A psychobiographical study of Presidents Taft through Carter with many illuminating anecdotes.

BURNS, JAMES MACGREGOR, *Roosevelt: The Lion and the Fox* (1956).

————, *Roosevelt: The Soldier of Freedom* (1970). A comprehensive political biography of Franklin Roosevelt.

Congressional Quarterly Service, *Watergate: Chronology of a Crisis*, 2 vols. (1973, 1974). A comprehensive review of the events and issues.

CRONIN, THOMAS E., *The State of the Presidency* (1975). Analysis of the so-called "institutionalization" of the presidency.

EVANS, ROWLAND, JR., and ROBERT D. NOVAK, *Nixon in the White House: The Frustration of Power* (1972). Emphasizes problems of staff coordination in the White House and Nixon's difficulty in trying to control the permanent bureaucracy.

————, *Lyndon B. Johnson: The Exercise of Power* (1968). A political biography useful for Johnson's career as Senate leader as well as his White House years.

FENNO, RICHARD F., JR., *The President's Cabinet* (1959).

FISHER, LOUIS, *The Constitution Between Friends: Congress, the President, and the Law* (1978).

GEORGE, ALEXANDER, and JULIETTE L. GEORGE, *Woodrow Wilson and Colonel House: A Personality Study* (1964). The best application of psychological insights to the study of political leadership.

HARGROVE, ERWIN C., *The Power of the Modern Presidency* (1974).

KESSEL, JOHN H., *The Domestic Presidency: Decision-Making in the White House* (1975).

KING, ANTHONY, "Executives," in *The Handbook of Political Science*, vol. 5, eds. Fred I. Greenstein and Nelson W. Polsby (1975).

KOENIG, LOUIS W., *The Chief Executive*, 3rd ed. (1975).

NEUSTADT, RICHARD E., *Presidential Power: The Politics of Leadership With Reflections on Johnson and Nixon* (1976). Influential analysis of the President's ability to impose his will on other politicians.

PIOUS, RICHARD M., *The American Presidency* (1979). A comprehensive reassessment of the post-Watergate presidency.

POLSBY, NELSON W., ed., *The Modern Presidency* (1973). A reader rich in details on recent presidents and presidencies.

REEDY, GEORGE E., *The Twilight of the Presidency* (1970). An account of presidential isolation and power by a former aide to Lyndon Johnson.

SCHLESINGER, ARTHUR M., JR., *The Imperial Presidency* (1973). The growth of presidential powers up to and through the Watergate period.

WAYNE, STEPHEN J., *The Legislative Presidency* (1978). Descriptions and analyses of those portions of the White House staff concerned with formulating and obtaining the passage of legislative programs.

WILDAVSKY, AARON, ed., *Perspectives on the Presidency* (1975).

CHAPTER 15 *The Politics of Administration*

The most useful source is the *United States Government Organization Manual,* published annually. It provides a complete picture of the organization and staffing of the federal bureaucracy. Regulations and orders of the federal agencies can be found in the *Code of Federal Regulations.* More current orders are in the *Federal Register.*

The *Budget in Brief* provides an overview of spending by each agency. A more detailed accounting of government expenditures can be found in *The Budget of the United States.* Most federal agencies publish annual reports and many other documents that provide voluminous information about their activities. *Congressional Quarterly Weekly Report* and the *National Journal* contain a good deal of current material on administrative developments.

BERNSTEIN, MARVER H., *The Job of the Federal Executive* (1964).

CAMPBELL, JOHN FRANKLIN, *The Foreign Affairs Fudge Factory* (1971). A critical study of the political and organizational troubles of the State Department.

DESTLER, I. M., *Presidents, Bureaucrats, and Foreign Policy,* 2nd ed. (1974).

DOWNS, ANTHONY, *Inside Bureaucracy* (1967).

HALPERIN, MORTON H., *Bureaucratic Politics and Foreign Policy* (1974).

HECLO, HUGH, *A Government of Strangers* (1977). An analysis, based on extensive interviews, of the "networks" of relationships between appointed public officials and civil servants in the executive branch.

HILSMAN, ROGER, *To Move a Nation: The Politics of Foreign Policy in the Administration of John F. Kennedy* (1967).

KAUFMAN, HERBERT, *Are Government Organizations Immortal?* (1976).

———, "Emerging Conflicts in the Doctrines of Public Administration," *American Political Science Review* (December 1956). Brief analysis of three different standards by which to judge bureaucratic performance.

LANDAU, MARTIN, "Redundancy, Rationality, and the Problem of Duplication and Overlap," *Public Administration Review* (July/August 1969). The positive functions of duplication and overlap for administrative agencies.

NADEL, MARK, and FRANCIS ROURKE, "Bureaucracies," in *The Handbook of Political Science,* vol. 5, eds. Fred I. Greenstein and Nelson W. Polsby (1975).

PRICE, DON K., *The Scientific Estate* (1965). Describes the growth of scientific agencies within the federal bureaucracy.

ROURKE, FRANCIS, *Bureaucracy, Politics, and Public Policy,* 2nd ed. (1976).

———, ed., *Bureaucratic Power in National Politics,* 3rd ed. (1978).

SEIDMAN, HAROLD, *Politics, Position, and Power: The Dynamics of Federal Organization,* 2nd ed. (1975).

SIMON, HERBERT A., *Administrative Behavior: A Study of Decision Making in Administrative Organizations,* 2nd ed. (1957).

STEINBRUNNER, JOHN, *The Cybernetic Theory of Decision: New Dimensions of Political Analysis* (1974). An attempt to explain atomic weapons decisions made by complex government organizations.

THOMPSON, VICTOR A., *Bureaucracy and the Modern World* (1976).

WEBER, MAX, "Bureaucracy," in *From Max Weber*, eds. Hans Gerth and C. Wright Mills (1946). A classic essay on the theory of bureaucracies.

WILDAVSKY, AARON, *The Politics of the Budgetary Process*, 3rd ed. (1979).

CHAPTER 16 *The Courts*

General information about the operation of the federal courts can be obtained from various reports and studies prepared by the Administrative Office of the U.S. Courts. Supreme Court opinions are published in three forms: (1) *United States Reports;* (2) *Supreme Court Reporter;* and (3) *United States Supreme Court, Lawyers' Edition*. Many libraries get only the bound volumes of one of these services, but law libraries and larger general libraries also receive the paperback supplements (called advance sheets) that appear only a few weeks after decisions are rendered. *United States Law Week* and *Supreme Court Bulletin* print opinions even before the advance sheets appear.

Decisions of lower federal courts are found in *The Federal Reporter* and *Federal Supplement*. The *Index to Legal Periodicals* indexes the articles that are published in law reviews. The *United States Code* contains an annotated list of all federal statutes. A wide range of legal dictionaries, encyclopedias, and digests are also available for tracing legal doctrines from case to case.

ABRAHAM, HENRY, *Justices and Presidents* (1974). An examination of the politics surrounding Supreme Court appointments.

BICKEL, ALEXANDER M., *The Least Dangerous Branch: The Supreme Court at the Bar of Politics* (1962).

CHASE, HAROLD W., *Federal Judges: The Appointing Process* (1972).

FUNSTON, RICHARD Y., *Constitutional Counter-Revolution?—The Warren Court and the Burger Court: Judicial Policy Making in Modern America* (1977).

GOLDMAN, SHELDON, and AUSTIN SARAT, *American Court Systems, Readings in Judicial Process and Behavior* (1978).

KRISLOV, SAMUEL, *The Supreme Court and Political Freedom* (1968).

MCCLOSKEY, ROBERT G., *The Modern Supreme Court* (1972).

MURPHY, WALTER F., and C. HERMAN PRITCHETT, eds., *Courts, Judges and Politics: An Introduction to the Judicial Process*, 3rd ed. (1979).

SHAPIRO, MARTIN, "Courts," in *The Handbook of Political Science*, vol. 5, eds. Fred I. Greenstein and Nelson W. Polsby (1975).

——, *Freedom of Speech: The Supreme Court and Judicial Review* (1966).

——, *Law and Politics in the Supreme Court* (1964). An analysis of the role of the Supreme Court outside the area of constitutional law.

——, *The Supreme Court and Administrative Agencies* (1968).

——, ed., *The Supreme Court and Public Policy* (1968).

——, "The Supreme Court: From Warren to Burger," in *The New American Political System*, ed. Anthony King (1978).

SCHMIDHAUSER, JOHN R., and LARRY L. BERG, *The Supreme Court and Congress* (1972).

SCHUBERT, GLENDON, *Judicial Policy-Making* (1965).

VOSE, CLEMENT E., *Constitutional Change* (1972). Describes the tactics that individuals and groups use in seeking changes in public policy through constitutional litigation.

WASBY, STEPHEN L., *Continuity and Change. From the Warren Court to the Burger Court* (1976).

——, *The Impact of the U.S. Supreme Court* (1970). Describes the influence of Supreme Court decisions on the behavior of other government officials and the public.

CHAPTER 17 *Public Policy Making*

The volumes published by the Congressional Quarterly Service are useful for the study of public policy. See *Congress and the Nation*, vols. I–III and the *Congressional Quarterly Almanac*. Also, the *United States Code* and the *Federal Register* list the actual rules emanating from the federal government.

ANDERSON, JAMES F., ET AL., *Public Policy and Politics in America* (1978).

DROR, YEHEZKEL, *Public Policy Making Reexamined* (1968).

HOROWITZ, DONALD L., *The Courts and Social Policy* (1977).

HITCH, CHARLES, *Decision Making for Defense* (1965). Describes program budgeting.

JONES, CHARLES O., *An Introduction to the Study of Public Policy*, 2nd ed. (1977).

LINDBLOM, CHARLES E., *The Intelligence of Democracy: Decision Making Through Mutual Adjustment* (1965).

———, *The Policy-Making Process* (1968).

LINEBERRY, ROBERT L., *American Public Policy: What Government Does and What Difference It Makes* (1977).

LOWI, THEODORE J., "Distrubution, Regulation, Redistribution: The Functions of Government," in *Public Policies and Their Politics*, ed. Randall B. Ripley (1966). An analysis of different types of policy outputs and the politics involved in the attainment of each.

MOYNIHAN, DANIEL P., *The Politics of Guaranteed Income* (1973).

PRESSMAN, JEFFREY L., and AARON WILDAVSKY, *Implementation: How Great Expectations in Washington Are Dashed in Oakland* (1973). "Or, why it's amazing that federal programs work at all, this being a saga of the Economic Development Administration as told by two sympathetic observers who seek to build morals on a foundation of ruined hopes."

SINDER, ALLAN P., ed., *America in the Seventies: Problems, Policies, and Politics* (1977). Case studies examining reform in the House of Representatives, the organization of the Nixon White House, school desegregation in San Francisco, reforms of delegate selection in the Democratic Party, the implementation of federal law enforcement policy by the state and local governments, and preferential admission of minorities to law school.

SUNDQUIST, JAMES L., *Politics and Policy: The Eisenhower, Kennedy and Johnson Years* (1968).

TALBOT, ROSS B., and DON F. HADWIGER, *The Policy Process in American Agriculture* (1968).

WILDAVSKY, AARON, *Speaking Truth to Power: The Art and Craft of Policy Analysis* (1979).

CHAPTER 18 *Evaluating the American Political System*

BARRY, BRIAN, and DOUGLAS W. RAE, "Political Evaluation," in *The Handbook of Political Science*, vol. 1, eds. Fred I. Greenstein and Nelson W. Polsby (1975).

COLEMAN, JAMES S., *Equality of Educational Opportunity* (1966). One of the most controversial of policy evaluation studies, on the relationships between school desegregation and educational achievement.

DAHL, ROBERT A., *After the Revolution: Authority in a Good Society* (1970). An analysis of the principal issues in political philosophy raised by the New Left.

GRUMM, JOHN G., "The Analysis of Policy Impact," in *The Handbook of Political Science*, vol. 6, eds. Fred I. Greenstein and Nelson W. Polsby (1975).

LINDBLOM, CHARLES E., *Politics and Markets*, (1977). A rigorous display of questions to ask in evaluating the American political system and the place of government in economic life.

LOWI, THEODORE J., *The End of Liberalism: The Second Republic of the United States*, 2nd ed. (1979). A controversial critique of the ability of liberal ideology and programs to solve social and economic problems.

MOSTELLER, FREDERICK, and DANIEL P. MOYNIHAN, *On Equality of Educational Opportunity* (1972). A review of some of the issues raised by the Coleman study.

PECHMAN, JOSEPH, ed., *Setting National Priorities* (1977, 1978, 1979). Annual reviews and evaluations of the federal budget by the Brookings Institution.

RIVLIN, ALICE M., *Systematic Thinking for Social Action* (1971). How the results of evaluation studies can be incorporated into subsequent policy decisions.

WATTS, WILLIAM, and LLOYD A. FREE, *State of the Nation* (1973). How the American public sees itself and the country's condition.

WHOLEY, JOSEPH S., ET AL., *Federal Evaluation Policy: Analyzing the Effects of Public Programs* (1970).

index

A

Abolitionists, 82
Abortion, 67
Abourezk, James, 216
Accountability, popular, 317–19
Accused persons, rights of, 62–65
Acheson, Dean, 427
Activists, political, 191, 198
  ideological gap between ordinary party
     members and, 219–21
  implications and consequences of, 222–24
  political participation by, 218–21
  regular and purists, 271–72
  socioeconomic composition of, 219

Activity, political, 189–90
  attitudes toward, 202
Adams, Abigail, 244, 245
Adams, John, 244
Adams, John Quincy, 293
Adams, Sherman, 425
Administration and policy, overview of, 473–75
Administrative branch, organization of, 440–45
Administrative law, 495
Administrative reorganization, politics of,
    466–72
Administrative responsibility, delegating,
    449–50
Affirmative action, 28, 70–73
Age, 30–31

Aged
  affirmative action and, 73
  federal benefits to, 31
  political power of, 31
Agency overlap and competition, 464–66
Agnew, Spiro, 167, 432–33
Agriculture, Department of, 351, 367, 368, 442
Agriculture Appropriations Subcommittee, 375
Agriculture Authorization Bill, 352
Agriculture Committee(s), 330–31, 367, 375
Agriculture and Related Agencies Appropriations Subcommittee, 371
Aid for Dependent Children (AFDC), 91, 92
Air Force, 375
Albert, Carl, 352
Amateur clubs, 201
Amendments to Constitution. *See specific amendments*
American associations, diversity of, 228–29
American Bankers Association, 328
American Bar Association, 489, 490
American Dental Association, 226
American Diabetes Association, 226
American Federation of Labor-Congress of Industrial Organization (AFL–CIO), 232, 236–37, 248
American Federation of Teachers (AFT), 240–41, 468
American Indians. *See also* Native Americans
  affirmative action and, 72–73
American Israel Public Affairs Committee (AIPAC), 243
American Medical Association, 231, 232
American Milk Producers, 236
American party system, 15. *See also* Parties, political
American people, makeup of, 38–39
Americans for Democratic Action, 248
American society, multilingual, 551
Amicus curiae, 499
Anderson, Jack 145
Anderson, Patrick, 425
Antiballistic missile (ABM) system, 123
Anti-Defamation League, 426
Appeal, 498
Appeals courts, 480
Appellate jurisdiction, 478
Appointments
  presidential, 415–28
  of Supreme Court Justices, 489–90
Appropriations Committee(s), 331, 368–69, 374
Appropriations process, 368–70
Appropriations subcommittee on health, 365
Aquinas, Saint Thomas, 103
Arab boycott bill, 426
Armed Services Committee, 375
Army Corps of Engineers, 250, 410, 534
Articles of Confederation, 42, 50–51
Asian-Americans, 72–73

Associated Corset and Brassiere Manufacturers, 234
Association
  anonymous, 61
  freedom of, 60–61
Attainder, bills of, 48
Attitudes. *See also* Political opinion; Public opinion
  how learned, 136–40
  shaping of, 140–42
Attractive incentives, 438
Auditing, 533

B

Balancing test, 57
Banking, Housing and Urban Affairs Committee, 327, 328
Barenblatt v. *United States,* 58
Bell, Griffin, 419, 493
Berkeley (California), 351
Bicameral legislatures, 303
Biden, Joseph R., Jr., 214, 215
Biemiller, Andrew, 366
Bill of Rights, 54, 73, 78
Birth control, 67
Birth rates, 31
Black, Charles, 506
Blacks (Black Americans), 24, 25–26
  affirmative action and, 72–73
Blue-collar jobs, 31
Board of Regents v. *Bakke,* 72
Boll Weevils, 347, 348
Box Association of America, 234
Boycott(s), 259
  consumer, 259
Branzburg v. *Hayes,* 61
Brief, 499
Brokered convention, 286
Brooke, Edward, 327
Brown, Edmund G., Jr., 283
Brown, Jerry, 408
Brown v. *Board of Education,* 68, 69, 500, 506
Brzezinski, Zbigniew, 427, 538
Buckley v. *Valeo,* 57, 61, 203
Budget(s), 469–73
  new congressional process, 371–72
  zero-based, 472
Budget Committee(s), 371, 372
Burger, Warren E., 500, 509
Burger Court, 496
Business, regulation of, 82
Business organizations, as interest groups, 233–36
Business Roundtable, 235, 426
Busing, 71
Byrd, Robert C., 340, 341, 342
Byrne, Jane, 194

C

Cabinet, United States, 421–23
   presidential role and, 422–23
Calhoon, Jesse, 238
Calorie Control Council, 226
Cambodia, 141, 388, 430
Campaign(s), presidential, 290–91
Campaign expenses
   disclosure of, 205
   public financing of, 205
Campaign finance, future issues in, 216–18
Campaign spending and candidate familiarity,
   213
Candidate appeal, 173–79
Candidate image, 297
Capacity, governmental, 547–48
Capitol, 321–22
Cargo preference, 238, 239
Carter, Jimmy, 126, 273, 275, 284, 291, 429,
   452, 513
   appointments to federal bench and, 495
   benefits from no-confidence in Ford voters,
     185
   big labor and, 237
   career patterns of first cabinet, 418–19
   and Catholic voters, 176
   coattail effect and, 311
   cronyism and, 436
   Democratic primaries in 1976 and, 286
   education program and, 468
   energy and, 126, 153
   issue voting and, 181
   Justice Department and, 493
   legislative veto and, 386
   liberalism and, 177
   maritime unions and, 192
   Middle Eastern peace negotiations and, 538,
     542
   as an outsider, 271
   and pork barrel legislation, 523
   and president-centered staff system, 407
   presidential appointees and, 420–21
   proposal to DNC about women delegates,
     287
   proposed Theodore C. Sorensen for CIA, 387
   public classification of, 178
   and publicly-financed congressional
     campaigning, 204
   public rating (1978), 312
   recognition of People's Republic of China by,
     395
   relations with Congress, 392
   relations with labor leaders, 238
   renomination vulnerability in 1979, 282
   rise from obscurity, 285
   and Senior Executive Service, 451
   southern voters and, 165
   State of the Union message, 50
   Supreme Court appointments and, 486
   as an unpopular president, 408

   veto power and, 415
   White House staff and, 424
   work day schedule of, 405
   zero-base budgeting and, 472
Castro, Fidel, 538
Categorical groups 34, 227
Catholics, 28, 29
Caucus-convention method, 280–81
Caucuses, party 343–44
Census Bureau, 122
Central cities, 37
Central Intelligence Agency (CIA), 369, 384,
   385, 444, 532, 536
Certiorari, 498
Chamber of Commerce, 234, 235, 238, 254,
   377
Checks and balances, 48–49, 109–10
Chewing Gum Manufacturers, National
   Association of, 234
Chicanos. *See* Mexican-Americans
Children, political information of, 138
China, People's Republic of (PRC), 395
China, Republic of (ROC), 395
Chocolate Manufacturers Association of the
   United States, 234
Church, Frank, 283
Cities, National League of, 242
Civil Aeronautics Board (CAB), 459–61
Civil disobedience, 260
Civil liberties, defender of, 403–4
Civil rights, 57
Civil Rights, Office of, 464
Civil Rights Act of 1964, 69, 113, 167, 251,
   377
Civil Rights Division, 464
Civil Service, United States, 101, 386, 450–52
   salaries, 451
Civil Service Act (1833), 450
Civil Service Commission, United States,
   450–51, 455
Civil services employees, protection of,
   452–53
Civil War amendments, 54, 68–69
Class actions, 258
Class consciousness, 35
Class structure of American society
   lack of clarity in, 35
   lower middle class, 34
   upper class, 34
   upper middle class, 34
   working class, 34
Cleavages, cross-cutting, 28
Clientelism, 457–62
   in the regulatory commission, 458–61
   specialization and, 458
Clifford, Clark, 385
Cloture, 358
Coattail effect, 311
Cohen, David, 343
Cohen, Richard, 197
Collective effort, 8–9

Colmer, William C., 311
Colored People, National Association for the
    Advancement of (NAACP), 243, 245,
    255, 256
Commerce, Department of, 236, 465
Commerce and Labor, Department of, 442–43
Commission for Public Education v. Nyquist, 64
Committee system, in Congress, 329–31
    appropriations process, 368–70
    assignments to committee, 331–32
    differences among committees, 332–34
    hearings, 353–55
    seniority system and committee chairmen,
        334–35
Common Cause, 232, 238, 246–48, 249, 343
    lobbying and, 252, 254
Common law, 41
Community Services Administration, 444
Comparative analysis, 550–52
Comprehensive Employment and Training Act
    (CETA), 93
Compromises, art of finding, 5
Conference committees, 358–60
Confirmation, of President's appointments,
        386–87
Conflict
    limiting, 548–49
    management of, 4–7, 555–56
    politics as a source of, 6–7
    religious, 555–56
    value, 5–6
Conflict resolution, 544
Confrontation strategies, by interest groups,
        258–61
Congress, United States
    appropriations process in, 368–70
    committee system in, 329–39
    controlled by conservative coalitions, 393
    ideological groups in, 347–48
    independence of, 46
    mail from constituents, 379–81
    members of
        outside income of, 327–28
        perquisites of, 323
        social life of, 325–26
    other ways to organize, 346–48
    parties in, 339–46
    party strength in, 362
    powers of, 46–48
    state delegations in, 346–37
    veto power, 363
Congressional Black Caucus, 348
Congressional Budget and Impoundment
        Control Act (1974), 371
Congressional Budget Office (CBO), 371, 372
Congressional candidates
    differ on issues, 294
    important influences on selection of, 318–19
    successful, 319–20
    voters knowledge of, 308
Congressional delegation, case study of, 531

Congressional elections, 307–19
    dynamic factors in, 312–13
Congressional ethics, 326–28
Congressional Record, 372, 379
Congressional Research Service (CRS), 373–74
Consciousness-raising, 241
Consensus, 115–16
Conservative, 129, 130
Conservative coalition, 361–63
Constituents
    desires of, 379–81
    influential, 414
Constitution, United States, 305–6, 565–74
    amendments to, 54. See also specific
        amendment
    as a contract, 41
    ideas behind, 41
    intent of framers of, 42–50, 54
    legislative power, 45
    limitations on Congress, 48
    role of, 107–11
Constitutional boundaries, maintaining, 503
Constitutional Convention, 54, 244, 305
Constitutional legitimacy, 54–55
Consumer movement, 246
Containment, 537
Continental Congress, 42
Continuity and crisis, in foreign policy-making
        process, 537–39
Contract Compliance, Office of, 464
Contracting, military, 447–49
Contractors, outside, 447–50
Convention delegates, 274
Convention of 1787, 54
Coordination, of foreign policy, 540
Corvair, 246
Cotton, Agriculture Subcommittees on, 384
Counsel, right to, 63, 66
Counties, National Association of, 242
Country teams, 540
Cox, Archibald, 387
Cranston, Alan, 208, 351, 352
Cruel and unusual punishment, 66
    prohibition of, 65
Cuba, 538
Cyprus, invasion of, 388

D

Dahl, Robert, 193
Debate(s), 357–58
Decentralization, 273
Decision-making
    administrators and governmental, 462–63
    styles, 515–22
Decisions, indivisible, 193
Dees, Morris, 211
Defeat, consequences of, 317
Defense, Department of, 384, 537, 540
Defense Intelligence Agency, 536

Delegate, instructed, 378
Delegations, 346
Dellums, Ronald V., 315, 351, 364
Democracy, 96–103
  American thoughts on, 102–3
  direct, 99–100
  and efficiency, 101
  Jacksonian, 100–101
  representative, 45–46, 99–100
Democratic Caucus, 338, 339, 344, 357, 368
Democratic identification, socioeconomic sources
  of, 164
Democratic National Committee (DNC), 275,
  287, 408
Democratic National Convention, 176, 194, 287
Democratic Party (Democrats)
  activists in, 218–21
  black loyalty to, 167–68
  ideological portrait of, 169–71
  percentage of total vote since 1952, 312–13
  social and economic bases of, 162–68
  voting behavior and identification with,
    157–62
Democratic Senators, seniority among, 338
Democratic Steering and Policy Committee, 338
Democratic Study Group (DSG), 347–48
Dennis v. *United States*, 58
Depression, 409, 410
Desegregation, school, 69
Direct mail solicitation, 210–11
Dirksen, Everett, 251, 342
Disability Examiners, National Association of,
  525
Disaffection, political
  sources of, 553
  trends in, 552
Discrimination, 22
  private, 69
  racial, 69, 113
  reverse, 72
Distant Early Warning (DEW) Line, 447
Distributive policy(ies), 522–23
  politicians' preference for, 524–26
District and circuit courts, policymaking in,
  495–96
District of Columbia Committee, 357
Diversity, geographical, 108
Double jeopardy, 65
Draft laws, justice of, 114–15
Drug industry, 411
Dualism of conflict, 269
Due process, 73–74
Due process clause, 68
Dunlop, John, 417

E

Eagleton, Thomas, 176, 432–33
Eastland, James, 411
Economic Advisers, Council of, 427, 517

Economic development, American, 19
Economic equality, evaluations of, 561
Economic exploitation, 22
Economic Opportunity, Office of (OEO), 85,
  444
Education
  as biggest single "industry," 32
  political opinions and, 134–36
Education, Arts, and Humanities Subcommittee
  of Senate Committee on Labor and
  Human Resources, 240
Education, Department of, study of, 467–69
Education, Office of, 375, 450, 461, 467
Educational levels of Americans, 127
Education and Labor Committee, House, 331,
  366, 524
Efficiency, 544
Eighth Amendment, 65
Eisenhower, Dwight D.
  heart attack, 397
  HEW and, 443–44
  landslide victories, 161
  legislative process and, 410, 411
  liberal backers of, 271
  mass media and, 144
  personal staff and, 406
  pledge to go to Korea, 182
  political magnetism of, 174
  popularity of, 176
  Schedule C appointees and, 453
  John Sirica and, 493
  veto and, 415
  working hours of, 405
Eizenstat, Stuart E., 238, 426
Election laws, 150–53
Elections, 108–9
  candidate appeal in, 173–79
  deviating, 161
  as mandates, 185–86
Electoral college, 50, 292–94
  attempts to abolish, 101
Elementary and Secondary Education Act
  (ESEA) (1965), 533
Eli Lilly Corporation, 200
Emergency School Assistance Act, 242
Employment Act of 1946, 106
Energy, Department of, 444
Energy crisis, 538
Energy and Natural Resources Committee, 328
Envelope Manufacturers Association, 234
Environmental impact statement (EIS), 256,
  528–29
Environmental Protection Act, 529
Environmental Protection Agency, 444
Equal Employment Opportunity Commission
  (EEOC), 457, 464
Equality, 111–13, 556–61
  learning about, 139–40
  of opportunity, 112
  political, 111
  racial, 113

Equality *(cont.)*
  social, 111–12
Equal protection clause, 68
Equal Rights Amendment, 34, 47, 73, 245
Equal treatment, 114
Erlichman, John, 423
Ethnic groups, 241–44
  largest, 25
  least prosperous, 25
  most prosperous, 25
  politically important, 24
Ethnicity and race, 22–28
Eucalyptus Bill, 352
Exclusionary rule, 63, 65
Exclusive committees, 330
Executive(s)
  career, 454–55
  political, 453–54
Executive agreements, 395
Executive branch
  budget-making process in, 470
  legislative control of, 383–89
  president and, 415–28
Executive Office of the President (EOP), 423,
    424, 431, 447
Executive power, 50–51
  kinds of, 51
  meaning of, 396
Executive privilege, 430–31
Expectations, increase in, 553
Expert(s)
  role of, 545–46
  rule by, 546

F

Faction, social and economic bases of, 162–68
Fair Campaign Practices Committee, 298
Fair procedure, 114
Fair trial rule, 505
Family income
  distribution of in 1977, 20
  median, 20
Farmers and Manufacturers Beet Sugar
    Association, 234
Feasibility, 544
Federal administration, indirect, 445
Federal agencies, 442–43
  coordination of, 467–69
Federal aid to states and cities, 89
Federal Bureau of Investigation (FBI), 369, 433,
    489, 532
Federal Communications Commission, 143, 445
Federal control of states, protection against, 87
Federal courts, lower, 491–95
Federal departments, presidential colonization
    of, 423
Federal Election Campaign Act, 57, 203
Federal Election Commission (FEC), 203, 205,
    209

Federal funding and public social welfare
    expenditures, 92
Federalism
  changes in, 82
  definition of, 76
  fiscal, 87–90
  new, 83–87
  principal impact of, 81
  results of, 81–82
  Supreme Court and, 77–78
Federalists, 268
Federalist Papers, The, 38, 108, 162
Federal judges
  appointment of, 492–95
  characteristics of appointees, 494
Federal matching funds, 217
Federal Power Commission, 445
Federal prosecutors, 493
Federal Register, 391, 531
Federal Regulation of Lobbying Act, 253
Federal-state relations, finances of, 87
Federal Trade Commission (FTC), 236, 257,
    445, 459, 460–61
Feminine Mystique, The (Friedan), 245
Fenno, Richard F., 317, 366, 380
Fifth Amendment, 65, 73
Fifteenth Amendment, 67, 68, 78, 111, 150
Filibuster, 357–58
Finance Committee, 328, 370
First Amendment, 57, 60, 255, 259
Flavor and Extract Manufacturers Association,
    234
Floor, the, 322
Floor leader, 341
Fogarty, John, 365
Food and Drug Administration (FDA), 225, 226,
    236, 246
Food Stamp Act (1977), 376
Food Stamp program, 91
Ford, Gerald
  big labor and, 237
  campaigning in Texas, 284
  Congress and, 392
  conservatism of, 177, 411
  energy conservation and, 126
  inability to accomplish, 429
  and lack of economic advances, 20
  lack of personal appeal, 291
  lack of popular appeal, 174
  pardon of Nixon, 265, 312
  presidential appointees and, 417
  presidential vulnerability and, 398
  public classification of, 178
  reelection nomination and, 282
  unclear position on issues, 181
  veto and, 415
  War Powers Resolution and, 430
  White House staff and, 424
Ford-Carter debates, 127, 144, 179
Foreign Corrupt Practices Act, 465
Foreign policy, 536

congressional oversight of, 388
  decisions, 538
Foreign Service, 536
Forestry Subcommittee, 351
Forest Service, 456
Fourteenth Amendment, 67, 68, 72, 73, 78, 256
Fourth Amendment, 62, 65
France, Anatole, 559
Franking privilege, 323
Freedom, 128
Freedom and equality, tension between, 562–63
Freedom of speech, 57–61
  education and support for, 135
  other aspects of, 59–61
  scope of, 60
Frick, Henry C., 215
Friedan, Betty, 245
Fugitive Slave Laws, 82

G

Gallup, George, 122
Gallup Poll, 123, 282, 312, 320, 398, 430. *See also* Public Opinion, American Institute of
Gandhi, Mohandas, 260
Gardening for Food and Fun, 323
Gardner, John, 365
Garner, John N., 432
Gay rights movement, 244
General Accounting Office (GAO), 373–74, 384, 533
General Motors, 234, 246
Georgia mafia, 426
Gerrymandering, 306
Gibb, Barry, 325
Gibb, Maurice, 325
Goal substitution, 548
Goldwater, Barry, 115, 161, 167, 174, 190, 199, 271, 273, 284, 289, 298
  direct mail solicitation and, 210, 211
  1972 primary and, 278
Governed, consent of, 96
Government, 16–17
  mixed, 44
  popular participation in, 99
  reorganization of, 386
Governmental Affairs Committees, 384
Governmental responsibility, 547
Government corporations, 446
Government employment, access to, 450–57
Government executives, 453–56
Government policies, local experimentation in, 80–81
Government reflected in federal budget, 473
Government and science, 449
Governors', National Association of, 242
Grants-in-aid, 83–85, 446
  legislation, 83

matching, 84
Grants and revenue sharing, impact of, 88–89
Great Compromise, 305
Great Depression, 20, 168
Great Society, 85, 393, 444
Greeley, Andrew M., 25
Griswold v. *Connecticut,* 67
Grocery Manufacturers of America (GMA), 235
Gross National Product (GNP), 19–20
Gulf Oil Company, 194, 195
Gulf of Tonkin Resolution, 429

H

Habeas corpus, writ of, 48, 67
Halperin, Morton, 385
Hamilton, Alexander, 392, 393
Handicapped
  affirmative action and, 73
  education of, 87
Harding, Warren, 397
Harris, Louis, 124, 125
Hays, Wayne, 327
Head Start program, 469
Health, Education, and Welfare, Department of (HEW), 365, 367, 417, 443–44, 467
  education programs and, 468
Health, National Institutes of, 365, 367
Health, Subcommittee on, 365
Health Research Group, 249
Hearings, congressional, 353–55
  purpose of, 354
Heinz, H. John III, 208
Helms, Jesse, 207
Hierarchy, 437
  limitations on control, 463
Highway Safety Act, 246
Hill, Lister, 365
Hispanic-Americans. *See* Spanish origin, persons of
Hoover, Herbert, 168, 397, 402, 405
Hopkins, Harry, 423
House Administration Committee, 327
House Appropriations Committee (HAC), 368–69
  Subcommittee on State, Justice, Commerce, and the Judiciary, 369
House Ethics Committee, 327
House Judiciary Committee, 310
House Merchant Marine and Fisheries Committee, 238
House of Representatives, 45
  election of members
    composition of vote in, 160
    Speaker of, 340–41, 343, 404
    voter turnout in, 152
Housing Act of 1949, 84
Housing and Urban Development, Department of (HUD), 85, 371, 444

Howar, Barbara, 325
Humphrey, Hubert, 180–81, 186, 191, 211, 265, 282, 289, 298, 404, 434
  Vietnam war and, 182–84
Hundred Days, 409

I

Ideological groups, in Congress, 347–48
Ideologues, 130, 198
Ideology
  defined, 129
  public opinion and, 129–30
  self-identification, 130–32
Ignorance
  level of, 126
  popular, 527–28
  technical, 528
Illegal aliens, 27
Immigrants, 21, 22
Immigration, 22–25
  Canadian, 23
  Latin American, 23
Impeachment, 48–49, 305, 396
  hearings in 1974, 310
Impoundment, 371, 431–32
Income
  distribution of, 19–21
    and federal tax burden, 560
  median family, 20
  real, 20
Incremental approach, to policymaking, 517–18
Incrementalism, 471
  objections to, 519–20
  reasons for, 471–72
Incumbency, advantages of, 309–11
Independent Progressive party, 172
Independents
  increase in, 173
  Pure, 172
Individual rights, 103–7
Infant Care, 323
Infant mortality, 551
Inflation, 20, 127
Information
  gathering, 372–77
  and policymaking, 527–29
  sources of, 373–77
Integration, 69
Intelligence, 536–37
  interpretation of, 537
Interest(s)
  conflicts of, 328
  economic, 105–6
Interest groups
  administration and, 461–62
  defined, 227
  economic, 231, 233–41
  facts about, 226–27
  government of, 248–49

membership, 229–31
  numbers and diversity, 228–29
  tactics, 251–61
  types of, 231–32
Interior, Department of, 440–41
Internal Revenue Service (IRS), 451, 530, 532
  Supreme Court and, 478
International Development, Agency for, 386
Internationals, 236
Interstate Commerce Commission, 255, 256, 445
  Supreme Court and, 478
Investigations Subcommittee, 384
Irish Catholics, 22, 25
Issue incentive group, 232
Issue voting, 179–85
  defined, 182
Italian-Americans, 25
Item veto, 363

J

Jackson, Andrew, 409, 477
Jackson, Henry, 243, 273, 283
Jacobson, Gary, 212, 217
Japan, 538
Japanese-Americans, 25, 547
Jaworski, Leon, 387
Jefferson, Thomas, 42, 267
Jeffersonian Democrats, 268
Jews, 24–25, 28, 29
Jim Crow laws. *See* Segregation laws
John Birch Society, 315
Johnson, Andrew, 42, 49, 396
Johnson, Lyndon
  Adam Yarmolinsky and, 347
  campaign funds, 209
  civil rights legislation and, 167
  Congress and, 408
  defeat of Barry Goldwater, 161
  Democratic majority and, 393
  Great Society and, 85
  lack of personal glamor, 291
  Model Cities program and, 85
  national party affairs and, 275
  1968 New Hampshire primary and, 185–86, 286
  personal role in Vietnam war, 395
  personal security of, 406
  political abilities of, 174
  popular opposition to, 392
  support by Baltimore blacks, 180
  veto and, 415
  as vice-presidential candidate, 432
  and war on poverty, 85, 447
Joint Chiefs of Staff, 540
Jordan, Hamilton, 407, 408
Judicial activism, 484
Judicial power, 51–54

Judicial review, 52, 478
Judicial modesty. *See* Judicial self-restraint
Judicial self-restraint, 484
Judicial supremacy, era of, 482–83
Judiciary Act (1789), 52
Judiciary Act (1925), 498
Jurisdiction, original, 498
Jury(ies), discrimination in selection of, 65
Justice, Department of, 327, 387, 465, 489, 492
Justice and the rule of law, 113–14

K

Kefauver, Estes, 411
Kennedy, Edward M., 282, 325, 326, 328
Kennedy, John F., 144, 166–67, 174, 176, 291, 377, 406, 408, 431–32, 447
   assassination of, 397
   as Catholic, 399
   drug legislation and, 412
   independent presidential action by, 392
   popularity of, 398–99
   presidential appointments and, 416, 419
   veto power and, 415
Kennedy, Robert, 198, 223, 527
King, Coretta, 291
King, Martin Luther, Jr., 261, 291
Kissinger, Henry, 427
Knowland, William, 353
Koreagate, 348
Korean War, 282, 503
Ku Klux Klan, 260

L

Labor and Public Welfare, Committee on, 365
Labor Statistics, Bureau of, 373
Labor unions, 236–38
   federal government and, 450–51
   membership, 34
La Follette, Robert, 172
Laissez faire doctrine, 104–6
   private property and, 104–5
Lance, Bert, 436
Land Management, Bureau of (BLM), 454, 461
Landon, Alfred M., 122
Latex Foam Rubber Council, 234
Law(s)
   ex post facto, 48
   rule of, 113, 115
Law clerks, 498
Law Enforcement Assistance Administration (LEAA), 86
Leadership
   congressional, 340–44
   role of, 141–42
League of Nations, 395

Legal Services Corporation, 257, 444
Legislation, coordination of, 370–72
Legislative appointment, 306–7
Legislative district, single-member, 269
Legislative oversight, 384–86
Legislative process, 353–64
   chart, 359
Legitimacy, Constitutional, 54–55
Libel, 60
Liberal, 129, 130
Liberal tradition, 103
Library of Congress, 373
Lindsay, John V., 194, 195
Line agencies, 440–44
Line departments, 440
Literary Digest, 122
Litigation, by interest groups 255–58
Lobbying, 252–55
   regulation of, 253–55
Lobbyists, 234, 237, 366, 367, 376–77
Location, 36–37
Locke, John, 41, 43, 44
Long, Russell, 328
Los Angeles Times, 143

M

MacArthur, Douglas, 174
McCarthy, Eugene, 185, 186, 198, 199, 209, 271
McCloskey, Paul N., 202
McDonald v. Sante Fe Trail Transport Co., 71
McFall, John, 351, 352
McGovern, George, 155, 271, 285, 288, 289, 432
   attracted idealists, 198–99
   campaign expenses and, 208
   defeated for presidency, 161
   Democratic primaries in 1976 and, 286
   direct mail solicitation and, 211
   labor unions and, 237
   lack of personal glamor, 291
   1972 primary and nomination of, 278
   party regulars and, 273
   popular recognition and, 282
   as a potential spoiler in 1972, 267
   regarded as liberal and indecisive by voters, 177
   as underdog candidate, 284
   as unpopular candidate, 176, 181
McKinley, William, 423
Machine politics, 197–98
   essence of, 197
Madison, James, 38, 108, 162, 392, 393, 413
Magazines, political influence of, 142
Mahoney, George, 180
Mail, as source of information, 379
Majorities
   local and national, 81–82
   of the moment, 110–11

Majority rule, 102, 107
  and minority rights, 107–8
Malapportionment, 306
Management and Budget, Office of (OMB), 367, 372, 410, 425, 427, 431, 469, 470–71, 472, 515, 523, 533
  basic purpose of, 471
Mandatory quotas, 287
Manufacturers, National Association of (NAM), 234, 235, 251, 254, 377
Marbury v. *Madison,* 482
Marijuana, 548, 549
Maritime Administration, 457
Markup session, 354–55
Marshall, John, 477, 482
Marshall, Ray, 417
Marshall Plan, 430
Mass media
  presidential use of, 414
  public opinion and, 142–46
  role of, in nomination process, 282–84
Mayors, U.S. Conference of, 242
Medicaid, 91, 92
Medicare, 91
  legislation, 550
Mental Health, National Institute of, 375
Mental Retardation Branch, 467
Merchant Marine and Fisheries Committee, 330
Mexican-Americans, 27, 243
Middle class, upper, 31
Middle Eastern crisis, 538
Military officers, 455–56
Milk Advisory Board, California, 460–61
Miller, Arthur, 272
Minimum wage laws, 106
Minorities
  fastest growing, 27
  majorities of the moment and, 110–11
  permanent, 111
Minority rights, 107–8
Minority rule, 364–70
  limits on, 365–67
Mitchell, John, 419
Model Cities program, 85, 444
Mondale, Walter, 50, 433
Muskie, Edmund, 399

∩

NAACP. *See* Colored People, National Association for the Advancement of
NAACP v. *Alabama,* 61
Nader, Ralph, 226, 238, 246, 249, 254, 255, 338
National contributions, private, 315–16
National convention, 286–89
  delegates, 287–89

National Direct Student Loan (NDSL) program, 449–50
National Education Association (NEA), 240–41, 468
National Endowments for the Arts and Humanities, 468–69
National Environmental Policy Act, 256, 528
National Gay Task Force, 244
National government, learning about, 137–39
National Highway Safety Act, 527
National Intelligence Estimate, 537
Nationality-group consciousness, 22
Nationality groups, misconceptions about, 25
National Labor Relations Act, 191
National Labor Relations Board (NLRB), 445, 555
National loyalty, learning, 137
National Maritime Engineers' Beneficial Association, 238
National Opinion Research Center, 125
National origins, 22–25
National party chairman, 274
National primary, 284
National Quota Act, 23
  revision of (1965), 23
National Science Foundation (NSF), 444, 468
National Security Agency (NSA), 536
National Security Council (NSC), 426, 427, 540
National Traffic and Motor Vehicle Safety Act, 246
National Women's Political Caucus, 319
Native Americans, 243. *See also* American Indians
Natural law, 41, 103
Natural rights, 103
Navy League, 368
Neighborhood Youth Corps, 195
Nelson, Gaylord, 333
Nelson, Rich, 414
Neustadt, Richard, 383
New Coalition, 242
New Deal, 411, 428, 445, 508
New Hampshire primary, 185, 186, 281, 283, 286
Newspapers
  leaks to, 144–46
  political bias of, 143
Newsweek (magazine), 143, 283
New York Civil Liberties Union, 203
New York Times, 143, 144, 195, 291, 372
New York Times v. *United States,* 59
Nineteenth Amendment, 102, 150
Nixon, Richard M., 155, 274, 406, 429, 486, 493
  black vote and, 167
  Catholic vote (1960) and, 176
  citizen groups and, 250
  conservatism of, 411
  direct mail solicitation and, 211
  ethics and, 247

executive power and, 428
executive privilege and, 430–31
idealists (1960) and, 199
impeachment hearings (1974) and, 310
impoundments by, 371
landslide victory in 1972, 126, 161, 345, 393
local issues and, 351
milk interests and, 240
1960 nomination of, 282
pardon of, 265, 312
party affairs and, 275
Pentagon Papers and, 509
photographers and, 398
plan to create superdepartments, 468
policy implementation and, 532
presidential appointments and, 416–17, 419
press and, 143
rejection of nominees of, 490
Republican Lambs and, 171
resignation of, 49, 495
revenue sharing and, 86
Rockefeller and, 290–91
Supreme Court appointments and, 489
Vietnam war and, 180, 182–83
Watergate scandal and, 345, 387, 392, 432
White House staff and, 406, 424
Nomination(s), 313–14. *See also* Presidential
    candidates, nominating of
evaluation of procedures, 289–90
routes to, 281–86
Noncareer executive assignments (NEAs), 453
North Atlantic Treaty Organization (NATO), 430
NOW. *See* Women, National Organization for
Noyes, Nicholas H., 200
Nuclear weapons, president's control of, 391

O

O'Brien, Lawrence, 412–13
Obscenity, 60
Occupation, 31–34
    of employed people in 1978, 32
    political opinion and, 134–36
Occupational Safety and Health Administration
    (OSHA), 459, 535
OEO. *See* Economic Opportunity, Office of
Officer Corps, 455–56
    aim of, 456
    weaknesses of, 456
Old people. *See* Aged
OMB. *See* Management and Budget, Office of
O'Neill, Thomas P., Jr., 50, 340, 341, 343, 352,
    357
Organizations
    characteristics of big 437–39
    membership in, 233
    membership and activity in, 230
    veterans, 232
Ottinger, Richard, 214

P

Page, Benjamin I., 170
Panama Canal Treaty, 250, 389, 395
Paper Bag Institute, 234
Parents of Gays, 244
Parochial schools, aid to, 64, 556
Participation, political. *See* Political participation
Parties, political
    defection, 173
    difference between, 294–98
    functions of, 265–67
    incumbency and, 207–8
    national structure of, 274–76
    organization of, 273–78
    as reference groups, 158
    relevancy of, 172–73
    state and local, 276–78
Party activists. *See* Activists
Party caucuses, 343–44
Party hybrids, 272
Party identification, 157–73, 297
    and attitudes on issues, 170
    bases of, 162–63
    direction of, 160
    incumbency and, 309
    1952–1978, 159
    stability of, 157–62
    strength of, 159–60
Party images, 311
Party legislator, responsible, 378
Party loyalties
    based on nationality, 166
    fundamental explanation for, 162
Party membership
    definitions of, 270–73
    meaning of, 157–58
Party organization
    leadership, 340–44
    local, 316
Party preferences, 139
Party professionals. *See* Party regulars
Party programs, 344–46
Party purists, 271
Party regulars, 271
Party spending, limits on, 204
Party voting, 360–61
Patent Office, United States, and Supreme
    Court, 478
Patman, Wright, 338
Patronage, 276, 413
    common types of, 197
    definition of, 194
    fact and fiction about, 195–96
    in federal government, 196
    growth of, 197–98
Patten, Edward J., 343
Peace Corps, 30
Pell, Claiborne, 240
Pennsylvania primaries, 283

Pentagon Papers, 493, 509
Phillips, David, 385
Policy
  analysis, 533–36
  effectiveness of, 532
  foreign and domestic, 540–42
Policy implementation, 529–32
  administration, ease of, 530–32
  overload and, 529–30
Policymaking, 17
  goals and priorities, 514–15
  information and, 527–29
  rational, 518–19
  status quo and, 519–20
  unanticipated consequences of, 528–29
Polish-Americans, 25
Political action
  collective, 15–16
  individual, 14–15
Political action committees (PACs), 206, 237
  funds, 209
Political authority, division of, 78–82
Political contributions, 193, 195, 200, 202–12
  effectiveness of, 212–14
  limits on, 204
Political enterpreneur, role of, 527
Political evaluation, 12–13, 17
Political influence, and money, 215–16
Political labor, division of, 559
Political machine, 276
Political opinion. See also Public opinion
  influences on, 134–36
  interrelations of, 132–34
Political participation, 101–2, 188–224
  active, 189–91
  definition of, 189
  ideological, 198–99
  incentive for, 191–212
  patronage-based, 194–98
  policy-oriented, 192–93
  rates of, 189–90
Political socialization, 137
  effect of change on, 138
Political Studies, Center for (CPS), 124, 125
Political system, evaluation of, 552–55
Politics
  American national, 11–13
  as an art, 10–11
  context of American, 13–14
  as a corrective, 549
  dynamics of, 12–13
  managing conflict, 4–7
  meaning of, 10–11
  organizing collective effort, 8–9
  as a source of conflict, 6–7
Politics without Power, 274
Polls, 379
  evaluation of, 124–25
  problems with, 125
  public opinion, 122–47
  straw, 122

Population, socioeconomic characteristics of, 26
Populism, 105
Pork barrel legislation, 413, 523
Postal Service, 450
Postindustrial businesses, 37
Post Office and Civil Service Committee, 330
Postwar baby boom, 30
Power(s)
  greater access to, 78–80
  separation of, 49–50, 80, 110
Prayer(s), in public schools, 63
Precedent, 439
Precinct caucus, 280, 281
  Iowa, 281, 283
President, of the United States
  advising the, 427–28
  appointments by, 415–21
  cabinet and, 421–23
  as chief legislator, 409–10
  Congress and, 408–15
  constitutional powers of, 394–96
  excessive power and, 430
  executive branch and, 415–28
  family backgrounds of, 402
  goals of, 403
  institutionalization of legislative role of,
      423–27
  legislative liaison, 412–13
  man and office, 399–407
  as party leader, 407–8
  party programs in Congress and, 345
  personality of, impact of, 405–7
  personal quality of, 404–5
  persuasion as task of, 404
  policy stance and initiative of, 410–12
  popularity of, 398–99
  power of, 428–32
  powers of, 391–94
  presence of, value of, 414
  primacy of, 402–3
  roles of, 402–5
  symbolic, 396–98
  time perspective of, 403–4
  twentieth-century American, 400–401
  use of military forces, 429–30
  veto power of, 415
  work day of, 405
Presidential appointees
  availability, 420–21
  expertise, 417
  loyalty of, 418–19
  political considerations, 417–18
Presidential candidate(s)
  feelings toward, 175
  nominating a, 278–90
    caucus-convention method, 279, 280–81
    growth in support for, 285
    legal framework, 278–81
Presidential election(s)
  composition of vote in, 160
  1936, 122

popular vote (1976), 268
third parties in, 268
voter turnout and, 152, 153, 156
Presidential Election Campaign Fund, 205
Presidential imperialism, 394
Presidential primaries, 279–80
Press, leaks to, 144–46
Primary
closed, 271
open, 271
Privacy, 67
Probability sampling, 122
Professional associations, 240–41
Professionals, 31–32
as civil servants, 457
Prohibition, 532
Property, private, 104–5
and equality, 105
Protestants, 28, 29
Protest demonstrations, 259
peaceful, 259–60
Proxmire, William, 207
Public Citizen, Inc., 246, 249
Public employment, growth in, 33
Public facilities, equal access to, 558
Public Health Research Group, 226
Public Health Service, 365
Public interest, 102
Public interest groups, 245–46
Public opinion. *See also* Political opinion
effectiveness of, 146–47
ideology and, 129–30
patronage and, 196
shaping of, 128–34
Public Opinion, American Institute of, 28, 125.
See also Gallup Poll
Puerto Ricans, 27, 243
Punishment, indirect, 59
Purism, 200

Q

Quotas
mandatory, 287
racial, 71

R

Race, influence of on opinions, 136
Race relations, 553
Racial discrimination, 68–69, 113
Racial gap, 547
Racial tolerance, 128
Ranney, Austin, 271, 272, 287
Rarick, John, 351, 352
Raw materials, abundance of, 19
Ray, Elizabeth, 327

Reagan, Ronald, 199, 200, 267, 271, 273, 282, 351, 353
Redistributive policies, 523–24
Re-elect the President, Committee to, 236
Reference group(s), 27, 158, 227
social class as, 35
Registration
laws, 153
purpose of, 270
Regulatory Analysis Review Group, 535
Regulatory Commissions, clientelism in, 458–61
Regulatory Commissions, Independent, 444–45
Rehabilitation Act (1973), 531
Religion, 28–29
as election issue, 399
establishment of, 61
freedom of, 61–62
Religious bigotry, 22
Religious conflict, 555–56
Representation, 377–79
bases of, 305–7
consent of the governed and, 96–99
proportional, 269
two theories of, 96–99
types of, 377
Republican National Committee, 275
Republican Party (Republicans)
activists in, 218–21
conservative, 434
ideological portrait of, 169–71
laissez-faire position of, 171
social and economic bases of, 162–68
voting behavior and identification with,
157–62
Republican Study Committee, 348
Research
federal sources of financial support for,
468–69
survey, 122–47
Respondents, 123
Restraint, prior, 59
Revenue sharing, 86–87
Ribicoff, Abraham, 216
Richardson, Elliot, 417
Riegle, Donald, 327
Right to life movement, 67–68
Right(s), 105–6
of the accused, 67, 504–5
to counsel, 63, 66
expansion of, 74
inalienable, 107
negative and positive, 106–7
and the states, 65–67
to vote, 67
Rockefeller, Nelson, 290, 433
Roe v. *Wade*, 67
Roman Republic, senate of, 45
Rooney, John J., 369
Roosevelt, Franklin D., 53, 122, 167, 314,
393–94, 398, 409, 423, 428–29, 432,
486

Roosevelt, Franklin D., *(cont.)*
death of, 397
independent presidential action by, 392
legislative liaison and, 412
legislative program of, 409–10
limited in foreign affairs, 395
Roosevelt, Theodore, 172, 405, 409
Rousseau, Jean-Jacques, 102
Rousselot, John, 315
Rule, defined, 356
Rules Committee, House, 343, 352, 356–57
Russia, 538

S

Saccharin, 226
ban on, 225
Salaries
federal executive, 420
by race and sex, 561
Sampling error, 123
Scales v. *United States,* 58
Scarcity, 4–5
Schattschneider, E.E., 273
Schedule C appointees, 453
Scheduling, legislative process and, 355–56
Scheuer, James H., 343
School systems, dual, 69
Schultze, Charles, 517
Science, National Academy of, 226
Search and seizure, 62
Secrecy, foreign policymaking and, 539–40
Securities and Exchange Commission, 445
Segregation
de facto (in fact), 70
de jure (by law), 70
Segregation laws, 69, 70
"Selection out" policy, 456
Selective incorporation, 505
Self-employed, 32
Self-incrimination, 63
Semi-exclusive committees, 330
Senate, United States, 45
confirmation of presidential nominees, 305
special powers of, 46
vice-president as presiding officer, 341
Senate Appropriations Committee, 388
Senate Appropriations Subcommittee, 369
Senate Finance Committee, 330, 331
Senate Judiciary Committee, 374, 377, 387,
411, 490, 495
Senators
incumbent, campaign contributions for, 213
popular election of, 45
staggered terms of, 109
Senior Executive Service (SES), 451–53
Seniority system, 335
changing biases of, 335–37
revolt against, 337–39

Seventeenth Amendment, 45, 101, 305
Seventh Amendment, 65
Sherwin-Williams Company, 226
Sierra Club, 254
Single-delegate district plan, 280
Sirica, John J., 249, 493
Sisk, Bernie, 351, 352
Situational factors, 150
Sixteenth Amendment, 485
Sixth Amendment, 65
Small Business Subcommittee, 351
Smith, Al, 165
Social class, 34–36
as basis for differences in political beliefs, 35
and party preference, relationship between,
163
as reference group, 35
Social cleavages, cross-cutting, 134
Social differences, 38
Social Security Act, 525
constitutionality of, 483
Social Security Administration, 90
Social Security Increment (SSI), 91
Soil Conservation Service, 375
Solidarity groups, 232, 241–45
Solid South, 37, 165, 311, 336
Sorensen, Theodore C., 387
Soul Sisters, 244
Sovereignty, popular, 99
Spanish origin, persons of, 27–28
affirmative action and, 72–73
Speaker of the House, 340–41, 343, 404
Specialization, 101, 437
clientelism and, 458
Speech
content of, 58–59
freedom of. *See* Freedom of speech
geography of, 59
symbolic, 59
Speedy trial, right to, 65
Spending, uncontrolled, 520–22
Staffs
committee and personal, 374–76
expanding, 376
Staff system, president-centered, 407
Standard Metropolitan Statistical Areas (SMSA),
36
Standards, Bureau of, 457
Stark, Pete, 351
State, Department of, 369, 373, 536, 538, 540
State Legislatures, National Conference of, 242
State and local budgets, dependence of on
federal funds, 89–90
State and national governments, cooperation
between, 83
States, powers of, 76–77
States' Rights Democratic party, 172
Stevenson, Adlai, 1–6, 161, 167, 191, 198,
199
Strategic Arms Limitation Treaty (SALT), 52,
389, 430

Strauss, Robert S., 239
Strikes, 259–60
Student aid, federal, 520, 521
Student Lobby, 368
Subcommittee Bill of Rights, 332, 334
Subgovernments, 367–68
Suburbs, 37
Superdepartments, 468
Support, sources of, 314–16
Supreme Court, 50, 256
    appellate jurisdiction of, 478
    as court, 479–84
    decision-making process and, 500–501
    democracy and, 484–87
    economic rights and, 508
    elections and, 506
    executive privilege and, 431
    federalism and, 77–78
    final disposition of cases by, 499
    finality of decisions, 487
    as highest court, 481–84
    imposition of national rules on states by, 78
    as instrument of government, 481
    justices, 109. *See also* Supreme Court
        Justices
    as lawmaker, 480–81
    legitimating role of, 506
    as one of three branches of government,
        483–84
    opinions, 501–3
        audiences for, 501–2
    overview of current state of, 508–9
    political questions and, 478
    presidential powers and, 395–96
    race relations and, 506–7
    rights of the accused and, 504–5
    roles of, 503–8
    routes to, 496–98
    school desegregation and, 69, 167, 241, 394
    separation of powers and, 50
    as third person, 480
    welfare and, 91
    work of, 491–501
    workload of, 498–500
Supreme Court Justices, 488–90
    appointment of, 489–90
    appointments, interval between, 486
    characteristics of candidate for, 489
    judicial attitudes of, 489
    years of service of, 485
Symbionese Liberation Army, 260
Synoptic approach, to policymaking, 515–16

T

Taft, William Howard, 172
Taxation, bills for, 305
Teague, Charles, 352, 353

Teamster, 237, 249
Technical Education Branch, 467
Technology Assessment, Office of, 374
Tennessee Valley Authority, 438
Test Ban Treaty, 430
Thalidomide, 411
Third parties, 172
Thirteenth Amendment, 68, 78
Thurmond, J. Strom, 155, 172
Time (magazine), 143, 283
Tocqueville, Alexis de, 111, 228
Tourism and Sugar, Subcommittee on, 331
Transportation, Department of, 444, 531
Treaties, Senate control of, 389
Truman, Harry S., 172, 286, 392, 406, 410,
        429, 430, 503
    legislative liaison and, 412
Trustee, 378
Twenty-fifth Amendment, 433
Twenty-fourth Amendment, 150
Twenty-sixth Amendment, 102, 150
Two-party system, 265–70
    alternative to, 171–73
    reason for, 267–70

U

Udall, Morris K., 195
Unemployment compensation, 90
Unions. *See* Labor unions
Unitary executive, 269
United Automobile, Aerospace, and Agriculture
        Implement Workers (UAW), 237
United Mineworkers, 237
United States v. *Nixon*, 431, 500
Unruh, Jess, 215
Unsafe at Any Speed (Nader), 246
"Up or out" policy, 456

V

Vagueness, 60
Value conflict, 5–6
Vance, Cyrus, 385, 538
Veterans' Administration, 444
Veterans benefits, 93
Veto(es)
    legislative, 385–86
    pocket, 415
    presidential, 49
    by twentieth-century presidents, 416
Vice-president, 432–34
    duties of, 433–34
    method of selection, 432–33
    as Senate's presiding officer, 341
Vietnam war, 127, 182–85, 282, 388, 509,
        519, 553

Vietnam war *(cont.)*
  opinions on, 141–42
Viguerie, Richard A., 211
Violence and disobedience, small-scale, 260–61
Vocational Education, Division of, 467
Volkmer, Harold L., 343
Volunteer campaign workers, 191
Vote, right to, 67
Voter differences, 163–68
  age, 168
  economic, 163–64
  racial, 166–67
  regional, 164–65
  religious, 165–66
Voters, analysis of, 153–55
Voter turnout
  by age and sex, 154
  decline of, 156–57
  factors influencing, 153
  influences on, 150–57
  most important influence on, 154
  personal economic misfortune and, 156
  in presidential and House elections, 152
Voting
  abstention from, 155–56
  issue, 179–85
  party influence on, 361
  residency requirements, 153
Voting Rights Act, 151

and 1974 primaries, 314
  tapes, 501
Ways and Means Committee, 330, 331, 366, 370, 374
Wealth, 19–21
  and ideology, in political finance, 208–9
Wednesday Group, 348
Welfare, 90–93
Well-being, 545
Wertheimer, Fred, 343
Whip, 341
White-collar jobs, 31
White House, major function of, 424
Wild, Claude C., Jr., 195
Wildavsky, Aaron, 517, 553
Will, general, 102
Will of the people. *See* Will, general
Wilson, Woodrow, 172, 395, 405, 409, 423
Wisconsin v. *Yoder*, 62
Witcover, Jules, 197
Women
  affirmative action and, 73
  rights of, 251
  in workforce, 34
Women, National Organization for (NOW), 245
Women's Bureau, 457
Women's movement, 244–45
Wright, Benjamin F., 550

W

Waldie, Jerome, 351
Wallace, George, 172, 209, 211, 267, 273, 282, 284
Wallace, Henry, 155, 172
Wall Street Journal, 143
War on poverty, 85, 444
War Powers Resolution (1973), 429, 430
Warren, Earl, 490
Warren Court, 496
Washington, George, 393–94
Washington Post, 143, 253
Watergate, 48, 143, 236, 247, 254, 265, 312, 384, 387, 393, 395, 468, 493

Y

Yarmolinsky, Adam, 347
Yates, Sidney R., 333
Yates v. *United States,* 58
Young people
  party affiliations of, 168
  political information of, 138

Z

Zero-base budgeting (ZBB), 520, 522
Zero-sum game. *See* Redistributive policies